THE **HR** SOLUTION

Print + Online

HR⁴

DENISI · GRIFFIN

HUMAN RESOURCES

4LTR PRESS · NOW WITH HR ONLINE
$85 US SUGGESTED RETAIL PRICE

MANAGE MY COURSE ⌄ · STUDENT

HR4

CHAPTER 1

The Nature of Human Resource Management

CHAPTER 2

The Legal Environment

HR⁴ delivers all the key terms and core concepts for the **Human Resources** course.

HR Online provides the complete narrative from the printed text with additional interactive media and the unique functionality of **StudyBits**—all available on nearly any device!

What is a StudyBit™? Created through a deep investigation of students' challenges and workflows, the StudyBit™ functionality of **HR Online** enables students of different generations and learning styles to study more effectively by allowing them to learn their way. Here's how they work:

COLLECT WHAT'S IMPORTANT
Create StudyBits as you highlight text, images or take notes!

WEAK

FAIR

STRONG

UNASSIGNED

RATE AND ORGANIZE STUDYBITS
Rate your understanding and use the color-coding to quickly organize your study time and personalize your flashcards and quizzes.

StudyBit™

TRACK/MONITOR PROGRESS
Use Concept Tracker to decide how you'll spend study time and study YOUR way!

85%

PERSONALIZE QUIZZES
Filter by your StudyBits to personalize quizzes or just take chapter quizzes off-the-shelf.

D1511512

INCORRECT

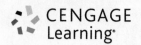

HR4
Angelo S. DeNisi, Ricky W. Griffin

SVP, GM, Science, Technology & Math:
    Balraj Kalsi

Product Manager: Laura Redden

Content/Media Developer: Sarah Keeling

Product Assistant: Eli J Lewis

Marketing Manager: Emily McLellan

Content Project Manager: Nadia Saloom

Manufacturing Planner: Ron Montgomery

Production Service: MPS Limited

Sr. Art Director: Bethany Casey

Internal Designer: Trish & Ted Knapke: Ke Design

Cover Designer: Lisa Kuhn: Curio Press, LLC/
    Trish & Ted Knapke: Ke Design

Cover Image: Dimitri Otis/DigitalVision/Getty
    Images and g-stockstudio/Shutterstock.com

Intellectual Property

    Analyst: Diane Garrity

    Project Manager: Carly Belcher

For product information and technology assistance, contact us at
Cengage Learning Customer & Sales Support, 1-800-354-9706

For permission to use material from this text or product,
submit all requests online at **www.cengage.com/permissions**
Further permissions questions can be emailed to
permissionrequest@cengage.com

Library of Congress Control Number: 2016955679

Student Edition ISBN: 978-1-337-11639-8
Student Edition with Access Card ISBN: 978-1-337-11638-1

Cengage Learning
20 Channel Center Street
Boston, MA 02210
USA

Cengage Learning is a leading provider of customized learning solutions with employees residing in nearly 40 different countries and sales in more than 125 countries around the world. Find your local representative at **www.cengage.com**

Cengage Learning products are represented in Canada by Nelson Education, Ltd.

To learn more about Cengage Learning Solutions, visit **www.cengage.com**

Purchase any of our products at your local college store or at our preferred online store **www.cengagebrain.com**

Printed in the United States of America
Print Number: 02   Print Year: 2017

DENISI / GRIFFIN
HR⁴

BRIEF CONTENTS

Dimitri Otis/DigitalVision/Getty Images

CONTENTS

4 The Competitive Environment 84

Part 2
DECISION-MAKING IN HUMAN RESOURCE MANAGEMENT

eddtoro/Shutterstock.com

5 Information for Making Human Resource Decisions 108

Part 3 MANAGING THE EXISTING WORKFORCE

Goodluz/Shutterstock.com

9 Compensation and Benefits   218

10 Performance Appraisal and Career Management   244

Part 4
ENHANCING PERFORMANCE

Francis Vachon/Alamy Stock Photo

1 | The Nature of Human Resource Management

lightpoet/Shutterstock.com

After finishing this chapter go to **PAGE 22** for **STUDY TOOLS**

LEARNING OBJECTIVES

1-1 Describe the contemporary human resource perspectives

1-2 Trace the evolution of the human resource function in organizations

1-3 Identify and discuss the goals of human resource management

1-4 Discuss the setting for human resource management

1-5 Describe the job of human resource managers from the perspectives of professionalism and careers

At first glance, Google, Hilcorp, and Quicken Loans appear to have little in common. After all, one is a software development company, one is an oil and gas producer, and one is a financial services business. They are headquartered in different states, use different resources, sell different products, have different organizational structures, and do not directly compete with one another. But they do share a few things in common: They have all been cited as among the most admired companies in the United States by *Fortune* magazine, they routinely appear on lists of the best places to work, and they are consistently profitable.

So, what do they have in common? They invest heavily in attracting the best employees and then work diligently to train them and offer them rewarding career opportunities. They pay well, offer good benefits, and strive to make their employees feel valued. And while many different things determine a firm's profitability, the relationships Google, Hilcorp, and Quicken Loans have with their employees has a strong impact on their success.

Google, for example, offers stock options and health care benefits to all of its employees, even those who only work part-time. The firm also keeps all of its employees informed about its business strategy, its profitability and growth goals, and career opportunities. In December 2010, the CEO of Hilcorp pledged to give every employee $100,000 if the firm doubled its equity value, net production, and reserves by the end of December 2015. The goal was met, and the firm made good on its promise. Quicken Loans offers a $20,000 forgivable loan when employees want to buy their first home and then adds another $5000 for decorating or improvements.

"In order to create better alignment across all employees, our bonus structure treats everyone equally. We have a culture that we are all in this together.[1]"

—GREG LALICKER, PRESIDENT OF HILCORP

In addition to Google, Hilcorp, and Quicken Loans, of course, there are many other businesses today that see their employees as a major contributor to their competitive advantage. For instance, Wegmans Food Markets, The Container Store, Genentech, USAA, Edward Jones, Marriott International, and KPMG are also among the firms that routinely appear on lists of good places to work and also consistently post strong growth, profit, and other indicators of financial success. The bottom line is that while there are many routes to business success, treating employees well is often the best way to go.[2]

THINK IT OVER

1. Given the success enjoyed by Hilcorp, Google, and Quicken Loans, why don't all firms use similar approaches to managing their employees?
2. If you were starting a new business, what kind of relationship would you want to have with your employees? How would you go about trying to achieve this?

Regardless of their size, mission, market, or environment, all organizations strive to achieve their goals by combining various resources into goods and services that will be of value to their customers. Economists traditionally thought in terms of concrete physical resources such as ownership investment, sales revenues, and bank loans to provide capital and to cover expenses necessary to conduct business. Material resources such as factories, equipment, raw materials, computers, and offices also play an important role in the actual creation of goods and services and are easy to think about when we discuss a firm's resources. But managers are beginning to view less tangible resources as the most critical for gaining a competitive advantage.

For example, successful organizations need information not only about consumers but also about the firm's competitive environment to help managers make decisions, solve problems, and develop competitive strategies. Many people refer to such resources as *knowledge-based resources*.[3] That is, organizations need to know how to get information and how to use that information. We discuss knowledge-based resources and knowledge workers later in this chapter and throughout the book, but for now it is sufficient to note that most (but not all) of this critical knowledge tends to reside in the people in the organization. Therefore, many experts in the field have come to recognize that no set of resources is more vital to an organization's success than its human resources.[4]

Human resources (HR) are the people an organization employs to carry out various jobs, tasks, and functions in exchange for wages, salaries, and other rewards. Human resources include everyone from the CEO, who is responsible for the overall effectiveness of the organization, to the custodian who cleans the offices after everyone else goes home. Each employee, in his or her own way, is a vital ingredient that helps determine the overall effectiveness—or lack of effectiveness—of the organization as it strives to accomplish its goals and objectives.

Human resource management (HRM) refers to the comprehensive set of managerial activities and tasks concerned with attracting, developing, and maintaining a qualified workforce—human resources—in ways that contribute to organizational effectiveness. As we will see, more and more organizations are coming to appreciate the dramatic impact that effective HRM can have on all aspects of the organization.[5] But in addition to organizations paying more attention to HRM in general, there are also several more recent developments in the field that may elevate the HRM function even higher. Several of these involve notions of talent management[6] and the idea of a differentiated workforce.[7] We will discuss these new developments as part of our broad discussion of the field of HRM in this chapter. This discussion will serve as the basis for more detailed discussions of specific aspects of HRM in subsequent chapters. We begin with a look at contemporary HRM and the current field and then briefly trace the history of the field. The goals of the HRM function are then identified and discussed before we examine how the responsibilities for HRM are shared as staff and management functions. The HR department in different kinds of organizations is then discussed. Finally, we focus on the professionalism and career development of HR managers themselves.

1-1 CONTEMPORARY HUMAN RESOURCE MANAGEMENT PERSPECTIVES

In most organizations today, the role of HRM has become quite important. This results partly from a growing realization of the importance of people as a source of competitive advantage, but there are also more practical reasons. For instance, the passage of Title VII of the Civil Rights

> Title VII of the Civil Rights Act of 1964 prohibits discrimination on the basis of an individual's race, color, religious beliefs, sex, or national origin.

Act of 1964 (and various court decisions that followed it) made it clear that organizations had to find ways to hire, reward, and manage people effectively within the limits of the law. As a result, the HRM function came to require dedicated professionals who could balance legal and ethical concerns with the need of organizations to survive and be profitable. If a firm did not employ qualified managers in these roles, then they faced increased risks of serious financial penalties and legal fees.

The view of HRM as part of the legal enforcement arm of an organization is largely applicable only in the United States. Yet managers around the world have come to understand that properly managed human resources can be an important source of competitive advantage in an increasingly competitive world. In fact, as noted earlier, human resources are the organization's most important resources. Hiring the right people, equipping them with the right skills, and then providing an environment in which they can truly contribute can substantially affect the quality and quantity of whatever goods or services the organization produces. Properly motivated and committed employees can add immeasurable value to an organization's bottom line. Given the shift in competitiveness, top executives in most firms now see that HRM practices and policies significantly affect their ability to formulate and implement strategy in any area and that other strategic decisions significantly affect the firm's human resources as well.

It was only natural, therefore, that HRM would eventually be elevated to the same level of importance and status as other major functional areas of the firm.[8] The top HR executive at most companies today has the status of vice president or executive vice president and is a fully contributing member of the firm's executive committee, the body composed of key top managers that makes major policy decisions and sets corporate strategy. Today, most firms use a term such as *human resource management* to reflect more accurately the sophistication and maturity of the function. But some people argue that even this term is outdated and does not do justice to the role the HR manager plays. Instead, some

Contemporary Challenges in HR

Labor Shortage? Or Labor Surplus?

During good times and bad, one thing is true: some businesses and industries will be cutting jobs and laying off workers. But other businesses and industries will be adding new jobs and hiring new employees. During challenging economic times like we've faced in the past decade or so, the press routinely reports large job cuts and predicts high unemployment. For example, plunging oil prices in 2015 and 2016 led many energy companies such as Shell, Schlumberger, BP, and Halliburton to impose significant job cuts. Many highly qualified engineers and geologists found themselves looking for work.

> "It's time to plan for a massive demographic shift. Discourage retirement, encourage retraining, and encourage immigration."[9]
>
> —USA TODAY

But at the same time, U.S. businesses in some sectors are facing a growing labor shortage. How can we explain this apparently contradictory trend? There are actually several reasons. First, we have entered the retirement bulge associated with the baby boomer generation. This means that there are more workers retiring than there are younger workers entering the workforce. Second, the U.S. workforce has a growing misalignment between what workers can and are willing to do and what employers need for them to do and between where jobs are located and where workers live.

Take construction, for example. During the economic downturn that started in 2008, literally hundreds of thousands of construction workers were laid off. Given the dearth of jobs and what they saw as limited prospects in the future, many of these workers decided to retire. Others moved to states where there was more demand for their services. Still others changed fields, taking jobs as truck drivers, factory workers, or roughnecks in what was then the booming oil and gas fields. But now that construction is coming back, many building contractors are having trouble finding carpenters, plumbers, electricians, and other skilled workers.

Even some professional jobs are facing the same challenges. Take airline pilots, for example. There are about 90,000 commercial pilot jobs in the United States. A growing number of retirements coupled with new work rules requiring that pilots have more time to rest between flights and projected growth in air traffic combine to predict a shortage in the very near future. Some experts, for instance, project that there will soon be 8,000 or so openings a year. The major airlines such as Delta and American will likely not be impacted much by this, but shortages will likely occur in the regional airlines, especially because those pilots will be among the most qualified for openings in the bigger airlines.

But, as noted previously, there are surplus of petroleum engineers and geologists right now due to the drop in oil and gas exploration and refining. It's quite likely, of course, that when energy prices begin to go up again, the demand for engineers and geologists will also grow. Further, it is also possible that forces may cause a drop in the demand for pilots. Who really knows what the future holds?[10]

THINK IT OVER

1. As an employee, how might you best prepare yourself for impending labor shortages in some fields? For potential labor surpluses in other fields?

2. As an HR manager, what might you do to entice workers where there is a labor shortage? What might you do to soften the impact of layoffs caused by an economic downturn?

Markus Mainka/Shutterstock.com

organizations have moved toward using more specialized terminology that fits their corporate culture more closely. The top HR executive at Southwest Airlines, for example, has the title of Vice President for People, while other firms, recognizing the importance of HR as knowledge resources, have started using titles such as chief knowledge officer. To keep things simple, though, we will use the human resource management terminology throughout this book.

Many aspects of the modern HRM function actually date back to the 1980s and 1990s. It became apparent to many firms then that they were not able to compete effectively in the global marketplace. Some of these firms went out of business, and employees lost their jobs. Some firms were acquired by other, more successful companies, and in the aftermath, many employees of the acquired firm were seen as redundant and let go. Still other firms sought mergers with former or potential competitors in the hope of forming a new joint enterprise that could compete successfully. But again, in most cases, merged companies often did not find the same need for as many employees, and many workers lost their jobs.

Instead of simply managing the layoffs following a merger or acquisition, HR executives were part of the team deciding which firms to merge with or to acquire outright. HR managers could help to identify the critical human resources that the firm would need in the future, and they could also help to identify other firms that might already have those resources and thus be prime targets for takeovers or mergers. As knowledge became more critical in gaining competitive advantage, HR managers helped define strategies to acquire or develop knowledge resources. They also developed strategies for ensuring that any knowledge acquired was fully dispersed throughout the organization. As firms compete more broadly on a global basis, these factors become even more critical as firms try to integrate work processes and employees from diverse cultures around the world.

At the same time that HR managers were taking on a more strategic role, many organizations began shrinking the more traditional roles played by HR managers. As these organizations looked for new ways to be competitive by reducing costs, they often looked for activities within the company that could be done more efficiently by outsiders. Cleaning and maintenance were easy functions to replace, but, for example, many international airlines outsource their on-board catering to Lufthansa.

This trend has spread to other areas as well. Today, many large organizations hire outside firms to handle payroll, insurance and benefits, and even recruitment and selection in some cases.[11] This practice, commonly known as **outsourcing**, has resulted in smaller internal HR staffs and more reliance on outside consultants to provide the services once provided by those staffs. Thus, although the importance of HRM activities is growing, the importance of HR departments may be shrinking, and the kind of work performed by HR managers is certainly changing as the size of the HR function is shrinking.

Outsourcing can indeed be an important competitive weapon for organizations. If done properly, outsourcing results in more efficient operations. Outside firms that are hired benefit from the fact that they perform the same tasks for many companies. In addition, outsourcing tends to eliminate jobs that are more repetitious and perhaps dull. As a result, the employees who work on these jobs are more likely to be dissatisfied at work, which can have a tremendous cost for the firms. But not all functions can be outsourced for competitive advantage. Thus, it is critical that a firm retain any function that is either of strategic importance in its own right (i.e., strategic planning) or can lead to some advantage because the firm is especially expert at this function (e.g., selection or training). Therefore, the issue for most firms today is not whether to outsource but what to outsource and what to keep in-house.

Michael D Brown /Shutterstock.com

Outsourcing is the process of hiring outside firms to handle basic HRM functions, presumably more efficiently than the organization could.

Furthermore, many firms are beginning to realize that not all positions and not all employees contribute equally to firm performance. This is the notion behind the idea of a differentiated workforce. Some positions are more critical to the firm's effective performance, and these positions should receive the lion's share of the attention. The best people must be recruited and trained for these positions, and turnover in these positions is especially costly. Likewise, not all employees are equally valuable to the firm, and the idea behind talent management is that extra care must be taken to attract and then retain "stars,"[12] including using large financial incentives to retain them. These movements are making HRM even more complex.[13]

In addition, the legal imperatives that in large part elevated the importance of the HRM function are changing and becoming more complex. In what has been termed a post–affirmative action world, issues regarding differential test performance of members of different ethnic and racial groups, especially in high-stakes situations (where jobs or entrance into academic institutions are involved), are becoming more rather than less complex. How do we address differences in test scores in a society where credentialing and accountability are becoming more important, and when we still haven't figured out how to deal with the diversity our society presents us?[14]

In addition, as laws and attitudes change relative to gay rights, including same-sex marriages, problems of benefits and legal protection suggest that diversity management will become even more complicated in the future.

Of course, the world has changed in many other ways over the past decades. Beginning with the attacks of September 11, 2001, issues of security have become much more important in the United States. These concerns manifest themselves initially in the need to attract, select, train, and motivate airport security personnel who serve as the first line of defense against terrorism. These tasks fall squarely in the domain of HRM, increasing the stakes involved in getting these practices right. Then, in 2005, Hurricanes Katrina and Rita devastated the Gulf Coast of the United States, and the results illustrated new demands for security of employee records and open lines of communication with employees. The arrival in 2012 of Hurricane Sandy reinforced the vulnerability of business operations to natural disasters and further emphasized the need for better HR information systems.

But more recent terrorist attacks in San Bernardino, CA; Paris, France; and Istanbul, Turkey; among others, have added further levels of complications. Not only has the need for security—at all levels—been made clear, but these attacks by radical Islamist groups have triggered new waves of fear and mistrust of all Muslims, which presents problems for HRM in terms of legal concerns and may also serve to limit immigration from certain parts of the world, which may further challenge HRM to find qualified people. Unfortunately, there are also threats that do not come from terrorists. An example occurred in February 2016, when an employee of a lawn care company in Kansas left after his shift was completed and then returned to shoot 14 people. The reasons for the shooting are not entirely clear, but the shooter had been served with a restraining order to keep away from his girlfriend, just before the shooting began. In any event, this incident was just one more example of the threat of workplace violence facing all employees at all locations.

There is also uncertainty of a different nature facing the United States and everyone doing business in this country. In February 2016, Supreme Court Justice Antonin Scalia died unexpectedly. Many of the more controversial decisions handed down in recent years have been 5-4 decision, with Scalia a leading proponent of a strict interpretation of the Constitution. His decisions have put him in opposition to gay marriage and the Obama health care reforms. Typically, this set of circumstances would allow President Obama to appoint a more liberal justice. But, given what occurred in the last year of the President's term of office, many Republicans are calling for the President to not try to appoint anyone to the court, and to allow the upcoming election to determine what kind of justice should be appointed. President Obama will likely make a nomination, and the Republican-controlled Senate will likely try to stop the appointment. That will leave the Court with eight justices and will almost certainly result in 4-4 ties in the interim. Interestingly, a 4-4 tie in a Supreme Court decision means that any lower court decision stands—as if the Supreme Court never heard the case. It will be interesting to see how all this plays out in the long run, but in March 2016, we saw the first real effect of the new court structure. A case dealing with public unions (discussed further in Chapter 11) was reviewed by the Supreme Court, but the court was divided, so the lower court decision held. But the lower court had ruled in favor of the California teachers' union, and conservatives had hoped to win a big victory in the Supreme Court where a 5-4 decision—against the union—was fairly certain. It is important for the HR manager to remember that the Supreme Court is also preparing to hear cases regarding immigration and affirmative action, among others, and a deadlocked Court could paralyze a number of HR initiatives.

Before moving on to a more detailed discussion of the tasks and functions of modern HRM, it is useful to consider how we arrived where we are today. The struggle of HRM for legitimacy within the organization and how that legitimacy came about is due in large part to the history of how HRM developed.

1-2 EVOLUTION OF THE HUMAN RESOURCE FUNCTION

Even though businesses have existed for thousands of years, the practice of management itself has only been of special interest and concern for about 100 years.[15] Many early businesses were small enterprises and farms run by families interested only in supporting themselves and providing security for family members. The Industrial Revolution of the eighteenth century, however, sparked a greater interest in business growth and expansion, and large-scale business operations began to emerge throughout Europe and the United States. As these businesses grew and became increasingly complex, owners began to step aside and turn the operation of their firms over to full-time professional managers. Owners who remained in control of their businesses still needed to rely on managers to oversee a portion of their operations. This transition, in turn, resulted in greater awareness of the various functions of management that were necessary for long-term organizational success.[16]

A few early management pioneers and writers such as Robert Owen, Mary Parker Follette, and Hugo Münsterberg recognized the importance of people in organizations, but the first serious study of management practice—set during the early years of the twentieth century—was based on scientific management.[17] **Scientific management** was concerned with structuring individual jobs to maximize efficiency and productivity. The major proponents of scientific management, such as Frederick Taylor and Frank and Lillian Gilbreth, had backgrounds in engineering and often used time-and-motion studies in which managers used stopwatches to teach workers precisely how to perform each task that made up their jobs. In fact, scientific management was concerned with every motion a worker made, and there were many examples of how changes in movements or in the placement of some piece of equipment led to increased productivity.

However, often laborers would use the production standards established by management as a way to work even more slowly. Other critics argued that individual workers were generally valued only in terms of their capacity to perform assigned tasks as efficiently and as productively as possible. Still, scientific management helped augment the concepts of assembly-line production, division of labor, and economies of scale that gave birth to the large businesses that transformed domestic and international economies throughout the twentieth century.[18]

1-2a Origins of the Human Resource Function

As businesses such as General Motors (started in 1908), Bethlehem Steel (1899), Ford Motor Company (1903), Boeing (1916), and other industrial giants launched during this era expanded rapidly and grew into big companies, they obviously needed to hire more and more workers. B.F. Goodrich was the first company to establish a corporate employment department to deal with employee concerns in 1900. National Cash Register (NCR) set up a similar department in 1902 to deal with employee grievances, wages and salaries, and record keeping. The need for an employment department at Ford became clear as the company increased its production from 800 cars a day in 1910 to more than 9,000 cars a day by 1925, and increased its workforce from less than 200 to several thousand employees.[19] This same pattern of growth and hiring was being repeated in literally hundreds of other businesses across dozens of industries. These workers were needed to perform operating jobs created to produce ever-greater quantities of the products sold by the businesses. In the early days of this business explosion, the foreman, or first-line supervisor, usually hired new workers. Office workers were also needed, so people with titles such as *office manager* hired clerks and secretaries.

As these businesses became more complex and their hiring needs more complicated, however, the task of hiring new employees was too time-consuming for a first-line supervisor or an office manager to perform. In addition, extra administrative duties were being added. For example, in 1913, Ford was paying its unskilled employees $2.34 per 9-hour day. Because the pay was so low and the work was

> **Scientific management,** one of the earliest approaches to management, was concerned with structuring individual jobs to maximize efficiency and productivity.

> "We cannot solve our problems with the same level of thinking that created them."
>
> —ALBERT EINSTEIN

both monotonous and tiring, the firm was also experiencing a turnover rate of almost 400 percent per year. Thus, the firm had to replace its average worker four times each year. It was hiring workers to fill new jobs while also hiring workers to replace those who quit. In 1914, Henry Ford made a dramatic effort to attract and retain higher-quality workers by boosting the firm's pay to a minimum of $5 for an 8-hour day.[20] This action attracted a groundswell of new job applicants and almost overwhelmed first-line supervisors, who were then hiring new employees while overseeing the work of existing workers.

As a result of growth and complexity, most large businesses, including Ford, began hiring new employees through newly created specialized units. Ford, for example, called this unit the *employment department*. Although these units were initially created to hire those new employees, they also began to help manage the existing workforce. For example, the emergence and growth of large labor unions such as the United Auto Workers and the passage of the Fair Labor Standards Act in 1938 (established a minimum wage) and the National Labor Relations Act in 1935 (dealt with unionization procedures) made it necessary for businesses to have one or more managers represent the interests of the business to organized labor and to administer the emerging set of laws and regulations that governed labor practices.

Meanwhile, other developments, many taking place in other parts of the world, provided organizations with some of the tools they would need to manage these employment processes more effectively. For example, in England, Charles Darwin's work was used by some theorists to popularize the idea that individuals differed from each other in important ways. In France, the work of Alfred Binet and Theophile Simon led to the development of the first intelligence tests, and, during the course of World War I, several major armies tried using these tests to assign soldiers to jobs. These efforts continued in the private sector after the end of World War I, and by 1923, books such as *Personnel Management* by Scott and Clothier were spelling out how to match a person's skills and aptitudes with the requirements of the job.

Another important ingredient in the origins of the HR function during this period was the so-called **human relations era**, which emerged following the **Hawthorne studies**. Between 1927 and 1932, the Western Electric Company sponsored a major research program at its Hawthorne plant near Chicago. This research, conducted by Roethlisberger and Mayo, revealed for perhaps the first time that individual and group behavior played an important role in organizations and that human behavior at work was something managers really needed to understand more fully. One Hawthorne study suggested, for example, that individual attitudes may have been related to performance, and another suggested that a work group may have established norms to restrict the output of its individual group members.[21] Before this work, many managers paid almost no attention to their employees as people but instead viewed them in the same way they viewed a machine or a piece of equipment—as an economic entity to be managed dispassionately and with concern only for resource output.

Stimulated by the Hawthorne findings, managers began to focus more attention on better understanding the human character of their employees. During this era, for example, Abraham Maslow popularized his **hierarchy of human needs** (see Chapter 13 for a more detailed discussion of this model).[22] In addition, Douglas McGregor's well-known **Theory X** and **Theory Y** framework also grew from the HR movement.[23] The basic premise of the HR era was that if

Ford revolutionized hiring at plants such as this one by boosting pay to a minimum of $5 a day and shortening the workday to 8 hours.

> The **human relations era** supplanted scientific management as the dominant approach to management during the 1930s.
>
> The human relations era was instigated by the **Hawthorne studies**.
>
> Abraham Maslow's **hierarchy of human needs** was developed during the human relations era.
>
> Douglas McGregor's **Theory X** and **Theory Y** framework grew from the human relations movement.

managers made their employees more satisfied and happier, then they would work harder and be more productive. Today, researchers and managers alike recognize that this viewpoint was overly simplistic and that both satisfaction and productivity are complex phenomena affecting and affected by many factors. Nonetheless, the increased awareness of the importance of human behavior stimulated during this period helped organizations become even more focused on better managing their human resources. These organizations saw effective management of human resources as a means of potentially increasing productivity and, incidentally, as a way of slowing the growth of unionism, which was beginning to gain popularity.

1-2b Personnel Management

We noted earlier that growing organizations began to create specialized units to cope with their increasing hiring needs, deal with government regulations, and provide a mechanism for better dealing with behavioral issues. During the 1930s and 1940s, these units gradually began to be called **personnel departments** (the word *personnel* was derived from an Old French word that meant "persons"). They were usually set up as special, self-contained departments charged with the responsibility of hiring new workers and administering basic HR activities such as pay and benefits. The recognition that human resources needed to be managed and the creation of personnel departments also gave rise to a new type of management function—**personnel management**.[24]

During this period, personnel management was concerned almost exclusively with hiring first-line employees such as production workers, salesclerks, custodians, secretaries, blue-collar workers, unskilled labor, and other operating employees. Issues associated with hiring, developing, and promoting managers and executives did not surface until later. The manager who ran the personnel department was soon called the **personnel manager**.

Personnel management evolved further during World War II. Both the military and its major suppliers became interested in better matching people with jobs. They wanted to optimize the fit between the demands and requirements of the jobs that needed to be performed and the skills and interests of people available to perform them. Psychologists were consulted to help develop selection tests, for example, to assess individual skills, interests, and abilities more accurately. During the 1950s, the lessons learned during the war were adapted for use in private industry. New and more sophisticated techniques were developed, especially in the area of testing, and companies also began to experiment with more sophisticated reward and incentive systems. Labor unions became more powerful and demanded a broader array of benefits for their members. In addition, government legislation expanded and continued to add complexity to the job of the personnel manager.

Still, from the first days of its inception until the 1970s, personnel management was not seen as a particularly important or critical function in most business organizations. Although other managers accepted personnel management as a necessary vehicle for hiring new operating employees, personnel management was also seen primarily as a routine clerical and bookkeeping function. For example, personnel was responsible for placing newspaper ads to recruit new employees, filling out paperwork for those employees after they were hired, and seeing that everyone was paid on time.

While other organizational units, such as marketing, finance, and operations, grew in status and importance, the personnel department of most organizations was generally relegated to the status of necessary evil that had to be tolerated but that presumably contributed little to the success of the organization. Its offices were often drab and poorly equipped and were often located away from the central activity areas of the organization. Personnel managers themselves were often stereotyped as individuals who could not succeed in other functional areas and were assigned to personnel either because the organization had nothing else for them to do or as a signal that the individual was not deemed to be a candidate for promotion to a higher-ranking position.

As noted earlier, the first real impetus for the increased importance of the HRM role came with the passage of the Civil Rights Act in 1964. This law made it illegal for employers to consider factors such as gender, religion, race, skin color, or national origin when making employment-related decisions. The 1964 Act, combined with several subsequent amendments, executive orders, and legal decisions, made the processes of hiring and promoting employees within the organization far more complex. Thus, it quickly became critically important to organizations that those responsible

Personnel departments, specialized organizational units for hiring and administering human resources, became popular during the 1930s and 1940s.

Personnel management, a new type of management function, grew from the recognition that human resources needed to be managed.

The manager who ran the personnel department was called the **personnel manager**.

for hiring and promoting employees fully understood the legal context within which they functioned. For example, ethical and moral issues aside, improper or inappropriate hiring practices left the organization open to lawsuits and other legal sanctions, accompanied by large fines, judgments, and new expenses. (We discuss the 1964 Civil Rights Act and related regulation more fully in the next chapter.)

But, as we noted earlier, the HR manager's role as a compliance officer has grown into the role of strategic partner, and this is the role we stress in this book. As firms continue to recognize the importance of human resources, they must do more than just obey the laws. Firms are increasingly competing to attract and retain the best talent they can and then to develop strategies or tactics that leverage those talented people into a competitive advantage. At the same time, however, HR management is changing in response to new technological innovations, so we must consider how the electronic age has affected the HRM function.

1-2c Human Resource Management in the Electronic Age

One of the most dramatic changes in our lives over the past 10 years or so has been the increasing presence of technology. Bigger, faster computers have allowed firms to compile large amounts of data and keep better track of employees, and new approaches to data analysis allow organizations to monitor patterns of behavior and preferences of those employees. Surveillance technology enables organizations to literally watch what employees do on the job (and in some cases, off the job as well).

Electronic systems for communication and monitoring present new challenges to the legal system and have led to new discussions about ethics and privacy.

The Internet is no longer a luxury, but a necessity, and we now read books, make restaurant reservations, and do research online, in addition to "talking" to our friends.

The widespread use of technology, however, has not affected the basic approach to how we manage human resources, as much as it has affected how we execute various HR functions. For example, in Chapter 5, when discussing methods for conducting job analysis, we note that the O*NET OnLine system, introduced several years ago, now makes it possible for an organizations to obtain the job analysis information they need from an online database. In Chapter 7, when discussing recruiting techniques, we note that organizations have changed the way they advertise jobs to recognize that, today, most potential applicants search for jobs by accessing one of the many job-search websites (e.g., Monster.com). Chapter 7 also discusses the use of online testing for selection and interviews being conducted by SKYPE and other new technology, rather than face to face. In addition, as also noted in Chapter 7, training programs can now be purchased from vendors and provided to employees online, allowing them to take classes and training at their own pace. Information about benefits and the ability to change benefits are also available to employees online, allowing more flexibility in how benefit plans are administered, as discussed in Chapter 9. Finally, in Chapter 10, we note that computer monitoring allows organizations to collect real-time performance data from employees on various jobs, especially those involving telecommunications such as customer service representatives or staff in a call center.

Have these new applications of technology made HRM easier? Clearly, management can now easily deliver information and communicate with employees, but the openness of communication also means that employees can communicate with management, and this presents new challenges to managers. Electronic systems for communication and monitoring also bring up new challenges for the legal system (discussed in Chapter 2) and have led to new discussions about ethics and privacy. Thus, the new technology has made HRM easier in some ways but more complicated in others. Have these new applications of technology made HRM more effective? This question is important, but little data has addressed it. Nonetheless, we will discuss the opportunities and challenges presented by new technology and the Internet throughout the book.

One other way in which technology has affected the HRM function needs to be mentioned. As organizations introduced new technologies for manufacturing, communication, and HRM, they also increased their need for more specialized employees. **Knowledge workers** are employees whose jobs are to acquire and apply knowledge, and they contribute to the organization by the nature of what they know and how well they can apply what they know. Although knowledge workers include more than workers who deal with computer technology (scientists and lawyers, for example, are usually considered knowledge workers), the explosion of technology at work has led to a huge increase in the need for workers who can learn and apply the management of this technology. These employees present special problems for recruitment, retention, and compensation, as well as for motivation; we will discuss these challenges throughout the book.

doglikehorse/Shutterstock.com

1-2d Emerging Human Resource Challenges

Like all managers, HR executives face new challenges on a daily basis. The financial crisis that swept the world in 2008–2009 created havoc in most businesses. Many firms—including several large organizations—went out of business or came close to it. As a result, many people lost their jobs, and it typically fell to the HRM department to determine how and when layoffs would take place, as well as to notify those employees who would be losing their jobs. As the stock market also fell during this time, most pension funds lost value, and some older workers decided that they could no longer afford to retire. These effects too had a profound impact on the HRM departments involved. In addition, uncertainty about the future led to even more stress in the lives of many employees. As we will discuss in Chapter 12, stress can have a significant effect on how people behave at work, and problems arising from this increased stress often become the HRM department's responsibility.

Of course, the economies of the United States and most of the rest of the world have slowly recovered from the recent financial crisis. For example, unemployment in the United States is now down to 5 percent versus 10 percent in 2009. But there are still many people who are unemployed or underemployed, and there are new, perhaps less dramatic, financial crises arising all the

> **Knowledge workers** are employees whose jobs are primarily concerned with the acquisition and application of knowledge. They contribute to an organization through what they know and how they can apply what they know.

time, causing a great deal of economic instability and having a major impact on HRM.

For example, from June to August 2015, the Shanghai stock market lost 40 percent of its value.[25] This plunge caused havoc with stock markets worldwide and shook confidence in the Chinese market. In January 2015, China announced that its economy had slowed causing markets to react again as the Chinese government indicated less demand for commodity goods, which most of the world exports to China. But in February 2015, the Dow Jones had jumped 300 points on news about lower interest rates in Japan. Meanwhile, the worldwide price of oil has been falling steadily[26] and was below $30 a barrel in January 2015, versus over $100 a barrel just a few years earlier. In addition, in 2016, Walmart announced that it was closing 269 stores worldwide,[27] including 154 in the United States and affecting more than 10,000 American workers. Although none of these crises has had the impact of the financial meltdown a few years ago, these mini-crises affect the demand for labor, the supply of labor, and the kinds of businesses that are most likely to thrive—all of which influence the management of human resources at work. As a result of some of these events, the Society for Human Resource Management (SHRM) predicts that hiring will grow but at a slower pace through 2016.

As mentioned earlier, there have been a number of U.S. Supreme Court decisions that have had a profound impact on HRM departments (these are discussed in more detail in the next chapter). For example, in June 2013, in the case of *Fisher v. University of Texas*, the Court decided (by a 7-1 margin) that a lower court had not adequately scrutinized the need for a race preference affirmative action program at the University of Texas and made it clear that any such program will have to be narrowly justified in terms of furthering the educational benefits of diversity.

> Like all managers, HR executives continue to face an array of new challenges on a regular basis ... and in most cases, it is the job of the HRM department to determine how and when layoffs take place.

The case was referred back to a lower court, but in December 2015, the case came back to the Supreme Court, and supporters of affirmative action fear that the Court may issue a broad ruling that may restrict any university (or any other institution) from considering race in any fashion when making selection decisions.

In addition, later in June 2013, the Supreme Court handed down two decisions dealing with gay marriage. One decision dealt a blow to Proposition 8, the California law that banned same-sex marriage. A lower court had overturned "Prop 8," and the case before the Supreme Court was about the legality of that lower court decision. The Court ruled, on technical grounds, that the lower court decision would stand, effectively allowing same-sex marriages in California, which became the thirteenth state to recognize such marriages.

In a more far-reaching decision, the Supreme Court also ruled that the federal Defense of Marriage Act (DOMA) was unconstitutional. The effect here was to say that same-sex couples, married in states that recognize such marriages, were entitled to all federal benefits that went to other married couples. From the perspective of HRM departments, this has potentially huge implications for insurance and pension benefits to same-sex spouses. In addition, many observers suspect that the Obama administration may clarify some of these benefits through a series of executive orders, and other states may be encouraged to recognize same-sex marriages.

Controversy and uncertainty also continue with reference to the Affordable Care Act (commonly referred to as "Obamacare"). Even with President Obama's reelection by a clear majority in 2012, the opposition to this law has not relented. There will be another presidential election in 2016, and several potential Republican candidates have called for a repeal of the law. Thus, the uncertainty of how to deal with the regulations of the Affordable Care Act will continue to haunt HRM departments. In addition, because there will be a presidential election in 2016, there has been a fair amount of rhetoric touching on issues that may be of concern to HRM departments. These range from stated concerns about immigration (which has the potential of reducing the size of applicant pools for some jobs) to proposals to seriously limit some financial activities of bank and brokerage firms (which has the potential to reduce employment opportunities in these industries).

Other, noneconomic developments around the world also have the potential to impact HRM departments. International terrorism is becoming a huge problem everywhere as Al Qaeda has been replaced by ISIS as the major perpetrator of terrorist acts, which has caused greater concern about security issues, as well as raising some concerns about potential discrimination.

Other world events have the potential to influence HRM departments, although some of them are still unfolding. For example, in June 2012, Mohamed Morsi became the fifth president of Egypt after an election that was far more democratic than any earlier Egyptian election. This followed months of protest that resulted in the resignation of Hosni Mubarak, and the relatively free election held promise for stability in Egypt and, perhaps, much of the Middle East. But, a year later, Morsi was overthrown in an Army coup, and the future of democracy in Egypt, and Egypt itself, is now unclear. Unfortunately, these events have destabilized the Middle East, affecting companies doing business there, and increased the likelihood of future terrorist activities.

> **Some evidence suggests that employees in green workspaces tend to be more satisfied and are healthier and more productive.**

Finally, around the world, many thought leaders are advocating the need for businesses to address social issues. This has taken, and continues to take, many forms. Some organizations elect to "go green." This might involve anything from paperless communications to designing buildings with smaller carbon footprints that will blend in with the environment. Other organizations have adopted "corporate social responsibility" as a goal, and some buy only from sustainable sources and make sure that they "do no harm" while conducting business. Still other organizations go beyond this and establish social goals in addition to profit-making goals. Sometimes this is called "conscious capitalism"[28] and refers to treating social outcomes and financial outcomes as complementary, rather than competing. Others refer to this as the "triple bottom line,"[29] where a firm tries to maximize the bottom line, the way people are treated, and the level of environmental responsibility (profits, people, and the planet). In any case, these new levels of concerns over social goals require different types of employees and different ways of treating those employees. As a result, these movements have major implications for HRM departments.

All of these changes mean that the job of the HR manager will continue to evolve. The role of these managers will continue to expand, and they will have to gain expertise in wider and wider sets of skills than ever before.

FIG 1.1 **GOALS OF HUMAN RESOURCE MANAGEMENT**

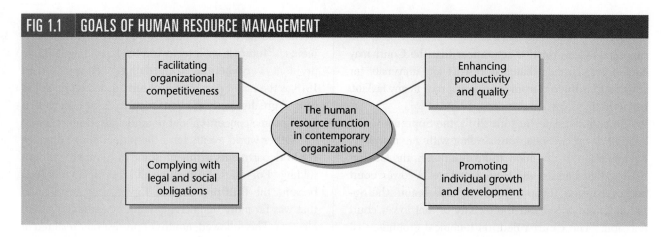

We will discuss the effects of some of these changes throughout the book, but in a few years, we will certainly have to revise our view of the HR manager as the job continues to evolve to deal with other changes in the world.

 ## GOALS OF HUMAN RESOURCE MANAGEMENT

This modern view of HRM has also meant that these departments have taken on increasingly important goals. Understanding the goals of HRM not only helps us put it in proper perspective but also provides a framework for evaluating any activities carried out by this area.[30] Figure 1.1 illustrates the four basic goals of the HRM function in most organizations today.

1-3a Facilitating Organizational Competitiveness

All organizations have a general set of goals and objectives that they try to accomplish. Regardless of the time horizon or the level of specificity involved in these goals, they are generally intended to promote the organization's ability to be competitive in fulfilling its purpose or mission. For example, business organizations such as General Electric, Walmart, Tata Industries, and Singapore Airlines exist primarily to make profits for their owners. Thus, their goals and objectives usually deal with sales or revenue growth, market share, profitability, return on investment, and so forth. Other organizations exist for different purposes and thus have goals other than increased profitability. Educational organizations such as The Ohio State University, Houston Community College, and the St. Louis Independent School District have their unique purposes. The same can be said for health care organizations such as the Mayo Clinic, governmental organizations such as the U.S.

Federal Bureau of Investigation (FBI) and the state of Missouri's revenue department, and charitable organizations such as the United Way.

People often associate competitiveness only with businesses, but each of these other types of organizations also must be managed effectively and compete for the right to continue to work toward fulfillment of its purpose. For example, a state university that misuses its resources and does not provide an adequate education for its students will not be held in high regard. As a result, the university will have difficulty competing for high-quality faculty and students, which are needed to enhance the university's reputation and thus make it more competitive. Similarly, a hospital that does not provide technical support for its doctors or adequate health care for its patients will find it more difficult to compete for the doctors and patients who might use and pay for its services.

Given the central role that HR play in organizational effectiveness, it is clear that organizations must hire and manage those individuals best able to help the firm remain competitive. Recently, some scholars and practitioners have therefore begun referring to *human capital* (rather than human resources). Human capital has been traditionally defined to include the knowledge, information, ideas, and skills of the individual,[31] but it has also been used to refer to the store of knowledge, and so on, available to an organization. This idea has been further expanded, however, to be called *human capital resources*,[32] which are defined as the human resource capacities accessible to a unit that help it gain some competitive advantage. HR analytics, also referred to as

> "Quality is everyone's responsibility"
>
> —W. EDWARDS DEMING

talent analytics, which will be discussed in several later chapters beginning with Chapter 5, makes it possible to take data from a wide variety of sources to help identify those unique resources and suggest ways to manage them better. From this perspective, a major goal of HRM functions in organizations is to translate potential capacities into actual capacities. This relates to attracting, developing, and managing human resources, and we will discuss these issues in more detail in Chapter 14. This also clearly relates to the strategic perspective, discussed further in Chapter 4. However, this perspective also suggests that the HR function move away from "silos" (e.g., compensation or training) to better appreciate how all the functions interact and need to be coordinated.

Facilitating organizational competitiveness must be the most important goal for modern HRM. This is the goal that sets the modern function apart even from the HRM function of 20 years ago. It is also the way in which the HRM function provides the most value to the organization. Of course, the second goal we will discuss also contributes to this goal of competitiveness.

1-3b Enhancing Productivity and Quality

A related but somewhat narrower concern for most organizations in the world today involves the issues, hurdles, and opportunities posed by productivity and quality. **Productivity** is an economic measure of efficiency that summarizes and reflects the value of the outputs created by an individual, organization, industry, or economic system relative to the value of the inputs used to create them.[33] **Quality** is the total set of features and characteristics of a product or service that bears on its ability to satisfy stated or implied needs.[34] In earlier times, many managers saw productivity and quality as being inversely related; the best way to be more productive was to lower quality and therefore costs. Most managers today realize that productivity and quality usually go hand in hand; that is, improving quality almost always increases productivity.

Organizations around the world have come to recognize the importance of productivity and quality for their ability not only to compete but also to survive. Actually improving productivity and quality, however, takes a major and comprehensive approach that relies heavily on HRM. Among other things, an organization that is serious about productivity and quality may need to alter its selection system to hire different kinds of workers. It will definitely need to invest more in training and development to give workers the necessary skills and abilities to create high-quality products and services, and it will need to use new and different types of rewards to

> "Good management is the art of making problems so interesting and their solutions so constructive that everyone wants to get to work and deal with them."
>
> —PAUL HAWKEN

help maintain motivation and effort among its employees. Thus, in most organizations, HRM also has the goal of helping to enhance productivity and quality through different activities and tasks.

1-3c Complying with Legal and Social Obligations

A third fundamental goal of the HRM function today is to ensure that the organization is complying with and meeting its legal and social obligations. As we noted earlier, the passage of the Civil Rights Act in 1964 really made this goal salient. Subsequent court cases made it clear that organizations which violated this law and discriminated in hiring, promotion, compensation, or other HR decisions, could face millions of dollars in fines and penalties. More recently, changes in the Americans with Disabilities Act (discussed in Chapter 2), as well as new legislation regarding equal pay for men and women (also discussed in the next chapter) brought new legal challenges to HRM departments. In most organizations, it is the role of the HRM department, along with the legal department, to ensure that business is conducted within the law so that financial penalties and bad press can be avoided.

Interestingly, the financial crisis of 2008–2009 introduced a new wrinkle into the role of government in the management of human resources. In several cases, the federal government made huge loans to private financial institutions to keep them solvent. But, in return, the government became a major stockholder in some of these firms. As such, the federal government had a lot to say about how employees were treated and paid (especially executives). Those loans have been

Productivity is an economic measure of efficiency that summarizes and reflects the value of the outputs created by an individual, organization, industry, or economic system relative to the value of the inputs used to create them.

Quality is the total set of features and characteristics of a product or service that bears on its ability to satisfy stated or implied needs.

> **Most managers today realize that productivity and quality usually go hand in hand—that is, improving quality almost always increases productivity.**

paid off, and the government is no longer a stockholder in those firms, but the level of intervention in 2008–2009 leaves the door open to possible government intervention in the future. Such intervention would require the U.S. government to take on substantial HRM responsibilities.

As noted earlier, beyond the strict legal parameters of compliance, more and more organizations today are assuming some degree of social obligation to the society in which they operate. This obligation goes beyond the minimum activities required to comply with legal regulations and calls for the organization to serve as a contributing "citizen." Earlier in the chapter, we discussed the ideas of corporate social responsibility, conscious capitalism, and the triple bottom line, which all speak to this enhanced citizenship role. But organizations do not need to go this far to express their desire to be good citizens. Some firms support volunteer activities by employees in the local community either by granting time off or by matching employee contributions to local charities. Others provide pro bono services, and some establish charitable foundations to deal with societal problems. Whatever the choice, it often requires some work by the HRM department that goes above and beyond its usual responsibilities.

1-3d Promoting Individual Growth and Development

Finally, a fourth goal for HRM in most contemporary organizations is promoting the personal growth and development of its employees.[35] As a starting point, this goal usually includes basic job-related training and development activities. But in more and more organizations, it is increasingly going far beyond basic skills training. Some firms, for example, now offer basic educational courses in english, math, and science for their employees. Many organizations also include some provision for career development—helping people understand what career opportunities are available

> A **psychological contract** is the overall set of expectations held by the employee with regard to what he or she will contribute to the organization and that are held by the organization with regard to what it will provide to the individual in return.

to them and how to pursue those opportunities. Formal mentoring programs are also commonly being used to help prepare women and minorities for advancement in the organization.[36]

Individual growth and development may also focus on areas that do not relate directly to job responsibilities. For example, some organizations provide stress-management programs to help their employees better cope with the anxieties and tensions of modern life. Wellness and fitness programs are also becoming more common as organizations seek new and different ways to help their employees remain physically, mentally, and emotionally fit and better prepared to manage their lives and careers. Still another common area for continuing education is personal financial planning, which may even include assistance in writing a will or retirement planning.

Organizations, however, are viewing this goal much more broadly. For many, it means that the firm should do everything it can to ensure that employees are personally fulfilled on the job. This may involve designing jobs that are more challenging and provide more personal satisfaction (see more in Chapter 14), or it may involve providing employees opportunities to be more creative at work (see Chapter 13). In general, more firms are seeing HRM as part of the psychological contract that they have with employees: Provide a personally rewarding work experience in return for the employees' working toward the firm's strategic goals. A **psychological contract** is the overall set of expectancies held by the employee with regard to what he or she will contribute to the organization and held by the organization with regard to what it will provide to the individual in return. These firms know that they will get the most out of employees as sources of competitive advantage when the employees feel that their work experience is meaningful and helps them meet their potential. It is worth noting that this has largely come full circle to the early days of HRM and the human relations movement.

> **Many organizations provide career development guidance—helping people understand the career opportunities available to them and how to pursue them. Formal mentoring programs are also commonly used to prepare women and minorities for advancement.**

1-4 THE SETTING FOR HUMAN RESOURCE MANAGEMENT

Another important factor to consider in the modern view of HRM is the setting in which the HR manager operates. Traditionally, all HR activities resided in a separate department, but this model is becoming rare. Instead, HR activities are carried out by both line and staff managers. Furthermore, we are seeing differences in the way HRM operates in larger versus smaller companies. We will explore some of these different settings.

1-4a Human Resource Management as a Staff versus Line Function

Organizations historically divided their managers into two groups: line management and staff management. HRM was traditionally considered to be a staff function. **Line managers** were those directly responsible for creating goods and services; that is, their contributions to the organization were generally assessed in terms of their actual contributions and costs to the organization's bottom line. The performance of a plant manager whose factory costs $2.5 million per year to support (for salaries, wages, materials, and machinery) and that generates $4 million per year in finished goods can be evaluated based on this information. Operations managers, financial managers, and marketing managers were generally considered to have line functions.

Staff managers, on the other hand, were those responsible for an indirect or support function that would have costs but whose bottom-line contributions were less direct. Legal, accounting, and HR departments were usually thought of as staff functions. Their role was to support line management's efforts to achieve organizational goals and objectives.

Today, however, many organizations have blurred this distinction. New forms of organizational design (e.g., teams and an emphasis on flatter and more decentralized organization) have made it more likely that many HRM activities are actually carried out by line managers. For example, it is fairly common today for line managers to be involved in evaluating the performance of subordinates and making recommendations about salary adjustments (although a staff member might help collect information used to support those decisions). Line managers are intimately involved in most of the interventions designed to enhance performance, and they often make decisions about pay raises and promotions.

Dusit/Shutterstock.com

Responsibilities for carrying out HR functions may reside in a separate HR department, but many smaller organizations do not have such departments and must deliver the required services in different ways.

In some organizations, the HRM function is structured in a completely different way. In these firms, the HRM department is structured around "centers of excellence." In these cases, the HR department is responsible for providing services only in those cases where it can provide higher-quality services than can be purchased on the outside (i.e., through the outsourcing discussed earlier). When they cannot provide higher-quality services, they are often asked to identify and then manage the outside consultants who are brought in to perform the services. In still other cases, the HR department itself functions as a consulting operation within the organization. These departments are expected to be responsive to the needs of the other functional areas, but they have to be able to demonstrate their added value, and they must actually "sell" their services to the line managers. In these arrangements, the HRM department budget is small, and the only way to hire and retain employees in that area is to provide services that other managers are willing to pay for. Thus, the HRM department becomes a self-funding operation, or it could even become somewhat of a profit center.

> **Line managers** are those directly responsible for creating goods and services.
>
> **Staff managers** are those responsible for an indirect or support function that would have costs but whose bottom-line contributions were less direct.

1-4b The Human Resource Department in Smaller versus Larger Organizations

There are also noteworthy differences in the way HRM operations are carried out in larger versus smaller organizations. As noted, responsibilities for carrying out HR functions may reside in a separate HR department, but many smaller organizations do not have such departments and must deliver the required services in different ways.[37] Most small organizations require line managers to handle their basic HR functions. In the case of a franchised operation such as a single McDonald's or Pizza Hut or an individual retail outlet such as an American Eagle or Abercrombie & Fitch clothing store, the store manager generally hires new employees, schedules and tracks working hours for all employees, and disciplines problem employees. The franchiser or home office, in turn, generally suggests or mandates hourly wages, provides performance appraisal forms for local use, and may handle payroll services.

A small independent business is generally operated in the same way, with the owner or general manager handling HR duties. Payroll and other basic administrative activities may be subcontracted to businesses in the local community that specialize in providing such services for other local organizations. Relatively little training is provided in these small organizations, and other HR issues are relatively straightforward. Very small organizations are exempt from many legal regulations (again, we cover this topic more fully in Chapter 2). Thus, a single manager can usually handle the HR function in smaller firms without too much difficulty.

As a firm grows beyond a certain size (usually around 250 employees), however, a separate HR unit becomes a necessity, and the issues involved become much more complicated. No standard approach exists, but a firm of this size might have one full-time manager and a single secretary or assistant to function as its HR department. These individuals handle all of the firm's HR administration.

As the firm continues to grow, however, more assistance is needed to staff the HR department, and so that department also grows. Infact, in the largest organizations, HR functions are themselves likely to have specialized subunits. For example, large firms might have separate departments to handle recruiting and selection, wages and salaries, training and development, and labor relations. Figure 1.2 shows how Shell Oil has organized its HR function.

1-4c The Human Resource Management System

The modern view of HRM is also a systems-oriented view. By its very nature, a strategic perspective requires the coordination of the various HRM activities to ensure that they are consistent with corporate strategy. If those services are provided primarily internally by the HRM department, this coordination can be fairly simple. As those activities move outside the organization, perhaps by contracting with outside vendors, the coordination problem becomes much more complex. But, in any case, a strategic perspective means understanding that a decision made in any one area of HRM will affect what happens in every other area. If an organization needs highly skilled, knowledgeable workers to carry out its strategy, then all staffing activities must be coordinated toward identifying and attracting such employees. After these employees join the firm, however, performance appraisals, compensation, and performance management systems must all be changed to reflect the nature of the new employee.

Thus, although we will often discuss various tasks and functions of HRM from the perspective of discrete, self-contained activities, this is not the case in practice. In fact, these tasks and functions are highly interrelated and do not unfold neatly and systematically. Each of the various tasks

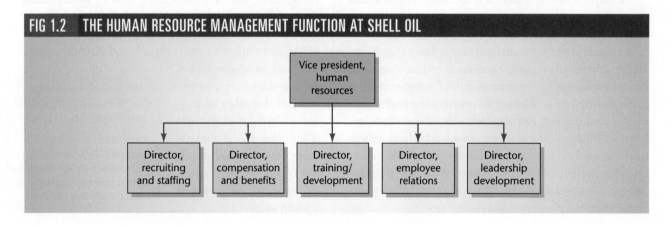

FIG 1.2 THE HUMAN RESOURCE MANAGEMENT FUNCTION AT SHELL OIL

FIG 1.3 A SYSTEMS VIEW OF HUMAN RESOURCE MANAGEMENT

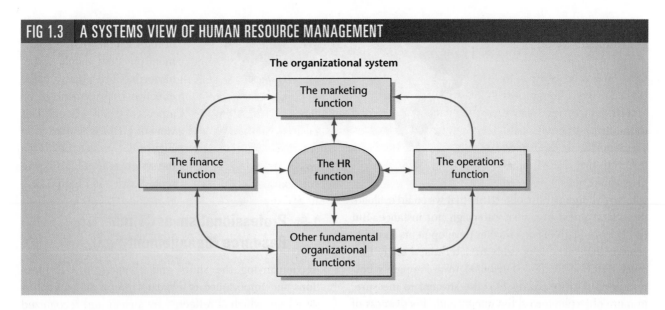

and functions can affect or be affected by any of the other tasks and functions. In addition, most basic HR functions are practiced on an ongoing and continuous basis.

In fact, It is appropriate to think of HRM as a system. A system is an interrelated set of elements functioning as a whole. A **human resource management system**, is an integrated and interrelated approach to managing human resources that fully recognizes the interdependence among the various tasks and functions that must be performed. This viewpoint is illustrated in Figure 1.3. The basic premise of this perspective is that every element of the HRM system must be designed and implemented with full knowledge and understanding of, and integration with, the various other elements. For example, poor recruiting practices will result in a weak pool of applicants. Even if the organization has sophisticated selection techniques available, it will not make much difference without a pool of qualified applicants to choose from. As a result, there will be a greater need for training before a new employee starts work to provide him or her with the necessary skills. Subsequent performance appraisals will also be more difficult because it may take longer for these employees to become proficient in their jobs, affecting how much they are paid.

Figure 1.3 also illustrates another useful systems-based perspective on HRM. Many systems are themselves composed of subsystems—systems within a broader and more general system. By viewing the overall organization as a system, HRM then can be conceptualized as a subsystem within that more general organizational system. As the figure shows, the HRM subsystem both affects and is affected by the other functional subsystems throughout the organization. This perspective can help to reinforce the idea that HRM must be approached from the same strategic vantage point afforded the other areas within the organization. Failure to do so can result in unanticipated consequences, poor coordination, and less-effective performance.

To illustrate, if the organization makes a strategic decision to compete on the basis of high-quality service, then it will almost certainly need to use several mechanisms to do so. For example, the organization will need to recruit and subsequently hire more-qualified new workers and provide more training to both new and current workers. Similarly, if the financial function of an organization dictates that major cost cutting be undertaken, some portion of those costs may come from the HR area. Thus, HR managers may need to reduce the size of the workforce, attempt to renegotiate labor contracts for a lower pay rate, defer payment of some benefits, and so forth.

The increasing globalization of business also reinforces the need to view the HRM function from a systems perspective; that is, HR managers must take a global perspective in managing people. Within the borders of their own country, HR managers must consider the social norms, individual expectations, and so forth that shape worker behaviors. Cross-national assignments for managers are also an important consideration for many businesses today. Thus, the global perspective on HRM includes the need to understand domestic similarities and differences in managing human resources in different countries and the role of international assignments and experiences in the development of HR skills and abilities.

A **human resource management system** is an integrated and interrelated approach to managing human resources that fully recognizes the interdependence among the various tasks and functions that must be performed.

This systems approach has also led to organizations becoming increasingly interested in ways to evaluate the effectiveness of HRM activities relative to the firm's strategic goals. Traditionally, many experts believed that HRM practices could not be assessed with anywhere near the objectivity that we could evaluate the effectiveness of a sales campaign, for instance. But the 1980s and 1990s saw further developments in utility analysis that made it possible to determine exactly how much HRM activities contributed to a company's bottom line.[38] **Utility analysis** is the attempt to measure, in more objective terms, the impact and effectiveness of HRM practices in terms of metrics such as a firm's financial performance. The advent of high-performance work systems resulted in broader metrics for evaluating HRM activities,[39] so it is now possible to develop fairly objective measures of the effects or effectiveness of HRM practices. It remains the role of the HRM department, however, to develop these metrics and apply them to all HRM activities undertaken on behalf of the organization.

Markovka/Shutterstock.com

1-5 HUMAN RESOURCE MANAGERS

Who are today's HR managers? Given the rapid and dynamic changes that have characterized this field, it should come as no surprise that HR managers represent a diverse set of professionals with a variety of backgrounds, experiences, and career objectives. An HR executive today needs to understand different specialized areas such as the legal environment, the process of change management, labor relations, and so forth. In addition, contemporary HR executives must also possess general management abilities that reflect conceptual, diagnostic, and analytical skills. It is important that they fully understand the role and importance of the HR function for their organization.[40] Thus, both a solid educational background and a foundation of experience are necessary prerequisites for success.[41]

Consistent with these changes, it is often more useful to conceptualize HR as a center of expertise within the organization. In other words, everyone in the organization should recognize HR managers as

> **Utility analysis** is the attempt to measure, in more objective terms, the impact and effectiveness of HRM practices in terms of such metrics as a firm's financial performance.

the firm's most critical source of information about employment practices, employee behavior, labor relations, and the effective management of all aspects of people at work. This view of HRM is illustrated in Figure 1.4, which builds on the systems view of HRM presented earlier in Figure 1.3.

1-5a Professionalism and Human Resource Management

Accompanying the shifts and changes in HR functions and importance is a greater emphasis on professionalism, which is reflected by a clear and recognized knowledge base and a generally understood way of doing business.[42] HR managers are no longer regarded as second-class corporate citizens, and more and more organizations are including a stint in HR as a normal step on a person's way to the top. Senior HR executives in large firms earn six-figure salaries and receive the same sorts of perquisites once reserved only for executives of operating units. In fact, the salaries for HR executives continue to rise at an impressive rate. HR departments are also being viewed more and more as cost centers, with the goal of providing clear and measurable financial benefits to the organization.[43]

Many HR managers today belong to the Society for Human Resource Management (SHRM), the field's largest professional HR association. SHRM publishes professional journals that help members stay abreast of the newest developments in the field, sponsor workshops and conferences, and so forth. SHRM has created the HR Certification Institute (HRCI). The HRCI is the recognized symbol of HR certification in much the same way that the accounting profession uses the certified public accountant exam and credential to designate those individuals who have formally achieved basic minimal competencies in prescribed areas.

The HRCI currently offers three core certifications: Professional in Human Resources (PHR), Senior Professional in Human Resources (SPHR), and Global Professional in Human Resources (GPHR). In addition, HRCI also offers a state-specific certification for California. To be eligible to take the PHR, SPHR, or GPHR exam, an HR professional must have a minimum of two years of professional (exempt-level) experience and pass a rigorous examination covering the body of HR knowledge as it relates to the particular certification.

FIG 1.4 HUMAN RESOURCE MANAGEMENT AS A CENTER FOR EXPERTISE

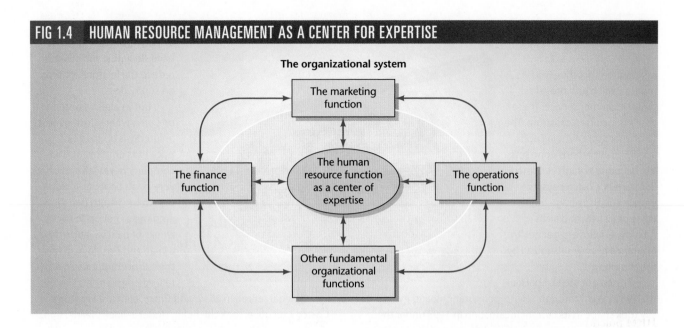

Beginning in 2011, eligibility requirements to take the exam were made more stringent. The HRCI website (www.hrci.org) has detailed information on the changes to the eligibility requirements.

1-5b Careers in Human Resource Management

How does one become an HR manager? Career opportunities in HRM continue to grow and expand and are expected to continue to do so. One obvious way to enter this profession is to get a degree in human resource management (or a related field) and then seek entry-level employment as an HR manager. Alternative job options may be as the HR manager for a small firm or as an HR specialist in a larger organization. Some universities also offer specialized graduate degree programs in human

resource management. For example, a master of science or master of business administration degree with a concentration in human resource management would likely lead to a higher-level position in an organization than would a bachelor's degree alone.

Another route to HRM is through line management. As described earlier, more and more firms are beginning to rotate managers through the HR function as part of their own personal career-development program. Thus, people who go to work in marketing or finance may well have an opportunity at some point to sample central HRM responsibilities. Regardless of the path taken, however, those interested in HRM are likely to have a fascinating, demanding, and rewarding experience as they help their organization compete more effectively through the power of the people who make up every organization in every industry in every marketplace in the world today.

CLOSING CASE
Low Prices, High Pay

Most major retailers follow a simple path—low prices made possible in part by low wages and minimal benefits for their employees. Walmart, for instance, is often criticized for its low wages (an average of $12.14 an hour) and the fact so many of its employees do not get health care benefits (about half, the company reports). Others, like Radio Shack, have run afoul of

the law by requiring their store managers to work extra hours doing nonmanagerial tasks (e.g., emptying trash cans and sweeping floors) for no extra pay.

But in recent years, another set of retailers has started to thrive, often using a different business model—paying employees more and treating them better, under the

(Continued)

(Closing Case – continued)

assumption that they will be more satisfied and provide better customer service. These retailers include Nordstrom, The Container Store, Whole Foods, and REI. But perhaps none sets the bar quite as high as Costco. For starters, Costco pays its employees an average hourly wage of $21.45, and all its full-time employees get health insurance heavily subsidized by the company.

Costco got its start back in the 1950s, went through several permutations, and eventually took shape in its current incarnation in 1993 under the leadership of James Sinegal. Sinegal developed the idea that superior customer service could be a distinctive competitive advantage in the discount retailing industry. Accordingly, he set Costco on a course toward mass-market, low-price, warehouse retailing (like Walmart) but with superior customer service (like Nordstrom). And today, Costco is the largest wholesale club operator in the United States with more than 600 members-only warehouse stores in 42 states. Costco also owns and operates warehouse clubs in Australia, Canada, Japan, Mexico, Puerto Rico, South Korea, Taiwan, and the United Kingdom. In 2015, the firm had more than $100 billion in revenues and employed 186,000 people.

Most merchandise in Costco stores is bulk-packaged and marketed to businesses and families. The firm doesn't carry multiple brands of the same product, instead offering only the one it can sell for the lowest price. Average markup is only 15 percent. Most products are carried to the sales area on pallets in their original boxes. Customers must bring their own shopping bags or else use the boxes products are

Ken Wolter/Shutterstock.com

displayed in. Costco stores have skylights, and sensors reduce the in-store lighting on sunny days.

But as already noted, one area where Costco most assuredly is on the right track is its employees. The company pays well and offers very good benefits. In addition to the health benefit, employees get up to five weeks of paid vacation time a year, and Costco matches their contributions to a 401(k) retirement plan.

Sinegal retired in 2012, and Craig Jelinek, a long-time Costco executive, took the helm. Under Jelinek's leadership, the retailing behemoth seems to have actually improved its trajectory. Its stock price has never been higher, for example, and sales are growing at a red-hot pace. Jelinek has vowed to not alter Costco's HR strategy. He recently commented, for example, "Could Costco make more money if the average wage was two or three dollars lower? The answer is yes. But we're not going to do it."[44]

Case Questions

1. Compare your shopping experiences at retailers such as Costco, Nordstrom, or Whole Foods with experiences you may have had at Walmart, Sears, or Kroger.

2. Under what circumstances might Costco have to start paying its workers less?

3. Costco has a policy of not hiring business school graduates because it wants employees to start at the bottom and work their way up. What are the advantages and disadvantages to this approach?

STUDY TOOLS 1

READY TO STUDY?
In the book, you can:

☐ Rip out the chapter review card at the back of the book for a handy summary of the chapter and key terms.

ONLINE AT CENGAGEBRAIN.COM YOU CAN:

☐ Collect StudyBits while you read and study the chapter.

☐ Quiz yourself on key concepts.

☐ Find videos for further exploration.

☐ Prepare for tests with HR4 Flash Cards as well as those you create.

2 | The Legal Environment

piksel stock/Shutterstock.com

After finishing this chapter go to **PAGE 55** for **STUDY TOOLS**

LEARNING OBJECTIVES

2-1 Describe the legal context of human resource management

2-2 Identify key laws that prohibit discrimination in the workplace, and discuss equal employment opportunity

2-3 Discuss legal issues in compensation, labor relations, and other areas in human resource management

2-4 Discuss the importance to an organization of evaluating its legal compliance

pikselstock/Shutterstock.com

OPENING CASE
Unequal Pay for Equal Work?

It seems logical. Men and women with comparable credentials, comparable experience, and comparable performance ratings performing the same tasks should make comparable pay, right? But while it may seem logical, in reality, men tend to make more than women even when there are no obvious reasons for the discrepancy. For instance, one recent study found an annual pay gap of $20,000 between comparably qualified professional men and women in the millennial generation. U.S. government statistics also report that, in general, women earn around 78 percent of what men earn for performing the same or similar jobs.

This pattern is not new. In fact, Title VII of the Civil Rights Act of 1964 broadly outlawed discrimination on the basis of gender in any aspect of the employment relationship (which obviously includes pay), and the Equal Pay Act of 1963 specifically stipulates that organizations must pay the same wages to men and women who are doing equal work. (Note, however, that both laws allow unequal pay if the basis for the differences are experience, performance, or other job-related factors.)

The question, then, is why, after more than fifty years of legislation outlawing disparate pay and widespread social awareness of this pattern, do such discrepancies still exist today? For years, experts attributed the problem to two things. First, some organizations have continued to practice outright discrimination. Some managers, for instance, either intentionally or unconsciously, may tend to reward men more if they are seen as the family "breadwinner" and reward women less if they are seen as providing only "secondary income." Obviously, this practice is illegal (and unethical) and can be grounds for legal action.

Another long-standing explanation is the so-called "mommy track" phenomenon. The premise here is that even if women and men start out the same, many women step away from their careers for periods ranging from a few months to as long as several years in order to have children. Even among families where both parents have careers, it is still more likely for a woman to make career sacrifices for the sake of family than it is for a man. Simplistically, if a woman suspends her career for, say, three years to start a family and then resumes her career, she has fallen three years behind her male peers in promotion opportunities and salary increases and may never catch up.

Recently, however, experts have come to believe that several other factors also play a role in the income gap. For

> "For women, success and likability are negatively correlated. As a woman gets more successful and powerful, she is less liked. . . . I don't know a senior woman in the workplace who hasn't been told she's too aggressive."
>
> —SHERYL SANDBERG, FACEBOOK COO

one thing, men are often more aggressive when they are first negotiating for a job. As a result, their initial salaries may be higher than their female counterparts. For another, this aggressiveness continues as men tend to ask for larger and more frequent salary adjustments than do their women peers. Hence, men may tend to start at a higher salary and then see their salaries grow faster than is the case for women.

Extending these ideas to a broader context, some evidence suggests that people tend to see aggressiveness and assertiveness positively in men but negatively in women. These positive or negative feelings can then easily translate into "likability." Likability, in turn, can then unconsciously begin to play a role in other elements of the employment relationship, including promotions, opportunities for career-enhancing assignments, and so forth. None of these explanations make it acceptable for a man to earn more than a woman, of course, but they do point to the need for complex and in-depth solutions.

THINK IT OVER

1. Suppose you offer a woman a job for $80,000, and she accepts it. You then offer a similar job to a man for $80,000. He demands $85,000, and you agree to pay him that amount. Should you now go back and adjust the woman's salary? Why or why not?

2. Richard Branson's Virgin Hotels Group has a policy that half of all management positions must be filled by women. Do you agree or disagree with this kind of policy? Why?

Organizations and managers must adhere to the laws and regulations that govern their employment practices. In general, organizations try to follow such laws and regulations for several reasons. One is an inherent commitment in most organizations to ethical and socially responsible behavior. Another is to avoid the direct costs and bad publicity that might result from lawsuits brought against the organization if those laws and regulations are broken. But as the opening case illustrates, these laws and regulations occasionally change or are reinterpreted by the courts. As we will see, failure to follow the law, even because of a well-intentioned misunderstanding, can be enormously costly to an organization.

As we noted in Chapter 1, the proliferation of laws and regulations affecting employment practices in the 1960s and 1970s was a key reason for the emergence of human resource management (HRM) as a vital organizational function. Managing within the complex legal environment that affects human resource (HR) practices requires a full understanding of that legal environment and the ability to ensure that others within the organization also understand it.[1] This chapter is devoted in helping you understand the legal environment of HRM. First, we establish the legal context of HRM and then focus on perhaps the most important area of this legal context—equal employment opportunity—and review several key court cases that have established the law in this area. Subsequent sections introduce legal issues in compensation and labor relations. Various emerging legal issues are also introduced and discussed. Finally, we summarize how many of today's organizations evaluate their legal compliance.

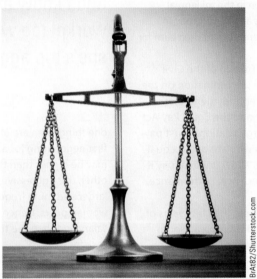

BrAt82/Shutterstock.com

2-1 THE LEGAL CONTEXT OF HUMAN RESOURCE MANAGEMENT

The legal context of HRM is shaped by different forces. The catalyst for modifying or enhancing the legal context may be legislative initiative, social change, or judicial rulings. Governmental bodies pass laws that affect HR practices, for example, and the courts interpret those laws as they apply to specific circumstances and situations. Thus, the regulatory environment itself is quite complex and affects different areas within the HRM process.[2]

2-1a The Regulatory Environment of Human Resource Management

The legal and regulatory environment of HRM in the United States emerges as a result of a three-step process. First is the actual creation of a new regulation. This regulation can come in the form of new laws or statutes passed by national, state, or local government bodies; however, most start at the national level. State and local regulations are more likely to extend or modify national regulations than create new ones. In addition, as we will see later, the president of the United States can also create regulations that apply to specific situations. Finally, court decisions, especially decisions by the Supreme Court of the United States, set precedence and so also play a major role in establishing the regulatory environment.

There are also numerous instances where court decisions have narrowed definitions of some laws and have reduced the ability of plaintiffs to bring charges under other laws. As a result, in some cases, activists have called for new laws to reestablish the original intent of a law that has been altered by various court decisions. For instance, the Civil Rights Act of 1991 was passed to reestablish certain provisions of the original Civil Rights Act passed in 1964 (we discuss these laws later).

The second step in the regulation process is the enforcement of these regulations. Occasionally, the laws themselves provide for enforcement through the creation of special agencies or other forms of regulatory groups. (We will discuss one important agency, the Equal Employment Opportunity Commission, later in the chapter.) In other situations, enforcement might be assigned to an existing agency, such as the Department of Labor. The court system also interprets laws that the government passes and provides another vehicle for enforcement. To be effective, an enforcing agency must have an appropriate degree of power. The ability to levy fines or bring lawsuits against firms that violate the law are among the most powerful tools provided to the various agencies charged with enforcing HR regulations.

The third step in the regulation process is the actual practice and implementation of those regulations in organizations. In other words, organizations and managers must implement and follow the guidelines that the government has passed and that the courts and regulatory agencies attempt to enforce. In many cases, following regulations is a logical and straightforward process. In some cases, however, a regulation may be unintentionally ambiguous or be interpreted by the courts in different ways over time. Regardless of the clarity of the regulation, the actual process of implementing and demonstrating adherence to it may take an extended period of time. Thus, organizations are sometimes put in the difficult position of figuring out how to follow a particular regulation or needing an extended period to fully comply.

"I've been speaking to my attorneys, Larson, and this time we think we've got you fired."

Danny Shanahan/Riley Illustration

2-2 EQUAL EMPLOYMENT OPPORTUNITY

Regulations exist in almost every aspect of the employment relationship. As illustrated in Figure 2.1, equal employment opportunity intended to protect individuals from illegal discrimination is the most fundamental and far-reaching area of the legal regulation of HRM. In one way or another, almost every law and statute governing employment relationships is essentially attempting to ensure equal employment opportunity. Such opportunity, however, has been interpreted to include protection that goes beyond ensuring that a person has a fair chance at being hired for a job for which the person is qualified. As also illustrated in Figure 2.1, this protection extends to preventing illegal discrimination against current employees with regard to performance appraisal, pay, promotion opportunities, and various other dimensions of the employment relationship. Several related legal issues warrant separate discussion as well.

Some managers assume that the legal regulation of HRM is a relatively recent phenomenon. In reality, however, concerns about equal opportunity can be traced back to the Thirteenth Amendment passed in 1865 to abolish slavery, and the Fourteenth Amendment passed in 1868 to provide equal protection for all citizens of the United States. The Reconstruction Civil Rights Acts of 1866 and 1871 further extended protection offered to people under the Thirteenth and Fourteenth Amendments, and together with those amendments, these laws still form the basis for present-day federal court actions that involve the payment of compensatory and punitive damages.[3]

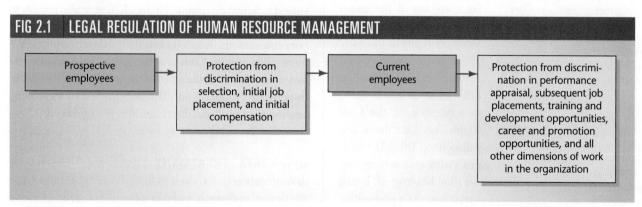

FIG 2.1 | LEGAL REGULATION OF HUMAN RESOURCE MANAGEMENT

Prospective employees → Protection from discrimination in selection, initial job placement, and initial compensation → Current employees → Protection from discrimination in performance appraisal, subsequent job placements, training and development opportunities, career and promotion opportunities, and all other dimensions of work in the organization

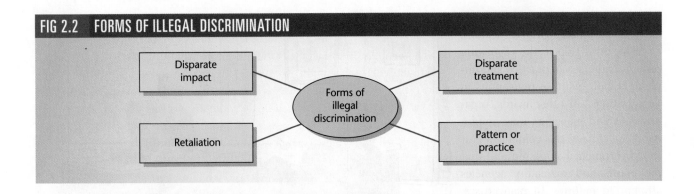

FIG 2.2 FORMS OF ILLEGAL DISCRIMINATION

Disparate impact

Disparate treatment

Forms of illegal discrimination

Retaliation

Pattern or practice

2-2a Discrimination and Equal Employment Opportunity

The basic goal of all equal employment opportunity regulation is to protect people from unfair or inappropriate discrimination in the workplace.[4] However, most laws passed to eliminate discrimination do not explicitly define the term itself. It is also instructive to note that discrimination per se is not illegal. Organizations routinely "discriminate" between effective and ineffective employees in how they are treated. As long as the basis for this discrimination is purely job related, however, such an action is legal and appropriate when based on performance or seniority and when applied objectively and consistently. Problems arise, though, when differentiation between people is not job related; the resulting discrimination is illegal. Various court decisions and basic inferences about the language of various laws suggest that **illegal discrimination** is the result of behaviors or actions by an organization or managers within an organization that cause members of a protected class to be unfairly differentiated from others. (We discuss protected classes later in this chapter.)

Although numerous laws deal with different aspects of equal employment opportunity, the Civil Rights Act of 1964 clearly signaled the beginning of a new legislative era in American business. The act grew out of the growing atmosphere of protest for equal rights in the early 1960s and contains several sections called *titles* that deal with different areas of application of the Civil Rights Act. Our discussion will focus on Title VII, which deals with work settings under the heading of Equal Employment Opportunity.

Illegal discrimination results from behaviors or actions by an organization or managers within an organization that cause members of a protected class to be unfairly differentiated from others.

Disparate treatment discrimination exists when individuals in similar situations are treated differently based on the individual's race, color, religion, sex, national origin, age, or disability status.

The Reconstruction Civil Rights Acts of 1866 and 1871 further extended protection offered to people under the Thirteenth and Fourteenth Amendments.

TITLE VII OF THE CIVIL RIGHTS ACT OF 1964 The most significant single piece of legislation specifically affecting the legal context for HRM to date has been **Title VII of the Civil Rights Act of 1964**. Congress passed the Civil Rights Act, and President Lyndon Johnson signed it into law in 1964 as a way to ensure that equal opportunities would be available to everyone. Title VII of the act states that it is illegal for an employer to fail or refuse to hire any individual, to discharge any individual, or to discriminate in any other way against any individual with respect to any aspect of the employment relationship on the basis of that individual's race, color, religious beliefs, sex, or national origin.

The law applies to all components of the employment relationship, including compensation, employment terms, working conditions, and various other privileges of employment. Title VII applies to all organizations with 15 or more employees working 20 or more weeks a year and that are involved in interstate commerce. In addition, it also applies to state and local governments, employment agencies, and labor organizations. Title VII also created the Equal Employment Opportunity Commission (EEOC) to enforce the various provisions of the law (we discuss the EEOC later in this chapter). Under Title VII, as interpreted by the courts, several types of illegal discrimination are outlawed. These types are discussed next and are illustrated in Figure 2.2.

DISPARATE TREATMENT Disparate treatment discrimination exists when individuals in similar situations are treated differently *and* when the differential treatment is based on the individual's race, color, religion, sex, national origin, age, or disability status. For example, if two people with the same qualifications for the job apply for a promotion, and the organization uses one individual's race or national origin to decide which employee to promote, then the individual not promoted is a victim of disparate treatment discrimination. To prove discrimination in this situation, an individual filing a charge must demonstrate that there was a discriminatory motive; that is, the individual must prove that the organization considered the individual's protected class status when making the decision.

One circumstance in which organizations can legitimately treat members of different groups differently is when a **bona fide occupational qualification (BFOQ)** exists for performing a particular job. This means that some personal characteristic, such as age, legitimately affects a person's ability to perform the job. For example, a producer casting a new play or movie can legally refuse to hire an older person to play a role that is expressly written for a young person. Few legitimate BFOQs exist, however. For example, a local bar cannot hire only young and attractive people as servers based on the argument that their customers prefer young and attractive servers. In fact, customer or client preference can never be the basis of a BFOQ. As we will see, this situation can become quite complex.

Under Title VII of the Civil Rights Act, it is illegal for an employer to fail or refuse to hire or to discharge any individual or to in any other way discriminate against any individual with respect to any aspect of the employment relationship on the basis of that individual's race, color, religious beliefs, sex, or national origin.

To claim a BFOQ exception, the organization must be able to demonstrate that hiring on the basis of the characteristic in question (e.g., age) is a **business necessity**; that is, the organization must be able to prove that the practice is important for the safe and efficient operation of the business. But what if customers at a casino would prefer female card dealers or if customers at an automobile dealership prefer male salespeople? These customers might go elsewhere if these preferences were not satisfied, and those decisions could surely hurt the business involved. In general, neither case would qualify as a BFOQ, but reality is rarely this simple.

The case of *Diaz* v. *Pan American World Airways*, for example, was filed after Celio Diaz (a male) applied for the job of flight attendant with Pan American Airlines (Pan Am).[5] He was rejected because Pan Am had a policy of hiring only women for this position (as did many airlines in 1971). Diaz filed suit for discrimination, but Pan Am argued that gender was a BFOQ for the job of flight attendant. This argument was based on Pan Am's own experience with male and female flight attendants and on the fact that Pan Am's customers over whelmingly preferred to be served by female attendants. A lower court accepted the airlines' argument that "an airline cabin represents a unique [and stressful] environment in which an air carrier is required to take account of the special psychological needs of its passengers. Those needs are better attended to by females."[6] The appeals court reversed that decision, however, citing that Pan Am's data on the relative effectiveness of male and female flight attendants was not compelling and that customer preference was not relevant because no evidence existed that hiring male flight attendants would substantially affect the business performance of the airlines. Although this may seem clear, consider that Asian restaurants are allowed to hire only Asian waiters because they add to the authenticity of the dining experience, and establishments such as Hooters are allowed to hire only attractive female waitresses because they are really selling the experience rather than the food; thus, these are considered business necessities.

A **bona fide occupational qualification (BFOQ)** states that a condition such as race, sex, or other personal characteristic legitimately affects a person's ability to perform the job and therefore can be used as a legal requirement for selection.

A **business necessity** is a practice that is important for the safe and efficient operation of the business.

DISPARATE IMPACT A second form of discrimination is **disparate impact** discrimination that occurs when an apparently neutral employment practice disproportionately excludes a protected group from employment opportunities. This argument is the most common for charges of discrimination brought under the Civil Rights Act. Examples include a rule that, in order to maintain cleanliness in a food service organization, no employee can have hair covering his or her ears (which will affect female applicants more than male applicants), or a rule that, in order to reach items on a high shelf, all employees must be at least 6 feet tall (which will also affect female applicants more severely, as well as applicants from certain ethnic groups). Note that even if an organization instituted these rules with no intention of discriminating against anyone, the intent to discriminate is irrelevant, and these would both be cases of disparate impact. Furthermore, any real concerns could be dealt with by rules that employees wear hairnets or use stepladders, respectively.

One of the first instances in which disparate impact was defined involved a landmark legal case, *Griggs* v. *Duke Power*. Following passage of Title VII, Duke Power initiated a new selection system that required new employees to have either a high school education or a minimum cutoff score on two specific personality tests. Griggs, a black male, filed a lawsuit against Duke Power after he was denied employment based on these criteria. His argument was that neither criterion was a necessary qualification for performing the work he was seeking. After his attorneys demonstrated that those criteria disproportionately affected blacks and that the company had no documentation to support the validity of the criteria, the courts ruled that the firm had to change its selection criteria on the basis of disparate impact.[7]

The important criterion in this situation is that the consequences of the employment practice are discriminatory, and thus the practice in question has disparate (sometimes referred to as *adverse*) impact. In fact, if a plaintiff can establish what is called a *prima facie case* of discrimination, the company is considered to be at fault unless it can demonstrate another legal basis for the decision.[8] This finding doesn't mean that the company automatically loses the case, but it does mean that the burden of proof rests with the company to defend itself rather than with the plaintiff trying to prove discrimination. Therefore, it is extremely important to understand how one establishes a prima facie case.

Several avenues can be used to establish a prima facie case, but the most common approach relies on the so-called **four-fifths rule**. Specifically, the courts have ruled that disparate impact exists if a selection criterion (e.g., a test score) results in a selection rate for a protected class that is less than four-fifths (80 percent) of that for the majority group. For example, assume that an organization is considering 100 white applicants and 100 Hispanic applicants for the same job. If an employment test used to select among these applicants results in 60 white applicants (60 percent) being hired, but only 30 Hispanic applicants (30 percent) being hired, then disparate impact is likely to be ruled because Hispanics are being hired at a rate that is less than four-fifths that of whites. At this point, the organization using the test would be required to prove that its differential selection rate of whites versus Hispanics could be justified (the basis for this justification will be explained below).

But demonstrating that an organization's policies have violated the four-fifths rule can sometimes be complicated. In the case of *Ward's Cove Packing* v. *Antonio*, the defendant, a salmon cannery in Alaska, had two distinct types of jobs for which people were hired.[9] Cannery jobs were seen as skilled (administrative and engineering), whereas noncannery jobs were viewed as unskilled. The plaintiff's attorneys argued that because the noncannery jobs were predominantly filled by Filipino and Native Alaskans, and the cannery

Disparate impact discrimination occurs when an apparently neutral employment practice disproportionately excludes a protected group from employment opportunities.

The **four-fifths rule** suggests that disparate impact exists if a selection criterion (e.g., a test score) results in a selection rate for a protected class that is less than four-fifths (80 percent) of that for the majority group.

jobs were held predominantly by whites, the company had violated the four-fifths rule and had therefore established a prima facie case for disparate impact. The defendant did not dispute the statistics but argued that the policies in place did not lead to apparent disparate impact and therefore there was no prima facie case. The Supreme Court agreed with the defendant, ruling that the statistical proof alone was not sufficient for establishing a prima facie case. Therefore, the burden of proof did not shift to the defendant but rested with the employee involved. Ward's Cove won the case. In addition to illustrating the problems with establishing a violation of the four-fifths rule, the Ward's Cove case was also widely seen as dealing a major blow to the enforcement of the Civil Rights Act of 1964—a topic to which we will return shortly.

A plaintiff might be able to demonstrate disparate impact by relying on **geographical comparisons**. These involve comparing the characteristics of the potential pool of qualified applicants for a job (focusing on characteristics such as race, ethnicity, and gender) with those same characteristics of current employees in the job. Thus, if the potential pool of qualified applicants in the labor market for the job of bank teller is 50 percent African American, then a bank hiring from that market should have approximately 50 percent African American tellers. Failure to achieve this degree of representation is considered a basis for a prima

facie case of disparate impact discrimination. This comparison requires a clear understanding of the labor market from which the organization typically recruits employees for this job because different jobs within the same organization might draw on different relevant labor markets with different characteristics. For instance, a university might rely on a national labor market for new faculty members, a regional labor market for professional staff employees, and a local labor market for custodial and food-service employees. It is also important to note that the definition of the "potential pool of qualified applicants" draws heavily on census data for the area.

Finally, the **McDonnell-Douglas test**, named for a Supreme Court ruling in *McDonnell-Douglas* v. *Green*, is another basis for establishing a prima facie case.[10] Four steps are part of the McDonnell-Douglas test:

1. The applicant is a member of a protected class (see below).

2. The applicant was qualified for the job for which he or she applied.

3. The individual was turned down for the job.

4. The company continued to seek other applicants with the same qualifications.

PATTERN OR PRACTICE DISCRIMINATION The third kind of discrimination that can be identified is **pattern or practice discrimination**. This form of disparate treatment occurs on a classwide or systemic basis. Although an individual can bring charges of practice discrimination, the question is whether the organization engages in a pattern or practice of discrimination against all members of a protected class instead of against one particular member. Title VII of the 1964 Civil Rights Act gives the attorney general of the United States express powers to bring lawsuits against organizations thought to be guilty of pattern or practice discrimination. Specifically, Section 707 of Title VII states that such a lawsuit can be brought if there is reasonable cause to believe that an employer is engaging in pattern or practice discrimination.

Gts/Shutterstock.com

Demonstrating that an organization's policies have violated the four-fifths rule can sometimes be complicated as was the case with *Ward's Cove Packing v. Antonio.*

Geographical comparisons involve comparing the characteristics of the potential pool of qualified applicants for a job (focusing on characteristics such as race, ethnicity, and gender) with those same characteristics of the present employees in the job.

The McDonnell-Douglas test is used as the basis for establishing a prima facie case of disparate impact discrimination.

Pattern or practice discrimination is similar to disparate treatment but occurs on a classwide basis.

A good example of pattern or practice discrimination allegedly occurred several years ago at Shoney's, a popular family-oriented restaurant chain with operations and locations throughout the South. A former assistant manager at the firm alleged that she was told by her supervisor to use a pencil to color in the "o" in the Shoney's logo printed on its employment application blanks for all African American applicants. The presumed intent of this coding scheme was to eliminate all those applicants from further consideration.[11]

To demonstrate pattern or practice discrimination, the plaintiff must prove that the organization intended to discriminate against a particular class of individuals. A critical issue in practice or pattern discrimination lawsuits is the definition of a statistical comparison group or a definition of the relevant labor market. A labor market consists of workers who have the skills needed to perform the work and who are within a reasonable commuting distance from the organization. The definition of labor market is a major issue in resolving lawsuits brought under pattern or practice discrimination claims.

RETALIATION A final form of discrimination that has become more prevalent in recent years is retaliation. Retaliation refers to an organization taking some action against an employee who has opposed an illegal employment practice or has filed suit against the company for illegal discrimination. Retaliation is expressly forbidden by Title VII of the Civil Rights Act, but several Supreme Court decisions have made it much less clear exactly how this protection might work.

In 2011, the Supreme Court, noting the sharp rise in claims filed with the EEOC by employees who allege retaliation for filing discrimination charges, handed down an important ruling that expanded protection against this type of retaliation. In *Thompson* v. *North American Stainless Steel*, the Court ruled unanimously that an employee could collect monetary awards from an employer for retaliating against her for her sexual harassment claim, broadening protection under the 1964 Civil Rights Act. What made the case more interesting is that the company didn't fire the woman who filed the charges but did fire her husband, and the ruling stipulated that he was covered against retaliation as well.

However, two years later, the Court handed down another ruling (this time 5-4) that seemed to make it more difficult for someone to bring suit over retaliation. In *Texas Southwestern Medical Center* v. *Nassar*, the Court ruled that in order for an employee to successfully sue for discrimination, the employee had to prove that "but-for" that retaliation, the person would have suffered no penalty. In other words, even if retaliation were part of the motivation for an action, the case would be successful only if retaliation were the only (or primary) motivation for the action.

This most recent decision seems to place such a serious burden of proof requirement upon the person claiming retaliation that few would be able to pursue such a complaint. It will be interesting to see if Congress reacts by passing additional legislation, but this seems unlikely given the gridlock in Congress. Thus, worker protection against retaliation seems to be compromised.

EMPLOYER DEFENSE Our discussion so far has focused on the types of illegal discrimination and the ways in which a plaintiff can establish a case of discrimination. As noted earlier, however, once a prima facie case has been established, the burden of proof shifts to the defendant; that is, the defendant has to provide evidence for nondiscriminatory bases for the decisions made. Therefore, it is critical to understand that just because a prima facie case has been established, the defendant (typically the company) will not necessarily be found liable. The company can defend itself by providing evidence that the selection decision (or employment decision of any type) was based on criteria that are job related. In other words, the defendant (usually an organization) must be able to prove that decisions were made so that the persons most likely to be selected (or promoted or given a pay raise) are those who are most likely to perform best on the job (or who have already performed best on the job). This situation is also referred to as *validation* of the practice in question. In Chapter 7, we will discuss how one validates a selection technique and therefore establishes that it is job related. Many of these issues are also based on the court ruling in the *Albemarle Paper Company* case, which is also discussed in Chapter 5.

2-2b Protected Classes in the Workforce

Now we turn our attention to what the term *protected classes* means in practice. Many of the discriminatory practices described earlier stemmed from stereotypes, beliefs, or prejudice about classes of individuals. For example, common stereotypes at one time were that African American employees were less dependable than white employees, that disabled individuals could not be productive employees, and that certain jobs were inappropriate for women or people who were overweight. Relying on these stereotypes, organizations routinely discriminated against African Americans, disabled people, women, and overweight individuals. Although such blatant cases of discrimination are now rare, it is clear that stereotypes persevere and discrimination continues, even if it is more subtle.

To combat this past discrimination, various laws have been passed to protect different classes or categories of individuals. Although it varies from law to law, a **protected class** consists of all individuals who share one or more common characteristics as indicated by that law. The most common characteristics used to define protected classes include race, color, religion, gender, age, national origin, disability status, and status as a military veteran. As we will see, some laws pertain to several protected classes, while others pertain to a single protected class. Class definition generally involves first specifying the basis of distinction and then specifying which degree or category of that distinction is protected. For example, a law may prohibit discrimination on the basis of gender—a basis of distinction—and then define the protected class as females. This distinction does not mean that an organization can discriminate against men, of course, and in some cases, men could even be considered members of a protected class. But the law was almost certainly passed on the assumption that most gender-based discrimination has been directed against women, and thus it is women who need to be protected in the future.

As the world becomes more complex, and different issues become more salient, questions of protected classes based on religion have become more important. A good case in point was the Supreme Court decision in *EEOC v. Abercrombie & Fitch*.[12] The company failed to hire Samantha Elauf, a 17-year-old Muslim girl, for a sales position because she wore a hijab, or head scarf, in observance of her deeply held religious beliefs. The store argued this violated its "look policy," which bans any head coverings. The company also argued that the plaintiff had not informed them of the reason for her wearing the "scarf." But the company *had* made other exceptions, and

the court ruled that a company's corporate image does not relieve a company's obligation to provide reasonable religious accommodations, even if they were not aware of the need for an accommodation, as long as the plaintiff could show that the accommodation was the reason for the failure to be hired.

Finally, an Executive Order passed in late 2015 and a New York City law passed in June 2015 have led discussions about discrimination against a group not usually considered as "protected." A proposed Federal Fair Chance Act, also referred to as the "Ban the Box" bill, prohibits employers from inquiring about a candidate's criminal records until they have been offered a conditional offer of employment. There are exceptions to the NYC law, including police and fire jobs, as well as jobs requiring certain types of licenses. Under this legislation, after a conditional offer of employment has been made, employers can conduct background checks but can only deny employment on the basis of criminal records in narrow cases (i.e., where it is proven to be job related). These laws exist in 17 states and 100 cities. The "box" in question is the box for checking if you have ever been convicted of a crime. In early 2016, there seems to be bipartisan support, and a federal law is likely to be enacted before the end of the year.

At the same time, an important issue is to what extent an organization can give preferential treatment to members of a protected class. Although exceptions can be made in certain circumstances, by and large, the intent of most equal employment opportunity legislation is to provide fair and equitable treatment for everyone, as opposed to stipulating preferential treatment for members of a protected class.[13] This interpretation becomes a bit complicated, though, and can result in charges of reverse discrimination, our next topic.

A **protected class** consists of all individuals who share one or more common characteristics as indicated by that law.

2-2c Affirmative Action and Reverse Discrimination

When charges of illegal discrimination have been supported, courts sometimes impose remedies that try to reverse the effects of past discrimination. Most frequently, these remedies have taken the form of some type of affirmative action. (As we will see below, some organizations are also required to file affirmative action plans even without charges of illegal discrimination.) **Affirmative action** refers to positive steps taken by an organization to seek qualified employees from underrepresented groups in the workforce. When affirmative action is part of a remedy in a discrimination case, the plan takes on additional urgency, and the steps are somewhat clearer. Three elements make up any affirmative action program.

The first element is called the **utilization analysis** and is a comparison of the racial, sex, and ethnic composition of the employer's workforce compared to that of the available labor supply. For each group of jobs, the organization needs to identify the percentage of its workforce with that characteristic (i.e., African American, female, etc.) and identify the percentage of workers in the relevant labor market with that characteristic. If the percentage in the employer's workforce is considerably less than the percentage in the external labor supply, then that minority group is characterized as being underutilized. Much of this analysis takes place as part of the discrimination case, if one is involved, and the affected groups are defined by the specifics of the case.

The second part of an affirmative action plan is the development of goals and timetables for achieving balance in the workforce concerning those characteristics, especially where underutilization exists. Goals and timetables generally specify the percentage of protected classes of employees that the organization seeks to have in each group and the targeted date by which that percentage should be attained; however, these are much more flexible than quotas, which are illegal (except in rare cases when these have been imposed by courts). The idea underlying goals and timetables is that if no discriminatory hiring practices exist, then underutilization should be eliminated over time.

The third part of the affirmative action program is the development of a list of action steps. These steps specify what the organization will do to work toward attaining its goals to reduce underutilization. Common action steps include increased communication of job openings to underrepresented groups, recruiting at schools that predominantly cater to a particular protected class, participating in programs designed to improve employment opportunities for underemployed groups, and taking all steps to remove inappropriate barriers to employment. In some cases, this third part might also include preferential hiring; that is, given two equally qualified applicants for a job, the organization would be required to hire the member of the underrepresented group in every case until its goals and targets are met.

In the late 1990s, the courts began to impose many more restrictions on what was acceptable (or required) in the way of preferential hiring and quotas. We will discuss representative relevant court decisions shortly, but the impetus for some of these decisions was the concern that affirmative action *could* in some cases appear to be a form of *reverse discrimination*, or a practice that has a disparate impact on members of *nonprotected* classes. Thus, charges of reverse discrimination typically stem from the belief by white males that they have suffered because of preferential treatment given to other groups.

The two most famous court cases in this area help to illustrate how complicated this issue can be. In one case, Allan Bakke, a white male, applied to medical school at the University of California Davis but was denied admission.[14] At issue was the fact that the university had set aside 16 of its 100 seats for an incoming class for minority students to promote diversity and affirmative action at the school. Bakke's attorneys argued that he was not necessarily more qualified than those admitted for the 84 "white" openings, but that he was more qualified than those admitted to the 16 openings set aside for minorities. Because the school had imposed this system on its own (to correct past injustice), the Court ruled that this "set-aside" program constituted reverse discrimination because it clearly favored one race over another and ruled in favor of Bakke.

In another case, Brian Weber, also a white male, applied for a temporary training program that would lead to a higher-paying skilled job at a Kaiser Aluminum facility.[15] He was not admitted into the program; he then sued because he claimed that African American applicants with less seniority were admitted into the program strictly due to their race. In fact, Kaiser and United Steelworkers had agreed to a contract whereby 50 percent of the openings for these programs would be reserved for African Americans in an attempt to address the fact that African

Affirmative action represents a set of steps taken by an organization to actively seek qualified applicants from groups underrepresented in the workforce.

A **utilization analysis** is a comparison of the racial, sex, and ethnic composition of the employer's workforce compared to that of the available labor supply.

Americans had been systematically excluded from these programs in the past. The Supreme Court found in favor of Kaiser and the union, acknowledging that a collective-bargaining agreement such as this one was binding and was a reasonable means of addressing past discrimination.

Given these two legal decisions, one might question the current status of reverse-discrimination cases. In fact, it is by no means clear. Within the space of a few years, the Supreme Court:

- ruled against an organization giving preferential treatment to minority workers during a layoff;[16]

- ruled in support of temporary preferential hiring and promotion practices as part of a settlement of a lawsuit;[17]

- ruled in support of the establishment of quotas as a remedy for past discrimination;[18] and

- ruled that any form of affirmative action is inherently discriminatory and could be used only as a temporary measure.[19]

It would appear that the future of affirmative action is unclear, suggesting that the courts will be leaning more toward interpretations in line with reverse discrimination in the future.

Indeed, the concept of affirmative action is increasingly being called into question. In 1998, California voters ratified a proposition called the California Civil Rights Initiative, which outlawed any preferential treatment on the basis of race, gender, color, ethnicity, or national origin for all public employment, education, and contracting activities. However, in 2003, the Supreme Court ruled that the University of Michigan could use diversity as one of several factors in making its admissions decisions, although it disallowed explicit rules that awarded extra points to underrepresented groups in the student population.

In *Ricci* v. *Stefano, 2009,* the Supreme Court ruled that the city of New Haven, Connecticut, violated the rights of a group of white firefighters when it decided to discard the results of a recent promotion exam that was shown to have disparate impact. The city developed and validated this test and administered it to group of candidates. Based on the test scores and corresponding job openings, no non-white firefighters would be promoted. This caused the city to throw out the results of the test and to order a new exam. The white firefighters subsequently sued the city for reverse discrimination. The city of New Haven argued that the test did not really measure what was needed to be successful as a lieutenant, but the Supreme Court, in a 5–4 decision, ruled that if the

In *Ricci* v. *Stefano*, 2009, the Supreme Court ruled that the city of New Haven, Connecticut, violated the rights of a group of white firefighters when it decided to discard the results of a recent promotion exam that was shown to have disparate impact.

city did not believe the test measured the right thing, it should not have been used and that the decision to throw out the results was simply a reaction to "racial statistics."

But there is a more interesting history involving various attempts by the University of Texas to include some type of affirmative action plan in the admission process. For many years, the University made admission decisions on the basis of a score based on standardized tests scores and high school academic performance, as well as applicant race. This plan was ruled unconstitutional in 1996, in *Hopwood* v. *Texas*,[20] because the Supreme Court ruled it violated equal protection laws and did not further any compelling government interests.

To comply with the *Hopwood* decision, the University then introduced a plan where, instead of considering race, the University considered a holistic measure of a candidate's potential contribution to the University, which would be used in conjunction with their academic achievements as above. This new "Personal Achievement Index" considered such factors as leadership, work experience, and community service, but also considered growing up in a single-parent home, speaking a language other than English at home, and the general socioeconomic conditions in the candidate's family. The University also expanded its outreach efforts to attract minority applicants. In addition, during this time, Texas passed a law stating that any student graduating in the top 10 percent of his or her high school class was automatically admitted to any public state college or University.

After the Supreme Court decision on the University of Michigan plan mentioned earlier,[21] the University adopted a new plan where race was again explicitly made part of the process as a "plus factor" in an overall admissions policy that considered an applicant's potential contribution to the University. This plan was implemented in 2004. However, the University of Michigan decision also included many restrictions on how the policy could be implemented, ultimately giving a great deal of weight to the University and its mission, but requiring the school to provide clear evidence of how their plan furthered government interests.

Ms. Fisher applied to the University of Texas in 2008, was denied admission, and sued for discrimination on account of her race (white). An appeals court upheld the University's plan, but, in 2013, the Supreme Court ruled that the University of Texas had not provided sufficient evidence that its plan furthered any government interests and so was not allowable, and the case was remanded back to a lower court for further consideration.[22] The lower court again sided with the University of Texas, and the case was sent back to the Supreme Court in late 2015.[23] All indications were that the Court was sharply divided on this issue, but, with the death of Justice Scalia in February of 2016, things changed. Justice Kagan recused herself because of earlier involvement in the case, and the Supreme Court then handed down a 4-3 decision upholding the admission plan from the University of Texas, which considers race as one factor in helping to increase diversity. The decision keeps limited affirmative action in university admissions alive, for the present.

2-2d Sexual Harassment at Work

One final area of coverage for the Civil Rights Act that is critical to the human resource manager is sexual harassment. This area is particularly important in this context because much of the litigation and the organization's liability in these cases depend on the initial responses to charges of sexual harassment, and these responses are typically the responsibility of someone in HR. Sexual harassment is defined by the EEOC as unwelcome sexual advances in the work environment. If the conduct is indeed unwelcome and occurs with sufficient frequency to create an abusive work environment, the employer is responsible for changing the environment by warning, reprimanding, or perhaps firing the harasser.[24]

The courts have ruled that there are two types of sexual harassment and have defined both types. One type of sexual harassment is **quid pro quo harassment**. In this case, the harasser offers to exchange something of value for sexual favors. For example, a male supervisor might tell or imply to a female subordinate that he will recommend her for promotion or provide her with a salary increase, but only if she sleeps with him. Although this type of situation definitely occurs, organizations generally have no problem in understanding that it is illegal and in knowing how to respond.

But a more subtle (and probably more common) type of sexual harassment is the creation of a **hostile work environment**, and this situation is not always so easy to define. For example, a group of male employees who continually make off-color jokes and lewd comments and perhaps decorate the work environment with inappropriate photographs may create a hostile work environment for a female colleague to the point where she is uncomfortable working in that job setting. Most experts would agree that this situation constitutes sexual harassment. But the situation becomes more complicated if an employee walks by a colleague's workstation and sees a suggestive website or photo on their computer screen.

In *Meritor Savings Bank v. Vinson*, the Supreme Court noted that a hostile work environment constitutes sexual harassment, even if the employee did not suffer any economic penalties or was not threatened with any such penalties.[25] In *Harris v. Forklift Systems*, the Court ruled that the plaintiff did not have to suffer substantial mental distress to receive a jury settlement.[26] Hence, it is critical that organizations monitor the situation and be alert for these instances because, as noted, it is the organization's responsibility for dealing with this sort of problem.[27]

> "But the issue of sexual harassment is not the end of it. There are other issues: political issues, gender issues, etc., that people need to be educated about."
>
> —ANITA HILL, AMERICAN ATTORNEY AND ACADEMIC

Quid pro quo harassment is sexual harassment in which the harasser offers to exchange something of value for sexual favors.

A **hostile work environment** is one that produces sexual harassment because of a climate or culture that is punitive toward people of a different gender.

It is also worth noting that the courts have indicated that a firm has differential liability for sexual harassment depending on the relationship between the parties involved. Basically, the firm's level of liability increases significantly if the harassing employee is a supervisor; if the harassing employee is a coworker, the employer is only liable if it was negligent in controlling working conditions. In 2012, in the case of *Vance v. Ball State University*, however, the Supreme Court (in a split decision) ruled that an employee would be considered as a supervisor only if he or she is empowered by the employer to take tangible employment actions against the victim. This decision has been widely viewed as limiting a firm's liability for sexual harassment and potentially dampening employee willingness to file such charges.

Therefore, the HR manager must play a major role in investigating any hint of sexual harassment in the organization. The manager cannot simply wait for an employee to complain. Although the Court had ruled in the case of *Scott* v. *Sears Roebuck*[28] that the employer was not liable for the sexual harassment because the plaintiff did not complain to supervisors, the ruling in the *Meritor* case makes it much more difficult for the organization to avoid liability by claiming ignorance (although this liability is not automatic). This responsibility is further complicated by the fact that although most sexual harassment cases involve men harassing women, there are, of course, many other situations of sexual harassment that can be identified. Females can harass men, and in the case of *Oncale* v. *Sundowner,* the Supreme Court ruled unanimously that a male oil rigger who claimed to be harassed by his coworkers and supervisor on an offshore oil rig was indeed the victim of sexual harassment.[29] Several recent cases involving same-sex harassment have focused new attention on this form of sexual harassment.[30] Regardless of the pattern, however, the same rules apply: sexual harassment is illegal, and it is the organization's responsibility to control it.

An interesting issue related to sexual harassment suits came to light in a case at Northwestern University in 2014. An undergraduate student (Student A) brought charges against a faculty member, alleging that the (male) Professor B, sexually assaulted the (female) student during an evening that started out at an art exhibit. The University found the faculty member guilty of violating its sexual harassment policy, but the faculty member was not fired. Instead he had to forgo a pay raise and avoid social contacts with students. The student involved then brought suit against the University arguing that it had not done enough to deal with harassment. During this process, another faculty member (Professor C) reported to the university that she had been informed about another case of harassment by a different student (Student D). As a result, Professor B sued both Student A and Professor C for defamation. The interesting angle here is that Professor C is indemnified by the university because she is an employee, but Student A is not, so she will be liable if the defamation charges are substantiated. Although we do not know the final outcome, the case raises interesting issues about the willingness of a student (or other low power individual) to file sexual harassment charges if he or she might then be open to defamation charges. In this regard, it is also interesting to note that the University of Notre Dame has been under recent investigation by the Department of Education for allegations that sexual harassment victims were tormented by the University's complicated system for handling such cases.[31]

Of course, issues regarding the "price" that can be paid when a person files such charges have been made even more salient in the case of comedian Bill Cosby. Mr. Cosby has responded to charges of sexual assault (not harassment) by suing several of his accusers for defamation of character and libel. Although the Cosby case is not about harassment, it only reinforces questions about the real-life consequences facing a person who files charges for sexual harassment.

2-2e Other Equal Employment Opportunity Legislation

In addition to the Civil Rights Act of 1964, a large body of supporting legal regulations has also been created in an effort to provide equal employment opportunity for various protected classes of individuals. Although the 1964 act is probably the best known and most influential piece of legislation in this area, a new civil rights act was passed in 1991, and numerous other laws deal with different aspects of equal employment or are concerned with specific areas of work; these are discussed in this section. Some of them apply only to federal contractors, and these are discussed separately, whereas others apply more widely. We will discuss each one briefly here and again in the chapters where they are most relevant.

THE LILLY LEDBETTER FAIR PAY ACT OF 2009 The **Equal Pay Act** clearly outlaws differential pay for male and female employees doing essentially the same job. But, in 2007, the U.S. Supreme Court ruled against Lilly Ledbetter, overturning a lower court finding in her favor. Ms. Ledbetter was a production supervisor at Goodyear for many years, but she came to realize that she was being

defines equality in terms of skill, responsibility, effort, and working conditions. Thus, an organization cannot pay a man more than it pays a woman for the same job on the grounds that, say, the male employee needs the money more because his wife is sick and is incurring large medical bills. Similarly, organizations cannot circumvent the law by using different job titles for essentially the same work: if the work is essentially the same, then the pay should be the same as well. The law does allow for pay differences when there are legitimate, job-related reasons for pay differences, such as difference in seniority or merit.[33]

paid 40 percent less than the lowest paid male supervisor. She sued in 1998, and, when her case finally came up for trial, a jury found that she had suffered from sex discrimination in her compensation and awarded her $3 million in back pay (this was reduced to $300,000 in accordance to a damages cap). But Goodyear appealed to the Supreme Court, where the company acknowledged that Ms. Ledbetter had been discriminated against *but* that the discrimination took place more than 180 days before the charges were filed. Thus, the case could not be raised because there was a 180-day limitation as part of the law. Goodyear furthermore argued that the 180-day limitation began when the discriminatory decision was actually made, rather than beginning when the employee received a paycheck. The Supreme Court agreed with Goodyear and took away Ms. Ledbetter's award. In a dissenting opinion, Judge Ginsburg pointed out that, after this decision, any firm, even admitting it was guilty of discrimination, would be free from suit if the discrimination occurred more than six months earlier. The new law corrected this and states that the clock for limitation begins with each paycheck—making it easier for employees to bring charges of discrimination. The new law also applies the same timetable to cases involving age discrimination or discrimination based on disability.[32]

THE EQUAL PAY ACT OF 1963 The **Equal Pay Act of 1963** requires that organizations provide the same pay to men and women who are doing equal work. The law

THE AGE DISCRIMINATION IN EMPLOYMENT ACT The **Age Discrimination in Employment Act** (**ADEA**) was passed in 1967 and amended in 1986. The ADEA prohibits discrimination against employees 40 years of age and older. The ADEA is similar to Title VII of the 1964 Civil Rights Act in terms of both its major provisions and the procedures that are followed in pursuing a case of discrimination. Like Title VII, enforcement of the ADEA is the responsibility of the EEOC.

The ADEA was felt necessary because of a disquieting trend in some organizations in the early 1960s. Specifically, these firms were beginning to discriminate against older employees when they had to lay people off or otherwise scale back their workforce. By targeting older workers—who tended to have higher pay because of their seniority and experience with the firm—companies were substantially cutting their labor costs. In addition, there was some feeling that organizations were also discriminating against older workers in their hiring decisions. The specific concern here was that organizations would not hire people in their forties or fifties because (1) they would have to pay those individuals more based on their experience and salary history, and (2) they would have a shorter potential career with the organization. Consequently, some organizations were found guilty of giving preferential treatment to younger workers over older workers. These concerns have been raised again as firms deal with the economic downturn by reducing the size of their workforce. Firms that are downsizing must be aware of the implications of this legislation to ensure that their efforts are not differentially affecting older workers.

Mandatory retirement ages is the other area in which the ADEA has generated a fair amount of controversy. The Supreme Court has indicated that an agency or an organization may require mandatory retirement at a given age only if an organization could demonstrate the inability of persons beyond a certain age to perform a given job safely. However, in several decisions, the Court has indicated that it will interpret this BFOQ exception very narrowly. In fact, in *Johnson* v. *Mayor and City of Baltimore*, the Court ruled that not even a federal statute requiring firefighters to retire at age 55 would qualify as an exception to the law.[34]

As the workforce continues to age, the number of age-discrimination complaints seems to be growing rapidly.[35] Statistics released by the EEOC, for instance, indicate that age-discrimination complaints increased from 19,000 in 2007 to more than 24,000 in 2008; they are now almost as common as race-discrimination complaints (the most common type of complaint filed with the EEOC). Thus, it is interesting to note that the Supreme Court recently ruled that in age-discrimination cases, it is up to the worker to prove that age was the decisive factor in a decision made by the employer—even if there is evidence that age played some role in the decision (*Gross* v. *FBL Financial Services 08-441*, in June 2009). By making it more difficult to file these so-called mixed motive cases in ADEA charges, the Court has essentially made it much more difficult to demonstrate age discrimination. Leaders in Congress soon began working on a revised ADEA to deal with this issue, but that new legislation is a long way from becoming law.

THE PREGNANCY DISCRIMINATION ACT OF 1979

As its name suggests, the **Pregnancy Discrimination Act of 1979** was passed to protect pregnant women from discrimination in the workplace. The law requires that the pregnant woman be treated like any other employee in

> The Civil Rights Act of 1991 makes it easier for individuals who feel they have been discriminated against to take legal action against organizations and provides for the payment of compensatory and punitive damages in cases of discrimination under Title VII.

the workplace. Therefore, the act specifies that a woman cannot be refused a job or promotion, fired, or otherwise discriminated against simply because she is pregnant (or has had an abortion). She also cannot be forced to leave employment with the organization as long as she is physically able to work. A doctor in Pennsylvania was recently fired by her employer (a clinic) after missing several days of work because of pregnancy-related complications. She filed suit under this act, while the clinic countersued using other laws as a basis.[36]

THE CIVIL RIGHTS ACT OF 1991 The **Civil Rights Act of 1991** was passed as a direct amendment of Title VII of the Civil Rights Act of 1964. During the 25 years following the passage of the original act, the U.S. Supreme Court handed down several rulings that helped define how the Civil Rights Act would be administered. But in the course of its 1989 Supreme Court session, several decisions were handed down that many people felt seriously limited the viability of the Civil Rights Act of 1964.[37] In response to this development, the Civil Rights Act of 1991 was passed essentially to restore the force of the original act. Although some new aspects of the law were introduced as part of the Civil Rights Act of 1991, the primary purpose of this new law was to make it easier for individuals who feel they have been discriminated against to take legal action against organizations. As a result, this law also reinforced the idea that a firm must remain within the limits of the law when engaging in various HRM practices.

Specifically, the Civil Rights Act of 1991 prohibits discrimination on the job and makes it easier for the burden of proof to shift to employers (to demonstrate that they did not discriminate). It also reinforces the illegality of making hiring, firing, or promotion decisions on the basis of race, gender, color, religion, or national origin; it also includes the Glass Ceiling Act, which established a commission to investigate practices that limited the access of protected class members (especially women) to the top levels of management in organizations. For the first time, the act provides the potential payment of compensatory and punitive damages in cases of discrimination under Title VII. Although the law limited the amount of punitive damages that could be paid to no more than nine times the amount of compensatory damages, it also allowed juries rather than federal judges to hear these cases.

This law also makes it possible for employees of U.S. companies working in foreign countries to bring suit against those companies for violation of the Civil Rights Act. The only exception to this provision is the situation in which a country has laws that specifically contradict some aspect of the Civil Rights Act. For example, Muslim countries often have laws limiting the rights of women. Foreign companies with operations in such countries would almost certainly be required to abide by local laws. As a result, a female employee of a U.S. company working in such a setting would not be directly protected under the Civil Rights Act. However, her employer would still need to inform her fully of the kinds of discriminatory practices she might face as a result of transferring to the foreign site and then ensure that when this particular foreign assignment was completed, her career opportunities would not have been compromised in any way.[38]

THE AMERICANS WITH DISABILITIES ACT OF 1990

The **Americans with Disabilities Act of 1990 (ADA)** is another piece of equal employment legislation that has greatly affected HRM. The ADA was passed in response to growing criticisms and concerns about employment opportunities denied to people with various disabilities. For example, one survey found that of 12.2 million Americans not working because of disabilities, 8.2 million would have preferred to work. Similarly, another survey found that almost 80 percent of all managers surveyed found the overall performance of their disabled workers to be good to excellent. In response to these trends and pressures, the ADA was passed to protect individuals with disabilities from being discriminated against in the workplace.[39]

Specifically, the ADA prohibits discrimination based on disability in all aspects of the employment relationship such as job application procedures, hiring, firing, promotion, compensation, and training, as well as other employment activities such as advertising, recruiting,

The Americans with Disabilities Act of 1990 (ADA) prohibits discrimination based on disability in all aspects of the employment relationship such as job application procedures, hiring, firing, promotion, compensation, and training, as well as other employment activities such as advertising, recruiting, tenure, layoffs, and leave and fringe benefits.

tenure, layoffs, leave, and benefits. In addition, the ADA also requires that organizations make reasonable accommodations for disabled employees as long as they do not pose an undue burden on the organization. The act initially went into effect in 1992 and covered employers with 25 or more employees. It was expanded in July 1994 to cover employers with 15 or more employees.

The ADA defines a *disability* as (1) a mental or physical impairment that limits one or more major life activities, (2) a record of having such an impairment, or (3) being regarded as having such an impairment. Clearly included within the domain of the ADA are individuals with disabilities such as blindness, deafness, paralysis, and similar disabilities. In addition, the ADA covers employees with cancer, a history of mental illness, or a history of heart disease. Finally, the act also covers employees regarded as having a disability, such as individuals who are disfigured or who for some other reason an employer feels will prompt a negative reaction from others. In addition, the ADA covers mental and psychological disorders such as mental retardation, emotional or mental illness (including depression), and learning disabilities.

On the other hand, individuals with substance-abuse problems, obesity, and similar non-work-related characteristics may not be covered by the ADA.[40] But because the ADA defines disabilities in terms of limitations on life activities, myriad cases continue to be filed. For example, in recent years, workers have attempted to claim protection under the ADA on the basis of ailments ranging from alcoholism to dental problems! These activities have led some critics to question whether the ADA is being abused by workers rather than protecting their rights.[41]

In fact, the definition of a disability and what constitutes a "reasonable accommodation" pose the greatest potential problems for the HR manager. Individuals who are confined to wheelchairs, visually impaired, or have similar physical disabilities are usually quite easy to identify, but many employees may suffer from "invisible" disabilities that might include physical problems (e.g., someone needing dialysis) as well as psychological problems (e.g., acute anxiety) and learning disabilities (e.g., dyslexia). It is not always obvious who among a group of employees is actually eligible for protection under the ADA.[42]

One area of coverage where the courts and the EEOC (the agency charged with the administration of the ADA) have taken a fairly clear position deals with AIDS and HIV in the workplace. Both AIDS and HIV are considered disabilities under the ADA, and employers cannot legally require an HIV test or any other medical examination as a condition for making an offer of employment. In addition, organizations must maintain confidentiality of all medical records, strive to educate coworkers about AIDS, and accommodate or try to accommodate AIDS victims.

In addition, the reasonable accommodation stipulation adds considerable complexity to the job of human resource manager and other executives in organizations. Clearly, for example, organizations must provide ramps and automatic door-opening systems to accommodate individuals confined to a wheelchair.

At the same time, however, providing accommodations for other disabilities may be more complex. If an applicant for a job takes an employment test, fails the test (and so is not offered employment), and *then* indicates that he or she has a learning disability (for example) that makes it difficult to take paper-and-pencil tests, the applicant probably can demand an accommodation. Specifically, the organization would likely be

> The ADA Amendments Act (or ADAAA) of 2008 broadens the protection offered to persons with disabilities at work by defining certain disabilities as "presumptive," thus negating several court cases that had ruled certain persons having disabilities as not qualifying for coverage under the ADA.

required either to find a different way to administer the test or provide the applicant with additional time to take the test a second time before making a final decision. Likewise, an existing employee diagnosed with a psychological disorder may be able to request on-site psychological support.

Recently, another issue involved with granting accommodations has been identified.[43] The nature of many accommodations granted to employees is such that other employees who are not disabled and not requesting an accommodation are unlikely to be envious or resentful about the accommodation. But this is not the case for all requested accommodations. For example, a woman claimed that having every Friday off was the only accommodation that would help to reduce her stress at work.[44] What if the organization granted her that accommodation? Surely other employees would wonder why they could not have Fridays off, especially since stress is not typically a visible disability. This situation would lead to resentment and potentially to other problems. Therefore, although the ADA does not consider coworker reactions as relevant to determining whether or not an accommodation is reasonable, the knowledgeable human resource manager will at least think about how others might react to an accommodation when trying to deal with the legal requests of employees with disabilities.

But a series of court decisions have worked to actually narrow the protection offered by the ADA.[45] For example, in 1999, the U.S. Supreme Court ruled that individuals who can correct or overcome their disabilities through medication or other means are not protected by the ADA. Similarly, in 1999 (*Sutton* v. *United Airlines*), the Court ruled that a person suffering from heart disease who was taking medication to control that heart disease was not covered by the ADA. In 2002, in *Toyota Motor Manufacturing Company, Kentucky Inc, v. Williams*, the Court ruled that for persons to be disabled, they had to have conditions that precluded them from doing activities central to one's daily life. Thus, they ruled that Ella Williams was not disabled, even though her carpal tunnel syndrome and tendinitis prevented her from performing the assembly-line job she was transferred to because she was able to attend to her personal hygiene.

In an attempt to return to the original intent of the ADA, in September 2008, President Bush signed into law the new **Americans with Disabilities Amendments Act (ADAAA)**. In June 2009, the EEOC finally voted on a set of guidelines to be used with the new law. The new guidelines broaden the definition of disability for the ADA, countering recent court decisions that have tended to narrow the definition of disability for cases brought forward (which was the original impetus for the law). For example, the changes would include specifying major life activities to include walking, seeing, bending, reading, and concentrating. The new guidelines also include a list of presumptive disabilities that will always meet the definition of disability under the AADA, including blindness, deafness, cancer, multiple sclerosis, limb loss, and HIV and AIDS. Also, under the new guidelines, persons will be "regarded as having a disability" if they can show that they have been discriminated against because of real or perceived disabilities. There has also been an interesting development in this area, relative to federal contractors and subcontractors, which will be discussed shortly.

THE FAMILY AND MEDICAL LEAVE ACT OF 1993 The **Family and Medical Leave Act of 1993** was passed in part to remedy weaknesses in the Pregnancy Discrimination Act of 1979. The law requires employers with more than 50 employees to provide as many as 12 weeks of unpaid leave for employees (1) after the birth or adoption of a child; (2) to care for a seriously ill child, spouse, or parent; or (3) if the employee is seriously ill. The organization must also provide the employee with the same or comparable job on the employee's return.[46]

The law also requires the organization to pay the health care coverage of the employee during the leave. However, the employer can require the employee to reimburse these health care premiums if the employee fails to return to work after the absence. Organizations are also allowed to exclude certain key employees from coverage (specifically defined as the highest paid 10 percent), on the grounds that granting leave to these individuals would cause serious economic harm to the organization. The law also does not apply to employees who have not worked an average of 25 hours a week in the previous 12 months.[47] The FMLA was also amended in 2009 with the passage of the Supporting Military Families Act, which mandates emergency leave for all covered active-duty members.

Recently, there has been renewed interest in the provisions of the FMLA. Some of this has been generated by activists who argue that few employees can afford to take any meaningful time off work without pay, with some arguing that having a baby is the leading cause of "poverty spells" (times when income dips below the level needed to pay for basics) in the United States.[48] Furthermore, among 21 high-income economies, the United States is alone in not having mandated paid leave for maternity.[49] Much of this new interest was generated by Netflix when, in August 2015, the firm announced that it would offer up to one year *paid* leave for both parents when a child is born or adopted. This time could be taken on any schedule the employee wanted, and the emphasis here was that the leave was paid. Virgin Airlines had already offered a one-year paid leave at two European offices, but, following the Netflix announcement, other firms in the United States followed suit. For example, by November 2015, Google, Microsoft, YouTube, and Amazon all introduced or increased paid maternity leave—for both parents. Whether or not the law will change in the United States depends, in part, on the results of the upcoming presidential election.

REGULATIONS FOR FEDERAL CONTRACTORS In addition to the various laws just described, numerous other regulations apply only to federal contractors. Note, however, that the definition of a federal contractor is quite broad. For instance, all banks (that participate in the U.S. Federal Reserve system) and most universities (that have federal research grants or that accept federal loans for their students) qualify as federal contractors.

Executive Order 11246 was issued by President Johnson who believed that Title VII of the 1964 Civil Rights Act was not comprehensive enough. The order mirrors the Civil Rights Act in terms of outlawing discrimination but also requires federal contractors and subcontractors with contracts greater than $50,000 to file written affirmative action plans.

> The Family and Medical Leave Act of 1993 requires employers having more than 50 employees to provide as many as 12 weeks unpaid leave for employees after the birth or adoption of a child; to care for a seriously ill child, spouse, or parent; or if the employee is seriously ill.

Executive Order 11478 was issued by President Nixon and required the federal government to base all employment policies and decision on merit and fitness, specifying that race, color, sex, national origin, and religion should not be considered. The threshold for this order was all contracts over $10,000.

Vocational Rehabilitation Act of 1973 requires that all federal agencies, as well as federal contractors and subcontractors receiving $2,500 a year or more from the federal government, are required to engage in affirmative action for persons with disabilities. A new wrinkle was introduced in in 2013, however, when the Office of Federal Contract Compliance Procedures (OFCCP), which oversees and enforces all these regulations, issued new guidelines, under Section 503 of the Vocational Rehabilitation Act. These new guidelines, which took effect in March of 2014, *only* apply to federal contractors and subcontractors (the definitions of which are also changing, as discussed later), but they require such contractors to implement affirmative action plans to recruit, hire, and improve job opportunities for individuals with disabilities. The guidelines also include a utilization goal of 7 percent individuals with disabilities for all job classifications. While these goals are not quotas, and there is no financial penalties if a firm does not meet these goals, any contractor not meeting the guidelines will be subject to closer scrutiny by the OFFCP. Finally, the guidelines stipulate that all employees can self-identify as having a disability at any time, before or after the employment offer. This information cannot be used for decision making and it cannot be used against the employer in any legal action. This information should be updated at least once every 5 years. The real challenge for contractors under these guidelines will be how to deal with persons with invisible disabilities, which were discussed earlier. These individuals are less likely to identify themselves as having a disability, and yet their doing so is critical for firms trying to reach the 7 percent utilization goals. It is interesting to note how these regulations move contractors in such a different direction than that which has been mandated by recent court decisions regarding other employers.

DISCRIMINATION ON THE BASIS OF SEXUAL ORIENTATION

Sexual orientation discrimination refers to being treated differently because of one's real or perceived sexual orientation—whether gay, lesbian, bisexual, or heterosexual. There is no federal law that prohibits discrimination on the basis of sexual orientation. Although federal employees are protected against such discrimination, any attempt to pass a law regarding all employees has failed.

> The Vocational Rehabilitation Act of 1973 requires that executive agencies and subcontractors and contractors of the federal government receiving more than $2,500 a year from the government engage in affirmative action for disabled individuals.

Several states, however, do have laws against this type of discrimination. California, Colorado, Connecticut, Hawaii, Illinois, Iowa, Maine, Maryland, Massachusetts, Minnesota, Nevada, New Hampshire, New Jersey, New York, Oregon, Rhode Island, Vermont, Washington, and Wisconsin, as well as the District of Columbia, all have laws prohibiting discrimination on the basis of sexual orientation for both public- and private-sector jobs. In addition, many city and county ordinances are dealing with this issue.

Recent Supreme Court decisions dealing with same-sex marriage, discussed in Chapter 1, may signal some changes in the situation—most critically in the case of *Windsor* v. *U.S.* regarding the Defense of Marriage Act (DOMA). In that case, Edith Windsor was the major beneficiary and executor of the estate of her late wife, Thea Clara Spyer. The IRS told her that she owed more than $350,000 in estate taxes because she could not inherit the way a spouse could in a traditional marriage (she would have paid nothing if she had been married to a man), citing the provision of DOMA as the basis for their decision. DOMA, signed into law in 1996 by Bill Clinton, states that for the purposes of deciding who receives federal benefits, marriage is defined as only between a man and a woman. The Supreme Court in a 5-4 decision ruled that DOMA placed an unfair burden on same-sex married couples and made a subset of state-sanctioned marriages unequal.

This decision did not make same-sex marriages legal in all states, but it did ensure that same-sex couples were entitled to all federal benefits (including tax benefits, pensions, and insurance benefits) afforded traditional couples. However, in June 2015, the Supreme Court ruled in *Obergefell v. Hodges*[50] that it is illegal for any state to refuse to allow, or to fully recognize same-sex marriages, this making the United States the

21st country to legalize same-sex marriages nationwide. The Supreme Court decision was split (5-4), with the late Justice Scalia calling the decision a "threat to American democracy," and reactions are also playing a role in the presidential race. Although much is still not clear, it seems as though pension rights and insurance benefits are two areas where this decision will have a significant impact upon HRM departments.

Currently, same-sex marriages are recognized in 13 states, plus the District of Columbia, and same-sex partnerships and unions are allowed in 10 more states, but 35 states still limit marriage to opposite-sex couples (New Mexico has no laws regarding same-sex marriages but recognizes out-of-state marriages). It will be interesting to see the real impact of this decision over time. It is clear that public opinion has swung (slightly) in favor of recognizing same-sex marriages, and the Supreme Court decisions open the door to more states recognizing these marriages and perhaps to federal equal rights protection on the basis of sexual orientation. We will discuss this final implication later in Chapter 9.

2-2f Enforcing Equal Employment Opportunity

The enforcement of equal opportunity legislation generally is handled by two agencies. As noted earlier, one agency is the Equal Employment Opportunity Commission, and the other is the Office of Federal Contract Compliance Procedures. The EEOC is a division of the Department of Justice. It was created by Title VII of the 1964 Civil Rights Act and today is given specific responsibility for enforcing Title VII, the Equal Pay Act, and the Americans with Disabilities Act. The EEOC has three major functions: (1) investigating and resolving complaints about alleged discrimination, (2) gathering information regarding employment patterns and trends in U.S. businesses, and (3) issuing information about new employment guidelines as they become relevant.

> Executive Order 11478 requires the federal government to base all of its own employment policies on merit and fitness and specifies that race, color, sex, religion, and national origin should not be considered.

The first function is illustrated in Figure 2.3, which depicts the basic steps that an individual who thinks she has been discriminated against in a promotion decision might follow to get her complaint addressed. In general, if an individual believes that she or he has been discriminated against, the first step in reaching a resolution is to file a complaint with the EEOC or a corresponding state agency. The individual has 180 days from the date of the incident to file the complaint. The EEOC will dismiss out of hand almost all complaints that exceed the 180-day time frame for filing. After the complaint has been filed, the EEOC assumes responsibility for investigating the claim itself. The EEOC can take as many as 60 days to investigate a complaint. If the EEOC either finds that the complaint is not valid or does not complete the investigation within a 60-day period, then the individual has the right to sue in a federal court.

If the EEOC believes that discrimination has occurred, then its representative will first try to negotiate a reconciliation between the two parties without taking the case to court. Occasionally, the EEOC may enter into a consent decree with the discriminating organization. This consent decree is essentially an agreement between the EEOC and the organization stipulating that the organization will cease certain discriminatory practices and perhaps implement new affirmative action procedures to rectify its history of discrimination.

On the other hand, if the EEOC cannot reach an agreement with the organization, then two courses of action may be pursued. First, the EEOC can issue a right-to-sue letter to the victim; the letter simply certifies that the agency has investigated the complaint and found potential validity in the victim's allegations. Essentially, that course of action involves the EEOC giving its blessings to the individual to file suit on his or her own behalf. Alternatively, in certain limited cases, the EEOC itself may assist the victim in bringing suit in federal court. In either event, however, the lawsuit must be filed in federal court within 300 days of the alleged discriminatory act. The courts strictly follow this guideline, and many valid complaints have lost standing in court because lawsuits were not filed on time. As already noted, the EEOC has recently become backlogged with complaints stemming primarily from the passage of the newer civil rights act. One recent court case that involved the implementation of a discriminatory seniority system was settled in such a way that it helped provide the grounds for amending Title VII to provide exceptions to the 300-day deadline for filing a lawsuit. In recent years, the EEOC has been working to better prioritize its caseload, giving the highest priority to cases that appear to have the potential for widespread or classwide effects.[51]

FIG 2.3 INVESTIGATING AND RESOLVING A DISCRIMINATION COMPLAINT

Amy Jones believes she has been discriminated against at work. She was passed over for a promotion to supervisor and believes it was because she is a woman, rather than because she is unqualified. Specifically, all candidates for promotion must be approved by their immediate supervisor, and most of these supervisors are older white men who have been heard to say that women should not be promoted. In fact, almost no women have been promoted to supervisor in this organization. What can Amy do?

STEP 1: Amy files a complaint with her local or state EEO agency.
STEP 2: Local/state EEO agency agrees to investigate Amy's claim on behalf of the EEOC, and the agency contacts Amy's employer to determine whether the claim has any merit.

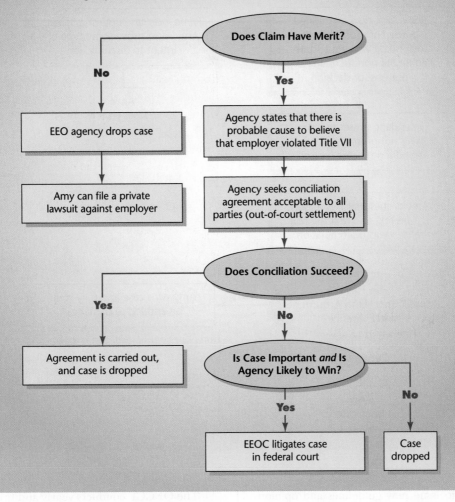

The second important function of the EEOC is to monitor the hiring practices of organizations. Every year, all organizations that employ 100 or more individuals must file a report with the EEOC that summarizes the number of women and minorities that the organization employs in nine different job categories. The EEOC tracks these reports to identify potential patterns of discrimination that it can then potentially address through class-action lawsuits.

The third function of the EEOC is to develop and issue guidelines that help organizations determine whether their decisions are violations of the law enforced by the EEOC. These guidelines themselves are not laws, but the courts have generally given them great weight when hearing employment-discrimination cases. One of the most important sets of guidelines is the uniform guidelines on employee-selection procedures developed jointly by the EEOC, U.S. Department of Labor, U.S. Department of Justice, and U.S. Civil Service Commission. These guidelines summarize how organizations should develop and administer selection systems to avoid violating Title VII. The EEOC also frequently uses the

FIG 2.3 (Continued)

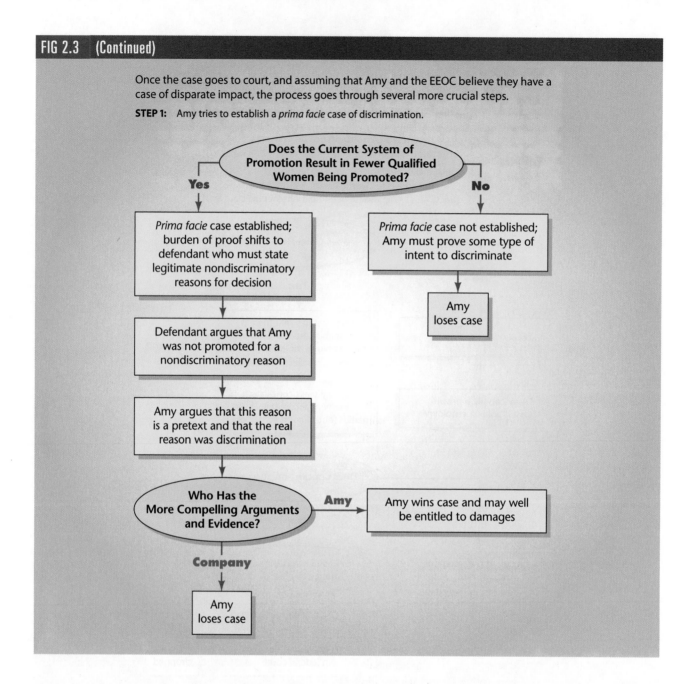

Once the case goes to court, and assuming that Amy and the EEOC believe they have a case of disparate impact, the process goes through several more crucial steps.

STEP 1: Amy tries to establish a *prima facie* case of discrimination.

Does the Current System of Promotion Result in Fewer Qualified Women Being Promoted?

Yes

No

Prima facie case established; burden of proof shifts to defendant who must state legitimate nondiscriminatory reasons for decision

Prima facie case not established; Amy must prove some type of intent to discriminate

Amy loses case

Defendant argues that Amy was not promoted for a nondiscriminatory reason

Amy argues that this reason is a pretext and that the real reason was discrimination

Who Has the More Compelling Arguments and Evidence?

Amy

Amy wins case and may well be entitled to damages

Company

Amy loses case

Federal Register to issue new guidelines and opinions regarding employment practices that result from newly passed laws.[52] This was the case discussed earlier relating to the new ADAAA.[53]

The other agency primarily charged with monitoring equal employment opportunity legislation is the Office of Federal Contract Compliance Procedures. The OFCCP is responsible for enforcing the executive orders that cover companies doing business with the federal government. Recall from our earlier discussion that businesses with contracts of more than $50,000 cannot discriminate based on race, color, religious beliefs, national origin, or gender, and they must have a written affirmative action plan on file.[54]

The OFCCP conducts yearly audits of government contractors to ensure that they have been actively pursuing their affirmative action goals. These audits involve examining a company's affirmative action plan and conducting on-site visits to determine how individual employees perceive the company's affirmative action policies. If the OFCCP finds that its contractors or subcontractors are not complying with the relevant executive orders, then it may notify the EEOC, advise the Department of Justice to institute criminal proceedings, or request that the labor secretary cancel or suspend contracts with that organization. This latter step is the OFCCP's most important weapon because it has a clear and immediate effect on an organization's revenue stream.

The EEOC and the OFCCP are the two primary regulatory agencies for enforcing equal employment legislation, but it is important to recognize that other agencies and components of our government system also come into play. The Departments of Labor and Justice, for example, are both heavily involved in the enforcement of equal employment opportunity legislation. The U.S. Civil Service Commission is also actively involved for government organizations where civil-service jobs exist. The U.S. judicial systems reflected by our courts also play an important role in enforcing all HRM legislation.

 2-3 OTHER AREAS OF HUMAN RESOURCE REGULATION

As noted earlier, most employment regulations are designed to provide equal employment opportunity, but some legislation goes beyond that and really deals more substantively with other issues. We will only touch on these different areas of legislation here and then discuss them in more detail when we discuss the content area involved. So, for example, we begin with a discussion of legislation dealing with compensation and benefits and then discuss these laws in more detail in Chapter 9.

2-3a Legal Perspectives on Compensation and Benefits

The most basic and yet far-reaching law dealing with compensation at work is the Fair Labor Standards Act. The **Fair Labor Standards Act** (**FLSA**), passed in 1938, established a minimum hourly wage for jobs. The rationale for this legislation was to ensure that everyone who works would receive an income sufficient to meet basic needs. The first minimum wage was $0.25 an hour but, as shown in Table 2.1, the minimum wage has been raised many times in the decades since as the law has been amended. The most recent increase in the federal minimum wage came in 2009 when the wage was raised to $7.25 per hour. President Obama had hoped to raise that to $10.10 in his last term, but that seems unlikely. He did, however raise the minimum wage for federal contractors and subcontractors to $10.15 in January of 2015. Also, several states, and even cities, have been more active in changing minimum wage laws over the past few years. For example, in California, the minimum wage is now $10.00 per hour,

TABLE 2.1 MINIMUM WAGE HISTORY	
Effective Date	Minimum Wage ($)
1938	0.25
1939	0.30
1945	0.40
1950	0.75
1956	1.00
1961	1.15
1963	1.25
1967	1.40
1968	1.60
1974	2.00
1975	2.10
1976	2.30
1978	2.65
1979	2.90
1980	3.10
1981	3.35
1990	3.80
1991	4.25
1996	4.75
1997	5.15
2007	5.85
2008	6.55
2009	7.25

but, in Los Angeles city and county, the minimum wage is set to increase to $15.00 by 2020. Also the minimum wage in Massachusetts is $10.00 per hour, while in Washington, D.C., it is $10.50 an hour as of 2016.

A new twist to state laws regarding minimum wages came in March of 2016, when Oregon governor Kate Brown signed a law calling for different minimum wages in cities than in rural areas.[55] Basically, the law will raise the minimum wage statewide through 2022, but that target wage will be $14.75 per hour in Portland, $13.50 an hour in other urban areas, and $12.50 in sparsely populated

Contemporary Challenges in HR

Working for Free?

Heather Jennings worked as a customer service representative for Verizon and was paid on an hourly basis. However, she was told that she needed to be at her workstation 10–15 minutes before her shift officially started in order to log in to her computer, open databases, and get her equipment adjusted so she could start work precisely on time. All of the other employees in her department were given the same instructions.

Jeffrey Allen was a sergeant in the Chicago police department. He left work each day at 5:00 pm but continued to receive dozens of text messages, e-mails, and calls on his department-issued BlackBerry until 10:00 pm or so each day. Allen felt compelled to respond to each contact, sometimes taking a matter of a few minutes but other times needing an hour or more. No one at his precinct told him he had to do this, but he felt subtle pressure to do so.

For years, Omar Belazi, a former RadioShack store manager, logged 65-hour workweeks, often staying late to clean the store's restrooms and vacuum the floor. He also felt pressured to work all weekend each week just to help meet the store's sales goals. Regardless of the hours he worked, however, he received the same monthly salary. Belazi gradually tired of the long hours, extra work, and stress, and he left RadioShack.

> "They called me a manager, but I was also a salesman, a janitor, and an errand boy. I spent as much time mopping as I did managing."
>
> —ANONYMOUS RADIOSHACK MANAGER

Each of these cases has something in common: what an employer can expect of its employees in relation to what it pays them. They have also each been the subject of a lawsuit. At the heart of the argument is a decades-old law that mandates overtime payments for hourly operating workers who work more than 40 hours a week but allows firms to pay salaries to professionals regardless of how many hours they work. The Fair Labor Standards Act (as discussed in the chapter) specifically

Jane September/Shutterstock.com

exempts those in executive, administrative, or professional jobs from overtime payments.

But because so many jobs have shifted from the manufacturing setting to service settings, and because the nature of so many jobs has changed, the lines between different kinds of work have blurred. That is, when someone works on an assembly line, it's pretty simple to step up to the line and start work, and the tasks themselves are clearly defined. Service jobs, though, often have more subjective "boundaries" and may require more start-up time.

Heather Jennings acknowledges that she was an hourly worker, but she lodged complaints in order to get paid for the extra 10–15 minutes she spent each day getting ready to work (her complaints were denied). Jeffrey Allen, meanwhile, filed grievances and requested overtime for the extra hours he worked each evening (his claims were also denied). RadioShack eventually settled a lawsuit filed by 1,300 current and former California store managers for $29.9 million. In similar fashion, Oracle recently paid $35 million to 1,666 workers who claimed they were misclassified. And Walmart was recently fined $4.8 million for denying overtime pay to employees working in store vision enters who were classified as managers but who were expected to work extra hours performing nonmanagerial jobs.

THINK IT OVER

1. How might you respond if your employer (current or future) directly or indirectly requires you to work extra hours with no additional compensation?

2. What might you as a manager do to insure your employees never feel compelled to work "off the clock"?

rural areas. Of course, as discussed in the Contemporary Challenges in HR feature, interpretations of the FLSA are still evolving.

The FSLA also established, for the first time, the workweek in the United States as 40 hours per week. It further specified that all full-time employees must be paid at a rate of one and a half times their normal hourly rate for each hour of work beyond 40 hours in a week. Note, however, that the law makes no provision for daily work time. Thus, a normal workday might be considered 8 hours, but an employer is actually free to schedule, say, 10 or 12 hours in a single day without paying overtime as long as the weekly total does not exceed 40 hours.

The FSLA also allows some employees to be considered "exempt" from the overtime provisions of the act, as will be discussed in more detail in Chapter 9. Thus, employees usually considered to be "salaried" do not qualify for overtime, and this has not traditionally been an area for controversy. However, in 2015, the Supreme Court ruled in *Perez v. Mortgage Bankers Association* that the Department of Labor was justified in reversing an earlier decision to consider mortgage bankers as being exempt employees. It is likely that the definition of who is and who is not exempt from overtime provisions will continue to be an issue in coming years. Finally, the FLSA also includes child labor provisions, which provide protection for persons 18 years of age and younger. These protections include keeping minors from working on extremely dangerous jobs and limiting the number of hours that persons younger than 16 can work.

Another important piece of legislation that affects compensation is the **Employee Retirement Income Security Act of 1974** (**ERISA**). This law was passed to protect employee investments in their pensions and to ensure that employees would be able to receive at least some pension benefits at the time of retirement or even termination. ERISA does not mean that an employee *must* receive a pension; it is meant only to protect any pension benefits to which the employee is entitled. (This topic will be discussed in somewhat more detail in Chapter 9.) ERISA was passed in part because some organizations had abused their pension plans in their efforts to control costs or to channel money inappropriately to other uses within the organization and in part due to corruption.

Two other emerging legal perspectives on compensation and benefits involve minimum benefits coverage and executive compensation. A few years ago, publicity about

President Obama signs the Health Care Reform Bill on March 23, 2010, in the East Room of the White House. Obama signed into law his historic health care reform, enacting the most sweeping social legislation in decades to ensure coverage for almost all Americans.

the poor benefits Walmart provides some of its employees, for example, led the Maryland General Assembly to pass a bill requiring employers with more than 10,000 workers to spend at least 8 percent of their payroll on benefits or else pay into a fund for the uninsured. At the time the bill was passed (in early 2006), Walmart was the only company to be affected. Moreover, several other states are exploring similar legislation. On another front, the Securities and Exchange Commission (SEC) is also developing new guidelines that will require companies to divulge more complete and detailed information about their executive-compensation packages.[56]

One of the major agenda items first tackled by President Obama was health care. Congress worked throughout 2009 in an attempt to pass legislation that would call for major reforms of health care in the United States. The Health Care Reform Bill passed in 2010 focused on benefits for employees who were not already covered by employer programs. The notion that employers who did not provide health care coverage would be required to pay a fine was part of the Affordable Care for America Act[57] proposed by the Democrats in 2009. The final bill did not include the much-debated "public option," but there is still debate about the constitutionality of the entire bill. During the 2012 Republican primaries, several

> The Fair Labor Standards Act (FLSA) established a minimum hourly wage for jobs.

candidates labeled the bill as "socialist," and the Republican Party platform includes a plank designed to kill the entire legislation. But the Supreme Court ruled, in June of 2012,[58] that President Obama's Health Care Bill was indeed constitutional, including the provision that companies either provide health insurance for their employees or pay a tax to help provide health care benefits for the unemployed. Other aspects of the bill were deemed unconstitutional, however, and so it will still take some time before we really know the complete implications of this legislation. We will discuss these regulations further in Chapter 9.

2-3b Legal Perspectives on Labor Relations

The **National Labor Relations Act**, or **Wagner Act**, was passed in 1935 in an effort to control and legislate collective bargaining between organizations and labor unions. Before 1935, the legal system in the United States was generally considered hostile to labor unions. The Wagner Act was passed in an effort to provide some sense of balance in the power relationship between organizations and unions. The Wagner Act describes the process through which labor unions can be formed and the requirements faced by organizations in dealing with those labor unions. The Wagner Act served to triple union membership in the United States and granted labor unions significant power in their relationships with organizations.

Following a series of crippling strikes, however, the U.S. government concluded that the Wagner Act had actually shifted too much power to labor unions. As a result, businesses had been placed at a significant disadvantage. To correct this imbalance, Congress subsequently passed the **Labor Management Relations Act (Taft-Hartley Act)** in 1947 and the **Landrum-Griffin Act** in 1959. Both of these acts regulate union actions and their internal affairs in a way that puts them on an equal footing with management and organizations. The Taft-Hartley Act also created the National

> The Employee Retirement Income Security Act of 1974 (ERISA) guarantees a basic minimum benefit that employees could expect to be paid at retirement.

> The Labor Management Relations Act (or Taft-Hartley Act) curtailed and limited union powers and regulates union actions and their internal affairs in a way that puts them on equal footing with management and organizations.

Labor Relations Board (NLRB), which was charged with enforcement of the act.

Although the basic issues of unionization and collective bargaining have become pretty well established, some legal issues have emerged in this area. The Taft-Hartley Act guarantees these rights but also guarantees that these unions should be independent. This issue has come up in two fairly recent cases. More important for the future, in both these cases, the company involved was setting up autonomous work teams that were empowered to make certain decisions about employees. In *Electromation* v. *NLRB*,[59] the NLRB ruled that the company's "action committees," which were formed to deal with employee working conditions and were staffed by employees, actually constituted a threat to the union already in place in the company. These action committees, which the NLRB ruled were dominated by management, were seen as an alternative way to deal with problems concerning working conditions and could allow the company to circumvent the union and the collective-bargaining process. As such, the company was found in violation of the Taft-Hartley Act. In a similar case, *E.I. Du Pont de Nemours* v. *NLRB*,[60] the board ruled that Du Pont's safety committees were essentially employer-dominated labor organizations and thus were in violation of the Taft-Hartley Act.

Controversy continues over what would amount to a major revision of the Taft-Hartley Act, and we will discuss this further in Chapter 11. The **Employee Free Choice Act**, also known as the Union Relief Act, was first proposed in 2009. The Act was passed by the House, but was voted down in the Senate, even though Democrats held a simple majority at the time. The bill has been reintroduced several times, and President Obama is said to support it, but it has failed to leave committee on subsequent attempts. Clearly, the outcomes of the 2016 election will have an impact on the future of this proposed legislation, but it is worth noting that, if it should pass, it would have a major impact on the process by which unions are certified in the United States, making that process much easier.

Finally, NLRB ruled, in August of 2015, in the case of the *Browning-Ferris Industries of California case*, that firms employing contractors to perform various HR functions are liable for any violations committed by those contractors. This decision dramatically expands the definition of "joint employer" so that firms employing contractors— such as staffing agencies to supply employees—would be considered joint employers and so would be potentially responsible for any unfair labor practices performed by the contractors, as well as for any collective bargaining obligations. This case may well go the Supreme Court, which, as noted earlier, may not have a full nine members in place in the near future.

2-3c Employee Safety and Health

Employees also have the right to work in safe and healthy environments, and these rights continue to be important in organizations. The Occupational Safety and Health Act of 1970 (OSHA) is the single most comprehensive piece of legislation regarding worker safety and health in organizations. OSHA granted the federal government the power to establish and enforce occupational safety and health standards for all places of employment directly affecting interstate commerce. The Department of Labor was given power to apply OSHA standards and enforce its provisions. The Department of Health was given responsibility for

> The Landrum-Griffin Act focused on eliminating various unethical, illegal, and undemocratic practices within unions themselves.

G.T. MCDONALD ENTERPRISES
GENERAL CONTRACTOR
CONSTRUCTION SITE
NO TRESPASSING
HARD HAT AREA
DRUG-FREE WORKPLACE

Marjorie Farrell/The Image Works

conducting research to determine the criteria for specific operations or occupations and for training employers to comply with the act itself. OSHA also makes provisions through which individual states can substitute their own safety and health standards for those suggested by the federal government.

The basic premise of OSHA (also known as the *general duty clause*) is that each employer has an obligation to furnish each employee with a place of employment that is free from hazards that can cause death or physical harm. OSHA is generally enforced through inspections of the workplace by OSHA inspectors, and fines can be imposed on violators. In fact, a bipartisan bill signed into law in 2015 will substantially increase those fines as of August 2016. The fines issued by OSHA are based on the consumer price index and haven't been adjusted since 1990. This new legislation will increase those fines and institute a "catch-up adjustment" so that fines can be brought more in line with costs (raising fines by as much as 80 percent) before further increases are implemented. We will deal with these issues in more detail in Chapter 12.

2-3d Drugs in the Workplace

The **Drug-Free Workplace Act of 1988** was passed to reduce the use of illegal drugs in the workplace. This law applies primarily to government employees and federal contractors, but it also extends to organizations regulated by the Department of Transportation and the Nuclear Regulatory Commission. Thus, long-haul truck drivers and workers at most nuclear reactors are subject to these regulations. The actual regulations themselves are aimed at establishing a drug-free workplace and include the requirement, in some cases, for regular drug testing.

Concerns over the problems of drug use at work have also led many other companies not covered by this law to establish drug-testing programs of their own. In fact, drug testing is becoming quite widespread, even though there is little hard evidence addressing the effectiveness of these programs.[61] The issue for the current discussion is whether these testing programs constitute an invasion of employee privacy. Many opponents of drug-testing programs argue that drug testing is clearly appropriate in cases in which there is some "reasonable" basis for suspected drug use, but not otherwise. Others argue that organizations that test for drug use often do not test for alcohol use, which, although not illegal, can cause problems on the job. Of course, what makes the privacy issues here even more salient is the method generally used to test for drugs on the job. Urinalysis (by far the most common method) is extremely invasive and has been known to result in a fair number of false-positive tests (i.e., employees are incorrectly identified as drug users). As a result, several alternatives have begun to appear in organizations, including testing an employee's individual hairs.[62] Perhaps these new technologies will reduce some of the concerns over drug testing while providing employers the protection they deserve from drug use on the job.

2-3e Plant Closings and Employee Rights

The **Worker Adjustment and Retraining Notification (WARN) Act of 1988** stipulates that an organization with at least 100 employees must provide notice at least 60 days in advance of plans to close a facility or lay off 50 or more employees. The penalty for failing to comply is equal to 1 day's pay (plus benefits) for each employee for each day that notice should have been given. An organization that closes a plant without any warning and lays off 1,000 employees would be liable for 60 days of pay and benefits for those 1,000 employees, which could translate into a substantial amount of money. The act also provides for warnings about pending reductions in work hours but generally applies only to private employers. There are exceptions to the WARN requirements that are related to unforeseeable business circumstances such as a strike at a major employer or a government-enforced shutdown.[63] The events of September 11, 2001, represent one such exception to this law.

A new wrinkle on this law was introduced in February of 2016, however. Under the leadership of Marissa Mayer, every employee at Yahoo receives a quarterly

> The Occupational Safety and Health Act of 1970 (or OSHA) grants the federal government the power to establish and enforce occupational safety and health standards for all places of employment directly affecting interstate commerce.

performance review and a ranking on a scale ranging from 1 to 15. In recent years, the bottom 5 percent of the workforce has been fired. This is not unusual for this type of appraisal system (often referred to as "rank and yank"), but, in this case, it resulted in more than 1,000 employees losing their jobs from late 2014 to early 2015. But now, one of the employees who was fired has brought suit against Yahoo claiming that this process is tantamount to a mass layoff and because Yahoo did not provide notice about such a layoff, the company is in violation of California's WARN Act. The case is still working its way through the system, but if Yahoo is found guilty, it would be required to pay each affected employee $500 a day plus back pay and benefits for each day of advance notice it failed to provide.[64]

2-3f Privacy Issues at Work

In recent years, issues of privacy have become more important to Americans, so it is not surprising that privacy at work has also become more important. The history of legislation dealing with privacy at work, however, actually goes back several years. The **Privacy Act of 1974** applies directly to federal employees only, but it has served as the impetus for several state laws. Basically, this legislation allows employees to review their personnel files periodically to ensure that the information contained in

> The Worker Adjustment and Retraining Notification (WARN) Act of 1988 stipulates that an organization employing at least 100 employees must provide notice at least 60 days in advance of plans to close a facility or lay off 50 or more employees.

them is accurate. Before this privacy legislation, managers could place almost any information they pleased in a personnel file, certain that only other managers could see those files.

But the larger concerns with privacy these days relate to potential invasions of employee privacy by organizations. For example, organizations generally reserve the right to monitor the e-mail correspondence of employees. Presumably, employees should be using company e-mail only for company business, so this practice may not be a problem, but it does mean that employees who receive unsolicited e-mails from suspect vendors (such as pornographic websites) may also have that information shared with their employers.

Late in 2009, Congress passed a law dealing with a different type of privacy. The **Genetic Information Nondiscrimination Act (GINA)** prohibits employers from collecting any genetic information about their employees, including information about family history of disease. This would mean that such information could not be obtained even during a medical examination, although there is some recognition that such information could be obtained "inadvertently" in some cases. One of the more interesting challenges posed by this new legislation is that some information about family medical history is often collected as part of determining whether or not a person requires an accommodation under the ADA. Such practices are now illegal, and it is not clear what effect this will have on the enforcement of the ADA.

The **PATRIOT Act** was passed shortly after the terrorist attacks on September 11, 2001, to help the United States more effectively battle terrorism worldwide. Many of the act's provisions expand the rights of the government or law enforcement agencies to collect information about and pursue potential terrorists. Some major provisions include those that allow law enforcement agencies to use surveillance to gather information related to a full range of terrorist crimes; those that allow law enforcement agencies to carry out investigations of potential terrorists without having to inform the targets of those investigations; and those that allow law enforcement agencies to obtain search warrants any place terrorist activity might occur. Congress passed a 4-year extension to the act in 2011, modifying some powers but not seriously changing the law.

The Genetic Information Nondiscrimination Act (GINA) of 2009 prohibits employers from obtaining genetic information about employees.

In the summer of 2013, however, several developments suggested that the trade-off between security and privacy in the United States was undergoing a new level of scrutiny. Over the course of the previous year, various sources revealed the full extent of surveillance being carried out by the government. Many citizens had long accepted the idea that certain persons suspected of terrorist activities outside the United States might be under surveillance, but it became clear that American citizens were also being subjected to surveillance under some circumstances. It also became clear that data concerning phone calls both to and from individuals on some "watch list" were being collected and stored, although the government indicated that no identifying information would be collected. Furthermore, there was some indication that unmanned drones were being used for domestic surveillance. In general, assumptions about privacy in the United States were no longer valid. In fact, in July 2013, the U.S. Congress came close to revoking some powers that had been granted to various security agencies. The bill to restrict those powers was defeated, but it was a strong signal that there would be

Iconico/Shutterstock.com

much more discussion about privacy rights being sacrificed in the name of national security.

2-4 EVALUATING LEGAL COMPLIANCE

Given the clear and obvious importance as well as the complexities associated with the legal environment of HRM, it is critically important that organizations comply with the laws and regulations that govern HRM practices to the best of their ability. The assurance of compliance can best be done through a three-step process. The first step is to ensure that managers clearly understand the laws that govern every aspect of HRM. In other words, all managers must understand and be intimately familiar with the various laws that restrict and govern their behavior vis-à-vis their employees.

Second, managers should rely on their own legal and HR staff to answer questions and review procedures periodically. Almost all larger organizations have a legal staff consisting of professionals trained in various areas of the legal environment of business. An HR manager or other manager with a legal question regarding a particular employment issue or practice is well advised to consult the firm's attorney about the legality of that particular action.

And third, organizations may also find it useful to engage occasionally in external legal audits of their HRM procedures. This audit might involve contracting with an outside law firm to review the organization's HRM systems and practices to ensure that they comply with all appropriate laws and regulations. Such an external audit will, of course, be expensive and somewhat intrusive into the organization's daily routine. When properly conducted, however, external audits can keep an organization out of trouble.

CLOSING CASE
Power Plays at Work

Recent research shows that more than 30 percent of female workers in the United States have been harassed at work—virtually all of them by men. Forty-three percent identified the male harasser as a supervisor, 27 percent as an employee senior to them, and 19 percent as a coworker at the same level. In 2012 (the last year for which there is complete data), nearly 13,000 charges of sexual harassment were filed with the EEOC, 84 percent of them by women.

Photographee.eu/Shutterstock.com

Why does sexual harassment (mostly of women) occur in the workplace? "Power," says researcher Debbie Dougherty, who conducted a study in conjunction with a large Midwestern health care organization. "It was the common answer. It came up repeatedly," says Dougherty, a specialist in communications and power in organizations. She also found that men and women understand the idea of power differently, and that difference in understanding may play an important part in the persistence of harassing behavior in the workplace:

- For most men, power is something that belongs to superiors—managers and supervisors—who can harass because they possess the power to do so. By definition, a male coworker cannot actually harass a female coworker who's at the same level because he doesn't possess sufficient power over her.

- Women, on the other hand, see power as something that can be introduced into a relationship as it develops; it's something more than the mere formal authority built into the superior's job description. Harassment can be initiated by anyone who's able to create the perception of power.

(Continued)

According to Dougherty, gender differences in the perception of power may account, at least in part, for gender differences in perceptions of behavior. "If a man," she suggests, "thinks that sexual harassment only comes from a supervisor, he may feel free to make sexual comments to a female coworker," reasoning that because he holds no power over her, she won't perceive the behavior as harassment. She, however, probably regards power as something that can be sought and gained in a relationship and may therefore "see the sexual comments as a quest for power and label it as sexual harassment."

The findings of another recent study tend to support Dougherty's conclusions. Researchers from the University of Minnesota discovered that women in supervisory positions were 137 percent more likely to be harassed than women in nonsupervisory roles. Although many of the harassers were men in superior positions, a large number were coworkers in equivalent positions. It would seem, then, that male coworkers felt free to behave in a harassing manner because they believed that their female targets would not perceive their behavior as efforts to exert power. As Dougherty predicts, however, they were wrong: The women perceived the harassing behaviors as power plays. "This study," says researcher Heather McLaughlin, "provides the strongest evidence to date supporting the theory that sexual harassment is less about sexual desire than about control and domination. . . . Male coworkers . . . and supervisors seem to be using harassment as an equalizer against women in power."

Case Questions

1. In light of the research discussed in this case, in your opinion, how should sexual harassment be punished?

2. What laws relate most closely to sexual harassment?

3. What legal protection, if any, should exist to protect an innocent individual from false charges of sexual harassment?

4. How might sexual harassment relate to bullying?

STUDY TOOLS 2

READY TO STUDY?

In the book, you can:

☐ Rip out the chapter review card at the back of the book for a handy summary of the chapter and key terms.

ONLINE AT CENGAGEBRAIN.COM YOU CAN:

☐ Collect StudyBits while you read and study the chapter.

☐ Quiz yourself on key concepts.

☐ Find videos for further exploration.

☐ Prepare for tests with HR4 Flash Cards as well as those you create.

3 | The Global Environment

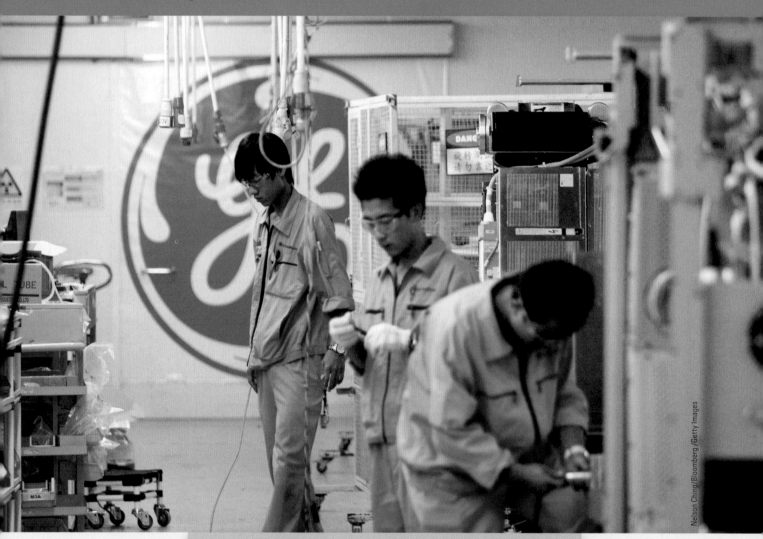

Nelson Ching/Bloomberg /Getty Images

After finishing this chapter go to **PAGE 82** for **STUDY TOOLS**

LEARNING OBJECTIVES

3-1 Describe the growth of international business

3-2 Identify and discuss the global issues in international human resource management

3-3 Discuss the human resource management function in international business

3-4 Identify and discuss the domestic issues in international human resource management

3-5 Describe the issues involved in managing international transfers and assignments

3-6 Summarize the issues in international labor relations

Nelson Ching/Bloomberg/Getty Images

OPENING CASE
On The Move

Businesses have long sought new and innovative ways to lower their costs for producing goods and services. Sometimes their quest includes buying raw materials and equipment from overseas suppliers for lower prices. Sometimes they might borrow from foreign lenders who are offering lower interest rates than can be obtained domestically. But for the last several decades at least, the focus has been on moving jobs to countries where labor costs are low. This practice is called *offshoring*. In fact, it seems like just yesterday that manufacturers were moving their production facilities to Mexico. A business-friendly government combined with an abundant supply of low-cost labor made the northern Mexican border a perfect place to set up shop. The North American Free Trade Agreement (NAFTA) made it relatively painless for businesses to move materials and finished goods back and forth across the U.S.-Mexico border as needed. But the good times slowed beginning around 2003 as Mexican wages crept higher and higher.

At the same time, though, China began to emerge as the world's newest low-cost manufacturing center. Low wages, combined with a nearly endless supply of potential workers, caused hundreds and hundreds of manufacturers to start shutting down their Mexican operations (as well as operations in other low-wage countries) and moving to China. For the next decade, China's burgeoning manufacturing prowess firmly established that country as *the* low-cost manufacturing hub.

But sometimes history has a way of repeating itself. As China's economy boomed, local workers demanded—and received—higher wages. For example, in 2003, Mexican wages were six times higher than comparable wages in China. By 2013, wages in China had escalated to the point where they were almost half of comparable wages in Mexico. Factoring in international shipping costs, manufacturers whose primary markets are in the Western Hemisphere came to see that total costs of producing in Mexico versus China were about the same.

Not surprisingly, then, some firms that once abandoned Mexico for China have started to reverse their course. Casabella, for example, makes cleaning supplies and kitchen

> "We thought moving to China was a good idea. It was good for a while, but now we need to move back to Mexico. Labor costs in China have grown a lot, and we can do just as well in Mexico now."[2]
>
> —MANUFACTURING MARVEL CEO

gadgets. It moved from Mexico to China in 2003 but moved back to Mexico in 2015. Similarly, the Manufacturing Marvel company has long produced toys and novelty items in both China and Mexico. But when the firm's Chinese contracts expired in 2015, the company closed its Chinese operations altogether and now centers all of its manufacturing in Mexico.

Mexico probably won't be the last stop for these firms, however, because for low-cost manufacturers, it generally pays to be where the lowest labor and materials costs are located. But now, at least, Mexico seems to be rising once again. Interestingly, too, some companies that once moved jobs from the United States to other low-wage countries have also started bringing those jobs back to the United States. Both General Electric and Caterpillar, for example, have recently shut down foreign factories and relocated that work back to the United States. In these cases, however, the impetus was not low wages but the inability of some foreign workers to meet rigid quality standards.[1]

THINK IT OVER

1. What can these examples tell us about the pros and cons of offshoring?
2. What conditions might cause a country's labor costs to remain low for an extended period of time?

International business is an ever-growing component of the global economy. During much of 2011 and 2012, this was made obvious to everyone as problems in Europe, ranging from a possible debt default by Greece to shaky credit in Italy to general problems with the euro, affected markets all over the world, and especially in the United States. Almost every large firm located anywhere in the world remains on the alert for new business opportunities anywhere else in the world. Such opportunities include new markets where products and services can be sold, new locations where products and services can be created for lower costs, and areas where new information, financing, and other resources may be obtained. To manage international expansion effectively, firms need skilled and experienced managers and employees who understand both specific individual foreign markets (e.g., Japan or Germany) and general international issues (e.g., exchange rate fluctuations, political risk, and the cost of labor). One of the fastest-growing and most important concerns for human resource managers in many companies today is preparing other managers for international assignments. In reality, however, this is only one part of international human resource management (HRM).

This chapter will explore international HRM in detail. We begin with a general overview of the growth of international business and then discuss global issues in international HRM. Next we examine the HR function in international business. We describe and identify domestic issues in international HRM and then discuss the management of international transfers and assignments. Finally, we summarize the basic issues in international labor relations.

3-1 THE GROWTH OF INTERNATIONAL BUSINESS

International business is not a new phenomenon. In fact, its origins can be traced back literally thousands of years to merchants plying their wares along ancient trade routes linking southern Europe, northern Africa, the Middle East, and Asia. Silks, spices, grains, jade, ivory, and textiles were among the most popular goods forming the basis for early trade. Even in more recent times, Columbus's voyages to the so-called New World were motivated by the economic goal of discovering new trade routes to the Far East. Wars have been fought over issues arising from international commerce, and the British Empire was built around the financial and business interests of the British nobility. In more recent years, however, several specific trends have emerged in international business that provide a meaningful context for the study of HRM.

The forces that shaped today's competitive international business environment began to emerge in the years following World War II. As a result of that global conflict, Japan and most of Europe were devastated. Roads and highways were destroyed, and factories were bombed. The United States was the only major industrial power

that emerged from World War II with its infrastructure relatively intact. Places not devastated by the war, such as South and Central America and Africa, were not major players in the global economy even before the war, and Canada had yet to become a major global economic power.

Businesses in war-torn countries had little choice but to rebuild from scratch. They were in the unfortunate position of having to rethink every facet of their business, including technology, productions, operations, finance, and marketing. Ultimately, however, this position worked to their advantage. During the 1950s, the United States was by far the dominant economic power in the world. Its businesses controlled most major marketplaces and most major industries. At the same time, however, Japan, Germany, and other countries were rebuilding their own infrastructures and developing new industrial clout.

During the 1960s, this newly formed Japanese and German industrial clout began to exert itself in the world marketplace. Such German firms as Siemens, Daimler-Benz, and Bayer, and Japanese companies such as Toyota, NEC, and Mitsubishi, began to take on new industrial strength and slowly but surely began to challenge the dominance of U.S. firms in markets ranging from automobiles to electronics. Firms from other parts of Europe had also fully recovered and were asserting themselves in areas ranging from petroleum and energy (e.g., Shell and British Petroleum) to food (e.g., Nestlé and Cadbury) and luxury goods (e.g., LVMH and Gucci).

By the late 1970s, businesses from other countries emerged as major players in the world economy, and by the 1980s, many of them had established dominant positions in their industries. At the same time, many U.S. firms had grown complacent, their products and services were not of high quality, and their manufacturing and production methods were outdated and outmoded.

Eventually, U.S. firms decided that they had little choice but to start over as well, so many of them practically rebuilt themselves in the late 1980s and early 1990s. They shut down or renovated old factories, developed new manufacturing techniques, and began to renew their emphasis on quality. By the mid-1990s, global competitiveness seemed to have become the norm rather than the exception. The United States, Japan, and Germany

> **Wars have been fought over issues arising from international commerce.**

remained the three leading industrial powers in the world. However, other western European countries such as France, England, the Netherlands, Spain, and Belgium were also becoming increasingly important. In Asia, Taiwan, Singapore, and Malaysia were also emerging as global economic powers. Of course, China and India are clearly emerging as global powers. Few events illustrate this fact better than the acquisition by Lenovo (a Beijing-based PC company) of IBM's PC division a few years ago and the growth of call-center operations in India.

Substantial developments in Europe (which we will discuss below) have strengthened the position of countries there. In North America, Canada and Mexico also began to show promise of achieving economic preeminence in the global marketplaces, and many countries in South America have also begun to globalize their operations. Figure 3.1 illustrates the regions of the world that are especially significant in today's global economy. It is also worth noting that, of the 100 largest firms in the world in 2015 (based on sales), 62 of them are headquartered outside the United States, and there are 15 different countries that have a business on the list. In each case, international business operations are a vital part of the firm's success.

Several other developments in the world also have affected the new global economy. First, many developed countries such as the United States, Japan, and the countries of Western Europe have experienced slowing rates of growth in their populations. This trend

has implications for the demand for certain types of consumer goods as well as for the availability of individuals to work producing those goods. On the other hand, countries such as Mexico, India, Indonesia, and China (despite its one-child-per-couple policy) continue to experience rapid population growth. This growth is fueling a demand for international goods and also makes these locations attractive sites for new businesses or joint ventures. Furthermore, the collapse of the Japanese markets in the late 1990s, the downturns in U.S. markets in 2009, and the various crises in the "eurozone" in 2011–12, made it clear exactly how interdependent global economies really are.

In recent years, there have been several clear illustrations of this interdependence. In 2008, the U.S. financial crisis, based largely on improperly evaluated mortgages, quickly spread to most of the Western world. A few years later, world markets were again threatened as Greece seemed to be ready to default on loans from the International Monetary. Then, in 2015, an inflated Chinese stock market lost some 35 percent of its total value in a few days, impacting markets everywhere. The Chinese economy once again demonstrated its role in world economies when, in 2016, China announced that its economy was not growing at the same rate as it had been, which plunged world markets into another spin as questions were raised about the sustainability of economies that depended on selling to China. In addition, beginning in 2015 and

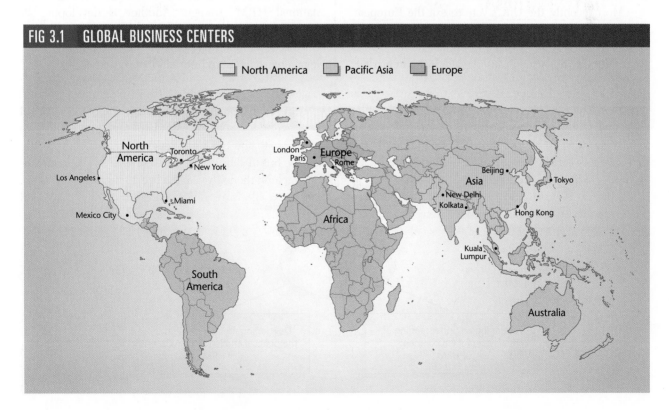

FIG 3.1 GLOBAL BUSINESS CENTERS

ildogesto/Shutterstock.com

all around the world, as no one could predict what a European Union without the United Kingdom would look like and be able to accomplish.

Today, no global organization can ignore elections in Iraq, the developments in the Gaza Strip, or the valuation of the Chinese renminbi. All of these events, once seen as far removed from the concerns of American businesses, now strongly and immediately affect how firms in this country and other countries around the world do business. Finally, as we discuss later, the growth of regional economic alliances has also had substantial effects on the global business community.

3-2 GLOBAL ISSUES IN INTERNATIONAL HUMAN RESOURCE MANAGEMENT

continuing through 2016, dropping prices for oil caused major disruptions to the Dow Jones in the United States as well as to other markets around the world.

Most recently, the U.K.'s vote to exit the European Union in June of 2016 caused the British pound to drop to its lowest level in 30 years, weakened the euro relative to the U.S. dollar, and caused major losses in markets

Various global issues in international HRM must be addressed by any international firm. As shown in Figure 3.2, one issue is the development of an international HRM strategy.[3] Another is developing an understanding of the cultural environment of HRM. A third is developing an understanding of the political and legal environment of international business.

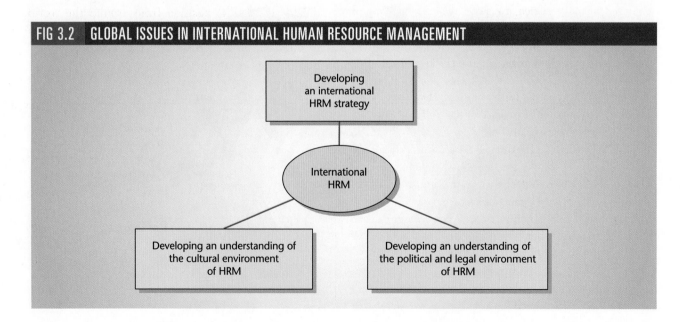

FIG 3.2 GLOBAL ISSUES IN INTERNATIONAL HUMAN RESOURCE MANAGEMENT

Developing an international HRM strategy

International HRM

Developing an understanding of the cultural environment of HRM

Developing an understanding of the political and legal environment of HRM

3-2a International Human Resource Management Strategy

The overall strategy of a business has to be logical and well conceived. The effective management of a firm's international human resources also must be approached with a cohesive and coherent strategy. As a starting point, most international businesses today begin by developing a systematic strategy for choosing among host-country nationals (HCNs), parent-country nationals (PCNs), and third-country nationals (TCNs) for various positions in their organization.[4]

Some firms adopt what is called an **ethnocentric staffing model**. Firms that use this model primarily use parent-country nationals (PCNs) to staff higher-level foreign positions. This strategy is based on the assumption that home-office perspectives and issues should take precedence over local perspectives and issues and that PCNs will be more effective in representing the views of the home office in the foreign operation.[5] The corporate HR function in organizations that adopt this mentality is primarily concerned with selecting and training managers for foreign assignments, developing appropriate compensation packages for those managers, and handling adjustment issues when the manager is reassigned back home. Local HR officials handle staffing and related HR issues for local employees hired to fill lower-level positions in the firm. Sony Corporation's operations in the United States follow this model. Sony Corporation of America, a wholly owned subsidiary of Sony Corporation, handles local HR issues, but top executives at the firm's operations around the United States are Japanese managers from the firm's Japanese home office.

Other international businesses adopt what is called a **polycentric staffing model** that calls for a much heavier use of host-country nationals (HCNs) from top to bottom throughout the organization. Thus, polycentric staffing is used with the assumption that such individuals (i.e., HCNs) are better equipped to deal with local market conditions. Organizations using this approach usually have a fully functioning HR department in each foreign subsidiary that is responsible for managing all local HR issues for lower- and upper-level employees alike. The corporate HR function in such companies focuses primarily on coordinating relevant activities with their counterparts in each foreign operation. U.S. energy

H.Kan/Shutterstock.com

companies operating in Asia often adopt this model, especially because these operations are often joint ventures between the U.S. company and one or more local companies.

Still other firms adopt what is called a **geocentric staffing model**. The geocentric staffing model puts PCNs, HCNs, and TCNs in the same category. The firm then attempts to hire the best person available for a position, regardless of where that individual comes from. The geocentric staffing model is most likely to be adopted and used by fully internationalized firms such as Nestlé and Unilever.[6] In many ways, the corporate HR function in geocentric companies is the most complicated of all. Every aspect of the HRM process—planning, recruiting, selection, compensation, and training—must be undertaken from an international perspective. Each foreign subsidiary or operation still needs its own self-contained HR unit to handle ongoing employment issues.

However, whatever model that is followed, there is growing awareness of the need to adopt a talent management approach to managing human resources internationally.[7] This means using analytics to better understand which resources are critical for operations across cultures and locations. The availability of large databases is especially critical for HR functions such as staffing. After a position is identified as critical for international operations, a multinational firm then needs access to possible candidates to fill this position from around the world. The firm also needs to understand constraints due to different laws, regulations and even religions. Therefore, international HRM may be the area that will be best served by new developments in the area of HR analytics.

3-2b Understanding the Cultural Environment

The cultural environment of international business also poses a variety of more applied challenges and

The **ethnocentric staffing model** primarily uses parent-country nationals to staff higher-level foreign positions.

The **polycentric staffing model** calls for the dominant use of host-country nationals throughout the organization.

The **geocentric staffing model** puts parent-country, host-country, and third-country nationals all in the same category, with the firm attempting to always hire the best person available for a position.

opportunities for HR managers. A country's **culture** can be defined as the set of values, symbols, beliefs, and languages that guide the behavior of people within that culture. A culture does not necessarily coincide precisely with national boundaries, but these two different constructs are sometimes similar in terms of geographic area and domain. All managers in an international business need to be aware of cultural nuances (by definition, HR managers are concerned with people), but they must be especially cognizant of the role and importance of cultural differences and similarities in workers from different cultures.

Cultural beliefs and values are often unspoken and may even be taken for granted by those who live in a particular country. When cultures are similar, relatively few problems or difficulties may be encountered. HR managers can extrapolate from their own experiences to understand their function in the other culture. Thus, U.S. managers often have relatively little difficulty doing business in England. Managers in both countries speak the same language, and a common framework exists for understanding both commercial and personal relationships.

More significant issues can arise, however, when considerable differences exist between the home culture of a manager and the culture of the country in which business is to be conducted. Thus, there is a higher likelihood of culturally related problems and difficulties between managers from, say, Canada and India. Differences in language, customs, and business and personal norms increase the potential for misunderstandings, miscommunication, and similar problems. In these instances, HR managers must be careful to avoid overgeneralizing from their own experiences or perspectives.

Cultural differences can also directly affect business practices in international situations. For example, the religion of Islam teaches that people should not make a living by exploiting the problems of others and that making interest payments is immoral. As a result, no outplacement consulting firms exist in Saudi Arabia and the Sudan (because outplacement involves charging a fee to help terminated workers cope with their misfortunes). As a result of these and myriad other cultural differences, then, managers may encounter unexpected complexities when doing business in countries where these sorts of cultural differences exist.

Language is another important cultural dimension that affects international HRM practices. Most obviously, differences in specific languages such as English, Japanese, Chinese, and Spanish dramatically complicate the issues involved in dealing with international business. Unfortunately, U.S. managers who are fluent in different languages still tend to be relatively rare. When a U.S. organization does find such an employee, that individual usually becomes a valuable asset. On the other hand, it is fairly common for Asian managers to learn English in school, and most European managers are multilingual. It is interesting to note that several years ago, many U.S. colleges and universities (and especially business schools) began dropping foreign-language requirements. As it turns out, those decisions may result in some competitive disadvantage for managers educated in the United States.

The roles that exist in different cultures make up another cultural factor that is directly related to HRM practices. The United States has seen considerable change over the past few decades regarding the role of women in our society. Women have made considerable strides in pursuing and achieving career opportunities previously closed to them. In some parts of the world, however, the situation is quite different. In Japan, for example, women may still find it fairly difficult to launch a successful career. Similar situations exist in some European countries, as well as in almost all the countries in the Middle East. Some role differences

Culture refers to the set of values that helps an organization's members understand what it stands for, how it does things, and what it considers important.

are related to status and hierarchy. In the United States, for example, relatively little psychological distance exists between managers and subordinates, resulting in a certain degree of familiarity and informality. But in many Asian countries, this psychological distance is much greater, resulting in more formalized roles and less informal communication across levels in the organization.

There have been at least two major studies of national values and how they influence behavior at work. The first of these, conducted by Dutch scholar Geert Hofstede, involved managers from 53 different countries.[8] He identified five dimensions of national culture:

1. power distance (or status and authority differences between a superior and a subordinate),

2. individualism versus collectivism (or the extent to which persons define themselves as individuals rather than as members of groups),

3. masculinity versus femininity (assertive, competitive, success-driven values versus quality of life, relationship-oriented values in society),

4. uncertainty avoidance (or preferences for structured rather than unstructured situations), and

5. time orientation (or emphasizing long-term values such as thrift and persistence versus short-term values such as fulfilling social obligations).

More recently, a group of scholars led by Robert House conducted a study of 62 different national cultures.[9] Their GLOBE project (Global Leadership and Organizational Behavior Effectiveness) was built upon the work of earlier scholars and proposed a rather comprehensive nine-dimension framework to explain cultural similarities and differences. Moreover, by further differentiating each value into "as it is" and "as it should be," this framework allows researchers to investigate cultural variations and their impact on managerial practices in a more refined way. Their nine cultural values are:

1. uncertainty avoidance: defined as Hofstede

2. power distance: defined as Hofstede

3. individualism versus collectivism: defined as Hofstede

4. assertiveness: defined the same as masculinity/versus femininity in Hofstede

5. in-group collectivism: how much pride people take in the groups and organizations to which they belong

6. gender egalitarianism: refers to equal opportunities for men and women in society

7. future orientation: degree to which people value long-term planning and investing in the future

8. performance orientation: degree to which people value and reward improvement and excellence in school, athletics, and at work

9. humane orientation: degree to which people value caring, altruistic, and generous behavior

Although Hofstede's work has been applied more widely and is generally better known, there are limitations to his work. Although the initial sample was quite large (100,000), it was drawn from a single organization (IBM). Thus, it is not always possible to know if the effects found in the study were due to country cultures or aspects of the corporate culture that all employees shared. The GLOBE project tried to overcome this limitation by sampling managers from a wide variety of

1000 Words/Shutterstock.com

Locating manufacturing facilities in countries with low labor costs can help a business lower its overall costs and therefore increase profits. However, this practice can also lead to worker exploitation.

organizations in each country, and they used scholars from each country to collect the data. But, while the results of both projects provide useful guidelines for what to expect when dealing with managers from different countries, they should be viewed as guidelines *only*. It is very difficult to make generalizations across the entire population of a country. This is especially the case in countries where there are two or more identifiable subgroups in the population (e.g., Walloon vs. Flemish in Belgium) or where there are strong regional differences based on factors such as race or religion (e.g., China, the United States). Therefore, it is difficult to discuss "the typical American" or "the typical Chinese" in any meaningful way. Nonetheless, the results of both Hofstede's work and the GLOBE project provide some useful ideas about cultural differences that are relevant to HR managers.

Yet another significant cultural factor has to do with children. In the United States, child labor is closely regulated, and children traditionally attend school until they become young adults. In other countries, however, this practice may be quite different. In Bangladesh, it is quite common for children to be a major source of income for their families. Many children do not attend school at all and begin seeking jobs at very young ages. A business operating in such an environment thus faces a significant dilemma. On the one hand, local cultural factors suggest that it is acceptable to hire young children to work for low wages because other businesses do the same. On the other hand, this practice would be illegal or unethical by the standards that exist in most industrialized countries.

The HR manager dealing with international issues thus faces two fundamental cultural challenges. The first challenge is simply understanding and appreciating differences that exist in different cultures. The value of work, orientation toward work, and common work-related attitudes and practices vary significantly from culture to culture, and the HR manager needs to develop an understanding of these differences to function effectively.[10]

The second challenge is more ethical in nature. On the one hand, many businesses relocate manufacturing facilities to other countries to capitalize on lower labor costs. For example, a business from a country such as Japan or the United States can set up a factory in Bangladesh, Pakistan, or other regions of the world and have minimal labor costs there. The ethical issue, however, is the extent to which this situation becomes exploitation. Many people, for instance, would agree that it is reasonable for a company to take advantage of low prevailing wages and benefit costs to achieve low-cost production. But if a company goes too far and truly begins to exploit foreign workers, then problems may arise.

3-2c Understanding the Political and Legal Environment

It is also important for HR managers in international businesses to understand the political and legal environment of the countries in which they do business. Figure 3.3 illustrates four fundamental aspects of the political and legal environment of international business that are of primary concern for HR managers: government stability, potential incentives for international trade, controls on international trade, and the influence of economic communities on international trade. In addition, laws that affect HRM are basic issues, but we will say more about those issues later.[11]

Government stability can be thought of as either the ability of a given government to stay in power against opposing factions or as the permanence of government policies toward business. In general, companies prefer to do business in countries that are stable in both respects because managers have a higher probability of understanding how those governments affect their business. Recent developments in the Middle East underscore the importance of a stable government. For years, several countries' governments faced pressure from

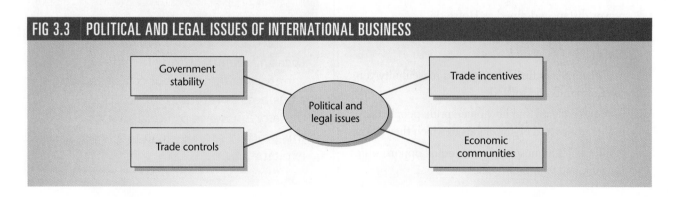

FIG 3.3 | POLITICAL AND LEGAL ISSUES OF INTERNATIONAL BUSINESS

Government stability — Political and legal issues — Trade incentives

Trade controls — Political and legal issues — Economic communities fundamentalist Muslims to establish governments more in line with the Koran. But, beginning in 2011, a new wave of instability struck the region. In January, Tunisian president Zine al-Abidine Ben Ali was overthrown, and elections were held. The Islamist party won the majority of seats, but soon faced pressure from secular Tunisians, leading the prime minister, Hamadi Jebali, to promise to replace Islamist supporters with qualified government technocrats in 2013. The situation there is still not completely stabilized. In August, the government of Muammar al-Gaddafi, the Libyan strongman, was replaced by the Libyan Arab Republic. The proposed economic and political reforms have still not been fully implemented, and there is still unrest. In fact, in September 2012, Libyan terrorists attacked the U.S. Consulate in Benghazi, killing U.S. Ambassador Christopher Stevens and three other Americans. The future of Libya is not only still uncertain, but there is evidence that it may again be a base of operations for terrorist groups, and the army seems to be once again in charge of Egypt following the election and subsequent overthrow of Mohammed Morsi.

> Some countries offer guaranteed labor contracts with local unions as a form of incentive designed to reduce the uncertainties that an entering foreign business faces in negotiating its own initial labor contract.

Unfortunately, the situation in the Middle East seems to be getting worse. Civil war in Syria and continuing violence in Iraq has apparently spawned a new terrorist group called ISIS (sometimes referred to as ISIL), which has taken credit for bombings in the region, in Europe, and in the United States. In addition, this group views itself as an actual state and has a large army that is fighting for territory in Syria. All of this has made this region of the world a much less attractive place to do business.

These developments, along with continuing violence in Iraq, the civil war in Syria, and the continuing conflicts between Israelis and Palestinians, have made this region of the world a less attractive place to do business.

A major HR issue relating to the topic of government stability is the extent to which expatriate managers, or any other representatives of a U.S. firm, may be put at risk as a result of political instability. For years, extremist groups have targeted U.S. executives for terrorist activities. But since September 11, 2001, these fears have grown considerably. Estimates are sketchy, but some experts suggest that at least a few hundred

people are kidnapped each year and are most often released in exchange for a ransom. In the post–September 11 world, many U.S.-based managers are more uncomfortable about traveling to parts of the world where they fear they may be threatened. Heightened security measures on planes and in airports have made these dangers salient to anyone traveling abroad.

In addition, some firms continue to face situations in which their managers are closely watched or even harassed by local government officials on the grounds that they are alleged illegal informants or spies for the U.S. government. Still another risk is the extent to which a business itself might become nationalized, or seized by a foreign government, which claims the company's facilities. Nationalization has occasionally occurred in the Middle East and in certain countries in South America.

Another aspect of the political and legal environment involves the incentives for international trade that are sometimes offered to attract foreign business. Occasionally, municipal governments offer foreign companies tax breaks and other incentives to build facilities in their area. Over the past few years, for example, BMW, Mercedes, and Toyota have built new assembly factories in the United States. In each instance, various state and local governments started what essentially became bidding wars to see who could attract the manufacturing facilities. Examples include reduced interest rates on loans, construction subsidies and tax incentives, and the relaxation of various controls on international trade. Some countries have also offered guaranteed labor contracts with local unions as a form of incentive designed to reduce the uncertainties that an entering foreign business faces in negotiating its own initial labor contract.

A third dimension of the political and legal environment of international business consists of those very controls that some countries place on international trade. Several different controls exist. One is a *tariff,* essentially a tax collected on goods shipped across national boundaries. Tariffs may be levied by the exporting country, countries through which goods pass, or the importing country. The most common form of trade control, however, is the *quota,* a limit on the number or value of goods that can be traded. The quota amount is typically designed to ensure that domestic competitors will be able to maintain a predetermined market share. Honda Motors in Japan,

> "People in China like to be able to say they have the title of manager.... We need a strong platform to attract those people and then develop them."
>
> —JOE HOSKIN, SENIOR HR MANAGER, MICROSOFT CHINA

Thinking Globally, Hiring Locally

When international businesses first began to aggressively move into China and India, they generally transferred expatriate managers from their home company to run these new operations. Among other reasons, the firms felt a need to try to export their corporate cultures and work procedures to the emerging markets they were entering. They also perceived a lack of local managerial talent.

jorisvo/Shutterstock.com

As recently as 25 years ago, for example, virtually every U.S. company doing business in China filled most of its middle and upper management positions in that country with Americans. The few positions not held by Americans were often filled with managers groomed in Singapore and Hong Kong, markets where these firms had operated for many years.

But in the 1990s, things began to change. In China, for instance, many locals sharpened their English language skills, developed more leadership and decision-making skills, and became increasingly familiar and comfortable with the international business world. As a result, more and more locals are entering the ranks of middle- and upper-level managers today. It's estimated, for instance, that around 70 percent of foreign firms' top management positions in China today are filled by Chinese managers. This trend is not restricted to China, the same pattern is also occurring in India.

Nor is this trend found only among U.S. firms in China. The German company Siemens, for instance, has Chinese nationals holding seven of its nine regional management positions there. And Ericsson, a Swedish telecommunications giant, currently fills 90 percent of its middle management positions and half of its top management positions in China with local managers.

Why are firms moving in this direction? There are several reasons. For one thing, hiring local managers is much cheaper. The company avoids costly relocation expenses and does not risk expatriate failure. Further, the compensation package for a local Chinese manager is only around 20 percent to 25 percent of that of a comparable manager transferred from a Western country. Local managers have a strong understanding of local market conditions, competitive behaviors, and government regulations. In addition, hiring locally can boost employee morale and motivation. The local manager has a rich understanding of cultural issues in the workplace and also serves as a symbol of advancement and success for other rising local managers.[12]

THINK IT OVER

1. What are the key HR issues faced by U.S. managers responsible for business activities in China and India?

2. How similar or different are the issues in this case for Chinese managers responsible for business activities in the United States?

for example, is allowed to export exactly 425,000 automobiles each year to the United States. Sometimes, however, companies can circumvent quotas. Honda has built assembly factories in the United States for this purpose because the automobiles they produce within the United States do not count against the 425,000-unit quota.

For the international HR manager, an important set of international controls involves the control of human resources. Some countries require that a foreign business setting up shop within its borders hire a minimum percentage of local employees to work there. For example, a country might require that 80 percent of the production employees and 50 percent of the managers of a foreign-owned business be local citizens. A less common but still salient factor is the control of international travel. Some countries, for instance, limit the number of trips that foreign managers can make in and out of their country in a given period of time. Contemporary Challenges in HR discusses some of the issues associated with hiring local managers versus transferring managers from other parts of the world.

A final aspect of the political and legal environment is the growing importance of the influence of economic communities. Economic communities consist of sets of countries that agree to reduce or eliminate trade barriers among their member nations. One of the most commonly cited economic communities is the European Union (EU). The original EU members were Belgium, France, Luxembourg, Germany, Italy, and the Netherlands. Denmark, Ireland, the United Kingdom, Greece, Portugal, and Spain joined later. Austria, Finland, and Sweden have also been admitted, and several nations have also recently joined, including Cyprus, Malta, and many former Soviet-bloc countries (Bulgaria, the Czech Republic, Estonia, Hungary, Latvia, Lithuania, Poland, Romania, Slovakia, and Slovenia). These countries have been relatively successful in working toward a unified market with no barriers, but, beginning in 2011, they also learned that they shared a certain amount of risk as several potential defaults threatened the stability of the euro and financial stability of each member country.

This EU became much more formidable with the introduction of the euro, a common currency designed to eliminate exchange-rate fluctuations and make cross-national transactions easier. Twelve early members of the EU (all except Denmark, Sweden, and the United Kingdom) officially converted their domestic currencies to the euro on January 1, 2002. These 12 countries now make up what is called the *eurozone*. From an HRM perspective, the advent of the euro brings up two issues: (1) Individuals and employers in the eurozone can more readily compare their compensation packages to those of their peers in other countries because they are all paid in the same currency, and (2) it is easier for firms in the eurozone to transfer managers to other countries.

Nonetheless, there are threats to the union. The admission to the EU of several economically weaker countries, such as Romania and Hungary, put a great deal of strain on the EU's ability to subsidize its members. Other financial risk came when Greece threatened to default in 2011, and when there was talk of default in Italy as well as in Spain. Although these financial threats continue, and the countries involved (especially Greece) continue to struggle with ways to strengthen their economies, in recent months, there have been perils from a different direction.

The decision of the United Kingdom to withdraw from the EU has highlighted problems in other countries with the basic structure of the union. British voters expressed their displeasure with EU rules and restrictions that they felt were limiting their country's ability to make decisions that were best for the UK. Nationalist parties in other EU countries have been voicing similar concerns so that some fear that entire union could unravel. Some of these concerns stem from the austerity measures that have been imposed on countries such as Greece in return for financial support, but there are also threats stemming from the tide of refugees coming to Europe. ISIS and civil war in Syria have produced an unprecedented number of people fleeing that region of the world, and many of them have fled to Europe. As a result, EU member countries are having to deal with huge numbers of refugees seeking asylum, and the administrative problems associated with this move have been staggering. In addition, there is fear that many of these refugees may actually be terrorists or terrorist sympathizers

who are using this mass migration as a way to sneak across borders. Terrorist attacks in Paris, Belgium, and Turkey have made this threat quite clear and real, so it is not surprising that there are groups all over Europe who are opposed to admitting any more refugees from the Middle East. As the groups opposing immigration become more vocal, the strains on the community will become more serious, and, in the long run, these strains may be a greater threat than those posed by weak economic performance.

Another less-comprehensive economic community was created by the North American Free Trade Agreement (NAFTA). NAFTA attempts to reduce the trade barriers that exist among Canada, the United States, and Mexico, making it easier for companies to do business in each of the three countries. Extending NAFTA to other countries in Latin America, especially Chile, has been discussed, but for now at least, it remains a three-country union. No plans for a single currency have been seriously discussed, and HRM practices and laws remain independent. But NAFTA also includes separate labor agreements, which have the potential to affect HRM practices dramatically. The Commission on Labor Co-operation, for example, was established to hear cases dealing with these labor agreements in areas such as child labor, occupational safety and health, and union–management relations. Some of these standards are more stringent than those imposed by U.S.-based legislation (see Chapter 2). Although it is not clear how much enforcement power the Commission on Labor Cooperation will have, it is possible that HR managers will have to deal with an even more complex set of regulations in

> The North American Free Trade Agreement (NAFTA) reduced trade barriers among Canada, the United States, and Mexico. NAFTA also includes separate labor agreements among the three countries.

the future. It is interesting to note that these standards would apply not only to U.S. companies doing business in Mexico or Canada but also to U.S. companies doing business solely in this country.

3-3 THE HUMAN RESOURCE FUNCTION IN INTERNATIONAL BUSINESS

All basic international functions—marketing, operations, finance, and HR—play a vital role in international business. The HR function, for example, must deal with several general, fundamental management challenges in international business.[13] These challenges are illustrated in Figure 3.4. In addition, specific HRM implications exist for the different forms of international business activity that firms can pursue.

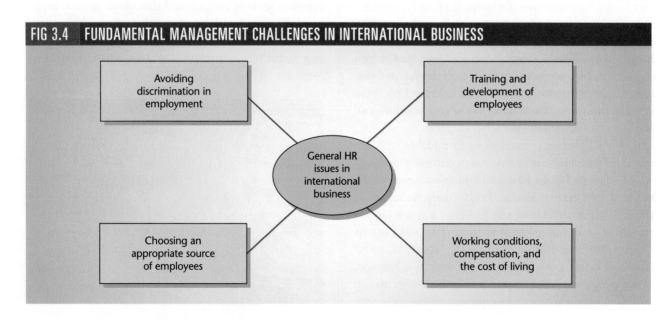

FIG 3.4 FUNDAMENTAL MANAGEMENT CHALLENGES IN INTERNATIONAL BUSINESS

- Avoiding discrimination in employment
- Training and development of employees
- General HR issues in international business
- Choosing an appropriate source of employees
- Working conditions, compensation, and the cost of living

3-3a General Human Resource Issues in International Business

One general set of challenges relates to differences that may exist in culture, levels of economic development, and legal systems that typify the countries where the firm operates. These differences may force an international organization to customize its hiring, firing, training, and compensation programs on a country-by-country basis. A particularly difficult set of issues arises when conflict exists between the laws or cultures of the home country and those of the host country.

The first issue of conflict is discrimination. For example, as described in Chapter 2, it is illegal in the United States to discriminate in an employment relationship on the basis of gender. In Saudi Arabia, on the other hand, such discrimination is not only allowed but also expected. Women are highly restricted in their career opportunities, and a firm doing business in that country has to balance its own affirmative action efforts with the legal and cultural restrictions imposed by that country. And overt discrimination is still actively practiced in many other countries as well.[14] As we noted, the Civil Rights Act of 1991 allows employees of U.S. firms working abroad to sue their employers if they violate the Civil Rights Act. But exception to this privilege exists when a country has a law that specifically contradicts the Civil Rights Act. For example, a woman could not sue a U.S. company operating in Saudi Arabia for sex discrimination because some discrimination against women is actually prescribed by law in that country. On the other hand, Japan has no laws institutionalizing such discrimination, so a woman could bring suit against a U.S. firm operating there if it were guilty of discriminatory practices.

The second fundamental HR challenge in international business (a topic introduced earlier) is the determination of the most appropriate source of employees: the host country, the home country, or a third country. The ideal combination of employees differs according to the location of a firm's operations, the nature of its operations, and myriad other factors. A company is more likely to hire local employees, for example, for lower-level jobs with minimal skill requirements and for which there is a reasonable local supply of labor. Again, it is also necessary to consider local laws or customs that may limit or constrain hiring practices. For instance, immigration laws may limit the number of work visas that a firm can grant to foreigners, and employment regulations may mandate the hiring of local citizens as a requirement for doing business in a particular country.

But this situation is changing to some extent. Twenty-five years ago, companies doing business in places such as Singapore would have relied on the local labor market for hourly employees only. Over the years, however, Singapore and other countries have made significant investments in their human capital. As a result, a large pool of well-educated (often at Western universities), highly motivated locals who are qualified for and interested in management positions now exists in these same countries. Some U.S.-based organizations are taking advantage of these relatively new labor pools by hiring local employees and then transferring them to the United States for training before returning them to their home country, where they can play a key role in managing the global enterprise. U.S.-based universities are increasingly opening branches for graduate study in places such as Singapore and China, as are European universities, especially INSEAD.

Third, international businesses must also deal with complex training and development challenges. At one level, for example, HR managers need to provide cross-cultural training for corporate executives who are chosen for overseas assignments. In addition, training programs for production workers in host countries must be tailored to represent the education offered by local school systems. Dramatic differences in the skill and educational levels within a labor force make it necessary for international businesses to pay close attention to the training and development needs of all its employees in foreign markets.[15] But again, the establishment of institutions of higher education from the United States, the United Kingdom, France, and Australia has changed the face of local training and education in many countries, especially in Asia.

The fourth important international HRM question relates to working conditions, compensation, and the cost of living. It costs more for people to live and work in some countries than in others. A general stance adopted by most international businesses is that an employee should not suffer a loss of compensation or a decrease in his or her standard of living by virtue of accepting an international assignment. Thus, HR managers must determine how to compensate executives who accept overseas assignments and who face higher costs of living, a reduction in their quality of life, or unhappiness or stress because of separation from family or friends. This stance, however, can create some additional complications that we will address later when dealing with issues for expatriate managers.

3-3b Specific Human Resource Issues in International Business

Organizations can adopt a wide variety of strategies for competing in the international environment. Each strategy poses its own unique set of challenges for HR managers. One common strategy is **exporting**, which is the process of making a product in the firm's domestic marketplace and then selling it in another country. Exporting can involve both goods and services. U.S. agricultural cooperatives export grain to Russia while major consulting firms sell their services to companies in Europe and Asia. Other businesses ship gas turbines to Saudi Arabia, locomotives to Indonesia, blue jeans to Great Britain, computers to Japan, disposable diapers to Italy, and steel to Brazil; others sell airline service, information-technology support, and various other service products.

Such an approach to international business has many advantages. First, it is usually the easiest way to enter a new market. In addition, it typically requires only a small outlay of capital. Because the products are usually sold "as is," there is no need to adapt them to local conditions. Finally, relatively little risk is involved. On the other hand, products exported to other countries are often subject to taxes, tariffs, and high transportation expenses. In addition, because the products are seldom adapted to local conditions, they may not actually address the needs of consumers in local markets, and consequently the products may not achieve their full revenue potential. The shipment of some products across national boundaries is also restricted by various government regulations. For example, it is not easy for ranchers from the United Kingdom to export beef into the United States because of complex regulations designed to protect U.S. domestic beef producers.

If the firm functions solely as an exporter, the HR function faces no meaningful differences in responsibilities from those in a domestic business. An exporting company usually has an export manager, and that manager likely has a staff to assist in the various parts of the exporting process. HR managers usually play a role in hiring people for these jobs and oversee other aspects of their employment, such as compensation and performance appraisal. But other than perhaps some exporting-specific skills required for workers in this department, these employees are treated the same as employees in the operations, sales, or finance departments. Thus, when a domestic firm begins to export to a foreign market, the HR function may be extended to include another set of employees, but it does not change in any other meaningful way.

Another popular form of international business strategy is called **licensing**. Under this agreement, a company grants its permission to another company in a foreign country to manufacture or market its products in the foreign country's local market. For example, a clothing manufacturer might allow a manufacturer in another country to use its design, logo, and materials to manufacture clothing under the original firm's name. Under such an agreement, the licensing firm typically pays a royalty or licensing fee to the original firm based on the number of units it actually sells. Microsoft licenses software firms in other countries to produce and distribute software products such as Office and Windows in their local markets.

The major advantage of this strategy is that it allows the firm to enter a foreign market with relatively little risk and to gain some market exposure and develop name recognition that will make it easier for it to enter the market more aggressively in the future. On the other hand, its profits are limited to those it receives from the royalty payment. Likewise, the firm must also be vigilant to ensure that its quality standards are upheld.

If a firm is involved in international business activities exclusively via licensing, the HR function is approached in the same way as in a pure exporting enterprise. In other words, no meaningful differences in the HR function likely exist, but HR managers need to extend their existing services and responsibilities to employees associated with the licensing activities. The HR function itself does not really change in any meaningful way.

A third international strategy for doing business is **direct foreign investment**. A direct investment occurs when a firm headquartered in one country builds or purchases operating facilities or subsidiaries in a foreign country; that is, the firm actually owns physical assets in the other country. Boeing, for example, constructed a composite materials factory in China. This business activity represents a direct investment on the part of Boeing. Other examples of direct investment include the Disney Corporation's construction of a new theme park near Hong Kong, a Mercedes Benz plant

Exporting is the process of making a product in the firm's domestic marketplace and then selling it in another country. Exporting can involve both goods and services.

Licensing involves one company granting its permission to another company in a foreign country to manufacture or market its products in its local market.

Direct foreign investment occurs when a firm headquartered in one country builds or purchases operating facilities or subsidiaries in a foreign country.

in Alabama, and Procter & Gamble's construction of a major new distribution center in Brazil.

As already noted, there are actually two different forms of direct investment. First, the firm can simply acquire an existing business in the foreign country. This has been the primary strategy used by Walmart as it entered the market in the United Kingdom—it bought existing retail chains and then converted them to Walmart stores. This approach provides nearly instant access to new markets, but it may require protracted negotiations over the acquisition; afterward, the firm also faces the challenge of how to integrate the new acquisition into its other operations. Alternatively, the firm can create or build a new wholly owned subsidiary, factory, or other unit. This takes much more time, carries much greater risk, and is much more expensive, yet it also represents the path to the greatest potential profits.

In either case, direct investment has the advantage that it provides the firm its own company-owned facilities in the foreign country, and allows it to become truly integrated in a particular foreign market. Considerably more profit potential can be realized in direct investment because the company itself keeps all the profits its investment earns in that country. On the other hand, considerably more risk is attached to this strategy. Just as the investing firm can keep all its profits, so too must it absorb any and all losses and related financial setbacks. In addition, of course, the costs of direct investment are also quite high and borne solely by the investing firm.

At this level of international business activity, the HR function changes substantially from that of a domestic firm or business using a pure exporting or licensing strategy. This difference stems from the fact that in a direct investment, employees of the firm are working in foreign locations. Depending on the nationalities reflected in the foreign workforce (i.e., whether the firm uses a polycentric, geocentric, or ethnocentric approach to hiring), the corporate HR function will need to extend and expand its scope and operations to provide the appropriate contributions to firm performance as determined by the philosophy used for staffing the foreign operations.

A fourth form of international strategy is a **joint venture** or **strategic alliance**. In this case, two or more firms cooperate in the ownership or management of an operation, often on an equity basis. *Joint venture* is the traditional term used for such an arrangement and describes a situation in which actual equity ownership exists. A strategic alliance might not involve ownership but still involves cooperation between firms. Both arrangements are rapidly growing in importance in the international business environment. They represent a way for two or more firms to achieve synergy from working together, they reduce risk, and they provide mutual benefit to both partners. The airline industry has seen several strategic alliances. One of the largest is known as the Star Alliance. This group includes United Airlines, Lufthansa, Swiss Air, Air New Zealand, South African Airways, Singapore Airlines, and Air China, among other airlines from all over the world. This alliance makes it easier for travelers to place reservations, purchase tickets, and make connections between any two or more partners in the alliance. This flexibility also makes the group itself more competitive relative to other airlines.

HR managers in a firm that uses this strategy face an even more complex set of issues and challenges. If the new operation is a separate legal entity that functions as a semiautonomous enterprise, the corporate HR staff of each strategic partner needs to determine how to link and coordinate with their counterparts in both the new venture (seen as a separate entity) and their partner. If the new venture is operated within the context of one of the existing partner's organization structures, the HR function becomes more complicated still because of the disparate relationships among the HR staff

> In a **joint venture (strategic alliance)**, two or more firms cooperate in the ownership or management of an operation on an equity basis.

for the new venture and its counterparts in both the partner within which it operates and the other partner (this latter relationship is somewhat more distant).

 3-4
DOMESTIC ISSUES IN INTERNATIONAL HUMAN RESOURCE MANAGEMENT

Regardless of their level of internationalization, all firms dealing in foreign markets must confront three sets of domestic issues in the management of their human resources. These domestic issues, shown in Figure 3.5, are local recruiting and selection, local training, and local compensation.

3-4a Local Recruiting and Selection Issues

Nonmanagerial employees, such as blue-collar production workers and white-collar clerical and office workers, are usually host-country nationals (HCNs) in international business. Basic and fundamental economic reasons explain this pattern. Simply put, HCNs are usually cheaper to employ than parent-country nationals (PCNs) or third-country nationals (TCNs). HCNs are also frequently used because local laws usually promote the hiring of locals.[16] Immigration laws, for example, may restrict jobs to citizens and legal residents of a country. Thus, an international business must develop and implement a plan for recruiting and selecting its employees in a host-country market. This plan must include assessments of the firm's HR needs, primary sources of labor in that country, labor force skills and talents, and training requirements. In addition, the plan should account for special circumstances that exist in the local markets. When firms hire PCNs for foreign assignments, they must obviously adhere to their home-country hiring regulations. But when hiring HCNs, they must also be aware of the regulations, laws, and norms that govern employment relationships within the host country. Thus, even though the reliance on PCNs may be less expensive, it adds complexity to the employment relationship.[17]

3-4b Local Training Issues

HR managers must also understand the training and development needs of the host country's workforce to help HCNs perform their jobs most effectively. These needs of a local workforce depend on several factors. One, of course, is the location of the foreign market. In highly industrialized markets such as England and Japan, organizations can usually find a cadre of capable employees who may need only a small amount of firm-specific training. But in a relatively underdeveloped area, training and development needs will be much more extensive.

For example, when Hilton first began opening hotels in Eastern Europe, it found that restaurant waiters, desk clerks, and other customer-service employees lacked the basic skills necessary to provide high-quality service to guests. Because Eastern European employees were accustomed to working in a planned economy in which they did not have to worry about customer satisfaction, they had difficulty recognizing why it was important to shift their focus. As a result, Hilton had

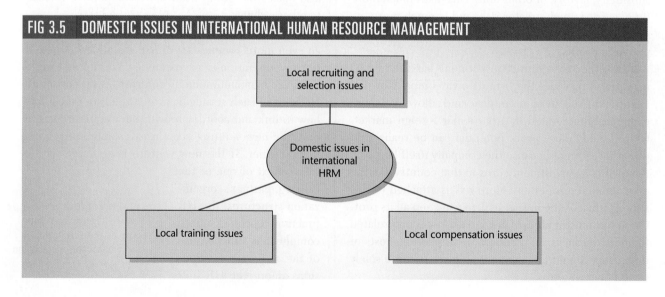

FIG 3.5   DOMESTIC ISSUES IN INTERNATIONAL HUMAN RESOURCE MANAGEMENT

Local recruiting and selection issues

Domestic issues in international HRM

Local training issues

Local compensation issues

to invest considerably more than originally planned in training employees to provide customer service. Training is also important if international business wants to take full advantage of locating production abroad. Many firms move production facilities to areas with low labor costs such as Malaysia and Mexico but then find that the productivity of the labor force is relatively low. Thus, they have to invest additional training and development dollars to bring the workforce up to the performance standards they expect.

Danilo Ascione/Shutterstock.com

3-4c Local Compensation Issues

Compensation must also be addressed at a local level for international businesses. Some countries, such as the United States, focus compensation on assessing an individual's performance and then compensating that individual accordingly. In other countries, however, such as Japan, the emphasis is based more on group work and less on individual performance. Dramatic differences in lifestyles, standards of living, and regulation also cause a wide variation in the way in which firms compensate their employees in different foreign locations.

Of course, dramatic differences in benefit packages are offered to workers in different countries as well. In countries with socialized medicine such as

the United Kingdom, firms do not have to worry as much about paying all or part of employee health-insurance premiums (although they pay higher taxes to help support the government program). In Italy, most workers expect to have several hours off in the afternoon. Also, Italy and Britain legally mandate 4 weeks of vacation a year, while France and Denmark mandate 5 weeks. In contrast, U.S. firms are not legally required to provide any vacation leave.[18]

It is also important for international HR managers to look at the total picture of compensation rather than on some simple index such as the hourly wage. For example, as already noted, some firms choose to move production to Mexico to take advantage of lower labor costs. Although labor costs in Mexico are cheaper than they are in the United States (when compared on an hourly basis), Mexican law requires employers to pay maternity leave to their employees, provide a Christmas bonus equal to 15 days' pay, and provide at least 3 months of severance pay for workers who are terminated. Lower labor costs thus may be at least partially lost because of these and other higher costs for other benefits.

> "Globalization means we have to re-examine some of our ideas, and look at ideas from other countries, from other cultures, and open ourselves to them. And that's not comfortable for the average person."
>
> —HERBIE HANCOCK, INTERNATIONALLY RENOWNED MUSICIAN

3-5 MANAGING INTERNATIONAL TRANSFERS AND ASSIGNMENTS

Another extremely important part of international HRM is the effective management of expatriate employees.[19] **Expatriates** are employees who are sent by a firm to work in another country; they may be either PCNs or TCNs. Particularly important areas here include selecting, training, and compensating expatriates. It is also important to understand how the management of expatriates is related to a firm's international strategy.[20]

> **Expatriates** are employees who are sent by a firm to work in another country; they may be either parent-country or third-country nationals.

3-5a Expatriates and Corporate International Strategy

To a large extent, how a firm deals with expatriates should depend on the strategy the firm is pursuing in terms of its international operations. We can best understand this relationship if we think about how expatriates help multinational corporations (MNCs) compete by playing a role in the knowledge-transfer process. This process involves the acquisition of knowledge as well as the diffusion of knowledge throughout the organization; some people have argued that MNCs exist primarily because they can transfer and exploit knowledge more efficiently and effectively than by using external market mechanisms.[21]

The expatriate manager is the key player in this knowledge-transfer and diffusion process; unfortunately, this manager may not have a real incentive to share the information he or she has acquired. If the expatriate manager does not share all the information acquired, then he or she will have a monopoly on that information, which can be to the manager's advantage (referred to as "opportunistic behavior"). Furthermore, the organization cannot possibly know all the information the expatriate manager has acquired. This then poses the classic agency problem[22] in which the incentives of the parties are not aligned, and there is an asymmetry in terms of who knows what. Furthermore, this problem can become more or less severe, depending on which international strategy the organization uses.

Table 3.1 shows the situation relative to potential agency problems for each of four international strategies proposed by Bartlett and Goshal.[23] Firms carrying out a global strategy rely heavily on direction from the home office, with one global strategy applied to all operations. Expatriate managers are not capable of making important decisions and so have less opportunity to behave opportunistically, and there is a low level of information asymmetry (lowest risk of agency problems). Firms employing an international strategy also rely heavily on headquarters expertise, although this expertise is adapted to local needs. The threat of opportunistic behavior and information asymmetry are also low here, but not as low as with the global strategy (low risk of agency problems). The threat of opportunistic behavior and information asymmetry are higher when a firm adopts a transnational strategy (higher risk of agency problems). Here the expatriate manager is expected to acquire, leverage, and transfer specialized knowledge. The only limit to the expatriate's opportunistic behavior is the need to get locals to go along with the behavior. Finally, firms using a multidomestic strategy face the greatest threats for opportunistic behavior and greatest information asymmetry (highest risk of agency problems) because all decision-making is decentralized.

For the MNC to manage the expatriate's information acquisition successfully in cases where there is a transnational or multidomestic strategy, the firm may implement a "knowledge contract" by which the organization systematically debriefs expatriate managers to make sure it has all the information acquired by the managers and can later diffuse that information throughout the firm. From this perspective, the success of an expatriate assignment depends on the volume and quality of the information acquired by the expatriate and shared with the organization and its members.[24]

3-5b Selecting Expatriates

Recruiting and selecting employees for an international business requires that the HR manager address two sets of questions.[25] The first set of questions involves the definition of skills and abilities necessary to perform the work that the organization needs to have done. The second set relates to defining the skills and abilities that are needed to work in a foreign location.

The first step, then, is to define the actual skills necessary to do the job. Different types of assignments typically require different types of skills for success. Traditionally, expatriate managers were sent abroad to provide some technical expertise that was not available in the local economy. In such cases, it is extremely important that the manager selected has the requisite technical skills and communication skills needed to work with less technically adept workers. Because these assignments are often for a limited time, however, it may be less critical that the manager possess extensive cultural skills. But multinational enterprises (MNEs) more and more often send managers overseas, not to help the overseas operation, but to

TABLE 3.1	THREAT OF OPPORTUNISM AND ASYMMETRY OF INFORMATION AS A FUNCTION OF INTERNATIONAL CORPORATE STRATEGY	
Strategy		**Risk for Potential Agency Problems**
Global (one strategy for all)		Lowest
International (one strategy adapted for local needs)		Low
Transnational (high transfer with much independence)		High
Multidomestic (strategy developed in each country)		High

help the manager. In other words, they see expatriate assignments as a critical developmental opportunity that is essential for career progress.[26] Clearly, success in these assignments is based less on technical skills, and cultural skills are far more critical because the expatriate manager is supposed to learn from his or her experience and carry this information back to the home country. Some of the more common skills and abilities assumed to be necessary in this regard include adaptability, language ability, overall physical and emotional health, relatively high levels of independence and self-reliance, and appropriate levels of experience and education. We will say more about required skills and abilities later in the chapter.

The recruitment of employees for international business is an important step in the HRM process. International businesses attempt to recruit experienced managers through various channels. One common source of recruits is the firm itself. A good starting place may be to seek employees already working for the firm and in the host country who might be prepared for international assignment. In some cases, the firm may be selecting individuals for their first international assignment, but in other cases, they may be selecting people for their second or third international assignment. Nestlé, for example, maintains a cadre of approximately 200 managers who are capable of and willing to accept an international assignment anywhere the firm does business.[27]

> "Together we can help transform the global economy into a global community."
> —ROBERT ALAN SILVERSTEIN, WRITER, ARTIST, AND SOCIAL ACTIVIST

International businesses also frequently look to other organizations as a source of prospective managers. These may be home-country managers who are qualified for an international assignment or managers already working in an international assignment for another firm. For higher-level positions in an organization, international businesses often rely on professional recruiting firms to help them identify prospective managerial candidates. These recruiters, often called *headhunters,* are recruiting firms that actively seek qualified managers and other professionals for possible placement in positions in other organizations. Headhunting has long been an accepted practice in the United States. In both Japan and Europe, headhunting was considered unethical until recently. Within the past decade or so, however, headhunting has become a more accepted practice in most industrialized countries.[28]

Increasingly, many firms are finding it necessary to hire new college graduates for immediate foreign assignment. Traditionally, this practice has been relatively unpopular because organizations believed that managers needed to develop experience in a firm's domestic operations before taking on an international assignment. Because of both the shortage of global managers and the recent emphasis that many colleges of business are placing on training international managers, however, firms are finding that they can hire younger managers and place them in foreign assignments more quickly than in the past. Potential managerial candidates with foreign-language skills, international travel experience, and course work in international business or related fields are especially attractive candidates for firms in this position.[29]

After a pool of qualified applicants has been identified, the organization must then select the managers that it needs for international assignments. In general, organizations look at three sets of criteria for selecting people for international assignments: managerial competence, language training, and adaptability to new situations. It is extremely important that organizations select managers for international assignments with deliberate care. The cost of a failed international assignment is extremely high.[30]

The real question, however, is how a firm should determine the failure—or the success—of an expatriate assignment. Traditionally, failure had been defined as an expatriate returning from an assignment before the scheduled time, but several scholars have pointed out why early termination may not be truly related to failure.[31] Newer perspectives on the success or failure of expatriate assignments means that failure rates may not be as high as had been previously suggested, but there is still some disagreement on how to best assess success and failure. Some experts have suggested that some type of performance evaluation be used,[32] but others have argued, instead, that the assessment of success or failure should be tied directly to the purpose for the initial assignment.

These scholars note that the efficient transfer of knowledge is one source of competitive advantage for MNEs and that expatriate assignments are an excellent means by which to transfer that knowledge, especially when that knowledge is more tacit (i.e., knowledge that cannot be easily codified). Thus, they suggest that success (or failure) be assessed relative to the knowledge that was successfully transferred, including knowledge that expatriates were supposed to disperse to subsidiary operations as well as knowledge that expatriates were supposed to gain and bring back to the headquarters, among other critical links.[33]

In any case, a number of factors seem to contribute to the success or failure of any international assignment. One factor is the inability of the manager or the manager's spouse and family to adjust to a new location. Evidence suggests that this inability interferes with the manager's ability to adjust to the new setting and subsequently contributes to failure.[34] As a result of this pattern, some firms are beginning to pay more attention to helping spouses and children adjust to the new environment, and many other firms are placing a greater emphasis on the non-technical aspects of a prospective manager's suitability for a foreign assignment. For example, they look closely at a person's cultural adaptability, as well as the adaptability of his or her family. It is also important to consider the perspective of an international manager's motivation for and real interest in the foreign assignment. Some managers are attracted to foreign assignments because they relish the thought of living abroad or perhaps they see the experience as being useful in their career plans.[35] In addition, personality and international experience (of any type) also seem to be important determinants of expatriate success.[36]

Regardless of their motives in seeking international assignments, and regardless of their skills and abilities to carry out those assignments, many managers who do not have a realistic preview of what an international assignment really is become disillusioned within a few months of accepting such an assignment. Thus, it is critical that organizations prepare managers completely for what they might expect when they move overseas. It is also becoming clear that once expatriate managers arrive at their new assignments, they must receive support and help from the HCNs with whom they will be working.[37] This realization is quite important because it may have far-reaching implications for other expatriate HR policies. Specifically, as we will see later, a great deal of attention is given to the problem of how to compensate expatriate managers. Most of the policies and practices result in expatriate managers earning considerably more than any host-country counterparts. In the past, this problem was not that serious because few local managers had the background and training of the expatriates. In fact, it was this very lack of local competence that led many organizations to assign expatriate managers. But, as noted earlier, organizations increasingly see expatriate assignments as helpful to the home-country manager. As a result, he or she may be

assigned to a foreign post even though other HCNs or local employees are capable of doing the same job. As many countries more routinely send potential managers abroad for training and education, the local employee may well be as qualified in every way as the expatriate. To date, however, most expatriate policies dictate that the expatriate manager would earn more than the local doing the same or a similar job. This situation can lead to resentment on the part of the HCN and can potentially lead the HCN to withhold the help and support the expatriate needs to be successful. Does this mean that expatriates should not be compensated for their overseas assignments? Surely not, but it does mean that organizations may have to take a closer look at their expatriate policies and practices and evaluate them in light of the importance of obtaining HCN support for the expatriate once he or she arrives in the new assignment.[38]

In this vein, it is also interesting to note that there may be other factors—in addition to pay differences—that might influence the willingness of HCNs to provide critical support to expatriates. Several studies have found that, when expatriates are categorized as belonging to the "out-group" (as opposed to the in-group) by HCNs, the local employees are reluctant to share critical information with the expatriates.[39] Subsequent research has suggested that ethnocentric attitudes (on the part of both parties) and general affect, as well as perceived differences in nationality and background, all play a role in this categorization process and result in less support and information sharing on the part of the HCNs.[40]

3-5c Training Expatriates

Given the potential costs involved in failure, it is not surprising that organizations also spend a great deal of time and money on training expatriate managers. General Motors spends almost $500,000 a year on cross-cultural training for 150 or so U.S. managers and

Monkey Business Images/Shutterstock.com

their families heading to international assignments. The firm reports that less than 1 percent of its expatriate assignments fail, and it attributes much of its success to its training program.[41] Training (as we will cover more fully in Chapter 14) is instruction directed at enhancing specific job-related skills and abilities and most often focuses on operating employees and technical specialists. For example, a training program might be designed to help employees learn to use a new software package as part of an international communication network. Development (also covered more fully in Chapter 14) is general education devoted to preparing future managers for higher-level positions or new assignments within the organization. For example, a development program might span several months or even years and be targeted to help managers improve their ability to make decisions, motivate subordinates to work harder, and develop more effective strategies for the organization.[42]

Training for expatriate managers may be as "simple" as language training (which is not especially simple if it involves a completely unfamiliar language such as Japanese or Arabic for the English speaker), or it can be rather involved. For example, language-training programs and other forms of language training from CD-ROMs, apps, videos, and similar media are common and fairly inexpensive.[43] In addition, it is common to have some type of classroom training dealing with the history of the country or the area and with daily living conditions (e.g., how to make a phone call or hail a cab). It is also typical to have some training component that deals with social manners and issues involved in social exchanges (e.g., when one should and should not shake hands, and how deeply to bow).[44]

The Cultural Assimilator is a more complex training program built around short case studies and critical incidents. It asks the manager how he or she would react to different situations and then provides detailed feedback on the correct responses.[45] In addition, firms are more often sending prospective expatriates to their ultimate foreign destination for short periods of time before their permanent move. This experience allows them to become

acculturated on a gradual basis and to obtain a truly realistic picture of what life will be like. But whatever the exact nature of the training, the goals of expatriate training are becoming clearer and more consistent. Increasingly, multinational organizations are recognizing that managers given overseas assignments must be able to communicate with others in the host country and be able to adapt to different lifestyles and values. When we consider all the factors that seem to go into expatriate success, it becomes clearer why some have suggested that a manager given an assignment in a foreign country must possess "the patience of a diplomat, the zeal of a missionary, and the language skills of a U.N. interpreter."[46]

3-5d Compensating Expatriates

As noted earlier, compensation is another important issue in international HRM. To remain competitive, an organization must provide compensation packages for its managers that are comparable to those in a given market. Compensation packages include salary and nonsalary items and are jointly determined by labor-market forces such as the supply and demand of managerial talent, professional licensing requirements, the standard of living, occupational status, and government regulations.[47]

Most international businesses need to provide expatriate managers with differential compensation to make up for differences in currency valuation, standards of living, lifestyle norms, and so on. When managers are on short-term assignments at a foreign location, their salaries are often tied to their domestic currency and home-country living standards. Of course, these managers are reimbursed for short-term living expenses such as the cost of hotel rooms, meals, and local transportation. If the foreign assignment is for a longer time period, however, compensation is usually adjusted to allow the manager to maintain her or his home-country standard of living. This adjustment is particularly important if the manager is transferred from a low-cost location to a high-cost location or from a country with a relatively high standard of living to one with a relatively low standard of living.[48]

Fotosearch/Jupiter Images

Differential compensation usually starts with a cost-of-living allowance. This basic difference in salary is intended to offset the differences in the cost of living between home and host countries. The logic is that if managers accept a foreign assignment, they should enjoy the same standard of living as they would have enjoyed had they remained in their home country. If the cost of living in the foreign country is higher than that at home, then the manager's existing base pay alone will result in a lower standard of living. The firm may therefore need to supplement the base pay to offset the difference. On the other hand, if the cost of living at a foreign location is lower than that at home, no such allowance is needed (few companies would actually lower the manager's salary).

Occasionally, organizations might have to provide an additional salary inducement simply to convince people to accept a foreign assignment. Many employees may be relatively interested in accepting assignments to countries such as England, France, Italy, or Japan, but it may be more difficult to entice people to accept a position in Haiti, Pakistan, or Vietnam. Thus, organizations sometimes find it necessary to provide what is called a **hardship premium** or a **foreign service premium**. Total Fina Elf S.A. is a large French oil company with substantial holdings in the African country of Angola. During a recent bloody civil war in the country, however, Total pulled its employees out. When the war ended, Total began to again assign managers to run its Angolan operations. But because of lingering violence and other concerns, the firm had to provide them with a 25 percent salary premium and many other incentives to get the desired mix of managers who would agree to accept their new assignments. Likewise, during the reconstruction efforts in Iraq in 2004–2007, U.S. contractors such as KBR (a large military contractor) also paid substantial premiums to attract and retain employees willing to work there. This premium (called an *uplift* by the firm) was sometimes more than the individual employee's base salary.

Many international businesses also find that they must set up a tax-equalization system for their managers on foreign assignments. This system ensures that the expatriates' after-tax income in the host country is comparable to what the after-tax income would have been in the person's home country.

A **hardship premium** (also called a **foreign service premium**) is an additional financial incentive offered to individuals to entice them to accept a "less than attractive" international assignment.

Every country has its own unique income tax laws that apply to the earnings of its citizens or to earnings within its borders by foreign citizens, and companies must develop plans to make sure that the tax burden for individuals is equalized relative to the amount of salary they earn.

The other part of compensation besides salary is benefits. Most international businesses find that, in addition to salary adjustments, they must also provide benefit adjustments. Special benefits for managers on foreign assignments usually include housing, education, medical treatment, travel to the home country, and club membership. Housing benefits are usually provided as a way to help equalize housing expenses in different areas. Equalizing the type of housing an executive enjoys in her or his home country may be expensive, so housing is usually treated as a separate benefit for expatriate managers. If a manager is going on a long-term or permanent foreign assignment, then the organization may buy the manager's existing home and help the manager buy a home in the host country.

Mr. Griffin & Mr. DeNisi

Flirt/SuperStock

Firms also find it increasingly necessary to provide job-location assistance for the spouse of an executive being transferred abroad and to help cover the education costs for their children. Children may need to attend private schools, and the firm would pay the tuition and perhaps other school fees. Medical benefits are also often adjusted for managers on international assignment. For example, some people consider medical facilities in Malaysia to be substandard; as a result, firms that transfer employees to that country often find it necessary to agree that their employees can travel to Singapore whenever they need something other than routine medical attention.

International businesses may also provide expatriates with a travel allowance for trips back to the home country for personal reasons such as visiting other family members or celebrating holidays. Managers and their families may typically be allowed one or two trips home per year for personal reasons at the company's expense. If the assignment is relatively short term, and a manager's family remains at home, then the manager may be provided with even more trips home to compensate for the fact that the manager and her or his family are separated.

Finally, it may be necessary to provide certain kinds of club memberships. In some cultures, for example, belonging to a specific club or participating in a particular activity is a necessary part of the business world. The Japanese, for instance, often conduct business during a round of golf. At the same time, golf-club memberships in Japan cost thousands of dollars, and a single round of golf costs many times more what it costs in the rest of the world. As a result, managers assigned to foreign posts in Japan may be given supplemental benefits to cover the costs of memberships in order to conduct business effectively.[49] When we take all these factors into consideration, it is easy to see how HCNs could become resentful of the salary and perks that expatriates receive. On the other hand, most companies believe that only by providing such inducements can they persuade qualified managers to accept overseas assignments.

Figure 3.6 illustrates how one company conceptualizes its compensation package for expatriates. The left side of its "balance sheet" summarizes what an employee currently earns and spends in the United States as broken down into taxes, consumption, and savings. The right side of the sheet provides more detail for these categories,

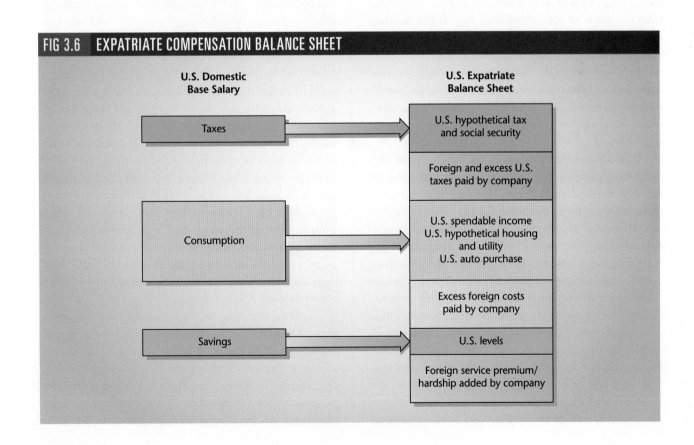

FIG 3.6 EXPATRIATE COMPENSATION BALANCE SHEET

U.S. Domestic Base Salary

- Taxes
- Consumption
- Savings

U.S. Expatriate Balance Sheet

- U.S. hypothetical tax and social security
- Foreign and excess U.S. taxes paid by company
- U.S. spendable income U.S. hypothetical housing and utility U.S. auto purchase
- Excess foreign costs paid by company
- U.S. levels
- Foreign service premium/ hardship added by company

allowing managers to provide comparable income to managers taking international assignments. Although more than 85 percent of North American companies use this approach, it is not without its critics.[50] Furthermore, the high costs associated with this approach have led some critics to call for shorter-term assignments and some forms of cost sharing by the expatriates.[51]

3-5e Repatriation

The final step in managing the human resources of global business involves bringing the expatriate manager home. This issue may seem quite simple, but it is much more involved than simply packing belongings and putting the manager and his or her family on a plane. A great deal of adjustment is often required (more or less depending on how long the assignment was) on both the personal and professional levels.[52]

On a personal level, the expatriate manager may have to become accustomed to living on less real income and going without perks such as club memberships or an assigned car. In addition, the manager and the manager's family may all have to become reaccustomed to U.S. practices, including driving on the right-hand side of the road, tipping at restaurants, and not bargaining over the price of everything they buy. If the overseas assignment was for a longer period of time, then the returning managers may also need to learn new styles in clothing, food, and music. For some managers who were not living in the United States before the tragedy of September 11, 2001, but who returned home afterward, there may be a need to adjust to a much different way of life.

The repatriation process could be even more difficult on a professional level. The expatriate manager has been out of sight for awhile and may have lost some status within the organization. The manager's old job may no longer exist, and he or she may be concerned about the nature of the new assignment and have questions about how much the company truly values the manager's overseas experience. Perhaps these are some of the reasons why roughly one-half of repatriated managers leave their companies within 2 years of repatriation.[53] In any event, most experts emphasize the importance of explaining the entire expatriation and repatriation process to managers before they are sent overseas. It is also critical to stay in touch with expatriates so that they can maintain their social and network ties within the company.

This step includes regular phone calls and visits, and it also means ensuring that expatriated managers are considered when other opportunities present themselves. Finally, most experts agree that some type of career counseling is helpful at the time of repatriation. Note, however, that few companies actually follow the advice of these experts and most fail to complete the process successfully.

The failure to successfully repatriate and retain expatriates is also more costly than had been realized, and this has resulted in much more attention paid to ways to retain returning experiates.[54] Specifically, if a returning expatriate fails to remain with the company, the company loses a presumably valuable employee who has now gained international experience. But, beyond that, if we adopt a view of expatriate success and failure that is tied to knowledge transfer, the firm also loses the knowledge that the expatriate was originally sent to bring back and disseminate.[55]

 ## 3-6 INTERNATIONAL LABOR RELATIONS

Labor relations, which we will discuss more fully in Chapter 11, are the processes of dealing with employees who are organized into labor unions. Labor relations are also heavily regulated by law, as we noted briefly in Chapter 2, and the actions of management toward labor and the actions of labor toward management are heavily restricted. However, different situations exist in other countries. In many countries throughout the world, labor parties seek to achieve the political goals of unions in those countries, and these parties are often quite powerful. Also, in many countries, labor unions are much more concerned with social issues than they are in the United States, so their political activism often extends beyond the wages and conditions of employment. In any case, union membership is quite large in many countries and continues to grow. In fact, more than half the world's workforce outside the United States belongs to labor unions.

Different norms or expectations exist in other countries about the relationships between unions and management. In England, labor "contracts" are not really legal contracts at all but are merely understandings that can be broken at any time by either party with no penalty. And throughout Europe, temporary work stoppages are frequently used by unions in a bid for public backing of their demands. In Paris, for example, 1-day work stoppages by employees who work in the city's buses, subways, and railroads are frequently used for this purpose. During recent contentious contract negotiations at French operations for Caterpillar, Sony, and 3M, angry labor officials actually took senior managers hostage in efforts to win better employment contracts.[56] In contrast to the situation in Europe, labor relations in Japan tend to be cordial. Unions are created and run by the businesses themselves. Because Japanese culture discourages confrontation and hostility, unions and management tend to work together cooperatively. Disputes are usually dissolved cordially and through mutual agreement, and it is rare that a third-party mediator must be consulted. Strikes are also rare in Japan.

CLOSING CASE
Training for Global Assignments

One of the biggest HR challenges facing global businesses today is how to most effectively train and develop a global workforce. In fact, there seems to be no single generally accepted approach for handling this increasingly important function. Even firms in the same industry adopt very different approaches. Take Chevron, for example. Chevron is a global energy company headquartered in California but with operations in more than 180 countries. Chevron uses a flexible approach to training in that it assesses each training opportunity as a unique activity and then develops it accordingly.

For instance, Chevron recently announced plans to open a new production facility in Angola and wanted to staff the facility with local employees and managers. However, the firm also felt that local employees lacked some of the technical skills needed for their new positions. Chevron also has a long-standing partnership with the Southern Alberta Institute of Technology (SAT) in Canada. SAT agreed to develop a custom training program to help train Chevron's employees for their new assignment. Forty five Chevron employees from Angola then spent 11 months in Alberta learning new technical skills.

Schlumberger, the world's largest energy services business, uses a different approach. All Schlumberger employees are trained locally. Sometimes relying on local expertise and sometimes relying on Schlumberger managers sent on temporary assignment, Schlumberger employees routinely receive classroom training on the newest job skills as well as managerial competencies without needing to travel.

Alexey Solodov/Alamy Stock Photo

(Continued)

(Closing Case – continued)

Meanwhile, Schlumberger's biggest competitor, Halliburton, uses a hybrid model for employee training. Like Schlumberger, Halliburton uses local experts plus its own managers to provide on-site technical training. However, managerial and leadership training activities are centralized at Texas A&M University's Mays Business School in the United States. Each year, several hundred Halliburton managers travel to Texas from around the world for training programs ranging from 1 to 5 weeks. This training is focused on management and leadership competencies and is intended to help prepare high-potential managers for future leadership roles.

Ironically, however, while most global firms do a reasonably effective job of preparing employees and managers for overseas jobs and assignments, most also do a somewhat less effective job of helping people on short-term foreign assignments prepare for their return home. Companies sometimes invest hundreds of thousands of dollars to help a manager prepare for and then execute a foreign assignment, but then devote virtually no attention to that manager when the assignment ends and the manager returns home. Unfortunately, though, about 20 percent of managers and other professionals leave their employer within 2 years from returning home after an extended overseas assignment. Consequently, it would seem that even globally successful companies still have a ways to go in developing comprehensive training and development strategies for their employees.[57]

Case Questions

1. Why do you think there is so much variation in how companies handle global training and development for their employees?

2. What kinds of additional training might be used for managers taking on a new overseas assignment?

3. Assume that you have been on an overseas assignment for 2 years but are now preparing to return home. What might you do to prepare for this transition?

STUDY TOOLS 3

READY TO STUDY?
In the book, you can:

☐ Rip out the chapter review card at the back of the book for a handy summary of the chapter and key terms.

ONLINE AT CENGAGEBRAIN.COM YOU CAN:

☐ Collect StudyBits while you read and study the chapter.

☐ Quiz yourself on key concepts.

☐ Find videos for further exploration.

☐ Prepare for tests with HR4 Flash Cards as well as those you create.

HR ONLINE

STUDY YOUR WAY WITH STUDYBITS!

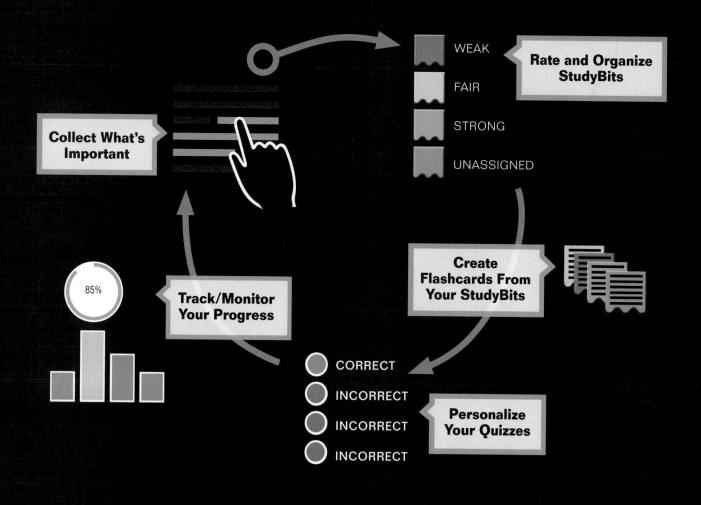

WEAK

FAIR

STRONG

UNASSIGNED

Rate and Organize StudyBits

Collect What's Important

Create Flashcards From Your StudyBits

Track/Monitor Your Progress

85%

CORRECT

INCORRECT

INCORRECT

INCORRECT

Personalize Your Quizzes

4LTR PRESS

Access HR ONLINE at www.cengagebrain.com

4 | The Competitive Environment

Caiaimage/Sam Edwards/Getty Images

After finishing this chapter go to **PAGE 106** for **STUDY TOOLS**

LEARNING OBJECTIVES

4-1 Describe the competitive environment of human resource management

4-2 Identify three types of strategies and relate each to human resource management

4-3 Discuss human resource strategy formulation and relevant organizational factors

4-4 Discuss the processes through which human resource strategy is implemented

4-5 Discuss how the human resource function in organizations can be evaluated

Caiaimage/Sam Edwards/Getty Images

OPENING CASE
Chief Social Media Officer?

The past few years have been big for social media digital platforms that allow users to create and exchange content. Twitter went public and introduced a video-sharing app called Vine. Facebook responded with Instagram, and YouTube rolled out a new layout feature called One Channel, which allows users to focus on developing bases of followers. Spending on social media advertising now exceeds $4.6 billion annually, and most marketers predict that this number will continue to grow.

Just what do social media managers do? It's a fairly new position, so job descriptions understandably vary. Here, however, is a generic description crafted by a veteran social media executive:

> The Social Media Manager will implement the Company's Social Media Strategy, developing brand awareness, generating inbound traffic, and encouraging product adoption. This role coordinates with the internal Marketing and PR teams to support their respective missions, ensuring consistency in voice and cultivating a social media referral network.

Primarily, social media managers handle information and communications through social media outlets—tracking trends and determining posting rates, creating positive communications, and maintaining a congenial media relationship with a company's community of customers. As you can also see from the job description, a key function of the position is coordination. Typically, social media managers work out of marketing departments and perform a variety of marketing-related tasks—replying to customer inquiries (sales), responding to customer complaints (customer service), and handling external communications (public relations). At the same time, however, because they often manage the use of social media among all of a company's employees and communicate information about all of its activities, the scope of responsibilities is company-wide.

"... social media managers [have] earned legitimacy.... Business owners began to realize that they could no longer hire their friend's daughter to do their social media just because she had a lot of friends on Facebook."

—ASHLEY COOMBE, SOCIAL MEDIA STRATEGIST FOR ALL INCLUSIVE MARKETING

Even so, some social media managers aren't quite sure how much "legitimacy" they've earned. "At the last place, I was a social manager," reports one brand specialist at a large corporation, "high-level VPs would come over and say I was messing around on the Internet too much." According to another veteran of corporate media management, "The biggest misconception is that, compared to other marketers, we don't understand analytics or don't have the education or background when it comes to the technical side." Old-school executives, charges a third social media strategist, "see [social media] as the warm and fuzzy side of marketing. In reality, it's a powerful revenue driver when it's given proper funding and attention.... When you show them the ROI, people start changing their minds."

THINK IT OVER

1. Would you want to be a social media manager? Why or why not?
2. In what ways, if any, has social media influenced your buying habits?

Most successful businesses do an effective job of blending strategy, operations, and people. This blending, in turn, requires that organizations carefully monitor and assess new trends, opportunities, and challenges. The emergence of social media as a cultural phenomenon in general and as a business function in particular certainly qualifies as a significant new trend. Most large businesses, many of which are led by older managers, seem to struggle with how to proceed. But other firms seem to be thriving. One key element in what is happening is how effectively—or ineffectively—businesses approach human resource management (HRM) from a strategic perspective.

Thus, this chapter is devoted to the strategic HR environment. The first section discusses the strategic context of HRM in terms of the organization's purpose, mission, and top management team. The next section focuses on corporate, business, and functional strategies and their relationship to HRM. We then address the increasingly important area of strategic HRM in terms of its formulation and its implementation. Important organizational characteristics that affect and are affected by these processes are also described. Finally, we provide a framework for how organizations evaluate the HR function.

 ## 4-1 THE COMPETITIVE ENVIRONMENT FOR HUMAN RESOURCE MANAGEMENT

HRM does not occur in a vacuum but instead occurs in a complex and dynamic milieu of forces within the organizational context.[1] A significant trend in recent years has been for HR managers to adopt a strategic perspective on their job and to recognize the critical links between organizational and HR strategies. In this way, an organization may be able to gain a competitive advantage through its management of human resources. Figure 4.1 illustrates the framework we will use in discussing strategic HRM. As the figure shows, this process starts with an understanding of the organization's purpose and mission and the influence of its top management team and culminates with the HR manager serving as a strategic partner to the operating divisions of the organization. Under this new view of HRM, the HR manager's job is to help line managers (at all levels) achieve their strategic goals. In this way, the HR manager adds value to the organization by providing expertise concerning how to use the firm's human resources to accomplish its objectives and gain competitive advantage.

This view also has important implications for how HR managers are trained and how HRM courses are designed. Traditionally, managers, scholars, and textbook authors have discussed the newest—and presumably the best—ways to interview candidates or select employees, as well as the best models for compensation and performance appraisal. But when we begin to consider the role of the HR department as being that of a strategic partner, does it still make sense to talk about the *single* best way to do anything? Are there truly "best practices" that all firms should adopt, or should the practices adopted by a firm depend exclusively on the firm's specific strategic goals? The "truth" probably lies somewhere between these two extremes, but there have been loud debates within the HR community over whether a best-practices approach or a contingency approach (based on the strategy pursued) is most logical.[2]

In reality, it seems that some general practices *are* better. If we examine fundamental HRM practices, it seems reasonable to suggest two points:

1. Formal performance appraisals are better than no appraisals (see Chapter 10).

2. Using systematic selection techniques is better than hiring based on intuition or some nonsystematic basis (see Chapter 7).

But, within some constraints, exactly *how* these practices are implemented probably should depend on the firm's strategic goals. In other words, although formal appraisals are better than no appraisals, exactly what is appraised should be consistent not only with a firm's strategic goals and missions but also with the other factors we discuss throughout this chapter.

Therefore, an organization must choose HR practices that fit its strategy and mission, and so the best practices for one firm may not be exactly the best for another. We will remind the reader of this fact throughout the book, but we recognize that this ambiguity can be a source of frustration. Students and managers alike often want to know what will work best in a particular organization. Although we will provide information and suggestions about general practices that should work (usually), the specific best solution or practice will depend on various characteristics of the organization such as strategic goals and top management values. There are few, if any, simple answers once we recognize the strategic role of HRM.

Recently, performance management systems (discussed in more detail in Chapter 14) have been discussed more broadly, and that discussion is relevant here. To begin with, instead of discussing specific HR practices, several authors have proposed that practices be described in terms of whether they are skill-enhancing practices, motivation-enhancing practices, or opportunity-enhancing practices.[3] Ability-enhancing practices, for example, include selection and training-related practices. Motivation-enhancing practices involve feedback and compensation-related policies; while opportunity-enhancing policies include mechanisms for voice and job rotation. After these practices have been implemented, the next step is to develop a "strong" HR system, which means all practices should be salient, valid, legitimate, consistent, and fair.[4] The notion here is that the message concerning what kinds of behaviors are desired should be clear and consistent so that everyone understands what is expected of them. This creates a climate for performance that enables generic knowledge, skills, and abilities (KSAs) to be transformed into the context-specific KSAs needed to improve firm performance.[5] We will discuss these ideas in more detail in Chapter 14,

FIG 4.1 STRATEGIC HUMAN RESOURCE MANAGEMENT

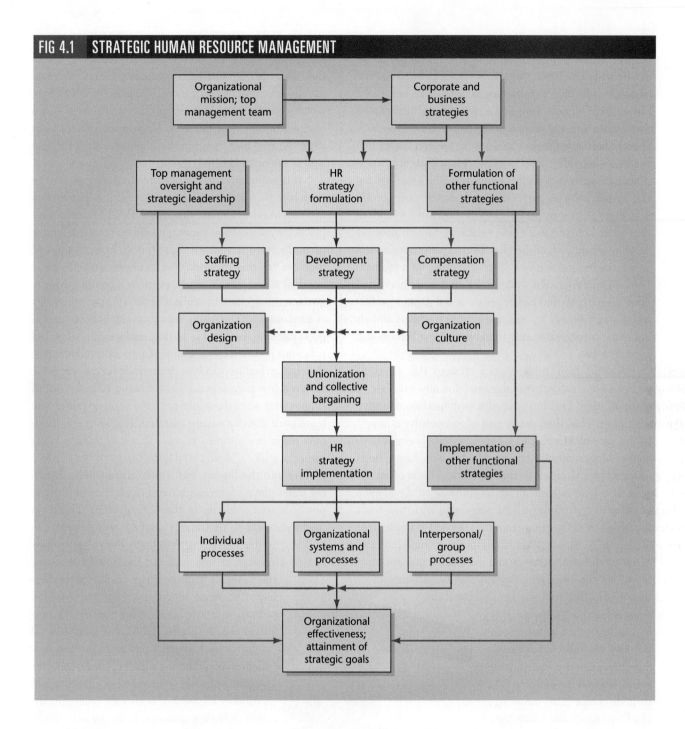

but several recent models have been suggested that attempt to better understand how HR practices can be used to gain real competitive advantage.[6]

4-1a A Strategic Perspective

We begin by explaining exactly what *strategy* and a *strategic* perspective mean. First, remember that all firms exist in a competitive environment. There are competitors who are trying to attract the same customers or sell the same goods and services, and each firm must fight to be successful; that is, each firm seeks to earn higher returns for its stockholders than do its competitors. Starbucks competes with Dunkin' Donuts and various local coffeehouses for its business. Southwest Airlines competes with Continental, Delta, United, and American Airlines to attract passengers who will fly with them. A basic tenet of capitalism is that there should be competition among different firms because this competition spurs each firm to try harder to provide better services, lower prices, or higher quality, and the public gains as a result.

Sometimes, though, a market is not large enough to support all the firms competing in it. For example, from the 1920s to the 1960s, New York City had two large department store chains competing for retail sales in the city. Macy's and Gimbels were fierce rivals (this rivalry played a role in the original version of the movie *Miracle on 34th Street*), and their flagship stores were located within two blocks of each other. But over time, Macy's was able to establish a more recognizable brand name (the Thanksgiving Day Parade was a big part of that) and reacted more quickly to changes in the way people liked to shop and the kinds of items they bought. As a result, established much stronger customer loyalty, which enabled the company to spend less on advertising and occasionally charge more for a product. Thus, Macy's created a strategy, and that strategy created value (lower costs and higher prices meant greater profits) and allowed Macy's to continue to thrive while Gimbels is a name recognizable only to old-time New Yorkers and some film fans.

When a firm implements a strategy that its competitors are unable to implement (for any number of reasons), that firm has gained a sustained competitive advantage. This, then, is the goal of competitive strategy. In the case of Macy's and Gimbels, Gimbels could have copied Macy's initially, but over time, it would have been too costly for Gimbels to shift its focus. This is often the case. If a firm is strategic in its thinking, it develops a strategy that it thinks will be successful and then finds the people and the other resources needed to implement that strategy. Any number of competitors could have decided on the same strategy and made the same attempts to gather the resources needed, but, assuming they made other choices, they could not easily switch strategies later.

Of course, for our discussion, we are most interested in how firms can use their human resources and the HR practices to gain competitive advantage. If a firm can do the following:

1. Hire the right people,
2. Train them to be effective,
3. Place them in the right jobs,
4. Motivate them to work hard, and
5. Retain them.

That same firm can gain a sustained competitive advantage over its competitors. These employees will work efficiently and effectively, and, if they are managed so that they also work toward the organization's strategic goals, the firm can reduce costs, increase quality, or develop innovative solutions to business problems. The only way a competitor can copy this is to hire the employees away from the firm and then manage them and treat them as well as the original firm.

It is not enough to simply hire similar employees or even hire the firm's employees away from it. Employees are important resources that are difficult to copy or replace; therefore, they are potentially an excellent source of competitive advantage. But all of the pieces must fit together for this to work. For example, assume that a baseball team (which surely exists in a competitive environment) decides to make a serious run at winning a championship. The team management believes it has good pitching, reasonable hitting, and solid fielding, but it has no power hitters. The first part of implementing the championship plan is to draft, trade for, or otherwise obtain a few players who can hit home runs instead of singles. But after these players have been acquired, the team must then formulate a strategy that leverages these new resources in order to win. This may include using something like a "designated hitter" to get more of these players into the lineup, but it may also include obtaining other players who can hit and reach base before the power hitters come up in the batting order. The team might also add to its training staff by hiring experts in building muscle and strength to further develop the new hitters. However, to fully leverage these new resources, the baseball team might go even further. Perhaps the team could refurbish the baseball stadium in a way that favors the team's new hitters. So, for example, if there were several right-handed sluggers on the team, the new stadium could have a slightly closer or shorter wall in left field, where these hitters would probably hit most of their long balls. Finally, in a defensive maneuver, the owners might instruct the ground crew to let the infield grass grow a bit longer to slow down opponents' ground balls.

Whether all these moves make sense in the context of a baseball team, they do illustrate the process of gaining a sustained competitive advantage. The organization must do more than acquire critical resources; it must also develop a

William Whitehurst/Media Bakery

complete strategy that leverages these resources. Even if the original team loses some of these new sluggers, it will be difficult for other teams to replicate the effects of the new strategy unless they also could rebuild their stadiums, recut their infield grass, and hire the other players and personnel needed to truly leverage the hitters. In general, an organization must acquire the best human resources it can, but it must then develop strategies to use those resources in the most effective manner. Every individual HRM practice and policy, then, must serve this larger goal.[7]

Although the strategy that is developed is the most important part of the strategic context for HRM, it is not the only one. Several other factors are important for determining this context, and we turn our attention to some of the more important factors next.

4-1b The Influence of Organizational Purpose and Mission

An organization's purpose and mission are among the most fundamental contextual forces that define the strategic context of HRM.

1. An organization's **purpose** is its basic reason for existence. The purpose of a business is to earn profit for its owners; the purpose of a university is to discover and disseminate new knowledge; the purpose of a museum is to preserve artifacts and historical relics.

2. An organization's **mission** is how its managers have decided to fulfill its purpose. A mission statement specifies how the organization intends to manage itself so it can pursue the fulfillment of its purpose most effectively. A mission statement attempts to specify the unique characteristics and strengths of an organization and identifies the scope of the business's operations in particular products and markets.[8]

Figure 4.2 shows the Starbucks mission statement. Note the prominence given to the firm's employees as the very first "guiding principle." This statement—and its placement—convey clearly the importance that Starbucks places on its employees.

Both its purpose and its mission affect an organization's HR practices in some obvious ways. A university, for example, must employ highly educated faculty members to teach courses and conduct research in specialized areas. A civil-engineering firm must employ people who understand construction and structural engineering; a natural history museum needs people who understand history and science; a marketing firm needs employees with sales expertise. But even finer gradations can be drawn within each type of organization as defined by their respective missions. For example, an oil-exploration firm such as Shell needs more petroleum engineers, while electronics firm Intel needs more electrical engineers, and construction firm Bechtel needs more civil engineers.

Mission statements often provide subtle cues about the importance that the organization places on its human resources. Many progressive firms today, such as Starbucks, refer to the importance of their human resources in their mission statement. Southwest Airlines and Walmart also stress the value of their employees in their mission statements. But some firms do not explicitly refer to employees in their mission statements. Most of these firms really do value the people who work for them, but the lack of specific reference to those people might be an indication that human resources are somehow not seen as being as important to the organization as other issues and goals. Although mission statements make a public commitment to some course of action (e.g., valuing human resources), we must recognize that, in some cases, the language of a mission statement is intended to placate a group of stakeholders, such as employees, rather than to signal an organization's true priorities.[9]

4-1c The Influence of the Top Management Team

The **top management team** of an organization is the group of senior executives responsible for the overall strategic operation of the firm. Common organizational positions that are assumed to be part of the top management team include

1. The chairperson of the board of directors,
2. The chief executive officer (CEO),
3. The chief operating officer (COO), and
4. The president.

> **Both its purpose and its mission affect an organization's HR practices in several different ways.**

An organization's **purpose** is its basic reason for existence.

An organization's **mission** is a statement of how it intends to fulfill its purpose.

The **top management team** of an organization refers to the group of senior executives responsible for the overall strategic operation of the firm.

FIG 4.2 STARBUCKS CORPORATE MISSION STATEMENT

Sorbis/Shutterstock.com

OUR STARBUCKS MISSION STATEMENT

Our mission: To inspire and nurture the human spirit – one person, one cup and one neighborhood at a time.

Here are the principles of how we live that every day:

Our Coffee

It has always been, and will always be, about quality. We're passionate about ethically sourcing the finest coffee beans, roasting them with great care, and improving the lives of people who grow them. We care deeply about all of this; our work is never done.

Our Partners

We're called partners, because it's not just a job, it's our passion. Together, we embrace diversity to create a place where each of us can be ourselves. We always treat each other with respect and dignity. And we hold each other to that standard.

Our Customers

When we are fully engaged, we connect with, laugh with, and uplift the lives of our customers – even if just for a few moments. Sure, it starts with the promise of a perfectly made beverage, but our work goes far beyond that. It's really about human connection.

Our Stores

When our customers feel this sense of belonging, our stores become a haven, a break from the worries outside, a place where you can meet with friends. It's about enjoyment at the speed of life – sometimes slow and savored, sometimes faster. Always full of humanity.

Our Neighborhood

Every store is part of a community, and we take our responsibility to be good neighbors seriously. We want to be invited in wherever we do business. We can be a force for positive action – bringing together our partners, customers, and the community to contribute every day. Now we see that our responsibility – and our potential for good – is even larger. The world is looking to Starbucks to set the new standard, yet again. We will lead.

Our Shareholders

We know that as we deliver in each of these areas, we enjoy the kind of success that rewards our shareholders. We are fully accountable to get each of these elements right so that Starbucks – and everyone it touches – can endure and thrive.

Nigel Reed QEDimages/Alamy Stock Photo

Other members of the top management team generally include the senior executive (usually having the title of vice president) responsible for each major functional area within the organization. For example, the senior vice presidents responsible for marketing, finance, and human resource management, respectively, are all likely to be considered part of an organization's top management team.

The top management team sets the tone for the organization and plays a major role in shaping its culture (as discussed later in this chapter). Some top management teams have a clear vision of where the

> Some views of leadership emphasize the importance of personal charisma in leadership and suggest that effective leaders need both a clear vision and a means of communicating that vision.

firm should go and how it should get there. They also do a good job of articulating this vision throughout the organization. In this case, middle- and lower-level managers know what is expected of them and can direct their own efforts and the efforts of members of their own division, department, or team toward this common goal. Other top management teams, however, present ambiguous, contradictory, or vague visions of where they see the organization headed. As a result, other managers in these organizations may be unsure about how to proceed and be unable to communicate effectively with their own employees.[10] In fact, views of leadership that emphasize the importance of personal charisma in leaders tend to suggest that effective leaders need both a clear vision and a means of communicating that vision. If an organization has top managers who are unable to accomplish both these goals, then the organization is less likely to be successful.[11]

Top managers can use speeches and proclamations to articulate the organization's vision and mission, but they communicate their true personal values and beliefs by their own behavior, thus setting the tone for the entire organization. Herb Kelleher, the legendary CEO of Southwest Airlines, knew many of his employees by name and insisted they call him Herb. Sam Walton, before his death, visited every Walmart store at least once a year and communicated with all his employees weekly. Steve Jobs was literally the face of Apple and its spirit as well, challenging himself and his employees to create and innovate, and treating all employees with the respect they needed in order to be creative. Of course, there are other top managers who send a much different message by their words and actions. James Dutt, a former CEO of Beatrice Foods, once told a subordinate that, if his wife and children got in the way of his working 24 hours a day, 7 days a week, he should get rid of them. In the late 1990s, Enron CEO Kenneth Lay created a culture that promoted internal cutthroat competition and a win-at-all-costs mentality.

But we should not assume from this discussion that the top management team or even the CEO will always have a major influence on what goes on in an organization. In many cases, serious constraints restrict the top management team's power and preclude it from having a great effect. Researchers who have examined this problem suggest that the ability of the top management team to influence the organization is constrained by the nature of the industry (commodity product industries tend to limit the influence of the top management team), the nature of the organization (more powerful boards of directors tend to constrain the influence of the top management team), and the nature of the individuals themselves.[12] This research, using the term *managerial discretion*, has found that the abilities of top management teams to influence their organizations and success can vary widely as a function of these constraints. We turn now to one of the determinants of managerial discretion: the model of corporate governance used by the organization.

4-1d The Role of Corporate Governance

Stockholders are the true owners of a modern corporation. These people, who often represent institutions such as pension funds, are not typically the same people who actually run the organizations on a day-to-day basis. That task is left to the CEO and the top management team. It is possible (and even likely), however, that the interests of the owners are different from those of the management. This produces a situation known as an *agency problem*. We will discuss agency theory again in Chapter 13, but for now, it is sufficient to note that stockholders prefer decisions that will increase the current value of the firm's cash flow. These decisions may carry a certain level of risk, but these owners are not overly concerned about risk because they can diversify their investments across several firms and so have a hedge against any one source of risk.

Managers, however, are much more risk averse because they cannot diversify their investments in people and equipment in the same way investors can diversify their investments. Thus, the best interests of the managers are somewhat different and might be at odds with the interests of the owners, creating an agency problem. This requires the owners to somehow monitor the actions of the managers to make sure they work for the best interests of the owners. One important means to accomplish this is through the operation of the board of directors. In most organizations, all officers and employees technically report to the board.[13]

Boards typically have 10–15 members. Some are members of the top management team, while others are major stockholders, and still others might be prominent members of the community. The role of the board is to monitor the actions of the top management team to ensure that stockholders' interests are protected. But boards differ not only in terms of their power but also in terms of their activity. Throughout the 1990s, there was an increase in the level of activism by boards in the United States,[14] but some still believed that there was not enough monitoring of top management, especially in terms of compensation. As a result, when major U.S. banks and investments firms turned to the government for financial assistance, many people blamed the boards for not being vigilant enough. One response to this was for the U.S. government to become an "owner" of some of these institutions and to try to use its power to rein in any abuse.

In March 2009, President Obama said he was outraged by the bonuses paid to AIG executives (after the firm received billions of dollars in funding from the government), but there was not much he could do about it; this suggests that government oversight may not be the answer.[15] In fact, it is increasingly clear that corporate governance mechanisms do not represent a serious constraint to managerial discretion when a sufficient number of insider managers are on the board. These and related issues are discussed more fully in Contemporary Challenges in HR.

4-2 CORPORATE, BUSINESS, AND FUNCTIONAL STRATEGIES

As indicated earlier, top managers are responsible for the strategic operations of their firms. The key to strategic operations, in turn, is developing and implementing effective strategies. These strategies may be at the corporate, business, or functional level, including the HR function.[16] In addition to strategy formulation (as shown earlier in Figure 4.1), the organization's top management team also provides oversight and strategic leadership for the organization on an ongoing basis. It should be clear by now that functional strategies should be consistent with and supportive of corporate strategy.

1. **Corporate strategy** deals with determining what businesses the firm will operate.
2. **Business strategy** deals with how the firm will compete in each market where it conducts business.
3. **Functional strategy** deals with how the firm will manage each of its major functions (e.g., marketing, finance, and HR).

Corporate, business, and other functional strategies can all affect and be affected by the HR function and its strategy.

4-2a Corporate Strategy and Human Resource Management

As noted earlier, the corporate strategy should be closely tied to the HRM practices within the firm, and only through this close relationship these practices can lead to higher corporate performance and competitive advantage.[17] There are several broad strategies that a firm might adopt at the corporate level, and each one has different implications for HRM practices. The first three we will discuss are all relevant for firms that decide to compete in a single market.

GROWTH STRATEGY When a business has identified a unique niche and is successfully and aggressively expanding within that particular market niche, it is pursuing what experts call a **growth strategy**. As the term suggests, a growth strategy focuses on the growth and expansion of the corporation. For example, Starbucks has been using a rapid growth strategy as it continues its geographic and brand expansion, opening on average at least one new store somewhere in the world every day.

Corporate strategy deals with determining what businesses the corporation will operate.

Business strategy deals with how the firm will compete in each market where it conducts business.

Functional strategy deals with how the firm will manage each of its major functions such as marketing, finance, and human resources.

Growth strategy focuses on growing and expanding the business. It can be pursued internally by opening additional locations or externally through mergers, joint ventures, or the acquisition of other businesses.

Contemporary Challenges in HR

Board Oversight or Board Negligence?

Among other things, corporate boards are responsible for setting the pay of a firm's top managers. They also have oversight of how efficiently the business is functioning and the strategic decisions being made by top managers. So, consider this example: A couple of years ago, having booked a record profit of $4.9 billion and with even better results projected for the next year, Caterpillar, the world's leading maker of engines, turbines, and construction and mining equipment, rewarded top executives with hefty bonuses. As for the blue-collar workforce at its plant in Joliet, Illinois, they were told to prepare for a 6-year wage freeze to keep the company competitive. Fair, or foul?

As a factor in U.S. economic calculations, meaningful wage increases appear to be a thing of the past. In January 1973, for example, the average hourly wage for nonmanagement private-sector workers was $4.03. Today, workers need to make $22.41 an hour in order to enjoy the same purchasing power as their 1973 counterparts. In December 2015, however, the average hourly wage for nonmanagement private-sector workers was $20.68. In other words, in terms of real wages—wages after inflation has been taken into account—the average hourly wage peaked more than 40 years ago.

It's not that the economy hasn't been generating enough wealth to pay workers. Between 1979 and 2014, U.S. productivity increased by 74.5 percent. Median hourly compensation (wages plus benefits), however, rose by a mere 5 percent to $12.85. One recent study conducted by the Economic Policy Institute (EPI) focused on the gap between wage and productivity growth in order to analyze economic pressures on the living standards of working families. The findings of the report reflect the effect of economic trends on wage percentiles: A worker in the bottom 70th percentile, for example, makes more than 70

> "For most U.S. workers real wages . . . have been flat or even falling for decades."
>
> —THE PEW RESEARCH CENTER, A WASHINGTON D.C. THINK TANK SPECIALIZING IN SOCIAL ISSUES AND DEMOGRAPHIC TRENDS

percent of the workforce and less than 30 percent of the workforce. During "the Great Recession and its aftermath" (2007–2012), for instance, productivity grew by 7.7 percent while wages declined for the entire bottom 70th percentile. In the previous period (2000–2007), productivity rose by 25 percent while wages for the bottom 70th percentile were either flat or declined. For the entire period (2000–2012), productivity grew by 22.2 percent while wages across the board rose by just 0.8 percent. In other words, the vast majority of U.S. wage earners "experienced a lost decade" in the battle to improve their standard of living.

Since 1979, reports the EPI, while productivity has grown 74.5 percent, wages for workers in the bottom 20th percentile actually declined by 0.4 percent. Meanwhile, 8 out of 10 American workers—those is the bottom 80th percentile—received only a very meager share of the new wealth, as their wages rose by merely 17.5 percent. The "central problem," according to the EPI, is that "the fruits of overall growth have accrued disproportionately to the richest households." Since 2000, according to Pew Research, those at the top of the income distribution have seen real-wage increases of 9.7 percent (as opposed to a decline of 3.7 percent for those in the bottom 10th percentile). During the Great Recession, 65 percent of the country's new wealth was garnered by the richest 1 percent of Americans.

For his part in returning profits of $4.9 billion, Caterpillar CEO Douglas R. Oberhelman, received a 60 percent raise to $16.9 million. The Joliet plant's unionized workforce went out on strike but was ultimately forced to accept a barely sweetened offer from the company. Needless to say, not everyone was happy about it: "We're the people who busted our butts to help them make record profits," said one worker. "We shouldn't be treated like this." And what did Caterpillar's board have to say about all this? They chose to remain silent.[18]

THINK IT OVER

1. Some social activists argue that there should be laws that limit the gap between the highest and lowest wages a firm can pay. What is your opinion on this issue?

2. Suppose you had to justify giving a CEO a 60 percent pay raise to almost $17 million. What information would you need to present your arguments?

A key challenge for HR managers with firms using a growth strategy is recruiting and training the large numbers of qualified employees to help operate growing operations. When organizations view the HR area as a true strategic partner, however, they also use input from HR managers in their initial formulation of corporate strategy. Thus, before the top management team of a firm decides to pursue a growth strategy, it consults with the HRM team to ensure that it has the capability to attract and train the large number of new employees needed to implement the anticipated growth. In other words, a true partnership requires both parties to consult with and support each other.

A growth strategy can also be pursued externally through mergers, joint ventures, and the acquisition of other businesses.[19] When these happen, a major initial challenge for HR managers is determining how to merge two existing workforces into a single cohesive and integrated unit. In some cases, for example, there will be unnecessary duplication of employees, and choices will have to be made about which overlapping employees to retain, which to transfer, and which to lay off. Similarly, it is likely that the two firms will be using different HR philosophies for issues such as training practices, promotion policies, and so forth. HR decision makers thus will have to decide which practices to retain and which to discard. When the Walt Disney Company acquired first Marvel Comics and then Pixar Animation, among the first questions that had to be answered were:

1. Who would manage various parts of the new enterprise?

2. How would the three firms' HR departments be integrated into one new operation?

In fact, there is reason to believe that the failure to integrate different strategies and cultures may be an important factor in the failure of some mergers and acquisitions.[20] Furthermore, because there is always a great deal of concern and speculation over what will happen to employees, the entire merger or acquisition process must be managed well relative to its effects on employees. Failure to do so can result in undue stress, the loss of valued employees, and long-lasting morale problems.[21]

RETRENCHMENT OR TURNAROUND STRATEGY
Sometimes, firms are forced to adopt, at least in the short run, a strategy usually referred to as a **retrenchment** or a **turnaround strategy**, which occurs when an organization finds that its current operations are not effective. For example, a firm might find that its dominant products are in declining markets, its technology is rapidly becoming obsolete, or in some other way its not performing as well as it should. Major changes are usually needed to rectify these kinds of problems. In most of these cases, organizations go through a period of *downsizing* (or *rightsizing*, as some managers prefer to call it) in an effort to get back on the right track (we will discuss this further in Chapter 6). They close operations, shut down factories, terminate employees, and take other actions to scale back current operations and reduce their workforces. Their ultimate goal is to take the resources generated as a result of these steps and reinvest them into other more promising products and markets.

Downsizing has become a common response to competitive problems. As more employees find their jobs at risk, the traditional psychological contract between the organization and the employee is changing. No longer can employees feel certain of keeping their jobs if they perform well, and the increased uncertainty makes it more difficult for employees to commit fully to their organizations. As a result of these problems, HR managers clearly need to be involved when the organization is eliminating jobs or decreasing the size of its workforce. They need to help

A **retrenchment** or **turnaround strategy** occurs when an organization finds that its current operations are not effective, and major changes are usually needed to rectify the problem. In most cases, this strategy involves rightsizing the organization by closing operations, shutting down factories, and terminating employees in order to get back on the right track.

manage the process so that employees continue to feel attached to and committed to the organization. In addition, HR managers must help ensure that decisions about who will be let go are made for job-related reasons as opposed to reasons that might reflect or suggest bias or illegal discrimination. Similarly, HR managers can help to optimize the transition process for displaced workers through practices such as equitable severance packages and outplacement counseling. International Harvester declared bankruptcy and was reborn as Navistar, a much smaller operation. HR managers were involved in all phases of this process and in making decisions about which employees would be most valuable to the new enterprise and how best to retain them.

STABILITY STRATEGY A third single-market strategy that might be adopted by some firms is a **stability strategy**, which essentially calls for maintaining the status quo. A company that adopts a stability strategy plans to stay in its current businesses and intends to manage them as they are already being managed. The organization's goal is to protect itself from environmental threats. A stability strategy is frequently used after a period of retrenchment or after a period of rapid growth. When the firm is using a stability strategy, HR managers play a major role in determining how to retain the firm's existing employees when the firm can offer little in the way of advancement opportunities, salary increases, and so forth.

DIVERSIFICATION STRATEGY In addition to the strategies focusing on one specific market, *diversification* is another widely used approach to corporate strategy.[22] A corporation that uses the **diversification strategy** usually makes the decision to own and operate several different businesses. For example, General Electric, one of the most successful practitioners of this strategy, owns varied businesses that manufacture aircraft engines, industrial products, major appliances, and technical products as well as financial services and insurance businesses.

1. The various businesses owned by a corporation are usually related to one another in some way, a strategy called **related diversification**.[23] The basic underlying assumption for using this strategy is that the corporation can achieve synergy among the various businesses it owns. For example, Limited Brands has an ownership stake in more than a dozen different retail chains, including Express, Victoria's Secret, and Bath & Body Works. A single group of buyers supplies all of the firm's chains, a single development operation seeks new locations for all chains, and so forth. This type of organization often adopts a policy of rotating managers across the various businesses so they develop an overall managerial perspective on the whole firm. A manager might start out with Express, get promoted to a new position at Bath & Body Works, and then move into yet another position with Victoria's Secret. The related aspects of the businesses presumably make such cross-business transfers easier. Because the markets for each business are similar, the firm can develop relatively uniform procedures for selection, compensation, training, and so forth.

2. Sometimes, however, an organization decides to expand into products or markets that are unrelated to its current products and markets. This approach is called **unrelated diversification**. A firm that pursues this strategy attempts to operate several unique businesses in different, unrelated markets. General Electric, as already noted, owns businesses that compete in different unrelated areas. The basic logic behind unrelated diversification is that a company can shield itself from the adverse effects of business cycles, unexpected competition, and other economic fluctuations. Because the various businesses are presumably unrelated, a downturn or setback in one does not necessarily suggest a corresponding downturn or setback in another. HR executives in a firm that uses unrelated diversification must approach the HR function in a very different way. In most cases, managers remain within a single business unit as they progress up the corporate ladder. Because each unrelated business is likely to have its own unique hiring, compensation, and training needs—as dictated by its own competitive

> **Stability strategy** essentially calls for maintaining the status quo. A company that adopts a stability strategy plans to stay in its current businesses and intends to manage them as they are already being managed. The organization's goal is to protect itself from environmental threats. A stability strategy is frequently used after a period of retrenchment or after a period of rapid growth.
>
> A **diversification strategy** is used by companies that are adding new products, product lines, or businesses to their existing core products, product lines, or businesses.
>
> **Related diversification** is used when a corporation believes it can achieve synergy among the various businesses that it owns.
>
> **Unrelated diversification** is used when a firm attempts to operate several unique businesses in different, unrelated markets. The basic logic behind unrelated diversification is that a company can shield itself from the adverse effects of business cycles, unexpected competition, and other economic fluctuations.

environment—these functions will likely be customized and decentralized for each business. Thus, even though the career tracks and compensation packages for managers at Express and Victoria's Secret will likely be similar to one another,

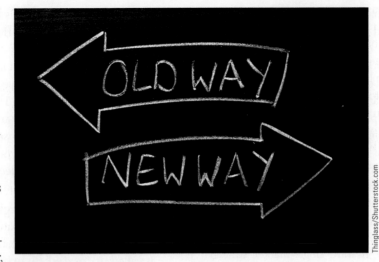

Thinglass/Shutterstock.com

variety of approaches can be used to develop a business-level strategy. One of these is the adaptation model.

THE ADAPTATION MODEL The adaptation model.[26] This model suggests that managers in an organization should try to match the organization's strategy with the basic conditions of its environment. Different levels of environmental complexity and change are expected to be matched most appropriately with different forms of strategy. The three basic strategic alternatives from which managers should select are the defender strategy, the prospector strategy, and the analyzer strategy.

the career tracks and compensation packages for managers at GE Jet Engines and GE Appliances may be quite different from one another. The GE Jet Engine compensation packages, for instance, will more closely resemble those at Rolls Royce, another large jet engine manufacturer, while the GE Appliance compensation packages may be more like those at Whirlpool and Maytag.

Organizations that use the diversification approach for managing their corporate strategy must also work to ensure close coordination between their corporate HR functions and the HR functions within each of their businesses or divisions. Essentially, the corporate HR group must interface with three sets of constituents. One set of constituents is the top management team or corporate management. Second, corporate HR can also be involved in representing the firm in its interactions with external constituents such as the government, labor unions, and benchmark companies (companies to which the organization compares itself). Third, corporate HR can also be involved with the division management, division human resources, and the employees of each division or business owned by the corporation.[24]

4-2b Business Strategy and Human Resource Management

As noted earlier, decisions must also be made about how to compete in each market where a firm operates. This question determines business strategy. A diversified corporation must therefore develop a business strategy for each operating unit.[25] A

The **adaptation model** is one popular approach to business strategy where a business seeks ways to adapt to its environment.

1. A *defender strategy* is assumed to work best when a business operates in an environment with relatively little uncertainty and risk and a high degree of stability. The goal of the defender is to identify for itself a relatively narrow niche in the market and then to direct a limited set of products or services at that niche. Although defenders may compete with other firms aggressively, their primary approach is to guard and secure their position within an existing market. Even though they monitor trends and developments outside their chosen domain, they focus primarily on their existing environment. Hershey Foods is a good example of a defender. The firm concentrates almost exclusively on the confectionery market. Another good example of a defender is Wrigley, the venerable chewing gum company founded in 1891. HR managers in organizations using this strategy are most likely to recruit and seek to retain stable employees who exhibit high levels of commitment and loyalty to the firm.

2. A second type of strategy used in this approach is the *prospector strategy*. This strategy anchors the other end of the continuum and works best when the environment is dynamic and growing and has considerable uncertainty and risk. Prospectors are advised to be on constant alert to discover and capitalize on new ideas and opportunities. They continually focus on new products and markets and try to avoid a long-term commitment to any single

type of technology, using multiple technologies instead. This strategy makes it easier for the organization to shift from one product market to another. General Electric is a good example of a prospector. As noted earlier, the firm owns everything from a jet-engine business to a financial services operation. For the right opportunity, the firm will buy any business that might be for sale or sell any business it currently owns. HR managers in organizations using this strategy may prefer to recruit and retain entrepreneurial employees who are highly flexible and more dedicated to their craft or profession than to the organization itself.

3. The *analyzer strategy* falls between the extremes of the defender and prospector strategies. The analyzer strategy is most appropriate in relatively stable conditions with a moderate degree of uncertainty and risk. An analyzer tries to identify and take advantage of new markets and products while simultaneously maintaining a nucleus of traditional core products and customers. The Walt Disney Company is a good example of an analyzer. The firm cautiously moved into television and video markets a few years ago, has expanded its movie division, and is currently investing in electronic games and virtual reality products, but it takes each step slowly and only after careful deliberation. HR managers in firms that pursue this strategy may seek to recruit and retain employees who might be moderately entrepreneurial and flexible but who will also be quite dedicated and loyal to the organization.

4. The adaptation model also identifies a fourth strategic alternative called the *reactor*. The reactor is really seen as a strategic failure, however, and is not held up as a model that any firm should emulate. A reactor is a firm that either improperly ignores its environment or else attempts to react to its environment in inappropriate ways. During the early 1980s, Kmart was guilty of using the reactor strategy. It failed to keep pace with Walmart, for example, and spread itself too thin by investing heavily in specialty retailing. HR managers in organizations functioning as reactors may lack a clear understanding of exactly what qualities they are seeking in their employees. This lack of understanding may contribute to the firm's poor performance.

OTHER COMPETITIVE STRATEGIES The other dominant approach to business-level strategies identifies three specific competitive strategies—namely, differentiation, cost leadership, and focus. These three are presumed to be appropriate for a wide variety of organizations in diverse industries.[27]

1. A company that uses a **differentiation strategy** attempts to develop an image or reputation for its product or service that sets it apart from its competitors. The differentiating factor may be real or objective, such as product reliability or design, or it may be more perceptual or subjective, such as fashion and appearance. Regardless of its basis, however, a firm that can differentiate its products or services from those of its competitors can charge higher prices for those products or services, thereby earning a larger profit. Rolex and BMW are both examples of firms that have used a differentiation strategy successfully. HR managers contribute to the successful use of a differentiation strategy by recruiting and retaining employees who can perform high-quality work or provide exemplary customer service. Likewise, employee training will likely focus on quality improvement, and reward systems may be based on factors such as quality of work and customer satisfaction.[28]

2. A **cost leadership strategy** focuses on minimizing the costs as much as possible. This strategy allows the firm to charge the lowest possible prices for its products, thereby presumably generating a higher overall level of revenue. Low cost may be achieved through production efficiencies, distribution efficiencies, or product design efficiencies. Timex and Hyundai are examples of businesses that have used a cost leadership strategy successfully. HR contributions here focus on recruiting and retaining employees who can work as efficiently and productively as possible. On the other hand, more experienced employees may demand higher wages, and so it might also be possible to reengineer jobs to require minimal skills and then select employees who can perform the jobs but may not remain with the organization long. Fast-food restaurants often control labor costs using an approach such as this one. In any case, training may emphasize efficient production methods, and reward systems may be based more on quantity than on quality of output. One

> A company that uses a **differentiation strategy** attempts to develop an image or reputation for its product or service that sets the company apart from its competitors.
>
> A **cost leadership strategy** is one that focuses on minimizing the costs as much as possible.

popular approach to reducing costs today is moving production to other countries where labor costs are lower.

3. Finally, when an organization uses the **focus strategy**, it tries to target a specific segment of the marketplace for its products or services. This focus may be toward a specific geographic area, a specific segment of the consuming population based on ethnicity or gender, or some other factor that segments the market. Within that focus, a firm may attempt to either differentiate or cost lead its products or services. Fiesta Mart is a Houston-based grocery store chain that has prospered by focusing its marketing on the large number of immigrants, especially Hispanics, who live in the Southwest. These stores sell Mexican soft drinks, cornhusks for wrapping tamales, and many other products that are not carried in general-purpose grocery stores. The key HR goal in this instance is recruiting and retaining employees who understand the focal market. For example, Fiesta Mart must recruit, hire, and retain employees who really understand the products they are selling and who speak Spanish, the language of most of its customers.

4-2c Functional Strategies and Human Resource Management

The third level of strategy formulation and implementation is at the functional level. Functional strategies address how the organization will manage its basic functional activities, such as marketing, finance, operations, research and development, and HR.

Olivier Le Moal/Shutterstock.com

Thus, at this level, HR strategy formulation formally begins to take shape. It is clearly important that an HR functional strategy be closely integrated and coordinated with corporate, business, and other functional strategies. In fact, without such integration and coordination, organizational competitiveness will clearly suffer.[29]

> The **focus strategy** is undertaken when an organization tries to target a specific segment of the marketplace for its products or services.

Much of our discussion throughout the remainder of this text explicitly or implicitly addresses the HR function from a contextual perspective that includes other fundamental business functions. As you saw in Figure 4.1, HR strategy is, of course, our primary concern. Keep in mind, however, that other functional strategies are also developed and (as shown in the figure) combine with the HR strategy and top management strategic leadership to determine the firm's overall performance.

4-3 HUMAN RESOURCE STRATEGY FORMULATION

Using the organization's overarching corporate and business strategies as context, managers can formally develop the organization's HR strategy, as noted previously. As illustrated in Figure 4.1, this strategy commonly includes three distinct components—a staffing strategy, a development strategy, and a compensation strategy. These dimensions are shown in more detail in Figure 4.3.

1. *Staffing* refers to the set of activities used by the organization to determine its future HR needs, recruit qualified applicants interested in working for the organization, and select the best of those applicants as new employees. Obviously, however, this process can be undertaken only after a careful and systematic strategy has been developed to ensure that staffing activities mesh appropriately with other strategic elements of the organization. For example, as already noted, if the business employs a growth strategy, then the staffing strategy must be based on the aggressive recruiting and selection of large numbers of qualified employees.[30] But if retrenchment is the expectation, then the staffing strategy will focus instead on determining which employees to retain and the best way to handle the process of terminating other employees.

2. Similarly, HR managers must also formulate an employee-development strategy for helping the organization enhance the quality of its human resources. This strategy usually involves performance management, the actual training and development

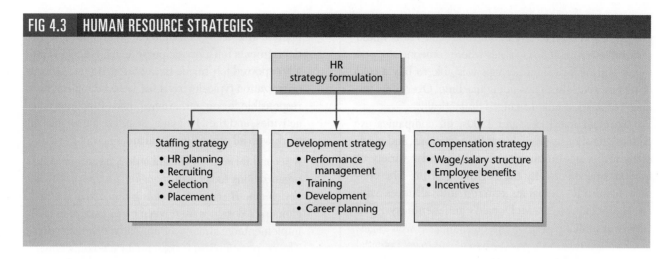

FIG 4.3 HUMAN RESOURCE STRATEGIES

HR strategy formulation

Staffing strategy
- HR planning
- Recruiting
- Selection
- Placement

Development strategy
- Performance management
- Training
- Development
- Career planning

Compensation strategy
- Wage/salary structure
- Employee benefits
- Incentives

of employees and managers, and career planning and development for appropriate employees. As with staffing, the development strategy must be consistent with corporate and business strategies. For example, if an organization uses a differentiation strategy, the firm needs to invest heavily in training its employees to produce the highest-quality products or provide the highest-quality service. Performance management must also be focused on recognizing and rewarding performance leading to improved quality. But if cost leadership is the strategy of choice, then the firm may choose to invest less in training (helping to keep overall costs low) and orient the training that is offered toward efficiency and productivity-improvement methods and techniques.

3. Third, the compensation strategy must likewise complement other strategies adopted by the firm. Basic compensation, performance-based incentives, and employee benefits and services—the major components of the compensation strategy—must all be congruent with their relevant strategic contexts to be effective. For example, if a firm uses a strategy of related diversification, its compensation system must be geared to (a) reward those employees with different skills that allow them to transition across businesses and to (b) be flexible enough to facilitate those same cross-business transfers. If a manager moves from one division to another, for instance, then that manager's pension plan should be readily portable to the new assignment. If the firm uses unrelated diversification, on the other hand, compensation may instead be focused on depth of knowledge and skills. Hence, the firm may choose to pay a premium salary to a highly talented expert with unusual skills relevant to one of the firm's businesses. The ability of this expert to

transition across businesses is less important and thus is not likely to be a factor in compensation.[31]

Of course, these components are not independent, but, as noted earlier, some have also argued that this model ignores the notion of opportunity. That is, even if employees have the skills and motivation to perform effectively, they must also be given the opportunity to demonstrate what they can do. In any case, proposed models of HR architecture suggest that not all employees possess capabilities of equal strategic value to a firm, and so they should be treated differently.[32] Specifically, the authors argue that a firm can have at least four types of employment modes—which they refer to as internal development, acquisition, contracting, and alliance—for its employees. The model suggests strategic imperatives for establishing these different relationships.

To explain the complexities of the interchange among these aspects of HR strategy and corporate strategy, we can consider a situation where an organization is moving into a new line of business or at least changing its emphasis within existing businesses. A good case in point is

> Basic compensation, performance-based incentives, and employee benefits and services—the major components of the compensation strategy—must all be congruent with their relevant strategic contexts to be effective.

the major oil companies in the United States. Someone growing up in this country in the 1960s and 1970s would remember gas stations as places where someone stopped to get gas for a car and perhaps was able to buy a cold drink or a snack from a vending machine. Over time, the image of the gas station changed dramatically.

Through the 1980s and 1990s, oil companies expanded the services available at these stations, and many of them became minimarts offering a wider variety of food and beverages. By the beginning of the 21st century, many oil companies entered into alliances with fast-food chains (e.g., McDonald's and Kentucky Fried Chicken) so that patrons could buy a meal as well as gas.

These services were viewed as a means to get potential customers to stop at a given gas station. Although the oil companies made money from products sold at the minimarts, they did not see these products as a primary line of business. At the end of the 1990s and in the early years of the 21st century, however, several large mergers occurred between major oil companies (e.g., British Petroleum and Amoco, Exxon and Mobil). Newly merged companies suddenly discovered they owned a large number of food marts around the country.

When attempting to formulate the HR strategy as well as its three basic components, HR managers must also account for other key parts of the organization. These components are important because they affect both how strategies are formulated and how they are implemented. Three critical components are organization design, the corporate culture, and unionization.[33] A fourth component, the labor force and how it relates to HR planning, will be discussed in more detail a bit later in the chapter.

4-3a The Impact of Organization Design

Organization design refers to the framework of jobs, positions, groups of positions, and reporting relationships among positions that are used to construct an organization.[34]

1. One form of organization design used by many smaller or newer organizations is the *functional design* (also called the *U-form organization*, with *U* representing *unitary*). The organization groups its members into basic functional departments such as marketing, finance,

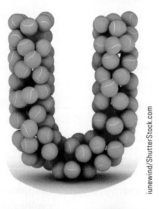

iunewind/ShutterStock.com

photobank.ch/ShutterStock.com

Gataki/ShutterStock.com

and operations. For this form of organization to operate effectively, considerable coordination across departments must exist. Senior management is usually expected to provide this coordination. A U-form organization typically has a single HR department responsible for organizationwide HR functions and activities, and the HR manager and department work with all other functional areas across the firm.

2. A second form of organization design used in some organizations today is the *conglomerate*, or *H-form design* (the *H* stands for *holding company*). A conglomerate design is used when an organization has implemented a strategy of unrelated diversification. The corporation itself is essentially a holding company that results from this unrelated diversification. Because the various businesses that make up the organization are unrelated to the others, each functions with a high degree of autonomy and independence. A corporate-level staff usually plays a key role in coordinating the activities of the various divisions, and HRM is a common staff function in an H-form organization. But each of the unrelated businesses within the corporation also has its own HR department that functions with relative autonomy within that specific business. The corporate-level staff provides broad and general oversight and links business-level and corporate-level issues.

3. A third form of fairly common organization design is the *divisional* or *M form* (the *M* stands for *multidivisional*). The divisional design looks similar to the H-form design except that the businesses are closely related to one another. The M-form design is especially popular because of the presumed synergies that can result from related business groupings. Coordination is usually decentralized down to the various operating companies where the work is actually being performed. Although M-form organizations may have a corporate HR staff, most of the basic HR functions are handled within each division.[35] The primary function of the corporate-level HR department is to facilitate synergy across businesses. Presumably, the U.S.-based oil companies discussed earlier are moving to this type of form.

Regardless of the specific design, in recent years, many firms have been moving toward becoming *flat organizations*. This involves eliminating levels of management, reducing bureaucracy, using wide spans of management, and relying heavily on teamwork and coordination to get work accomplished. Flatter organizations are believed to be more flexible and more easily adaptable to changing conditions. The HR function in these organizations is likely to be diffused so that operating managers take on more of the responsibility for HR activities, with a somewhat smaller HR staff providing basic services and playing more of a consultative role.

4-3b The Impact of Corporate Culture

The culture of the organization also affects how it formulates and implements its HR strategy. An organization's **culture** refers to the set of values that helps its members understand what the organization stands for, how it does things, and what it considers important.[36] Culture is a complex and amorphous concept that defies objective measurement or evaluation. Nevertheless, it is the foundation of an organization's internal environment and thus plays a major role in shaping managerial behavior and is a strong element in how the organization manages its human resources.

> As an organization grows, its culture is modified, shaped, and refined through a variety of forces, including symbols, stories, slogans, heroes, and ceremonies.

Although there is no such thing as an ideal culture, an organization should have a strong and well-articulated culture. This type of culture enables people within the firm to know what the organization stands for, what it values, and how they should behave with regard to the organization.[37] The HR department often plays a key role in helping new employees learn about the culture through orientation and through the telling and retelling of stories and corporate history. For current organizational employees, culture can be communicated through training, consistent behavior, and other organizational activities. Sometimes something as simple as a slogan can be used to manage culture. In 2011, KFC changed its traditional slogan of "Finger Lick'n Good" to "So Good" to embrace a trend toward healthier fast-food options and to communicate a breadth of different attributes about the brand, such as the firm's sense of community and its people.

Although an organization's culture is shaped by several different forces, one important force is the founder of the organization. Organizations with strong-willed and visionary founders often find that the remnants of that founder's vision remain a central part of their culture today. Walt Disney's influence is still found throughout the corporation that bears his name. Even though Sam Walton died almost two decades ago, his values and approach to doing business will likely remain a part of Walmart for decades to come. As an organization grows, its culture is modified, shaped, and refined through other forces. These forces include symbols, stories, slogans, heroes, and ceremonies. Shared experiences also play a role in determining and shaping the culture of an organization. Members of teams who work long hours together to develop a major new product such as the latest version of the Ford F150 pickup truck or who jointly experience a major crisis such as the aftermath of September 11, 2001, often develop a common frame of reference and become a more cohesive work group.

HR managers may find that, depending on the circumstances, corporate culture may either facilitate or impede their work. If the firm has a strong and well-understood culture that seems attractive to people, then recruiting qualified applicants is often easier. Southwest Airlines and Starbucks fall into this category, with each firm receiving large numbers of applications from prospective employees. But organizations that have and want to maintain strong cultures tend to select people who have values consistent with that culture. We will discuss the role of fit later in Chapter 7, but for now, note that some organizations select individuals who are qualified enough to do the job (even if they are not the *most* qualified) but who also share the values and beliefs of the firm's culture. In other words, they select the person who best fits the organization's culture and image.

Finally, managing culture is important

Organization design refers to the framework of jobs, positions, clusters of positions, and reporting relationships among positions that are used to construct an organization.

An organization's **culture** refers to the set of values that helps its members understand what the organization stands for, how it accomplishes what it wants to accomplish, and what it considers important.

goodluz/Shutterstock.com

for the success of corporate mergers and acquisitions, which we will discuss further in Chapter 6. The ability to integrate two cultures—in fact, to form a new unique corporate culture and identity for the merged organization—is critical for the overall success of any merger or acquisition and is the role of the HRM area. Several scholars have noted that the failure to deal with the HR implications of mergers and acquisitions leads to their failure far more frequently than do problems with finances.[38] An interesting example of these culture problems occurred several years ago when Philip Morris acquired General Foods. The employees of General Foods considered themselves part of a benevolent company that made family-oriented products such as Jell-O and Maxwell House coffee. Imagine their surprise when their new employers (who also owned Miller Brewing Company) continued *their* usual practice and distributed cartons of cigarettes to each employee every Friday!

4-3c The Impact of Unionization and Collective Bargaining

Other important aspects of the workforce that affect the development and

---

implementation of strategy in the HRM function are unionization and collective bargaining. Labor relations is the process of dealing with employees who are represented by an employee association, usually called a *union*. Union membership in the United States has been declining gradually for the past few decades, but it remains an important force in many industries, as we will see in Chapter 11. In fact, the AFL-CIO has recently been linking living-wage issues to larger social movements, introducing new sources of pressure on HRM.[39] In any case, unions can play an important role in formulating and implementing HR strategy. Unionized firms tend to have more rules and formal procedures that might limit a firm's ability to formulate an ideal strategy, and, if management and union leaders do not work together, the union can be a major obstacle in implementing any strategic change. On the other hand, a strong union can actually facilitate these changes, if its leaders and the firm's management are working together productively.

 ## INTERPERSONAL PROCESSES AND STRATEGY IMPLEMENTATION

The formulation of an HR strategy is clearly important and can be affected by many factors. Ultimately, the best formulated strategy will not help unless it is properly implemented.[40] We will discuss strategy implementation in more detail in the next chapter, where we, will consider strategy as a major source of information for decision-making in the arena of HRM. For now, it is also important to consider the role that interpersonal processes play in the implementation of strategy.

Interpersonal processes are especially important because of the role they play in affecting the performance effectiveness exhibited by each employee in a firm.[41] The starting point for understanding these processes is the psychological contract that an organization has with its employees. A **psychological contract** is the overall set of expectations held by an individual with respect to what he or she will contribute to the organization and what the organization, in turn, will provide to the individual.[42] Individuals see themselves as contributing their time, energy, effort, experience, and talent, and they expect to receive compensation, benefits, security, challenge, opportunities for promotion, and similar forms of rewards. Properly established and maintained psychological contracts are a fundamental starting point in ensuring that employees are committed to working toward

A **psychological contract** is the overall set of expectations held by an individual with respect to what he or she will contribute to the organization and what the organization will provide the individual in return.

organizational goals and contributing to organizational effectiveness by implementing the strategies that managers have developed. Special problems arise when the implementation of a new strategy involves a change in the terms of the psychological contract.[43]

Individual personality traits and attitudes are also important parts of individual processes in an organization. Personality is the relatively stable set of psychological attributes or traits that distinguish one person from another. Some organizations believe that one or more particular personality traits may relate to how well an employee can perform a certain job or type of job. Personality traits such as self-esteem and agreeableness may be important for someone who will be working in a job that requires regular interaction with the public; conscientiousness appears to be important for performance in a wide variety of jobs.[44] HR managers are usually responsible for determining the best way to measure relevant personality traits in job applicants and for being able to verify that those measures—as well as the underlying traits themselves—do indeed relate to job performance.

Attitudes also play an important role in implementing strategy in an organization. If people have positive attitudes toward their work and organization, then they will be more committed to making contributions to organizational effectiveness and will help to achieve strategic goals. Workers with negative attitudes, on the other hand, are less likely to make this commitment and may be more inclined to be absent frequently or seek alternative employment. HR managers are often called on to help other managers assess the attitudes of their workers by developing attitude surveys, administering those surveys to employees, and then interpreting and evaluating the results.

Perhaps the most important individual process in organizations, however, is motivation, or the set of forces that cause people to behave in certain ways. Individual motivation is also a major determinant of individual performance, but motivation is at the heart of what causes an employee to choose to expend the effort that will support any organizational activity. Unfortunately, the process of motivating employees to behave in desired ways is quite complicated, and there is a great deal we do not understand about it. Nonetheless, theories and models of motivation attempt to explain the phenomenon, and we will discuss several in Chapter 13.

Still another important individual process in organizational settings is stress, or a person's adaptive response to a stimulus that places excessive psychological or physical demands on him or her. Important considerations for HR managers include an understanding of the causes of stress, the processes by which stress affects individuals,

and how organizations and individuals can cope better with stress in organizational settings. HR managers are increasingly being called on to help employees cope with stress, and we will discuss some of the issues involved in these efforts in Chapter 12.

Finally, because little behavior in organizations takes place in isolation, HR managers also need to consider interpersonal processes that develop from the relationships an employee has with coworkers, supervisors, and subordinates. These processes are becoming even more important as organizations move more and more toward having employees work as part of a team instead of as individuals. HR managers must deal with various issues rising from the emphasis on teams, ranging from deciding who should be part of a team to how to evaluate the performance of team members and reward them. Clearly, in this new work environment, the management of interpersonal processes is important for implementing HR strategy.

Leadership is also an important priority for many organizations. Most experts believe that effective leadership is vitally important to organizational success, yet they cannot agree on how to define, measure, or predict leadership. HR managers are expected to help identify potential leadership qualities among existing employees and then to help structure procedures for developing and enhancing those qualities.[45] Obviously, these managers must have a basic understanding of leadership to help the organization achieve its goals.

A final important interpersonal process that is directly related to the implementation of HR strategy is communication. Communication is the process by which two or more parties exchange information and share meaning. Written communication, oral communication, and nonverbal communication are all pervasive in organizations. E-mail has become an especially important method of communication in recent years. In many organizations, the HR department is responsible for

Personality is the relatively stable set of psychological attributes or traits that distinguish one person from another. Some organizations believe that one or more particular personality traits may relate to how well an employee can perform a certain job or type of job.

Motivation is the set of forces that causes people to behave in certain ways. Individual motivation is also a major determinant of individual performance, but motivation is at the heart of what causes an employee to choose to expend the effort that will support any organizational activity.

Stress is a person's adaptive response to a stimulus that places excessive psychological or physical demands on that person. It is important for HR managers understand the causes of stress, the processes by which stress affects individuals, and how organizations and individuals can cope better with stress in organizational settings.

coordinating communication among employees through newsletters, bulletin boards, intranets, and so forth. Clearly, HR managers need to understand how to enhance communication to make sure that their efforts are indeed helping implement their strategies.

HR managers obviously must have a keen understanding of the behavioral processes that are critical in determining the relative effectiveness of various HR functions such as compensation, rewards, performance appraisal, and training and development. All managers need to understand and appreciate these behavioral processes to understand the actions of those with whom they work. Finally, HR managers are often charged with the responsibility of developing and implementing programs aimed at improving various behavioral processes. For example, they may be asked to overhaul the reward system to boost motivation and productivity, develop training programs for workers to cope better with stress, or help identify ways to improve interpersonal communication or resolve interpersonal conflict.

4-5 EVALUATING THE HUMAN RESOURCE FUNCTION IN ORGANIZATIONS

Evaluating the effectiveness of the HR function has become an important trend in recent years. HRM was historically seen as an organizational cost or expense; that is, the organization budgeted a certain amount of money to spend on the management of its HR function. As long as the HR manager stayed within this budget and the employees seemed generally happy, everything was assumed to be fine. More recently, however, many organizations have become more concerned with the cost as well as the benefits of HRM for two seemingly contradictory reasons.

First, as we discussed in Chapter 1, many organizations are now subcontracting or outsourcing some of their HRM functions to external vendors. Whether or not to outsource a function depends on the actual cost of keeping the function in-house.

At the same time, many organizations are coming to view effective HRM as a source of competitive advantage, so they are focusing on its potential benefits and examining the costs and benefits to see which ones actually contribute to competitive advantage and which should be outsourced. Functions that add little value are likely to be outsourced, even if they are not terribly expensive, and functions that add competitive advantage are likely to be retained, even if they are relatively expensive. Of course, the functions themselves may or may not contribute to competitive advantage, but it is the way the organization chooses to allocate its resources to manage those functions that will determine where the firm derives its competitive advantage.

In any event, line managers may even be allowed to decide between the corporation's HR department or an outsider vendor when they need HRM help. Traditionally, organizations relied primarily on indirect measures of the effectiveness of their HRM practices. For example, high turnover or high absenteeism indicated low satisfaction with the job, and this predicament was seen as a problem with HRM. Low levels of absenteeism and turnover or low costs were associated with positive HRM practices, and, as noted previously, costs were not seriously considered. Later, as we noted in Chapter 1, more sophisticated methods of utility analysis allowed organizations to put a dollar value on the contributions of various HRM practices and consider costs as well.

In addition to the evaluation of specific HR functions, there has been a recent trend toward evaluating entire systems of HR activities. Instead of determining if any one HRM practice can produce value, this approach examines the relationship between "bundles" of practices and the overall performance of the organization in terms of factors such as profitability, stock price, and productivity. Although the specific practices that have been investigated differ somewhat from study to study, and despite issues raised about the measurement of effectiveness,[46] the evidence seems to show that organizations which adopt more enlightened HRM practices actually do better than other organizations.[47] Although, as noted, we need to know exactly which practices work, these sets of practices have generally become known as *high-performance work systems*, and they include practices such as those illustrated in Table 4.1.

Of course, several questions must be answered before we can fully understand the importance of these HRM

TABLE 4.1	HUMAN RESOURCE MANAGEMENT PRACTICES THAT MAY LEAD TO IMPROVED FIRM PERFORMANCE
Self-directed work teams	
Total quality management (TQM)	
Contingent pay	
Attitude surveys	
Formal performance appraisals	
Continuous training	

practices. For example, there is some question about whether these practices are truly universally effective. There are also questions about the mechanisms through which these practices lead to firm performance; clearly the practices listed in Table 4.1 (which are derived from several research studies and are typical of the work in this area) are quite broad and cover several different elements. For example, formal performance appraisals can take many different forms, as we will see later in Chapter 10. Although it may be better to have some formal appraisal than none at all, it is also probably true that different types of appraisal systems will lead to different outcomes. Although it might be preferable to make pay contingent on something, exactly what that is may be important as well. In general, however, there is reason to believe that an organization can be more competitive if it adopts these practices, and this represents a new way of evaluating a firm's HR practices.

We will return to discussion of this "strategic" approach to HRM in the final chapter. There, we will discuss how this approach may provide some insight into the process of moving from individual-level performance improvement to firm-level performance improvement. That discussion will also cast some of the issues raised here in a different light.

CLOSING CASE
Using Strategic Goals to Drive Diversity

In 2015, Sodexo came in second on DiversityInc's list of Top 50 Companies for Diversity. Coming on the heels of #1 finishes in 2010 and 2013 and #2 finishes in 2011, 2012, and 2014, Sodexo's 2015 ranking made it the only company to make DiversityInc's top two for six straight years. The company's press release promised that "sustaining its efforts to engage a diverse workforce and foster an inclusive culture . . . is essential" to its strategy, adding that Sodexo "has a long commitment to diversity in the workplace."

Kristoffer Tripplaar/Alamy Stock photo

Strictly speaking, that commitment began in earnest in 2005, when Sodexo, a French-based multinational provider of food and facilities-management services, agreed to pay $80 million to settle a lawsuit filed in 2001 by black employees who charged that they weren't being promoted at the same rate as white coworkers. After fighting the case all the way to the U.S. Supreme Court, Sodexo (whose American arm is headquartered in Gaithersburg, Maryland) also agreed to implement a more structured hiring program and to set up a monitoring panel partly appointed by the plaintiffs. "We are pleased this case has been resolved," said U.S. CEO Richard Macedonia. "We are a stronger and better organization as a result of this process."

"It was a very painful thing for the company," recalls Dr. Rohini Anand, Global Chief Diversity Officer. Indian-born Anand, whose doctoral degree in Asian Studies from the University of Michigan focused on cross-cultural interactions, was hired in 2003, just over a year after the employee suit had first been filed. A specialist in multicultural issues, she began evaluating the experiences not only of African American

(Continued)

(Closing Case – continued)

employees, but those of Hispanics, Asians, and gays and lesbians. She also instituted a program of metrics to measure the performance of every diversity-related initiative, including a diversity scorecard to align the results of such efforts as promotion and retention with organizational strategy.

By 2005—the year of the class-action settlement— Sodexo had pronounced itself "a leader in diversity," but the self-congratulations were a little premature. In fact, complaints about promotion practices—and even about incidents violating basic respect and dignity—continued to surface right up to the time that federal oversight over Sodexo employment practices came to an end. Issued in April 2010, a report entitled, "Missing the Mark: Revisiting Sodexo's Record on Diversity," charged that, between 2004 and 2009, the number of African American managers had increased by only 1 percent and that of minority managers as a whole by only 2 percent. Reported one African American employee: "I worked with a chef who would pull down his pants and use the 'n' word and had this thing about 'you people.' I brought it up with Human Resources, but they said since he was part black, it was okay."

As suggested, however, by the run of DiversityInc citations from 2010 to 2015, Anand's efforts may have begun to pay off. Anand likes at least some of the latest scorecard numbers. Today, for example, 10–15 percent of total bonuses for about 16,000 managers is tied to the attainment of diversity-related goals, as is 25 percent of upper-management bonuses. According to former Sodexo North America CEO George Chavel, they were trying to drive change and "not just pointing to those metrics but using them."[48]

Case Questions

1. Do you think diversity goals should be a part of a company's strategy? Why or why not?

2. Over the past few decades, a number of firms that were sued for discriminatory employment practices ended up becoming exemplars for promoting diversity. What might explain this pattern?

3. Describe the link between developing strategies for increasing diversity and then implementing those strategies.

STUDY TOOLS 4

READY TO STUDY?
In the book, you can:

☐ Rip out the chapter review card at the back of the book for a handy summary of the chapter and key terms.

ONLINE AT CENGAGEBRAIN.COM YOU CAN:

☐ Collect StudyBits while you read and study the chapter.

☐ Quiz yourself on key concepts.

☐ Find videos for further exploration.

☐ Prepare for tests with HR4 Flash Cards as well as those you create.

HR ONLINE

PREPARE FOR TESTS ON THE STUDYBOARD!

CORRECT

INCORRECT

INCORRECT

INCORRECT

Personalize Quizzes from Your StudyBits

Take Practice Quizzes by Chapter

CHAPTER QUIZZES

Chapter 1
Chapter 2
Chapter 3
Chapter 4

4LTR PRESS

Access HR ONLINE at www.cengagebrain.com

5 | Information for Making Human Resource Decisions

eddtoro/Shutterstock.com

After finishing this chapter go to **PAGE 130** for **STUDY TOOLS**

LEARNING OBJECTIVES

5-1 Describe human resource planning as a source of information for decision-making

5-2 Discuss strategy as a source of information for making human resource decisions

5-3 Discuss economic conditions as a source of information for making human resource decisions

5-4 Describe job analysis as a source of information for making human resource decisions

5-5 Discuss the job-analysis process, and identify and summarize common job-analysis methods

OPENING CASE
Forecasting the Future

Information plays a vital role in all organizational activities. Marketing managers need information about customer preferences and competitor products. Operations managers need information about inventories and product demand. Financial managers need information about interest rates and cash flows. And human resource managers need information about all of these areas so they can insure they have the right employees with the right skills in the right places at the right times.

Consider, for example, three recent developments related to employment in the United States. In one, major employers in the U.S. pharmaceutical, financial services, and energy sectors cut more than 100,000 jobs in 2014 and 2015. Some of these cuts were due to industry slowdowns and corporate restructuring. But surprisingly, some of the cuts were also related to improvements in the economy. Some banks, for example, had hired extra loan officers to help process a surge in home refinancing. But an improving economy was pushing interest rates up; higher rates, in turn, led to a drop in home refinancing and a reduced need for extra loan officers. Meanwhile, plunging oil prices led firms such as Chevron, Shell, Schlumberger, and Halliburton to lay off thousands of workers.

On the other hand, during the last three months of 2015 and again in 2016, following an annual ritual, major U.S. retailers and related businesses announced that they were planning to hire hundreds of thousands of temporary workers for the holiday season. For example, Kohl's typically adds more than 50,000 seasonal workers; Macy's added 75,000 in 2015; and Target added almost 90,000. Similarly, both FedEx and UPS also hire thousands of seasonal

> "The banking sector is cutting workforce levels as a direct result of an improving economy."
>
> —JOHN CHALLENGER, SENIOR HUMAN RESOURCE CONSULTANT[1]

workers to help keep up with sharp increases in package deliveries. And, as each holiday season ends, some of these workers are offered permanent employment, some are extended (temporarily), but most see their temporary jobs come to an end.

Finally, Starbucks recently announced a long-term plan of increasing its global workforce from around 200,000 now to more than 500,000. Within this total, the firm will seek to hire at least 10,000 veterans and active-duty spouses. Similarly, Walmart indicated that it intended to hire around 100,000 new permanent employees within the next 5 years. What do these examples have in common? They each illustrate that human resource managers must rely on a variety of information sources as they make plans to hire new employees, either temporarily or permanently.[2]

THINK IT OVER

1. What industry sectors are most likely to add jobs during a down economy? During an improving economy?

2. Are there employment sectors that are essentially unaffected by economic fluctuations?

Walmart executives face a continuous challenge of hiring and retaining workers in a low-wage environment. But as with most things, Walmart does an outstanding job of forecasting its needs for employees. These forecasts come from a logical and systematic analysis of the firm's current and projected human resource (HR) needs. And as the ongoing hiring process continues, it will be critical that company officials monitor the environment and the firm itself and make any required midcourse adjustments. Both current hiring goals and their implementation have one major thing in common: information. It is critical that

firms have the information they need to make informed human resource management (HRM) decisions.

With an understanding of the nature of HRM and the HR environment as a foundation (as provided in Chapters 1 through 4), it is now possible to begin a more focused and detailed analysis of the kinds of decisions HR managers must make and the information they need to make those decisions. This chapter opens this part of the book with a discussion of the critical information needs of the HR manager. Chapter 6 begins dealing with the decisions themselves and addresses decisions concerning size and structure of the organizational form, including who to let go, who to retain, and how to make sure that the right people are retained and separated. Finally, Chapter 7 deals with staffing by discussing issues involved in recruiting and selecting employees. These are critical decisions for the HR manager because they determine the nature of the workforce available to try to meet strategic objectives.

We will discuss various types of information that HR managers have traditionally relied on for making decisions, but we will end the chapter with a discussion of what has been termed "big data" or "data analytics." The move toward big data analytics has meant that all managers are now looking at larger sets of data in order to make decisions, and HR managers are included in this trend. At the simplest level, analytics refers to the discovery and communication of meaningful patterns in data. This is especially useful in areas rich with recorded data, and analytics employ statistics, computer programs, and operations research to help describe, predict, and improve all areas of business performance. First, though, we turn to the most basic type of information used by HR managers—information about the supply and demand for labor—which forms the basis for HR planning.

5-1 HUMAN RESOURCE PLANNING AS A SOURCE OF INFORMATION

Probably the most important factor that affects the HRM function is the labor force (also referred to as the *workforce*). An organization may pursue a growth strategy, and the HR manager may attempt to recruit and hire new employees, but if there are not enough people in the labor force with the required skills or background, then efforts to recruit and hire will fail, as will the overall growth strategy. Thus, the composition of the labor force is a major limiting factor in pursuing strategic goals. The successful management of this component requires **human resource planning**, which can often make the difference between organizational success and failure.[3] HR planning, illustrated in Figure 5.1, can be defined as the process of forecasting the supply and demand for human resources within an organization and developing action plans for aligning the two. This section examines that process in more detail.

> **Human resource planning** is the process of forecasting the supply and demand for human resources within an organization and developing action plans for aligning the two.

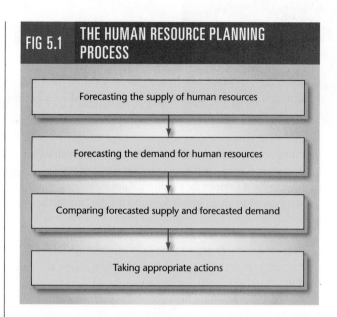

FIG 5.1 **THE HUMAN RESOURCE PLANNING PROCESS**

- Forecasting the supply of human resources
- Forecasting the demand for human resources
- Comparing forecasted supply and forecasted demand
- Taking appropriate actions

5-1a Forecasting the Supply of Human Resources

An important first step in HR planning is forecasting the future supply of human resources—predicting the availability of current or potential employees with the skills, abilities, and motivation to perform jobs that the organization expects to have available. Several mechanisms can help managers forecast the supply of human resources in regard to current employees. By looking internally at its own records, the organization is likely to be able to draw on considerable historical data about its own abilities to hire and retain employees. In addition, the organization can glean information about the extent to which people leave their jobs voluntarily or involuntarily. All of this information is then useful in predicting the internal supply of human resources in the future.

Suppose, for example, that Moyer Industries, a regional manufacturing and supply business serving the aviation industry, has averaged 15 percent turnover for each of the past 10 years, with little variation from year to year. When Moyer's HR manager attempts to predict the future supply of existing workers, at least initially, it seems reasonable to predict a relatively similar level of turnover for the forthcoming year. Thus, the internal supply of the human resources at Moyer will likely decline by about 15 percent during the next year. Assuming the firm plans to maintain its current operations and will need a workforce comparable to what it has today, the organization needs to plan to replace those individuals who will depart by recruiting and hiring new employees.

An increasingly important element in this part of the HR planning process for most organizations is the effective use of the organization's **human resource information system**. A human resource information system is an integrated and increasingly automated system for maintaining a database regarding the employees in an organization. For example, a properly developed human resource information system should have details on each and every employee regarding date of hire, job history within the organization, education, performance ratings, compensation history, training and development profile, and various special skills and abilities.[4] Of course, the HR manager also needs to look carefully at impending retirements and the firm's experiences with involuntary turnover. We will discuss these issues more fully in Chapter 6.

Because a firm often expects to need new employees in the future, it is also important to forecast the supply of human resources outside the firm that will be potentially available for it to recruit and hire. Here it is important to consider both general trends in the population and the workforce while simultaneously generating specific data about availability as it relates to the specific firm. Specifically, these trends and issues serve as valuable information related to forecasting the supply of human resources.

5-1b Labor Force Trends and Issues

Several changes in the labor force continue to emerge and affect HRM. Decades ago, the labor force in the United States was primarily male and white. Now, however, the workforce is much more diverse in numerous ways.[5] For example, most people once followed a fairly predictable pattern of entering the workforce at a young age, maintaining a stable employment relationship for the period of their work lives, and then retiring at the fairly predictable age of 65. But today, these patterns and trends have all changed. For example, the average age of the U.S. workforce is gradually increasing and will continue to do so. Several reasons have contributed to this pattern:

1. The baby boom generation continues to age.

2. Declining birthrates for the post-baby boom generation are simultaneously accounting for a smaller percentage of new entrants into the labor force.

3. Improved health and medical care also contribute to an aging workforce. People are now simply able to be productive at work for longer periods of their lives.

4. Mandatory retirement ages have been increased or dropped altogether, allowing people to remain in the labor force for longer periods.

Gender differences in the workforce also play an important role. More women have entered the workforce, and their presence is felt in more and more occupational groupings that were traditionally dominated by men. In 2017, the composition of the workforce in the United States was almost 50 percent female, although some critics claim that a glass ceiling—an invisible barrier that keeps women from progressing to higher levels in a firm—still exists in some organizations.

Changing ethnicity is also reflected in the workforce today. The percentage of whites in the workforce is gradually dropping, while the percentage of Hispanics is climbing at an almost comparable rate. The percentage of African Americans and Asians in the workforce is also growing but at a much smaller rate. In addition to age, gender, and ethnicity, other diversity forces are also affecting the labor force. For example, country of national origin is an important diversity dimension. Physically challenged employees and employees with other disabilities are also an important part of workforce trends. Many other dimensions of diversity, such as single-parent status, dual-career couples, gays and lesbians, people with special dietary preferences, and people with different political ideologies and viewpoints also are each playing an important role in organizations today. We cover diversity more fully in Chapter 8.

In addition, external data can also be used to predict the supply of labor in specific regions. Over the past several years, for example, there has been a gradual population shift away from the northern and northeastern

Lisa S/Shutterstock.com

> A **human resource information system** is an integrated and increasingly automated system for maintaining a database regarding the employees in an organization.

parts of the United States and toward the southern, southeastern, and southwestern parts of the country. Thus, the supply of labor in the north and northeast is gradually declining, and the supply of labor in the southern parts of the United States is gradually increasing. In other parts of the world, wherever immigration rules permit, workers are gradually shifting away from developing parts of the world and toward industrialized and economically prosperous regions. For instance, many workers in eastern regions of Europe continue to move into western areas in anticipation of better employment prospects, even given recent problems with Western European financial systems.[6]

In any case, immigration patterns are important inputs for forecasting the supply of labor. But borders are not as open as they once were, even in the United States. Concerns over homeland security have made it much more difficult for individuals from certain parts of the world to even visit the United States. Young males from predominantly Arab countries have had an especially hard time coming to the United States to work, or even study, and some business leaders have become concerned about this and argue that security concerns are taking precedence over the need for qualified people to fill jobs. Furthermore, several critics, including Robert Gates (Secretary of Defense for George W. Bush and for President Obama for the first 2 years of his first term), have warned that these policies can hurt the long-term productivity of the United States and cut the country off from an important pool of talent.

Future labor supplies are typically forecast by developing mathematical trend models using data from the past, with appropriate adjustments for migratory trends and predictions. These models, which essentially assume that trends will continue in a linear (i.e., straight-line) fashion, are usually reasonably accurate. But they can be far less accurate

> **Immigration patterns are important inputs for forecasting the supply of labor.**

when some unforeseen event or trend disrupts expectations. An example was the unexpected increase in the labor force participation rates for women during the 1980s. Although women's participation rates had been climbing for years, statistical predictions based on simple trend lines substantially underestimated the growth rates in the 1980s. In retrospect, observers realized that new (i.e., first-time) entries by women into the labor force were being substantially supplemented by other women already in the labor force but who were previously underemployed.

But major economic upheavals, such as those experienced in the United States and much of the rest of the world in 2009, can present major challenges to predictive models. Many organizations actively cut the size of their workforces, which dramatically increased the supply of labor in the market. Because stock prices initially tumbled, many employees who had planned to retire found that they could no longer afford to do so, further increasing the supply of labor in the market. These forces, of course, also lowered the "price" of labor (i.e., what a firm had to pay), but many firms were too busy dealing with the new financial realities to be able to take advantage of lower labor costs. In any case, events such as this cannot be predicted by any linear model, which makes planning much more difficult.

Finally, we should also note the special forecasting situation generally known as **executive succession**. Executive succession involves systematically planning for future promotions into top management positions. This process is far more complicated because it is often critical that exactly the right type of person is selected for a top position, the development costs to groom this person are very high, and the actual decision may have major effects on the firm's future. Thus, many organizations try to bring as much order and logic to the process as possible. For example, senior executives usually indicate well in advance when they expect to retire—sometimes several years in advance. The firm can then draw on its cadre of up-and-coming managers for replacement candidates. Sometimes a specific set of individuals may be moved into special high-profile jobs, with the expectation that whoever does the best job will receive the promotion when the senior person steps down. In other cases, the most likely successor is moved into the second spot to eliminate all uncertainties and allow this person to concentrate on learning as much as possible about the senior position.[7] For example, a few years ago, Apple's board of directors and CEO Steven Jobs realized that continued concerns about Jobs' health might weaken confidence in the firm and could lead to confusion if he needed to step down from his leadership position. So, working together, they identified Tim Cook as Jobs' heir apparent. When Jobs did find it necessary to step down a few months before his death in 2011, Cook was well prepared to take over, and the transition was seamless.

5-1c Forecasting the Demand for Human Resources

In addition to supply, strategic planning requires that HR managers must also develop forecasts about future demand. In other words, they need to ascertain the numbers and types of people the organization will actually need to employ in the future. One important ingredient in this assessment is the organization's own strategic plans regarding anticipated growth, stability, or decline, which are described later in the chapter.

It is also necessary to consider larger, broader trends in the economy when forecasting the demand for human resources. For example, the chart illustrated in the Contemporary Challenges in HR box shows how some jobs, such as retail sales, have remained in high demand since 1900. But other jobs, such as tailors, masons, tobacco factory workers, and butchers, have dropped sharply. Still others, such as nurses, waiters and waitresses, and customer service representatives, have seen demand

increase significantly. These general demand trends influence the availability of human resources for two reasons. First, employees for jobs in high demand will be more difficult to hire and will be more expensive to hire. In addition, students and future employees who track these demand trends often make decisions about what majors to pursue in college based on their anticipated employability. Thus, general trends such as the ones described here must be part of the planning process.

Clearly, the planning process, and the associated forecasting of supply and demand relative to labor, is an important source of information for the HR manager. Information about what kinds of people will generally be in demand, as well as information about what kinds of people will be available, is critical as the HR manager begins thinking about staffing decisions, downsizing or rightsizing decisions, and how to develop a diverse organization. This information not only will serve as a set of constraints on what the manager can accomplish but also help the manager identify ways to meet the organization's strategic goals. A related source of information for the HR manager comes out of the strategic-planning process itself.

5-2 STRATEGY AS A SOURCE OF INFORMATION

We discussed the relationship between strategic planning and effective HRM in Chapter 4, but clearly the need for human resources in an organization depends to a large extent on the organization's overall strategy. As noted in Chapter 4, if an organization intends to grow, then it will most likely need to hire additional human resources in the future.[8] Likewise, if the organization expects to enter a period of stability, its HR demand is also likely to be relatively stable.[9] Finally, if a period of decline or retrenchment is anticipated, then the organization may be confronting a decreased demand for human resources. In each case, it is up to the HR manager to implement the chosen strategy. Therefore, we will discuss the implications of each strategy for HRM decisions.

5-2a Implications of a Growth Strategy

A strategy of growth indicates growing sales, increasing demand, and expanding operations for the organization. When

> **Executive succession** involves systematically planning for future promotions into top management positions.

Contemporary Challenges in HR

Coming and Going

Managers attempting to forecast the future supply of and demand for jobs and employees face numerous uncertainties. One major uncertainty for long-term planning is the extent to which any given job may become more or less popular in the future. This graph, which rank orders the top 30 jobs (by millions of workers) for the years 1900, 1960, 1995, 2010, and 2014, clearly illustrates the point. Only a few job categories among the most popular in 1900 are still on the list by 2014. Some jobs, such as carpenter, have consistently dropped further down the list, whereas others, such as police officer and

TOP 30 JOBS (millions of workers)

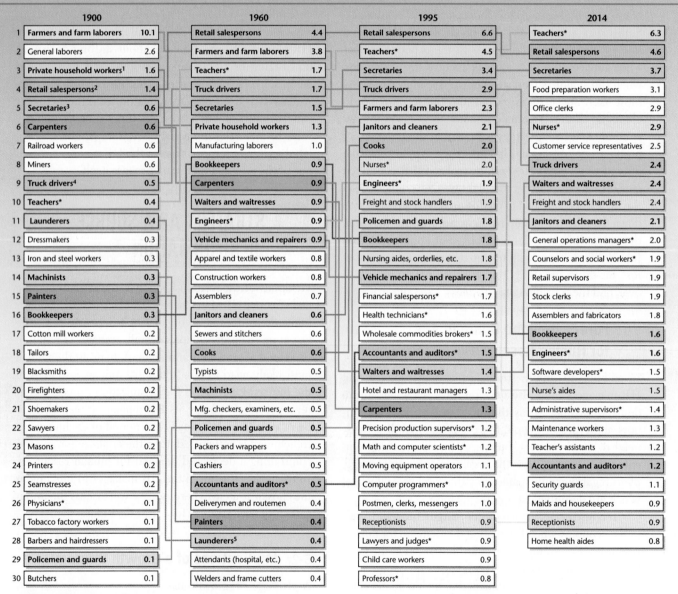

	1900		1960		1995		2014	
1	Farmers and farm laborers	10.1	Retail salespersons	4.4	Retail salespersons	6.6	Teachers*	6.3
2	General laborers	2.6	Farmers and farm laborers	3.8	Teachers*	4.5	Retail salespersons	4.6
3	Private household workers[1]	1.6	Teachers*	1.7	Secretaries	3.4	Secretaries	3.7
4	Retail salespersons[2]	1.4	Truck drivers	1.7	Truck drivers	2.9	Food preparation workers	3.1
5	Secretaries[3]	0.6	Secretaries	1.5	Farmers and farm laborers	2.3	Office clerks	2.9
6	Carpenters	0.6	Private household workers	1.3	Janitors and cleaners	2.1	Nurses*	2.9
7	Railroad workers	0.6	Manufacturing laborers	1.0	Cooks	2.0	Customer service representatives	2.5
8	Miners	0.6	Bookkeepers	0.9	Nurses*	2.0	Truck drivers	2.4
9	Truck drivers[4]	0.5	Carpenters	0.9	Engineers*	1.9	Waiters and waitresses	2.4
10	Teachers*	0.4	Waiters and waitresses	0.9	Freight and stock handlers	1.9	Freight and stock handlers	2.4
11	Launderers	0.4	Engineers*	0.9	Policemen and guards	1.8	Janitors and cleaners	2.1
12	Dressmakers	0.3	Vehicle mechanics and repairers	0.9	Bookkeepers	1.8	General operations managers*	2.0
13	Iron and steel workers	0.3	Apparel and textile workers	0.8	Nursing aides, orderlies, etc.	1.8	Counselors and social workers*	1.9
14	Machinists	0.3	Construction workers	0.8	Vehicle mechanics and repairers	1.7	Retail supervisors	1.9
15	Painters	0.3	Assemblers	0.7	Financial salespersons*	1.7	Stock clerks	1.9
16	Bookkeepers	0.3	Janitors and cleaners	0.6	Health technicians*	1.6	Assemblers and fabricators	1.8
17	Cotton mill workers	0.2	Sewers and stitchers	0.6	Wholesale commodities brokers*	1.5	Bookkeepers	1.6
18	Tailors	0.2	Cooks	0.6	Accountants and auditors*	1.5	Engineers*	1.6
19	Blacksmiths	0.2	Typists	0.5	Waiters and waitresses	1.4	Software developers*	1.5
20	Firefighters	0.2	Machinists	0.5	Hotel and restaurant managers	1.3	Nurse's aides	1.5
21	Shoemakers	0.2	Mfg. checkers, examiners, etc.	0.5	Carpenters	1.3	Administrative supervisors*	1.4
22	Sawyers	0.2	Policemen and guards	0.5	Precision production supervisors*	1.2	Maintenance workers	1.3
23	Masons	0.2	Packers and wrappers	0.5	Math and computer scientists*	1.2	Teacher's assistants	1.2
24	Printers	0.2	Cashiers	0.5	Moving equipment operators	1.1	Accountants and auditors*	1.2
25	Seamstresses	0.2	Accountants and auditors*	0.5	Computer programmers*	1.0	Security guards	1.1
26	Physicians*	0.1	Deliverymen and routemen	0.4	Postmen, clerks, messengers	1.0	Maids and housekeepers	0.9
27	Tobacco factory workers	0.1	Painters	0.4	Receptionists	0.9	Receptionists	0.9
28	Barbers and hairdressers	0.1	Launderers[5]	0.4	Lawyers and judges*	0.9	Home health aides	0.8
29	Policemen and guards	0.1	Attendants (hospital, etc.)	0.4	Child care workers	0.9		
30	Butchers	0.1	Welders and frame cutters	0.4	Professors*	0.8		

Over the century, the structure of U.S. employment has changed enormously. Only eight top job categories have survived throughout. And many more top job categories now require substantial education.

* Requires education. [1]Servants and housekeepers in 1900. [2]Merchants and salespeople in 1900. [3]Clerks in 1900. [4]Teamsters and coachmen in 1900. [5]Launderers and dry cleaners in 1960.

Sources: http://www.bls.gov/news.release/pdf/ocwage.pdf; (accessed February, 2016); "Top 30 Jobs" *Forbes*, May 6, 1996, p. 17. (Accessed April 26, 2016).

guard, have steadily risen. But most striking is simply the array of jobs on the 2014 list that did not appear previously such as customer service representative, general operations manager, and home health aide. Over the course of the 20th century, the structure of U.S. employment clearly changed enormously, and this change continued (and perhaps even accelerated) in the first decade a of the twenty-first century.[10]

THINK IT OVER

1. What are some very new kinds of jobs of which you are aware?

2. What jobs on the 2014 list may be in danger of disappearing in the near future?

the organization is growing and expanding, it most likely needs to hire new employees in the future.[11] In some cases, the organization may be able to hire employees readily without additional work. If, for example, a firm is currently receiving 100 qualified applicants per month but has only been hiring 5, the firm may be able to meet any targeted growth by simply hiring 10 people per month.

In other situations, implementing a growth strategy may be more difficult. Market conditions may be such that qualified employees are hard to find. For example, a firm receiving 100 qualified applications per year and hiring as many as 90 of them is not likely to hire dramatically larger numbers of them without taking additional actions. The organization may have to increase its recruiting efforts to attract more job applicants and even perhaps begin to provide additional support to apprentice or training programs. Support of various college and university programs might also be a way of increasing the future supply of available labor talent.

A related incident involved United Parcel Service (UPS), the giant delivery business. UPS is based in Louisville, Kentucky, and maintains a huge operation there. The firm recently wanted to launch a major expansion but was concerned about its ability to attract enough new workers, especially those who might be interested in working the night shift. The firm threatened to build its expansion in another state unless Kentucky would help. Facing the threat of losing such a big employer, the state passed and funded major job-training legislation and programs to help it attract and develop capable workers of the type that UPS needed.[12]

5-2b Implications of a Stability Strategy

In many ways, a stability strategy may be the easiest for the HR manager to implement because the organization presumably must do what it has been doing all along. But, even here, specific and subtle planning nuances

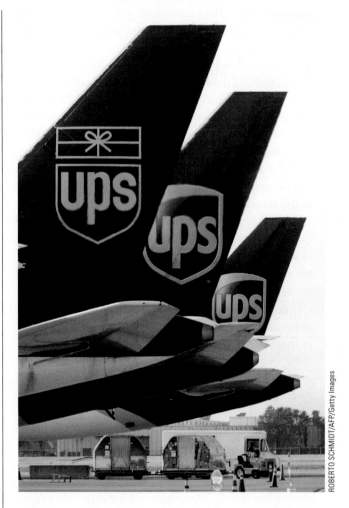

ROBERTO SCHMIDT/AFP/Getty Images

must be considered. For example, the organization will naturally experience a certain amount of attrition in its employee ranks each year. As noted earlier, some people will leave for better jobs, some people will retire, some will leave because of poor performance, and others will leave for reasons such as career relocation on the part of a spouse or significant other. Thus, even an organization that is projecting a period of stability is likely to need to augment its labor force to replace those individuals who leave the organization for various reasons. In such cases, the organization can implement programs such as training to upgrade the skills of current employees, making them more valuable to the organization. Alternatively, the organization might implement programs that help reduce turnover among current employees, making stability easier to maintain.

5-2c **Implications of a Reduction Strategy**

In some cases, an organization may find itself facing reductions. Perhaps an organization is experiencing cutbacks, such as many organizations in the United States have faced over the past several years. As the economy gradually began to recover from the 2008–2009 recession, some businesses slowly started to hire again. But even those firms adding jobs have done so cautiously.[13]

Sometimes these reductions can be handled through normal attrition processes as described earlier. For example, if the organization currently has 1,000 employees and knows from experience that approximately 100 of those individuals will retire, resign, or be fired next year, and if it forecasts that it will need only 900 employees following next year, then it may need to do little. But if the actual forecast calls for only 700 employees, the organization must figure out how to eliminate the other 200 jobs in addition to the 100 that will disappear automatically. This sort of situation may call for laying people off, and we will discuss some important issues associated with this downsizing process in Chapter 6.

A popular alternative to terminations and layoffs, especially for managers, is early retirement. The idea is to make offers to employees to enhance their retirement benefits so that people might consider retiring at an earlier age than they would have done otherwise. Of course, this process involves costs to the organization. The organization may be forced to pay additional benefits to those employees above and beyond what they would have ordinarily expected to pay. It is also possible that the organization might lose people that it would have preferred to keep; that is, its highest-performing employees may be those who opt for early retirement. In fact, they may see early retirement as an opportunity for increasing their income by taking retirement benefits from their current employer but using their high-performance credentials to gain new employment with another organization. On the other hand, lower-performing employees are less likely to have this option and thus may be more likely to remain with the current organization.

The **rate of unemployment** is calculated by the Bureau of Labor Statistics as the percentage of individuals looking for and available for work who are not currently employed.

Clearly, the actual strategy chosen is an important source of information for decision-making because it determines what kinds of decisions will need to be made. It will determine whether the HR manager needs to be concerned with recruiting new talent or finding ways to reduce the workforce. Strategy will also determine whether the HR manager needs to worry about reducing turnover or encouraging it. Another source of information operates at this macro level: the general state of the economy. We discussed this briefly earlier, but we now need to consider more seriously how the state of the economy is an important source of information for HR decision-making.

5-3 ECONOMIC CONDITIONS AS A SOURCE OF INFORMATION

We noted previously how the economy influenced the supply of and demand for different types of employees, but the economy also has a more general effect on the workforce that the HR manager must consider. To understand this, think about an employee as having a valued asset (his or her effort at work) and as having to make some decision about how to use that asset. The employee could decide to keep the asset for himself and not work for anyone else. The employee may start her own business or find some other way to support herself. On the other hand, the employee may decide to enter the marketplace and see how much her effort is worth and so decide for whom to go to work. Although this example is oversimplified, it illustrates the importance of economic-based decisions by potential employees and how these might affect HRM decisions. Many factors could affect a person's decision to enter the labor market and seek employment. We will discuss some of these next.

5-3a **Unemployment Rates**

The **rate of unemployment** (or the *rate of employment*) is an important determinant of an individual's employment choices. The national unemployment rate is, of course, relevant, but the local unemployment rate is more closely linked to an individual's choices. Most people who live in, say, Denver, cannot just pack up and move to Miami just because there are more jobs available there. This lack of mobility means that people respond more to local labor market conditions. There is considerable evidence that turnover rates are better predicted by unemployment statistics than by any other variable (see Chapter 6 for a discussion of these other variables).[14]

Therefore, if unemployment is relatively high, then individuals are less likely to leave their current jobs to look for alternatives. As a result, firms may be able to find many willing applicants among the unemployed but are unlikely to be able to lure desirable employees from a different company. In addition, during times of high unemployment, individuals who are contemplating entering the labor market are less likely to do so because they see their chances of finding a job lower than they prefer. Finally, some people might decide to move to a more attractive location from an employment perspective. Such options had been limited in the United States for a few years, so retention was not really a problem, but things have been changing. After several years of relatively high unemployment in the United States (as high as 10 percent in 2010), the unemployment rate began to fall in 2012 and has hovered around 7.5 percent since then. But the unemployment rate rose a bit in the summer of 2013 (to around 7.6 percent) as people became more optimistic about the economy and reentered the job market seeking employment, and in 2016, the rate was 4.9 percent. Throughout these fluctuations, the picture differs from state to state. By July 2016, the states with the highest unemployment rates were New Mexico (6.4 percent), Nevada (6.5 percent), and Alaska (6.7 percent). The states with the lowest unemployment rates, on the other hand, were South Dakota (2.8 percent), New Hampshire (2.9 percent), and Nebraska (3.1 percent).[15]

On the other hand, when there are few attractive jobs available, there may be a short-term shortage of qualified workers if people get discouraged and stop looking for work. It is interesting to note that, if a person stops looking for work, he or she is considered to have withdrawn from the labor market and is no longer considered "unemployed." But, as noted earlier, the U.S. economy has been improving, so that the unemployment rate in March 2016 was 4.9 percent. This was the lowest level in 8 years, and it has provoked some interesting discussions and behaviors. First of all, while the unemployment rate has remained more or less steady for several months, the number of new job seekers has been increasing. Presumably, potential employees see new possibilities and so are reentering the job market. This development, of course, puts more pressure on the economy because new jobs must be created to meet this new demand. But, in addition, some economists are wondering whether we are getting closer to "full employment." The term does not refer to a situation where unemployment is zero, but instead refers to a situation where the number of job seekers roughly equals the number of job openings. Traditionally, the jobless rate at such a point is 4–6 percent. Some people in HR[16] argue that "full employment" is really a meaningless term to everyone except economists and politicians and that, as long as people are out of jobs there are issues. It is interesting to realize, however, that once "full employment" is reached, some politicians will call for reducing programs aimed at increasing job growth. As the United States still works it's way out of the last recession, any such policies may be met with serious resistance.

5-3b Market Wage Rates

A related factor that will influence decisions about joining the labor force is the **market wage rate**. Most people are aware that wages are generally higher in a place such as New York City than in a place such as Houston. The differences in salaries and wage rates partly result from differences in the cost of living, but they also are caused by different levels of competitiveness for talent in the market. Thus, teachers in university towns are often paid poorly because there is a surplus of qualified teachers looking for jobs in those locations. On the other hand, civil service jobs pay almost no premium for cost of living, so a mail carrier in New York City makes almost exactly what a mail carrier makes in Houston or in West Lafayette, Indiana. Figure 5.2 illustrates the range of salaries paid for different jobs in different parts of the United States.

An individual is more likely to decide to enter the labor force when the higher relative wage rate is available to him or her. Again, limited mobility makes it difficult for individuals to find the optimal wage rate for their skills, but some movement is possible. Thus, it is important to understand some determinants of local wage rates.

The simplest explanation relies on supply and demand. Given a certain level of demand for firefighters, for example, in any area, the average wage paid will be higher if the supply is lower; likewise, if the supply for firefighters remains the same, the wage rate will go up as the demand for firefighters increases. But some firms try to attract the best employees they can. These organizations seek to be "the employer of choice" in their market and will pay more than the going market rate to attract the best employees. These "efficiency wages" are believed to be justified by the fact that the best employees are assumed to be more productive and that the higher wages will bind the employee more tightly to the firm,

FIG 5.2 WAGES AND SALARIES ACROSS THE UNITED STATES (HOURLY BASIS)

North Dakota

All Occupations:	$21.20
Financial Manager:	$50.39
Substitute Teacher:	N/A
Registered Nurse:	$27.94
Firefighter:	$18.83
Retail Salesperson:	$14.05

Illinois

All Occupations:	$23.45
Financial Manager:	$60.33
Substitute Teacher:	$16.31
Registered Nurse:	$32.71
Firefighter:	$23.70
Retail Salesperson:	$12.43

New York

All Occupations:	$26.75
Financial Manager:	$84.18
Substitute Teacher:	$17.23
Registered Nurse:	$37.07
Firefighter:	$35.19
Retail Salesperson:	$12.75

California

All Occupations:	$25.91
Financial Manager:	$69.55
Substitute Teacher:	$18.41
Registered Nurse:	$47.31
Firefighter:	$34.44
Retail Salesperson:	$12.98

Texas

All Occupations:	$21.79
Financial Manager:	$64.71
Substitute Teacher:	$10.27
Registered Nurse:	$32.98
Firefighter:	$22.36
Retail Salesperson:	$12.48

Florida

All Occupations:	$20.11
Financial Manager:	$61.80
Substitute Teacher:	$10.90
Registered Nurse:	$30.15
Firefighter:	$25.02
Retail Salesperson:	$11.88

Source: Bureau of Labor Statistics, February 2016 State Occupational Employment and Wage Estimates.

thus reducing turnover. Of course, these benefits will need to offset the higher labor costs associated with the higher wages in order for the firm to remain competitive. Thus, although local wage rates can affect an individual's decision to enter the labor market, efficiency wages can influence which firm the individual decides to join.

5-3c Human Capital Investments

Just as a firm can differentiate itself by paying higher wages, individuals can differentiate themselves as well by making **human capital investments**. In other words, individuals can invest in themselves, through training and education, to increase their value to employers.[17] These investments must be made in areas that an employer considers valuable enough to pay more for, but general education is usually a worthwhile investment and will yield a higher wage. This happened in 2009 and 2010; as unemployment rose to historic levels, many universities saw an increase in the number of applications. But by 2012 and 2013, although unemployment levels remained high, applications generally returned to more traditional levels, as some potential students apparently began to question the value of additional education.

In fact, employers often make decisions about where to locate a facility based on the human capital available in a market. For example, in the 1960s, the Boston area was suffering through a minor regional recession as traditional employers shifted operations elsewhere or went out of business. But the population of the Boston area was highly educated and considered to have a strong work ethic. As a result, it made sense for the early computer and technology firms to locate in the area and take advantage of the availability of a highly educated workforce, and so Boston enjoyed a real boom in the early 1970s as it became the hub of the new computer industry. Thus, human capital investments can increase wages for an individual and so influence decisions to enter the labor market, and the

The **market wage rate** is the prevailing wage rate for a given job in a given labor market.

Human capital investments are investments people make in themselves to increase their value in the workplace. These investments might take the form of additional education or training.

> Employers often make decisions about where to locate a facility based on the human capital available in a market.

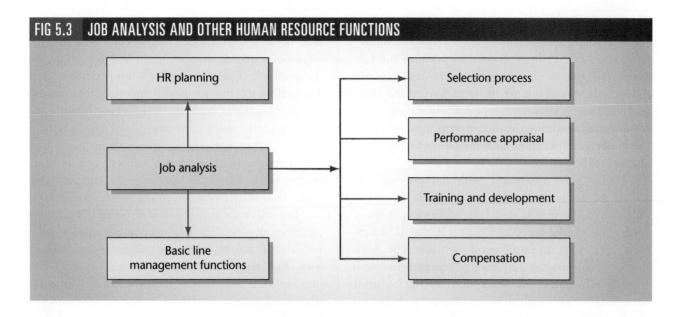

FIG 5.3 JOB ANALYSIS AND OTHER HUMAN RESOURCE FUNCTIONS

HR planning

Job analysis

Basic line management functions

Selection process

Performance appraisal

Training and development

Compensation

availability of persons who have already made human capital investments can affect a firm's location strategies.

Thus, the state of the economy (both local and national) is an important source of information for the HR manager. Economic variables will influence how many potential employees will be available and what kinds of employees those will be. Such variables will also influence the wages that will need to be paid to attract employees to the labor force or to a specific firm. Decisions about what kinds of activities should be conducted in an area should depend on what kinds of people will be willing to enter the labor force and what kinds of people a given firm will be able to attract. Only by understanding the economic forces operating can the HR manager make the decisions that need to be made.

The Americans with Disabilities Act prohibits discrimination based on disability and all aspects of the employment relationship such as job-application procedures, hiring, firing, promotion, compensation, and training, as well as other employment activities such as advertising, recruiting, tenure, layoffs, and leave and fringe benefits.

The types of information we have discussed thus far operate at the level of the organization, or even the region of the country. Each type of information is important for the HR manager who will need to make critical decisions. But the HR manager also needs information at a much more basic level—information about what is required on each of the jobs that will be staffed, evaluated, compensated, and so on. That information comes from job analysis.

 5-4
JOB ANALYSIS AS A SOURCE OF INFORMATION

Job analysis is the process of gathering and organizing detailed information about various jobs within the organization so that managers can better understand the processes through which the jobs are performed most effectively.[18] Generally, job analysis is an effort to study and understand specific jobs in the organization so that managers can have a full sense of the nature of those jobs and the kinds of skills and abilities needed to perform them. As we already noted, job analysis is a fundamental input and building block of the planning process, but, as illustrated in Figure 5.3, it also relates to other HRM processes.

As shown in the figure, job analysis affects selection or hiring decisions because the job-analysis process indicates

> **Job analysis** is the process of gathering and organizing detailed information about various jobs within an organization so that managers can better understand the processes through which they are performed most effectively.

the tasks to be performed by the person to be hired. Job analysis results in assessments about the underlying skills and abilities needed to perform the job, and it leads to logical and appropriate plans to recruit individuals who are most likely to have these skills and abilities. Selection techniques, for instance, can be designed and administered to determine which of the applicants recruited have the necessary skill and ability levels.

Under the Americans with Disabilities Act (ADA), job analysis has taken on an even more important role in the selection of new employees in many companies. As we noted in Chapter 2, the ADA outlaws discrimination based on disabilities. The ADA does not require an organization to hire someone who cannot perform the job in question, of course, but it does require an organization to hire a "qualified individual with a disability," specified as "an individual with a disability who, with or without a reasonable accommodation, can perform the essential functions of the employment position that such an individual holds or desires" (Americans with Disabilities Act, Title 1, section 101).

Further, imagine the implications of an organization refusing to hire a disabled applicant because a manager assumes that the individual cannot perform the job. The individual might have grounds for a discrimination claim if ambiguity exists about exactly which job elements are essential to the organization and which are less essential or optional and if the applicant can demonstrate a capacity for performing the job. Thus, it becomes more important than ever for managers to determine the essential functions of the jobs within the organization because they must identify those parts of jobs (e.g., tasks, duties) that must be carried out effectively for the person to be successful in performing the job. This information can best be obtained through job analysis.

Figure 5.3 also indicates that job analysis relates to performance appraisal. This relationship stems from the understanding of what an employee should be capable of doing in a job before one can assess how well that employee is actually performing. Job analysis similarly affects training and development because it provides information that

> The knowledge, skills, and abilities (KSA) requirements may be similar for a set of jobs.

Knowledge, skills, and abilities (KSA) are the fundamental requirements necessary to perform a job.

helps managers better understand the kind of training and development programs that are necessary to enhance employee competencies and capabilities so the employees can achieve ideal levels of performance. Job-analysis information is also important for compensation (job-analysis methods used for establishing compensation rates are often referred to as *job evaluation*) because work behaviors have traditionally been a primary basis for compensation. (As we will see later, however, compensation based on knowledge or competencies, rather than behaviors, is becoming more common.)

In addition to its fundamental role in HR planning and other aspects of the HR function, job analysis is also important to line managers for various general reasons. First, they must thoroughly understand the work-flow processes that characterize their particular work units. They must understand how work flows from employee to employee, from job station to job station, and from work group to work group. To develop this understanding, of course, they must also have a fundamental insight into the basic mechanics, character, and nature of each job. Job analysis provides this. In addition, because line managers are often involved in hiring and appraisal decisions, they must rely on the information provided by job analysis to help determine who should be hired and how well employees are doing their jobs.

Job analysis provides fundamental input to the HR manager by defining the kinds of both general work and specific jobs that the organization currently relies on and will be relying on in the future.[19] Whereas the focus of job analysis is typically an individual job, in many organizations, the tasks and responsibilities on some jobs may be similar to those on other jobs. Likewise, the **knowledge, skills, and abilities (KSA)** requirements may be similar for a set of jobs. As a result, for planning purposes, organizations often try to form *job families*—groups of jobs that have task and KSA requirements that are quite similar.

These job families can be quite useful in several ways. First, if the jobs within a job family have similar KSA requirements, then it might be possible to train employees so that they can apply what they have learned to the entire family of jobs, making them much more flexible resources for the organization. In addition, this training for job families rather than for specific jobs can help employees remain useful to the organization even if their current jobs become obsolete.[20]

Well-conceived job families can also be used to help organizations in career planning. The jobs within a family represent jobs that have similar patterns of requirements. If they occur at different levels within an organization, then those jobs can represent a typical career path for an employee. Thus, managers can plan where an employee might go as his or her career builds, and they might also discover where to find replacements when a job opening occurs.

Finally, job families can be used in selection decisions. For instance after an organization establishes the selection requirements for one job within a family, managers may be able to use this information to predict requirements in other jobs within the family.[21] In fact, if it is reasonable to believe that an employee will progress through all the jobs in a job family, then the organization might well choose to select individuals based on the needs of the *highest-level* job within the family rather than on those of the specific job for which an individual is applying. For example, suppose Microsoft needs to hire technicians for customer support teams. The HR manager in charge of this hiring might determine that each technician will rotate across several groups over a 4-year period, performing different functions for each. The astute manager might therefore set as the performance requirements for all such support roles as the hiring standard for all technicians, even though some technicians may start out in less-demanding roles.

5-5 THE JOB-ANALYSIS PROCESS

The job-analysis process itself is generally clear and straightforward. As a starting point in this process, it is helpful to understand the steps involved, including who is responsible for job analysis. As illustrated in Figure 5.4,

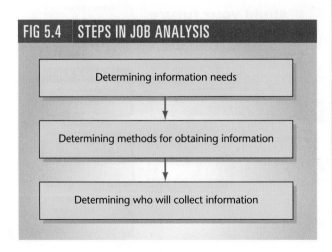

FIG 5.4 STEPS IN JOB ANALYSIS

Determining information needs

↓

Determining methods for obtaining information

↓

Determining who will collect information

the job-analysis process generally follows three steps: (1) determining information needs, (2) determining methods for obtaining information, and (3) determining who will collect information.[22]

The first step is determining the organization's precise information needs. A wide range of information on various jobs may be obtained during the course of job analysis. The exact type and nature of the information obtained, however, depend on both the intended purposes of the job-analysis information and various constraints imposed by the organization such as time and budget limitations. Regardless of constraints, the job analysis must provide enough information about what someone does on a job to allow a determination of the KSAs necessary to perform the job. Job-analysis information might include general work activities (e.g., a description of the specific tasks that are carried out, how the job interfaces with other jobs and equipment, the procedures used in the job, behaviors required on the job, and the physical movements and demands of the job) and the machines, tools, equipment, and work aids used to perform the job.

Other useful information that may be collected includes details regarding the job context (physical working conditions such as exposure to dust, heat, and toxic substances; the indoor environment versus outdoor environment; etc.). Information may also be collected regarding the organizational context and social context of the job. In addition, details regarding work schedule, various financial and nonfinancial incentives, and personal requirements (job-related attributes such as specific skills, education, and training; work experience and related jobs; physical characteristics and aptitudes) are usually desirable pieces of information.[23]

The next step in the job-analysis process is to determine how that information will be collected. The most common methods of collecting job-analysis information include the observations of task and job behaviors, interviews with job incumbents, and the use of questionnaires and checklists. For example, the individuals who perform the job analysis—**job analysts**—can sometimes gather the desired information on jobs simply by observing people performing them. This method is especially useful for unskilled manual jobs but is less relevant for jobs involving creative thought and analytic skills. In many cases, it is also beneficial to interview individuals who are performing the jobs being analyzed.[24] These individuals are in a position to explain both the

Job analysts are individuals who perform job analysis in an organization.

nature of the work they are performing and the qualifications and credentials they believe are necessary for the successful performance of those jobs. Of course, these individuals may overstate the skills and qualifications needed to perform the job and the complexities and sophistication of the job, especially if the employee believes (correctly or not) that the job analysis is being conducted to determine compensation rates.

Someone other than the incumbent who is also knowledgeable about the job can also be interviewed. Any such person, whether the incumbent or someone like the supervisor, is referred to as a **subject matter expert (SME)**. SMEs are the individuals from whom job analysts obtain data for the job analysis; they may be existing job incumbents, supervisors, or other knowledgeable employees such as higher-level managers, or industrial engineers. For the job analysis to be successful, the employees selected to provide the job-analysis information must be intimately familiar with the nature of the jobs themselves. Thus, participants in job analysis tend to be experienced and high-performing individuals who thoroughly understand the job.[25] Of course, if critical job-analysis information must be collected through the interview process, then it is best to interview multiple individuals who have different perspectives on the actual job and then integrate or average the information collected.

The job analyst could be a specialist within the HRM function or a consultant hired from the outside. Many times, however, firms (especially smaller ones) do not actually collect their own job-analysis information at all. When they need to obtain information about jobs, they may instead refer to available reference

materials. The major source of such information is a system known as the **Occupational Information Network (O°NET)**, a computerized job classification system that contains continually updated information regarding the KSAs required for virtually every job in the U.S. economy. O°NET is technically not a job-analysis procedure; it is a database that provides both basic and advanced job-analysis information. As such, it can be viewed as an alternative to conducting job analysis.[26] O°NET currently has information for more than 1,000 occupations and is organized according to a system known as the *standard occupational classification*.

For each occupation, information is provided about the relative importance of worker characteristics, including 52 separate abilities for effective job performance. These abilities are classified as representing (1) cognitive abilities such as oral comprehension, deductive reasoning, and spatial orientation; (2) psychometric abilities such as manual dexterity and reaction time; (3) physical abilities such as explosive and static strength and stamina; and (4) sensory abilities such as peripheral vision, heat sensitivity, and speech clarity. Also classified are occupational interests (e.g., interests in artistic occupations, realistic occupations, and social occupations), values (e.g., achievement, status, and comfort), and work styles (e.g., achievement orientation, conscientiousness, and practical intelligence). Information is also included regarding general occupational characteristics and occupation-specific requirements.

In addition, information is provided about appropriate worker requirements such as knowledge

A **subject matter expert (SME)** is an individual presumed to be highly knowledgeable about a particular job and who provides data for job analysis. An SME may be an existing job incumbent, a supervisor, or another knowledgeable employee.

Occupational Information Network (O*NET) is technically not a job-analysis procedure but a database that provides both basic and advanced job-analysis information; as such, IT can be viewed as an alternative to conducting job analysis.

Source: O*Net

(52 cross-occupation knowledge areas), skills (including 10 basic skills such as writing and speaking, and 36 cross-functional skills such as negotiating, persuading, and time management), and education. There is also information about the experience requirements (including requirements regarding training and licensure), as well as occupational requirements, including general work activities (e.g., getting information needed to do the job and thinking creatively), work context (e.g., environmental conditions), and organizational context (e.g., type of industry, organizational structure, and organizational culture). Links to other resources are provided, and they yield information about legal requirements, job hazards, and environmental conditions.

Although this is quite an array of information, and, in fact, new information is being added all the time, it is still possible that the O*NET does not have information that an organization needs about a specific job. In addition, the match between the job as it exists in a given firm and the job as it is classified in the O*NET may not be perfect. Nonetheless, the O*NET provides a valuable resource for anyone interested in doing job analysis, and it is likely to become even more important as various branches of the U.S. government move toward implementing the system. However, there are still many cases where more traditional job-analysis methods are needed because more detailed information is desired. Many such methods are available.

5-5a Job-Analysis Techniques

Several job-analysis techniques are used in organizations, although the trend is away from these more traditional methods and toward competency modeling, which we will discuss later. The most commonly used methods are the straight narrative, the Fleishman job-analysis system, task-analysis inventory, functional job analysis, the Position Analysis Questionnaire, the Managerial Position Description Questionnaire, and the critical incidents approach.[27]

1. **Narrative Job Analysis.** The most common approach to job analysis is simply to have one or more SMEs prepare a written narrative or text description of the job. These narratives can vary in terms of length and detail. To some extent, the quality of the information depends on the writing skills of the job analyst. Although it is possible to specify the format and structure of these narratives, they are typically individualistic, making it difficult to compare the tasks on one job with the tasks on another. They are relatively inexpensive, however, and it generally does not require a great deal of training for someone to complete a narrative job analysis.

2. **Fleishman Job-Analysis System.** Another popular method of job analysis is the Fleishman job-analysis system.[28] This approach defines abilities as enduring attributes of individuals that account for differences in performance. The system itself relies on the taxonomy of abilities that presumably represents all the dimensions relevant to work. The taxonomy includes a total of 52 abilities that are presumed to reflect cognitive, psychomotor, and sensory abilities. Examples of the specific abilities included in the Fleishman system include oral comprehension, written comprehension, oral expression, written expression, fluency of ideas, night vision, depth perception, auditory attention, and speech clarity. The actual Fleishman scales consist of descriptions of each ability followed by a behavioral benchmark example of the different levels of the ability along a seven-point scale. An organization using this job-analysis technique relies on a panel of SMEs (again, incumbent workers or supervisors are most commonly used) to indicate how important the ability is for the job and the actual level of ability required for a particular job. Because of its complexity, job analysts who use this method require training, but it is also much closer in operation to the notion of competency modeling, which we will discuss a bit later in this chapter.

3. **Task-Analysis Inventory.** Another method of job analysis is the task-analysis inventory. The task-analysis inventory method actually refers to a family of job-analysis methods, each with unique characteristics.

> The **Fleishman job-analysis system** is a job-analysis procedure that defines abilities as the enduring attributes of individuals that account for differences in performance; it relies on the taxonomy of abilities that presumably represents all the dimensions relevant to work.
>
> The **task-analysis inventory** is a family of job-analysis methods, each with unique characteristics; each focuses on analyzing all the tasks performed in the focal job.

Alexander Gospodinov/ShutterStock.com

However, each one focuses on analyzing all the tasks performed in the focal job. Any given job may have dozens of tasks, for example. Again relying on SMEs, this method requires the generation of a list of tasks performed in a job. After the list has been developed, a job analyst—frequently the job incumbent—evaluates each task on dimensions such as the relative amount of time spent on the task, the frequency with which the task is performed, the relative importance of the task, the relative difficulty of the task, and the time necessary to learn the task. Task inventories require a fair amount of effort to develop, but afterwards they are relatively easy to use. This approach to job analysis is often used in municipal and county governments and is also the most common form of job analysis used in the U.S. military. The information generated by this approach to job analysis is often detailed, and it is useful for establishing KSAs and training needs. The military has used these inventories to establish career paths and job families where the jobs clustered together have a large amount of overlap in terms of important tasks.[29] Managers then use a single task inventory to analyze all the jobs in the family. It is more difficult, though, to make comparisons across job families, and this drawback reduces the usefulness of task inventories to some degree.

4. **Functional Job Analysis.** One attempt to have a single job-analysis instrument that can be used with a wide variety of jobs resulted in the development of functional job analysis.[30] According to this approach, all jobs can be described in terms of the level of involvement with *people*, *data*, and *things*. For example, employees on a job at a General Motors manufacturing site might be said to *set up* machines (things), *mentor* people, and *synthesize* data. All are high levels of involvement and indicate a complex job. The exact definition of each term is provided to the job analyst. The U.S. Department of Labor relies on functional job analysis for some of its classifications of jobs, but it is not used widely in private industry. Nonetheless, this approach is important because it represents the first attempt to develop a single instrument that can describe all jobs in common terms.

enciktepstudio/Shutterstock.com

5. **Position Analysis Questionnaire.** One of the most popular and widely used job-analysis methods is the **Position Analysis Questionnaire (PAQ)**. Developed by Ernest McCormick and his associates, the PAQ is a standardized job-analysis instrument consisting of 194 items. These items reflect work behavior, working conditions, and job characteristics that are assumed to be generalizable across a wide variety of jobs.[31] The items that make up the PAQ are organized into six sections. *Information inputs* include where and how a worker gets information needed to perform his or her job. *Mental processes* represent the reasoning, decision-making, planning, and information-processing activities involved in performing the job. *Work output* refers to the physical activities, tools, and devices used by the worker to perform the job. *Relationships with other people* include the relationships that are required in performing the job. *Job context* represents the physical and social contacts where the work is performed. Finally, *other characteristics* include the activities, conditions,

and characteristics other than those previously described that pertain to the job.

Job analysts are asked to determine whether each scale applies to the specific job being analyzed. The analyst rates the item on six scales: extent of use, amount of time, importance of the job, possibility of occurrence, applicability, and special code. *Special code* refers to unique and special rating scales that are used with a particular item. These ratings are then submitted to a centralized location indicated on the questionnaire where computer software compiles a report regarding the job scores on the job dimensions.

A major advantage of the PAQ is that, like functional job analysis, its dimensions are believed to underlie all jobs. This feature allows a wide variety (although probably not all) jobs to be described in common terms. In the case of the PAQ, this feature results from the items and dimensions of the PAQ that describe what a worker does on the job rather than what gets done. So, for example, many different jobs may obtain critical information from dials and gauges, such as jobs ranging from truck driver to mechanic to engineer. The persons doing these jobs use this information for different reasons, and they accomplish much different outcomes, but they do obtain information in similar ways.

Unlike functional job analysis, the PAQ can provide information on 187 separate items, allowing a much richer picture of what happens on a job (the PAQ actually includes 194 items, but the remaining items deal with methods of pay). Finally, another strength of the PAQ is that because it has been widely used for many years, a considerable database of information exists that attests to its validity and reliability.

In general, research supports the validity and reliability of the instrument. Research also suggests that the PAQ measures 32 dimensions and 13 overall job dimensions. A given job score on these dimensions can be useful in job analysis.[32] Because the instrument has been so widely used, it has also been statistically related to other measures, including the scores of job applicants on standardized selection tests, compensation rates on various jobs, and even the importance of various abilities.[33]

Even though it is widely used, however, the PAQ also has some noteworthy shortcomings. The PAQ instrument itself is relatively complex, and an employee must have the reading level of a college graduate to be able to complete it. Although the PAQ is supposed to be applicable to most jobs, there is reason to believe that it is less useful for higher-level managerial jobs and less useful for describing white-collar jobs.[34] Despite these limitations, the PAQ remains the most popular standardized job-analysis instrument available and is commonly used by firms such as Exxon, Utah Power and Light, and Delta Air Lines.

6. **Management Position Description Questionnaire.** The **Management Position Description Questionnaire (MPDQ)** is a standardized job-analysis instrument similar in approach to the PAQ and also containing 197 items. The focus here, however, is on managerial jobs, and the analysis is done in terms of 13 essential components of all managerial jobs.[35] These essential components are supervision, staff service, internal business control, complexity and stress, coordination of other units, public and customer relations, HR responsibility, autonomy of action, advanced consulting, advanced financial responsibility, approval of financial commitments, product and service responsibility, and product market and financial planning. The information generated by the MPDQ can be used to classify managerial positions as well as estimate reasonable compensation for them.

7. **Critical Incidents Approach.** Critical incidents are examples of particularly effective or ineffective performance.[36] When used for job analysis, the **critical incidents approach** focuses on the critical behaviors that distinguish effective from ineffective performers. Although this approach to job analysis is most widely used in connection with the development of appraisal instruments, it is generally useful because it focuses the organization's attention on aspects of the job that lead to more or less effective performance.

Although these techniques are the most commonly used in industry, we should

Management Position Description Questionnaire (MPDQ) is a standardized job-analysis instrument, similar in approach to the PAQ, that also contains 197 items. The MPDQ's focus, however, is on managerial jobs, and the analysis is done in terms of 13 essential components of all managerial jobs.

The **critical incidents approach** to job analysis focuses on critical behaviors that distinguish effective from ineffective performers.

note that, in many cases, the organization simply develops its own job-analysis technique or instrument. This is especially true for managerial jobs and for jobs performed by teams rather than by individuals. In both cases, no widely accepted standardized job-analysis instruments are available. Regardless of which job-analysis technique an organization employs, however, at some point, a narrative description of the job will probably be needed. Therefore, it is important to draw a distinction between a job description and a job specification, which we discuss in the next section.

Syaheir Azizan/Shutterstock.com

5-5b Job Descriptions and Job Specifications

A **job description** lists the tasks, duties, and responsibilities that a particular job entails. Observable actions are necessary for the effective performance of the job. The job description specifies the major job elements, provides examples of job tasks, and provides some indication of their relative importance in the effective conduct of the job.[37] A **job specification** focuses more on the individual who will perform the job. Specifically, a job specification indicates the knowledge, abilities, skills, and other characteristics that an individual must have to perform the job. Factual or procedural capabilities and levels of proficiency refer more to skills. In general, enduring capabilities that an individual possesses can be thought of as abilities. Job specifications may include general educational requirements (e.g., having a high school degree or a college degree) as well as the specifications of job-related skills (e.g., the ability to use Microsoft Word, fluency in a foreign language, or even knowledge of Facebook).

Taken together then, the job description and the job specification should provide a parallel and mutually consistent set of information and details that focuses on the job itself and the individual most likely to be successful performing that job. This information should then inform all subsequent recruiting and selection decisions. Figure 5.5 illustrates an actual job description and job specification for a particular kind of accountant at Johnson & Johnson. This description and specification were created as part of a job analysis and are used to communicate to job applicants and managers what skills and abilities are necessary to perform the job.

5-5c Modeling Competencies and the End of the "Job"

Given the rate of change in work, some scholars and other HR experts have argued that the nature of work is changing so much that the concept of a "job" is becoming obsolete. Although many people will continue to have "jobs" for some time to come, in some work settings, it may well be true that the traditional view of jobs and work is no longer applicable. In these settings, people usually work on teams where the focus is on getting tasks accomplished rather than on specific task requirements. Thus, there is reason to suggest that we should think about roles that have to be filled within the organization and how employees will need to emphasize flexibility, teamwork, and accomplishing tasks, rather than job descriptions and sets of duties. In light of these developments, then, some critics have argued that traditional methods of job analysis (including the O*NET) have little place in the modern organization, and that the information needed by HR managers can be better provided by modeling competencies instead of by describing jobs.

In fact, a study of competency modeling published in 2000 reported that between 75 and 80 percent of companies surveyed were using some type of competency modeling.[38] Nonetheless, there is little agreement about what exactly is meant by the term *competency*. Some view competencies as being broader than abilities, and others suggest that competencies exist at a

A **job description** lists the tasks, duties, and responsibilities for a particular job. It specifies the major job elements, provides examples of job tasks, and provides some indication of their relative importance in the effective conduct of the job.

A **job specification** focuses on the individual who will perform the job and indicates the knowledge, abilities, skills, and other characteristics that an individual must have to be able to perform the job.

FIG 5.5   EXAMPLE JOB DESCRIPTION AND JOB SPECIFICATION

Job Title: Accounts Payable and Payroll Accountant, Johnson & Johnson Corp.

Job Description: Business partner with Accounts Payable and Payroll Departments to develop expense forecasts and commentary; prepare Accounts Payable and Payroll shared services charge-outs to affiliates; ensure Accounts Payable and Payroll inputs are posted weekly; perform account analysis/reconciliations of Cash, Liability, and Employee Loan accounts related to Accounts Payable and Payroll; submit routine reports to Corporate; identify and implement process improvements relative to all responsibilities listed above.

Job Specification: BS degree in accounting or finance; 2+ years of accounting/finance experience; sound knowledge of Integral Accounts Payable and General Ledger Systems; working knowledge of Hyperion Software, PACT; good communication skills; able to work independently at off-site location.

deeper level and really underlie abilities. Generally, however, experts view competencies as characteristics of employees (or teams of employees) that lead to success on the job. Thus, abilities such as decisiveness and adaptability are seen as competencies that might underlie more specific abilities such as decision-making or coping with change.[39]

Clearly, this approach has the potential for providing critical information to the HR manager in a more useful form because it emphasizes what a person needs to be successful. Thus, it may not be important to know whether an employee will type letters or run a lathe, but it may be critical to know that an employee needs to be adaptable.

Competencies are determined in several ways, but typically teams of top managers, working with consultants, identify the competencies necessary to compete in the future. These competencies are then described in clear behavioral terms, measures are designed, and each is rated according to its relative importance for future success. Employees who have these competencies are then sought through the recruiting and selection process, or current employees are provided training opportunities to acquire these competencies and are then rewarded when they do acquire them. (See the discussion of skill-based pay and knowledge-based pay in Chapter 9.) The critical difference is that the HR manager no longer focuses on what is needed to be successful at one job but instead focuses on what is needed to

> "The measure of intelligence is the ability to change."
>
> —ALBERT EINSTEIN, NOBEL PRIZE–WINNING THEORETICAL PHYSICIST

be successful at any and all jobs within the organization. There are also some applications of competency modeling to selection, which we will discuss in Chapter 7.[40]

Finally, this is another area where HR analytics is making a difference and will probably play a bigger role in the future. For example, companies such as The Container Store have begun using wearable computers to track employees at work. Although this could be viewed as the ultimate in monitoring, the company uses the data to better understand how employees communicate with coworkers and employees and where they actually spend most of their time.[41] Thus, new technologies and the ability to use the data they can generate make it possible to learn exactly how employees spend their time without depending on surveys, potentially providing much more useful job analysis data.

5-5d Legal Issues in Job Analysis

Because job analysis is a critical building block for much of the HRM process, it should not be surprising that numerous legal issues have been raised with regard to job analysis. In fact, federal guidelines on selection include discussion of the appropriate ways to conduct job analysis and the statement that any attempt to establish the job relatedness of a selection instrument must begin with a careful analysis of the jobs in question. Most of the specific cases, in fact, have been concerned more with the *failure* of an organization to perform a job analysis.

For example, in *Albemarle* v. *Moody*, the Albemarle Paper Company argued that tests found to be job related for one set of jobs could be used to select employees for another set of jobs that they argued were similar.[42] The Court found that, in the absence of clear job-analysis information to support such a claim (and there was no job-analysis information), it was unacceptable to assume that the jobs in question were the same.

The Americans with Disabilities Act of 1990 (ADA), and its recent modification (the American with Disabilities Amendment Act of 2009) raise additional legal issues associated with job analysis. As noted in Chapter 2, the ADA states that an employer must offer a reasonable accommodation to any employee who has a disability and who can perform the "essential functions" of the job. Basically, essential functions are those that take up a significant part of the employee's time, are performed regularly, and have consequences for other parts of the job. Organizations need to rely on careful job analysis to determine exactly what those essential functions are and thus determine if the employee is entitled to an accommodation under the law.

Several issues regarding the accuracy of job-analysis information have potential legal implications.[43] Perhaps the most troubling of these issues relates to potential gender discrimination in job analysis. Specifically, evidence suggests that jobs occupied primarily by male incumbents are more likely to be rated as more complex and of a higher level than similar jobs occupied primarily by female incumbents.[44] One striking result that has been published relates to different job-analysis information generated for the jobs of prison guard and prison matron, which are simply the traditional titles for persons of different gender doing the same job (these different titles are no longer used, incidentally). Because the information from job analysis can be used for determining appraisal systems as well as compensation rates, this problem is potentially serious.

> Evidence suggests that jobs occupied primarily by male incumbents are more likely to be rated as more complex and of a higher level than similar jobs occupied primarily by female incumbents.

Finally, as discussed in Chapter 2, the creation of autonomous work teams has presented a new legal challenge. In the *Electromation* decision, the National Labor Relations Board ruled that the autonomous work teams and action committees created at the company were illegal labor organizations.[45] In other words, they were labor organizations because they scheduled work, determined wages, and made selection and promotion decisions—and they were illegal because they were created and controlled by management.

In summary, job analysis can provide extremely important information for the HR manager because it reveals what a person does on the job. This information can be used for a variety of applications, and it can be collected using different types of job analysts using a variety of job analysis techniques. Recently, many organizations have moved toward competency modeling to replace traditional job analysis, and this approach has the potential to provide even more useful information about what is required for someone to be successful on the job. Finally, because job-analysis information is a basic building block for HRM decisions, several legal issues have been raised relative to the applications of job-analysis information.

5-6 DATA ANALYTICS AND BIG DATA

As noted at the beginning of this chapter, in recent years, there has been a growing interest in what has been termed data analytics or sometimes referred to as big data. This refers, not so much to a different type of data for decision-making, but more to a different way of thinking about data.[46] This approach to business information has been more popular in areas such as marketing, rather than in HRM, but it certainly has implications for decision-making in the HR area as well. We should begin with some definitions and clarification of concepts, but these terms are used quite loosely.

Analytics is simply the discovery and communication of meaningful patterns in data. In the past, this activity was at times referred to as "data mining," and it can be especially valuable in areas rich with recorded information. Generally, analytics relies on statistics, computer programing, and operations research to quantify performance data, and data visualization is often used to describe how information is communicated.[47]

The primary goal of data analytics is to help companies make more informed decisions by enabling data scientists and other analytics professionals to analyze large volumes of transactional data, as well as other forms of data that might go untapped by conventional business information systems. These data can be either structured or unstructured, which is why data visualization tools are often used in the process. But, when we begin to discuss big data analytics, we are simply referring to applying these processes to very large databases. In fact, the size of some of these databases is so large that they may not fit in traditional data warehouses, and traditional methods may not be able to keep up with the constant updating that is required. Therefore, a newer class of technologies, such as HADOOP[48] and related tools are being used as staging areas for large data sets before they are analyzed.

One area where big data can make a real difference is by allowing companies to look beyond mere transactions (where, by the time they are recorded, it is too late to do anything about them) and look instead at signals data, which can help a company anticipate what is going to happen and do something about it before it happens. Examples might include tracking "likes" for your product on social media (a decline is a signal that sales will fall) or using complex algorithms to predict when an aircraft part will need to be replaced (rather than wait until a breakdown delays a flight for hours). For example, Williams–Sonoma uses data on its 60 million customers to generate different versions of its catalogs based on family income and preferences, and Amazon claim that almost a third of sales are generated by recommendations from their website (e.g., "you might also like"). These applications are important in the gaming industry as well, as Harrah's uses data from its loyalty program (where members enter their card before they start playing any machine or game) to determine everything from where different types of games should be located, to who should be invited for different free ("comped") events and activities.

But big data is not without risks. Companies interested in exploiting these data must have the analytical skills needed to deal with those data. Hiring or training such talent may be expensive, and because the term "big data" is often used loosely, there are vendors who are selling services that are not really very different from what was available before. In addition, the bigger the data set is, the bigger the risk when a company uses unreliable or inaccurate data. And, there is a danger that focusing on granular data can result in a decision maker missing the big picture by pursuing even more granular data. Finally, though, there is no substitute for intuition and wise judgment. Big data and data analytics may provide companies with information they could not obtain before, but it still requires someone to ask the right questions of the data available and to use the answers wisely.

Although big data techniques have not been used as widely in the HR area as in some other areas, the idea of HR analytics, sometimes referred to as talent analytics, is gaining popularity, and this appears to be a major area for HR spending in the near future. We will discuss some specific applications and examples in the next chapter. The issue, going forward, however, is not so much concerned with how to manage and analyze the large data sets that are involved, but to make sure that data are being collected on the metrics that best help HR managers make decisions. We will discuss those decisions, and some of the metrics that can be useful for making them, in the next two chapters.

CLOSING CASE
Low Pay for Hazardous Work

Business magazines and newspapers regularly publish articles about the changing nature of work in the United States and about how many jobs are being changed. Because so much has been made of the shift toward service-sector and professional jobs, many people might assume that the number of unpleasant and undesirable jobs has declined.

In fact, nothing could be further from the truth. While many Americans work in gleaming air-conditioned facilities, millions of others work in dirty, grimy, unsafe settings. For example, many jobs in the recycling industry require workers to sort through moving conveyors of trash, pulling out those items that can be recycled. The trash, though, may contain used syringes, old razor

(Continued)

(Closing Case – continued)

blades, and other sharp objects. Other relatively unattractive jobs include cleaning hospital restrooms, washing dishes in a restaurant, and handling toxic waste.

Consider the jobs in a chicken-processing facility. Much like a manufacturing assembly line, a chicken-processing facility is organized around a moving conveyor system. Workers call it the chain. In reality, it's a steel cable with large clips that carries dead chickens down what might be called a "disassembly line." Standing along this line are dozens of workers who do, in fact, take the birds apart as they pass.

Even the titles of the jobs are unsavory. Among the first set of jobs along the chain is the skinner. Skinners use sharp instruments to cut and pull the skin off the dead chicken. Toward the middle of the line are the gut pullers. These workers reach inside the chicken carcasses and remove the intestines and other organs. At the end of the line are the gizzard cutters, who tackle the more difficult organs attached to the inside of the chicken's carcass. These organs have to be individually cut and removed for disposal.

The work is obviously distasteful, and the pace of the work is unrelenting. On a good day, the chain moves an average of 90 chickens a minute for 9 hours. And the workers are essentially held captive by the moving chain. For example, no one can vacate a post to use the bathroom or for other reasons without the permission of the supervisor. In some plants, taking an unauthorized bathroom break can result in suspension without pay. But the noise in a typical chicken-processing plant is so loud that the supervisor often can't hear someone calling for relief unless the person happens to be standing close by.

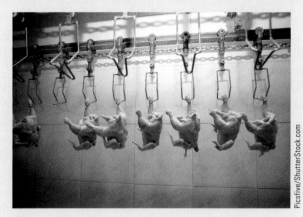

Picsfive/ShutterStock.com

Besides being unpleasant and dirty, many jobs in a chicken-processing plant are dangerous and unhealthy. Some workers, for example, have to fight the live birds when they are first hung on the chains. These workers are routinely scratched and pecked by the chickens. And the air inside a typical chicken-processing plant is difficult to breathe. Workers are usually supplied with paper masks, but most don't use them because they are hot and confining.

The work space itself is so tight that the workers often cut themselves—and sometimes their coworkers—with the knives, scissors, and other instruments they use to perform their jobs. Poultry processing ranks third among industries in the United States for cumulative trauma injuries such as carpal tunnel syndrome. The inevitable chicken feathers, feces, and blood also contribute to the hazardous and unpleasant work environment.

Jobs such as these in the chicken-processing facility are actually becoming increasingly common. Fueled by Americans' growing appetites for lean, easy-to-cook meat, the number of poultry workers has almost doubled since 1980, and today they constitute a workforce of around a quarter-million people. The chicken-processing industry has become a major component of the state economies of Georgia, North Carolina, Mississippi, Arkansas, and Alabama.[49]

Case Questions

1. How relevant are the concepts of competencies to the jobs in a chicken-processing plant?
2. What information sources would be of most significance regarding jobs in a chicken-processing plant?
3. Are dirty, dangerous, and unpleasant jobs an inevitable part of any economy?

STUDY TOOLS 5

READY TO STUDY?
In the book, you can:
☐ Rip out the chapter review card at the back of the book for a handy summary of the chapter and key terms.

ONLINE AT CENGAGEBRAIN.COM YOU CAN:
☐ Collect StudyBits while you read and study the chapter.
☐ Quiz yourself on key concepts.
☐ Find videos for further exploration.
☐ Prepare for tests with HR4 Flash Cards as well as those you create.

6 | Human Resource Decision-Making in Organizations

Bloomberg/Getty Images

After finishing this chapter go to **PAGE 155** for **STUDY TOOLS**

LEARNING OBJECTIVES

6-1 Discuss the role of ethics in human resource decision-making

6-2 Describe the concept of rightsizing, and identify organizational strategies for rightsizing

6-3 Describe how to manage termination and retention

6-4 Describe the elements of voluntary turnover

6-5 Discuss the key human resource issues during mergers and acquisitions

Bloomberg/Getty Images

Employee engagement is a popular topic these days. In general, engagement refers to the extent to which an employee feels committed to and a part of the organization. What's the difference between engaged and disengaged employees? Gallup's Jim Harter puts it this way: "When you ask people about their intentions during a recession, it's pretty clear that disengaged workers are just waiting around to see what happens. Engaged workers, though, have bought into what the organization is about and are trying to make a difference. This is why they're usually the most productive workers."

Best Buy, the giant consumer electronics retailer, has been using annual surveys to track levels of employee engagement since 2003. Best Buy's strategy calls for providing customers with individualized shopping experiences, and top management realized early on that this strategy depended on the company's most important asset—the employees who engaged with its customers. It also stood to reason that if its customers were motivated by the company's ability to respond to their individual needs, then its employees could be motivated by its willingness to respond to their individual needs as well. In 2003, Best Buy thus launched a fairly radical initiative allowing employees to shape their own jobs and define their own career paths according to their own needs and talents. In 2010, an independent study concluded that Best Buy had "doubled the rate of increase in employee engagement." In the same year, another study linked increased employee engagement to increased productivity: The researchers found that a 0.1 percent increase in employee engagement at a given store correlated with an annual increase in sales of $100,000.

Findings like those at Best Buy have been confirmed on a much broader scale by a wealth of independent research. In 2015, for example, Gallup examined nearly 50,000 work units (groups of workers assigned to perform specific tasks) across 192 organizations in 34 countries. The purpose of the study was to provide statistical correlations between employee engagement and performance outcomes. According to Gallup, the study "confirmed the well-established connection between employee engagement and nine performance outcomes" ranging from profitability and customer ratings to absenteeism and workplace theft.

Among other things, Gallup found that work units in the top quartile (those that scored better than 75 percent of all organizations in the study) outperformed those in the bottom quartile (those outscored by 75 percent of all organizations) by 10 percent on customer ratings, 22 percent on profitability, and 21 percent on productivity. Units in the top quartile had significantly lower levels of turnover (25–65 percent depending on industry-wide turnover rates), absenteeism (37 percent), safety incidents

> "When you ask people about their intentions during a recession, it's pretty clear that disengaged workers are just waiting around to see what happens. Engaged workers, though, have bought into what the organization is about and are trying to make a difference. This is why they're usually the most productive workers."
>
> —JIM HARTER, GALLUP EXECUTIVE

(48 percent), and quality defects (41 percent). Meanwhile, a study by Towers Watson, a global professional services firm, showed that organizations with high employee engagement enjoyed a 1-year average increase in operating income of 19 percent and 28 percent growth in earnings per share (EPS); companies with low levels of engagement experienced an average decline of 32 percent in operating income and an 11 percent drop in EPS.

Gallup translated such data into some bottom-line numbers: Actively disengaged employees—about 26 percent of all workers—cost U.S. organizations between $450 and $550 billion in lost productivity every year.

It may seem fairly obvious at this point, but according to Gartner, a consulting firm specializing in information technology research, "the positive correlation between employee engagement and organization performance suggests that there is a substantial upside for organizations that focus on enhancing employee engagement." More specifically, however, what do all of these numbers mean for top managers when it comes to implementing changes in practices affecting employee engagement? For one thing, they need to appreciate the numbers. "Many executives and line managers," says Gartner, "still view improving employee engagement as a soft and fuzzy concept," failing to understand "why it's important and what a vital role it plays in driving business success."[1]

THINK IT OVER

1. What might the role of HR be in promoting employee engagement?
2. How easy or difficult would you expect it to be to transform disengaged workers into engaged workers?

In Chapter 5, we discussed some of the sources of information for making human resource management (HRM) decisions. In this chapter and the next, we will discuss the details of some of those decisions that are made on a regular basis. Chapter 7 will describe the details of how organizations recruit and select employees. This chapter looks at decisions about the size of an organization; that is, our focus here is the decisions about how many employees should be on the payroll at any time. This is often referred to as the head count. We will discuss both temporary and more permanent decisions that can be made about head counts, and we will also discuss some special problems about the size of an organization's workforce after a merger or acquisition. Before dealing with any of these decisions, we begin by discussing the importance of ethics in decision-making.

6-1 ETHICS AND HUMAN RESOURCE MANAGEMENT

In Chapter 2, we discussed how the legal framework provided a set of parameters for HRM decisions, and, as noted above, we discussed various sources of information for these decisions in the previous chapter. But ethics is another important aspect of decision-making for all managers, not just human resource (HR) managers.[2] Ethics is a separate concept from the law but is closely intertwined. **Ethics** refers to an individual's beliefs about what is right and wrong and what is good and bad. Ethics are formed by the societal context in which people and organizations function. In recent years, ethical behavior and ethical conduct on the part of managers and organizations have received considerable attention, usually fueled by scandals at firms such as Enron, WorldCom, Imclone, and Tyco International and unscrupulous managers such as Kenneth Lay, Jeffrey Skilling, and Bernard Madoff. The basic premise is that laws are passed by governments to control and dictate appropriate behavior and conduct in a society. The concept of ethics serves much the same purpose because of its premise about what is right and what is wrong.

> **Managers must take steps to ensure that their behavior is both ethical and legal.**

Ethics refers to an individual's beliefs about what is right and wrong and what is good and bad. Ethics are formed by the societal context in which people and organizations function.

> "The biggest risk is not taking any risk. . . . In a world that is changing really quickly, the only strategy that is guaranteed to fail is not taking risks."
>
> —MARK ZUCKERBERG, CO-FOUNDER OF FACEBOOK

But ethics and law do not always coincide precisely. For example, it may be perfectly legal for a manager to take a certain action, but some observers might find his or her action to be unethical. For example, an organization undergoing a major cutback might be legally able to terminate a specific employee who is nearing retirement age, but if that employee has a long history of dedicated service to the organization, then many people could consider termination to be ethically questionable. Managers from every part of the organization must take steps to ensure that their behavior is both ethical and legal. Some organizations develop codes of conduct or ethical statements in an attempt to communicate publicly their stance on ethics and ethical conduct.

The various scandals of the 1990s raised many public questions about the ethical training and orientation of managers. A survey published in *USA Today* created even more questions. In that survey of 443 master's of business administration (MBA) students, more than 50 percent responded that they would buy stock based on insider information, more than 25 percent said they would allow a gift to influence a company purchasing decision, and more than 10 percent said they make a payoff to help close a deal.[3] Even more serious questions of business ethics emerged in the aftermath of the financial meltdown of 2009 and the financial crises of 2010–2011.

Following the near collapse of several major banks and financial institutions, the U.S. government instituted its Troubled Asset Relief Program (TARP) to provide billions of dollars in loans to institutions such as Bank of America and JPMorgan Chase. By the end of 2011, every one of these firms had repaid the loans and were, for the most part, reasonably healthy financially. It does seem clear, however, that many of these institutions would never have survived without the federal funds. The problems really arose, however, over the year-end bonuses the companies were paying to their executives. We will discuss executive compensation more fully in Chapter 9, but suffice it to say that Wall Street firms paid multimillion dollar bonuses to top executives in early 2010. There was no question that these bonuses were perfectly legal, but questions were raised about the ethics of paying out huge bonuses to executives while many Americans were unemployed or struggling financially—especially when the firms were in a position to pay those bonuses only because of government bailout dollars. In fact, in early 2010, Andrew Cuomo, New York's attorney general, sent a letter to eight of the nation's largest banks demanding to know how they structured those bonus payouts.[4]

One interesting ethical challenge facing an organization became apparent when Internet search provider Google announced that it was going to close its operations in China.[5] The huge company had formally entered China in 2005 (although it had provided a Chinese-language version of Google since 2000). As the company saw its market share shrink, however, Google's executives realized they must formally enter the Chinese market. The problem was that Google considered itself a company that was socially responsible; to enter the Chinese market, the company had to agree to a certain level of censorship required by the government. Not only the information that was critical of government policies censored but also there was evidence that the Chinese government used Internet access to track down and prosecute dissidents within China.

To access the hundreds of millions of Chinese Internet users, Google agreed to this censorship, even though it was clearly at odds with Google's corporate philosophy and what most Americans would consider ethical behavior.[6] As a result, in January 2010, Google announced that it had uncovered a Chinese government plot to use e-mail attachments to get access to sensitive information and to identify political dissidents, and this was seen as going too far. The source of the attacks has been speculated to be students at Chinese universities. In March 2010, Google transplanted its Chinese operations to Hong Kong. This case illustrates how some companies must balance ethics with profits, and how complicated it is to maintain a real balance. (In late 2016, Google announced plans to reenter China in the near future but gave no details as to when or how.) These questions became very complicated for Apple. The FBI recovered three cell phones belonging to the alleged shooters in the San Bernardino terror attack in December of 2015. Two had been destroyed, while one was intact but the FBI could not access the data on the cell phone (e.g., who did the assailants call and who else might have been involved) because they do not have the right password. The FBI has asked for Apple's help in dealing with the encryption, but Apple has refused. At issue is whether, after the FBI gets access to cell phone data in this case, it could set the precedent for other cases. In addition, Apple has stated they guarantee that cell phone data cannot be "hacked" and if they create a way around the safeguards (they claim that none exists currently), it would open the door for others to hack other phones. Apple is not backing down, and the FBI is threatening further legal action, but as of March 2016, this issue has not been resolved. It does represent a new wrinkle battle between privacy and protection, and it also raises the stake on Apple's stated ethics and privacy policies.[7] It is also worth noting that Bill Gates (of Microsoft) has suggested that there is a way for Apple to provide the access requested by the FBI without compromising its integrity. Gates has argued that the FBI is simply seeking access to one phone and not that Apple create a "back door" that can be reused.[8] Interestingly, his position is somewhat at odds with the official Microsoft position, which has supported Apple's decision.

These cases also help to illustrate how the scope of business ethics can be even more complicated when one thinks about the global environment of modern business. Different countries and different cultures have different values and norms, and this translates into different ideas about what kinds of behaviors are ethical and what kinds are unethical. Specifically, nations and cultures differ in what they see as acceptable behaviors relative to corruption, exploitation of labor, and environmental impact. Transparency International, a global coalition fighting corruption, publishes a list of the countries perceived to be the least and the most corrupt in the world. In their latest survey, they found Denmark, Finland, New Zealand, Sweden, and Singapore to be perceived as the least corrupt countries in the world. Somalia, North Korea, Afghanistan, Sudan, and Myanmar were perceived to be the most corrupt. The United States was ranked as being perceived to be the nineteenth least corrupt country.[9] Thus, it is important to recognize that one's sense of ethics is always part of any decision made, but that individuals as well as countries can differ in terms of their sense of what constitutes ethical behavior. We will refer back to questions of ethics throughout these next two chapters.

6-2 RIGHTSIZING THE ORGANIZATIONS

One of the more basic decisions an organization must make concerning human resources is the size of the workforce. Whether a company is forecasting revenue growth or decline, the number of its employees must be adjusted to fit the changing needs of the business. In all cases, therefore, it is essential that the organization, through the HRM function, manage the size of its workforce effectively. This process is called **rightsizing**, and it is the process of monitoring and adjusting the organization's workforce to its optimal size and composition.

Managing the size of the workforce may, in turn, involve layoffs or early-retirement programs to reduce the size of the workforce, retention programs to maintain the size of the workforce, and temporary workers as a bridge between the current state of affairs and either growth or reduction. In any case, the organization must ensure that it has the "right" people. Reduction, retention, or any other strategy affecting the size and composition of the workforce must target the specific types of employees the organization wants to eliminate or keep. For the most part, organizations choose to retain highly committed, highly motivated, and productive employees, and they prefer to lose less committed and less productive employees. How an organization achieves this goal while staying within the limits of the law is one major focus of this chapter.

Over the past three-plus decades, people in the United States have witnessed first-hand the cyclical nature of economic forces. In the 1980s, numerous layoffs and workforce reductions occurred at U.S. firms, primarily as the firms adjusted to increased global competition. Both academic researchers and the popular press discussed at length the best ways to manage layoffs and the challenges of dealing with their survivors. Then the economy began to grow at an unprecedented rate in the 1990s, and expert opinion began to focus more on recommendations for recruiting and retaining valuable employees. Then came September 11, 2001, and its aftermath: The economy slowed, and workforce reductions began again. By the middle of 2002, the Dow Jones Industrial Average had its sharpest decline since the Great Depression, and layoffs and reductions were again the order of the day. This time, however, most organizations took a more strategic approach than they had in the 1980s; as a result, many were in a good position to capitalize when markets rebounded again in 2006. In late 2008 and early 2009, however, things took a turn for the worse. Problems with bad mortgages led to foreclosures, banks that had invested in mortgage-backed securities began to have serious problems, and there were massive layoffs. In fact, as noted earlier in the chapter, if it had not been for the intervention of the U.S. government, many large banks and financial institutions would have failed during 2009. The economy began showing signs of recovery by 2010, but unemployment problems lingered and did not drop below 9 percent until 2012. By June 2013, the unemployment rate was hovering around 7.6 percent. The Dow Jones Industrial Average set a new record high in July 2013, and by then, the housing market had demonstrated several months of steady improvement. Throughout the first half of 2014, the stock market continued to get stronger, there was continued job growth, and unemployment claims went down to their lowest levels since 2007. Nonetheless, the United States was still plagued by economic uncertainty in 2017, and this uncertainty caused many companies to take a very cautious approach to expanding their operations in general and their hiring in particular.

How, then, do organizations manage the size of their workforces to deal with their current needs and potential future economic realities? One important, short-term

> If not for the intervention of the U.S. government, many large banks and financial institutions would have failed during the recent recession.

Norman Chan/Shutterstock.com

Rightsizing is the process of monitoring and adjusting the composition of the organization's workforce to its optimal size.

solution is the use of temporary or contingent workers, who provide a buffer for the organization. When facing declining needs for employees, the organization can simply decide not to renew the contracts of temporary workers or end their relationship with contingent workers in other ways. When facing increasing demand for employees, the organization can increase overtime or hire contingent workers until it determines if it will need more permanent workers. After the need for permanent employees is established, companies must deal with the recruitment and selection issues discussed in the next chapter. This chapter is more concerned with temporary fixes for increased demand and the special issues that face an organization with declining demands for employees: These are the true focus of any discussion of rightsizing. We begin with an examination of the increased demands for employees.

Fuzzbones/Alamy Stock Photo

6-2a Dealing with Increased Demand for Employees

When an organization anticipates an increased need for employees, the traditional approach has been to recruit and hire new permanent employees. In recent years, that model has changed. Specifically, if the demand for new employees is not expected to last, or if it would take a long time to find the needed permanent employees, then a firm may try a more temporary solution—at least for awhile. This is the case, for example, when the increased need for employees is part of a normal and well-understood cycle such as the practice of retailers hiring temporary help during November and December.

The easiest way to deal with a temporary increase in the demand for employees is to offer **overtime** opportunities, which simply means asking current workers to put in longer hours for extra pay. As noted, this alternative is especially beneficial when the increased need for human resources is short term. For example, a manufacturing plant facing a production crunch might ask some of its production workers to work an extra half-day, perhaps on Saturday, for 2 or 3 weeks to get the work done. An advantage to this approach is that it gives employees the opportunity to earn extra income. Some employees welcome this opportunity and are thankful to the organization for making it

available. In addition, it keeps the organization from having to hire and train new employees because the existing employees already know how to do their work.

On the other hand, labor costs per hour are likely to increase. The Fair Labor Standards Act (described earlier in Chapter 2 and discussed further in Chapter 9) stipulates that employees who work more than 40 hours a week must be compensated at a rate of one and a half times their normal hourly rate. Furthermore, if the organization doesn't really need all the members of a work group for overtime, then it may face a complicated situation in deciding who gets to work the overtime. Unionized organizations often have contracts that specify the decision rules that must be followed when offering overtime. Finally, there is the problem of potential increased fatigue and anxiety on the part of employees, particularly if the overtime is not particularly welcome and if they have to work the overtime for an extended period of time.

Another increasingly popular alternative to hiring permanent employees is a growing reliance on temporary employees. The idea behind temporary employment is that an organization can hire someone for only a specific period of time, and a major advantage to the organization is that such workers can usually be paid a lower rate, although they are now more likely to be entitled to the same benefits as full-time workers.[10] Considerable flexibility comes from the fact that employees themselves realize their jobs are not permanent, so the organization can terminate their relationship as work demands mandate.[11] On the other hand, temporary employees tend not to understand the organization's culture as well as permanent employees. In addition, they are not as likely to be as productive as permanent full-time employees of the organization.

Employee leasing is yet another alternative. An organization can pay

Overtime refers to hours worked above the normal 40-hour workweek, for which there is usually a pay premium.

Employee leasing involves an organization paying a fee to a leasing company that provides a pool of employees who are available on a temporary basis. This pool of employees usually constitutes a group or crew intended to handle all or most of the organization's work needs in a particular area.

a fee to a leasing company that provides a pool of employees to the client firm. This pool of employees usually constitutes a group or crew intended to handle all or most of the organization's work needs in a particular area. For example, an organization might lease a crew of custodial and other maintenance workers from an outside firm specializing in such services. These workers appear in the organization every day at a predetermined time and perform all maintenance and custodial work. To the general public, they may even appear to be employees of the firm occupying the building. In reality, however, they work for a leasing company.

The basic advantage to the organization is that it essentially outsources to the leasing firm the HR elements of recruiting, hiring, training, compensating, and evaluating those employees. On the other hand, because the individuals are not employees of the firm, they are likely to have less commitment and attachment to it. In addition, the cost of the leasing arrangement might be a bit higher than if the employees have been hired directly by the firm itself.

Our final alternative to hiring permanent workers is to rely on **part-time workers**, or individuals who routinely expect to work fewer than 40 hours a week. Among the major advantages of part-time employment is the fact that these employees are usually not covered by benefits, thus lowering labor costs, and the organization can achieve considerable flexibility. The part-time workers are routinely called on to work different schedules from week to week, thereby allowing the organization to cluster its labor force around peak demand times and have a smaller staff on hand during downtimes. Part-time workers are common in organizations such as restaurants. Wait staff, bus persons, kitchen help, and other employees might be college students who want to work only 15 or 20 hours a week to earn spending money. Their part-time interest provides considerable scheduling flexibility to the organization that hires them.

Each group of employees described in the preceding can be considered part of the *contingent workforce,* which includes (1) all temporary employees, (2) all part-time employees, and (3) all part-time employees who are employed by organizations to fill in for permanent employees during peak demand. Thus, these contingent workers are considered alternatives to recruiting, but usually as less-desirable alternatives. Some recent views of staffing take a more strategic perspective, however, and suggest that there may be situations when it would be preferable to hire temporary or contingent workers instead of permanent employees.[12]

In this view, whenever a firm requires additional human resources unrelated to its core competencies or required to have skills or knowledge that is generally available in the marketplace, then it may be to the firm's competitive advantage to add resources through some other arrangement besides permanent hires. Eventually, though, it may become clear that the firm needs to hire more permanent employees, which is the focus of the next chapter. For now, we turn instead to the situation in which rightsizing requires the firm to reduce the number of employees.

> The Fair Labor Standards Act stipulates that hourly workers must be compensated at a rate of one and a half times their normal hourly rate for work in excess of 40 hours per week.

Part-time workers refers to individuals who are regularly expected to work less than 40 hours a week. They typically do not receive benefits and afford the organization a great deal of flexibility in staffing.

6-2b Dealing with a Declining Need for Employees

There are also cases in which an organization needs fewer employees. If the organization employs a large contingent workforce, then the easiest solution is to cut those workers and simply retain its core of permanent employees. This approach works best in cyclical industries in which demand increases and decreases with the time of year, such as farming and its use of migrant farmworkers. But dealing with more permanent decreases in the demand for employees is more problematic, although there are some approaches we can discuss for this possibility as well.

Early retirements and natural attrition can be used when it is possible to plan systematically for a gradual decrease in the workforce. In some cases, organizations can even conduct planning exercises that may suggest the need to reduce the workforce over the next few years. This reduction may result from anticipated changes in technology or customer bases or even from anticipated changes in corporate or business strategies. The organization can attempt to manage the reduction by simply not replacing workers who leave voluntarily, by providing incentives for other employees to retire early, or both.

Clearly, a certain number of employees will retire every year in any mature organization, which can reduce the size of the workforce by simply not replacing those retired employees. But what if normal retirement rates are not expected to be enough to produce the necessary reductions? In those cases, the organization can offer certain types of incentives to convince some employees to retire earlier than they had planned.

For example, in an organization that has a defined benefit retirement plan (see Chapter 9), the pension that an employee earns at retirement is a function of (among other things) the number of years that person has worked and her or his salary. An organization could simply announce that those who are thinking about retiring will automatically have, say, 3 years added to their years of service if they make a decision to retire by a certain date. As a result, employees could feel comfortable about retiring 3 years earlier than they had planned. An organization could also increase the rate at which it matches employee contributions to 401(k) plans (also discussed in Chapter 9) or in some other way make it financially more attractive for employees to retire early. Some firms actually provide employees with opportunities to learn more about wealth management so they are better able to take advantage of early retirement opportunities. But, in all cases, these plans must truly be voluntary or the organization may encounter legal problems. By definition, early-retirement plans target older workers, so any attempt—real or perceived—to coerce them into leaving can be construed as age discrimination. As noted in Chapter 2, age discrimination toward older workers is illegal.

6-2c Strategies for Layoffs

In many cases, there is not enough warning to rely on early retirements, or the early retirement strategy simply does not result in enough decrease in employee numbers. In these cases, it is usually necessary to reduce the workforce through layoffs. Layoffs are not popular for obvious reasons. When notified of a layoff, some employees decide to sue the organization for wrongful termination. In these cases, the former employee alleges that the organization violated a contract or a law in deciding who to terminate. Even if an employee does not pursue legal remedies, many employees who have lost their jobs develop negative feelings toward their former employer. These feelings usually manifest themselves through negative comments made to other people or refusing to conduct personal business with their former employer. In some extreme cases, they may even result in aggressive or violent responses directed at those perceived to be responsible. Hundreds of such attacks occur each year, and several dozen result in the loss of life. For these reasons, it is critical that layoffs be carried out humanely and carefully.

A critical determinant of an employee's reaction to being laid off is his or her perceptions of the justice involved in the layoff process. Three types of justice—distributive, procedural, and interactional—seem to be related to reactions to layoffs.[13]

1. **Distributive justice** refers to perceptions that the outcomes a person faces are fair when compared to the outcomes faced by others. This type of justice is often important in determining an employee's reactions to pay decisions, for example. Most experts believe that these perceptions are based on both the actual outcomes faced (e.g., how much I am paid, whether or not I lose my job) and the perceptions of what others have contributed.[14] For example, a person may be paid less than his coworker, but if he can see that she contributes more to the company than he does and that

> Perceptions of distributive, procedural, and interpersonal justice affect reactions to layoffs.

Distributive justice refers to perceptions that the outcomes a person faces are fair when compared to the outcomes faced by others.

Kheng Guan Toh/Shutterstock.com

TABLE 6.1 CRITICAL DIMENSIONS OF PROCEDURAL JUSTICE

Voice: The perception that the person had some control over the outcome or some voice in the decision.

Consistency: The perception that the rules were applied the same way to everyone involved.

Free from bias: The perception that the person applying the rules had no vested interest in the outcome of the decision.

Information accuracy: The perception that the information used to make the decision was accurate and complete.

Possibility of correction: The perception that some mechanism exists to correct flawed or inaccurate decisions.

Ethicality: The perception that the decision rules conform to personal or prevailing standards of ethics and morality.

Representativeness: The perception that the opinions of the various groups affected by the decision have been considered in the decision.

Source: Adapted from Jason Colquitt, Donald Conlon, Michael Wesson, Christopher Porter, and K. Yee Ng, "Justice at the Millennium: A Meta-Analytic Review of 25 Years of Organizational Justice Research," *Journal of Applied Psychology* (2001), 86: 425–445.

the difference in the pay is proportional to the difference in contributions each makes, then he can still view the outcome as fair. Others argue, however, that unequal outcomes alone lead to perceptions of low distributive justice, and when someone loses his or her job but someone else does not, then it is difficult to see how this difference in outcome can be linked to differences in contribution.[15]

2. Nonetheless, those who lose their jobs may still react reasonably as long as they feel that the organization has not also violated another type of justice—**procedural justice**—or perceptions that the process used to determine the outcomes was fair. Thus, an employee who loses his or her job may be less angry if everyone in a department also lost their jobs or if layoffs were based on objective and accepted criteria. Several models of procedural justice have been proposed, and these models have yielded the dimensions of procedural justice presented in Table 6.1.

It is also clear, however, that an employee (or any other observer) will judge a process to be fair when it leads to an outcome that is favorable.[16] This perspective explains why most students generally consider fair tests to be the ones they perform best on. It is also why employees who do not lose their jobs are more likely to view the basis for layoff decisions as being more just (see, however, the discussion on the survivor syndrome).

Procedural justice refers to perceptions that the process used to determine the outcomes were fair.

Interactional justice refers to the quality of the interpersonal treatment people receive when a decision is implemented.

3. Finally, a third dimension of justice, **interactional justice**, refers to the quality of the interpersonal treatment people receive when a decision is implemented.[17] Thus, employees losing their jobs will feel that the decision was more just if it is communicated to them in a considerate, respectful, and polite manner. In fact, scholars have proposed more recently that there are two separate dimensions to interactional justice. The first dimension deals with the extent to which the person was treated with respect and dignity when he or she was told about the decision, while the second dimension refers to the extent to which the decision maker provides information about the decision rules used and how they were applied. These two dimensions have been called *interpersonal justice* and *informational justice*, respectively.[18]

The HR manager who has to deal with layoffs should consider these justice issues. Basically, they suggest that necessary layoffs should be implemented using a well-formulated strategy that can be communicated to and understood by the employees and follows the rules implied by the dimensions of procedural justice in Table 6.1. Finally, the decisions should be communicated in a way that conveys respect and caring for the people involved.

Of course, the actual strategy used for determining who will be laid off must also be reasonable. As noted earlier, a layoff strategy that targets older workers is probably illegal and would rarely be considered as fair. Sometimes, layoff decisions are made on the basis of performance; that is, the organization decides to lay off its poorest performers. But how does an organization decide who these employees are? Typically,

Contemporary Challenges in HR

Making Good Decisions

Managers today use more information to make decisions than ever before. Perhaps the most obvious example comes from the retailing sector. Point-of-sale technology helps managers know exactly how many units of every product in a store are sold every day. They can correlate this information with sales of other

> "Our analysis provides management with another data point before they make their decision."

— BOB BENNETT, FORMER CHIEF LEARNING OFFICER AND VICE PRESIDENT OF HR FOR FEDEX[19]

products; track it on daily, weekly, monthly, seasonal, and annual bases; and monitor the effects of price fluctuations on customer demand. Similarly, hotel managers can track occupancy rates in real time, website administrators know how many people view their sites every day, and airline managers know how many reservations are made, how many people are on each flight, and how much luggage is on every airplane.

It should come as no surprise, then, that HR managers are also getting into the act. HR managers essentially use two kinds of data. One type they gather themselves: For instance, they can collect, store, and access objective data related to employee education, skills, experience, demographics, and so forth. In addition, they can conduct

employee surveys to assess attitudes, job satisfaction, engagement, and the like. In most cases, they can also access organizational data related to finance, operations, marketing, and so forth.

HR managers also often rely on the second type of information, from external sources. For instance, salary surveys, cost-of-living data, projected population shifts (migration), and labor force profiles can all be useful. This and related information can be obtained from government sources, consulting firms, and so forth.

FedEx is a great example of a firm that relies heavily on HR information in making decisions. For instance, if FedEx is considering acquiring a company, it first analyzes data from the target company related to employee engagement surveys, turnover rates, experience, education, and diversity to compare with its own workforce information. This helps FedEx understand what additional investments (if any) it will need to make in human capital if it completes the acquisition. The firm is also looking into ways to compare data its employees provide on engagement surveys with the information they share on various social media platforms.[20]

THINK IT OVER

1. Can a manager ever have too much information? Why or why not?

2. What issues arise when a firm looks at its employees' posts on social media sites to gain information about them?

this decision is based on past performance appraisals, but, as we will see in Chapter 10, performance appraisals are far from perfect and are prone to various biases. When layoff decisions are based on performance ratings, those ratings take on the role of employment tests. In other words, because the organization is making a decision based on the performance ratings, the courts consider the performance ratings to be employment tests. Thus, if there is evidence of disparate impact in the layoffs, the organization will need to demonstrate that the performance ratings are job related or valid. This process is not always simple, as we will see in the

next chapter. In addition, the layoff strategy must also include some plan for callbacks if the demand for labor increases again. For example, a strategy that states the first to be laid off will also be the first to be called back will often be perceived as a fair strategy.

Finally, as noted in Chapter 2, when an organization is about to undertake a large-scale layoff or site closure, it is necessary to announce this step far enough in advance to allow employees (and others) to take some action to adjust to the coming changes. The Worker Adjustment and Retraining Notification (WARN) Act requires at least 60 days' notice for a facility closure or a mass layoff. Failure to provide this notification can result in serious financial penalties, especially for a firm facing pressure to reduce costs. From the organization's perspective, however, some potential costs come with announcing planned layoffs. After this plan is made known, many employees will seek alternative employment to avoid being out of work (which is the intention of the law). The employees most likely to find alternative employment are the best employees, however, and the firm is most likely to want to retain these employees. It is difficult to balance the requirements of the law (and of the individual employees) with the needs of the organization that desires to retain its top talent. This chapter's closing case presents additional information about exporting jobs.

6-2d Is Downsizing Effective?

Given the prevalence of downsizing as a way to reduce labor costs and make a firm more efficient, it would seem that the effectiveness of downsizing as a strategy would get a lot of support. Why else would so many firms turn to this strategy as a means of becoming more competitive? The data on the effectiveness of downsizing is rather mixed, however, and most of the data suggests that downsizing is *not* an effective strategy.

A major study of the effects of downsizing was conducted in the 1990s.[21] The authors compared several groups of companies that were tracked from 1980 through 1994, but we will focus on only three for the current discussion. "Stable employers" were defined as those firms where changes in employment throughout these years fell between plus and minus 5 percent (this was the largest group in the study). "Employment downsizers" were firms where the decline in employment was more than 5 percent, *and* the decline in plant and equipment was less than 5 percent during the same period. "Asset downsizers" were defined as firms where the decline in employment was less than 5 percent during this time, but the decline in plant and assets was at least 5 percent greater than the decline in employment. The authors examined the impact of these strategies over time on two indexes of performance: return on assets (a financial index of profitability) and common stock prices.

The results clearly showed that employment downsizers had the lowest levels of return on assets over time and also did quite poorly on stock price. In both cases, the asset downsizers produced the greatest performance over the period. Most of the pressure on management to downsize the workforce comes from stockholders, who believe that this method is a good way to cut costs and increase profitability. But the results of this study suggest that firms facing increased competition or some other need to downsize should consider reducing plants and assets rather than their workforce.

Other studies have also reported negative effects on stock prices and other financial indexes as a result of downsizing.[22] Given these findings, why do firms continue to downsize as a reaction to the need to cut costs? Some evidence suggests that, in the short run, the stock market reacts positively to these cuts, and so managers are reinforced for their decisions. But other potential costs, not only potential direct financial costs, are also associated with downsizing.

Earlier in this chapter, we emphasized issues that can occur in conjunction with those employees who lose their jobs in a layoff, but issues related to those who avoid losing their jobs in the layoff also crop up. A phenomenon known as *survivor syndrome* can counteract many of the presumed cost savings that led to the layoffs in the first place.[23] This syndrome describes employees who feel guilty over keeping their jobs (i.e., they survived) when others lost their jobs. Their morale and commitment to the organization drop dramatically. One study from the 1990s found that HR managers reporting layoffs reported steep declines in morale and increased levels of voluntary turnover.[24] A more recent study found that 72 percent of respondents had gone through layoffs or restructuring since 2008, and these firms reported that top performers were less likely to see a link between their own goals

> The Worker Adjustment and Retraining Notification (WARN) Act requires at least 60 days' notice for a facility closure or a mass layoff.

> **Most of the pressure on management to downsize the workforce comes from stockholders.**

and company goals, while almost half the employees reported that these changes resulted in declines in quality and customer service.[25] This data may underestimate the total costs of increased layoffs. Evidence suggests that the increasing rates of layoffs and the resulting joblessness are causing serious emotional problems for employees—both those actually affected by layoffs and those who think they *might* be affected by layoffs.

Given this data, we must close with a discussion of alternatives to layoffs as ways of reducing costs. Downsizing the number of employees is a tangible way of demonstrating that a firm is serious about cutting costs, but it may not be the most effective. Reducing assets is an alternative. This could include reducing investments in new machinery, stretching out maintenance schedules for equipment, or actually getting out of some lines of business. Although closing plants will also result in job loss, a firm might be able to sell some of its less productive assets. Thus, some alternatives to layoffs may also result in job loss, but that outcome isn't a foregone conclusion. Some firms find even more productive ways to reduce costs. Some years ago, one of the authors of this textbook learned about a DuPont plant that was facing layoffs or closure because of high labor costs. The plant manager (subsequently promoted several times) asked the employees to get involved in the decision about reducing costs. The employees suggested a combination of job sharing, salary reductions (the plant was nonunion), early-retirement plans, and part-time work, which resulted in almost no employees losing their jobs. At the same time, the plant became extremely profitable, and the employees developed a loyalty to the company that was the envy of the manufacturing sector.

Tino Mager/Shutterstock.com

6-3 MANAGING TERMINATIONS AND RETENTION

Not all decisions regarding who remains with a firm result from changes in the demand for human resources. There are times when an organization wants to sever the employment relationship not with a large number of employees but with specific employees. There are also times when an organization is concerned over the loss of critical employees (or group of employees) and must instead focus on ways to retain them. We begin this discussion by turning our attention to the various issues involved in terminating employees whose services are no longer desired—also known as **involuntary turnover**.

6-3a Managing Involuntary Turnover

Effective HR practices are supposed to ensure that employees perform their job satisfactorily. But even the most sophisticated recruitment and staffing practices can still result in hiring an employee who is simply not capable of or is not willing to perform up to acceptable standards or who presents enough of a disciplinary problem that he or she must be terminated. We should note, first, however, that any time an employee is terminated, it represents a failure of some part of the HR system. It can also be costly because the firm must then seek to recruit, hire, and train a replacement. Therefore, in all the situations we describe in this section, termination should be seen as the last resort. Before terminating an employee, managers should always start with an effort to rectify the problem. These attempts begin with trying to ascertain the reasons for poor performance.

For example, in some cases, the poorly performing employee might have the potential to perform effectively, but he or she was never properly trained or is not properly supervised. In such cases, the employee's performance may be brought up to standard by retraining or reassignment to a supervisor who is better at developing employees. In other cases, the employee may be suffering from various physical or psychological problems such as excessive stress or problems associated with alcohol or drug abuse. Most organizations have some type of employee assistance program (EAP) designed to either help such employees directly or refer them to competent professionals who can provide that help. Originally, many EAPs focused on alcoholism, but more recently they have expanded to deal with drugs and more general problems of mental health.[26] Considerable evidence suggests that effective EAPs can help employees and reduce the costs associated with lost workdays and poor productivity.[27] These plans can also save costs by serving as gatekeepers for employee health plans because they

Involuntary turnover is terminating employees whose services are no longer desired.

> **Before terminating an employee for poor performance, managers should start with an effort to rectify the problem—trying to ascertain the reasons for the poor performance.**

determine what types of services are best suited for each employee.[28] But, more important, these programs make it possible for potentially valuable employees to be brought back to productive levels, thus ensuring their continued employment and yielding savings for the organization.

In many cases, the reason for an employee failing to perform up to standard is that he or she simply does not know how or cannot perform at that level. It may be a lack of ability or a lack of fit between the person's abilities and the job requirements. In these cases, it is in everyone's best interests for the employee to leave the company or be reassigned to another job, and this is what most termination decisions deal with. But, in other cases, poor performance is a motivational problem, not a personal or ability problem. For whatever reason, the employee chooses not to perform at expected levels, even though he or she is capable of doing so. This may be the result of poorly designed incentives for performance, which we will discuss in Chapters 13 and 14, but sometimes it is possible to convince the employee to exert greater effort by taking some type of disciplinary action.

6-3b Progressive Discipline

Disciplinary programs in organizations are designed to try to improve performance through the use of punishment.

Punishment simply refers to following unacceptable behavior with some type of negative consequences.

Discipline refers to the system of rules and procedures for how and when punishment is administered and how severe the punishment should be.

Progressive disciplinary plans are organizational disciplinary programs where the severity of the punishment increases over time or across the problem.

1. **Punishment** simply refers to following unacceptable behavior with some type of negative consequences.

2. **Discipline** refers to the system of rules and procedures for how and when punishment is administered and how severe it should be.

In all cases, the goal of the disciplinary program is to convince the employee to stop the ineffective or undesired behavior and engage in more accepted or desired behavior. The goal is not to terminate the employee unless that becomes the only viable alternative.

We refer to these programs as **progressive disciplinary plans** because, almost invariably, the severity of the punishment increases over time or across the seriousness of the problem. A list of typical steps in the progressive disciplinary program is provided in Table 6.2. Each infraction, as well as the schedule of penalties, should be spelled out clearly to employees, both in the form of an employee handbook and orally at employee orientation. Whatever the infractions, the steps in the disciplinary process are almost always the same. It is also true, however, that some types of problems might incur more severe penalties from the outset. For example, if a bank teller fails to balance at the end of the day, and this pattern continues for several days, the bank may simply send the teller for further training. If the pattern continues, the bank may suspend the teller and, eventually, dismiss the teller, but this will take some time. On the other hand, if the teller is found to be stealing money, the penalty is immediate dismissal for the first infraction.

TABLE 6.2	TYPICAL DISCIPLINARY PROBLEMS
Problems with performance	• Failure to complete work on time • Errors in work products • Work products that do not meet established tolerances
Problems with attendance	• Repeated unexcused absences • Tardiness • Leaving work early
Problems with ethics or honesty	• Taking credit for the work of others • Falsifying records • Soliciting or accepting bribes or kickbacks
Other behavior problems	• Gambling • Vandalism • Use of drugs or alcohol on the job • Sexual harassment
Problems that could lead to immediate termination	• Major theft • Sleeping on the job • Selling narcotics on the job

TABLE 6.3 EXCEPTIONS TO THE DOCTRINE OF EMPLOYMENT AT WILL

1. **The termination would violate a specific law.** Various laws forbid termination for a specific reason. Some of the most common reasons are termination based on gender or race (violates the Civil Rights Act) or termination because of union activity (violates the Taft-Hartley Act).

2. **The employee has a contractual right to his or her job.** The contract might be a formal contract or an implied contract guaranteeing or implying a guarantee of employment.

3. **The employee's rights of due process have been violated.** For example, if an employee is accused of theft, the employee has the right to know of the charges and to refute those charges—in a court of law if necessary.

4. **Public–policy exception.** This exception has been less common but involves cases in which an employee is discharged for refusing to commit a crime or for reporting a crime or unethical or unsafe behavior on the part of the organization. Thus, whistle-blowers are protected under this exception.

5. Breach-of-good-faith exception. This is the most difficult exception to establish because it involves a breach of promise. In one of the best-known cases, an employee claimed that he was terminated after 25 years of employment so that the company could avoid paying him his sales commission.

Note: These exceptions have been cited in various court cases, but there is no guarantee that any specific state will recognize any one of these exceptions in its jurisdiction.

Source: *Fortune* v. *National Cash Register*, 364 Massachusetts 91, 36 N.E. 2d 1251 (1977).

1. Typically, the first step in a progressive disciplinary program is a **verbal warning**, or a caution conveyed to the employee orally rather than in writing. The supervisor or manager should keep a written record of the fact that a verbal warning was given to document the fact that all required steps were taken in dealing with an employee.

2. **Written warnings** are more formal and are the second step in the process. Here the supervisor gives the warning to the employee in writing and provides a copy to the HR department. As a result, a written warning becomes part of the employee's permanent record.

3. **Suspension**, or a temporary layoff, is the next step in the process. The suspension could last a day or a few weeks; it may be with or without pay. At each step, the supervisor should discuss the performance problems with the employee and seek ways for the employee to improve.

4. If all else fails, the final step in the process is **termination**. At this point, the organization faces potential legal problems as well as potentially violent reactions by the employee. This final step should be taken only after serious consideration and the decision that the employee cannot be salvaged.

6-3c Employment at Will

It is not always easy to terminate an employee, no matter how problematic he or she may be. Considerable publicity has surrounded the issue of employees suing organizations for wrongful termination, so we might suspect that the formal law dealing with this issue is quite complicated. It might be surprising, therefore, to learn that the only real legal perspective on employee termination is a nineteenth-century common-law rule known as **employment at will**. Basically, this view asserts that, because an employee can terminate an employment relationship at any time (i.e., quit a job), the employer should have similar rights. Therefore, employment at will states that an employer can terminate any employee at any time for any reason (good or bad)—or for no reason at all. This view differs dramatically from the situation in many European countries, where employees can be terminated for criminal behavior only.[29]

In the United States, companies are relatively free to terminate employees anytime they wish, so in most cases, an employee has no legal recourse if he or she is terminated. Several important exceptions to the employment-at-will doctrine exist. These exceptions define situations in which an employee who is discharged can sue for wrongful termination and thus get his or her job back. These exceptions are important to keep in mind and are presented in Table 6.3.

Verbal warnings—the first step in most progressive disciplinary programs—are cautions conveyed orally to the employee.

Written warnings—the second step in most progressive disciplinary programs—are more formal warnings. They are given to the employee in writing and become part of the employee's permanent record.

As part of a progressive disciplinary program, a **suspension** is a temporary layoff, usually with pay, when there is an ongoing investigation.

As part of a progressive disciplinary program, **termination** is an act by the organization to end the employment relationship.

Employment at will states that an employer can terminate any employee, at any time, for any reason (good or bad), or for no reason at all.

Even with these exceptions, employers can still usually terminate employees *for cause*; that is, if the employee violates a written company rule or policy or is an objectively documented poor performer, then he or she can be terminated in virtually every case. The key to successful termination of an employee is documentation. An organization can terminate any employee at any time, but if the employee claims that the termination was wrong, the employer may have to prove otherwise. If an employee is dismissed for poor performance, then it may be necessary to document that most (if not all) of the employee's recent performance appraisals were poor or below standard. If the employee has received generally acceptable evaluations, then it will be extremely difficult to terminate the employee for poor performance. In any case, if a company has a progressive disciplinary program, it must show that each step was followed before the employee was terminated.

If an employer does not follow the proper steps and document each one, the employee may well get his or her job back. This situation may be annoying to the employer, but it is actually far more serious than annoyance. Progressive discipline can work only if the employee truly believes that he or she will be fired without improved performance. If the threat of termination is not credible because procedures were not followed correctly or for some other reason (perhaps the employee is a civil-service employee), it is extremely difficult to correct a problem employee. The credible threat of termination is actually an important part of the process by which an organization can turn a poorly performing employee into a productive one.

Some organizations have begun to adopt an approach referred to as *positive discipline*, which has a somewhat different orientation.[30] This approach integrates discipline with performance management. (We will discuss this more fully in Chapter 14). Positive discipline emphasizes positive changes rather than punishment. Typically, the process is still somewhat progressive in nature, with warnings leading to eventual termination if the problem is not corrected. The major difference, however, is that a great deal of counseling and problem solving are integral to the process. The employee is given as much help as is reasonable to help him or her identify the behaviors desired by the organization and to eliminate undesirable behaviors.

6-3d Employee Retention

Sometimes the focus of HR decisions is on ways to retain valued employees instead of on ways to terminate undesired employees. In fact, the two work together: Organizations must seek ways to eliminate poorly performing employees while at the same time find ways to retain highly performing employees. Thus, termination is about ways to ensure the involuntary turnover of undesired employees, and retention is about ways of reducing the voluntary turnover of desired employees.

One of the authors of this book works at a university in New Orleans where this problem was played out in dramatic fashion following Hurricane Katrina and the breaching of the New Orleans levee system in August 2005. As a result, the university had to close for a semester, and it lost a great deal of money. When the university was ready to reopen, it became clear that it would be necessary to reduce the size of the staff (and the faculty) to survive. Deans and heads of programs were therefore asked to determine which staff positions were critical for the future of the university and to prioritize layoffs among the remainder of the staff. Lists of potential layoffs were thus generated across the university, and hundreds of staff members were scheduled to lose their jobs. But no one really understood the situation from the perspective of the staff employees. Many of them had been forced to evacuate New Orleans, and they had to enroll their children in schools in other cities. Many of them had lived in areas that had been flooded and could not be rebuilt in time to return to work in January 2006. Still others had found jobs elsewhere or had spouses who had found jobs elsewhere and were not planning to return to New Orleans. As a result, hundreds of staff employees voluntarily left their jobs. Unfortunately, these were often not the same people the university had planned to lay off. Instead, these were valued employees whose jobs were critical to the future of the organization. As a result, all the planned layoffs had to be canceled (with a few exceptions), and the university had to scramble to make sure that all critical positions were filled.

This is also an area where HR analytics can play a role. As noted earlier, the goal is not simply to understand why people leave, but to be able to predict why they leave and then do something to retain them. At the simplest level, regular employee satisfaction surveys (more on this below) as well as exit interviews can provide valuable information about why people stay and why they leave. This is an area, though, where a great deal of data may be available, and the organization has to decide what to focus on and how to use the data. In addition, an author discussing HR big data,[31] reported that Xerox reduced voluntary turnover at call centers by 20 percent simply by focusing on the "right" metrics. Instead of relying only on survey data, Xerox began focusing on data from social media to learn more about what led to turnover and employee engagement. Again, there is often a great deal of such data available, so this is not a trivial undertaking, but by searching for a new source of employee data, XEROX was able to take actions that helped reduce turnover and increase engagement.

This example, as well as the Katrina story, help illustrate that there are two sides to every rightsizing effort: retaining people who are critical for the future and terminating those that are not. Therefore, we turn our attention now to the problems of retaining valued employees. These strategies are always important if the firm hopes to gain competitive advantage through its human resources, but they are especially critical as part of any rightsizing.

 ## 6-4 MANAGING VOLUNTARY TURNOVER

Managers cannot always control who leaves the organization or why they leave, but they should not assume that all turnover is negative even in the case of voluntary turnover. In fact, although the organization does not want to force someone out, management may not be totally disappointed that the person left, and a certain amount of voluntary turnover is probably healthy for the organization.[32] Yet it is important to manage this turnover as much as possible. High rates of turnover cost the organization a great deal in terms of the expense associated with employee replacement, and such turnover can hurt the organization's reputation as a good place to work.

To manage turnover, it is important to understand why people leave. A major cause for turnover is **job dissatisfaction**, or being unhappy with one's job.[33] We will discuss some causes for job dissatisfaction later in the chapter (as well as some additional consequences of dissatisfaction), but for now, it is enough to say that the HR manager plays a major role in ensuring that employees remain reasonably satisfied with their jobs. It is also the role of HR to help reduce turnover and retain valued employees. As we will see, job dissatisfaction is often the key to turnover. Different views explain why dissatisfied workers decide to leave.

6-4a Models of the Turnover Process

The basic reason people leave their jobs is because they are unhappy with them. Thus, the simplest view of the employee turnover process would suggest that if we increase job satisfaction, then we will decrease turnover.

> A certain amount of voluntary turnover is probably healthy for the organization.

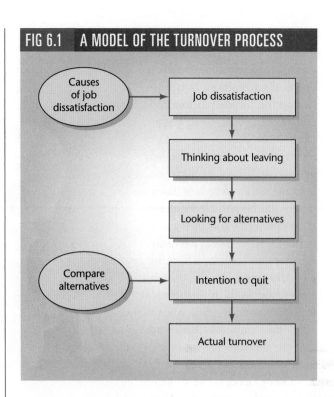

FIG 6.1   A MODEL OF THE TURNOVER PROCESS

Although this basic view is essentially correct, the processes involved are somewhat more complex.

First, the economy and the labor market play a role. It has been noted that the prevailing unemployment rate is as big a factor in whether a person leaves a job at the level of dissatisfaction.[34] Clearly, this explanation makes a great deal of sense. Even if an employee is extremely dissatisfied, he or she is not likely to quit without real prospects of finding another job.

Recognizing this fact, several turnover models emphasize the role of dissatisfaction in the decision to look for alternatives, and it is seen as a necessary (but not sufficient) first step in the decision to quit. At least two major streams of research have proposed models that incorporate these ideas, and the basic concepts of these models are present in Figure 6.1.[35] As you can see in the figure, the process begins with factors leading to job dissatisfaction (which will be discussed below). Job dissatisfaction causes the employee to begin thinking about quitting, which leads to a search for alternatives. Only if those alternatives look better does the employee decide that he or she will quit, a decision first manifested by an intention to quit.

> **Job dissatisfaction** is the feeling of being unhappy with one's job. It is a major cause of voluntary turnover.

Of course, the implication of this type of model is that managers should reduce the sources of job dissatisfaction. It is best to stop the turnover before the employee begins searching for alternatives because he or she might find a more attractive alternative. Even if an employee begins searching for alternatives, it may still be possible to retain the employee by convincing him or her that the current job really is better than the alternatives. In fact, the search for alternatives sometimes leads to increased satisfaction on the current job after the employee discovers that the alternatives were not as positive as once believed.

Other models have proposed similar mechanisms but have also suggested that job dissatisfaction must reach a critical level before anything happens, and, at that point, it may be too late to do anything. In other words, this approach suggests that increasing job dissatisfaction does little to change the employee's intentions to leave. Those levels of job dissatisfaction finally reach a critical level, however, and the intention to leave becomes so strong that the employee is almost guaranteed to leave.[36]

Another interesting model that deviates a bit from the basic model in Figure 6.1 focuses on "shocks" to the individual.[37] First, this model proposes that several paths can lead to turnover, and they do not all require shocks. Nonetheless, the major focus is on a shock—an event that can be either positive or negative but is so profound that it causes the employee to think about the organization, the job, and how he or she fits with both. This model begins with shock and not with job dissatisfaction. In fact, the dissatisfaction occurs only because the employee started thinking about the job in response to the shock. The decision to leave is largely based on the perception that the employee does not really fit with the company—that is, the current job in the current company is not consistent with the image the employee has of himself or herself. In some cases,

UpperCut Images/Alamy Stock Photo

the employee will leave without even considering alternatives, but in all cases, the decision to leave takes place over time.

The model includes other aspects of cognitive processing, but the shocks include events such as winning the lottery or losing a loved one, as well as job-related events such as missing a promotion or receiving an offer from another company. This model has interesting implications for understanding how difficult it is to manage the turnover process, but recently the authors of the model have added one more wrinkle. Although the model was originally proposed as a way of understanding why people leave their jobs, it can also help understand why others stay. The notion of **job embeddedness** has been proposed as an explanation for why some people stay on their jobs, even when they decide they are unhappy and should leave.[38] Some employees are simply tied too strongly to their jobs to leave. Perhaps they are deeply involved in the neighborhood, or perhaps they cannot sell their houses. Whatever the reason, they feel that they cannot quit. These employees may be quite unhappy, which can cause other problems. This state is not always desirable. Nonetheless, the notion of job embeddedness adds a great deal to our potential understanding of the turnover process.

6-4b The Causes of Job Dissatisfaction

A common thread in these models of the turnover process is job dissatisfaction. Wherever and however in the process job dissatisfaction occurs, reducing it is likely to reduce turnover. Therefore, it is important to understand the causes of job dissatisfaction. Although most sources of job dissatisfaction that have been studied are related to the job, some of the more creative approaches have focused on factors that have little or nothing to do with the job. For example, one line of research, using identical twins, has (cautiously) suggested that a certain component of job satisfaction may be genetic.[39] A related line of research has suggested that some individuals are simply disposed toward being satisfied, while others are

Job embeddedness refers to the fact that some people stay in their jobs, even when they decide they are unhappy and should leave. Other ties in the community or obligations keep the employee in the job.

disposed toward being dissatisfied, and that, although conditions on the job play a role, these tendencies are as important in determining levels of job dissatisfaction.[40] More typical approaches to job dissatisfaction, however, tend to focus on the following job-related factors.

1. **Nature of the Work.** One of the most important sources of dissatisfaction on the job is the nature of the work that a person does.[41] For example, a consistent relationship exists between job complexity (and job challenge) and job satisfaction such that employees with more complex and challenging jobs are more satisfied. We will discuss how jobs can be redesigned to make them more motivating and satisfying in Chapter 14.

   In addition, job satisfaction tends to be higher when the job is less physically demanding. We don't want to suggest that a boring job is preferred—quite the contrary—but a job that requires constant physical exertion and strain tends to lower levels of job satisfaction. jobs that help employees achieve something of value also tend to result in higher levels of job satisfaction; that is, if an employee feels that he or she is accomplishing some good on the job, satisfaction tends to be higher. In addition, if an employee values status, and a job provides him or her with more of it, then levels of satisfaction are also likely to be higher.[42]

2. **Pay and Benefits.** It may not be a surprise that an employee's level of satisfaction on the job is affected by the extent to which he or she is satisfied with pay and benefits. In general, higher levels of pay and more attractive benefits tend to result in greater satisfaction, and we will discuss issues of both compensation and benefits in Chapter 9. But another important factor in determining satisfaction with pay is what other people make. Basically, we compare ourselves with similar others, and we gauge what we contribute to an organization versus what a comparison person contributes. We then compare how much we are paid, and, if the ratio of rewards to contributions is better for the other person, we tend to be dissatisfied. Note that these calculations are all based on perceptions, which may be incorrect, and note also that this comparison person could be working in the same organization or in another organization.

3. **Supervisors and Coworkers.** Supervisors and coworkers represent two additional potential sources of job dissatisfaction. An employee may be satisfied (or dissatisfied) with coworkers for several reasons. An important factor for job satisfaction is that the employee believes he or she shares certain values and attitudes with coworkers—that everyone has some shared vision of the world and can work together as a team.[43] Clearly, the impression that coworkers do not share values and attitudes can lead to dissatisfaction. In addition, coworkers can be seen as sources of social support, which can also lead to increased job satisfaction. Employees can be satisfied with supervisors for many of the same reasons. In other words, shared values and social support can be important determinants of satisfaction with a supervisor as well as with a coworker. In addition, an employee can be satisfied (or dissatisfied) with a supervisor's leadership ability. How a supervisor leads (i.e., his or her leadership style) and the effectiveness of the work group are important determinants of satisfaction with the supervisor.[44]

Each source of job dissatisfaction can be measured and thought of independently or as part of a whole; that is, studying and considering satisfaction with pay in its own right has some value, whereas others consider it simply as one source of overall satisfaction with the job. We will return to this issue later when we discuss methods of measuring satisfaction. Before turning to that topic, however, we turn our attention to some of the outcomes of dissatisfaction on the job.

> Happier workers are healthier workers. Dissatisfied employees are more likely to be absent for health reasons.

6-4c The Effects of Job Dissatisfaction

We began our discussion of job satisfaction by noting that it is a major determinant of voluntary turnover and thus our major reason for discussing job satisfaction. However, job dissatisfaction can have other negative effects, and some of these effects are related to topics we discuss later in the text.

For now, our primary concern with job dissatisfaction is that it leads to increased voluntary turnover. As noted earlier, job dissatisfaction is a major determinant of turnover, but it is also predictive of other types of withdrawal behavior. For example, a strong relationship exists between job dissatisfaction and absenteeism,[45] partly because employees who are dissatisfied may not always be able to leave their jobs (due to a lack of alternatives); thus, they choose to withdraw partially by being absent. In addition, it is possible to withdraw even more gradually (or partially) by simply being late.

A more subtle form of withdrawal that does not involve being away from the job is a reduction of commitment to the organization. **Organizational commitment** is the degree to which an employee identifies with an organization and is willing to exert effort on behalf of the organization.[46] Employees who lack organizational commitment are excellent candidates for turnover when a workable alternative presents itself. They are also unlikely to exert extra effort or even to encourage others to join the organization.

Dissatisfied employees are also more likely to join unions. Several studies support this relationship, and, although the process of joining a union is fairly complex, job dissatisfaction has consistently been found to be a good predictor of who joins unions.[47] We will discuss the implications of this relationship in more detail in Chapter 11.

Finally, dissatisfied employees are less likely to engage in behaviors on the job known broadly as *organizational citizenship behaviors*,[48] or sometimes as *contextual performance*.[49] **Organizational citizenship behaviors (OCBs)** include those behaviors that are beneficial to the organization but are not formally required as part of an employee's job. These behaviors include activities such as volunteering to carry out extra tasks, helping and cooperating with others, following rules even when such behavior is inconvenient, and endorsing and supporting organizational goals. We discuss contextual performance further in the next chapter, but clearly the organization benefits when employees engage in these types of behavior, and dissatisfied employees are simply less likely to do so.

In addition, considerable evidence suggests that job dissatisfaction imposes a different type of cost on an organization.

Career Advancement · Flexibility: work/life · Satisfactory Salary · Job Satisfaction · Working Conditions · Work Itself · Job Security

Job dissatisfaction has been found to be strongly linked to stress (discussed more fully in Chapter 12), job burnout (the condition of physical, emotional, and mental exhaustion on the job[50]), and (through the first two processes) employee health.[51] Thus, happier workers are healthier workers. Dissatisfied employees are more likely to be absent for health reasons.

The most intriguing possibility, however, is the link between job satisfaction and productivity. The notion that happy workers may be productive workers has attracted scholars for almost 100 years. Although there are cases in which performance and satisfaction have common determinants, and even some in which the most productive employees are also the most satisfied, no consistent causal relationship between job satisfaction and performance has been found. Thus, higher levels of job satisfaction do not necessarily lead to higher levels of performance, and an organization should not target increases in job satisfaction in the hope of raising productivity.

6-4d Measuring and Monitoring Job Satisfaction

As should be clear by now, job satisfaction is extremely important for managing workforce size and effectiveness. As a result, organizations spend a fair amount of time and effort monitoring the levels of their employees' job satisfaction, primarily through the use of attitude surveys that are distributed to employees once or more a year. The responses from these surveys are used to track changes in employees' attitudes—such as job satisfaction—so that the organization can respond to them before they become problematic.

Although many organizations design their own attitude surveys (or hire consulting firms to design them), some widely used measures of job satisfaction often show up as part of these surveys. By using standard measures of job satisfaction, an organization not only tracks changes in its employees' levels of satisfaction but also is able to compare satisfaction levels with other organizations that use the same measures.

Organizational commitment is the degree to which an employee identifies with an organization and is willing to exert effort on behalf of the organization.

Organizational citizenship behaviors (OCBs) include employee behaviors that are beneficial to the organization but are not formally required as part of an employee's job.

The job descriptive index (JDI) is the most commonly used measure of job satisfaction.[52] It assesses satisfaction with specific job aspects such as pay, the work itself, and supervision, but it does not have a single overall measure of job satisfaction (although it is easy to assess overall satisfaction using the JDI). For each aspect of the job, a series of descriptors might apply. For example, for the work itself, adjectives such as *routine* and *satisfying* are listed, among others. Employees are asked to indicate if each adjective "describes your work," "does not describe your work," or if the employee "can't decide." The employee indicates the level of agreement by placing a Y, N, or ? next to each item, with the question mark (?) assumed to indicate a moderate level of dissatisfaction.

Other instruments do include direct measures of job satisfaction, and some include questions about the levels desired versus what is experienced. One instrument, the *faces scale*, presents a series of faces that are either happy or sad, and the employee is instructed to check the face that best reflects his or her feelings about the job.[53]

Whatever the measure, most organizations are interested in changes in the levels of job satisfaction over time. Before leaving this discussion, it is important to make a final note. The primary reason to measure job satisfaction is because dissatisfied employees tend to quit their jobs; over time, those employees who are the most dissatisfied will quit the soonest. The next time the organization surveys its employees, the survey will not include those employees who have already quit. As a result, it is quite likely that the overall levels of job satisfaction will go up, even if the organization does nothing to improve job satisfaction, because only the more satisfied employees are still on the job. The others have already left, indicating a serious problem that the organization could overlook if managers are not paying attention.

Alex Mit/Shutterstock.com

6-4e Retention Strategies

The purpose of discussing job satisfaction is to provide insights into how to manage voluntary turnover. At the simplest level, one could say that the way to manage turnover is to increase the levels of satisfaction among employees. But the key is in understanding exactly how to do that. When an organization learns of a potential problem, most likely through a survey, it is important that *something* be done. Employees are less likely to respond honestly to survey questions if they feel that no one will respond to their concerns. More specifically, two other types of interventions (both discussed previously in different contexts) have been found to increase levels of job satisfaction.

Job enrichment, discussed in Chapter 14 as a strategy for enhancing performance, has been consistently linked with higher levels of job satisfaction. By making employees' work more challenging and meaningful and by granting them more autonomy and more opportunity to use their skills, the work itself becomes both motivating and satisfying (and more satisfied employees are also more productive). This in turn reduces turnover rates.

Realistic job previews (RJPs) are preemployment previews that provide accurate and realistic information to the job applicant. They are often used with new employees as a means of socializing them in their new job roles (and they will be discussed further in this context in the next chapter), but they are also effective in reducing turnover. The link to turnover reduction is the result of several aspects of RJPs. First, because potential employees who receive RJPs have more complete information about the job (including the nature of the work, supervision, and pay), those who are more likely to be dissatisfied with the job characteristics are less likely to accept the jobs. Therefore, RJPs help ensure that the people on the job are those most likely to be satisfied and thus remain. In addition, when new employees are made aware of potential sources of dissatisfaction before encountering them, the employees can prepare themselves (psychologically or even physically) so that, when they encounter the problem, they are ready to deal with it. In fact, when employees learn that they can cope with various

Realistic job previews (RJPs) are preemployment previews that provide accurate and realistic information to the job applicant. They can also be used with new employees as a means of socializing them in their new job roles, and they are effective in reducing turnover.

problems on the job by preparing for them beforehand, this knowledge alone can be a source of job satisfaction and promote retention.

Another retention strategy involves issuing stock options to new employees at all levels of the organization (these options have typically been given to executives only). **Stock options** are rights, given to employees, to purchase a certain number of shares of stock at a given price. That stock-option price is often just slightly lower than the selling price of the stock when the option is issued. If the stock appreciates in value, then these options can become very valuable. The employee can exercise the option, buy the stock at an option price that is lower than the current selling price, and then sell the stock for an immediate profit (some firms do not even require the employee to purchase the stock at that point but simply pay out the profit). By the end of the 1990s, however, some firms added a new wrinkle aimed specifically at employee retention. Although an employee was issued stock options early in the employment relationship, the options were restricted so that the employee could not exercise the options for 5 or so years. If the stock was climbing, then the employee who left before he or she had completed 5 years of employment would forgo potentially large profits because he or she would not be able to exercise the stock options. Thus, there was a real incentive for the employee to remain with the firm (at least long enough to exercise stock options). Of course, if the stock price falls below the option price (and the option is said to be "underwater"), there is no reason to exercise the option, and the incentive to remain with the company is lost.

As noted earlier, HR analytics can be useful in determining exactly what kinds of approaches will work best. Recently, however, a new development came to light in the area of retention. It is not about retention per se but about noncompete clauses. In jobs where there is a great deal of proprietary information involved, it is common to have executives sign noncompete clauses. These clauses prevent the executive from working for a competitor for some period of time. But, in 2015, it was reported[54] that Amazon actually forced even temporary warehouse workers to sign noncompete clauses that are good for 18 months after their brief stay at Amazon. Because the clause actually included firms that develop, sell, or market any product or service that competes with any product or service provided by Amazon, this covers a lot of territory. Furthermore, permanent warehouse workers who were subsequently laid off, were asked to reaffirm their noncompete contract

as a condition of receiving severance pay. Earlier, it had also been reported that Jimmy Johns forced permanent workers to sign noncompete clauses preventing them from working at any sandwich shop within 3 miles. We should note that Amazon removed its noncompete clause from the contracts of all hourly works, later in 2015, but there is clearly a trend to rely more on noncompete clauses, even for nontechnical employees. Although this is not typical of approaches designed to retain employees, such clauses could reduce turnover, especially in tight labor markets.

 6-5 MANAGING HUMAN RESOURCES DURING MERGERS AND ACQUISITIONS

Managing human resources during mergers or acquisitions is the last issue we address concerning decisions regarding the size and nature of the workforce. Every few years, we seem to experience another wave of mergers and acquisitions. During the past decade, for example, the six largest U.S. airlines merged—Delta joined with Northwest Airlines, United with Continental, and American with U.S. Airways—to form three mega-airlines that control most of the long-haul air travel industry in this country. We have also seen many acquisitions in the casino industry so that now two companies, MGM and Harrah's, control almost 60 percent of all the casino business in the United States. More recently, following the financial crisis of 2009 and the so-called subprime crisis, several banks and financial firms acquired large but financially less viable firms. These included Wells Fargo acquiring Wachovia, Chase buying Washington Mutual, and Merrill Lynch taking over what was left of Bear Stearns.

Although a lot of attention is paid to big mergers and acquisitions, the public is less aware that many of these mergers and acquisitions actually fail. Failure (or success) can be assessed by looking at stock prices, accounting measures, or indicators such as research-and-development (R&D) expenditures. For each of these measures, data usually has shown that mergers and acquisitions typically fail; that is, they result in lower stock prices, lower returns, and lower levels of R&D expenditures.[55] This pattern ended quite quickly, but there is some evidence that restructuring in the financial sector will continue, as evidenced by Aabar Investments (representing the Abu Dhabi sovereign fund) increasing its share of Uni-Credit, a troubled Italian bank, in early 2012.

Stock options are rights given to employees to purchase a certain number of shares of stock at a given price.

There is considerable speculation and some limited research on why mergers and acquisitions fail, but much of the attention has been paid to a deal's financial elements (e.g., the acquiring firm paid too much) or to strategic elements (e.g., the new business was too far from the firm's areas of expertise). Although these issues are certainly important, it is also becoming increasingly clear that the successful management of human resources during the merger and acquisition process is also quite important for the overall success of the project.[56] In fact, several HRM aspects may be critical for successful mergers and acquisitions.

When a merger or acquisition is announced, several interesting processes begin. The most obvious is that employees in the firms involved become concerned about their jobs, especially employees of the firm that is being acquired by another company. In many cases, for example, a merger or acquisition results in a certain amount of redundant human resources, so it is not unusual for layoffs to occur following the merger or acquisition. This awareness causes employees to become more stressed and to worry about their security, and it leads some employees to seek other employment before they become victims of a layoff. Unfortunately, in these cases, it is often the more valued employees who have the market value that makes such a job change easy.

Mergers and acquisition also threaten the way employees think about themselves. This core belief is known as a person's *self-identity*, and a great deal of our self-identity is tied up with what we do and for whom we work. For example, there has been a lot of recent discussion about the merger between Internet giant AOL and media titan Time Warner. When it was announced in 2000, it was valued at $350 billion, and it remains today the largest merger in U.S. business history. By the time that Time Warner spun off AOL in April 2009, billions of dollars had been lost (Ted Turner personally lost a reported $8 billion), and everyone declared the merger a disaster. What went wrong? Clearly, the nature of the Internet business changed, and the bursting of the dot-com bubble was a factor. But most analysts see the real issue as having been that the cultures of the two companies never joined to form one new entity.[57] Few

people were involved in doing the deal, so almost no one felt they had a stake in making it work, and no one at the top of the new company really tried to persuade the people in charge of their brands that they needed to try to make this deal work. The fact that the two cultures were never blended was clearly a critical, if not *the* critical issue in explaining the failure of this giant merger.

The problems at AOL and Time Warner are not unique. Employees involved in mergers and acquisitions must abandon one self-identity and then develop a new one: an employee of the acquiring firm or an employee of the new, merged firm. This is not a trivial manner. When people perceive threats to their self-identity, they actually work to reinforce that self-identity. In this case, an employee in a firm about to be acquired would feel his or her identity threatened and, as a reaction, would develop even stronger feelings of identity with the firm about to be acquired. Then, when employees of the acquiring firm were there, they would be seen as the "enemy"—as the people responsible for threatening the employee's self-identity. Intergroup research shows that these feelings are associated with an "us versus them" mentality that results in competition between groups and even dislike for the other group members.[58]

Of course, this is exactly what the organizations want to avoid. They must move to integrate the two firms into one and create a new self-identity for all employees: employees of the newly merged firm. In other words, for a merger or acquisition to be successful, all the employees should identify with the new firm and therefore work with one another and cooperate to help make the new firm the best it can be—especially because it is even more rewarding to be associated with a really successful firm.

The situation thus far does not sound promising. It would seem as if all mergers and acquisitions are doomed to fail because of identity issues, yet we know that many mergers and acquisitions are successful. Moreover, we believe that in successful cases, HR managers functioned in such a way as to increase the likelihood that the mergers or acquisitions were successful. One critical role the HR manager can play during this process is to serve as the center of communications. As noted previously, there is a great deal of uncertainty for everyone during a merger or acquisition, and the HR manager can work to communicate openly, honestly, and frequently with the employees. Research has shown that realistic information during the merger or acquisition process can reduce stress, increase job satisfaction and commitment, and even reduce turnover, so this communication process can be extremely useful.[59]

In addition, it is important to build employee identification with the new corporate identity. This can be accomplished with simple measures such as distributing shorts or caps with the new corporate logo, or it might involve orientation sessions in which all of the reasons and details of the merger or acquisition are explained. It is easier to do this when the policies and procedures in the new firm are not based solely on the policies and procedures of one party in the merger or acquisition. If some policies are based on one firm's

> "Take risks. Ask big questions. Don't be afraid to make mistakes; if you don't make mistakes, you're not reaching far enough."
>
> —DAVID PACKARD, CO-FOUNDER OF HEWLETT-PACKARD

policies, some on the other firm's policies, and still other policies are blends of the two, then it is easier for employees from both firms to retain good feelings about their former employers and also feel good about the newly created firm.[60]

Through programs such as these, the HR manager can be an important player in the merger and acquisition process and thus can add value to the organization in yet another way. Perhaps the HR manager should never become the final arbiter of which mergers or acquisitions should be pursued, but input from that manager might be useful. For example, input from HR might help decide how much should be paid for an acquisition or what terms should be agreed to for a merger—with an eye toward how easy it would be to implement the merger or acquisition from the perspective of dealing with the problems identified in this chapter. In any event, after a merger or acquisition begins, the close involvement of the HR manager is obviously critical for the ultimate success of the endeavor.

CLOSING CASE
Hard Facts and Half-Truths

Stanford University professors Jeffrey Pfeffer and Bob Sutton, authors of *Hard Facts, Dangerous Half-Truths, and Total Nonsense*, have put out a call for a renewed reliance on rationality in managerial decision-making—an approach that they call evidence-based management (EBM). "Management decisions," they argue, "[should] be based on the best evidence, managers [should] systematically learn from experience, and organizational practices [should] reflect sound principles of thought and analysis." They define evidence-based management as "a commitment to finding and using the best theory and data available at the time to make decisions," but their "Five Principles of Evidence-Based Management" make it clear that EBM means more than just sifting through data and crunching numbers. Here's what they recommend:

1. Face the hard facts and build a culture in which people are encouraged to tell the truth, even if it's unpleasant.

2. Be committed to "fact-based" decision-making—which means being committed to using the best evidence to guide actions.

3. Treat your organization as an unfinished prototype— encourage experimentation and learning by doing.

4. Look for the risks and drawbacks in what people recommend (even the best medicine has side effects).

5. Avoid basing decisions on untested but strongly held beliefs, what you have done in the past, or on uncritical "benchmarking" of winners.

Pfeffer and Sutton are particularly persuasive when they use EBM to question the outcomes of decisions based on "untested but strongly held beliefs" or on "uncritical 'benchmarking.'" Take, for instance, the popular policy of paying high performers significantly more than low performers. Pfeffer

(Continued)

(Closing Case – continued)

and Sutton's research shows that pay-for-performance policies get good results when employees work solo or independently. But it's another matter altogether when it comes to the kind of collaborative teams that make so many organizational decisions today. Under these circumstances, the greater the gap between highest- and lowest-paid executives, the weaker the firm's financial performance. Why? According to

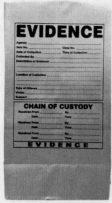

Shawn Hempel/Shutterstock.com

"Management decisions [should] be based on the best evidence, managers [should] systematically learn from experience, and organizational practices [should] reflect sound principles of thought and analysis."

Pfeffer and Sutton, wide disparities in pay often weaken both trust among team members and the social connectivity that contributes to strong, team-based decision-making.

Or consider another increasingly prevalent policy for evaluating and rewarding talent. Pioneered at General Electric by the legendary Jack Welch, the practice of "forced ranking" divides employees into three groups based on performance—the top 20 percent, middle 70 percent, and bottom 10 percent—and terminates those at the bottom. Pfeffer and Sutton found that, according to many HR managers, forced ranking impaired morale and collaboration and ultimately reduced productivity. They also concluded that automatically firing the bottom 10 percent resulted too often in the unnecessary disruption of otherwise effective teamwork. That's how they found out that 73 percent of the errors committed by commercial airline pilots occur on the first day that reconfigured crews work together.[61]

Case Questions

1. Do you think evidence-based management seems like common sense? If so, why wasn't it advocated earlier?
2. Are there circumstances in which evidence-based management might not be the best approach?
3. Could automated evidence-based management ever replace human decision makers? Why or why not?
4. Would you want to work under Jack Welch's system at General Electric? Why or why not?

STUDY TOOLS 6

READY TO STUDY?
In the book, you can:

☐ Rip out the chapter review card at the back of the book for a handy summary of the chapter and key terms.

ONLINE AT CENGAGEBRAIN.COM YOU CAN:

☐ Collect StudyBits while you read and study the chapter.

☐ Quiz yourself on key concepts.

☐ Find videos for further exploration.

☐ Prepare for tests with HR4 Flash Cards as well as those you create.

7 | Recruiting, Selecting, Training, and Developing Employees

epa european pressphoto agency b.v./Alamy Stock Photo

After finishing this chapter go to **PAGE 187** for **STUDY TOOLS**

LEARNING OBJECTIVES

7-1 Describe the recruiting process, including internal and external recruiting and the importance of realistic job previews

7-2 Discuss the steps in the selection process and the basic selection criteria used by most organizations

7-3 Identify and discuss popular selection techniques that organizations use to hire new employees

7-4 Describe the selection decision, including potential selection errors and reliability and validity

7-5 Discuss how organizations train and develop new employees to better enable them to perform effectively

cpa european pressphoto agency
b.v./Alamy Stock Photo

OPENING CASE
The Coaching Carousel

It's called the coaching carousel. Every year when football season ends, coaches get fired, and new coaches get hired. And because every team needs a head coach, there is precisely one job at each team and that job has to be filled—and quickly. Take the National Football League for example. Every team wants to make the playoffs, so that becomes the critical measure of success. The day after the regular season ends is known as Black Monday, and most firings take place that day or a few days after. Of course, not all teams failing to make the playoffs fire their coach. Sometimes a team has a long history of success, and one bad year is considered an aberration. In other cases, a team is in the midst of a planned rebuilding, so expectations are low to begin with.

At the end of the 2015 season, seven head coaches were fired. So where do new head coaches come from? Some come from a pool of former head coaches who were previously fired but are still considered viable head coaching prospects. For example, in early 2016, the Tennessee Titans hired Mike Mularkey as their coach. Mularkey had been fired from two previous head coaching positions but subsequently had been performing well as an assistant coach. Other teams look to the college ranks. The Houston Texans hired Bill O'Brien a year earlier. O'Brien had several years of experience as an NFL assistant and then spent 2 years as head coach at Penn State University. Still other teams look for respected up-and-coming assistant coaches. The Miami Dolphins hired Adam Gase, formerly offensive coach for the Chicago Bears.

The same situation exists at the college level as well, but given the larger number of teams involved, things are even more complicated. Consider just these examples. As noted above, the NFL's Houston Texans hired Bill O'Brien from Penn State University, so Penn State needed a new coach. The school ended up hiring up-and-comer James Franklin, at the time the head coach at Vanderbilt. Vanderbilt then needed a coach and hired Stanford's defensive coordinator. Similarly, after legendary head coach Mack Brown was eased out at the University of Texas, the school hired Charlie Strong, at the time head coach of Louisville. Louisville, in turn, turned to former coach Bobby Petrino as their next head coach.

What do teams look for when hiring a new coach? Most of all, they want someone who can win. Team success is measured by wins and losses, and a coach who consistently fails to win will not be employed very long. The San Francisco 49ers, for example, fired head coach Jim Tomsula after a single season (actually, a rare event). NFL teams want coaches who can win (obviously) and whose offensive and defensive philosophies match those of the team's general manager and owners

"[Bill O'Brien is] … respected and he won in a very tough situation at Penn State. He's been an offensive coordinator in the NFL, a position coach, he's called plays, he's recruited. He's got the right pedigree."

—NFL LEAGUE EXECUTIVE[1]

and fit the team's players. Colleges want winners too but also have to put an emphasis on recruiting skills (to entice talented high school players to join their team) and public relations skills (to schmooze with important alumni and donors).

Some hiring decisions are applauded by the fans and media, while others attract dubious scrutiny. For instance, after the 2013 season, the Tampa Bay Buccaneers fired Greg Schiano and hired Lovie Smith. Smith had spent several years coaching the Chicago Bears, leading them to the playoffs several times and to the Super Bowl once, even being named Coach of the Year in 2005. He was fired in 2012 after a disappointing season and a change in top management. His hiring by Tampa Bay was widely hailed as a great move. Unfortunately, though, things didn't work out, and Smith was among the seven coaches fired after the 2015 season.

In contrast, consider Louisville and Bobby Petrino. Petrino is considered an offensive genius and enjoyed great success at Louisville for 4 years. He was then enticed to take on the NFL's Atlanta Falcons. He quit that job before his first season ended, a move that was criticized for both the timing and the manner in which he departed (informing his players via a printed note in their lockers) and took the head coaching job at the University of Arkansas. He was subsequently fired from that job for having an "inappropriate relationship" with a subordinate and then lying about it to his boss. After spending one season coaching at a lower-tier school, he was rehired by Louisville after Charlie Strong left for Texas. This move was widely criticized, given Petrino's public conduct, and was seen by some critics as a "win at any cost" move.

While we've focused on head football coaching jobs at the professional and college levels here, the coaching carousel also extends across other sports and other levels, as well as the ranks of assistant coaches and coordinators. Basketball, soccer, and baseball coaches and assistant coaches at the high school, college, and professional levels also move on a regular basis. Indeed, it's rare for a coach to have an extended career in the same job.[2]

THINK IT OVER

1. In what ways are recruiting and hiring coaches similar to and different from recruiting and hiring corporate managers?

2. If you were a coach, what would be important to you in considering a new coaching position?

In this chapter, we examine the processes used by organizations to attract, hire, and develop new employees. We begin by examining the goals of recruiting and then discuss some recruiting methods. We next turn to the selection process by which organizations decide which of those persons recruited should be offered employment with the organization. Finally, the chapter ends with a discussion of methods and models of training those new employees so that they can perform their jobs most effectively.

7-1 RECRUITING EMPLOYEES

In Chapter 6, we discussed how organizations reduce the size of their workforces to optimize their form and structure, but we also noted we would discuss organizations desiring to increase their workforce. If an organization is growing, it almost certainly needs to hire new employees. But even when it is stable, it will still likely need to hire new employees to replace those who leave voluntarily and involuntarily. The processes of recruitment and selection are the means whereby organizations acquire new human resources. The two processes work together, and if they are carried out effectively, the organization will have not only the number but also the type of human resources it needs to carry out its overall strategy. These two processes are the focus of this chapter, and we begin with the recruitment process.

Recruiting is the process of developing a pool of qualified applicants who are interested in working for the organization and from which the organization might reasonably select the best individual or individuals to

hire for employment.[3] As we will see, however, and as illustrated in Figure 7.1, recruiting is a two-way street; that is, just as the organization is looking for qualified job applicants, those applicants are also likely to be looking at various potential employment opportunities. Thus, both organizations and individuals have recruiting goals.[4] The best hiring opportunities for organizations and employment opportunities for job seekers emerge when these different goals match.

Both parties in the recruiting process—the organization and the prospective employee—have goals they are trying to accomplish in the recruiting process. The most basic and fundamental goal of an organization's recruiting effort is essentially to fulfill the definition of recruiting: to develop a pool of qualified applicants. This overriding goal, however, also suggests three specific related goals that are important to the recruiting process.

1. The organization wants to optimize the size of the pool of qualified applicants, that is, have enough candidates to be able to have choices but not so many that processing would become overwhelming.

2. The recruiting process should generate a pool of applicants that is both qualified and interested in working for the organization.

3. The process should give prospective applicants an honest and candid assessment of the kinds of jobs and opportunities that the organization can potentially make available to them. (We examine this issue in more detail later when we discuss realistic job previews.)

FIG 7.1 ORGANIZATIONAL AND INDIVIDUAL GOALS IN RECRUITING

Organizational Goals		**Individual Goals**
• Attract a pool of qualified applicants • Keep pool at a manageable size • Provide realistic job previews	← **?** →	• Meet work-related goals • Meet personal goals • Address personal needs

Of course, it is important for the organization to remember that the prospective employee in the recruiting pool also has goals that affect the process. HR managers must never forget that recruiting is a two-way process. As stated previously, just as the organization is seeking qualified applicants who are interested in employment with the firm, so too are individuals likely to be approaching several organizations and trying to entice as many of them as possible to offer employment.[5]

In many cases, a prospective employee's goals are relatively straightforward. Individuals work for several reasons, but the most common are the following:

- Financial income
- Job security
- Promotion opportunities
- Benefits
- Challenging work assignments

In addition to these goals, however, individuals can also have idiosyncratic goals. For example, some people put extra emphasis on the location of a particular job opportunity. They may want to work close to their hometown, close to where they went to school, in a big city, in a small city, near family, near the ocean, or near recreational opportunities.[6]

One fundamental decision that an organization must make as part of its recruiting strategy is whether to focus recruiting efforts internally or externally. As summarized in Table 7.1 and discussed below, both internal and external recruiting have unique advantages and disadvantages.

7-1a Internal Recruiting

Internal recruiting is the process of looking inside the organization for existing qualified employees who might be promoted to higher-level positions. This situation may not seem particularly useful for increasing the size of the workforce, but internal recruiting can play a role even in growth strategies. If an organization can fill higher-level openings with current employees who are ready to move up, it will have to fill lower-level positions from the outside later. These lower-level positions would presumably be easier and less costly to fill. Using this approach in an ideal situation, the organization could fill all of its needs, except those for entry-level jobs, from the inside and then recruit externally for entry-level job openings.

In any event, it is generally important that an organization use internal recruiting as part of its overall planning process because, as noted in Table 7.1, internal recruiting has several advantages over external recruiting. Perhaps the most important of these advantages is employees can see that there is really an opportunity for advancement when a firm relies on internal recruiting. This is likely to serve as a major source of motivation for those employees to perform their jobs as best they can. Employees recruited internally also bring the advantage of familiarity with the company—its heritage, culture, policies and procedures, strategies, and ways of doing business-making transitions to new positions easier. Yet, as shown in Table 7.1, there are also disadvantages when internal recruiting is the only type a firm uses. This can result in stagnation and stifle creativity. It is unlikely that new ideas will be proposed for how to deal with challenges if everyone in the firm has only been familiar with one way of doing things. Finally, internal recruiting creates a ripple effect in the organization. Every time a person is promoted, a new opening must be filled, and a relatively few promotions can sometimes result in a large-scale set of transfers and movements from position to position within the organization. The two most common methods used for internal recruiting are job posting and supervisory recommendations.

JOB POSTING Perhaps the most common method that organizations use for internal recruiting is a process called **job posting**. This is a relatively simple procedure. Vacancies in the organization are publicized through various media such as the company intranet, newsletters, bulletin boards, and/or internal memos. Interested individuals simply file an application with the HR department. Some organizations that rely heavily on internal recruiting go so far as to require that jobs be

TABLE 7.1	ADVANTAGES AND DISADVANTAGES OF INTERNAL AND EXTERNAL RECRUITING	
	Advantages	**Disadvantages**
Internal recruiting	• Increases motivation • Sustains knowledge and culture	• May foster stagnation • May cause a ripple effect
External recruiting	• Brings in new ideas • Avoids the ripple effect	• May hurt motivation • Costs more

Recruiting is the process of developing a pool of qualified applicants who are interested in working for the organization and from which the organization might reasonably select the best individual or individuals to hire.

Internal recruiting is the process of looking inside the organization for existing qualified employees who might be promoted to higher-level positions.

Job posting is a mechanism for internal recruiting in which vacancies in the organization are publicized through various media such as company newsletters, bulletin boards, internal memos, and the firm's intranet.

posted internally before any external recruiting is undertaken. Note that a candidate hired through a job posting could be applying for a promotion or merely for a lateral transfer.

SUPERVISORY RECOMMENDATIONS Another method of internal recruiting is **supervisory recommendations**. In this case, when a new position needs to be filled, a manager solicits nominations or recommendations for the position from supervisors in the organization. These supervisors look at the employees for whom they are responsible, and if any are particularly well suited for the new job opening, the supervisors recommend those individuals to the higher-level manager. It is important, however, that supervisors give equal consideration to all potential candidates in these cases. In a landmark decision, *Rowe* v. *General Motors*, the Supreme Court found General Motors (GM) guilty of discrimination because, under a system in which supervisory recommendations were needed for promotions, supervisors failed to recommend qualified African American candidates as frequently as they recommended white candidates. As a result, almost no African American supervisors were working at most GM facilities at the time of the suit.

We should also point out that, given the large number of layoffs and workforce reductions (from downsizing) in recent years, some potential applicants are somewhere between the classifications of internal and external candidates. Individuals who have been laid off (as opposed to terminated) are usually considered first when openings occur in the organization (and this procedure may be mandated by certain union contracts). These individuals may not be active employees at the time, but they are still considered internal candidates. On the other hand, individuals who actually lost their jobs during downsizing— that is, were officially terminated—are technically no longer employees of the organization and are considered external candidates. Because they had worked for the organization previously, however, they often

share more characteristics in common with internal candidates and might constitute a good source of potential applicants.

7-1b External Recruiting

External recruiting involves looking to sources outside the organization for prospective employees. As noted in Table 7.1, external recruiting has advantages and disadvantages that are directly counter to those of internal recruiting. For example, external recruiting has the advantage of bringing in new ideas, new perspectives, and new ways of doing things. Hence, the organization can enhance its vitality, creativity, and potential ability to innovate by routinely bringing in people from the outside. External recruiting also avoids the ripple effect. In some cases, no internal employees may be able to fill new positions, thereby making external recruiting the only option.

Several years ago, the managers and owners of a small software company in Iowa were frustrated because they could not make the major breakthroughs necessary to fuel growth for their firm. After considerable discussion, they decided that no one inside the firm had the managerial skills to take the company to the next stage in its growth. All current managers were professional engineers, and none really had much managerial experience. Consequently, the firm decided to hire an outsider to run the business. Within a couple of years, he had increased the firm's sales from $750,000 a year to more than $11 million.[7]

On the other hand, external recruiting may result in motivational problems in the organization. Current employees may feel that they have been denied opportunities and that outsiders who are brought into the organization at higher levels may be less qualified than the current employees themselves. External recruiting also tends to be a bit more expensive than internal recruiting because of the advertising and other search processes that must be undertaken.

Many organizations prefer to rely on both internal and external recruiting strategies. This combined approach allows an organization to match the advantages and disadvantages of each particular recruiting effort to its own unique context. For example, during a recent dramatic growth period, Walmart recruited both

Using **supervisory recommendations**, a mechanism for internal recruiting, a manager solicits nominations or recommendations for a position that needs to be filled from supervisors in the organization.

External recruiting is the process of looking to sources outside the organization for prospective employees.

internally and externally. The firm wanted to ensure that current employees had ample promotion opportunities, but it also felt that it needed to hire people at a faster rate than could be accommodated by internal recruitment alone. Thus, each major hiring phase was carefully assessed, and decisions were made in advance about the sources to be used. In some instances, almost all recruiting was done internally, whereas only external recruiting was used in others. In still other cases, the firm looked both inside and outside at the same time for new recruits.

7-1c Methods for External Recruiting

Somewhat different methods are likely to be used by an organization engaged in external recruiting because the organization needs to reach potential applicants from outside the company.

WORD-OF-MOUTH RECRUITING Referrals come to an organization via **word-of-mouth recruiting**. In most cases, the organization simply informs current employees that positions are available and encourages them to refer friends, family members, or neighbors for those jobs.[8] From the organization's perspective, this method is an inexpensive way to generate a large number of applicants. In addition, if we assume that the current employees are satisfactory and that people generally associate with people who are similar to them, then the organization should have a reasonable chance of generating high-quality applicants with this method. If an organization relies on this recruiting technique exclusively, however, problems may arise if the current workforce is almost completely white and male, so that the individuals referred will most likely be primarily white males as well.

ADVERTISEMENTS Advertisements on websites and in newspapers and related publications are also popular methods for external recruiting. Any local newspaper is likely to have help-wanted sections ranging from perhaps a few listings to as many as several pages, sometimes organized by different kinds of job openings such as sales, health care, professional, nonprofessional, technical, and so forth. Depending on the job, these advertisements might be placed in local newspapers or national newspapers such as the *Wall Street Journal*.

Some professional periodicals and publications also have space set aside for help-wanted recruiting ads. This form of advertising tends to be relatively expensive and, perhaps surprisingly, attracts somewhat fewer qualified applicants than do some other recruiting methods. It does enable the organization to cast a wide net, however, in its efforts to publicize its affirmative action programs and to reach every sector of the labor market. By targeting specialized publications that might appeal primarily to members of groups that are underrepresented in the workforce, the organization might also advance its affirmative action goals. On the other hand, restricting advertisements to publications that are not widely available could be considered discriminatory.

EMPLOYMENT AGENCIES Reliance on employment agencies is another common method for external recruiting, but there are different types of employment agencies that serve different purposes. *Public employment agencies* became a formal part of the recruiting process with the passage of the Social Security Act of 1935. This law requires that anyone who is paid unemployment compensation must register that fact with a local state employment office. These state agencies work closely with the U.S. Employment Service to get unemployed individuals off state aid as quickly as possible and back in permanent jobs. Employers register their job openings with the local state employment agency, and the agency collects data (mostly regarding skills, experience, and abilities) from unemployed persons and uses this data to match qualified individuals with available jobs.

Private employment agencies are more likely to serve the white-collar labor market (although some serve specialized niches such as office workers), and they charge a fee for their services. Sometimes this fee is paid by the individual; sometimes it is paid by the organization if it hires an individual referred to it.

> In **word-of-mouth recruiting**, the organization simply informs current employees that positions are available and encourages them to refer friends, family members, or neighbors for those jobs.

In a public employment agency, all potential employee job applicants are currently unemployed, but many employed individuals use the services of private employment agencies in an effort to find other work while maintaining their current jobs. Because private employment agencies are supported by the firms and individuals that use their services, however, they may be able to devote more resources to performing their function.

NAN728/Shutterstock.com

firms may visit many different colleges and universities scattered across the country, or they may choose to visit only regional or local colleges and universities.

An advantage of this method for the organization is that it can specify qualifications such as major, grade point average, work experience, and so forth. It is also a relatively inexpensive method of recruiting because colleges and universities typically provide the facilities, schedule the appointments, and so forth. The organization sends the interviewer to the campus, and that individual sits in the interview room during the course of the day and meets prospective applicants. For students, this job search method is also quite efficient. The student can visit his or her local placement office on a regular basis, be apprised of which companies are coming to interview, and sign up for interviews using whatever methods and protocols the college or university has established.

Finally, *executive search firms* specialize in finding applicants for high-level positions. An individual working for an executive search firm is also known as a **headhunter**. An organization that wants to hire a top-level manager can go to an executive search firm and describe exactly what kind of individual it is looking for. This description, for example, might specify the kind of work experience the organization wants the individual to have, the degree that is necessary, the number of years of experience, and perhaps a salary profile as well. The executive search firm then attempts to locate individuals who fit this profile for the organization. Typically, the search firm screens potential candidates and then presents the organization with a small number of candidates, all of whom are highly qualified and interested. As a result, this is the most expensive method of external recruiting.

Regardless of the type of employment agency involved, if an organization engages the services of an agency that discriminates, the organization will also be held responsible for the discrimination, so it is important to make sure that any employment agency truly offers equal opportunity to all.

COLLEGE PLACEMENT OFFICES Another method of external recruiting is to use the placement offices that most colleges and universities sponsor. Most large organizations visit college campuses every year to interview graduates for jobs within the organization. Large

A **headhunter** is an individual working for an executive search firm who seeks out qualified individuals for higher-level positions.

Microsoft relies heavily on college recruiting in its efforts to bring in new talent every year. The firm has a staff of 22 full-time campus recruiters who visit schools each year. These recruiters conduct half-hour interviews with thousands of prospective employees, selecting about 450 for follow-up visits to company headquarters.

DIGITAL RECRUITING The Internet has affected many human resource management (HRM) activities, but there are few areas where it has had greater impact than on the recruiting function. In fact, many of the techniques discussed previously for external and internal recruiting can be and are being replaced by the Internet. The importance of digital recruiting is hard to overestimate. In 1998, 29 percent of the *Fortune 500* companies generated applicants through their websites, but that rate rose to 88 percent in less than 3 years, and 34 percent of these companies accepted applications only through their websites.[9] And today, all require that applications be submitted online.

Perhaps the most important reason for the growing reliance on digital recruiting is that it is cost effective. It does not cost much to post job openings on online job boards (e.g., Monster .com), which are visited by literally millions of people annually. In addition, many organizations that start their own websites for recruiting find that they can reach potential applicants more easily and use these sites as marketing tools.[10] Thus, exposure is another important reason for the growth of digital recruiting. Not long ago, the effectiveness of digital recruiting was somewhat limited by the number of potential job applicants who had easy access to the Internet, but data now suggests that there are 280 million Internet users in the United States and 3.5 billion Internet users worldwide. In the United States, approximately 74 percent of those with access to the Internet use it to search for jobs.[11] In other countries, this percentage is even greater because applicants do not have access to other information about jobs. Thus, it is not surprising that many organizations report that Internet advertising has resulted in a more diverse group of applicants and job seekers than they had reached using more traditional methods.[12] Finally, digital recruiting saves time. A potential applicant who sees an interesting opening can e-mail questions and answers as well as electronically submit résumés—all in a matter of minutes.

Of course, there are some potential problems associated with digital recruiting as well. Ease of access also means that many people may apply for a job who are not really qualified, and this means more time spent sifting through the résumés of unqualified applicants. In addition, although digital recruiting has the potential to generate a more diverse group of applicants, differences in access to computers and the Internet still exist in the United States. For example, a study by the Department of Labor notes that fewer Hispanic American and African American applicants have regular access to computers; as a result, members of both groups are more likely to rely on more traditional sources of job information.[13] Finally, although digital recruiting can offer a company many advantages, it seems that potential job seekers who visit company websites do

not always come away happy. Many users report that company websites are difficult to navigate or are sloppy, while others complain that it is difficult to apply for a job at the site.[14] It is important for organizations to recognize that, in this electronic age, a company websites may actually be the first point of contact for applicants, and it is important for the firm to make a good impression.

7-1d Internships: A Mixed Model

Although it is easier to think about recruiting having either an internal or external focus, it is possible to take an approach that really combines elements of the two. Many students try to obtain internships that will provide real-world experience, but internships are also quite useful from the organization's perspective. Of course, an internship is a form of temporary employee (discussed in Chapter 6) who can help respond to work demands in the short term. More important, internships can be an important recruiting tool.

The intern is hired, in essence, on approval. In other words, if the organization does not think that the person is someone who will be able to contribute to the organization or that the person is a good fit, then the organization simply allows the internship to end. The intern is not really rejected because he or she has never really applied. On the other hand, if the intern interests the organization, it can offer that person permanent employment. Even if the intern is a student who must

> "Great vision without great people is irrelevant."
>
> —JIM COLLINS, MANAGEMENT EXPERT AND AUTHOR

complete his or her studies, the organization might want to offer a contract that would become effective on graduation.

7-1e Realistic Job Previews

A final topic for discussion concerning external recruiting is the use of the **realistic job preview (RJP)**. In the past, many recruiters were guilty of painting a glowing picture of what a particular job might entail. They made the job sound glamorous, exciting, fun, challenging, and rewarding in different ways. After employees accepted the job, however, they found just the opposite: The job they were hired to fill proved to be boring, tedious, monotonous, and routine. Because their expectations were set so high, and because the reality they faced proved to be so different, they were extremely dissatisfied with their work and consequently were prone to high turnover. These problems can be partly minimized if recruiters paint a more realistic picture of the job.[15] Thus, RJPs were first discussed in the previous chapter as a method of retaining valued employees.

Realistic information about the job can be presented via video, online presentations, or brochures and printed materials. An applicant can also get realistic information by observing people at work on the job in question. Disney, for one, has found that using RJP has greatly improved its recruiting and selection processes. At its vast Disney World complex, the firm has an employment office it calls its *casting center*. Before being interviewed or asked to complete a job application, people who visit the center seeking employment are instructed to watch a short video. The video informs job seekers about the firm's strict appearance guidelines and the difficult and rigorous working conditions. The goal is to provide a candid and realistic introduction to the working conditions at Disney.[16]

How RJPs seem to work is interesting. If applicants are given realistic previews before they make a decision, some potential applicants will be discouraged and withdraw from consideration.[17] But these potential applicants would likely have become dissatisfied if they joined the firm and later learned what the job was really like. At the same time, however, those who know what to expect and still choose to join the organization generally are more successful and more likely to remain with the company. A meta-analysis of several studies of RJPs reported that they are generally associated with higher performance, higher levels of trust in the organization, and lower turnover.[18] Not only do RJPs seem to work, but their effectiveness has been demonstrated with jobs as diverse as bank teller,[19] army recruit,[20] and prison guard.[21]

7-1f Evaluating the Recruitment Process

The final issue to discuss is how an organization might go about evaluating its recruiting efforts. This evaluation requires metrics that a firm might use in that evaluation. Several industry leaders[22] suggest that these metrics should include time to fill a position, vacancy rates, turnover rates, selection ratios, quality of hire, and retention rates. Another, overall metric is the recruitment cost ratio, which includes all the costs associated with a new hire, from advertising through recruiter salaries and to compensation for the new hire, including bonuses. The idea here is to compare these metrics for different recruitment sources to see which are the most effective. For example, an organization might learn that external recruiting using Agency A, results in less time to fill a clerical position, higher retention rates, higher quality hires, and so on when compared to any other agency. This suggests that the organization should focus its recruiting efforts for clerical positions on Agency A in the future. Using these metrics will obviously involve large amounts of data so that this is another area where HR analytics can contribute to decision-making in HRM.

7-2 THE SELECTION PROCESS

After the recruiting process has identified a pool of qualified applicants, it is time to begin the selection process. **Selection** is concerned with identifying the best candidate or candidates for a job from among the pool of qualified applicants developed during the recruiting process.

7-2a Steps in Selection

At a general level, the selection process involves three distinct steps (see Figure 7.2).[23]

1. The first step is gathering information about the members of the pool of qualified recruits (as created by the recruiting process described earlier) regarding the levels of requisite knowledge, skills, and abilities (KSAs) possessed by each applicant. In addition,

A **realistic job preview (RJP)** is an effective technique for ensuring that job seekers understand the actual nature of the jobs available to them.

Selection is concerned with identifying the best candidate or candidates for a job from among the pool of qualified applicants developed during the recruiting process.

FIG 7.2 STEPS IN THE SELECTION PROCESS

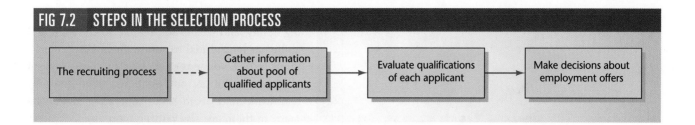

| The recruiting process | - - -> | Gather information about pool of qualified applicants | -> | Evaluate qualifications of each applicant | -> | Make decisions about employment offers |

information is collected about factors such as education and experience, as well as attitudes of the individuals toward work and the impressions of current managers about their likelihood of success.

2. The second step is evaluating the qualifications of each applicant from among the recruiting pool. This evaluation process occurs through the application of explicit or implicit standards to the information gathered in step 1, with the manager assessing how closely the individual fits the desired profile. Such standards could refer to the number of keyboard strokes a person can enter in a minute or a specific personality type. But sometimes applying standards is not so straightforward. For example, if the standard is 10 years of relevant work experience, someone must make the decision about whether a person who exceeds that standard is more qualified than a person who simply meets it, or if these two candidates are to be treated as equal on this dimension because they each meet the standard. We will discuss important implications of decisions such as this one later in the chapter.

3. The third step is making the actual decision about which candidate or candidates will be offered employment with the organization. This decision involves careful assessment of the individuals' qualifications relative to the standards of the job and the extent to which those qualifications best prepare and provide an individual the requisite skills and abilities for the position. In some cases, an organization may need to select a large number of people to hire simultaneously. For example, a firm opening a new factory may be hiring hundreds of operating employees from a pool of thousands of applicants, or a rapidly growing restaurant chain may need to hire dozens of management trainees to assume management positions in new restaurants in a year or two. In both cases, the manager does not necessarily have to make fine gradations between, say, candidate number 11 and candidate number 12. The only decision is determining the extent to which a

candidate is in the set of desirable people to hire or is outside that set because of job-relevant characteristics.

But if the selection decision involves hiring a specific single individual for a specific position in the organization, such as a new director of marketing or a vice president of HR, then one individual must be selected. It is sometimes helpful at this point to rank-order the candidates who are being considered for the job. If the organization does not succeed in hiring its top choice for the job, then decisions will have already been made regarding the relative acceptability of candidate number 2, candidate number 3, and so on. In some cases, if the recruiting process has been handled effectively, the organization may want to hire more than one qualified applicant in the pool. Thus, it may be helpful to develop a backup plan in case the top choice cannot be employed.

Also, we noted earlier that recent approaches to talent management suggest that not all positions are equal. That is, some positions are more critical for competitive advantage and require special efforts. These efforts begin with the selection process. It is essential that an organization hire the best people it can for all positions, but for critical positions, it is vital that they hire the best candidates. Therefore, filling these positions may require more detail in terms of what is expected and may also require additional steps in the decision-making process (e.g., an additional interview with a member of senior management) to make sure that the right person is hired.

7-2b Basic Selection Criteria

What exactly are the bases for evaluating applicants during the selection process? Several possible criteria can be used in the selection decision, and these often differ in terms of how objectively they can be assessed.

EDUCATION AND EXPERIENCE Education and experience are relatively straightforward criteria to assess.

Jirsak/Shutterstock.com

In a selection context, **education** refers to the formal classroom training an individual has received in public or private school and in a college, university, or technical school. Some jobs require high school diplomas; others require advanced degrees. For some jobs, the educational fields (a person's major) are open; in other cases, they must be within a specified area such as mechanical engineering, French, or HRM.

Experience refers to the amount of time the individual may have spent working in either a general capacity or a particular field. Experience is presumably an indicator of an individual's familiarity with work and his or her ability to work, and it is a surrogate measure of a person's competencies as an employee. In some cases, it may be necessary that the individual have a predetermined level of experience in a certain field of study. For example, if a large organization is looking to hire a director of advertising, it will quite likely expect applicants to have substantial experience in the advertising field. In other cases, however, the experience requirement may be more general. Simply having a certain number of years of experience in full-time work activities might be sufficient evidence of an individual's employability. And some entry-level jobs may require no experience at all.

SKILLS AND ABILITIES

The assessment of skills and abilities, on the other hand, is rather mixed in terms of objectivity. It is relatively straightforward to assess someone's typing ability, and it is even possible to measure an ability such as spatial relations (the ability to manipulate three-dimensional objects in one's mind) objectively. But as organizations move toward teamwork and team-based operating systems, many of them are also putting more emphasis on hiring individuals with the skills necessary to function effectively in a group situation.[24] These skills are much more subjective and therefore more difficult to assess accurately.

PERSONAL CHARACTERISTICS Some personal characteristics, which are believed to reflect the applicant's personality, are also difficult to assess objectively. Assessments of characteristics such as friendliness, the ability to deal with others, and perseverance are usually quite subjective and are obtained as part of the interview process (discussed later). More recently, however, a great deal of attention has been paid to assessing applicants in terms of the **big five personality traits**. These traits tend to be more behavioral than cognitive or emotional and so can be assessed in a fairly objective manner. Furthermore, recent research has suggested that they are likely to be more important for job performance than more traditional personality traits.[25] The big five traits are *neuroticism* (disposition to experience states such as anxiety and guilt rather than being better adjusted emotionally), *extraversion* (tendency to be outgoing, sociable, and upbeat), *openness to experience* (tendency to be imaginative and intellectually curious), *agreeableness* (tendency to be altruistic and cooperative), and *conscientiousness* (tendency to be purposeful and dependable and to pay attention to detail).

HIRING FOR "FIT" A rather unique and interesting criterion for selection is referred to as "fit." When a firm decides to hire someone on the basis of fit, it hires that person not because he or she is the most qualified for a specific job, but because she or he is a good fit for the larger organization. Thus, rather than hire someone for a programming position because of his or her computer skills alone, the firm might consider hiring persons whose personal values or personalities align with the organization. Note that the firm likely would not hire an unqualified person simply because of fit, but it would select the person who it thought would fit in best from among a group of reasonably qualified persons. But fit for a specific job is likely to be based on KSAs, and it can probably be assessed rather objectively, whereas organizational fit is likely to be based on values and personality, which are more difficult to

Education refers to the formal classroom training an individual has received in public or private schools and in a college, university, or technical school.

Experience is the amount of time the individual has spent working in either a general capacity or a particular field of study.

The **big five personality traits**—neuroticism, extraversion, openness to experience, agreeableness, and conscientiousness—tend to be more behavioral than cognitive or emotional and are likely to be more important for job performance than more traditional personality traits.

assess objectively.[26] In some cases, the organization might assume that the requisite KSAs can actually be learned after the person has been hired, resulting in even more reliance on selection based on fit. This trend has developed into a growing controversy in selection today. HR managers traditionally believed that they should hire the person with the best set of job-specific skills relative to the work that needed to be performed, but today many argue that the best hires are those who fit into the overall organization based on personal characteristics, values, and so forth.[27]

 7-3 ## POPULAR SELECTION TECHNIQUES

Organizations use different techniques for gathering information that reflects an individual's education and experience, skills and abilities, and personal characteristics.

Most organizations rely on a comprehensive system of multiple selection techniques to ensure that they gather all the relevant data and assess this data rigorously, objectively, and without discrimination. A fundamental requirement of any technique is that it be reliable and valid. Reliability and validity are so important that we devote an entire section to these properties later in this chapter. In this section, we identify and discuss some of the more popular and commonly used selection techniques. Logic may underlie the sequence in which organizations use these techniques, but at the same time, many organizations vary the order to fit their own particular needs, circumstances, and beliefs. Figure 7.3 illustrates one example selection sequence that an organization might use.

7-3a Applications and Background Checks

A first step in most selection systems is to ask applicants to complete an employment application or an application

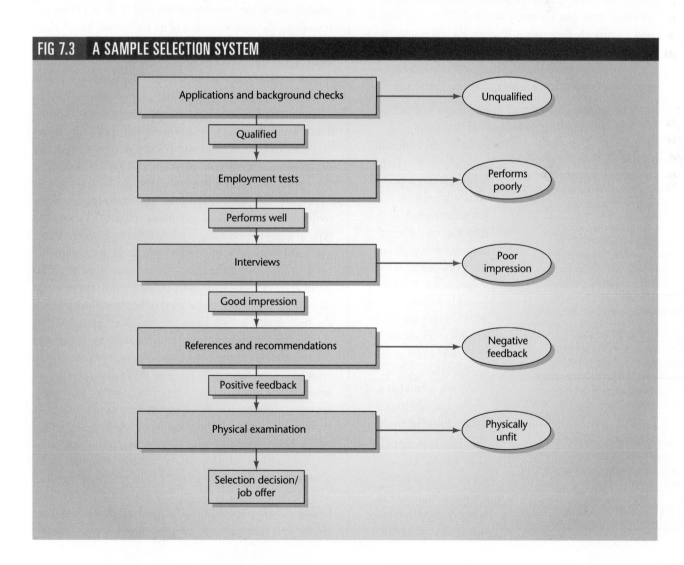

FIG 7.3   A SAMPLE SELECTION SYSTEM

- Applications and background checks → Unqualified
- Qualified
- Employment tests → Performs poorly
- Performs well
- Interviews → Poor impression
- Good impression
- References and recommendations → Negative feedback
- Positive feedback
- Physical examination → Physically unfit
- Selection decision/ job offer

blank. An **employment application** asks individuals for various facts and information pertaining to their personal background. Commonly asked questions include details such as name, educational background, personal career goals, and experience.

Of course, all questions on an employment application must relate to an individual's ability to perform the job. An employment application cannot ask for a person's gender, age, or marital status because these questions have no bearing on that person's ability to perform specific jobs. Such questions could even serve as a basis for an applicant's claims of discrimination on the basis of age or gender. An organization may need this information after someone is hired, but it is illegal to make selection decisions based on these variables, and they should be avoided on application blanks. Figure 7.4 presents an example of an application blank.

Application blanks, when used in typical selection systems, provide a quick and inexpensive mechanism for gathering several kinds of objective information about an individual that can be easily verified. They can also be used to quickly determine if an applicant meets minimum selection criteria (e.g., years of experience).

A number of innovations have extended the usefulness of application blanks, including the following:

1. The so-called **weighted application blank**[28] relies on statistical techniques to determine the relative importance of various personal factors for predicting a person's ability to perform a job effectively. Using information gathered from current high and low performers in the organization, it is often possible to determine whether specific levels of education, experience, and so on gathered on the application blank are related to a person's ability to perform a job effectively.

2. The **biodata application blank** focuses on the same type of information found in a regular application, but it also goes into more complex and detailed assessments about that background.[29] For example, in addition to asking about an applicant's college major, a biodata application might ask questions about which courses the applicant enjoyed most and why a particular field of study was chosen. As with weighted application blanks, responses to these questions are then studied to see if they differentiate between employees who have done well and those who have done poorly on the job. This information is then used to predict the performance of new applicants from their application blanks. Thus, in both cases, the organization is interested in determining if any of the information collected on application blanks can be used to provide direct predictions of performance on the job.

7-3b Employment Tests

Another popular selection technique used by many organizations is an **employment test**,[30] or a device for measuring the characteristics of an individual. These characteristics may include personality, intelligence, or aptitude. Although employment tests are generally traditional question-and-answer exercises that applicants complete on paper or online, the courts consider any device used to make an employment decision, including interviews, to be a test. Typically, though, employment tests per se are either on paper or computer administered. For a paper test, the organization scores the employment test itself or sends it to the agency from which it acquired the test for scoring. For a computer-administered test, the applicant enters answers to questions via keyboard and mouse. Figure 7.5 shows the type of items typically found on various employment tests.

Different types of employment tests are commonly used. Before identifying them, however, we want to distinguish aptitude tests from achievement tests. These terms often refer to how the test is used rather than the nature of the test. Aptitude tests focus on predicting future performance. Achievement tests focus on the mastery of some set of learned skills. For example, keyboarding tests are usually seen as achievement tests because they focus on whether an applicant has basic proficiency or mastery in using a keyboard. Cognitive ability tests are seen as aptitude tests because they focus on the question of whether the person will be able to perform some specific task in the future.

Cognitive ability tests measure mental skills. The applicant is not required to do anything physical, only to demonstrate some type of knowledge. Therefore, knowing how a specific tool is used reflects a cognitive ability, and being able to use the tool is a psychomotor

---

An **employment application** asks individuals for various bits of information pertaining to their personal background.

A **weighted application blank** relies on numerical indexes to determine the relative importance of various personal factors for predicting a person's ability to perform a job effectively.

Biodata application blanks focus on the same type of information that is found in a regular application but go into more complex and detailed assessments about that background.

An **employment test** is a device for measuring the characteristics of an individual such as personality, intelligence, and aptitude.

Cognitive ability tests measure mental skills.

FIG 7.4 **A SAMPLE EMPLOYMENT APPLICATION**

Notes: This application will be considered active for 90 days. If you have not been hired within 90 days of submitting this application, and you wish to be considered for employment, you must complete a new application. Applicants' right to privacy will be observed in accordance with applicable law.

APPLICATION FOR EMPLOYMENT
PLEASE PRINT REQUESTED INFORMATION – USE ONLY BLACK OR BLUE INK

Date of Application   **Date Available**   **Location #** (Company Use Only)

PERSONAL INFORMATION

First Name   **MI**   **Last Name**

Social Security Number (Utah Applicants: Do not provide social security number on this application.)

Current Address

	Street & Apt #	City	ST	Zip Code	County	Telephone No.
1						

Previous Address

If you have not lived at your current address for 7 years, please list all prior residential addresses (most recent first) for the 7 years before the date this application is submitted. (Note: if more space is needed, use page 3 of this application.)

	Street & Apt #	City	ST	Zip Code	County	Dates From: mm/yy To: mm/yy
2						
3						
4						
5						

EMPLOYMENT DESIRED

Position Applying for: _____

Number of hours you would prefer to work each week: _____   Maximum number of hours you can work each week: _____

Number of evenings you can work each week: _____   Number of weekends you can work each month: _____

Are you able to work national holidays: Yes ☐   No ☐

Please list the earliest time and the latest time you are available to work each day:

	Sunday	Monday	Tuesday	Wednesday	Thursday	Friday	Saturday
Earliest Time							
Latest Time							

EDUCATION

School Attended	No. of Years	Name of School	City/State	Graduate? (Yes/No)	Course or College Major
High School					
College					
Other (Name and Type)					

FIG 7.4 **(CONTINUED)**

PRIOR EXPERIENCE

Have you ever been employed by this Corporation or any of its subsidiaries?   Yes ☐   No ☐

If yes, list when and where were you last employed: | List termination date and reason for leaving: | List job position worked:

Do you have any relatives in the employment of this Corporation or any of its subsidiaries?

Yes ☐   No ☐

If Yes:
Provide name: _____ Relationship: _____ Job: _____ Job Location: _____

RECENT EMPLOYERS

List your three most recent employers, beginning with the most recent one. If you have had fewer than three employers, use the remaining space for personal references. Also list any periods of unemployment in the boxes below.

Name and address of former employers, beginning with the most recent

	NOTE: State reasons for and length of inactivity between present application date and last employer	Your Job Title	Employment Dates		Reason for leaving
1	Employer's Name		From	To	
	Address Telephone No.	Supervisor	Rate of Pay		
			Start	Final	
	City State Zip Code				

	NOTE: State reasons for and length of inactivity between employers	Your Job Title	Employment Dates	Reason for leaving
2	Employer's Name		From	To
	Address Telephone No.	Supervisor	Rate of Pay	
			Start	Final
	City State Zip Code			

	NOTE: State reasons for and length of inactivity between employers	Your Job Title	Employment Dates	Reason for leaving
3	Employer's Name		From	To
	Address Telephone No.	Supervisor	Rate of Pay	
			Start	Final
	City State Zip Code			

I authorize the employers listed above to give our company any and all information (except information that cannot be obtained as a matter of law) concerning my previous employment and release all parties from all liability that may result from furnishing the same.

If you were employed under or have otherwise used another name, please provide name(s) _____

ADDITIONAL INQUIRIES

To assist the Company in properly placing you if hired, please list any special skills, ability to speak/read a foreign language, training, licenses, certifications, or degrees that qualify you for the position for which you are applying. (Exclude all information that indicates your membership in any of the protected groups listed at the top of page 1 of this application.) Check the applicable response:

_____

If hired, can you furnish proof that you meet your state's minimum work age requirement?   Yes ☐   No ☐

If hired, can you furnish proof that you are legally entitled to work in the United States?   Yes ☐   No ☐

Answer the following , only if the position for which you are applying requires driving:

Are you licensed to drive a car?   Yes ☐   No ☐

If yes, which state(s)? _____

BEFORE answering the following questions, please refer to the instructions at the top of the next page if you are applying for a position in California, Connecticut, Georgia, Hawaii, Massachusetts, Nevada, or New York.

Have you been convicted of a crime within the past seven (7) years (answer "no" for expunged and sealed records, arrests, and minor traffic offenses)?   Yes ☐   No ☐

If yes, provide details: _____

(This information will be kept confidential. A conviction will not automatically bar employment but will be considered as it relates to the applicant's suitability for the job in question.)

FIG 7.5   SAMPLE ITEMS FROM AN EMPLOYMENT TEST

1. Mathematical Skills Tests:
   If an item at a store has a list price of $24.00 and has been reduced 15% for a sale, what is the sale price of the item?

2. Clerical Skills Tests:
   For each of the pairs below, indicate if the two entries are EXACTLY the same (S) or different (D)

6482 Park Avenue	_____	6482 Park Place
77654832	_____	77645832
James McCarthy	_____	James MacCarthy

3. Cognitive Reasoning (verbal reasoning)
   FACTS:
   Joan is a widow
   Mary works for Company A
   Joan's only child is a girl
   Company B makes auto parts
   Company B employs no women

   CONCLUSIONS:

Joan does not work for Company B	TRUE	FALSE	CANNOT TELL
Joan's son is ill	TRUE	FALSE	CANNOT TELL
Joan works for Company C	TRUE	FALSE	CANNOT TELL
Joan has never been married	TRUE	FALSE	CANNOT TELL
Joan inspects auto parts	TRUE	FALSE	CANNOT TELL

4. Cognitive Reasoning Tests (analogies):
   Tournament is to golf as regatta is to

   a. Racing
   b. Boating
   c. Boxing
   d. None of the above

Source: Minnesota Paper Form Board Test, Revised. Copyright © 1995 NCS Pearson, Inc. Reproduced with permission. All rights reserved. Minnesota Clerical Test. Copyright © 1979 NCS Pearson, Inc. Reproduced with permission. All rights reserved. Bennett Mechanical Comprehension Test (BMCT). Copyright © 1942, 1967-1970, 1980-1981 NCS Pearson, Inc. Reproduced with permission. All rights reserved.

ability (which we discuss later). Intelligence is an extremely important cognitive ability. General intelligence, or *g*, refers to reasoning or problem-solving skills, but it is typically measured in terms of the information one learns in school. The Scholastic Aptitude Test (SAT) is a test of general intelligence. Scores on these tests can be expressed in terms of intelligence quotient (IQ). The way these quotients are computed is beyond the scope of this discussion, but it reflects performance on a test relative to other people of the same age.

Two important facts make the use of intelligence tests in selection controversial. First, IQ is related to performance on a wide variety of jobs because more intelligent people perform better.[31] This feature makes the use of intelligence tests in selection procedures popular and is consistent with the ideas discussed earlier about

> **Bias in employment test construction and fundamental cultural differences can result in different frames of reference and lead to disparate impact.**

the value of a more educated workforce. The second fact is that, on average, African Americans tend to score lower on these tests than do white Americans. Therefore, using intelligence tests as selection criteria will likely result in disparate impact. Many explanations have been offered about why these differences exist and what they should mean for selection.[32] Among the most common explanations are bias in test construction and fundamental cultural differences that result in different frames of reference. The key point vis-à-vis our discussion is simply that intelligence tests are potentially useful but controversial tests of a special cognitive ability.

Other cognitive abilities include vocabulary and reading comprehension (verbal ability) and mathematics (quantitative ability), clerical ability (such as the ability to put names in alphabetical order and to recognize when two names are alike or different from each other), and spatial relations (defined earlier). These cognitive abilities are important for performance on a wide variety of jobs, and they are widely used in selection settings. As noted earlier, auto manufacturers are seeking to improve the general intelligence of their workers. Ford and Chrysler both now rely on cognitive ability tests to assess basic reading and mathematical abilities.

Psychomotor ability tests measure physical abilities such as strength, eye–hand coordination, and manual dexterity. These abilities can be practiced and perfected, and they are usually measured by some type of performance test. For example, the O'Connor Tweezer Dexterity Test requires an applicant to pick up and move small parts with a pair of tweezers (eye–finger coordination). (The popular children's game Operation requires the same essential skills as those tapped by this test.) Psychomotor tests are popular because they apparently measure what is important for performance on the job (HR experts say that these tests have high "face validity"). In addition, they often measure skills that are important for jobs (e.g., eye–hand coordination is important for any job requiring someone to drive a vehicle), and little evidence of disparate impact occurs when they are used.

Personality tests measure traits, or tendencies to act, that are relatively unchanging in a person. Some tests are designed to measure a wide spectrum of personality traits or dimensions; as noted earlier, however, measures of the big five personality dimensions have become extremely popular in recent years and seem useful for predicting who will do well on jobs. Personality can be measured in two ways: self-report inventories and projective techniques.

iStockphoto.com/Devonyu

1. A **self-report inventory** is a paper-and-pencil measure in which an applicant responds to a series of statements that might or might not apply to that applicant. Some of these inventories such as the Minnesota Multiphasic Personality Inventory (MMPI) focus on "abnormal" personality traits such as schizophrenia, paranoia, and psychopathology. Others, such as the California Personality Index (CPI), focus on "normal" personality traits such as introversion versus extraversion, dominance, and masculinity versus femininity. Most attention these days, however, is focused on measures of the big five personality variables so that instruments such as the Personnel Characteristics Inventory[33] are becoming very popular.

2. The other type of personality measure is known as a **projective technique**. This approach involves showing an individual an ambiguous stimulus such as an inkblot or a fuzzy picture and then asking what he or she "sees." Because there is nothing representative to see, whatever the applicant reports is presumed to reflect his or her personality. The best-known projective technique is the Rorschach Inkblot Test, which requires trained clinicians to interpret the results.

Psychomotor ability tests measure physical abilities such as strength, eye–hand coordination, and manual dexterity.

Personality tests measure traits, or tendencies to act, that are relatively unchanging in a person.

A **self-report inventory** is a paper-and-pencil measure in which an applicant responds to a series of statements that might or might not apply to him or her.

The **projective technique** involves showing an individual an ambiguous stimulus, such as an inkblot or a fuzzy picture, and then asking what he or she "sees."

Personality tests are somewhat controversial. Some critics believe they can lead to legal problems,[34] whereas others disagree on whether cognitive ability tests (especially intelligence tests) or personality tests provide the most useful information for selection decisions.[35] Regardless of the merits of these arguments, however, both personality and cognitive ability remain popular criteria in selection techniques, as do all employment tests in general.[36]

A somewhat different but related approach to testing prospective employees is the use of an integrity test. Integrity tests attempt to assess an applicant's moral character and honesty. Most of these tests are fairly straightforward and include questions such as "Do you think most people would cheat if they thought they could get away with it?" and "Have you ever taken anything that didn't belong to you at work?" Other tests are less obvious and are based more on personality measures. The use of integrity tests is growing dramatically, with several million administered annually in the United States.[37] The likelihood is that the number will continue to increase as the cost of employee theft rises.[38] Despite their popularity, however, important issues are involved with their use in selection settings. First, most of the evidence about their accuracy has been supplied by the publishers of the tests, which raises the possibility of a conflict of interest. Second, these tests may do a good job of identifying potential "thieves," but many other individuals not identified by the tests steal and simply do not get caught. Finally, some applicants find these tests invasive and respond negatively to them.[39]

7-3c Work Simulations

Work simulations (sometimes referred to as work samples) require an applicant to perform tasks or job-related activities that simulate or represent the actual work for which the person is being considered. For example, suppose an organization needs to hire a new data-entry specialist. The organization has determined that the data-entry specialist must be proficient with Microsoft Office software and be capable of keyboarding 75 words a minute. A relatively easy method for assessing a candidate's qualifications, then, is to seat the individual at a computer, ask him or her to perform various data-entry tasks and activities using Microsoft Office, and then keyboard a letter or document to measure how quickly the person can keyboard. Other jobs for which work simulations are appropriate might be machinist jobs in which an individual can work on a machine under close supervision, a driving test for taxi drivers or school-bus drivers, and an audition for a performing-arts organization such as a musical group. In-basket exercises, which consist of collections of hypothetical memos, letters, and notes that require prioritization and responses, are sometimes used in management simulations.

7-3d Personal Interviews

Although tests are popular, the most widely used selection technique in most organizations is the employment interview. Interviews have traditionally been defined as face-to-face conversations between prospective job applicants and representatives of the organization.[40] But in our digital age, employment interviews are not always technically face to face. Instead, many are done using tools such as Skype, which make it possible to conduct interviews without needing the two participants in the same location. As organizations recruit globally to a greater extent, this ability becomes increasingly important. These new tools also pose new issues for interviewers, which we will discuss below.

In any case, three different types of interviews are commonly encountered.

In a structured employment interview, the interviewer works from a list of standard questions that are presented to every candidate, by every interviewer. If the questions are based on a careful study of the job (as they should be), they will be more pertinent than those that many interviewers would generate on their own. Furthermore, it is possible to generate potential answers for these questions, and the interviewer can assign overall grades based on a scoring key.

In the semistructured employment interview, major or key questions are decided in advance and provided for each interviewer, but the interviewer is also given the prerogative to ask follow-up questions to probe the interviewee's specific answers. For example, a popular strategy used in some firms today, especially high-tech firms, is to ask challenging and unusual

Integrity tests attempt to assess an applicant's moral character and honesty.

Work simulations (or **work samples**) involve asking the prospective employee to perform tasks or job-related activities that simulate or represent the actual work for which the person is being considered.

In-basket exercises are special forms of work simulations for prospective managers. They consist of collections of hypothetical memos, letters, and notes that require responses.

In the **structured employment interview** the interviewer either prepares or receives from others a list of standard questions to be asked during the interview. All interviewers ask the same questions of each candidate to achieve consistency across interviews.

A **semistructured employment interview** involves advance preparation of major or key questions that all applicants will be asked. However, the interviewer is also given the prerogative to ask additional follow-up questions to probe the interviewee's specific answers.

questions designed to assess creativity and insight. For example, Microsoft interviewers sometimes ask applicants, "Why are manhole covers round?" This question has four different, relatively correct answers, each of which allows the interviewer to probe more in different areas.[41]

Finally, there are no predetermined questions in the **unstructured employment interview**. The interviewer may have a general idea about what she or he wants to learn about the job applicant, but the interview is more spontaneous, more wide ranging in its focus, and more likely to cover a variety of topics.

In addition to these basic types, another form of interview has been gaining popularity. A **situational interview** asks the applicant questions about a specific situation to see how he or she would react. For example, an interviewer might ask the applicant something like:

- Think back to a situation when a personal conflict between a supervisor and a subordinate was interfering with the work of both parties. How did you deal with this conflict? Was the problem resolved?

In other cases, rather than ask about something that has already happened, the interviewer might ask the applicant to imagine a situation that has not yet occurred. In such cases, the interviewer might ask something like:

- Suppose you had a subordinate who you knew had the abilities to perform his or her job but who simply chose not to exert any effort on the job. How would you address this problem? What kinds of approaches might you try?

Research results indicate that situational interviews are better predictors of future job performance than are more traditional interviews.[42] They also change the focus of the interview more explicitly from a KSA approach to a job-fit approach.

Interviewers generally prefer unstructured interviews because they believe these interviews allow them to gather richer information and provide the freedom to make employment decisions on their own. But evidence suggests that structured interviews are much better predictors of subsequent job performance (i.e., they are more valid or job related) than are unstructured interviews, and situational interviews are even better at predicting future job performance.[43] None of them do as well predicting future performance as some paper-and-pencil tests, but only interviews are effective at assessing KSAs such as interpersonal skills, and interviews are generally effective at allowing organizations to decide who fits best.

For these and other reasons, interviews will continue to be a popular means for making selection decisions. Note, however, that the Supreme Court, in *Watson v. Forth Worth Bank & Trust*, ruled that interviews used for making selection decisions had the same requirements concerning demonstrating job relatedness as did any other selection technique.[44] As we noted earlier, however, it is more difficult to establish the job relatedness of interviews, partly because of the prevalence of interview errors.

1. Interviewers who make the **first-impression error** tend to make a decision early in the interview process.[45] For example, the candidate being interviewed might arrive a minute or two late or might have a few awkward moments at the beginning of the interview. Such events, in turn, may cause the interviewer to make a negative judgment about that individual, even though later evidence in the interview may have been more positive.

2. The **contrast error** occurs when the interviewer is unduly influenced by other people who have been interviewed. For example, suppose an interviewer meets with one candidate who is extremely good or extremely bad. The next person interviewed may suffer or benefit by the contrast with this person.

An **unstructured employment interview** involves relatively little advance preparation. The interviewer may have a general idea about what she or he wants to learn about the job applicant but has few or no advance questions that are formally constructed.

The **situational interview** is a type of interview, growing in popularity, in which the interviewer asks the applicant questions about a specific situation to see how the applicant reacts.

A **first-impression error** occurs when an interviewer makes a decision too early in the interview process. This error may significantly affect a decision even when subsequent information indicates the first impression may have been wrong.

A **contrast error** occurs when the interviewer is unduly influenced by other people who have been interviewed. For example, suppose an interviewer meets with one candidate who is extremely good or extremely bad. The next person interviewed may suffer or benefit by the contrast with this person.

3. **Similarity errors**, on the other hand, occur when the interviewer is unduly influenced by the fact that the interviewee is similar to the interviewer in one or more important ways. For example, an interviewer might be biased in favor of someone because he or she is from the same hometown or attended the same university.

4. Another type of error interviewers can make is that of **nonrelevancy**. For example, the interviewer may be influenced by information that is irrelevant to the job, such as dress, appearance, or posture.

5. A final type of error that is common in interview situations has to do with the interviewer's knowledge of the job. Some organizations do not pay adequate attention to selecting appropriate interviewers. They may select employees to interview candidates for a particular job even though the interviewers know little or nothing about that job. Thus, the interviewer may base her or his assessment of the individual's abilities to perform the job on incomplete or inaccurate assessments of the nature of that job.

These problems exist in all interviews to a greater or lesser extent. Their effects can be minimized, however, with proper training of interviewers. Experience itself is not a good substitute for training. This training should focus on the occurrence of the problems outlined above, making the interviewer aware of what he or she says and does. In addition, the training should provide interviewers with the means to replace behaviors that lead to errors with behaviors more likely to lead to their deciding on the best person for the job.

7-3e Other Selection Techniques

Application blanks, tests, and interviews are part of most selection systems, but these techniques are often enhanced by several other techniques that are part of the selection process.

REFERENCES AND RECOMMENDATIONS One of these other techniques is the use of references and recommendations. The job applicant is usually asked to provide either letters of recommendation or the names and addresses of individuals who may be contacted to write such letters. Presumably, the organization can use this information as a basis for assessing a person's past experiences and work history. References and recommendations, however, are often of little real value. For instance, if the applicant selects the people to write recommendations (which is standard practice), he or she is likely to pick people who will write positive letters. Thus, the organization must be somewhat skeptical about a set of glowing recommendation letters that a job applicant submits for consideration.

There is also a growing concern about legal liability in the preparation of recommendation letters. Job applicants have sued people who wrote negative letters of recommendation that were, in turn, the bases for the individuals not being offered employment. Organizations themselves have sued people who wrote favorable recommendations for job candidates who were then found to be highly unsuitable. As a result of these legal concerns, many individuals have begun to take the position that they will provide only objective information about a job candidate as part of a reference letter. Thus, they might be willing to verify dates of employment, salary, history, job title, and so forth, but unwilling to provide any assessment regarding the person's performance, capabilities, or the likelihood for success in a new setting.[46]

ASSESSMENT CENTERS Another selection technique that is used widely, but only for the selection of managers, is the assessment center.[47] An assessment center is not a physical location but is instead an approach to selecting managers based on measuring and evaluating their ability to perform critical work behaviors. Individuals participating in an assessment center are likely to be either current managers who are being considered for promotion to higher levels or in a pool of external recruits such as upcoming college graduates whom the firm is considering hiring for management positions.

A **similarity error** occurs when the interviewer is unduly influenced by the fact that the interviewee is similar to the interviewer in one or more important ways. As a result of the perception of similarity, the interviewer may be more favorably disposed toward the candidate than the candidate's credentials warrant.

Nonrelevancy is a type of error that occurs when an interviewer is influenced by information that is not relevant to an individual's ability to perform the job.

ehammer/Shutterstock.com

> **Almost all of the 100 best companies to work for in America (as determined by *Fortune* magazine), ranging from Southwest Airlines to The Container Store, rely heavily on multiple predictors when making hiring decisions.**

The individuals to be assessed are brought together in a single place such as the company's training headquarters or perhaps a conference facility at a hotel. While there, they undergo a series of tests, exercises, and feedback sessions. A normal assessment-center schedule lasts 2–3 days and involves 10–15 individuals at any one time. During the assessment center, these individuals may undergo experiential exercises; group decision-making tasks; case analyses; individual employment tests, such as personality inventories and so forth; role-playing exercises; and other methods for assessing their potential skills and abilities. Current managers oversee the assessment and serve as evaluators. At the conclusion of the assessment center, each evaluator provides an in-depth evaluation of each attendee and makes an overall evaluation about the person's suitability for promotion.

AT&T was one of the first companies in the United States to use the assessment-center concept, and since 1956, more than 200,000 of its employees have attended various assessment centers. AT&T's evaluation of its assessment centers indicates that this method for selecting managers is fairly effective in differentiating between those who are more and those who are less likely to be successful in the organization. This suggests that assessment centers may be quite useful, but there are some disadvantages as well. The most critical is that assessment centers are rather expensive to run, especially when we consider the lost productivity of both the candidates and the assessors.[48]

 ## 7-4 THE SELECTION DECISION

The final step in the selection process is deciding whom to hire. If there is only one position to fill, the decision is relatively easy: The organization can simply hire the highest-ranked candidate. Likewise, if there is a need to hire dozens of employees for similar kinds of positions, the selection decision may simply consist of choosing where to draw the line between those who qualify for employment and those who do not.

7-4a Multiple Indicators

Because every selection technique has its limitations, most organizations actually rely on several selection techniques and, in fact, may use all or most of the selection techniques discussed earlier. Hence, a person who applies for a job may be subjected to a preliminary screening interview to make sure that she meets the minimum qualifications necessary for the job. Then she may have to complete an application and be subjected to background checks, followed by employment tests, work simulations, or both. For example, almost all of the 100 best companies to work for in the United States (as determined by *Fortune* magazine), ranging from Southwest Airlines to The Container Store, rely heavily on multiple predictors when making hiring decisions.[49]

By using multiple approaches, the organization is able to counterbalance the measurement error in one selection technique against another, and it is also able to base decisions on the basis of more complete information. This fact can complicate matters, however. The organization must decide if a candidate must pass some minimum requirement on every selection technique (i.e., "multiple hurdles"), or if a high score in one area can compensate for a lower score somewhere else (i.e., a compensatory model). Thus, when an organization uses multiple approaches, it is not always clear who the "best" candidate really is.

The hiring decision may also be complicated by the fact that the person hired may not be the one who is ranked first on the selection criteria. As noted earlier, an organization might select a person who has "acceptable" levels of the requisite KSAs but who is a better "fit" with the culture and style of the organization. Furthermore, it is fairly common for organizations to cluster applicants who differ somewhat in terms of KSAs but not enough to be critical. Thus, the organization can use any decision rules it wants to select among the people in such a cluster without sacrificing performance on the job. This procedure, known as *banding*, allows an organization to select an applicant, for example, from some underrepresented group in the organization while still ensuring high performance standards. A variation on this approach can also be used to ensure that candidates selected because they fit can also perform the jobs in question. Finally, regardless of what step is used as the initial selection screen (especially if it is a telephone interview, as discussed in Contemporary Issues in HR), organizations typically used multiple follow-up procedures to verify a candidate's job worthiness before making a final offer.

HR analytics are making the selection process even more complicated by considering even more metrics. Perhaps the most famous example of this process came, first with the book (and movie) *Moneyball* and then with the book *The Numbers Game*, dealing with baseball and soccer, respectively.[50] In these examples, the authors noted that traditional statistics concerning players were not telling enough of the story. For example, in baseball, it was not simply batting averages that mattered, but hitting with men on base and in clutch positions. This, of course, involved huge amounts of data, but the Oakland Athletics were able to win a World Series with a low budget by acquiring players with the "right" set of skills. In a similar fashion, the soccer book indicates that not giving up goals is actually more important than scoring goals and that the emphasis should be placed on defensive players, rather than offensive players if a team wants to win. Therefore, by identifying and collecting metrics related to sales, productivity, absenteeism, or a wide variety of other outcomes, and then utilizing those data, an organization can be much more effective in their hiring decisions.

7-4b Selection Errors

No selection system is perfect, and an organization will always make at least an occasional selection error and hire the wrong person. Actually, two basic types of selection errors can be made: **false positives** and **false negatives**. In each case, the decision maker examines the information available, predicts whether the applicant will ultimately succeed or fail on the job, and then decides to hire or reject (not hire) the person on that basis. In each case, some of the predictions are correct, and others are incorrect; these situations are illustrated in Figure 7.6.

The figure shows that some of the people who are predicted to be successful and are subsequently hired will in fact succeed. These are "hits" (shown in quadrant II) because the right decision was made. The bottom-left quadrant (quadrant III) also shows hits. These people are rejected; if they were hired, they would fail. But the other two quadrants illustrate the two types of selection errors. Quadrant I represents the false positives: the applicants who are predicted to be successful and who are therefore hired, but who ultimately fail. Quadrant IV represents the false negatives: the applicants who are predicted to fail and so are not hired. If they had been hired, however, they would have been successful.

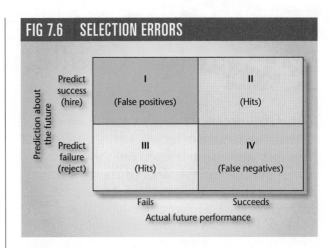

FIG 7.6 SELECTION ERRORS

It would seem obvious that selection systems which minimize selection errors will be more effective for the organization, but it is not possible to minimize both types of errors at the same time, so decisions must be made concerning which type of decision is more costly for the organization. Specifically, it is possible to minimize the number of poor performers that are hired by using more rigorous tests or more challenging interviews to make selection decisions; however, this will also result in fewer people, overall, being hired, and the organization will miss opportunities by rejecting people who could have done the job and been successful. Again, it depends on which error the organization sees as more costly. The information in Figure 7.6 also provides some insight into the issue of *test validity*, discussed more fully in the next section. If a test is valid, then there should be many more "hits" than errors. As noted, there are trade-offs between the types of errors we can make, but a test cannot be valid unless it predicts subsequent success more often than it misses.

7-4c Reliability and Validity

Reliability and validity are important concepts for any psychological type of measurement, and they are especially important for establishing the "job relatedness" of a selection technique. Hence, the selection decision must rely on measures and indicators that are both reliable and valid. Any organization that does not have information about the reliability and validity of its selection techniques is exposed to charges of discrimination, as described in Chapter 2. Specifically, if there is evidence of disparate impact,

False positives are applicants who are predicted to be successful and are hired but who ultimately fail.

False negatives are applicants who are predicted to fail and are not hired, but if they had been hired would have been successful.

Contemporary Challenges in HR

The Converse of In-Person Communication

News flash: *Interviews are stressful* with the uncomfortable dress clothes, the need to make an instant good impression, and the unexpected questions. Surely phone interviews are easier, right? Wrong. A job interview is a job interview, and interviews conducted on the phone pose all the challenges of a face-to-face interview—and then some. You need to take phone interviewing seriously because today, many corporations use them to prescreen applicants and, more importantly, because some HR departments rely on phone interviews exclusively. So, if you get invited to a telephone interview, here are a few tips to remember:

> "I'm not looking to be sold. [I want] to get an accurate view of your experience."
>
> —MATT ABERHAM, TELEPHONE RECRUITER FOR MICROSOFT [51]

- *Be flexible.* When scheduling the call be aware of both your time constraints and those of the interviewer.

- *Prepare for the interview.* Do your homework in advance, and make notes. Know as much as possible about the organization and the job for which you are interviewing.

- *Be positive.* Talk about the positive aspects of your present job and what you're looking forward to in a new one.

- *Know what you're talking about and be specific.* In other words, hold the interviewer's interest by taking charge of context cues. "Because [interviewers] don't have an image of your face to set you apart from others," says one job counselor, "you need to draw pictures with your words." Back up general statements with good examples; people prefer good (economical) stories to dissertations, and they get a better impression of what you've done in your work life.

- *Refer to your notes.* Don't be embarrassed about asking to look at your notes. It shows confidence and preparation to ask to refer to notes.

- *Take the initiative.* If there's something that you feel it's important to talk about but that doesn't come up, bring it up. Don't waste any opportunity to sell yourself.

- *Know when a topic has been covered (and when the conversation is over).* Don't be tempted to fill in silences by simply continuing to talk.

Let's also review a few things to avoid. Matt Aberham, who interviews would-be program managers and engineers for Microsoft's Online Services Business, offers the following list of five good ways to avoid failing a telephone interview (at least one that he's in charge of):

- *Keep track of the time.* Because most interviews are slated for 30–45 minutes, there's time to cover several topics thoroughly and a couple in fairly deep detail. But no matter what you're talking about, be conscious of how long you've been talking about it. Err on the side of conciseness—if the interviewer wants to know more, he or she will be sure to let you know.

- *Answer the question instead of trying to sell yourself.* Don't be afraid to discuss areas where you need (and want) further development. "I'm not looking to be sold," says Aberham. "[I want] to get an accurate view of your experience."

- *Talk about "me," not "we."* Don't get into the habit of saying "we" instead of "I" throughout the interview unless you're trying to show how you *led* a group in accomplishing its goals. Take "ownership" of what *you* did. "Showing ownership," explains Aberham, "helps me figure out if . . . your contributions are appropriate for the work we're thinking of having you do."

- *Be concrete instead of abstract.* Don't give a hypothetical answer to a specific question. "The quickest way to fail a 'Tell-me-about-a-time-when . . .' question," advises Aberham, "is to give me a 'Here's-what-I-would-do-in-that-situation . . .' answer. . . . If [I ask you] to describe a situation you've never handled, let me know, and I'll pick a different question."

- *Don't ask "How'd I do?"* Interviewers usually don't mind giving you some feedback about the match between your skills and experiences and the employer's needs, but they're rarely ready at the end of a phone interview to tell you what they're going to do next about you. And Aberham particularly doesn't like it when something like, "How'd I do?" is the only question you have for him.[52]

iStockphoto.com/Sharon Dominick

THINK IT OVER

1. As a job seeker, would you prefer a telephone interview or a face-to-face interview? Why?

2. The preceding advice is directed at the job seeker. What advice might be useful for the person conducting the telephone interview?

the organization must prove it is not discriminating by demonstrating that the selection technique is job related. In practice, this means demonstrating that the selection technique is a valid predictor of performance on the job. But even outside the United States, in countries where there might be no civil rights legislation, it is important for firms to pay attention to issues of reliability and validity. As we discussed and illustrated in Figure 7.6, if the selection techniques result in too many errors, then it is not helping the organization and is probably not worth the cost, regardless of legal requirements.

RELIABILITY Reliability refers to the consistency of a particular selection device. Specifically, it means that the selection device measures whatever it is supposed to measure, without random error. Systematic error may be present, though, so reliability is not the same as accuracy. For example, if your true weight remained constant across 3 days at precisely 135 pounds, but your bathroom scale indicated you weighed 137 pounds one day, 134 the next day, and 135 pounds, the third day, you would have an unreliable scale. It is unreliable not because the scale is usually not accurate, but because the amount and direction of error are random—the error is +2 pounds on the first day, −1 pound on the second day, and 0 on the third day. If the scale indicated your weight was 2 pounds more than it actually was every single day, your scale would still be inaccurate, but now it would be reliable—it is always off by 2 pounds in the same direction. You could always learn your true weight by simply subtracting 2 pounds from the weight indicated on your scale.

No selection technique used today is perfectly reliable. Every one of them is prone to some degree of random error,

but most professionally developed tests and selection devices have sufficient reliability to make any results obtained with their use interpretable. In other words, in the selection context, most measures are reliable enough that we can be sure that if Mary scores higher on math test than John, Mary is better at math than John. We would be in a better position to determine how much better Mary is, the more reliable the test. Logically, if most of the differences in scores on a test resulted from random error (i.e., the test is not reliable), it cannot be valid because it obviously does not measure what it is supposed to measure—unless it was designed to measure random error!

The fact that a test is relatively free of random error should also indicate that the test can produce consistent scores. There are different ways of assessing reliability, depending on whether we are concerned with scores that are consistent over time (test–retest reliability); across different forms of the same test (alternate-forms reliability), as with different forms of the SAT or Graduate Management Admission Test (GMAT); or consistent across all the different items of the same test (internal consistency reliability—i.e., all the items on the test are measuring the same thing). We discuss test reliability because reliability is a necessary but not sufficient condition for test validity.

VALIDITY Validity refers to the extent to which a measure or indicator is in fact a real reflection of what it is assumed to be. There

> **Reliability** is the consistency of a particular selection device—that is, it measures whatever it is supposed to measure without random error; this is not the same as accuracy.
>
> **Test validity** means that scores on a test are related to performance on a job. This must be determined empirically, and it is critical to defending against charges of discrimination in hiring.

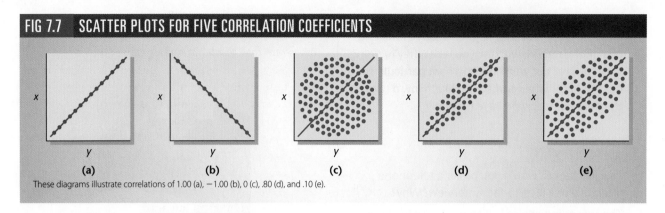

FIG 7.7   SCATTER PLOTS FOR FIVE CORRELATION COEFFICIENTS

x	x	x	x	x
y	y	y	y	y
(a)	**(b)**	**(c)**	**(d)**	**(e)**

These diagrams illustrate correlations of 1.00 (a), −1.00 (b), 0 (c), .80 (d), and .10 (e).

are actually different forms of test validity, although one is far more important than the others in a selection setting. Therefore, we will focus on what is known as *criterion-related validity*. The other two—*content validity* and *construct validity*—are less relevant, although they can be helpful at times in selection settings.

Criterion-related validity refers to the extent to which a particular selection technique can accurately predict one or more elements of performance. Criterion-related validity is most typically demonstrated by establishing a correlation between a test or measured performance in a simulated work environment with measures of actual on-the-job performance. In this approach, the test or performance measure represents a predictor value variable, and the actual performance score itself is the criterion (there can be other criteria of interest in selection settings such as retention rates, but performance is the most commonly used). If this correlation is meaningful (i.e., statistically significant), then a relationship exists between test scores and performance, and the test is job related.

Different relationships, or correlations, are illustrated in Figure 7.7. The first diagram in the figure, labeled (a), illustrates a perfect positive correlation (+1.00), which means perfect prediction. If we were to superimpose the four quadrants from Figure 7.6 on this figure, we would see that we make *no* errors; that is, everyone we predict will succeed will be successful, and everyone we predict will fail will fail. Figure 7.7 (b) also illustrates a perfect correlation, but this one is negative (−1.00). In this case, higher predictor scores predict lower performance and vice versa. Figure 7.7 (c) shows no correlation (0); in this case, there is no relationship whatsoever between the predictor and performance.

Figures 7.7 (d) and (e) present positive correlations of different strength, with (d) being a better predictor than (e).

Because selection decisions are most closely related to criterion-related validity, it is worth noting factors that can influence the strength of the relationship between scores on a test and performance on the job—factors other than the idea that the test is simply not related to job performance.

1. As noted previously, it is important that both the test and other selection devices be reliable and that the measure of performance or success be reliable. Unfortunately, as we discussed earlier in this chapter, some commonly used selection techniques such as the interview are often not reliable; and, as we will discuss in Chapter 10, many measures of performance are also not reliable. Even in the case where a selection technique should be able to predict performance perfectly, if the technique does not use a reliable measure, or if the measure of performance is not reliable, then the correlation we obtain will be much less than perfect (exactly how much less depends on how unreliable each measure actually is).

2. Correlations between predictor scores and job performance will also be maximized if we have the complete range of both scores on the predictor (selection technique) and scores on the criterion (job performance). But this requires hiring people, regardless of their scores on the predictor and then keeping them employed long enough to collect performance data. Although this is exactly what some firms do (by making selection decisions on the basis of something other than the predictors to be validated), this is a costly way to go about the validation process. Instead, many organizations attempt to validate selection techniques with their current employees (referred to as *concurrent validation*), giving the test or other selection technique

Criterion-related validity is the extent to which a selection technique accurately predicts elements of performance. It is most typically demonstrated by establishing a correlation between a test or measured performance in a simulated work environment and measures of actual on-the-job performance.

to current employees, and then simply using their most recent performance appraisal as a measure of performance. Although cost-effective, this practice does have the effect of restricting the range of scores on both sides of the equation and thus reducing the size of the obtained correlations.

7-4d Legal and Effectiveness Issues in Recruiting and Selection

Two final issues of importance for selection decisions, as well as recruiting, are an awareness of legal issues and the importance of evaluating the effectiveness of these activities.

LEGAL ISSUES IN RECRUITING AND SELECTION The Civil Rights Act (and other nondiscrimination legislation) applies to all employment decisions, but this legislation is clearly most critical for selection decisions. We noted in Chapter 2 that an organization faced with a prima facie case of discrimination must prove that the basis for the selection decision was job related, and this is demonstrated by establishing the validity of a selection instrument as described previously.[54] But as far back as the *Griggs* v. *Duke Power Co.* decision, the courts have become more insistent that validation studies should be conducted in order to be acceptable.[55] More recently, in *Ricci* v. *De Stefano*, the Supreme Court reversed a lower court decision and ruled that the City of New Haven could not throw out a test just because it would lead to decisions that would promote no minority firefighters. Thus, the Court has moved from imposing guidelines about how to validate tests to guidelines about how test scores could be used. Even though the *Ricci* decision would seem to make it easier for companies to defend selection practices in some ways, it also indicates a willingness on the part of the court system to get quite involved in how tests are used in practice. This trend suggests that it will become even more important for HR managers to be familiar with the law and recent court decisions in order to guide organizations to select the best employees without violating the law.[56]

EVALUATING RECRUITING AND SELECTION Because recruiting and selection are such vital parts of the HRM process for most organizations, it stands to reason that

Rawpixel.com/Shutterstock.com

organizations will periodically evaluate their effectiveness. As far as recruiting is concerned, an effective process is one that results in a reasonable pool of qualified employees who are available to the organization and from which the organization can hire people to perform various jobs at a reasonable cost. Therefore, if the organization is having problems attracting qualified candidates or filling jobs, this would suggest that the recruiting process is not working. In addition, it is possible to assess the effectiveness of different recruiting sources the organization might be using in terms of providing successful employees who remain with the firm.[57]

There are also formal methods available for evaluating the success of the selection system, beyond detraining if the selection technique is job related. Most of these represent some variation on what is known as *utility analysis*. **Utility analysis** is an attempt to determine the extent to which a selection system provides real benefit to the organization. This method assesses the practical payoff for any selection system in terms of the percentage of selection decisions that are correct (or the "hit rate"; see earlier discussion about selection errors). The actual formulas for assessing utility are beyond the scope of the current discussion, but it is worth noting that an assessment of utility requires calculating the cost involved in improving the hit rate, and the benefit of that improved hit rate, as well as the costs of making selection errors. This allows an HR manager to show exactly how an improved selection system contributes to the bottom line.

7-5 TRAINING AND DEVELOPMENT

After new employees have been hired, HR managers must take steps to ensure that they can perform to their full potential as soon as possible. This generally involves training and development. Training and development, then, represent a fundamental investment in the employees who work for an organization, with the overall goal of improving their ability to make contributions to the firm's

> **Utility analysis** is an attempt to determine the extent to which a selection system provides real benefit to the organization.

effectiveness. Employee **training** can be defined as a planned attempt by an organization to facilitate employee learning of job-related knowledge, skills, and behaviors. **Development**, on the other hand, usually refers to teaching managers and professionals the skills needed for both present and future jobs. Thus, each has a slightly different orientation, but both have the goal of increasing an employee's potential contributions.

Training usually involves teaching operational or technical employees how to do their jobs more effectively and more efficiently. Teaching telephone operators to help customers more efficiently, showing machinists the proper way to handle certain kinds of tools, and demonstrating for short-order cooks how to prepare food orders systematically are all part of training, and all these activities are aimed at helping the organization function more effectively.

Rather than focusing on specific job-related skills, development is more generally aimed at helping managers better understand and solve problems, make decisions, and capitalize on opportunities.[58] For example, some management development programs have a component dealing with effective time management. Other management development programs may help managers better understand how to motivate employees (e.g., how to get the employees discussed earlier to exert extra effort). Thus, managers do not necessarily return from development programs with a specific new operational method for doing their job more effectively. Instead, they may return with new skills that may be relevant to them in a general sense at some point in the future. They may have a better understanding of how to work more effectively, how to better motivate their employees, and how to make better decisions. They may possess a more complete understanding of how the overall organization functions and their role within it. Development is considered an HR function in most organizations, but because of its strategic nature and importance, one or more senior executives are usually given specific responsibility to ensure that management development is approached systematically and comprehensively.

IBM helps develop its new first-line managers with an extensive 9-month training program called Basic Blue, which covers such topics as people management, HR policies, and leadership development. Program participants complete 6 months of online e-learning before traveling to this Learning Center next door to headquarters in Armonk, New York, for the continuation of the program. Almost 20,000 IBM managers worldwide have attended the program since its inception in 1999. Similarly, Halliburton provides 6 weeks of development annually for its top executives under its Presidential Leadership Seminar program.

Several basic steps in the design of any training or development program are illustrated in Figure 7.8. The process should begin with a needs analysis where HR managers responsible for training and development determine the organization's true needs vis-à-vis training. This analysis generally focuses on two issues: the organization's job-related needs and the capabilities of its current workforce. The organization's needs are determined by the nature of the work that the organization performs—that is, what KSAs must the organization's workforce have to perform the organization's work most effectively?

As part of this analysis, the manager must carefully assess the company's strategy, the resources it has available for training, and its general philosophy regarding employee training and development. By "philosophy," we mean the extent to which the organization views training as a true investment in human resources or simply as a necessity to alter or change a specific outcome or criterion measure. Workforce analysis involves a careful assessment of the capabilities, strengths, and weaknesses characterizing the organization's current workforce. That is, it is important to understand the extent to which the organization's workforce is skilled or unskilled, motivated or unmotivated, committed to the organization or not, and so forth. Furthermore, it is important that the organization decide whether it wants to train employees for the present or more proactively train them for what is expected in the future.

After these needs are assessed, whether through direct observation or some type of survey or interview process, the organization must determine its goals for

Training is a planned attempt by an organization to facilitate employee learning of job-related knowledge, skills, and behaviors.

Development refers to teaching managers and professionals the skills needed for both present and future jobs.

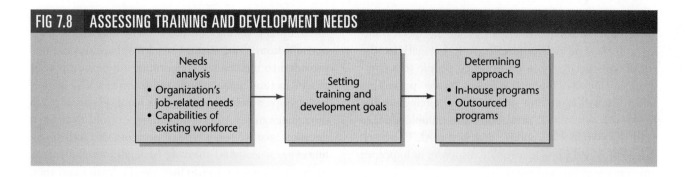

FIG 7.8 ASSESSING TRAINING AND DEVELOPMENT NEEDS

Needs analysis
• Organization's job-related needs
• Capabilities of existing workforce

Setting training and development goals

Determining approach
• In-house programs
• Outsourced programs

training and development. Unless a manager knows what to expect from the training, it is difficult (if not impossible) to determine how effective any training or development activity has been. For example, consider the case of an insurance claims office. Assume that claims adjusters are processing insurance claims at an average rate of 6 business days per claim. Responses and feedback suggest that some customers are becoming unhappy because they would like to have their claims processed more quickly. Using this information and other relevant data, the HR manager—working in conjunction with operating managers—might decide that an appropriate and reasonable goal would be to cut the average processing time from 6 to 4 days. Thus, a "4-day processing average" becomes the goal of this particular training endeavor.

The next step in the process is to decide between in-house versus outsourced training. Many larger organizations such as Texas Instruments and Exxon Mobil have large training staffs and assume the responsibility for training and developing their employees, thus assuring that the content of its training and development efforts are precisely and specifically tailored to fit the organization's needs. Alternatively, outsourcing training activities enables a firm to draw upon expertise not available inside in order to maximize training effectiveness. But outsourced programs tend to be more general and even generic, and thus have less applicability and direct relevance to the organization's needs.

Finally, after the organization has decided on whether to conduct training and development in-house or through outsourcing, it must determine the specific techniques to be used. For some situations, organizations might prefer to rely upon various **work-based programs**. *Work-based programs* tie the training and development activities directly to performance of the tasks. The most common method of work-based training is *on-the-job training*. This approach to training can help an organization achieve a return on the labor cost of the employee almost immediately, assuming that the individual is

capable of performing at a minimal level of competency. In addition, direct training costs may be lower because the organization may not need to hire dedicated trainers or send employees to training programs. Two other types of work-based training are apprenticeship programs and vestibule training. **Apprenticeships** involve a combination of **on-the-job training** and classroom instruction. **Vestibule training** involves a work-simulation situation in which the job is performed under a condition that closely simulates the real work environment.

Instructional-based programs are also quite common, especially the *lecture or discussion approach*. In these situations, a trainer presents the material to those attending the program in a lecture format; although lectures continue to play a role in most training programs, there is evidence that their use has been declining, and they are being replaced with training outside the classroom, primarily using electronic technologies.

Another instructional-based program for training and development is *computer-assisted instruction*. In this situation, a trainee sits at a computer and operates software that has been developed specifically to impart certain material to the individual. The major advantage of this method is that it allows self-paced learning, and immediate feedback can be given to the trainee.[59]

Another method that involves basic instruction as a training device is *programmed instruction*. In recent years, these activities have become computerized but remain self-paced with self-assessment. Additionally, in recent years, all of these approaches have been affected by changes in training technology. Video teleconferencing allows a

Work-based programs tie training and development activities directly to performance of the tasks.

Apprenticeships involve a combination of on-the-job training and classroom instruction.

On-the-job training involves having employees learn the job while they are actually performing it.

Vestibule training involves a work-simulation situation in which the job is performed under a condition that closely simulates the real work environment.

trainer in a centralized location to deliver material live via satellite hookup to multiple remote sites; the training can thus be delivered effectively but without the travel costs necessary in transporting people to a common training site. Interactive videos involve presenting information on a monitor from a central serving mechanism, such as via DVD or website. The trainee interacts with the system via a mouse and keyboard. Feedback can be provided when inadequate responses or improper answers are given, and the trainee can skip material that has already been learned.

7-5a Management Development

The training and development issues discussed thus far are applicable to both standard training programs and development programs. However, some specialized issues and techniques come into play in management development. This process involves more generalized training for future managerial roles and positions rather than training that is specific to an immediately relevant task. As a result, managerial training usually involves attending a series of training programs over a period of time rather than attending a single program.

Techniques may be more or less applicable to management development as opposed to more traditional training. For example, the lecture method may not be very well suited for this type of training because it is critical that that the learner be an active participant in any development program. On the other hand, techniques such as the *in-basket* and *leaderless group* may be more appropriate for management development. In an in-basket exercise, the participant is confronted with a hypothetical in-basket full of letters, memos, reports, phone messages, and e-mail messages associated with a particular manager. The trainee must then play the

> **Organizational development** is a system-wide effort, managed from the top of the organization, to increase the organization's overall performance through planned interventions.

role of the manager by reading and evaluating each of the materials, noting how he or she would handle each one and prioritizing them. Useful feedback can then be provided to the trainee concerning the best responses as well as time management and priorities. The leaderless group exercise, on the other hand, places a group of trainees in a setting where they are told to make a decision or solve some type of problem. No individual, however, is assigned the role of leader or chair. It is up to the group to decide they need a leader and then identify and select a member who must function in that role.

7-5b Organizational Development

Technically, learning is a process that only occurs at the level of the individual, and so it may make little sense to talk about change or learning at any other level. But, in fact, there are processes at the organizational level that are related to learning and development. Even though the actual changes that might take place occur at the level of the individual, collections of individuals can change in such a way that it actually does make sense to talk about organizational development and learning.

Organizational development (OD) is a system-wide effort, managed from the top of the organization, to increase the organization's overall performance through planned interventions. The technique relies heavily on behavioral science technology, and, although the development activities target the

iStockphoto.com/Curt Pickens

individual, the purpose is to ultimately change the way the entire organization operates. In addition, OD assumes that people have a need to grow and develop, as well as a desire to be accepted by other members of the organization. As a result, collaboration between managers and employees is necessary to take advantage of the skills and abilities of the employees and to eliminate aspects of the organization that limit employee growth, development, and group acceptance. Most such programs also involve an OD consultant to implement and manage the program.

Different OD techniques are widely used. *Survey feedback* involves having employees respond to questionnaires about attitudes and perceptions of leadership styles, and then sharing the results of the survey with everyone involved, including managers and supervisors. The purpose is to change the behavior of managers or supervisors by making them aware of how everyone perceives them. Following the feedback are usually workshops designed to help managers evaluate the feedback and suggest constructive changes.

When OD is undertaken to solve a specific problem, such as interpersonal conflict, techniques such as *third-party peacemaking* might be used. Here a neutral third party, often an OD consultant from outside the organization, hears both sides in a conflict. He or she then helps the parties develop satisfactory solutions or compromises so that everyone can win (also known as integrative bargaining). Active listening—where a person pays attention to both verbal and nonverbal information—is extremely valuable in these settings.

Finally, in *process consultation,* the OD consultant observes managers in the organization to develop an understanding of their communication patterns, decision-making and leadership processes, and methods of cooperation and conflict resolution. The consultant then provides feedback and recommendations to the managers about how to improve these procedures. It is worth noting that, although there is evidence that such interventions are successful in improving communications, there seems to be a real question about whether there is any improvement in organizational effectiveness as a result.[60]

At some point, when change begins to spread throughout the organization, we can actually talk about "**organizational learning**" taking place. This topic, as well as the related topic of organizational memory, will be discussed in the next chapter. These two topics go beyond the traditional boundaries of either training or development, and they are more closely related to managing the knowledge function in organizations, which is discussed in Chapter 8.

7-5c Evaluating Training and Development

There is a long tradition of evaluation for training and development activities—much longer than for most areas of HRM. This is because it is easier to evaluate these activities than some other practices. The purpose of training and development is to enact fundamental change in individual performance behavior (or other outcomes), and it is relatively easy to quantify such changes, making evaluation more straightforward. For example, sales training should result in increased sales; training of repair persons should result in greater customer satisfaction and fewer call backs; and safety training should result in fewer accidents.

This type of evaluation might be relatively simple, but that doesn't mean there are no issues to consider. The most important is to determine if there is an actual change in the behavior being targeted. That is, we hope the trained salesperson will sell more than he or she had sold before. This requires some type of pretraining measure to make sure that there has generally been change. In addition, we want to be sure that any changes we observe are really due to the training program, not just the passage of time (i.e., the employee could just get better with more time on the job). Therefore, it is often useful to have a "control group" of employees who work on the same job, but do not receive the training. In this way, it is possible to assess the change in the performance of the trained employees, not only relative to their performance before training but also relative to a similar group of employees who did not receive any training.

Evaluating management development programs is a bit more problematic because the training is really geared at helping managers prepare for future jobs. Therefore, it may require a longer period of time and outcome measurement to evaluate these programs. In addition, management development programs tend to target more complex types of behaviors that are to be changed. The fact that the evaluation of management development programs is more difficult is not an excuse for not conducting an evaluation. Because these programs tend to be more expensive and involve higher level employees, it is even more important that an organization knows if the programs are effective.

> **Organizational learning** refers to the process by which an organization "learns" from past mistakes and adapts to its environment.

CLOSING CASE
The Temptation of Temping

Several years ago New Yorker Diana Bloom logged on to Craigslist, an online network that posts free classified ads, and offered her services as a tutor, editor, and translator. She's been making a living on the short-term jobs that come her way from the website ever since. A former English professor who couldn't find secure long-term employment, Bloom works out of her home in order to take care of a young son. Temp work is also appealing, she says, because "I'm not very outgoing, and getting my foot in the door to companies would have been hard."

Craigslist works in the other direction, too, with employers posting openings for jobs both permanent and temporary. Another New Yorker, Simone Sneed, scours the Craigslist "Gigs" section for jobs that last for perhaps a day, often for just a few hours. Whether as a backup singer or a grants writer, she's turned the strategy of patching together "gigs" into a convenient way to supplement the income from her full-time job. "I'll use the extra money to pay off my school loan," she says. "Every little bit helps."

In the current economic climate, unfortunately, overall job postings are down on Craigslist and everywhere else, except for short-term jobs—gigs that usually include no health benefits, sick days, or paid vacations. If you're employed short term or part-time for economic reasons (probably because you got laid off), the Bureau of Labor Statistics (BLS) classifies you as "underemployed."

Naturally, most people who are "underemployed" are, by definition, overqualified. In fact, they often have years of professional experience but are willing to take jobs that don't call for their levels of training or experience. Take the case of Gloria Christ. As national project manager for an information-technology company in the Chicago area, Christ used to co-ordinate the installation of Wi-Fi hotspots all over the country. She has several years of managerial experience but is also been willing to put it to use as a temporary office manager. Of course, she'd like something with a little more long-term promise: "At this point in time," she says, "I think even if there was something that was temporary, it could become full time later on. . . . Sometimes," she explains, "you can go in at a low level to interview just to get your foot in the door."

It may be small compensation (so to speak), but because of the recent economic situation, although many companies are reluctant to add costly permanent jobs, they are increasingly willing to open up temporary positions to tide them over. Often, of course, you'll have to take a job that isn't exactly what you've trained for or set your sights on, but as one employment-services manager observes, job seekers today "are more than willing to try new occupations—much more willing than they were even a year ago."

Interestingly, for a lot of people, the adjustment to current labor-market conditions isn't necessarily as traumatic as you might think. A recent survey conducted by the temporary-staffing agency Kelly Services found that as many as 26 percent of employed American adults regard themselves as "free agents" when it comes to the type of job that they're willing to take (up from 19 percent in 2006). Of all those polled, only 10 percent said that they're doing temporary work because they've been laid off from permanent jobs; 90 percent said that they're doing it because they like the variety and flexibility that temping afford them.

Kelly client Jaime Gacharna's first assignment was packaging products for a light-industrial wholesaler—"putting doorknobs into little bags," he recalls. Since then, he's worked for eight different employers, working at a job for a few days, a few weeks, or a few months. He doesn't mind the constant adjustments because the variety in his work life compensates for the drawbacks. "If I want to try something out, and I like it," says Gacharna, "I can stay with [the company]. If I don't, I can always just call up Kelly and say I want something different."

In fact, temping offers several advantages. It can, for example, provide income during career transitions, and it's a good way to exercise a little control over the balance between your work and the rest of your life. In 1995, for example, when she was 7 months pregnant with her first child, veteran retail manager Stacey Schick accepted a two-week data-entry job with the Orange County (New York) Association of Realtors. "I didn't know how to turn on a computer," she remembers, but "they needed bodies." Now the mother of two, Schick is still with the Association as its education coordinator. "I would never have considered it," she says, if a job in her field had come up, but the job she landed in has turned out to be a much better fit with her lifestyle: "It's afforded me the opportunity to have a family and be able to have time with them."

The path taken by Schick is called "temp-to-perm," and it offers employers several advantages as well. Companies that are hesitant to make commitments to untested employees can try before they buy—they get a chance to see employees in action before finalizing hiring decisions. Because there are no fees to pay when an employee goes from temp to perm, trying out temps is

(Continued)

(Closing Case – continued)

also cheaper than paying an agency outright to find a hire. The big savings, of course, come from benefits, which can amount to one-third of the total cost of compensating a permanent position.

Then there's the economy. While many employers have laid off full-time workers, many have tried to compensate by turning over some of the work to temp staff. Ironically, of course, many of those who've been laid off are highly qualified, and as they hit the job market willing to accept lower-level positions, the ranks of job hunters are being joined by a substantial number of highly qualified (which is to say, overqualified) workers. "The quality of candidates," says Laura Long of Banner Personnel, a Chicago-area staffing agency, "is tremendous. . . . As an employer, you can get great employees for a great price."

As a matter of fact, if you're a U.S. employer, you've always been able to get temp workers at a relatively good price. As of December 2015, according to the BLS, the average cost of a full-time worker in private industry was $24.19 per hour in wages plus $10.95 in benefits, for a total of $35.14 in compensation. By contrast, the average wages for

leungchopan/Shutterstock.com

a temp were $14.59 and the average benefits were $4.31, for total compensation of $18.90. One of the results of this cost differential has been a long-term increase in the number of temp workers, which, over the past 25 years, has far outstripped the increase in jobs occupied by full-time workers. [61]

CASE QUESTIONS

1. You're a senior manager at a growing business, and you're ready to add employees. Your HR manager has recommended a temp-to-perm policy. You know the advantages of this approach, but what might be some of the disadvantages?

2. Assume that you're a prospective job seeker (which you may very well be). What do you personally see as the advantages and disadvantages of taking a temp-to-perm position? Under what circumstances are you most likely to take a temp-to-perm position?

3. What sort of challenges are likely to confront a manager who supervises a mix of temporary and permanent employees? In what ways might these challenges differ if the temporary workers have been hired on a temp-to-perm basis rather than on a strictly temporary basis?

STUDY TOOLS 7

READY TO STUDY?

In the book, you can:

☐ Rip out the chapter review card at the back of the book for a handy summary of the chapter and key terms.

ONLINE AT CENGAGEBRAIN.COM YOU CAN:

☐ Collect StudyBits while you read and study the chapter.

☐ Quiz yourself on key concepts.

☐ Find videos for further exploration.

☐ Prepare for tests with HR4 Flash Cards as well as those you create.

8 | Managing a New and Diverse Workforce

After finishing this chapter go to **PAGE 216** for **STUDY TOOLS**

LEARNING OBJECTIVES

8-1 Discuss the nature of diversity and distinguish among diversity management, equal employment opportunity, and affirmative action

8-2 Identify and describe the major dimensions of diversity in organizations

8-3 Discuss the primary impact of diversity on organizations

8-4 Describe individual and organizational strategies and approaches to coping with diversity, and discuss the multicultural organization

8-5 Discuss the basic issues in managing knowledge workers

8-6 Relate human resource management to social issues

Goodluz/Shutterstock.com

OPENING CASE
Dealing with Differences

As noted in Chapter 2, the Americans with Disabilities Act of 1990 (ADA) forbids discrimination on the basis of disability and further requires that employers make reasonable accommodation for disabled employees. Not surprisingly, some employers see this requirement as an extra cost and see disabled employees as liabilities. But many other employers have come to see that people with disabilities are often capable of being productive and committed employees and that accommodations are often relatively easy and inexpensive. Moreover, by employing a diverse workforce, they are often better able to engage with and understand a larger customer base. To illustrate this point, consider two examples.

Rick, a construction engineer who broke his back in an auto accident, is a paraplegic suffering from vocal-cord damage. However, he also holds a productive job, managing complaints for building-construction projects. At both home and office, Rick uses a mouse activated by one finger and an on-screen keyboard because his voice is too soft for most voice-recognition software. David, whose job requires speech-recognition software and a trackball mouse to compensate for impaired manual dexterity and verbal communication, coordinates health care strategies and operations at the Department of Defense.

Both Rick and David depend on employer-provided *assistive technology*, and according to David, it's "a real equalizer for people with disabilities. . . . It not only raises your productivity but also your expectations for yourself. That's a good feeling for the individual and good for the employer, too." In addition to the sort of hardware, software, and peripherals that help people like Rick and David perform jobs requiring computer access, assistive technology includes such lower-tech equipment as walkers and wheelchairs—much of which makes accommodating disabled workers less expensive than you might think. Low-tech, low-cost accommodation for a visually impaired person might entail nothing more than adjusting the lighting, supplying magnification devices, and/or fitting the work schedule to mass transit. More severely impaired individuals may need higher-tech assistance,

"We have to keep up with their declining abilities, or we'll find ourselves in the position of not being able to serve our customers or leverage employees' talents."

—DIANA BURKE, VP FOR INFORMATION SECURITY, RBC FINANCIAL GROUP[1]

but the technology is usually reasonably priced. (Dragon NaturallySpeaking, for example, the speech-recognition software that David uses, sells for $199.)

Both Rick and David suffer from permanent disabilities, but experts estimate that as many as 20 percent of us will experience some form of physical disability at some point in our careers or lives. In addition, it's worth remembering that currently employed baby boomers are getting older. "The population is aging," says Diana Burke, VP for information security at RBC Financial Group, "and people are losing hearing, vision, and mobility as the years progress. This affects employees and customers. We have to keep up with their declining abilities, or we'll find ourselves in the position of not being able to serve our customers or leverage employees' talents." Adds Dinah Cohen, director of the Department of Defense's Computer/Electronic Accommodations Program (CAP), "It's not just people born with disabilities who need assistive technology. More and more, [CAP is] serving people who acquire disabilities later in life. . . . We're all potential users."[2]

THINK IT OVER

1. Can you identify examples of ADA accommodations in general and assistive technology in particular at your school or employer?
2. What are the implications of assistive technology for a large business with global operations?

Diversity is an important part of contemporary human resource management (HRM). Most organizations have come to realize that increasing the diversity of their workforce can contribute to their effectiveness and add value in many different ways. At first blush, people tend to equate diversity with gender, skin color, and/or national origin. But as our opening case illustrates, diversity is actually a very broad concept encompassing many kinds of differences. As such, diversity poses both challenges and opportunities to managers.

This chapter is primarily about workforce diversity in organizations. Other new challenges also face organizations today, and some of these will be addressed here as well. We begin by exploring the meaning and nature of diversity. We distinguish between diversity management and equal employment opportunity. Next we identify and discuss several common dimensions of diversity. The impact of diversity on the organization is explored. We address how diversity can be managed for the betterment of both individuals and organizations, and we describe the fully multicultural organization. We then turn to some other types of challenges. One of these is managing knowledge in organizations, so we will discuss issues involving managing knowledge workers. Finally, we will turn to concerns over social issues in today's organizations. We will discuss challenges involved with managing human resources while trying to address social concerns, including some discussion of HRM and social entrepreneurship.

8-1 THE NATURE OF WORKFORCE DIVERSITY

Workforce diversity has become an important issue in many organizations in the United States and abroad. A logical starting point in better understanding this phenomenon is establishing the meaning of the word *diversity* and then examining why such diversity is increasing today.

8-1a The Meaning of Workforce Diversity

Diversity exists in a group or organization when its members differ from one another along one or more important dimensions.[3] If everyone in the group or organization is exactly like everyone else, no diversity exists. But if everyone is different along every imaginable dimension, then total diversity exists. In reality, of course, these extremes are more hypothetical than real; most settings are characterized by a level of diversity somewhere between. Thus, diversity is not an absolute phenomenon wherein a group or organization is or is not diverse. Instead, diversity should be conceptualized as a continuum and thought of in terms of degree or level of diversity along relevant dimensions.[4]

These dimensions of diversity might include gender, age, and ethnic origin, among many others. A group composed of five

Diversity exists in a group or organization when its members differ from one another along one or more important dimensions.

middle-aged white male U.S. executives has relatively little diversity. If one member leaves and is replaced by a young white female executive, then the group becomes a bit more diverse. If another member is replaced by an older African American executive, then diversity increases a bit more. And when a third member is replaced by a Japanese executive, the group becomes even more diverse.

8-1b Trends in Workforce Diversity

As we noted earlier, organizations today are becoming increasingly diverse along many different dimensions. Several different factors have accounted for these trends and changes. Changing demographics in the labor force is one such factor. As more women and minorities have entered the labor force, for example, the available pool of talent from which organizations hire employees has changed in both size and composition. If talent within each segment of the labor pool is evenly distributed (e.g., if the number of talented men in the workforce as a percentage of all men in the workforce is the same as the number of talented women in the labor force as a percentage of all women in the workforce), then it follows logically that proportionately more women and fewer men will be hired over time by an organization compared to the employees who were hired in the past.

A related factor that has contributed to diversity has been the increased awareness by organizations that they can improve the overall quality of their workforce by hiring and promoting the most talented people available regardless of gender, race, or any other characteristics. By casting a broader net in recruiting and looking beyond traditional sources for new employees, organizations are finding more broadly qualified and better qualified employees from many different segments of society. Thus,

> **Most organizations have come to realize that they can improve the overall quality of their workforce by hiring and promoting the most talented people available, regardless of gender, race, or any other characteristic not related to performance.**

these organizations are finding that diversity can be a source of competitive advantage.

Another reason for the increase in diversity has been legislation and legal actions that have forced organizations to hire more broadly. Organizations in the United States were once free to discriminate against women, African Americans, and other minorities. Thus, most organizations were dominated by white males. Over the past 30 years or so, however, various laws have outlawed discrimination against these and other groups. As we detailed in Chapter 2, organizations must hire and promote people today solely on the basis of their qualifications.

A final contributing factor to increased diversity in organizations has been the globalization movement. Organizations that have opened offices and related facilities in other countries have had to learn to deal with different customs, social norms, and mores. Strategic alliances and foreign ownership have also contributed because managers today are more likely to have job assignments in other countries or to work with foreign managers within their own countries. As employees and managers move from assignment to assignment across national boundaries, organizations and their subsidiaries within each country become more diverse. Closely related to this pattern is a recent increase in immigration into the United States. As illustrated in Figure 8.1, for example, immigration declined steadily from 1900 to around 1940 but then started to slowly pick up again. The pace of new immigration jumped in the 1980s and has been increasing ever since.

As a result of recent trends, immigration has become a hot issue in the United States. According to statistics published by the Department of Immigration (part of the Department of Homeland Security), in 2013, there were more than 14 million immigrants in the United States from Mexico, followed by about 7 million each from China and India, and over 5 million each from the Philippines and the Dominican Republic. But, more critically, the Pew Hispanic Center estimates that 56 percent of all illegal immigrants in the United States come from Mexico and that other Latin American countries account for an additional 22% of illegal immigration. In fact, there is a great deal of variance in estimates of illegal immigration, but it is clearly an issue for many people. In fact, in the 2016 Republican primary, this issue was front and center. Although all candidates stated that illegal immigration was a problem, some, such as Marco Rubio, seemed to favor a path to citizenship for illegals, while other, such as Ted Cruz, were opposed to it.

But Donald Trump went a bit further than any other candidate, vowing to deport more than 10 million (estimated) illegal immigrants currently in the United States and then building a wall along the Mexico-U.S. border to keep out illegal immigrants from Mexico. It is clear that debate over this issue will continue, and that dealing with illegal immigration will continue to be a serious challenge for anyone doing business in the United States.[5]

8-1c Diversity Management Versus Other Concepts

Many managers, as well as many in the public, often confuse diversity management with several other concepts. One common misperception is that diversity management is the same thing as equal employment opportunity. In fact, they have completely different meanings. **Equal employment opportunity** means treating people fairly and equitably and taking actions that do not discriminate against people in protected classes on the basis of some illegal criterion. But **diversity management** places a much heavier emphasis on recognizing and appreciating differences among people at work and attempting to provide accommodations for those differences to the extent that is feasible and possible.

The distinction between diversity management and affirmative action has also led to confusion, and recent Supreme Court decisions (especially *Fisher* v. *University of Texas*), discussed in Chapter 2, have made the distinction even less clear. In the University of Texas case, as well as in the earlier case involving the University of Michigan, the stated goal of the university's affirmative action plan was to increase the diversity of the student body. That is, they proposed to work to increase the number of students from underrepresented groups in order to make the learning environment richer because of the more diverse student body. The courts have supported this goal of diversity but have made it clear that affirmative action may not be the only (or the best) way to accomplish the goal of greater student diversity. Thus, although affirmative action plans could serve to increase diversity, these plans are different

Equal employment opportunity means treating people fairly and equitably and taking actions that do not discriminate against people in protected classes on the basis of some illegal criterion.

Diversity management places a much heavier emphasis on recognizing and appreciating differences among people at work and attempting to provide accommodations for those differences to the extent that is feasible and possible.

FIG 8.1 IMMIGRATION TRENDS INTO THE UNITED STATES

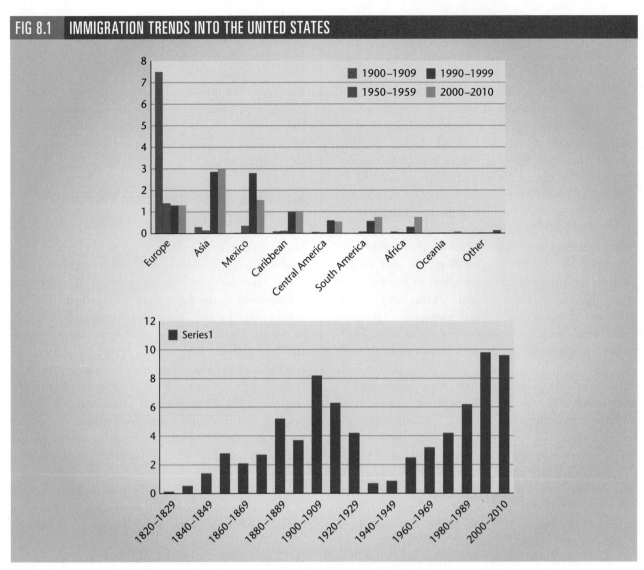

Source: 2010 Yearbook of Immigration Statistics, published by Office of Immigration Statistics http://www.dhs.gov/xlibrary/assets/sttistics/yearbook/2010/ois.

from plans focusing on diversity management alone. Recent history makes it very clear that a narrow pursuit of diversity will not be accepted as a defense for affirmative action without strong evidence that this is the best way to proceed.

SIMILARITIES AMONG PEOPLE AT WORK Regardless of how different people appear to be, almost all employees share some fundamental similarities.[6] For example, most people work to satisfy some set of needs that almost always have financial bases. Most people have a basic desire to be treated with respect and dignity by their employer. And, most people have a capacity for being reasonable and understanding when confronted with reasonable behavior by others.

DIFFERENCES AMONG PEOPLE AT WORK Although many people share some basic set of similar characteristics, they also display various fundamental differences, a topic that will be discussed more fully in the next major section of the chapter. Common differences include gender, ethnicity, and age. But the list of differences among individuals is much longer and ranges from religious beliefs to dietary preferences to political philosophies.

IDENTICAL TREATMENT VERSUS EQUITABLE TREATMENT In the years immediately after Title VII of the 1964 Civil Rights Act was passed, many human resource (HR) managers operated under the assumption that they were required by law to treat everyone equally. In reality, that assumption is neither the intent of the law nor even truly possible. The real essence not only of Title VII but also of the more contemporary perspective on workforce diversity is that it is appropriate to acknowledge differences among people as long as people are treated fairly.

Consider religion, for example. A typical company in the United States routinely gives days off to employees for basic Christian holidays such as Christmas. But people who have different religious beliefs may not acknowledge the sanctity of these religious holidays and instead have different sets of days that they associate with strong religious beliefs. Thus, an employer who provides Christian holidays off should also be sensitive to the need to provide important religious holidays off for various employees of different beliefs and faiths. The Whirlpool appliance factory near Nashville, Tennessee, for example, employs about 200 Muslims (about 10 percent of its workforce). The factory found it necessary to adjust its work schedules, cafeteria menus, and dress codes to accommodate workers who pray several times a day, do not eat pork, and wear loose-fitting clothing, head coverings, and sandals.[7]

Men and women are also fundamentally different in various ways that cannot be ignored. On average, men have greater muscle mass than do women and can therefore lift heavier weight. And women have the biological capacity to bear children. Consequently, men and women may need fundamentally different treatment in work organizations. For example, women may need to be given longer periods of time off during the time immediately preceding and after the birth of a child. When a woman chooses to return to work after birth, the organization may need to provide a transitional period during which her work-related demands are lessened at first but then gradually increased over time.

The Americans with Disabilities Act (ADA) presents a serious challenge to managers who try to balance treating everyone the same with treating everyone equitably. The ADA specifically states that an organization cannot discriminate against a person with a disability as long as he or she can perform the essential functions of the job *with or without a reasonable accommodation.* Therefore, requested employee accommodations must be addressed. At first glance, this situation may not appear problematic because the employee presumably needs this accommodation to perform his or her job. Many of the accommodations requested and granted, such as large-print computer screens, allowances for guide dogs, wheelchair ramps, and amplified phones, do not present a problem.

But what about an accommodation requested by a person with a disability that would be desirable or useful to other employees who do not have a disability? An interesting example of this dilemma occurred about 10 years ago when the Professional Golf Association ruled that Casey Martin, whose serious leg problems made walking a golf course dangerous, would be allowed to use a golf cart in tournament play. Although there was disagreement over exactly how much of a difference this accommodation would make, many other golfers claimed that if they too were allowed to ride around the course, they would be less tired and so would play better. In this case, other golfers not only wanted the same accommodation that had been granted to Martin but also felt that it gave him an unfair competitive advantage.

Although Martin's case may be a particularly dramatic example of the problem, we can easily imagine other accommodations requested by a person with a disability that also would be valued by other employees or that other employees might perceive the accommodation as providing an unfair advantage. Even in classroom settings, students often perceive it as unfair when a student with a disability is granted extra time for a test. Coworker resentment over the granting of accommodations can be a problem for all concerned. For the able-bodied employee, these accommodations may be perceived as unjust, leading to dissatisfaction on the job. For the disabled employee, the anticipated resentment may discourage him or her from asking for the accommodation needed to perform the job effectively. The manager's perspective, of course, focuses on the problem of balancing the concerns of the different parties.[8]

Again, the important message is for managers to recognize that differences among people exist. It is important first to acknowledge the differences and then to make reasonable accommodation to deal with these differences. The key issue, however, is to make sure that the acknowledgment and the accommodation are equitable: Everyone needs to have an equal opportunity to contribute to and advance within the organization.

Torian/Shutterstock.com

FIG 8.2 AGE AND FATAL ACCIDENT RATES (2014)

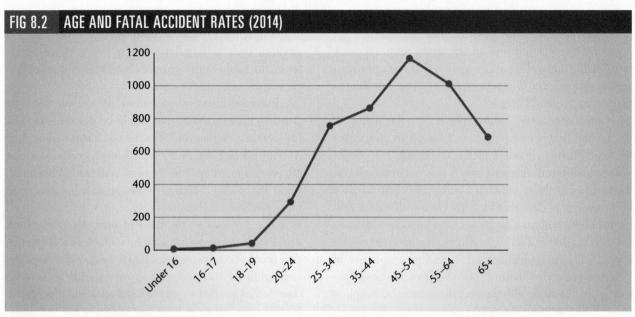

Source: Bureau of Labor Statistics, CFOI, 2014.

DIMENSIONS OF DIVERSITY

As indicated earlier, many different dimensions of diversity can be used to characterize an organization. In this section, we discuss age, gender, ethnicity, disability, and other dimensions of diversity.

8-2a Age Distributions

One key dimension of diversity in any organization is the age distribution of its workers.[9] The average age of U.S. workers is gradually increasing and will continue doing so for the next several years. Several factors contribute to this pattern. The baby boom generation (the unusually large number of people who were born in the 20-year period following World War II) continues to age. Declining birthrates among the post–baby boom generations simultaneously account for smaller percentages of new entrants into the labor force. Another factor that contributes to workforce aging is improved health and medical care, which enables people to remain productive and active for longer periods of time. Combined with higher legal limits for mandatory retirement, more and more people are working beyond the age at which they might have retired just a few years ago.

How does this trend affect HRM? Older workers tend to have more experience, may be more stable, and can make greater contributions to productivity.

The **glass ceiling** describes a barrier that keeps many females from advancing to top management positions in many organizations.

On the other hand, despite improvements in health and medical care, older workers are nevertheless likely to require higherlevels of insurance coverage and medical benefits. As shown in Figure 8.2, accident rates are substantially higher for older workers than for younger workers up to age 54. In most years, accident rates continue to increase; however, for the year shown (2014) accident rates actually dropped a bit for workers 55 and older. Further, the overall number of retirees combined with fewer younger members of the workforce may lead to future labor shortages, even though some workers are staying in the workforce longer.

8-2b Gender

As more and more females have entered the workforce, organizations have subsequently experienced changes in the relative proportions of male to female employees. Figure 8.3 highlights these trends in gender composition (as well as ethnicity) in the workplace. Census data indicate that in 2010, women constituted 47.9 percent of the workforce, up from 45.2 percent in 1990 and 46.6 percent in 2000.

These trends aside, a significant gender-related problem that many organizations face today is the so-called **glass ceiling**, which was introduced in Chapter 5. The term describes a real and subtle but nonphysical barrier that keeps many females from advancing to top management positions in many organizations. Although women make up almost 50 percent of all managers, female chief executive officers (CEOs) head only 10 of the 500 largest businesses in the United States. Similarly, the average pay of females in organizations is lower

FIG 8.3 CHANGING COMPOSITION OF THE U.S. WORKFORCE

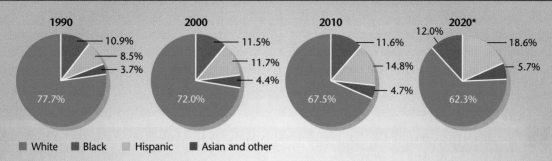

■ White ■ Black ▒ Hispanic ■ Asian and other

The shifting racial and ethnic makeup of the U.S. workforce: number of workers by race and ethnic origin and their share of the total civilian labor force.

Numbers (thousands)	1990	2000	2010	2020*	Percent	1990	2000	2010	2020*
Total	125,840	142,583	153,889	164,360	Total	100.0	100.0	100.0	100.0
Men	69,011	76,280	81,985	87,128	Men	54.8	53.5	53.3	53.0
Women	56,829	66,303	71,904	77,232	Women	45.2	46.5	46.7	47.0
White, non-Hispanic	97,818	102,729	103,947	102,371	White, non-Hispanic	77.7	72.0	67.5	62.3
Men	53,731	55,040	55,116	53,867	Men	42.7	38.6	35.8	32.8
Women	44,087	47,689	48,831	48,504	Women	35.0	33.4	31.7	29.5
Black, non-Hispanic	13,740	16,397	17,862	19,676	Black, non-Hispanic	10.9	11.5	11.6	12.0
Men	6,802	7,702	8,415	9,393	Men	5.4	5.4	5.5	5.7
Women	6,938	8,695	9,447	10,283	Women	5.5	6.1	6.1	6.3
Hispanic origin	10,720	16,689	22,748	30,493	Hispanic origin	8.5	11.7	14.8	18.6
Men	6,546	9,923	13,511	17,859	Men	5.2	7.0	8.8	10.9
Women	4,174	6,767	9,238	12,634	Women	3.3	4.7	6.0	7.7
Asian and other, non-Hispanic	4,653	6,270	7,248	9,430	Asian and other, non-Hispanic	3.7	4.4	4.7	5.7
Men	2,570	3,362	3,893	4,968	Men	2.0	2.4	2.5	3.0
Women	2,083	2,908	3,355	4,462	Women	1.7	2.0	2.2	2.7

*Projection

Source: U.S. Department of Labor, Bureau of Labor Statistics, *Monthly Labor Review*, January 2012, http://www.bls.gov.

than that of males. Although the pay gap is gradually shrinking, inequalities are still present.

Why does the glass ceiling exist? One reason is that some male managers are still reluctant to promote female managers. Another is that many talented women choose to leave their jobs in larger organizations and start their own businesses. And some women choose to suspend or slow their career progression to have children.

8-2c Ethnicity

A third major dimension of cultural diversity in organizations is **ethnicity**, or the ethnic composition of a group or organization. Within the United States, most organizations reflect varying degrees of ethnicity and are composed of whites, African Americans, Hispanics, and Asian Americans. Figure 8.3 also shows the current ethnic composition of the U.S. workforce.

The biggest changes, over the years, have involved whites and Hispanics. In particular, the percentage of whites in the workforce dropped to 69.2 percent in 2010, down from 73.1 percent in 2000 and 77.7 percent in 1990. Also, the percentage of Hispanics has climbed to 13.3 percent in 2010, up from 10.9 percent in 2000 and 8.5 percent in 1990. The percentage of African Americans has remained relatively stable (10.9 percent in 1990, 11.8 percent in 2000, and 12.7 percent in 2010), while Asian Americans and others

Ethnicity refers to the ethnic composition of a group or organization.

represent 6.1 percent of the U.S. workforce in 2010, up from 4.7 percent in 2000 and 3.7 percent in 1990.

As with women, members of the African American, Hispanic, and Asian American groups are generally underrepresented in the executive ranks of most organizations today, as well as in several different occupational groups. Their pay also is lower than might be expected. As is the case for women, however, the differences are gradually disappearing as organizations fully embrace equal employment opportunities and recognize the higher overall level of talent available to them. Table 8.1 shows trends in different occupations for African Americans and

TABLE 8.1	EMPLOYMENT OF AFRICAN AMERICANS AND HISPANICS/LATINOS IN SELECTED OCCUPATIONS, 2010 AND 2015			
	African Americans		Hispanics and Latinos	
	2010	2015	2010	2015
Total workforce, ages 16 and older	10.8	11.7	14.3	16.4
Occupation				
Executive, administrative, and managerial	8.4	9.2	7.3	9.1
Financial managers	6.7	7.2	8.1	9.4
HR managers	—	11.9	—	11.9
Purchasing managers	7.6	11.4	7.8	10.8
Managers in marketing, advertising, and public relations	5.9	6.2	5.1	9.7
Managers in medicine and health care	12.4	13.1	7.2	8.0
Accountants and auditors	8.6	9.5	5.8	7.4
Management analysts	7.2	9.3	6.7	5.9
Architects	2.1	5.8	7.8	5.7
Physicians	5.8	6.4	6.8	6.4
Dentists	0.3	2.9	5.7	8.6
College and university teachers	—	5.1	—	7.6
Psychologists	3.9	4.1	7.3	5.8
Lawyers	4.3	4.6	3.4	5.1
Authors	3.8	4.9	1.5	5.3
Musicians and composers	13.9	10.5	8.7	8.8
Editors and reporters	4.9	6.5	3.9	13.7

Source: Modified from (http://www.bls.gov/cps/cps_aa2009.htm) for 2015

Source: Modified from (http://www.bls.gov/cps/cps_aa2010.htm) for 2015

Source: Modified from (http://www.bls.gov/cps/cps_aa2011.htm) for 2015

Hispanics. For example, the percentage of African Americans and Hispanics comprises several different kinds of business roles plus various professional specialties and increased in most categories between 2010 and 2015.

8-2d Disability

Disability is another significant dimension of diversity. Disabilities can range from hearing impairments to missing fingers or limbs, blindness, and paralysis. The presence of a disability represents another aspect of diversity in organizations, but among persons who have disabilities, some differences are important as well. Unlike other dimensions of diversity, reactions to persons with disabilities vary dramatically as a function of several dimensions of the disability. One of these dimensions is termed "origin"; that is, if the disability is perceived as being avoidable (e.g., someone who has been injured while driving drunk), coworkers are likely to react more negatively to the disability than when the problem was unavoidable (e.g., a person who was born blind).

A second dimension is the aesthetic aspect of the disability, with disabilities that are more disfiguring being perceived more negatively. A third and critical dimension refers to the nature of the disability itself. For example, although mental disabilities might be easier to conceal, they are also more frightening to coworkers. Disabilities related to stress or to back injuries are not as physically obvious and so, when individuals with these disabilities request and are granted an accommodation, resentment by coworkers is more likely.[10]

8-2e Other Dimensions of Diversity

In addition to age, gender, ethnicity, and disability status, organizations are also confronting other dimensions of diversity. One of these is sexual orientation. Although as discussed earlier, the Supreme Court has upheld the right for same-sex couples to be married, in fact, there is no federal law generally prohibiting discrimination against persons because of sexual orientation, and state laws exist in only 22 states. Several years ago, Rep. Barney Frank (D-Mass.) introduced the Employment Non-Discrimination Act (ENDA), but it still

Racorn/Shutterstock.com

has not been passed by Congress. There have been a few important developments, however. First, in 2012, the EEOC ruled that discrimination against transgendered persons was prohibited by the Civil Rights Act because that act prohibited discrimination on the basis of sex. But, in July of 2015, the EEOC went one step further and ruled that existing federal laws regarding sex discrimination should cover lesbian, gay, and bisexual employees as well.[11]

There may be attempts to pass legislation that overturns this EEOC decision, although sentiment in the United States seems to be moving clearly toward support for the LGBT community. Furthermore, there have been a series of executive orders, beginning in 1998, that gradually prohibited discrimination against LGBT employees working for the federal government. Finally, the Society for Human Resource Management (SHRM) called for more training regarding dealing with LGBT employees.[12] SHRM cited recent charges made by EEOC as evidence that the agency intends to stamp out this form of discrimination, and the organization suggests that training helps anti-gay employees to check their personal prejudices at the door and learn to treat all fellow employees with respect. In any case, it is clear that sexual orientation and identity will continue to be an issue in the American workplace, and one that will become even more important as more Americans are willing to "come out of the closet" concerning their sexual orientations.

Over the past few years, in the United States, rights for gays and lesbians have been increasing. A noted in Chapters 1 and 2, there have been a number of court decision that have recognized the rights of same-sex couples,

Contemporary Challenges in HR

Serving the Guests

Tourism is projected by some experts to be the world's largest employer within the next decade. While most think of the travel and tourism industry as consisting of young people who are greeters at airports, servers at restaurant, or front desk agents at hotels, the impact of the growing number of visitors ripples out across national economies to unexpected areas such as jobs in retail, construction, and manufacturing. The challenge for any international destination is to teach employees about the key differences that a nonnative traveler will have that should be accommodated when that traveler arrives at a service experience. Whether the issue is one of language, customs, or service expectations, the employee serving the international customer must be alert to the many variations that different travelers will bring. HR often plays a major role in addressing these issues.

The post-9/11 period in the United States is a good example. This tragic act of terrorism created a surge of patriotism that spanned nearly all Americans in all jobs. This became an especially important issue for the American travel and tourism industry as American employees needed to display special sensitivity to international travelers, especially those from countries that had been publicly hostile to the United States. Some of those travelers, when encountering this patriotism, found it at least mildly uncomfortable and sometimes frighteningly hostile.

This problem was more likely after the travelers left entry cities such as New York or Los Angeles and traveled to other locations perhaps less accustomed to dealing with international guests. Even at portal destinations, however, travelers reported checking into hotels after a long flight and being confronted with a desk agent wearing an American flag and a lapel button displaying an aggressively patriotic slogan. On the streets, people were flying flags on private residences and commercial buildings, and patriotic auto bumper stickers were everywhere. To some foreign travelers coming to the United States to conduct business or vacation, this display was at least a little intimidating.

iofoto/Shutterstock.com

"Crossing the border to a foreign country is always a little stressful. It seems like some countries make it stressful on purpose, while others try hard to make you feel welcome."

—ANONYMOUS INTERNATIONAL TRAVELER

An astute manager of a business-class hotel in New York, Los Angeles, or Washington, DC, might anticipate this situation and provide extra training to sensitize employees to the impact these strong visual might have on guests. Unfortunately, not every manager is astute, and outside the major ports of entry to the United States, there have been reports of situations where the hospitality to ensure a welcoming atmosphere for all visitors was not so well done. If an organization is supposed to be providing a service to all customers, then it is incumbent on managers to ensure that employees are prepared for the variations in customers.

For example, Houston hosts many business and tourist visitors from Mexico and other countries in Latin America and South America. To help ensure proper hospitality, most large hotels in the city have Spanish-speaking employees available at all times. Similarly, large car rental operations such as Hertz and Avis try to have multilingual employees on hand at major airports in cities greeting lots of international visitors. In general, organizations that serve international customers are well-advised to ensure that their employees are provided training and other assistance in managing those customers' experiences so that they and those around them are satisfied.

and attitudes toward gays and lesbians are clearly changing. But that does not mean that discrimination against persons for sexual orientation has been eradicated. In fact, recently, there has been an increased focus on transgendered persons and their rights.

Issues relating to transgendered persons received a great deal of attention in September of 2015 when the former Bruce Jenner became a woman and officially changed her name to Caitlyn. However, from an HR perspective, this focus became much more important as several states passed laws forbidding municipalities from passing LGBT anti-discrimination suits. The states of Georgia and Indiana passed laws that essentially allowed discrimination against gay individuals if that discrimination was based on religious beliefs,[13] although Georgia's governor vetoed the bill after considerable pressure. The state of North Carolina, however, went one step further and passed a bill (North Carolina House Bill 2) that stated individuals must use bathrooms that correspond to the gender listed on their birth certificate. This bill was passed, in part, in response to a law enacted by the city of Charlotte that allowed transgendered persons to use the bathroom corresponding to their consistent gender presentation.

Aside from raising questions about which bathrooms transgendered individuals really should use, it appears that this kind of legislation may be illegal. In May of 2016, the EEOC stated that denying an employee access to a restroom that corresponds to the employee's gender identity is sex discrimination and violates Title Vii of the Civil Rights Act,[14] and further stated that any state laws to the contrary could not be used as a defense. Furthermore, the U.S. Department of Justice asked the State of North Carolina to respond as to whether it will remedy these violations of the law. When the State indicated an unwillingness to make those changes, the Department of Justice brought suit against the State. There were

quickly a series of suits and countersuits among all those involved, with the governor arguing that the new law is not in violation of federal legislation. It is clear that this battle is not over. There will be continuing fights over a person's "right" to discriminate because of religious reasons and the civil rights of all individuals, but it would also appear that the rights of transgendered persons may become the next focus of those fights.

Most of the dimensions of diversity we have been discussing are of particular interest to Americans, but they may not be as critical to employers and employees around the world. Religious diversity is, of course, a more universal concern. In recent years, one religious group has been the target of considerable discrimination in many parts of the world, so religion presents a special challenge for diversity. Ever since September 11, 2001, Americans and Europeans have become much more sensitized to religious differences, with special attention paid to Muslims. Estimates of the total number of Muslims in the world vary greatly, but at approximately 1.6 billion, they represent about 23 percent of the world's population, second in number to Christians, who are 32 percent of the world's inhabitants.[15] Furthermore, Islam is growing about 2.9 percent per year, which is actually faster than the total world population, which increases about 2.3 percent annually. Clearly, Islam is attracting a progressively larger percentage of the world's population. Estimates of the number of Muslims in the United States vary considerably, but according to the U.S. Census Bureau,[16] approximately 2.6 million Americans self-identified as Muslims, which would represent about 1 percent of the population.

Unfortunately, much of the attention paid to and concern over the number of Muslims stems from fears about terrorism. All around the world, there are regular reports about extremist Muslim groups who plot and carry out terrorist attacks, and this leads to a concern that "all" Muslims are potential terrorists. Such a concern, of course, is baseless, but the fact remains that many people are becoming more guarded about interactions with Muslims and are more willing to discriminate against them. Of course, this is illegal in the United States, but recent attitudes about Muslims present new challenges for developing truly diverse workforces.

In addition to sexual orientation and religion, other dimensions of diversity are also relevant. For instance, single parents, people with special dietary preferences (e.g., vegetarians), and people with different political ideologies and viewpoints also represent meaningful dimensions of diversity in today's organizations. Another dimension of diversity that is seldom discussed, Native American standing, is explored in this chapter's Closing Case feature.

 ## 8-3 THE IMPACT OF DIVERSITY ON ORGANIZATIONS

No doubt organizations are becoming ever more diverse. But what is the impact of this diversity on organizations? As we will see, diversity provides both opportunities and challenges and plays several important roles in organizations today.

8-3a Diversity and Social Change

Diversity can significantly affect an organization as a force for social change. This change generally occurs as the composition of an organization's workforce gradually begins to mirror the composition of the surrounding labor market. For example, if a manager in an organization learns to interact effectively with a diverse set of people at work, then she or he will be better equipped to deal with a diverse set of people in other settings. Conversely, an individual who is comfortable interacting in diverse settings should have little problem dealing with diversity at work. Thus, diversity in organizations both facilitates and is facilitated by social change in the environment.

Another way in which organizations affect social change is through the images they use to promote themselves and their products. An organization that runs print ads showing nothing but white male executives in its workplace conveys a certain image of itself. In contrast, an organization that uses diverse groups as representatives conveys a different image.

8-3b Diversity and Competitiveness

Many organizations are also finding that diversity can be a source of competitive advantage in the marketplace. In general, six arguments have been proposed for how diversity contributes to competitiveness.[17] These six arguments are illustrated in Figure 8.4.

1. The *cost argument* suggests that organizations which learn to cope with diversity will generally have higher levels of productivity and lower levels of turnover and absenteeism. Organizations that do a poor job of managing diversity, on the other hand, will suffer from problems of lower productivity and higher levels of turnover and absenteeism. Ortho Pharmaceuticals estimates that it has saved $500,000 by lowering turnover among women and ethnic minorities.

2. The *resource acquisition argument* for diversity suggests that organizations which manage diversity

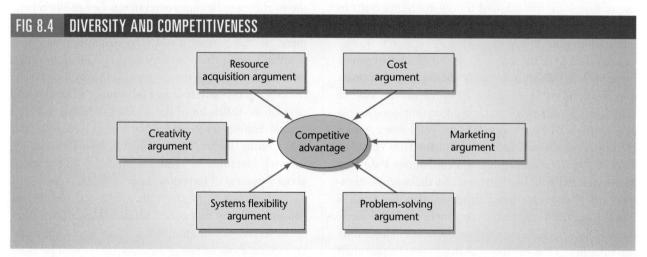

FIG 8.4 DIVERSITY AND COMPETITIVENESS

Source: Ricky W. Griffin, *Management*, 10th ed. © 2011 South-Western, a part of Cengage Learning, Inc. Reproduced by permission. www.cengage.com/permissions.

effectively will become known among women and minorities as good places to work. These organizations will thus be in a better position to attract qualified employees from among these groups. Given the increased importance of these groups in the overall labor force, organizations that can attract talented employees from all segments of society are likely to be more competitive.

3. The *marketing argument* suggests that organizations with diverse workforces will be able to understand different market segments better than will less diverse organizations. For example, a cosmetics firm such as Avon that wants to sell its products to women and African Americans can better understand how to create such products and market them effectively if women and African American managers are available to provide input into product development, design, packaging, advertising, and so forth.

4. The *creativity argument* for diversity suggests that organizations with diverse workforces will generally be more creative and innovative than will less diverse organizations. If an organization is dominated by one population segment, then its members will generally adhere to norms and ways of thinking that reflect that population segment. They will have little insight or few stimuli for new ideas that might be derived from different perspectives. The diverse organization, in contrast, will be characterized by multiple perspectives and ways of thinking and is therefore more likely to generate new ideas and ways of doing things.

5. Related to the creativity argument is the *problem-solving argument*. Diversity

carries with it an increased pool of information. In almost any organization, there is some information that everyone has, and other information is unique to each individual. In an organization with little diversity, the larger pool of information is common, and the smaller pool is unique. But in a more diverse organization, the unique information is larger. Thus, if more information can be brought to bear on a problem, there is a higher probability that better solutions will be identified.[18]

6. Finally, the *systems flexibility argument* for diversity suggests that organizations must become more flexible as a way of managing a diverse workforce. As a direct consequence, the overall organizational system will also become more flexible. Organizational flexibility enables the organization to respond better to changes in its environment. Thus, by effectively managing diversity within its workforce, an organization simultaneously becomes better equipped to address its environment.[19] As we will see below, however, the truth is a bit more complex than these arguments suggest.

8-3c Diversity and Conflict

Diversity in an organization can also become a major source of conflict for various reasons.[20] One potential avenue for conflict is when an individual thinks that someone has been hired, promoted, or fired because of her or his diversity status.[21] For example, suppose a high-performing younger manager loses a promotion to an older manager who happens to be an average performer. If the younger manager believes that the promotion was based solely on age and seniority rather than merit and performance, then he or she will likely feel resentful toward the organization and be less motivated to perform at a high level in the future.

Conflict among whites and African Americans within the ranks of the Federal Aviation Administration (FAA) has been a recurring problem. Some blacks have charged that

"We all should know that diversity makes for a rich tapestry, and we must understand that all the threads of the tapestry are equal in value no matter what their color."

—MAYA ANGELOU,
AMERICAN AUTHOR AND POET

their white supervisors are prejudiced and that African Americans are subject to various subtle forms of discrimination. Some whites, however, believe that the government agency has hired some blacks who are not really qualified for the job of air traffic controller because the agency cannot attract a significant number of qualified employees.[22]

Another source of conflict stemming from diversity is through misunderstood, misinterpreted, or inappropriate interactions between or among people of different groups. For example, suppose a male executive tells a sexually explicit joke to a new female executive. He may intentionally be trying to embarrass her, he may be trying clumsily to show her that he treats everyone the same, or he may think he is making her feel like part of the team. Regardless of his intent, however, if she finds the joke offensive, she will justifiably feel anger and hostility. These feelings may be directed only at the offending individual or more generally toward the entire organization if she believes that its culture facilitates such behavior. Of course, sexual harassment itself is both unethical and illegal.

Firms that have resisted efforts to diversify their workforce often argue that a diverse workforce can hurt a strong corporate culture. Sometimes diversity is impacted indirectly through various poorly conceived employment practices. For example, Pepsi Beverages, PepsiCo's largest bottling unit, recently settled a lawsuit by paying a claim of $3.1 million to more than 300 African American applicants who had been denied jobs at the company. A few years ago, Pepsi Beverages adopted a new criminal background screening process. This process inadvertently screened out people who had been arrested for certain minor offenses, but these offenses had no relevance to Pepsi Beverages employment criteria. In addition to the payments, Pepsi Beverage offered jobs to those applicants who had been denied employment due to the faulty background check process but who were otherwise employable, and the company agreed to establish new job training programs.

Some evidence suggests that conflict may be especially pronounced between older and younger women in the workplace. Older women may be more likely to have sacrificed family for career and to have overcome higher obstacles to get ahead. They were, in a sense, trailblazers. Younger women, on the other hand, may find that organizational accommodations make it relatively easy for them to balance multiple roles and also may have a less-pronounced sense of having to fight to get ahead.[23]

Conflict can also result from other elements of diversity. For example, suppose a U.S. manager publicly praises a Japanese employee for his outstanding work. The manager's action stems from the dominant cultural belief in the United States that such recognition is important and rewarding. But because the Japanese culture places a much higher premium on group loyalty and identity than on individual accomplishment, the employee will likely feel ashamed and embarrassed. A well-intentioned action thus may backfire and result in unhappiness.

Conflict can arise as a result of fear, distrust, or individual prejudice. Members of the dominant group in an organization may worry that newcomers from other groups pose a personal threat to their own position in the organization. For example, when U.S. firms have been taken over by Japanese firms, U.S. managers have sometimes been resentful or hostile to Japanese managers assigned to work with them. People may also be unwilling to accept people who are different from themselves. And, personal bias and prejudices are still very real among some people today and can lead to potentially harmful conflict.

8-3d The Bottom Line on Diversity

Despite the arguments, the data supporting the positive effects of diversity on organizational outcomes is not as clear as one might believe. In fact, several studies have found that diversity leads to positive outcomes such as better firm performance and the absence of harmful conflict. Other studies have found that diversity results in poorer performance and more conflict, and still others find no relationship between diversity and outcomes such as these.[24] This has led some scholars to propose a nonlinear relationship between diversity and such outcomes as conflict and firm performance.[25]

The arguments all follow lines similar to the following: When diversity is low (i.e., most employees are similar to each other), organizations obtain no benefits from diversity (e.g., creativity) but also suffer no penalties (e.g., greater conflict). As diversity increases, positive gains increase, but the problems increase at a greater rate so that the most problematic situation occurs when there is a moderate amount of diversity. However, when a firm becomes truly diverse, to such an extent that there really are no identifiable "minority groups" within the workforce, the positive results of diversity can be truly maximized while most of the problems disappear. The key here is that when a firm reaches true diversity, the conflicts and subgroup dynamics disappear as everyone begins to view themselves as members of the same organization rather than members of a subgroup within the organization. Thus, firms experiencing problems because of workforce diversity would be advised to further increase diversity to make the firm truly diverse. A growing body of research supports exactly this recommendation.[26]

8-4 MANAGING DIVERSITY IN ORGANIZATIONS

Because of the tremendous potential that diversity holds for competitive advantage, as well as the possible consequences of diversity-related conflict, much attention has been focused in recent years on how individuals and organizations can manage diversity better. In the following sections, we first discuss individual strategies for dealing with diversity and then summarize organizational approaches to managing diversity.

8-4a Individual Strategies for Dealing with Diversity

One key element of managing diversity in an organization consists of four actions that individuals themselves can take. Individuals can strive for understanding, empathy, tolerance, and communication.

1. The first element in the strategy is *understanding* the nature and meaning of diversity. Some managers have taken the basic concepts of equal employment opportunity to an unnecessary extreme. They know that, by law, they cannot discriminate against people on the basis of gender, race, and so forth. Thus, in following this mandate, they come to believe they must treat everyone the same. But this belief can cause problems when it is translated into workplace behaviors among people after they have been hired. As noted earlier, people are not the same. Although people need to be treated fairly and equitably, managers must understand that differences do exist among people. Thus, any effort to treat everyone the same, without regard to their fundamental human differences, only leads to problems. It is important, then, for managers to understand that cultural factors cause people to behave in different ways and that these differences should be accepted.

2. Related to understanding is *empathy*. People in an organization should try to understand the perspective of others. For example, suppose a group that has traditionally been composed of white males is joined by a female member. Each male may be a little self-conscious about how to act toward the group's new member and may be interested in making her feel comfortable and welcome. But each one may be able to do this even more effectively by empathizing with how she may feel. For example, she may feel disappointed or elated about her new assignment or confident or nervous about her position in the group, and she may be experienced or inexperienced in working with male colleagues. By learning more about these and similar circumstances, the existing group members can facilitate their ability to work together effectively.

3. A third related individual approach to dealing with diversity is *tolerance*. Even though managers learn to understand diversity, and even though they may try to empathize with others, the fact remains that they may still not accept or enjoy some aspect or behavior on the part of others. For example, one organization recently reported that it was experiencing considerable conflict among its U.S. and Israeli employees. The Israeli employees always seemed to want to argue about every issue that arose. The U.S. managers preferred a more harmonious way of conducting business and became uncomfortable with the conflict. Finally, after considerable discussion, it was learned that many Israeli employees simply enjoy arguing and see it as part of getting work done. The firm's U.S. employees still do not enjoy the arguing but are more willing to tolerate it as a fundamental cultural difference between themselves and their Israeli colleagues.

4. A final individual approach to dealing with diversity is *communication*. Problems often become magnified over diversity issues because people are afraid or otherwise unwilling to discuss issues that relate to diversity. For example, suppose a younger employee has a habit of making jokes about the age of an elderly colleague. Perhaps the younger colleague means no harm and is just engaging in what she sees as good-natured kidding. But the older employee may find the jokes offensive.

If the two do not communicate, then the jokes will continue, and the resentment will grow. Eventually, what started as a minor problem may erupt into a much bigger one. For communication to work, it must be two-way. If a person wonders if a certain behavior on her or his part is offensive to someone else, the curious individual should probably just ask. Similarly, if someone is offended by the behavior of another person, then he or she should explain to the offending individual how the behavior is perceived and request that it stop. As long as such exchanges are handled in a friendly, low-key, and non-threatening fashion, they will generally have a positive outcome. Of course, if the same message is presented in an overly combative manner or if a person continues to engage in offensive behavior after having been asked to stop, then the problem will escalate.

Sergey Nivens/Shutterstock.com

At this point, third parties within the organization may have to intervene. In fact, most organizations today have one or more systems in place to address questions and problems that arise as a result of diversity.

We now turn our attention to the various ways that organizations can manage diversity better.

8-4b Organizational Strategies for Dealing with Diversity

Individuals can play an important role in managing diversity, but the organization itself must also play a fundamental role. Through its various policies and practices, people in the organization come to understand which behaviors are and are not appropriate. Diversity training is an even more direct method for managing diversity. The organization's culture is the ultimate context that diversity must address.

ORGANIZATIONAL POLICIES Managing diversity starts with the policies that an organization adopts because they directly or indirectly affect how people are treated. Obviously, the extent to which an organization embraces the premise of equal employment opportunity determines to a large extent the potential diversity within an organization. But differences exist between the organization that follows the law to the letter and practices passive discrimination and the organization that actively seeks a diverse and varied workforce.

Another aspect of organizational policies that affects diversity is how the organization addresses and responds to problems that arise from diversity. Consider the example of a manager charged with sexual harassment. If the organization's policies put an excessive burden of proof on the individual being harassed and invoke only minor sanctions against the guilty party, then the organization is sending a clear signal about the importance of such matters. But the organization that has a balanced set of policies for addressing questions such as sexual harassment sends its employees a different message about the importance of diversity and individual rights and privileges.

Perhaps the major policy through which an organization can reflect its stance on diversity is its mission statement. If the organization's mission statement articulates a clear and direct commitment to diversity, everyone who reads that mission statement will grow to understand and accept the importance of diversity, at least to that particular organization.

As a result of some of the issues raised here, people have argued that increased diversity should not be a major goal of most organizations. These individuals are not necessarily arguing that diversity is not worth achieving but simply that so many problems are associated with increased diversity that it should not be a major focus of organizations.

ORGANIZATIONAL PRACTICES Organizations can also help manage diversity through various ongoing practices and procedures. Avon's creation of networks for various groups represents one example of an organizational practice that fosters diversity. In general, the idea is that diversity is characterized by differences among people, so organizations can manage that diversity more effectively by following practices and procedures based on flexibility rather than rigidity.

Benefits packages, for example, can be structured to accommodate individual situations. An employee who is part of a dual-career couple and has no children may require relatively little insurance (perhaps because his spouse's employer provides more complete coverage) and would like to be able to schedule vacations to coincide with those of his spouse. Another employee who is a single parent may need a wide variety of insurance coverage and prefer to schedule his vacation time to coincide with school holidays.

Flexible working hours can help an organization accommodate diversity. Differences in family arrangements, religious holidays, cultural events, and so forth may each require that employees have some degree of flexibility in their work schedules. For example, a single parent may need to leave the office every day at 4:30 to pick up the children from their day-care center. An organization that truly values diversity will make every reasonable attempt to accommodate such a need.

Organizations can also facilitate diversity by making sure that it exists in key committees and executive teams. Even if diversity exists within the broader organizational context, an organization that does not reflect diversity in groups such as committees and teams implies that diversity is not a fully ingrained element of its culture. In contrast, when all major groups and related work assignments reflect diversity, the message is quite different. Most U.S. corporations have boards of directors with few, if any, African American directors. Moreover, the trend does not appear to be improving. Increasing board diversity would be a useful step in making any company more inclusive.

DIVERSITY TRAINING Many organizations are finding that diversity training is an effective means for managing diversity and minimizing its associated conflict. **Diversity training** is specifically designed to

iQoncept/Shutterstock.com

enable members of an organization to function better in a diverse workplace. This training can take various forms.[27]

Men and women can be taught to work together more effectively and can gain insights into how their own behaviors affect and are interpreted by others. In one organization, a diversity training program helped male managers gain insights into how various remarks they made to one another could be interpreted by others as being sexist. In the same organization, female managers learned how to point out their discomfort with those remarks without appearing overly hostile.

Similarly, white and black managers may need training to understand each other better. Managers at Mobil noticed that African American colleagues never seemed to eat lunch together. After a diversity training program, they realized that the black managers felt that if they ate together, their white colleagues would be overly curious about what they were talking about. Thus, they avoided close associations with one another because they feared calling attention to themselves.

Some organizations go so far as to provide language training for their employees as a vehicle for managing diversity. Motorola, for example, provides English-language training for its foreign employees on assignment in the United States. At Pace Foods in San Antonio, Texas, staff meetings and employee handbooks are translated into Spanish for the benefit of the company's 100 Hispanic employees (out of a total payroll of 350 employees).

ORGANIZATIONAL CULTURE The ultimate test of an organization's commitment to managing diversity is its culture. Unless there is a basic and fundamental belief that diversity is valued, it cannot become a truly integral part of an organization, regardless of what managers say or put in writing. An organization that really wants to promote diversity must shape its culture so that it clearly underscores

> **Diversity training** is specifically designed to enable members of an organization to function better in a diverse workplace.

top management commitment to and support of diversity in all of its forms throughout every part of the organization. With top management support, and reinforced with a clear and consistent set of organizational policies and practices, diversity can become a basic and fundamental part of an organization.

other group better. Thus, African American employees try to understand white employees, and white employees try just as hard to understand their black colleagues. In addition, every group represented within an organization has the potential to influence the organization's culture and its fundamental norms.

8-4c The Multicultural Organization

Many organizations today are grappling with cultural diversity, but others are succeeding admirably. For instance, some people think of UPS as a somewhat old-fashioned company, and it certainly isn't as splashy as some of its competitors in the shipping industry. But that doesn't mean that UPS is behind the curve in multiculturalism. Jovita Carranza, the company's highest-ranking Hispanic female executive, began working at UPS 30 years ago. She says she never asked for a promotion, but more responsibility came as a result of doing a good job. She now oversees the daily loading and unloading of 1.6 million packages and the 9,000 employees who handle them as they come through UPS Worldport, a 5.2-million-square-foot facility, in Louisville. She notes that there is no diversity officer or diversity committee at UPS. Instead, she notes that diversity and multiculturalism are just part of the way UPS does business.

Even though organizations such as UPS are becoming more diverse, there are few truly multicultural organizations. The multicultural organization is one that has achieved high levels of diversity, one that can capitalize fully on the advantages of the diversity, and one that has few diversity-related problems.[28] A multicultural organization is one in which diversity and the appreciation of all cultures is simply the way business is done. One recent article described the six basic characteristics of such an organization.[29] This perspective is shown in Figure 8.5.

1. The multicultural organization is characterized by pluralism. Every group represented in an organization works to understand every other group better. Thus, African American employees try to understand white employees, and white employees try just as hard to understand their black colleagues. In addition, every group represented within an organization has the potential to influence the organization's culture and its fundamental norms.

2. The multicultural organization achieves full structural integration. Full structural integration suggests that the diversity within an organization is a complete and accurate reflection of the organization's external labor market. If about half of the labor market is female, then about half of the employees are female. This same proportion is reflected at all levels of the organization. No glass ceilings or other subtle forms of discrimination exist in the organization.

3. The multicultural organization achieves full integration of its informal networks. This characteristic suggests that no barriers to entry and participation in any organizational activity exist. For example, people enter and exit lunch groups, social networks, communication grapevines, and other informal aspects of organizational activity without regard to age, gender, ethnicity, or other dimension of diversity.

4. The multicultural organization is characterized by an absence of prejudice and discrimination. No traces of bias exist, and prejudice is eliminated. Discrimination is not practiced in any shape, form, or fashion. Discrimination is nonexistent not because it is illegal but because of the lack of prejudice and bias. People are valued, accepted, and rewarded purely on the basis of their skills and what they contribute to the organization.

5. In the multicultural organization, no gap in organizational identification is based on a cultural identity group. Many organizations tend to make presumptions about organizational roles based on group identity. For example, some people walking into an office and seeing a male and female conversing tend to assume that the female is the

The **multicultural organization** is one that has achieved high levels of diversity, can capitalize fully on the advantages of the diversity, and has few diversity-related problems.

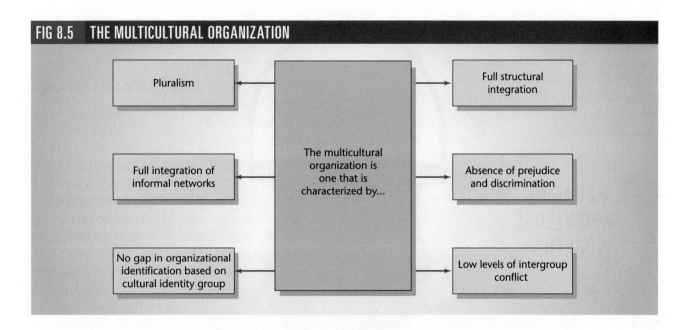

FIG 8.5 THE MULTICULTURAL ORGANIZATION

Pluralism

Full structural integration

Full integration of informal networks

The multicultural organization is one that is characterized by...

Absence of prejudice and discrimination

No gap in organizational identification based on cultural identity group

Low levels of intergroup conflict

secretary and the male is the manager. No such tendencies exist in the multicultural organization. People recognize that males and females are equally likely to be managers and secretaries.

6. The multicultural organization experiences low levels of intergroup conflict. We noted earlier that conflict is a likely outcome of increased diversity. The multicultural organization has evolved beyond this point to a state of almost no conflict among different people. People within the organization fully understand, empathize with, have tolerance for, and openly communicate with, everyone else. Values, premises, motives, attitudes, and perceptions are so well understood by everyone that any conflict that does arise involves meaningful and work-related issues as opposed to differences in age, gender, ethnicity, or other dimensions of diversity.

We began this chapter by discussing how population and immigration patterns in the United States have made the management of diversity such a critical issue. We have also noted recent arguments that suggest moving to a truly multicultural organization might help firms enjoy all the potential benefits of a diverse workforce while avoiding most of the potential problems that can come with increased diversity. But can these same arguments be used to address the issues of diversity in the larger society? The history of the United States has not been characterized by multiculturalism relative to any group. Traditionally, the United States has characterized itself as a "melting pot" in which immigrants from many countries (who have always fueled the growth of the United States) gradually abandoned their identities as Italians or Hondurans or Vietnamese and developed identities as Americans. Perhaps they began by developing a "hyphenated identity" such as Italian-Americans, but the ultimate goal was to become an American. In fact, one of the authors regrets never learning Italian at home—because his parents were raised to be Americans by their immigrant parents.

Thus, foreigners were told that they would be accepted as "Americans" if they simply abandoned their old identities. But until they developed this American identity, immigrants were often pressured to live among others like themselves. Because of this, many cities in the United States developed neighborhoods in which different cultures thrived; many of these became tourist attractions and colorful places to visit such as Little Italy in New York City and Chinatown in San Francisco. But these did not begin as tourist attractions. In fact, these were the only places where the Italians of New York or the Chinese of San Francisco were allowed to live—that is, they were really ghettos. It is instructive to realize that so-called ghettoization has often been the first reaction to dealing with diverse populations until they could become part of the melting pot. Even gay populations, in many cities, tend to be concentrated in certain neighborhoods.

But perhaps our studies of diversity in organizations lead us to an alternative way of dealing with immigrant groups. Is a model of pluralism better in the long run than a melting pot model? Although the traditional model seems to have worked well in the past, perhaps the reasons for immigration have changed and, with them, the effectiveness of the melting pot model.

8-5 MANAGING KNOWLEDGE WORKERS

As should be clear, managing an increasingly diverse workforce is one of the major challenges facing HR managers today. But the workplace also has changed in other ways. One important change has been in the very nature of the organizations we have and the kinds of services they provide. Traditionally, most organizations thought of their products as tangible types of goods; that is, steel companies produced steel, and auto companies produced autos. Over time, however, the economies in many countries, including the United States, shifted from manufacturing to services, and so the orientation shifted to the production of goods *and* services. In today's economy, many organizations are now really trading in knowledge, and this presents a special set of challenges for the HR manager. Investment firms are selling their special knowledge about how to manage a portfolio and plan for retirement or some other goal, consulting firms are selling expertise in dealing with the many management problems that face organizations, and many other types of businesses are actually dealing primarily in knowledge rather than goods or services.

With these shifts also came the recognition that knowledge was also a commodity within an organization that needed to be managed and leveraged. Furthermore, as the nature of work and business changed, many organizations found that they were employing larger numbers of "knowledge workers" who required special handling. In this section, we focus on the notion of organizational learning, which is an important part of the internal knowledge management function, as well as some issues associated with the management of knowledge workers.

8-5a Organizational Learning

Organizational learning refers to the process by which an organization "learns" from past mistakes and adapts to its environment. Over time, rules and procedures change based on experience, but this change, is still based on individual learning; that is, individuals learn how to adapt, change, and then interact with one another so that the new information gained can be shared and distributed throughout the organization. As a result, a shared vision and interpretation of the information is developed, and the change permeates the entire organization. At this point, the organization can be said to have "learned" how to be more effective.

A few points are important to remember. First, the process begins with individual learning and change. If there is no individual learning, then there can be no organizational learning. Second, whereas the individual learning process is cognitive, organizational learning depends more on social processes and sharing of information. Thus, individual learning is a necessary but not sufficient condition for organizational learning to occur.[30]

The process of organizational learning, then, involves the acquisition of new knowledge by the organization. Again, it is not enough that individuals acquire this knowledge; they must then communicate with other organizational members to ensure that this knowledge is available throughout the organization. The organization must then use this information to adapt. There is a strong belief that organizations that can manage this change—that is, organizations that can acquire information and adapt—can gain significant competitive advantage over their competitors.[31]

For example, large conglomerates such as General Electric or Viacom typically grow by acquiring other firms. Each time these firms make an acquisition, they must figure out how to best integrate the new employees into the firm and marry the cultures of the acquired and parent firms. Presumably, these large conglomerates made mistakes over the years in both the targets of their acquisitions and how they managed the

Robert Wroblewski/Shutterstock.com

Organizational learning is the process by which an organization "learns" from past mistakes and adapts to its environment.

acquisitions after they were completed. But they also probably learned from their experiences and got better at it over time. This is a case of organizational learning, and learning how to better target and manage acquisitions would clearly give a conglomerate an advantage over its competitors.

Furthermore, a firm can gain important new knowledge as a result of a merger or acquisition. Thus, for example, a large firm may be contemplating entering a new market in China, but the firm lacks the expertise (or knowledge) on how to enter that difficult market successfully. The large firm (company A) could acquire the needed information by sending key employees to some source where they can learn the needed skills, or it can acquire those skills directly by acquiring individuals who already possess the needed skills. In other words, the large firm can look for another firm (company B) that has already mastered the China market. Then company A can either try to hire the experts away from company B or, if the expert knowledge is widely held throughout company B, access the expertise throughout the firm via a merger, a joint venture, or a complete acquisition of company B.

Finally, we should note the concept of organizational memory and the role it plays in organizational learning. **Organizational memory** refers to the collective, institutional record of past events. For an organization to "learn" from past events, it must be possible to "recall" those events in some way. Some of these events and processes are written down or stored electronically so that a physical record exists for a merger, a change caused by legislation, or any other event from which someone might have learned a lesson. These physical records then serve as the organizational memory. In many cases, however, such information is not formally recorded. Instead, one or more people who were there when the event happened become the organizational memory. These individuals are the repository for information that can help the organization learn from experience and avoid repeating mistakes.

An organization thus can gain access to new information in a variety of ways. After this information is shared and distributed throughout the organization so that all employees now share a view of what this information means and how it can be used to change, organizational learning is said to have occurred. When this information and its interpretation also become part of the organizational memory, change and adaptation can continue for some time. This type of learning and the adaptation involved will clearly be critical to firms as they try to compete effectively in the 21st century.

Monitoring the behavior of banks and other financial firms in the United States in the coming years will be interesting. After the financial crisis of 2009, there was a great deal of criticism about the way banks handled mortgage-backed securities and how these securities were rated and monetized.* Early in 2010, many of these same institutions were criticized because of planned bonus payments. As noted earlier, there is growing sentiment to have the government limit bonuses or at least monitor executive pay policies (which will be discussed in more detail in the next chapter). The question is, will these firms "learn" from their experience? Will they be able to avoid similar financial meltdowns in the future, and will they be able to modify their compensation policies to avoid closer government scrutiny?[32]

8-5b Knowledge Workers

Traditionally, employees were seen as adding value to organizations because of what they did or because of their experience. As we enter the information age in the workplace, however, many employees add value simply because of what they know.[33] This new reality creates new problems and challenges for managing work relationships. Employees who add value simply because of what they know are usually referred to as **knowledge workers**, and how well these employees are managed is seen as a major factor in determining which firms will be successful in the future.[34] Knowledge workers include computer scientists, engineers, and physical scientists, and they provide special challenges for the HR manager. They tend to work in high-tech firms and are usually experts in some abstract

> **Organizational memory** is the collective, institutional record of past events.
>
> **Knowledge workers** are employees who add value simply because of what they know.

---

*In the midst of these discussions about bailouts and bonuses, it was revealed that several G-S employees were short-selling investments they were recommending to their clients. Nothing concrete came of this, but it fueled the arguments that the government should do more to regulate the financial sector.

Megainarmy/Shutterstock.com

knowledge base. They often believe they have the right to work autonomously, and they identify more strongly with their profession than they do with any organization—even to the extent of defining performance in terms recognized by other members of their profession.[35]

As the importance of information-driven jobs grows, so will the need for knowledge workers. But these employees require extensive and specialized training, and not everyone is willing to make the human capital investments necessary to move into these jobs. In fact, even after knowledge workers are on the job, retraining and training updates are critical so that their skills do not become obsolete. It has been suggested, for example, that the "half-life" for a technical education in engineering is about 3 years. Failure to update the required skills by the end of that time not only results in the organization losing competitive advantage but also increases the likelihood that the knowledge worker will go to another firm that is more committed to updating these skills.[36]

Compensation and career-development policies for knowledge workers must also be specially tailored. For example, in many high-tech organizations, engineers and scientists have the option of entering a technical career path that parallels a management career path. This option allows the knowledge worker to continue to carry out specialized work without taking on management responsibilities; at the same time, the organization offers the knowledge worker compensation that is equivalent to the compensation available to management. In addition, in many high-tech organizations, salary adjustments within various classifications for management workers are most frequently based on maturity curves rather than on performance; that is, because performance is difficult to quantify for these employees and because a great deal of research-and-development activity may not have an immediate payoff, salary is based on the employee's years of work experience. The assumption is that, in a technical area, more experience makes the employee more valuable to the organization.[37]

In other high-tech firms, though, the emphasis is on pay for performance, with profit sharing based on projects or products developed by the knowledge workers. In addition, the tendency in most firms employing these workers is to reduce the number of levels of the

> **The growing demand for knowledge workers results in organizations going to extreme measures to attract and retain them.**

organization to allow the knowledge workers to react more quickly to the external environment and reduce the need for bureaucratic approval.[38]

Perhaps the biggest challenge facing firms that employ knowledge workers is figuring out how to attract and retain them. The growing demand for knowledge workers has resulted in firms introducing regular market adjustments to pay in order to retain those employees. Financial firms have used exactly the same argument in defense of the high bonuses paid to employees in 2010. They argue that, despite overall economic conditions, they need to retain their best employees because these are the people responsible for the profits that were made even when economic times were bad. Without such adjustments or bonuses, after an employee accepts a job with a firm, he or she is more subject to the internal labor market, which is not likely to grow as quickly as the external market for knowledge workers. As a result, the longer an employee remains with a firm, the further behind the market rate his or her pay falls—unless it is regularly adjusted.

Of course, the growing demand for these workers also results in organizations going to rather extreme measures to attract them in the first place.[39] When the boom for knowledge workers really began in the 1990s, high starting salaries and signing bonuses were common. At one point, British Petroleum Exploration paid petroleum engineers with undersea-platform-drilling knowledge (not experience, just knowledge) salaries in the six-figure range with signing bonuses of more than $50,000 and immediate profit sharing. The market for knowledge workers is not as hot as it once was, and these bidding wars are a thing of the past. Furthermore, recent high unemployment rates have further depressed salaries in many industries. As the U.S. economy comes out of the recent recession, however, some of these issues may be with us again. In early 2010, the problems Wall Street had experienced produced a soaring demand for a new type of knowledge worker, one who knew how to assess and manage risk for financial institutions. JPMorgan's $6 billion loss reported in June 2012 due to faulty trading decisions underscores that Wall Street still has a long way to go in effectively managing risk. Clearly, the need to better manage knowledge workers is not going away, and organizations can build competitive advantage if they can learn how to better use and manage the knowledge resources they have.[40]

8-6 HUMAN RESOURCE MANAGEMENT AND SOCIAL ISSUES

We turn now to yet another way in which the world of work has changed. Employees, especially younger employees in the 21st century, are more interested in social issues than employees have been for quite some time. These interests affect how potential employees decide where to work and what issues they will get involved in after they are working. Thus, they are extremely important for managing a new generation of human resources. Furthermore, around the world, many organizations are becoming more concerned with the effects of their practices on the larger world around them, and these concerns also have implications for the HR manager. In fact, one study conducted a few years ago found that HR executives in the United States (as well as in Australia, China, and India) are more likely to be in charge of implementing and monitoring areas associated with social issues and social responsibility than any other functional executive.[41]

There is an increasing awareness that the needs of the organization can be met even while addressing the needs of the employees or of society as a whole,[42] and there is also an increasing concern with social issues in general. In fact, this is one area in which management and organized labor can often come together. Furthermore, labor unions in the United States have been especially successful at using these issues to change their image as that of a group of people concerned about conditions around the world, which we will discuss further in Chapter 11. For now, however, we will discuss several social issues that have begun playing a role in the lives of HR managers. These key social issues are shown in Figure 8.6.

8-6a Prison Labor

Most of us do not spend a lot of time thinking about what prison inmates do with their time, but, in most cases, they work at jobs inside the prisons. Traditionally, these jobs included manufacturing automobile license plates, repairing roads, or doing the laundry for other state institutions, but that situation has been changing. As we note in Chapter 11, this is a source of concern for the U.S. labor movement, but it is increasingly a source of concern for HR managers as well.

First, the number of prisoners involved has been changing. In 1990, there were approximately 66,000 federal prisoners and 708,000 state and local prisoners. By 2014, those numbers had risen to approximately 185,000 federal inmates and 2.15 million state and local inmates. Many of these inmates work at paid jobs, but they earn somewhat less than workers on the outside. In fact, in 1991, prison wages ranged from $0.23 to $1.15 per hour on a federal pay scale, although more than half these workers earned $0.40 per hour or less.[43] Second, the laws regulating where and how the goods produced by inmate labor can be sold have been changing, thus making it easier to sell products produced by inmates on the open market. Since 1980, the number of people in prison has increased 458 percent.

The fact that goods produced at such a low cost can compete openly with goods produced by workers who are paid a minimum wage is potentially a serious threat to the jobs of low-paid, unskilled workers in the general population.[44] In fact, some critics argue that prison labor

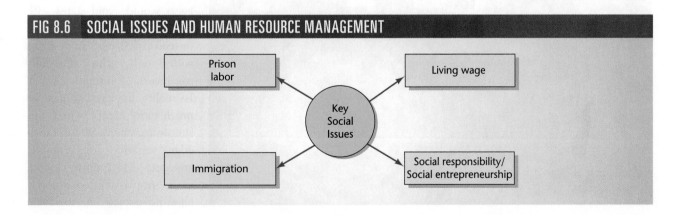

FIG 8.6 SOCIAL ISSUES AND HUMAN RESOURCE MANAGEMENT

contributes little to the gross domestic product but substantially affects the employment opportunities and wages of high school dropouts in this country.[45] These same critics also argue that these jobs do not prepare prison inmates for outside jobs after they are released and so do not lessen the rates of subsequent arrest and incarceration.

What should we do? Clearly, several different issues are involved. One relates to the problem of allowing products produced by prisoners (who are paid less) to compete with products that are produced by employees who earn a legal wage. Although companies may need incentives to hire prison workers, allowing these goods to compete more freely in the open market may actually be a problem. Other organizations can see this as a way to gain some advantage, and eventually, we can see a very heavy reliance on prison labor. In addition, we must think about what we would like to have inmates do while they are in prison. For those who will never be released, this may not be a problem, but for others it may be important that the work they do in prison will help them get and keep jobs on the outside. Furthermore, the employees should probably be paid what their work is really worth.

8-6b A Living Wage

In Chapter 2, we discussed the minimum wage and noted that there is some controversy over whether the minimum wage should be raised (we discuss overall compensation in Chapter 9). But how does a person earning the national minimum wage of $7.25 actually live? That person will earn less than $300 per week or slightly more than $15,000 per year. It is difficult to imagine how someone would support a family on that much money. Instead, there are proponents in our country who suggest that we should work instead toward paying employees a "living wage"—that is enough to allow a family to live above the poverty level. In fact, this is exactly what several states have done. For example, the minimum wage in Connecticut is more than $9.00 per hour, and the minimum wage in the District of Columbia is more than $10.00 per hour. These are attempts to ensure that working people can live at some reasonable level, but they may not be enough.

In New Orleans after Hurricane Katrina, there was a shortage of workers for jobs in fast-food restaurants. As a result, Burger King was offering $10 an hour to start and a $5,000 signing bonus if the employee worked for 1 year. But Katrina destroyed much of the lower-middle-class housing that had been available in New Orleans, and the housing that remained was expensive even at these higher wages. Therefore, even these wages could not attract a sufficient number of employees for some time.

The challenge, then, is how we should determine what someone is paid. The traditional HRM approach is either to conduct some type of job evaluation (we discuss some of these in Chapter 9) or do a survey to determine the "going rate" in a given market. The living wage movement suggests that this is not adequate and that organizations owe their employees the ability to live a reasonable life. Of course, opponents argue that if a state (or a firm) pays above market rate, then it will need to either charge more for its goods (making them less competitive) or accept lower profits. Therefore, the argument continues that rational managers would avoid states with higher minimum wages and instead locate in states with only the federally mandated minimum wage. In reality, however, things are much more complex than this simple argument. Many knowledge workers, for example, are located in California, and, as a result, high-tech may have no choice but to locate

L. Kragt Bakker/Shutterstock.com

there despite the higher minimum wage simply due to labor market conditions. In fact, many different factors, such as quality of life, quality of health care, weather, state regulation, and so forth are also considered in addition to labor costs as businesses look for places to locate.

But should HR managers be social activists? Should they argue for a living wage as opposed to a more competitive wage? In fact, that is exactly what some states and cities have done. As also noted in Chapter 2, the minimum wage in California and Massachusetts is $10.00 per hour, while, in Los Angeles, the minimum wage is set to increase to $15.00 by 2020. This became a big issue in the Democratic Party primaries leading up to the 2016 presidential election. Representative Bernie Sanders (I-Vt.) has proposed raising the national minimum wage to $15.00 an hour and expanding Social Security benefits for retired persons as well.

An interesting development in this area was the decision announced by Walmart to raise its minimum wage to $9.00 an hour. This raise went into effect immediately, and before the end of 2016, this minimum was raised to $10.00 an hour. However, for employees who earn more than this minimum, there are no raises. Thus, Walmart now has many unhappy employees who are complaining that they did not receive any raise, and so new hires were making what they (more experienced workers) were making.[46] In October of 2014, Walmart announced that, because of these wage hikes (and a strong dollar causing slow sales), Walmart operating profits would plunge about $1.5 billion in fiscal 2017.[47] In response, Walmart's stock dropped 10 percent the next day, suggesting that dealing with the problem of a living wage is not easy, and the stock continued to struggle at more than 20 percent below its' price in early 2015. For some of our readers, it will be difficult not to speak out.

8-6c Immigration

We noted earlier that immigration had become a major issue for Republicans vying for the 2016 presidency of the United States. Much of this actually began back in 2006, when Congress was trying to deal with the problems of illegal immigrants. People were angry, and they continue to be so, and this is an issue that has a great impact on HR mangers who must deal with sometimes both legal and illegal immigrants.

The concerns during 2006 were specifically with illegal immigrants. These are people who have entered the country illegally but who are living (and often working) in this country. These workers are typically willing to accept lower wages, and they are usually in no position to complain about their working conditions, which makes them perfect targets for anyone who wants to exploit them. Why would someone do that? There are several reasons.

First, as noted, these workers are willing to work for lower wages. This allows organizations and employers to hold down labor costs. These workers are also usually quite willing to work hard, so they may be especially productive. In some cases, these workers are also willing to perform jobs that other workers are unwilling to do. In addition, even if they are paid exploitative wages, they are probably earning more than they could earn in their home countries. So what is the problem?

As with several of the issues we have been discussing, one problem is that U.S. citizens (or legal immigrants) who need to work to support a family will either not find jobs or will be forced to work for lower wages because an employer can always go to illegal immigrants if necessary, even though these illegal immigrants cannot really support their families on the wages they earn. But the immigration problem is actually even more complex. Congress tried to come up with legislation that would make it more difficult for illegal immigrants to enter the United States but would also allow a "path to citizenship" for those that were already here illegally—a plan supported by then President Bush. But this idea of a path to citizenship became political dynamite, and no real action was taken.

> "If we cannot end now our differences, at least we can help make the world safe for diversity. For, in the final analysis, our most basic common link is that we all inhabit this small planet. We all breathe the same air. We all cherish our children's future. And we are all mortal."
>
> —JOHN F. KENNEDY, 35TH PRESIDENT OF THE UNITED STATES

Several years later, President Obama took executive action that would force some rules about illegals and allow a path for citizenship, but his actions have been frozen by several court decisions. Meanwhile, on the political front, this has become a defining difference between the Republican and Democratic parties during the presidential primaries. Democratic candidates favor a path to citizenship for illegal immigrants, while Republican candidates generally do not, and, as mentioned earlier, Donald Trump has proposed building a wall to keep Mexican immigrants out. All candidates favor tougher rules and enforcement of the U.S. borders to keep illegal immigrants from entering the country, but they cannot agree how this would best be accomplished. This debate will go on for some time, and, in some ways, it strikes at the core of the character of the United States as this a nation of immigrants.

But dealing with immigration problems is not only the case for the United States. In the wake of the Syrian civil war and the rise of Muslim extremists such as ISIS, there has been a hug outflow of people from Syria and the surrounding territory. The United Nations estimated that, in 2015, more than 360,000 immigrants have entered Europe from Iraq, Syria, and Afghanistan. European countries such as Germany and Austria, which have welcomed these refugees now feel overwhelmed by the sheer numbers.[48] Other countries in Europe have begun taking some of the load, and the United States had agreed to take in some 10,000 refugees as well. This was not well-received by all Americans, however, as some believed that many of the refugees were actually terrorists. Unfortunately, issues of immigration and dealing with refugees will be a problem for the foreseeable future. There remains, however the question of how do organizations find employees to perform undesirable, unskilled, and relatively low-paying jobs that need to be done? Could older, retired workers perform some of them? What do we owe employees, even if they are guests? Do we owe them full benefits? Job security? Education? Is the solution simply to make sure that everyone is paid a living wage so that there would be no advantage to a firm hiring illegal immigrants? Finally, how do all of these issues affect those who have entered the United States legally and are pursuing normal channels to become citizens? In closing, it is interesting to note that as unemployment rates began to rise to 10 percent in the United States in 2010 and as major financial institutions struggled or died, illegal immigration to the United States also seems to have subsided.

8-6d Social Responsibility and Social Entrepreneurship

Our discussion about the role of social issues has focused to this point on specific social issues that present challenges for HR managers. But broader social issues also affect the way entire corporations do business and also affect how they manage their people.

Corporate social responsibility (CSR) is one label that has been frequently used to describe a dedication to build organizations that are accountable, responsible, transparent, and ecologically sustainable.[49] In the United States, much of the impetus for CSR grew out of a series of Supreme Court decisions in the 1950s that allowed corporations to participate in philanthropic enterprises. In the 1960s, much of the attention turned to consumer safety and consumer protection, as well as environmental issues. By the 1980s, CSR became much more concerned with corruption, but beginning in the 1990s, the focus broadened to consider every aspect of a company's strategy, business model, and business practices. Today, there is recognition that we must integrate environmental concerns with every aspect of a firm's strategic management.[50]

The ongoing challenge is balancing these concerns for the environment with the responsibility to other stakeholders to make a profit, but recent years have seen much more emphasis on being "green"—that is, reducing carbon footprints and finding ways to actually help the environment while still making a profit. In fact, in recent years, several analysts have demonstrated that it is feasible to be socially responsible and profitable by reducing costs while at the same time gaining access to new markets and being able to differentiate one's products from those of others.[51]

John Mackey, co-CEO of Whole Foods, does not like the term *corporate social responsibility*. Instead, he prefers to describe his company's approach as *conscious capitalism*. He believes that a corporation should make a profit, but it should use that profit to further worthwhile social causes around the globe. Mackey and his employees (who make their own commitments) fund projects ranging from microloan programs to schools. Many of these are in Latin America, where Whole Foods buys many of its products.[52] Whole Foods' entire corporate philosophy and corporate culture is guided by Mackey's ideas, so a person who does not share his views probably will not fit comfortably into the Whole Foods organization.

Finally, we should note the concept of *social entrepreneurship*. Many scholars and writers use this term differently (in fact, John Mackey has described Whole Foods as a corporation that follows this concept), but it generally refers to applying business and entrepreneurial skills and tools to deal with social problems. In practice, this might manifest as a business school program designed to train managers for not-for-profit organizations, or it might simply refer to taking a more businesslike approach to dealing with charity. Organizations such as Whole Foods are becoming more active in transferring what they have learned about doing business to deal with social problems, and this is likely to continue as a trend. There is a lot of speculation that the new generation of university students is more socially conscious and so more interested in how to apply business models to social problems. For the HR manager, this may mean recruiting a different breed of employees or at least finding a way to lead and motivate a new generation of employees. It may also mean that business will be run differently, so human resources will have to be managed differently to support these new strategic directions. In any event, social issues are clearly changing the nature of the workplace and the people working there.

CLOSING CASE
(Native) American Diversity

Diversity conversations seldom include Native Americans. There is even disagreement over how these individuals should be identified. But whether we use the terms "American Indian" or "Native American," or refer to their tribal affiliation (Cherokees are the largest, with more than 800,000 members), the prevailing perception is that Native Americans are a relatively homogeneous group. But while different tribes each have their own issues and are actually quite heterogeneous, there are some issues that face all Native Americans.

According to current census data, there are 5.2 million Native Americans living in the United States (including American Indians and Alaska Natives), and this number is projected to grow to 8.6 million by 2050. The largest Native American populations are in Oklahoma and California, but another nine states each have more than 100,000 Native American residents. Furthermore, with a median age of 29 (compared to 37 for the general population), Native Americans will become increasingly important for the workforce.

Since 1871, American Indians have been considered wards of the U.S. government, and, although we are now more sensitive to the history of how the U.S. government treated Native Americans, images of "cowboys and Indians" are still part of society—as reflected in recent debates over using names and images associated with their culture as names, mascots, and logos for sports teams. And while relations between the U.S. government and Native Americans have certainly improved, conflicts are still often solved by actions of the U.S. military or are referred to the Bureau of Indian Affairs, a non-Indian Federal organization.

As a result, diversity initiatives aimed at Native Americans face unique challenges. One grows out of the

Kobby Dagan/Shutterstock.com

tension between assimilation and the desire to maintain a strong Native American and tribal identity. This drives discussions over the role of tribal courts and tribal governments relative to issues of child custody, sentencing

(Continued)

(Closing Case – continued)

guidelines, and general policies aimed at "mainstreaming" Native American children. Another challenge stems from the fact that for many Native Americans, there is no clear definition of religion—religious beliefs are part of their way of life and cannot be separated. Consequently, it is not clear what protections are afforded to Native Americans under the First Amendment, or what religious rights they have (although in one case employees at Oglala Lakota College are granted 5 days of leave for their Sun Dance ceremony).

Native Americans face many of the same challenges confronting other minority groups, including stereotypes, prejudice, and bias, as well as the relative lack of quality education, poverty, early parenthood, and substance abuse. But while all Civil Rights legislation applies to Native Americans (Native Americans were granted citizenship rights in 1924), few cases have been brought on behalf of Native Americans. In fact, it was only in 1997 that the Civil Rights Division of the U.S. Department of Justice first enforced the education statues on behalf of Native Americans by ordering a Utah school district to build a new high school in a remote community populated mostly by Navajo and Paiute tribe members.

Diversity efforts targeted at Native Americans deserve more attention because Native Americans have a great deal to offer modern business. Native Americans are much more likely to be bilingual when compared with the general population—over 70 percent of the Navajo nation is bilingual, for instance. Even though the second language involved is often a tribal language, these statistics suggest that Native Americans have strong language skills. They also appear to have strong entrepreneurial skills: There are now more than 400 tribal gaming casinos, operated across 30 states, generating $15.5 billion dollars in annual revenues. It therefore seems clear that Native Americans represent a growing yet vastly underutilized group of employees who have a strong cultural tradition combined with strong entrepreneurial skills. They clearly deserve more attention as the target of diversity initiatives.[53]

CASE QUESTION

1. Why do you think Native Americans are so seldom discussed in the context of diversity?

2. If you were an HR manager, what special strategies might you adopt to recruit more Native Americans to apply for positions in your organization?

STUDY 8
TOOLS 8

READY TO STUDY?

In the book, you can:

☐ Rip out the chapter review card at the back of the book for a handy summary of the chapter and key terms.

ONLINE AT CENGAGEBRAIN.COM YOU CAN:

☐ Collect StudyBits while you read and study the chapter.

☐ Quiz yourself on key concepts.

☐ Find videos for further exploration.

☐ Prepare for tests with HR4 Flash Cards as well as those you create.

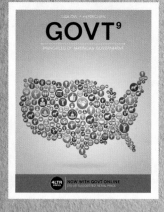
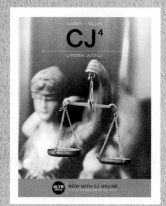

9 | Compensation and Benefits

After finishing this chapter go to **PAGE 243** for **STUDY TOOLS**

LEARNING OBJECTIVES

9-1 Describe the basic issues involved in developing a compensation strategy

9-2 Discuss how organizations develop a wage and salary structure

9-3 Identify and describe the basic issues involved in wage and salary administration

9-4 Discuss the basic considerations in understanding benefit programs

9-5 Identify and describe mandated benefits

9-6 Identify and describe nonmandated benefits

9-7 Discuss contemporary issues in compensation and benefits

AP Images/Jacquelyn Martin

If you're looking for the best Parmesan cheese for your chicken parmigiana recipe, you might try Wegmans, especially if you happen to live in the vicinity of Pittsford, New York. Cheese department manager Carol Kent will be happy to recommend the best brand because her job calls for knowing cheese as well as managing some 20 subordinates. Kent is a knowledgeable employee, and Wegmans sees that as a key asset. Specifically, Wegmans believes that its employees are more knowledgeable than are the employees of its competitors.

Wegmans Food Markets, a family-owned East Coast chain with more than 80 outlets in six states, prides itself on its commitment to customers, and it shows. It consistently ranks near the top of the annual *Consumer Reports* survey of the best national and regional grocery stores. But commitment to customers is only half of Wegmans' overall strategy, which calls for reaching its customers through its employees. "How do we differentiate ourselves?" asks Danny Wegman, who then proceeds to answer his own question: "If we can sell products that require knowledge in terms of how you use them, that's our strategy. Anything that requires knowledge and service gives us a reason to be." That's the logic behind one of Kent's recent assignments—one which she understandably regards as a perk. Wegmans sent her to Italy to conduct a personal study of Italian cheese. "We sat with the families" that make the cheeses, she recalls, "broke bread with them. It helped me understand that we're not just selling a piece of cheese. We're selling a tradition, a quality."

Kent and the employees in her department also enjoy the best benefits package in the industry, including fully paid health insurance. And, that includes part-timers, who make up about two-thirds of the company's workforce of more than 37,000. In part, the strategy of extending benefits to this large segment of the labor force is intended to make sure that stores have enough good workers for crucial peak periods, but there's no denying that the costs of employee-friendly policies can mount up. At 15–17 percent of sales, for example, Wegmans' labor costs are well above the 12 percent figure for most supermarkets. But according to one company HR executive, holding down labor costs isn't necessarily a strategic priority: "We would have stopped offering free health insurance [to part-timers] a long time ago," she admits, "if we tried to justify the costs."

Besides, employee turnover at Wegmans is about 6 percent—a mere fraction of an industry average that hovers around 19 percent (and can approach 100 percent

> ## "We would have stopped offering free health insurance [to part-timers] a long time ago," she admits, "if we tried to justify the costs."
>
> —WEGMANS HR MANAGER[1]

for part-timers). And, this is an industry in which total turnover costs have been known to outstrip total annual profits by 40 percent. Wegmans employees tend to be knowledgeable because about 20 percent of them have been with the company for years, and many have logged at least a quarter century. Says one 19-year-old college student who works at an upstate New York Wegmans while pursuing a career as a high school history teacher, "I love this place. If teaching doesn't work out, I would so totally work at Wegmans." Edward McLaughlin, who directs the Food Industry Management Program at Cornell University, understands this sort of attitude: "When you're a 16-year-old kid, the last thing you want to do is wear a geeky shirt and work for a supermarket," but at Wegmans, he explains, "it's a badge of honor. You're not a geeky cashier. You're part of the social fabric."

Wegmans usually ranks high on *Fortune* magazine's annual list of 100 Best Companies to Work For. "It says that we're doing something right," says a company spokesperson, "and that there's no better way to take care of our customers than to be a great place for our employees to work." In addition to its health-care package, Wegmans has been cited for such perks as fitness center discounts, compressed work weeks, telecommuting, and domestic partner benefits, which extend to same-sex partners.

Finally, under the company's Employee Scholarship Program, full-time workers can receive up to $2,200 a year for 4 years and part-timers up to $1,500. Since its inception in 1984, the program has handed out $80 million in scholarships to more than 24,000 employees. Like most Wegman policies, this one combines employee outreach with long-term corporate strategy: "This program has made a real difference in the lives of many young people," says President Colleen Wegman, who adds that it's also "one of the reasons we've been able to attract the best and the brightest to work at Wegmans."

Granted, Wegmans, which has remained in family hands since its founding in 1915, has an advantage in being as generous with its resources as its family of top executives wants to be. It doesn't have to do everything with quarterly profits in mind, and the firm likes to point out that taking care of its employees is a long-standing priority. Profit sharing and fully funded medical coverage were introduced in 1950 by Robert Wegman, son and nephew of brothers Walter and John, respectively, who opened the firm's original flagship store in Rochester, New York, in 1930. Why did Robert Wegman make such generous gestures to his employees way back then? "Because," he says simply, "I was no different from them."

THINK IT OVER

1. Why does Wegman's approach to compensation seem to work so well?

2. In your opinion, why don't other grocery chains use the same compensation model as Wegman's?

The amount of value people create for an organization and what the organization gives them as compensation for that value are important determinants of organizational competitiveness. If employers pay too much for the value created by workers, then profits (and hence competitiveness) will suffer. But if they pay too little or demand too much from their workers for what they are paying, they will suffer in different ways: lower-quality workers, higher turnover, or employee fatigue and stress. Clearly, then, managing compensation and benefits are important activities for any organization. And just as clearly, Wegmans' managers have a keen understanding of the relationship between worker compensation and company performance.

Compensation and benefits refer to the various types of outcomes employees receive for their time at work. **Compensation** is the set of rewards that organizations provide to individuals in return for their willingness to perform various jobs and tasks within the organization. **Benefits** are the various rewards, incentives, and other items of value that an organization provides to its employees beyond wages, salaries, and other forms of financial compensation. The term *total compensation* is sometimes used to refer to the overall value of financial compensation plus the value of additional benefits that the organization provides.

In this chapter, we cover the basic concepts of compensation and benefits. We start by examining how compensation strategies are developed, and then we turn to the administration of compensation programs and how organizations evaluate their compensation programs. We look at benefits, discussing the basic reasons for benefit plans and describing different types of benefit plans typically found in organizations. Next we consider the often controversial topic of executive compensation, discussing the basic components of executive-compensation packages and why they are so controversial. We conclude with a discussion of legal issues associated with compensation and benefits and the ways in which organizations can evaluate their compensation and benefit programs.

 9-1 ## DEVELOPING A COMPENSATION STRATEGY

Compensation should never be a result of random decisions but instead the result of a careful and systematic strategic process.[2] Embedded in the process is an understanding of the basic purposes of compensation, an assessment of strategic options for compensation, knowledge of the determinants of compensation strategy, and the use of pay surveys.

9-1a **Basic Purposes of Compensation**

Compensation has several fundamental purposes and objectives. First, the organization must provide appropriate and equitable rewards to employees. Individuals who work for organizations want to feel valued and be rewarded at a level commensurate with their skills, abilities, and contributions to the organization. In this regard, an organization must consider two different kinds of equity. In addition, compensation serves a "signaling" function. Organizations signal to employees what they feel is important (and less important) for an employee to focus on by paying for certain kinds of activities or behaviors (and not for others). As we discuss in more detail in the next chapter, compensation can serve as an incentive to employees to increase their efforts along desired lines. We turn first to the issues of fairness and equity.

Internal equity in compensation refers to comparisons made by employees to other employees within

Compensation is the set of rewards that organizations provide to individuals in return for their willingness to perform various jobs and tasks within the organization.

Benefits generally refer to various rewards, incentives, and other things of value that an organization provides to its employees beyond their wages, salaries, and other forms of direct financial compensation.

Internal equity in compensation refers to comparisons made by employees to other employees within the same organization.

the same organization. In making these comparisons, the employee is concerned that he is equitably paid for his contributions to the organization relative to the way other employees are paid in the firm. For example, a female account manager learns that most other account managers in the firm are paid more than she is. By looking closely at the situation, she may determine that these other account managers have similar experience and responsibilities, and she may become unhappy with her compensation and ask for a raise. In this case, she may also threaten to sue for pay discrimination. Of course, on the other hand, when the female account manager looks more closely, she may determine that she has fewer responsibilities and less experience, and so she concludes that there is no equity problem. In any case, problems with internal equity can result in conflict, feelings of mistrust, low morale, and even legal action in some cases.

External equity in compensation refers to comparisons made by employees with similar employees at other firms performing similar jobs. For example, an accountant may experience internal equity relative to her accounting colleagues in her work group because she knows they are all paid the same salary. But if she finds out that another major employer in the same community is paying its accountants higher salaries for comparable work, then she might be concerned about external equity. Problems with external equity may result in higher turnover (because employees will leave for better opportunities elsewhere), dissatisfied and unhappy workers, and difficulties in attracting new employees.

How does an employer learn about compensation rates at other firms? In some cases, an HR manager might simply ask a colleague for such information, but there are potential charges of "price-fixing" if such discussions are too detailed. More commonly, much of the information concerning external equity comes from a pay survey, or a survey of compensation paid to employees by other employers in a particular geographic area, industry, or occupational group. Some such surveys, especially for executive and managerial jobs, are conducted by professional associations such as the Society for Human Resource Management, and the results are then made available to all members. Individual

employees may have access to this information, or they may seek their own comparative data on the Internet. In fact, as discussed more fully in this chapter's Contemporary Challenges in HR feature, "Negotiating Salaries on the Web," the Internet is making this practice increasingly common and easy today.

Other organizations also routinely conduct wage surveys. Business publications such as *Business Week*, *Fortune*, and *Nation's Business* routinely publish compensation levels for various kinds of professional and executive positions. In addition, the Bureau of National Affairs and the Bureau of Labor Statistics also are important sources of government-controlled wage and salary survey information. To obtain the *exact* data they need, however, many larger firms design their own pay surveys, which allows the firm to take advantage of the expertise available in such firms and minimize their own risk and the prospects of making a significant error or mistake in the conduct of the survey.[3] Figure 9.1 presents a sample section from a pay survey.

A survey such as this one is sent to other organizations in a given region. In this case, the survey would go to organizations in various industries, but other surveys might be targeted to a specific industry. The jobs that are the focus of the survey should be benchmark jobs—that is, everyone understands the nature of the job, the content is fairly stable, and the job is likely to be found in a wide variety of organizations. In some surveys, specific benchmark jobs are coded to ensure that everyone reacts to the same job. In addition, some surveys ask more specific questions about other areas of compensation. Data from surveys such as this are then summarized for each job.

Both internal and external equity are clearly important for an organization's compensation strategy. Perceptions of external inequity can lead to the type of job search that results in the voluntary turnover problems

External equity in compensation refers to comparisons made by employees to others employed by different organizations performing similar jobs.

Pay surveys are surveys of compensation paid to employees by other employers in a particular geographic area, industry, or occupational group.

Contemporary Challenges in HR

Negotiating Salaries on the Web

For decades, negotiations about individual wages and salaries were typically handled in a meeting between the employee and his or her manager. The same approach was used both for individuals who were being offered their first job with the company and for existing employees who felt they deserved a raise. But in both cases, the supervising manager and the organization itself usually had the upper hand. This situation stemmed from the fact that both prospective and current employees generally had relatively little knowledge about prevailing wage and salary levels. They usually did not know what others in the firm were being paid, for example, or what similar companies were paying for similar jobs in different parts of the region or country.

To make things worse (for the employee), locating this kind of information was difficult. National and regional data were sometimes published in government reports, but the information was often dated and/or incomplete. Local information could sometimes be located more efficiently, but it too was likely to be dated or flawed. For example, when coworkers ask one another what they are being paid, they may be reluctant to provide details. And, they may even inflate or deflate their answers to either make themselves look better or avoid creating resentment.

But the Internet has rapidly changed all that. For instance, several free websites, such as Glassdoor.com, now provide salary information for interested parties. Among other information, these sites include salary survey data,

job listings with specified pay levels, and even customized compensation analyses. Other sites provide even more detailed information for a fee. Armed with such detailed information, more and more people today are negotiating better deals for themselves with their employers.

Sometimes the Web can also provide even more insights, especially for crafty negotiators. For example, some people have been known to use Internet bulletin boards to track down other individuals who have recently been offered employment with a particular firm, find out how much they were offered, and then use that information as leverage in their own negotiations. That is, they can confidently discuss with their prospective employer what that employer has been offering to other job candidates.

In another interesting development, the big-time recruiting firm of Korn Ferry recently set up its own salary site called Futurestep. But the firm faced internal negotiations when some of its own employees used the site to determine that they themselves were being underpaid! On balance, then, it seems like the Internet will be playing a major role from now on in the kinds of wages and salaries that employees expect and that companies pay.[4]

THINK IT OVER

1. How do you foresee using the Internet in your initial job search after you finish school?

2. Are there drawbacks to using the Internet to search for salary information?

---

discussed in Chapter 6. But when a female employee, for example, perceives internal inequity vis-à vis a male employee, this can also lead to a lawsuit. Recall from Chapter 2 that the Equal Pay Act of 1963 stipulates that men and women who perform essentially the same job

> **Under the Equal Pay Act of 1963, men and women who perform essentially the same job must be paid the same.**

must be paid the same. If there are differences in the compensation paid to men and women, then such differences may be defensible if they are based on factors such as performance differentials. In any case, the organization may well find itself in court defending these decisions when there are perceptions of internal inequity.

Compensation can also serve a *motivational purpose*— that is, individuals should perceive that their efforts and contributions to the organization are recognized and rewarded. Individuals who work hard and perform at a high level should be compensated at a level higher than individuals who do just enough to get by and who perform at only an average or below average rate.[5] If everyone perceives this

FIG 9.1   EXAMPLE OF A PAY SURVEY

Organization: ABC Trucking
Location: Dallas, TX

Benchmark Jobs	No. of workers (this title)	No. of workers (total)	Average weekly hours	Base Pay			Median total compensation (base pay + benefits)	Industry			
				25th %-tile	50th %-tile	75th %-tile		Mfg.	Trans.	Utilities	Trade
File clerk	10	300	40	$15,000	$20,000	$25,000	$28,000		✓		
Order clerk											
Accounting clerk											

A survey such as this one is sent to other organizations in a given region. In this case, the survey would go to organizations in various industries, but other surveys might be targeted to a specific industry. The jobs that are the focus of the survey should be benchmark jobs, where everyone understands the nature of the job, the content is fairly stable, and the job is likely to be found in a wide variety of organizations. In some surveys, specific benchmark jobs are coded to ensure that everyone reacts to the same job. In addition, some surveys ask more specific questions about other areas of compensation. Data from surveys such as this one are then summarized for each job.

situation to be true, then employees will believe that the reward system is fair and just and that internal equity exists, and they will be more motivated to perform at their highest level. Clearly, then, organizations must adequately and effectively manage compensation. Underpayment can cause the problems discussed previously, although it is also important for organizations to control costs and not overpay individuals for the value of their contributions (which could lead to problems with internal equity) or provide excess or superfluous benefits or rewards.[6] Thus, the ideal compensation system reflects an appropriate balance of organizational constraints, costs, budgets, income, and cash flow relative to employee needs, expectations, demands, and market forces. We will discuss specific models of motivation in Chapter 13 and incentive pay plans in Chapter 14.

> The Fair Labor Standards Act established a minimum hourly wage for jobs and further stipulated that wages for hourly workers must be paid at a rate of one and a half times the normal rate for work in excess of 40 hours per week.

The fundamental purpose of compensation, then, is to provide an adequate and appropriate reward system for employees so that they feel valued and worthwhile as organizational members and representatives. Compensation represents more than the number of dollars a person takes home in her or his pay envelope. It also provides a measure of the employee's value to the organization and functions indirectly as an indicator of the employee's self-worth.[7]

9-1b Wages versus Salaries

An important distinction in the field of compensation is the difference between wages and salaries. **Wages** generally refer to hourly compensation paid to operating employees. Time is the basis for wages—that is, the organization pays individuals for specific blocks of their time such as payment by the hour. Most jobs that are paid on an hourly wage basis are lower-level or operational jobs within the organization. These employees are also eligible for the overtime provisions of the Fair Labor Standards Act (discussed in Chapter 2), which means they are eligible for extra pay if they work more than 40 hours a week. These employees are typically paid every 1 or 2 weeks. **Salary**, on the other hand, describes

Wages generally refer to hourly compensation paid to operating employees; the basis for wages is time.

Salary is income paid to an individual on the basis of performance, not on the basis of time.

FIG 9.2 STRATEGIC OPTIONS FOR COMPENSATION

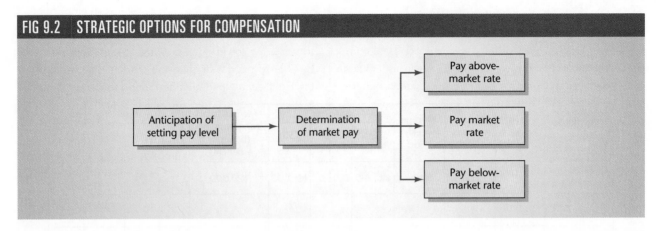

compensation on a monthly or annual basis and compensates employees not for how much time they spend in the organization but for their overall contributions to the organization's performance. In general, salaries are paid to professional and managerial employees within an organization. Plant managers, product managers, and professional managers in areas such as marketing, finance, and accounting, for example, are all likely to be paid on an annual basis; most of these employees are exempt from the overtime provisions of the Fair Labor Standards Act.

9-1c Strategic Options for Compensation

Most organizations establish a formal compensation strategy that dictates how they will pay individuals. Several decisions are embedded within such a strategy. The first relates to the basis for pay. Traditionally, most organizations based pay on the functions performed on the job, but more recently they have begun to rely on skill-based pay and pay-for-knowledge programs. In this way, organizations signal to their employees the relative importance of what someone does on the job versus what they bring to the job.

The second decision in developing a compensation strategy focuses on the basis for differential pay within a specific job. In some organizations, especially those with a strong union presence, differences in actual pay rates are based on seniority: With each year of service in a particular job, wages go up by a specified amount, so the longer one works on the job, the more that person makes, regardless of the level of performance on the job. Most public school systems use a seniority system to pay teachers: They get a base salary increase for each year of service they accumulate. As already noted, unions have historically preferred pay based at least in part on seniority.

> A **maturity curve** is a schedule specifying the amount of annual increase a person will receive.

Sometimes, the relationship between seniority and pay is expressed as something called a **maturity curve**, which is a schedule specifying the amount of annual increase a person receives. This curve is used when the annual increase varies based on the actual number of years of service the person has accumulated. Organizations that use maturity curves might argue that a new person tends to learn more (in part because there is more to learn) than more experienced employees and thus may deserve a larger increase. Meanwhile, more senior people may already be earning considerably higher income anyway and also have fewer new tasks to learn. In any event, the assumption under a seniority-based pay system is that employees with more experience can make a more valuable contribution to the organization and should be rewarded for that contribution. These systems also encourage employees to remain with the organization.

In other organizations, differences in pay are based on differences in performance, regardless of time on the job. These systems are generally seen as rewarding employees who are good performers rather than those who simply remain longer with the organization. For such systems to succeed, however, the organization has to be certain that it has an effective system for measuring performance (as will be discussed in Chapter 10). Most major companies base at least a portion of individual pay on performance, especially for managerial and professional employees. Performance-based incentives will be discussed in more detail in Chapter 14.

A third decision in developing a compensation strategy deals with the organization's pay rates relative to going rates in the market. As shown in Figure 9.2, the three basic strategic options are to pay above-market compensation rates, market compensation rates, or below-market compensation rates.[8] This decision is important because of the costs it represents to the organization.[9]

A firm that chooses to pay above-market compensation, for example, will incur additional costs as a result.

This strategic option essentially indicates that the organization pays its employees a level of compensation that is higher than that paid by other employers competing for the same kind of employees. Of course, it also anticipates achieving various benefits. Some organizations believe that they attract better employees if they pay wages and salaries that are higher than those paid by other organizations; that is, they view compensation as a competitive issue. They recognize that high-quality employees may select from among several different potential employers and that they have a better chance of attracting the best employees if they're willing to pay them an above-market rate. Above-market pay policies are most likely to be used in larger companies, particularly those that have been performing well.

In addition to attracting high-quality employees, an above-market strategy has other benefits. Above-market rates tend to minimize voluntary turnover among employees. By definition, above-market rates mean that an employee who leaves a company paying such wages may have to take a pay cut to find employment elsewhere. Paying above-market rates also might be beneficial by creating and fostering a culture of elitism and competitive superiority. Google and Netflix both pay higher-than-average salaries as a way to retain their most valued employees in industries where turnover and mobility are high.

The downside to above-market compensation levels, of course, is cost. The organization simply has higher labor costs because of its decision to pay higher salaries to its employees. After these higher labor costs become institutionalized, employees may begin to adopt a sense of entitlement, coming to believe that they deserve the higher compensation, making it difficult for the organization to be able to adjust its compensation levels downward.

Another strategic option is to pay below-market rates. The organization that adopts this strategy is essentially deciding to pay workers less than the compensation levels offered by other organizations competing for the same kinds of employees. Thus, it is gambling that the lower-quality employees it is able to attract will more than offset the labor savings it achieves. Organizations most likely to pursue a below-market rate are those in areas with high unemployment. If lots of people are seeking employment, and relatively few jobs are available, then many people are probably willing to work for lower wages. Thus, the organization may be able to pay lower than the market rate and still attract reasonable and qualified employees. In other situations, employers may be able to pay below-market rates because of various offsetting factors. For instance, some employers in Hawaii find that the state's beautiful setting and mild weather allow them to pay below-market salaries—some people are willing to work for less money just to be able to live in Hawaii. Again, the benefit to this strategy is lower labor costs for the organization.

On the other hand, the organization will also experience several negative side effects. Morale and job satisfaction might not be as high as the organization would prefer. Individuals are almost certain to recognize that they are being relatively underpaid, and this situation can result in feelings of job dissatisfaction and potential resentment against the organization. In addition, turnover may also be higher because employees will be continually vigilant about finding better-paying jobs. Compounding the problem even further is the fact that the higher-performing employees are among the most likely to leave, and the lower-performing employees are among the most likely to stay.

Finally, a third strategic option for compensation is to pay market rates for employees—that is, the organization may elect to pay salaries and wages that are comparable to those available in other organizations, no more and no less. Clearly, the organization that adopts this strategy is taking a midrange perspective. The organization assumes that it will get higher-quality human resources than a firm that takes a below-market strategy. At the same time, it is willing to forgo the ability to attract as many high-quality employees as the organization that takes an above-market strategy.

The advantages and disadvantages of this strategy are also likely to reflect midrange comparisons with the other strategies. The organization will have higher turnover than a firm paying above-market rates but lower turnover than an organization paying below-market rates. An organization that adopts a market-rate strategy is likely to believe it can provide other intangible or more subjective benefits to employees in return for their accepting a wage rate that is perhaps lower than they

Georgios Kollidas/Shutterstock.com

might be paid elsewhere. For example, job security is one important subjective benefit that some organizations provide.

Employees who perceive they are being offered an unusually high level of job security may therefore be willing to take a somewhat lower wage rate and accept employment at a market rate. Universities frequently adopt this strategy because they believe that the ambience of a university environment is such that employees do not necessarily expect higher salaries or higher wages. Microsoft also uses this approach. It offsets average wages with lucrative stock options and an exceptionally pleasant physical work environment.

9-1d Determinants of Compensation Strategy

Several different factors contribute to the compensation strategy that a firm develops. One general set of factors has to do with the overall strategy of the organization itself. As detailed in Chapter 4, a clear and carefully developed relationship should exist between a firm's corporate and business strategies and its human resource strategy.[10] This connection, in turn, should also tie into the firm's compensation strategy. Thus, a firm in a high-growth mode is constantly striving to attract new employees and may find itself in a position of having to pay above-market rates to do so. On the other hand, a stable firm may be more likely to pay market rates given the relatively predictable and stable nature of its operations. Finally, an organization in a retrenchment or decline mode may decide to pay below-market rates because it wants to reduce the size of its workforce anyway.[11]

In addition to these general strategic considerations, several other specific factors determine an organization's compensation strategy. One obvious factor is simply the organization's ability to pay. An organization with a healthy cash flow or substantial cash reserves is more likely to be able to pay above-market wages and salaries. On the other hand, if the organization suffers from a cash flow crunch, has few cash reserves, and is operating on a tight budget, it may

> A firm pursuing a strategy of stability will likely pay market rates given the relatively predictable and stable nature of its operations.

be necessary to adopt a below-market wage strategy. The organization's ability to pay is thus an important consideration. During the economic stagnation of recent years, many firms have found themselves in this predicament. In response, several major companies reduced the pay increases they granted to their employees.[12]

In addition, the overall ability of the organization to attract and retain employees is a critical factor. For example, if the organization is located in an attractive area, has several noncompensation amenities, and provides a comfortable, pleasant, and secure work environment, it might be able to pay somewhat lower wages. But if the organization is located in, for example, a high-crime area or a relatively unattractive city or region, and if it has few noncompensation amenities that it can provide to its employees, it may be necessary to pay higher wages simply as a way of attracting and retaining employees.

Union influences are another important determinant of an organization's compensation strategy. If an organization competes in an environment that is heavily unionized, such as the automobile industry, then the strength and bargaining capabilities of the union influence what the organization pays its employees. On the other hand, if the organization does not hire employees represented by unions or if the strength of a particular union is relatively low, then the organization may be able to pay somewhat lower wages, and the union influence is minimal or nonexistent.

9-2 DETERMINING WHAT TO PAY

After a compensation strategy has been chosen, it is necessary to determine exactly what employees on a given job should be paid. The starting point in this effort has traditionally been job evaluation. We will briefly describe this more traditional method first, but then discuss a more innovative and strategic approach to determining what to pay.

9-2a Job-Evaluation Methods

Job evaluation is a method for determining the relative value or worth of a job to the organization so that individuals who perform that job can be compensated adequately and appropriately. In other words, job evaluation is mostly concerned with establishing internal pay

Job evaluation is a method for determining the relative value or worth of a job to the organization so that individuals who perform that job can be compensated adequately and appropriately.

equity. Several job-evaluation techniques and methods have been established.[13] Among the most commonly used are classification, point, and factor-comparison systems.

CLASSIFICATION SYSTEM An organization that uses a **classification system** attempts to group sets of jobs together into classifications, often called *grades*. After classifying is done, each set of jobs is then ranked at a level of importance to the organization. Importance, in turn, may be defined in terms of relative difficulty, sophistication, or required skills and abilities necessary to perform that job. A third step is to determine how many categories or classifications to use for grouping jobs. The most common number of grades is anywhere from 8 to 10, although some organizations use the system with as few as 4 grades and some with as many as 18.

The U.S. postal system is a good example of an organization that uses the classification system. The U.S. postal system has 16 job grades, with nine pay steps within each grade. After the grades have been determined, the job evaluator must write definitions and descriptions of each job class. These definitions and descriptions serve as the standard around which the compensation system is built. After the classes of jobs are defined and described, jobs that are being evaluated can be compared with the definitions and descriptions and placed into the appropriate classification.

A major advantage of the job-classification system is that it can be constructed relatively simply and quickly. It is easy to understand and easy to communicate to employees. It also provides specific standards for compensation and can easily accommodate changes in the value of various individual jobs in the organization. On the other hand, the job classification assumes that a constant and inflexible relationship exists between the job factors and their value to the organization, which sometimes results in jobs within a grade not fitting together very well. Figure 9.3 presents an example of a job-classification system.

Job-classification systems require clear definitions of classes and benchmark jobs for each class. The most widely known example of a job-classification system is the General Schedule (GS) system used by the federal government. This system has 18 grades (or classes). Most federal employees fall into one of 15 grades; the top 3 grades have been combined into a single "supergrade" that covers senior executives.

Figure 9.3 describes three grades from the GS system. An example of a job classified as a GS-1 is a janitor; a GS-6 job example is a light truck driver; and an example of a GS-10 job is an auto mechanic. Within each grade are 10 pay steps based on seniority so that the range of salaries for a GS-6 job starts at just under $20,000 a year and goes up to more than $25,000 a year.

POINT SYSTEM The most commonly used method of job evaluation is the point system.[14] The point system is more sophisticated than the classification system and is also relatively easy to use. The **point system** requires managers to quantify, in objective terms, the value of the various elements of specific jobs. Using job descriptions as a starting point, managers assign points to the degree of various *compensable factors* that are required to perform each job—that is, any aspect of a job for which an organization is willing to provide compensation.

For instance, managers might assign points based on the amount of skill required to perform a particular job, the amount of physical effort needed, the nature of the working conditions involved, and the responsibility and authority involved in the performance of the job. Job evaluation simply represents the sum of the points allocated to each of the compensable factors for each job.

Point systems typically evaluate 8–10 compensable factors for each job. The factors chosen must not overlap one another, and they must immediately distinguish between substantive characteristics of the jobs, be objective and verifiable in nature, and be well understood and accepted by both managers and employees. Not all aspects of a particular job may be of equal importance, so managers can allocate different weights to reflect the relative importance of these aspects to a job. These weights are usually determined by summing the judgments of various independent but informed evaluators. Thus, an administrative job within an organization might result in weightings of required education, 40 percent;

The **classification system** for job evaluation attempts to group sets of jobs together into clusters, which are often called grades.

The **point system** for job evaluation requires managers to quantify, in objective terms, the value of the various elements of specific jobs.

Visions of America, LLC / Alamy Stock Photo

FIG 9.3   JOB-CLASSIFICATION SYSTEM

Grade GS–1

Grade GS–1 includes those classes of positions the duties of which are to perform, under immediate supervision, with little or no latitude for the exercise of independent judgment:

    A. the simplest routine work in office, business, or fiscal operations; or

    B. elementary work of a subordinate technical character in a professional, scientific, or technical field.

Grade GS–6

Grade GS–6 includes those classes of positions the duties of which are:

    A. to perform, under general supervision, difficult and responsible work in office, business, or fiscal administration, or comparable subordinate technical work in a professional, scientific, or technical field, requiring in either case:
        1. considerable training and supervisory or other experience;
        2. broad working knowledge of a special and complex subject matter, procedure, or practice, or of the principles of the profession, art, or science involved; and
        3. to a considerable extent the exercise of independent judgment; or

    B. to perform other work of equal importance, difficulty, and responsibility, and requiring comparable qualifications.

Grade GS–10

Grade GS–10 includes those classes of positions the duties of which are:

    A. to perform, under general supervision, highly difficult and responsible work along special technical, supervisory, or administrative lines in office, business, or fiscal administration, requiring:
        1. somewhat extended specialized, supervisory, or administrative training and experience which has demonstrated capacity for sound independent work;
        2. thorough and fundamental knowledge of a specialized and complex subject matter, or of the profession, art, or science involved; and
        3. considerable latitude for the exercise of independent judgment; or

    B. to perform other work of equal importance, difficulty, and responsibility, and requiring comparable qualifications.

Source: U.S. Office of Personnel Management

experience required, 30 percent; predictability and complexity of the job, 15 percent; responsibility and authority for making decisions, 10 percent; and working conditions and physical requirements for the job, 5 percent.

Because the point system is used to evaluate jobs, most organizations also develop a point manual. The **point manual** carefully and specifically defines the degrees of points from first to fifth. For example, education might be defined as follows: (1) first degree, up to and including a high school diploma, 25 points; (2) second degree, high school diploma and 1 year of college education, 50 points; (3) third degree, high school diploma and 2 years of college, 75 points; (4) fourth degree, high school education and 3 years of college, 100 points; and (5) fifth degree, a college degree, 125 points. These point manuals are then used for all subsequent job evaluation.

FACTOR-COMPARISON METHOD A third method of job evaluation is the **factor-comparison method**. Like the point system, the factor-comparison method allows the job evaluator to assess jobs on a factor-by-factor basis. At the same time, it differs from the point system because jobs are evaluated or compared against a standard of key points; instead of using points, a factor-comparison scale is used as a benchmark. Although an organization can choose to identify any number of compensable factors, commonly used systems include five job factors for comparing jobs: responsibilities, skills, physical effort, mental effort, and working conditions. Managers performing a job evaluation in a

The **point manual**, used to implement the point system of job evaluation, carefully and specifically defines the degrees of points from first to fifth.

The **factor-comparison method** for job evaluation assesses jobs, on a factor-by-factor basis, using a factor-comparison scale as a benchmark.

factor-comparison system are typically advised to follow six specific steps.

1. The comparison factors to be used are selected and defined. The five universal factors are used as starting points, but any given organization may need to add factors to this set.

2. Benchmark or key jobs in the organization are identified. These jobs are typically representative of and common in the labor market for a particular firm. Usually, 10–20 benchmark jobs are selected.

3. The benchmark jobs are ranked on each compensation factor. The ranking itself is usually based on job descriptions and job specifications determined by a job analysis.

4. Part of each benchmark's job wage rate is allocated to each job factor based on the relative importance of the job factor. Each manager participating in the job evaluation might be asked to make an independent allocation first, without consulting with other managers. Then the managers would meet as a group to develop a consensus about the assignment of monetary values to the various factors.

5. The two sets of ratings are prepared based on the ranking and the assigned wages to determine the consistency demonstrated by the evaluators.

6. A job-comparison chart is developed to display the benchmark jobs and the monetary values that each job received for each factor. This chart can then be used to rate other jobs in the organization as compared to the benchmark jobs.

The factor-comparison system is a detailed and meticulous method for formally evaluating jobs. Thus, it provides a rigorous assessment of the true value of various jobs, which is one of its advantages. It also allows managers to recognize fully how the differences in factor rankings affect the compensation that the organization allocates to various jobs. On the other hand, the factor-comparison method is also extremely complex, difficult to use, time-consuming, and expensive for an organization that chooses to adopt it. A fair amount of subjectivity is involved, and it is possible that people whose jobs are evaluated with this system may feel that inequities have crept into the system through either managerial error or politically motivated oversight.

Hay and Associates is a well-known compensation consulting firm that often does job evaluations for large organizations. It uses a factor-comparison system based on three factors: know-how, problem solving, and accountability.

9-2b Pay for Knowledge and Skill-Based Pay

The steps, decisions, and processes outlined previously still apply in many organizations, but recent proposals have suggested a whole different approach to compensation: Employees should be rewarded for what they know rather than what they are specifically required to do on the job.

Pay for knowledge involves compensating employees (usually managerial, service, or professional employees) for learning specific material. This approach might include paying programmers for learning a new programming language or rewarding managers who master a new manufacturing system. These systems can also be designed to pay for learning supervisory skills or for developing more in-depth knowledge about a topic relevant to the organization. Pay-for-knowledge systems reward employees for mastering material that allows them to be more useful to the organization in the future and are based on mastering new technology or mastering information that relates to global issues. These systems tend to be fairly expensive to start because the organization needs to develop methods for testing whether the employee has mastered the information in question, but once in place, the costs are usually not excessive. These plans also have the potential to clash with more traditional incentive systems (see Chapter 14) because employees might choose to perfect and apply knowledge they already have rather than learn new material.[15]

Skill-based pay operates in much the same way as a pay-for-knowledge system, but these plans are more likely to be associated with hourly workers. Instead of rewarding employees who master new material, employees are rewarded for acquiring new skills. Under such a plan, for example, an administrative assistant would be paid for learning how to use spreadsheets. The skills involved can be either for the same job (or in the same job family) or relevant for other jobs in the organization. For example, in manufacturing plants, it is often useful for employees to be cross-trained so that they have the skills to do several different jobs in the plant. This approach affords management a great deal of flexibility in scheduling, and it benefits employees because they can rotate through different jobs (providing some variety) and acquire skills that may increase their market value if they choose to seek another job.

Pay for knowledge involves compensating employees for learning specific information.

Skill-based pay rewards employees for acquiring new skills.

9-3 WAGE AND SALARY ADMINISTRATION

After wages and salaries have been determined, the resulting compensation system must be administered on an ongoing basis. Most organizations call this process **wage and salary administration** or *compensation administration*. Much of this administration involves making adjustments to wages and salaries as the result of pay raises or changes in job responsibilities. In addition, in organizations where jobs are arranged in a more hierarchical structure, programs should be implemented to maintain progression to a higher-level job within a job class. Certain issues related to compensation must also be addressed as part of this administration process. Two of the most important involve pay secrecy and pay compression.

9-3a Pay Secrecy

Pay secrecy refers to the extent to which the compensation of any individual in an organization is secret or the extent to which it is formally made available to other individuals. Each approach has merit.[16] On the one hand, advocates of pay secrecy maintain that what an individual is paid is his or her own business and not for public knowledge. They also argue that if pay levels are made known to everybody else, then jealousy or resentment may result. In fact, most businesses practice pay secrecy, sometimes to the point of formally forbidding managers from discussing their pay with other people.

On the other hand, some organizations adopt a more open pay system in which everyone knows what everyone else makes. The logic is that this promotes equity and motivation. If high performers are known to make more money than low performers, then it logically follows that people throughout the organization will be motivated to work harder under the assumption that they too will be recognized and rewarded for their contributions. Many publicly funded organizations such as state universities and public schools have open pay systems whereby interested individuals can look at budgets or other information to determine how much any employee is being paid.

9-3b Pay Compression

pictafolio/Getty Images

Another problem that some organizations must confront occasionally during wage and salary administration is pay compression. **Pay compression** occurs when individuals with substantially different levels of experience or performance abilities are being paid wages or salaries that are relatively equal. Pay compression is most likely to develop when the market rate for starting salaries increases at a rate faster than an organization can raise pay for individuals who are already on the payroll. As a result, an employee with experience may find himself or herself not making much more than an entry-level employee. In some cases, the external market can change so rapidly that new employees are actually paid more than experienced employees; this is known as **pay inversion**.

9-4 THE NATURE OF BENEFITS PROGRAMS

As noted earlier, in addition to wages and salaries, most organizations provide their employees with an array of other indirect compensations, or *benefits*. Although these benefits were once called *fringe benefits* (and a few people still use this expression today), when managers began to fully realize that they were spending more than one-third of wages and salaries in additional expenses on benefits they decided that the word *fringe* might have been understating the true value of these benefits.

9-4a The Cost of Benefits Programs

Data from the U.S. Chamber of Commerce provides some insights into the composition of the total compensation paid to a typical employee in the United States. According to these figures, the typical employee costs the company just over $50,000 a year in total

Wage and salary administration is the ongoing process of managing a wage and salary structure.

Pay secrecy refers to the extent to which the compensation of any individual in an organization is secret or the extent to which information on compensation is formally made available to other individuals.

Pay compression occurs when individuals with substantially different levels of experience, performance abilities, or both are paid wages or salaries that are relatively equal.

In **pay inversion**, the external market changes so rapidly that new employees are actually paid more than experienced employees.

compensation. Of this, just over $30,000 is paid for time worked, and the remainder paid is for something other than time worked such as vacation time, mandated benefits, pensions, insurance, and so forth.[17]

Hence, it is quite clear that organizations are spending huge amounts of money on benefits. It also appears that many organizations are trying to hold the tide, or even reverse it, by asking employees to bear more of the costs of these benefits. But certainly benefits costs will continue to be a large part of labor costs in the United States. Note that despite these statistics, however, the United States actually ranks rather low in terms of the relative costs of benefits around the world.

Rufous/Shutterstock.com

These global differences result almost entirely from mandated benefits, which are based on the different social contracts (guarantees made by the government in return for higher taxes) in place in the respective countries, and they are substantial. For example, the German workweek is 35 hours (on average). The German worker works 1,685 hours per year, has 34 days off, and has mandated benefit costs alone that equal almost 30 percent of wages. For comparison purposes, the average U.S. worker spends 40 hours a week at work, spends 1,847 hours a year working, has 13 days off a year, and has mandated benefits costs equal to about 10 percent of wages. When Ford acquired Swedish automobile maker Volvo, several years ago, Volvo workers immediately started to express their concerns about the potential loss of their relatively lavish benefits. These included an Olympic-size swimming pool, tanning beds, and tennis courts at the main manufacturing plant in Gothenburg, Sweden. Ford's strong U.S. benefits program paled in comparison to the program at Volvo.[18] This clash may well have been part of the reason why Ford finally decided to divest itself of Volvo and brokered a deal to sell the company to Chinese brand Zhejiang Geely Holding Group Co. Ltd.

As you can see, the exact benefits offered differ substantially from one country to the next, but in each case, the benefits are designed to meet the specific needs (relative to balancing work and family) in the host country. For example, in Egypt, resorts are quite expensive, so offering short vacations for families to spend together is helpful. Because Muslims are expected to make the pilgrimage to Mecca at least once during their life (if at all possible), vacation time is a valuable benefit. Another example involves a multinational oil company, which operates in countries such as Norway, Trinidad, and the United Kingdom, where drilling operations tend to be off-shore or in rather remote regions of the country. As a result, employees do not see their families every day and do not generally live at home. Under these circumstances, compressed workweeks are extremely important to employees, as are other benefits such as family days, where families are brought to work sites for visits at company expense.

9-4b Purposes of Benefit Programs

In general, benefit programs serve several purposes for the organization. First, many experts believe that organizations willing to spend more money on total compensation are able to attract better-qualified people and convince employees to work harder, saving the company money. The general concept underlying this approach is known as *efficiency wage theory*. Little data exists to support or refute this position, but some organizations appear to view wages and benefits as a means of attracting better applicants.

Most experts also argue that money spent on benefits affects job satisfaction and subsequent turnover. Even if employees do not work harder in response to better benefits, they are more likely to remain with a firm that provides better benefits and are more satisfied with that firm. In part, an employee's reactions to specific benefits programs reflect that individual's belief about the value of benefits at the current company compared with the value of benefits at other companies. As a result, the need to remain competitive with other firms in an industry is a major force driving up the price of benefits. Just as when one airline in a market lowers fares, and all others follow suit, when one visible organization in an industry starts offering a given benefit, it is usually not long until its competitors offer similar benefits.

In addition, various social, cultural, and political forces may promote the introduction of new and broader benefits programs. For example, increases in the number of women in the workforce and the rising costs of health care have each affected benefits programs in recent times. Because of the growth in the numbers of female workers, more and more companies offer on-site day care, dual-parent leave for the birth of a child, and other benefits that make it easier for people to work and have productive careers. Likewise, the health-care environment has prompted growth in benefits programs, including health maintenance organizations, managed health care, and so forth.

Finally, employee expectations are a driving force in determining what benefits a firm must offer. For example, even though an organization is not legally required to offer any vacation time, this benefit is so desirable and has become so common that almost every person who accepts a new job expects that he or she will be given vacation time. Most people today would be unlikely to accept a permanent full-time job without this basic benefit. A major implication of these issues, then, is the strategic importance of employee benefits. Their costs are high, and their effects are great. Thus, careful planning, monitoring, and communication about benefits are of paramount importance.

9-5 MANDATED BENEFITS

Some common benefits are mandated by law. Specifically, in the United States, several laws have been passed that require organizations to offer certain types of benefits to their employees or that legislate the way benefit plans are administered. In Chapter 2, we discussed several of these, including the Pregnancy Discrimination Act, the Employee Retirement Security Act, and the Family and Medical Leave Act. Relative to this last piece of legislation, we also noted that the law requires only unpaid maternity leave of 12 weeks. However, in the past year or so, several firms have begun offering up to 1 year of paid maternity leave. In 2016, this has also become an issue for politics, as Democratic candidates have called for some type of mandated paid maternity leave, while Republican candidates have been silent on the issue. Another significant law, the Social Security Act of 1935, is discussed later. Each of these laws has resulted in mandated benefits or legally restricted the way organizations treated certain benefits. Protection plans are benefits designed to provide protection to employees when their income is threatened or reduced by illness, disability, death, unemployment, or retirement. Unemployment insurance was created in the United States as part of the Social Security Act of 1935. The rationale for the act was to protect those people who were experiencing the high levels of unemployment that were pervasive in the United States during the 1930s.

Unemployment insurance is intended to provide a basic subsistence payment to employees who are between jobs—that is, for people who have stopped working for one organization but who are assumed to be seeking employment with another organization. Employers pay premiums to the unemployment insurance fund. In addition, in the states of Alabama, Alaska, and New Jersey, employees also contribute to the fund. The premium payment is increased if more than an average or designated number of employees from the organization are drawing from the fund at any given time. To be covered by unemployment insurance, an individual must have worked a minimum number of weeks, must now be without a job, and must be willing to accept a suitable position if one is found through a state's unemployment compensation commission or department.

Furthermore, if a covered employee is out of work through no fault of his or her own (as in the case of a layoff), then benefits start almost immediately. If the employee quits or is fired for cause (e.g., for poor performance), there is usually a waiting period before the individual can collect unemployment benefits. Regardless of the starting time, compensation is normally available for no more than 26 weeks. But beginning in 2010, as unemployment began to rise, Congress authorized extensions of unemployment benefits to as much as 99 weeks. In early 2012, however, as unemployment started to ease, there was an announcement that the maximum period for unemployment benefits would go down to 73 weeks by midyear. Payments are generally about half of what individuals might have been earning in their former jobs, although an upper limit is placed on the benefit paid. As noted previously, this program is funded through employer contributions, but there are considerable variations in how these laws are administered from state to state.

9-5a Social Security

A second mandated benefit created by the same law is **Social Security** itself. What most people think of as Social Security is officially the **Old Age Survivors and Disability Insurance Program**. The initial purpose of this program was to provide some limited income to retired individuals to supplement their own personal savings, private pensions, part-time work,

Unemployment insurance, a mandated protection plan, is intended to provide a basic subsistence payment to employees who are between jobs.

Social Security (officially the **Old Age Survivors and Disability Insurance Program**), another mandated program, was originally designed to provide limited income to retired individuals to supplement their personal savings, private pensions, part-time work, and so forth.

and so forth. Unfortunately, many people have come to view Social Security as their primary source of retirement income. Problems associated with this assumption are discussed later in this section.

Currently the maximum taxable earnings amount for Social Security is $118,500. The tax rate is 6.2 percent each, for both the employer and the employee. An extra 1.45 percent is taken to cover Medicare (although some high-income individuals are required to pay an additional 0.9 percent). Self-employed individuals rare required to pay 12.4 percent for Social Security and 2.9 percent for Medicare. Individuals are eligible for partial benefits beginning at age 62, and they are eligible for full benefits at age 66. In 2016, the maximum monthly benefit for a worker retiring at full age was $2639. This is roughly twice the amount considered to be at the poverty line for a family of two, under various federal programs. Effective in 2027, however, individuals will not be able to retire with full benefits until they reach age 67. If an employee dies before reaching retirement age, then a family with children under age 18 receives survival benefits, regardless of the employee's age at the time of her or his death. In addition, an employee who becomes totally disabled before age 65 is also eligible to receive insurance benefits; Medicare benefits are also provided under this act.

The amount of money any individual is eligible to be paid from the Social Security system is a function of the average monthly wage that individual earned, weighted toward the latter years of a person's career. In addition, an individual has to have worked a minimum period of time and made a minimum amount of contributions to the system to be eligible to draw full benefits. Actual

funding for Social Security benefits, however, comes from the withholdings of current employees. They do not directly depend on the withholdings assessed against the employee who is retiring. This is a potential problem for the Social Security system because retirees are living longer, and it takes more current employees to fund the benefits of each retiree. It is therefore not surprising that Social Security has also become an issue for the 2016 presidential election. Suggestions have gone anywhere from privatizing the entire system, to putting stricter earnings caps on who can received benefits, to dramatically increasing the withholding tax so that Social Security benefits can be expanded.

9-5b Workers' Compensation

Workers' compensation is also an important legally mandated benefit available to most employees. **Workers' compensation** is insurance that covers individuals who suffer a job-related illness or accident. Employers pay the cost of workers' compensation insurance. The exact premium paid is a function of each employer's past experience with job-related accidents and illnesses. About 100 million workers in the United States are protected under the Workers' Compensation Insurance Program.

In addition to these major forms of mandated benefits, a few others are also mandated by most states. For example, in most instances, organizations must give employees time off to vote and when they have been summoned for jury duty. The organization might or might not choose to pay the employee for the time off, but the employee cannot be penalized or otherwise sanctioned for taking the time.

9-5c Mandated Health Care

The Patient Protection and Affordable Health Care Act (or the Affordable Care Act) was signed into law on March 23, 2010. Although most see this

Workers' compensation, another mandated protection program, is insurance that covers individuals who suffer a job-related illness or accident.

legislation as the biggest regulatory overhaul of the country's health-care system since the passage of Medicare and Medicaid (in 1965), not everyone agrees that this change is for the best. Governor Mitt Romney and many other Republicans campaigned, during the 2012 elections, on the notion that they would work to repeal the law. In response to various lawsuits, the Supreme Court ruled on the constitutionality of the law, and, although they upheld most of its statutes, they also ruled that states could not be forced to participate in the act's Medicaid expansion. Other legal challenges to the law continue to evolve on a regular basis. As a result, there is a great deal of uncertainty about exactly how the Affordable Care Act will impact employers. Furthermore, President Obama postponed the implementation of some provisions of the Act, causing further confusion. To complicate things further, in late 2016, some large health insurance carriers indicated that they were going to drop out of the national health insurance "market" that serves as a cornerstone of the program.

The basic aim of the Act is to increase the quality and affordability of health-care insurance, lower the number of uninsured employees, and reduce the cost of insurance for all involved. How is this supposed to work? The goal is to expand some type of health-care coverage to the 47 million Americans who are currently uninsured, according to the AARP.[19] A few major provisions need to be discussed in order to understand that, as illustrated in Table 9.1.

As can be seen, most of the Act deals with providing insurance for the uninsured, either through Medicaid (federally funded) or mandated employer policies. Funding for these provisions will come through higher Medicare taxes on incomes over $250,000 (for joint filings), a special assessment on insurance companies with policies that charge more than $10,200 a year for an individual premium, various other taxes, and proposed reductions in Medicare and Medicaid spending. But, despite estimates by the Congressional Budget Office that the changes will significantly reduce the deficit and increase health-care coverage, many critics are concerned about the real costs. Some of these concerns are baseless (the new legislation will *not* require any insurance company to fund abortions), but others are more complicated. For example, Delta Airlines recently announced that their health-care costs for next year would increase by $100 million.[20] This increase is due to rising costs and later retirements, but it is also due to several provisions from the new health-care legislation. Delta is especially concerned with the need to insure children of dependents up to the age of 26, and the airline also believes that employees who previously turned down health-care insurance will now sign up. In addition, there are further complications associated with the fact that Delta funds its own health-care insurance for employees. That is, the plan is self-funded as opposed to being run through an insurance company.

TABLE 9.1 MAJOR PROVISIONS OF THE AFFORDABLE HEALTH CARE ACT

1. **Preexisting Conditions**—Insurers cannot refuse someone and cannot charge them a different rate (as compared to others of the same age in the same geographical area) because of preexisting conditions (except for tobacco use). The purpose here was to extend health care to a larger portion of the population and to eliminate perceived abuses by insurance companies regarding the role of preexisting conditions.

2. **Minimum Standards**—Minimum standards for health insurance policies are established, called "essential benefits," and lifetime coverage caps are banned.

3. **Individual Mandate**—All individuals NOT covered by an employer-sponsored health plan, Medicaid, Medicare, or some other public insurance program must secure an approved private insurance policy or pay a penalty (there are exceptions for members of certain religious groups and in financial hardship cases). The purpose here was to prevent individuals from waiting until they were sick to procure insurance. If insurance companies could not turn them down (as per the provision above), this could result in unfair costs to the insurance company, which would be insuring unhealthy individuals.

4. **Subsidies**—Individuals and families below certain income levels would receive federal subsidies (in the form of tax credits) to ensure that their health-care costs stay below a certain percentage of their income.

5. **Small Businesses**—Small businesses can get subsidies if they purchase insurance through an exchange (see below).

6. **Medicaid Extensions**—The eligibility requirements for Medicaid were significantly expanded so that more people would qualify. The Supreme Court ruled, however, that individual states could opt out of this portion of the legislation and set their own Medicaid requirements (which are generally lower than the new federal thresholds). Several states have indicated their plans to exercise this option.

7. **Employer Mandate**—Firms employing 50 or more people but NOT offering health insurance will pay a shared responsibility requirement if the government has to subsidize an employee's health care.

8. **Health Insurance Exchanges**—A marketplace will be created in each state so that individuals and small businesses can compare policies and premiums and buy insurance.

Regardless of the accuracy of the estimates made by the airline, it is clear that companies—even large companies—are concerned that their health-care costs will rise. To some, this is the price we must all pay to ensure that everyone has adequate health-care insurance, but to others, it is an unreasonable intervention by the federal government. Estimates place the total cost of this overhaul of the health-care system at more than $1 trillion.[21] Hopefully, as all the provisions of the new law are put in place, we will know more about the true costs and benefits, but for now many organizations feel a great deal of uncertainty and apprehension. It does appear, however, that some form of health-care insurance coverage is now mandatory for most U.S. firms. In addition, as of 2016, anyone who does not have a qualified health insurance plan is required to pay a $500 penalty to the IRS.

During the 2016 presidential campaign, Donald Trump vowed to repeal the Affordable Health Care Act if elected. After his victory, however, he indicated that he was open to retaining parts of the Act but revising other parts. President Trump has also gone on record as being in favor of allowing insurance companies to compete across state lines. This has the potential to reduce health care premiums, although some have warned that it will make it more difficult to regulate insurance companies if that is the case. In any event, we can anticipate that there will be changes in the rules and regulations regarding health care in the near future. President Trump has also been in favor of increased incentives for employers to provide child care and the requirement of six weeks *paid* maternity leave under the FMLA. Finally, his proposed lowering of the corporate tax rate from 35 to 15% is aimed at increasing employment. Thus, it is clear that there are changes coming and a number of them will impact the HR function although the exact nature of that impact is not yet clear.

9-6   NONMANDATED BENEFITS

Most organizations today provide other benefits in addition to those mandated by law. Businesses may elect to provide these benefits in order to attract more qualified workers. However, even if offering the benefit is elective, if a business does make the decision to offer that benefit, there are laws or regulations that must be followed.

9-6a   Private Pension Plans

In addition to the pension benefits guaranteed under the Social Security Act, many companies elect to establish **private pension plans** for their employees. These

> The Employee Retirement Income Security Act of 1974 guarantees a basic minimum payment that employees could expect to be paid on retirement.

prearranged plans are administered by the organization that provides income to the employee at her or his retirement. Contributions to the retirement plan may come from either the employer or the employee, but, in most cases, they are supported by contributions from both parties. Different retirement plans are available, including individual retirement accounts (IRAs) and employee pension IRAs. In addition, a 401(k) plan allows employees to save money on a tax-deferred basis by entering into salary deferral agreements with their employer.

There are two basic types of pension plans: defined benefit plans and defined contribution plans. Under **defined benefit plans**, the size of the benefit is precisely known and is usually based on a simple formula using input such as years of service and salary. This type of plan is often favored by unions and is closely monitored under the Employee Retirement Income Security Act of 1974, or ERISA (as discussed in Chapter 2). Although the employee may contribute to these plans, the amount of the contribution has little or no bearing on the actual pension payments. Under **defined contribution plans**, the size of the benefit depends on how much money is contributed to the plan. This money can be contributed by either the employer alone (noncontributory plans) or the employer and the employee (contributory plans). Most new pension plans are contributory, defined contribution plans, and there are legal restrictions concerning how the money is invested.

9-6b   Paid Time Off

Most organizations also provide their employees with some amount of time off with pay. No U.S. laws mandate this type of benefit, but most employees now expect it. One major type of paid

Private pension plans are prearranged plans administered by the organization that provides income to employees at their retirement.

Defined benefit plans are private pension plans in which the size of the benefit is precisely known and is usually based on a simple formula using input such as years of service.

Defined contribution plans are private pension plans in which the size of the benefit depends on how much money is contributed to the plan.

time off is the paid holiday. Most full-time employees receive about 10 paid holidays per year. The most common holidays for which workers are paid without having to work include New Year's Day, Memorial Day, Independence Day, Labor Day, Thanksgiving Day, and Christmas. In addition, religious holidays (in addition to Christmas) are also often given. Organizations have to be careful with this practice, however, because growing diversity in the workplace is accompanied by an increasingly diverse set of religions and thus religious holidays, requiring clear policies about religious holidays, which are enforced equitably.[22]

Paid vacations are also common but are likewise not required by law. They are usually periods of 1, 2, or more weeks when an employee can take time off from work and continue to be paid. Most organizations vary the amount of paid vacation according to an individual's seniority with the organization, with newer employees receiving 1 week of paid vacation, and the most senior employees receiving as many as 4 weeks of paid vacation a year. One part of the rationale for such long vacation breaks is that senior management employees need a break to escape from the stress of their jobs.[23] But, as can be seen in Table 9.2, some countries actually mandate extensive vacation benefits for all employees. Moreover, these vacation breaks are in addition to public holiday time. For example, Finnish workers get not only a mandated 25 days of vacation time per year but also an additional 15 public holidays.

Another common paid time-off plan is sick leave. This benefit is provided when an individual is sick or otherwise physically unable to perform his or her job duties. Most organizations allow an individual to accumulate sick time on the basis of some schedule, such as 1 sick day per month worked. Some organizations require that employees submit a doctor's note verifying illness in order to be paid for the day, but others do not. Further, some organizations extend sick day coverage when the employee needs to help with a spouse, child, or parent who is sick. In addition, some organizations require the employee to use his or her allocation of sick days within a certain period of time (such as by December 31) or lose them. Under such a system, it would seem illogical for an employee not to take all the sick days allocated during the year. Finally, another form of paid time off is personal leave. Sometimes an organization allows an employee to take a small number of days off for personal business such as funerals and weddings.

But a report by the Bureau of Labor Statistics[24] reveals an interesting fact about paid time off in the United States. Paid time off was the most prevalent benefit provided by employers in the private sector throughout the United States in 2012, with 72 percent of all employees receiving both paid holidays and paid vacation. This percentage has remained virtually unchanged since 1992. However, while vacation benefits have remained unchanged, benefits such as sick leave and personal leave have actually grown during the same period. But a new trend is also emerging, referred to as "consolidated leave." Under these plans, workers are allocated a specified amount of time off that they can use for any purpose, although the plans usually allow days off in small increments of one or two days. According to Bureau data, about one-fourth of all workers in the United States were enrolled in consolidated leave plans in 2012. It will be interesting to see how these plans develop and what their implications are for employees. For example, if an employee used her or his allotted time for vacation and then became seriously ill, what would happen? Could the employee be fired for nonattendance? These matters will sort themselves out in the coming years.

TABLE 9.2	MINIMUM ANNUAL VACATION BY LAW IN DIFFERENT COUNTRIES	
Country	**Minimum Vacation Time (Days per Year)**	
United Kingdom	28	
Poland	26	
Finland	25	
France	25	
Sweden	25	
South Africa	21	
Australia	20	
Hong Kong	14	

Source: Mercer (www.mercer.com/press-releases/holiday-entitlements-around-the-world), accessed on September 18, 2016.

> "Preparation for old age should begin not later than one's teens. A life which is empty of purpose until 65 will not suddenly become filled on retirement."
>
> —ARTHUR E. MORGAN, PROMINENT AND INFLUENTIAL 19TH CENTURY ADVOCATE FOR EDUCATION

9-6c Other Benefits

Private pensions, pay for time not worked, and health insurance are the most common nonmandated benefits, but many other benefits also are available. For example, disability insurance pays for employees who cannot work because of some injury or disability. In addition, in an attempt to reduce health-care costs, some companies have introduced a different type of benefit known as a **wellness program**. Wellness programs concentrate on keeping employees from becoming sick rather than simply paying expenses when they do become sick.[25] In some organizations, these programs may be simple and involve little more than organized jogging or walking during lunch breaks, but some organizations have full-fledged health clubs on site and provide counseling and programs for fitness and weight loss. These plans are either paid for by the company or heavily subsidized because they are attractive to employees who appreciate the ease and low costs; at the same time, they can reduce costs by reducing the number of sick days, cut medical costs, and improve productivity as the organization gains a more physically fit workforce.[26]

An additional group of benefits is often referred to collectively as *life-cycle benefits*, or benefits targeted at different stages in an employee's life. The most common are child-care and elder-care benefits. Child-care benefits are becoming more popular because the changing nature of the workforce and the fact that being considered a family-friendly organization (which must, at a minimum, have some type of child-care benefits) is increasingly viewed as a competitive advantage in attracting talented workers.[27] These plans might include scheduling child-care help, referrals to various types of child-care services, or reimbursement accounts for child-care expenses. Company-paid day care has been found to strongly affect employee attitudes and job performance.[28] Elder-care benefits are also growing in popularity. These typically take the form of referrals for employees with a disabled parent or one who needs constant care. Long-term health-care insurance is also becoming a more common benefit, and these plans provide for nursing homes or at-home care.

A somewhat different type of service is contained in what are referred to as *employee assistance plans*. These programs are designed to assist employees who have chronic problems with alcohol or drugs or who have serious domestic problems. An increase in the number of programs for mental problems and stress, as well as for bereavement, have also been part of a recent trend.[29] These programs are typically voluntary, and referrals are confidential. Yet the needs of the organization (especially when the personal problem is causing performance problems on the job) must be balanced with the needs of the individual to avoid any stigma attached to having the specific problem.[30]

Finally, employee perquisites are sometimes provided. A *perquisite*, or *perk*, as it is more informally known, is an extra benefit that may or may not have any direct financial value but is considered an important reward by employees. A perk might include a bigger office, a company car, membership in a country club, stock-purchase options, premium insurance coverage, and so forth. Perks are usually made available only to members of top management or to certain especially valuable professionals within the organization.

Sometimes organizations provide special perks that might be available to all employees. For example, Google provides free transportation from many remote locations to its headquarters, and the company also provides free meals for employees in its various cafeterias.

Although most benefits programs are designed for all the employees in an organization, **cafeteria-style benefits plans** allow employees to choose the benefits they really want. Under these plans, the organization typically establishes a budget indicating how much it is willing to spend per employees on benefits.[31] The employee is then presented with a list of possible benefits and the cost of each; they are free to choose the benefits in any combination they wish. Such an approach should maximize the effectiveness of the benefits program for achieving the organizational goals discussed at the beginning of the chapter, and some evidence suggests that cafeteria-style benefits programs can lead to increased satisfaction and reduced turnover.[32]

Nonetheless, these programs are not without

Wellness programs are special benefits programs that concentrate on keeping employees from becoming sick rather than simply paying expenses when they do become sick.

Cafeteria-style benefits plans allow employees to choose those benefits they really want.

elisekurenbina/Shutterstock.com

problems. One challenge is the cost of administering such plans. Because every employee has a potentially unique set of benefits, someone has to keep track of what benefits each employee has chosen, and these choices can usually be changed over time. Another problem is what is known as *adverse selection*. This refers to the fact that the employee most likely to select a benefit, such as children's braces, is also most likely to use the benefit, which tends to drive up benefit costs. Finally, given a choice of benefits, employees are not always rational in their choices. A younger employee may elect to contribute less to his or her retirement because retirement seems like a distant future event and wait until later in life before increasing the contribution. But given the power of compounding interest, a larger contribution early in life, followed by a smaller contribution later, is actually worth much more at retirement age than a smaller contribution made early in life followed by a larger contribution made later. It is thus extremely important for employees to have full information about the available benefits, and in some cases it may be necessary for the organization to mandate minimum benefits levels in some areas.

For quite some time, one of the more controversial issues for benefit programs involve the question of whether to extend benefits to same-sex partners. However, after the Supreme Court decisions regarding marriage equality, it has become clear that benefits extended to heterosexual couples must also be extended to same-sex couples.

 ## 9-7 CONTEMPORARY ISSUES IN COMPENSATION AND BENEFITS

Three contemporary issues in compensation and benefits include executive compensation, growing legal issues, and how best to evaluate compensation and benefits programs.

9-7a Executive Compensation

Quite simply stated, many human resource management (HRM) practices and techniques do not work well with top executives. Selection and appraisal of these executives cannot be accomplished using the methods used for other employees. But the area of HRM that is most important for executives deals with their compensation. Therefore, we will concentrate primarily on the issue of executive compensation, discussing techniques and methods as well as some of the issues that arise in this area.

Most senior executives receive their compensation in two forms: base salary and some form of incentive pay. The traditional method of incentive pay for executives is in the form of bonuses, which can exceed their base pay by some

multiple. Bonuses are typically a function of the performance of the organization and are less dependent on the perceived performance of the executive. Near the end of a fiscal year, some portion of a corporation's profits are diverted into a bonus pool, and the share received by each executive is determined partially by perceived performance but mostly in advance as part of the executive's employment contract.

For example, in 2009, Goldman Sachs set aside $16.7 billion for compensation, most of which was paid out in year-end bonuses. As a result, the average salary of a Goldman employee was reported to be $595,000 in 2009. This figure may be shockingly high for some readers, but the fact that Goldman also reported record profits for the year suggests that executives may well have earned their huge paychecks.[33] All of these announcements took place, however, against the backdrop of the highest unemployment rate (10 percent) in living memory in the United States. Furthermore, many financial firms, including Goldman, had accepted large amounts of government support to keep the company viable after the financial meltdown in late 2008. Although Goldman had repaid that money, the outcry over the size of the payouts led the firm to actually consider requiring that some portion of the bonus money be donated to charity.[34]

New York's State Attorney General Andrew Cuomo released a report in July 2009 that described how many employees in each of several large financial firms received bonuses of at least $1 million in 2008—before most of the funds had been repaid. These figures indicated that more than 150 employees of Citigroup, Bank of America, JPMorgan Chase, Merrill Lynch, and Goldman Sachs each received a bonus in 2009 of more than $1 million.[35]

There was a temporary dip in average CEO bonuses in 2010, as a result of the outcry over the size of these bonuses, especially in the banking industry. However, they rebounded in 2011, when the average cash bonus paid to a CEO increased by 30.5 percent. But bonuses are not the whole story. A large component of CEO compensation is the stock bonus, which can be worth huge sums of money.

A stock-option plan is established to give senior managers the option to buy the company stock in the future at a predetermined, fixed price. The basic idea underlying stock-option plans is that if the executives contribute to higher levels of organizational performance, then the company stock should increase. Then the executive can purchase the stock at the predetermined price that, theoretically, should be lower than its future market price. The difference then becomes profit for the individual. These options can be worth huge sums of money, such as the case for Steve Jobs in 2006 when his then fully vested stock options were valued at $646 million (his total compensation was only $14.6 million in 2007).

Of course, in 2009 many of these stock options were not worth as much as they had been as stock prices plummeted. However, by 2010, most of the lost value of the stock market had been recouped, presumably making stock options once again a viable form of compensation. In fact, in a report issued several years ago, KPMG Peat Marwick stated that, for all of top management (managers with annual salaries of more than $750,000), stock options constituted a full 60 percent of their total compensation. The KPMG Peat Marwick report also indicated that even among exempt employees at the $35,000-a-year level, stock options represented 13 percent of total compensation.

Agency theory arguments are often cited as the rationale for stock-option plans. The owners of the firm (typically the stockholders) want to increase the firm's profitability, but the CEO does not necessarily have any incentive to work toward maximizing profits. By basing a considerable portion of the CEO's compensation on stock, however, the interests of the CEO are presumably aligned more closely with the interests of the owners, and everyone works toward the same goal. But some critics have noted that CEO and firm interests are not really aligned, however, until the CEO or executive actually exercises the stock option. Up to that point, the executive might actually even have an incentive to lower stock prices in the short run in the hope of being offered more options at the lower price of the stock.[36] Moreover, stock options generally tend to have relatively short time line, so managers may be motivated to make short-term decisions that are likely to drive up stock prices even though a different decision might have been better for the firm's long-term success.

Of course, some companies also include other types of executive compensation such as membership in private clubs and low-cost (or even no-interest) loans, but it is difficult to put a true value on these. In addition, in any given year, a CEO may be able to exercise certain stock options that will significantly impact his or her earnings for the year. Table 9.3 presents some data on the 10 highest paid CEOs in the United States in 2016 (which make them the highest paid in the world), considering only cash, stock, and stock options.

One notable fact from the table is that, despite concerns over Wall Street, many of the highest paid CEOs don't work on Wall Street (although CEOs from big banks and investment firms still do very well). In fact, at the end of 2015, the CEOs from consumer-discretionary firms were actually the highest paid, followed by information technology firms, with financial firms coming in third.[37] It is also worth noting that a few CEOs saw a slight drop in their total compensation for 2015, although none of the CEOs involved are facing financial ruin.

Given the money involved, it is not surprising that executive compensation continues to be a controversial topic. CEO compensation now runs almost 100 times the average wage rate of an hourly employee. Thus, it is not surprising that many people ask why CEO compensation

TABLE 9.3 TOTAL COMPENSATION FOR TOP CEOS IN 2015

CEO (Company)	Cash (in Millions)	Stock and Options (in Millions)	Change in Total Pay from 2014
David Zaslav (Discovery Communications)	$11	$145	+368%
Michael Fries (Liberty Global)	$16	$95.9	+140%
Mario Gabelli (GAMCO Investors)	$88.5	–	+4%
Satya Nadella (Microsoft)	$4.5	$79.8	(Mr. Nadella became CEO in 2014)
Nick Woodman (GoPro)	$2.7	$74.7	+4,079%
Greg Maffei (Liberty Media & Liberty Interactive)	$8.5	$65.3	+1,077%
Larry Ellison (Oracle)	$2.3	$65	−14%
Steve Mollenkopf (Qualcom)	$2.7	$58	(Mr. Mollenkopf became CEO in 2014)
David Hamamoto (NorthStar Realty Finance)	$11.6	$48.7	+227%
Les Moonves (CBS)	$29.9	$24.5	−6%

Source: Gabriel Solomon, "15 Top Paid CEOs," *CNN Money*, May 16, 2015.

remains so high when CEOs seemed to be responsible for many of the country's financial woes a few years earlier. It is clear that CEO compensation can be reduced, and it is true that some CEOs have already seen their pay cut as company fortunes faltered, but CEOs in the United States are still well paid.

Furthermore, executive compensation in the United States seems far out of line with that paid to senior executives in other countries. For example, compensation for foreign CEOs has only recently crept into the seven-figure range, their annual bonuses are much smaller, and they seldom participate in lavish stock-option plans like those enjoyed by their U.S. counterparts. That is not to suggest that CEOs from other countries are deprived. In fact, top executives in places such as Hong Kong are also likely to receive paid housing, and executives in Germany get twice as many vacation days as their U.S. counterparts. The total perquisite package is worth about 28 percent of a U.S. executive's salary, but packages in France and Hong Kong, for example, are also estimated to be valued at more than 20 percent of the executive's base salary. However, regardless of the value of anyone's perquisites, there is still outrage when we learn about cases such as that of the Gordons, who run Tootsie Roll industries. The company spent $1.2 million in 2011, to fly the couple (aged 92 and 80) from their home to corporate headquarters in Chicago—where the company also pays $120,000 to rent them an apartment.[38]

Compounding the problem created by perceptions of executive compensation is the fact that little or no relationship seems to exist between the performance of the organization and the compensation paid to its

Phil Cantor/SuperStock

senior executives.[39] Certainly, if an organization performs at an especially high level, and its stock price is increasing consistently, then most observers would agree that the senior executives responsible for this growth should be entitled to attractive rewards.[40] However, it is more difficult to understand situations in which executives are paid huge salaries and other forms of rewards when their companies are performing at only a marginal level or even poorly, yet this is fairly common today. A few years earlier, Oracle's CEO Lawrence Ellison pocketed more than $700 million from the sale of previously granted stock options, but during the same year, the value of Oracle stock dropped by 57 percent.

Several highly publicized bankruptcies in 2001–2002 further raised concerns over executive pay and especially over stock options. Enron, for example, declared bankruptcy even as CEO Ken Lay enjoyed the gains from the stock options he had recently exercised. Similar tales from other companies led to a strong belief for many people that something should be done about how stock options were treated.

Finally, there is some concern about the effects the huge gap between CEO pay and everyone else's pay might have on those other employees. On the one hand, he or she may not believe that the CEO is making 100 times the contribution made by the typical employee, or at least that no one could be working 100 times as hard. This perception may lead to resentment and other problems on the job, and evidence suggests that such large dispersions result in decreased satisfaction, willingness to collaborate, and overall productivity.[41] On the other hand, the typical employee may view this huge salary as a prize worth aiming for. From this perspective, pay structures are seen as tournaments, and the bigger the prize, the more intense the competition, and so the greater the effort and productivity. In fact, some evidence supports this position, indicating that managers cannot really be sure of the effects of these income gaps.[42]

9-7b Legal Issues in Compensation and Benefits

The major legal issues involved in compensation and benefits were discussed in Chapter 2, but we will review them briefly here. The Fair Labor Standards Act includes provisions for the minimum wage, overtime, and child labor. It also specifies which employees are covered by the overtime provisions and which are exempt; this usually affects whether an employee is paid wages or a salary. Even nonexempt workers are sometimes asked to work more than 40 hours with no overtime pay; in exchange, they are offered time off, which is usually referred to as *comp time.*

Thus, someone who has to work 45 hours one week might be assigned only 35 hours the next week but still receive full pay. Comp time is often not as beneficial to the employee, who would otherwise earn more in total pay, but it is more cost-efficient for the organization. And, it does give employees something that many of them value: time away from work.

But there is a good chance that some of this clarity is about to disappear. In May of 2016, companies were still awaiting the details on the proposed changes in the overtime provisions from the Department of Labor. These proposed regulations will address how an employee is classified as being exempt or nonexempt (i.e., hourly), which has clear implications for overtime pay. The new overtime rule is expected to raise the threshold for white-collar exemptions to at least $47,000 a year versus $23,650 at present.[43] There is also discussion of adding duties that would be required before an employee could be classified as white-collar and exempt. The effect of these changes would be to force organizations to reclassify many employees as hourly, meaning that they would be entitled to overtime for work over 40 hours a week. These employees might well feel "demoted" as a result, but, in any case, would be forced to punch a clock at work and keep track of their hours worked. The potential costs, then, are both financial and psychological, and we will have to wait to see what the final guidelines specify and how firms deal with these changes.

The legal issues related to benefits are a bit more complicated. Organizations typically seek to ensure that their benefit plans are qualified; that is, where the employer receives an immediate tax deduction for any contributions made, the employee does not incur a tax liability at the time of the employer deduction, and investment returns (such as from stocks and bonds) are accumulated tax-free. Although the requirements for qualification differ for different types of benefits plans, it is critical that the plan be nondiscriminatory: The plan cannot disproportionately favor employees with higher income levels.[44]

Of course, the most important legal issue in this area deals with the Employee Retirement Income Security Act (ERISA) of 1974. We introduced this law in Chapter 2, but it deserves additional attention here. As noted earlier, this law was passed to protect employees who had contributed to their pensions but were unable to collect those benefits later. This situation occurred primarily because of the restrictions that the organizations had placed on employees before they could receive retirement benefits. Specifically, organizations required that employees remain with the company as long as 30 years before they were vested. (**Vesting rights** are guaranteed rights to receive pension benefits.) For example, before 1974 a 60-year-old employee with 29 years of service would not be entitled to pension benefits if he or she left the company—or even if he or she died—before his or her 30-year anniversary. Under ERISA, however, vesting rights become operational after 6 years *at the most*, and employees with less service are still usually eligible to receive some portion of their retirement benefits.

ERISA also provides protection for the funding underlying the pension plan. The Pension Benefit Guaranty Corporation oversees how pension plans are funded, and it can seize corporate assets to support underfunded plans. In addition, ERISA allows an employee to carry a portion of his or her benefits to another job. This notion of portability is especially important when employees change jobs frequently. ERISA also imposes some minimum requirements for how pension plans are communicated to employees. If an organization does not follow ERISA guidelines, its pension plan will not be qualified as just defined.

Finally, we discussed the recent Supreme Court decision regarding the Defense of Marriage Act, in Chapter 2. Although the decision is discussed most widely in terms of allowing states to recognize same-sex marriages, the original case was filed on the basis of rights for spouses, and this decision may well have important implications for benefits plans.

It seems clear that same-sex partners will have access to the same federal benefits as any other spouses. This means that Social Security benefits and Medicare benefits would accrue to same sex-partners the same as to any other spouses. In the case of inheritances, same-sex partners would be considered the same as any other spouses. But what about state benefits, and, more to the point, what about nonmandated benefits offered by companies? If an organization offers certain health-insurance benefits to employees, would same-sex partners be eligible for the same benefits to which other spouses are eligible? More and more firms are extending benefits to same-sex partners, but would they be required to do so under the law? This is not clear at present and will take time and some cases to sort out. Clearly, though, the trend is growing toward offering same-sex partner benefits, and, even if the law does not require companies to do this, they may be required to do so simply to remain competitive.

9-7c Evaluating Compensation and Benefit Programs

Given the enormous cost to an organization of compensation and benefit

Vesting rights are guaranteed rights to receive pension benefits.

packages, its managers clearly must carefully assess the benefit of these packages for the organization. Although it may not be easy to assess the effectiveness (or even the "right" level) of executive compensation, it is easier to deal with the other aspects of compensation and benefits. Organizations that do not offer competitive pay and benefit packages will find it increasingly difficult to attract employees—especially the best potential employees. Furthermore, because satisfaction with pay and benefits is an important part of overall job satisfaction, noncompetitive packages will lead to higher rates of voluntary turnover as well.

In any case, many organizations may find that their benefit programs do not seem to be as much as they could be simply because the organization has not communicated effectively with employees about those benefits. In fact, many organizational surveys suggest that many employees are not fully informed about their benefits. For example, some evidence suggests that awareness about benefits could be increased through communication via several media and that, as awareness increased, so would satisfaction with benefits.[45] The reason for this relationship is underscored by the results of another study in which employees were asked to estimate the value of the employer's contribution to their benefits. When asked about family coverage, the average estimate was only 38 percent of the actual cost of those benefits to the employer.[46] It seems clear that an organization can never expect to appreciate the full advantage of its benefits program when employees underestimate the cost of their benefits by such a large amount.

CLOSING CASE
Holding True at Nucor Steel

Nucor Steel

For the most part, the watchwords in U.S. business since the 2008–2011 recession have been cutting payroll, reducing head count, and eliminating jobs. But Nucor, the country's largest steelmaker, still has *all* its jobs. Hit by a 50-percent plunge in output that had begun in September 2008, the U.S. steel industry laid off some 10,000 workers by January 2009 and another 25,000 by 2010. Nucor, however, has refused to follow suit in laying anyone off. Whenever they don't have enough steel orders to fill their workweek, Nucor employees have been performing other tasks: rewriting safety manuals, getting a head start on maintenance jobs, mowing the lawns, and cleaning the bathrooms, but they're still drawing paychecks. "Financially," says one employee at the company's facility in Crawfordsville, Indiana, "Nucor workers are still better off than most."

As far as top management is concerned, the company's ability to weather the recent economic downturn is based on several factors, most importantly, the firm's employees and culture. What's that culture like? It originated in the 1960s as the result of policies established by Ken Iverson, who brought a radical perspective on how to manage a company's HR to the job of CEO. Iverson figured that workers would be much more productive if an employer went out of its way to share authority with them, respect what they accomplished, and compensate

Studio 37/Shutterstock.com

them as handsomely as possible. Today, the basics of the company's HR model are summed up in its "Employee Relations Principles":

1. Management is obligated to manage Nucor in such a way that employees will have the opportunity to earn according to their productivity.
2. Employees should feel confident that if they do their jobs properly, they will have a job tomorrow.
3. Employees have the right to be treated fairly and must believe that they will be.
4. Employees must have an avenue of appeal when they believe they are being treated unfairly.

The Iverson approach is based on motivation, and the key to that approach is a highly original pay system. Step 1, which calls for base pay below the industry average, probably doesn't seem like a promising start, but the Nucor compensation plan is designed to get better as the results of the work get better. If a shift, for example, can turn out a defect-free batch of steel, every worker is entitled to a bonus that's paid weekly and that can potentially triple his or her take-home pay. In addition, there are one-time annual bonuses and profit-sharing payouts. In 2005, for instance, Nucor had an especially good year; it shipped more steel than any other U.S.

(Continued)

(Closing Case – continued)

producer, and net income hit $1.3 billion, up from $311 million in 2000. The average steelworker took home $79,000 in base pay and weekly bonuses, plus a $2,000 year-end bonus and an average of $18,000 in profit-sharing money.

The system, however, cuts both ways. Take that defect-free batch of steel, for example. If there's a problem with a batch, workers on the shift obviously don't get any weekly bonus. And, that's *if* they catch the problem before the batch leaves the plant. If it reaches the customer, they may lose up to three times what they would have received as a bonus. "In average-to-bad years," adds HR vice president James M. Coblin, "we earn less than our peers in other companies. That's supposed to teach us that we don't want to be average or bad. We want to be good." During fiscal 2009, total pay at Nucor was down by about 40 percent.

Everybody in the company, from janitors to the CEO, are covered by some form of incentive plan tied to various goals and targets. We've just described the Production Incentive Plan, which covers operating and maintenance workers and supervisors and may boost base salaries by 80 percent to 150 percent. Bonuses for department managers are based on a return-on-assets formula tied to divisional performance, as are bonuses under the Non-Production and Non-Department-Manager Plan, which covers everyone, except senior officers, not included in either of the first two plans; bonuses under both manager plans may increase base pay by 75 percent to 90 percent. Senior officers don't work under contracts or get pension or retirement plans, and their base salaries are below industry average. In a world in which the typical CEO makes more than 400 times what a factory worker makes, Nucor's CEO makes considerably less. In the banner year of 2005, for example, his combined salary and bonus (about $2.3 million) came to 23 times the total taken home by the average Nucor factory worker. His bonus and those of other top managers are based on a ratio of net income to stockholder's equity.

Nucor needs just four incentive plans because of an unusually flat organizational structure—another Iverson innovation. There are only four layers of personnel between a janitor and senior management: general managers, department managers, line supervisors, and hourly personnel. Most operating decisions are made at the divisional level or lower, and the company is known for its tolerance of honest mistakes made in the line of decision-making duty. The Nucor website points out that workers are allowed to fail if that failure comes as a result of logical initiative and idea sharing. That is, if a worker approaches a problem in a logical manner and makes a sound decision that is defensible but turns out to be wrong, he or she is not punished. The reasoning behind this approach is that it promotes creativity and initiative.

The Nucor system works not only because employees share financial risks and benefits but also because, in sharing risks and benefits, they're a lot like owners. And, people who think like owners are a lot more likely to take the initiative when decisions have to be made or problems solved. What's more, Nucor has found that teamwork is a good incubator for initiative as well as idea sharing. John J. Ferriola, who managed the Nucor mill in Hickman, Arkansas, before becoming COO, remembers an afternoon several years ago when the electrical grid at his facility went down. His electricians got on the phone to three other company electricians, one in Alabama and two in North Carolina, who dropped what they were doing and went straight to Arkansas. Working 20-hour shifts, the joint team had the plant up and running again in 3 days (as opposed to an anticipated full week). There was nothing in it (at least financially) for the visiting electricians, but they knew that maintenance personnel get no bonuses when equipment in their facility isn't operating. "At Nucor," says one frontline supervisor, "we're not `you guys' and `us guys.' It's all of us guys. Wherever the bottleneck is, we go there, and everyone works on it."

THINK IT OVER

1. Would you want to work under a compensation system like Nucor's? Why or why not?
2. Why don't more firms use approaches to compensation along the lines of Nucor's model?

STUDY TOOLS 9

READY TO STUDY?
In the book, you can:

☐ Rip out the chapter review card at the back of the book for a handy summary of the chapter and key terms.

ONLINE AT CENGAGEBRAIN.COM YOU CAN:

☐ Collect StudyBits while you read and study the chapter.

☐ Quiz yourself on key concepts.

☐ Find videos for further exploration.

☐ Prepare for tests with HR4 Flash Cards as well as those you create.

10 | Performance Appraisal and Career Management

After finishing this chapter go to **PAGE 269** for **STUDY TOOLS**

LEARNING OBJECTIVES

10-1 Describe the purposes of performance appraisal in organizations

10-2 Summarize the performance-appraisal process in organizations

10-3 Identify and describe the most common methods that managers use for performance appraisal

10-4 Discuss other general issues involving performance appraisal in organizations

10-5 Describe the nature of careers in organizations

10-6 Discuss human resource management and career management

10-7 Identify and discuss basic career-development issues and challenges

Dennis MacDonald/Alamy Stock Photo

OPENING CASE
Counting Seconds, Measuring Scans

One of the most important jobs in retailing is the person who takes the customer's money, in part because paying for their items is about the last thing customers do before leaving. An efficient and pleasant experience can leave a customer walking out of the store with a smile, and a slow or unpleasant experience can leave a bad taste in the customer's mouth. There is also a lot of variation in how checkout operators work. Some are fast and efficient, and others are plodding and never seem to get in a hurry.

Meijer, a family-owned discounting chain, operates 203 huge megastores in Michigan, Illinois, Indiana, Kentucky, and Ohio. The company has recently installed a new performance-measurement system for its checkout operators that might potentially revolutionize those jobs. Essentially, the system works like this:

1. Meijer has established minimum baseline performance metrics for the job based on the number of units a person should reasonably be able to scan and bag in a specified amount of time.

2. When a checkout operator scans a customer's first item, a timer in the scanning system is activated.

3. This timer runs until a customer's last item is scanned.

4. The operator's "score" is adjusted for the kinds of items being purchased (large, bulky items take longer to scan than small, tightly packed ones) and how the customer is paying (checks usually take longer than cash or credit).

5. Each checkout operator's score is averaged across an entire shift.

6. The minimum performance expectation at Meijer is 95 percent of the standard. If an operator falls below this standard too many times, the person is either demoted to a lower-paying job or fired.[1]

> "An efficient and pleasant checkout experience can leave a customer walking out of a store with a smile."

Interviews with Meijer cashiers suggest mixed results. On the one hand, they all agree that the new system causes them to work faster. On the other hand, they feel more stress. Moreover, several suggested that they avoid conversations with their customers because that can detract from their work and slow them down.

Feedback from customers is also mixed. Some think the new system is great. One woman, for instance, said, "A lot of the [cashiers] like to stop and chat, and I don't really have the time for it." But another suggested that "elderly people . . . feel so rushed at checkout that they don't want to come here."

But the Meijer system, developed by Accenture, may be the wave of the future. Gap, Office Depot, Limited Brands, and Toys "R" Us are all testing it. On the other hand, other retailers such as Kroger and Abercrombie & Fitch have said, "Thanks, but no thanks," because they are afraid the new system will detract from customer service.[2]

THINK IT OVER

1. How would you feel about working under the Meijer system?

2. What other kinds of jobs might be amenable to this sort of performance-measurement technology?

Virtually all businesses must focus some degree of attention on performance management. In fact, the effective management of performance may be the difference between success and failure. Many firms, such as Boeing, find it necessary to occasionally adjust how they approach performance management. Performance-appraisal systems are designed to provide organizations with the information to manage performance improvement. To develop employees to their full potential, however, organizations also must help employees manage their careers. Career management and career development enable employees to grow both personally and professionally. Further, performance appraisals help provide employees with information on how they can best manage their own careers. This chapter is about performance-appraisal systems and their implications for how individuals manage their careers. We also cover careers from other perspectives.

Performance appraisal is the specific and formal evaluation of an employee to determine the degree to which the employee is performing his or her job effectively. Some organizations use the term *performance appraisal* for

> A **performance appraisal** is the specific and formal evaluation of an employee to determine the degree to which the employee is performing his or her job effectively.

this process, and others prefer to use different terms such as *performance evaluation, performance review, annual review, employee appraisal*, or *employee evaluation*. The outcome of this evaluation is some type of score or rating on a scale. These evaluations are typically conducted once or twice a year. A related topic, **performance management**, refers to the more general set of activities carried out by the organization to change (improve) employee performance. Although performance management typically relies heavily on performance appraisals, performance management is a broader and more encompassing process and is the ultimate goal of performance-appraisal activities. We will touch on some concepts of performance management in this chapter but will discuss these ideas much more fully in Chapter 14. It is important to realize, however, that efforts to improve performance appraisal alone, without a larger performance-management program, are unlikely to produce the improvements that organizations seek.

Interestingly, though, some firms have begun separating the two processes and focusing more on performance management than on performance appraisal (if that is possible). We will discuss these developments later in this chapter. Finally, it probably is not surprising that over the years, there has been a great deal of research conducted on various issues associated with performance appraisals and performance management. Although it is difficult to sum up all that has been done, there is a recent review paper that attempts to organize and critique the past 100 years of appraisal research.[3]

10-1 WHY ORGANIZATIONS CONDUCT PERFORMANCE APPRAISALS

Most people involved in performance appraisals tend to be dissatisfied with them. This is true for both the person being rated and the person doing the rating. We will discuss some of the major reasons for this dissatisfaction in this chapter. But the fact that performance appraisals are so widely used in spite of this dissatisfaction is a strong indicator that managers believe performance appraisals are important and have a meaningful role to play in organizations. In fact, managers conduct performance appraisals for several reasons. Organizations also hope to achieve several goals with performance appraisals.[4]

Performance management is the general set of activities carried out by the organization to change (improve) employee performance.

10-1a The Importance of Performance Appraisals

Although most managers are dissatisfied with the appraisal process, most would also agree that performance appraisal is an important part of human resource management (HRM). The results of performance appraisals serve many important functions in organizations, and this is why they are still prevalent despite their problems.

1. For example, appraisal results provide a benchmark for assessing the extent to which recruiting and selection processes are adequate; that is, appraisal results help managers assess the extent to which they are actually recruiting and selecting the most appropriate employees. When this information is used in conjunction with performance-management techniques (described in more detail in Chapter 14), it can lead to real improvements in the performance of individual employees and, ultimately, the entire organization.

2. Performance appraisals are also important for legal reasons. Organizations must be able to demonstrate that their promotions, transfers, terminations, and reward allocations are based on merit (or the lack thereof), as opposed to discriminatory factors such as gender or race. Performance appraisal, therefore, is the mechanism by which the organization can provide this documentation.

3. Appraisals play a role as part of the larger performance-management process. The goal of performance management is to improve employee performance. Part of this process is letting employees know how well they are currently doing so they can correct their deficiencies, capitalize on their strengths, and improve their overall contributions to their jobs.[5] Performance appraisal should provide this information to employees.

4. Finally, performance-appraisal information should be the basis of incentive pay systems and other performance-management interventions designed to improve motivation and performance.

10-1b Goals of Performance Appraisal

The preceding discussion makes the goals of appraisals almost self-evident. A basic goal of any appraisal system is to provide a valid and reliable measure of employee performance along all relevant dimensions. In other words, the appraisal results should reflect the true picture of who is and is not performing well, and they should indicate the areas of specific strengths and weaknesses for each person being rated. Although it is extremely difficult to assess the extent to which an appraisal system accomplishes these goals, it is probably just as important that employees perceive appraisals to be fair and accurate.[6]

Sergiy Telesh/Shutterstock.com

Although documentation, as discussed, is another important goal of the appraisal process, the ultimate goal for any organization using performance appraisals is to improve performance on the job. Accomplishing this goal requires that employees receive useful and accurate feedback about their job performance, as well as guidance on how to improve. The goal also relies on the organization's ability to make decisions about things such as raises and promotions on the basis of performance on the job. When these two requirements are met, managers can generally assume that when employees get feedback about areas needing improvement, they will be motivated to make these improvements if they recognize that improving their performance will improve their chances for a promotion, pay increase, or other important outcome or benefit. At the same time, employees should also gain a clear understanding of where they stand relative to the organization's expectations of them vis-à-vis their performance.

10-2 THE PERFORMANCE-APPRAISAL PROCESS

Several tasks are necessary for the performance-appraisal process to be successful. Some should be done by the organization, some by raters (the individuals who will be conducting the performance appraisal), and, in many organizations, by the ratee (the individual whose performance is evaluated). In addition, follow-up and discussion should accompany the process. Although some of this follow-up and discussion may be more accurately considered performance management rather than performance appraisal per se, it is still an integral part of how organizations manage the entire process. Figure 10.1 illustrates the actual performance-management system of one major corporation. Although some firms might make minor modifications to reflect their philosophies more closely, these general steps are almost always followed. The performance-appraisal part of this overall process is highlighted and will be the framework for much of the discussion that follows. In later sections of this chapter, we will address and discuss the remaining parts of the process.

10-2a The Role of the Organization

The organization, primarily through the work of its human resource (HR) function, develops the general performance-appraisal process for its managers and employees to use. One of the first considerations relates to how the information gained from performance appraisals is to be used. For example, will it be used for developmental feedback only? Or will decisions about merit pay or other outcomes be based on these ratings as well? It is obviously important that everyone understand exactly what the ratings are to be used for and exactly how they will be used. The organization also generally determines the timing of the performance appraisals. Most organizations conduct formal appraisals only once a year, although some organizations conduct appraisals twice a year or even more frequently for new employees. However frequent the appraisals, the organization and its HR managers must decide when they will be conducted. The most common alternatives are for appraisals to be done on the anniversary date of each individual employee's hiring (which spreads out the need to do appraisals throughout the year but makes budgeting for raises more problematic) or for all appraisals throughout the organization to be conducted during a specified period of time each year (which makes budgeting and comparisons easier but requires a great deal of work during a short period of time).

The organization is also responsible for ensuring that clear and specific performance standards are available to managers. The organization should also ensure that these standards are communicated carefully to the

FIG 10.1 | THE PERFORMANCE MANAGEMENT PROCESS IN A TYPICAL ORGANIZATION

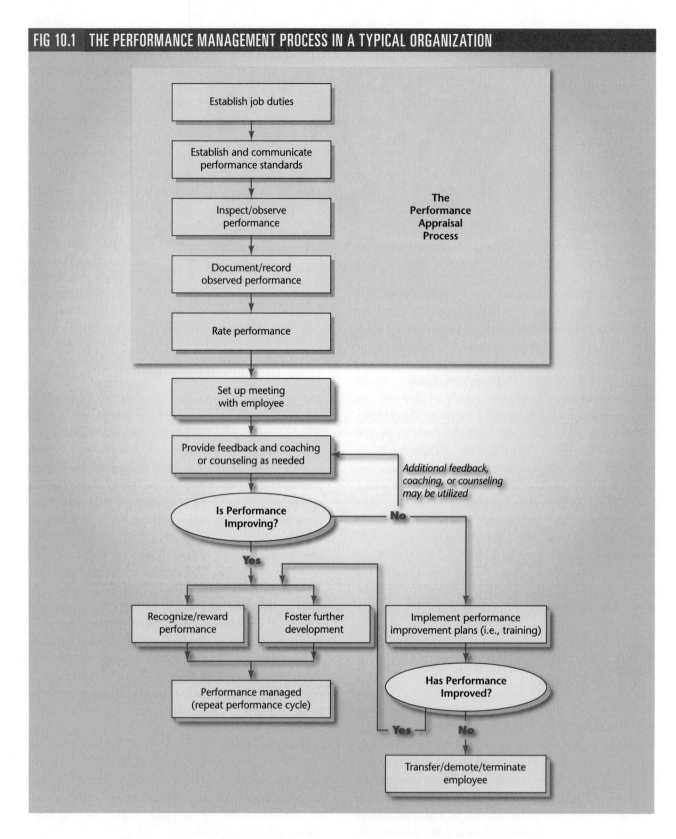

employees. Although this step involves those individuals performing the ratings as well, the organization must ensure that everyone rates performance using the same set of standards and that employees know what is expected of them. Otherwise, performance appraisal cannot accomplish its goals, and the organization may have serious problems by creating a disgruntled workforce or by exposing itself to legal liabilities.

10-2b The Role of the Rater

The rater (traditionally and most typically the supervisor of the employee being appraised) plays the largest role in the appraisal process. As noted earlier, the organization is responsible for making sure that all raters have clear performance standards, but raters have to help develop and learn those standards. As performance information is acquired about a ratee, the rater also has to compare the information acquired with these standards as a way of evaluating the employee's performance. When making these decisions, the rater must consider the context in which performance occurs so that any extenuating conditions can be taken into consideration. In addition, the rater has to communicate those standards to the ratees so that each individual will know what is expected.

The rater has a more critical role to play as well. On a day-to-day basis, an employee behaves, or performs, on the job and exhibits many behaviors that might be relevant to performance on that job. The rater's task is to collect information about those behaviors and translate that information into the ratings themselves. Therefore, the rater truly becomes a decision maker who must observe ratee performance and process the information gleaned from the observations. Because most formal appraisals are conducted only once a year, the rater must also somehow store this information in memory, recall what has been stored at the appropriate time, and use the information to provide a set of ratings. This task is potentially difficult and time-consuming.[7]

After ratings have been completed, it is also usually the rater who must then communicate the results and consequences of the appraisal to the ratee. When the results are somewhat negative, this task may be uncomfortable, and it is often stressful for managers. This communication process should also include goals for the future and a performance plan for helping the employee improve, thus adding a positive element. This set of activities, of course, is really part of the performance-management process. Finally, the rater is ultimately responsible for preparing the employee to perform at desired levels. In other words, the supervisor must be sure that the employee knows what is required on the job, has the needed skills, and is motivated to perform at the level desired.

10-2c The Role of the Ratee

Although attempts to improve appraisals often focus on the organization or the rater, the ratee also has responsibilities in the appraisal process. First, for performance appraisals to work most effectively, a ratee should have a clear and unbiased view of his or her performance. Problems can occur during the appraisal process if there is disagreement between the rater and the ratee, so it is essential that both parties have all the information they can collect about the ratee's performance. This approach may require the ratee to acquire information about the performance of coworkers and requires the ratee to gain an understanding about how his or her behavior affects performance. This approach should also allow the ratee to be more receptive to feedback from the rater (especially if it is somewhat negative), which in turn makes it more likely that the ratee will change his or her behavior in response to that feedback.

10-2d Who Performs the Performance Appraisal?

Another important aspect of performance appraisal is the determination of who conducts the appraisal and what information will be used. The most common appraisers are shown in Figure 10.2.

As noted earlier, the individual's supervisor is the most likely rater. Supervisors are perhaps the most frequently used source of information in performance appraisal. The assumption underlying this approach is that supervisors

One weakness of annual performance reviews is that managers tend to be biased toward the most recent behaviors of their subordinates.

FIG 10.2 SOURCES OF INFORMATION FOR PERFORMANCE APPRAISAL

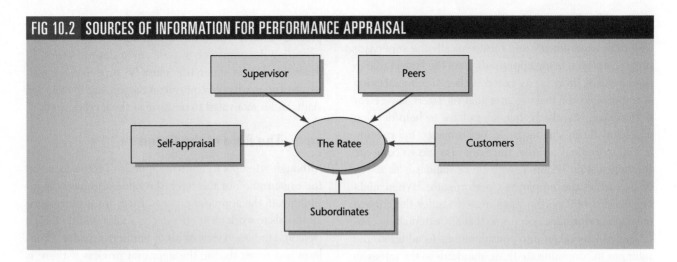

usually have the most knowledge of the job requirements and the most opportunities to observe employees performing their jobs. In addition, the supervisor is usually responsible for the performance of his or her subordinates and thus is both responsible for employees' high performance and accountable, perhaps, for their low performance.[8]

At the same time, it should also be recognized that supervisors are not necessarily a perfect source of information. A supervisor may have been promoted from another part of the organization and thus may have never performed the jobs that she or he is supervising, and, in some job settings (e.g., outside sales jobs), the supervisor may not really have an adequate opportunity to observe employees performing their work. But in addition to these potential constraints on the supervisor's *ability* to provide a meaningful appraisal, we must also consider the supervisor's *motivation* to provide such ratings. Stated simply, supervisors are not always motivated to give the most accurate ratings they can. For example, there is always the possibility that the supervisor is biased (either for or against) the person being rated. Only mixed evidence of systematic bias against members of identifiable groups based on race,[9] age,[10] gender,[11] and disability exists.[12] Nonetheless, a supervisor may be negatively or positively biased toward various workers because of personal liking, attitudes, personal relationships, and so forth. As a result, favoritism or negative bias may be possible.

Supervisors might also choose to be inaccurate in their ratings because they feel threatened by a particular subordinate and want to prevent him or her from getting ahead. In another scenario, the supervisor might want to get rid of a problem subordinate by getting her or him promoted into a different department. In addition, supervisors may be concerned about team member relations and decide to rate all team members the same, regardless of what they deserve, to avoid jealousy or conflict.

These and other motivational factors that affect supervisory ratings are beyond the scope of this discussion but are treated in detail in various specialized sources.[13] The main point here is to recognize that supervisors may choose to be inaccurate in their ratings for a wide range of reasons.

Peers, colleagues, and coworkers represent other potential sources of information for performance-appraisal systems. An advantage of using peers in such a process is that, by definition, they have expert knowledge of job content and may also have more opportunities than the supervisor to observe the performance of a given worker on a day-to-day basis. Peers also have a different perspective on the performance of their work in that they really understand their own opportunities and limitations regarding performance. Halliburton and PepsiCo both use peer evaluations as a major component of their performance-appraisal process.

Of course, friendship, group norms, and other personal factors may intervene in this situation. And individuals may see their own performance as being significantly different than others in the group may see it.[14] In some situations, coworkers might be competing with each other for a promotion (or some other reward), which may affect their motivation to be accurate in their peer evaluations. Because peers or coworkers remain in an ongoing relationship with each other, someone who received poor ratings from his or her coworkers may try to retaliate and rate those coworkers poorly during subsequent evaluations.[15] Nevertheless, peer evaluation is particularly useful in professional organizations such as law firms, architectural firms, academic departments, and so forth. As more and more organizations begin to use work teams for production work, peer evaluations are becoming more widely used in those contexts as well.

A third source of information in the performance-appraisal process is subordinates of the individual being appraised. Subordinates are an especially important source of information when the performance of their own manager is being evaluated, and this information is perhaps most useful when the performance appraisal is focused on the manager's leadership potential. If top-level managers in an organization are appraising the performance of a certain middle manager on the basis of his or her leadership potential, for example, then the subordinates of that manager are perhaps the best source of information for evaluating that person's performance. Of course, a major problem with using subordinates as input to the performance-appraisal process is that this approach may influence the manager's behavior in the sense that she or he may be more focused on making workers happy and satisfied than in making them perform at a high level.[16] Nonetheless, there has been a great deal of recent interest in so-called upward appraisals and in the ways to make them more effective.[17]

Occasionally, appraisal information is obtained from the employees themselves. Although few (if any) organizations rely on self-evaluations for decision-making, it is often useful to have the ratee consider his or her own performance as part of the overall appraisal process. Finally, in some service organizations (e.g., Chili's and Red Lobster), customers are formally brought into the process when they fill out feedback forms or respond to mail surveys after using the services of an organization. In any event, it is important to realize that each source of performance-appraisal information is subject to various weaknesses and shortcomings. As a result, many organizations find it appropriate and effective to rely on different information sources when conducting a performance appraisal. In fact, in a number of companies, ratings are obtained from supervisors, peers, and subordinates; these are then compared with self-ratings. Such systems are known as *360-degree appraisals*.

Organizations that use **360-degree appraisals** gather performance information from people on all sides of the manager: above, beside, below, and so forth.[18] By focusing on 360-degree feedback, they obtain information on a person's performance from all perspectives. This approach allows them to match the strengths and weaknesses, the benefits and shortcomings, from each perspective and gain a more realistic, overall view of a person's true performance.[19] Recognize, however, that the feedback from the different sources could be inconsistent. Otherwise, there is no value in obtaining evaluations from different sources. But this approach means that the manager has to reconcile different feedback and that the organization probably needs to use these ratings for feedback and development purposes only. If decisions are to be based on these evaluations, then the organization would have to decide how to weight the ratings from the different sources.[20] Although it is not a panacea (and few studies have evaluated its effectiveness), variations on 360-degree appraisal systems are likely to continue to be popular for some time.

Regardless of who conducts the appraisals, it is important to remember that most organizations do performance appraisals only once a year. As a result, the rater must observe and then remember the relevant performance information that occurred over that entire time,[21] but memories are not perfect. Raters forget what happened, especially if something happened many months earlier. Rater memory is therefore a critical factor and limits the accuracy and effectiveness of performance appraisals. If a rater cannot remember a performance incident, then he or she cannot rate it. Fortunately, there may be a rather simple solution to this problem, such as having raters keep performance diaries (or performance logs).[22] Performance diaries (electronic or otherwise) record the relevant performance information when the behavior actually occurs, so the rater does not have to rely on an imperfect memory to provide ratings. In addition, the diary information can help raters provide

> In conducting performance appraisals, many organizations rate traits—abstract properties that cannot be observed directly but can be inferred from behavior.

In a **360-degree appraisal**, performance information is gathered from people on all sides of the manager: above, beside, below, and so forth.

detailed feedback to ratees, which should increase the perceptions of procedural fairness. Finally, if an employee is discharged for poor performance and subsequently sues the organization, these diaries can serve as the documentation of performance that the organization needs to defend itself in court.

10-2e **What Gets Rated?**

Another important decision to make regarding the design of appraisal systems is what should be rated. The choice of appraisal instruments (discussed below) is related to this issue because some systems are clearly designed to measure some aspects of performance rather than others. But the decision of what to rate should be based more on the needs of the organization than on the choice of rating instrument. Although the decision about what to rate can probably include many factors, three are most commonly encountered.

Many organizations choose to rate traits in conducting appraisals. Traits are abstract properties of individuals that generally cannot be observed directly but can be inferred from behavior. Ratings of attitude, leadership, and initiative are particularly popular traits for appraisals. Rating traits allows an organization to use the same appraisal instrument for all or most employees, and this approach is based on the assumption that similar traits underlie effective performance for all jobs. Note, however, that an analysis of court cases involving performance appraisals suggests that trait-based appraisals are the most difficult to defend because the courts tend to see them as more subjective than other systems.[23] In

addition, feedback concerning rating traits is often less instructive and helpful than other types of feedback.

In some cases, organizations base their appraisals on behaviors. These appraisals tend to be based on job analysis, and they tend to be tailored for specific jobs. For example, a ratee may be evaluated on how well he or she follows up on sales leads. These appraisals are still subjective, but they require the rater to evaluate behaviors that he or she can physically observe, so they seem more objective. Reliance on behaviors can also lead to an emphasis on processes underlying effective performance. In the preceding example, one might assume that following up sales leads is part of the process of being an effective salesperson. Providing feedback about behaviors and processes can be instructive and useful because it can help employees understand how to improve their performance.

The final commonly encountered option is to rate performance based on outcomes. For example, rather than evaluating whether the salesperson has a good attitude or follows up on leads, an organization could simply tally actual sales. Focusing on outcomes has the advantage of emphasizing the most objective measures of performance available. In addition, these systems are usually tied to specific goals, which have added benefit (discussed below). Feedback can be relatively straightforward and easy to interpret (i.e., you did or did not meet your sales goal), although feedback is even more useful if it includes information on how to improve future performance. Goals can be stated in terms of absolute amounts or in terms of improvement (e.g., increase sales by 10 percent over last year). It is important to set the right goals (goals that help the organization achieve its objectives), and it is important to monitor the means by which employees meet their goals (i.e., to make sure they act ethically and legally). Appraisal systems built around outcome measures are a reasonable alternative for organizations to consider.[24]

10-2f **Who Should Be Rated?**

A final issue to consider is exactly who should be rated in the appraisal process. Specifically, this issue is connected with the use of work teams. With work teams, the organization must decide whether to evaluate individual performance or team performance, and this issue can become quite complicated.

Andresr/Shutterstock.com

If individuals are rated and rewarded based on their individual performance, they have less reason to cooperate with other team members to accomplish the team's goals. In some cases, there may be no basis or reason for cooperation. For example, one of the authors recently learned that his university's bowling team was competing in a major tournament. But each team bowls at their own alley, and each teams' score is simply the average of the scores of each individual team member. Therefore, there is no opportunity to cooperate, and each team member helps the team by maximizing his or her own performance. In such settings, either the team captain (or leader) or fellow team members can provide team member evaluations.

In other team settings, though, it is critical that team members work together toward a common goal. In these cases, it is critical that performance be measured and rewarded only at the team level. One person's performance should not be considered except as part of the whole. Some employees are uncomfortable with this kind of system and believe they should be recognized for their individual efforts. In such settings, it is also possible for one employee to relax and let the other team members carry the workload. This free-rider problem is a real challenge to work teams. Nonetheless, if the team functions as a team rather than as a set of individuals, it is essential that the team's performance is appraised and rewarded.[25]

 ## 10-3 METHODS FOR APPRAISING PERFORMANCE

Different performance-appraisal methods and techniques are used in organizations. By their very nature, most appraisals are subjective—that is, we must rely on a rater's judgment of an employee's performance. As a result, performance appraisals are also prone to problems of bias (some of which were discussed earlier) and rating errors (which are discussed later in this chapter). Raters tend to be uncomfortable passing judgment on employees, and employees generally do not care to be judged in this way. The question then becomes, why don't managers simply use objective measures of performance in evaluating employee performance?

The simplest answer is that, for most jobs, and for all managerial jobs, straightforward objective measures of perfomance do not exist. Moreover, even when such measures do exist, they are usually contaminated by factors such as locations of sales territories. In many other cases where objective measures exist, they are meaningful

only at the level of the team (or an assembly line) and not at the level of the individual. Of course, objective data that does reflect conditions under the control of the individual employee are sometimes available. These data could be sales figures for outside sales employees. In other cases, a rater could measure outcomes such as reductions in complaints. These examples are best suited for outcome-based appraisal methods. But as shown in the Contemporary Challenges in HR box, even objective outcome-based methods may not always tell the full story. In many other cases, however, organizations have no choice but to rely on judgments and ratings. Therefore, a great deal of effort has been spent in trying to make these subjective evaluations as meaningful and as useful as possible. Some of the methods that have been proposed are based on relative rankings, while others rely more on absolute ratings.

10-3a Ranking Methods Versus Rating Methods

Probably the simplest method of performance appraisal is the **simple ranking method**, which involves having the manager simply rank-order, from top to bottom or from best to worst, each member of a particular work group or department. The individual ranked first is presumed to be the top performer, the individual ranked second is presumed to be the second-best performer, and so on. The ranking is generally global or based on overall performance. A variation on the ranking method is the **paired-comparison method** of performance appraisal, which involves comparing each individual employee with every other individual employee, one at a time. This technique is simply an alternative way to generate rankings, however.

Although ranking techniques are simple and easy to implement, there are some serious shortcomings. It is true that organizations seeking to make relatively simple decisions (e.g., which person to promote) can obtain clear and useful information about the "most promotable," but even in such cases where an organization must then turn to the "second-most promotable," ranking methods provide no information about the difference between the persons ranked first and second. The absence of such information is even more problematic

> The **simple ranking method** involves having the manager rank-order each member of a particular work group or department from top to bottom or from best to worst.
>
> In the **paired-comparison method** of performance appraisal, each individual employee is compared with every other individual employee, two at a time.

Contemporary Challenges in HR

When Is Acceptable Unacceptable?

For years, General Electric (GE) had used a ruthlessly efficient method for evaluating the performance of its employees. The system was widely known informally as the ABC approach. Each year, managers were required to sort all of their subordinates into one of three categories. The best, as much as 10 percent of the workforce, made up the A group; the next set, as much as 80 percent, included those in the middle and was called the B group (this large group subsequently were broken down into smaller groups).

The lowest 10 percent, though, was called the C group—and these workers lost their jobs even if they were generally seen as exhibiting acceptable performance! GE executives argued that this allowed the firm to continuously elevate the quality of the firm's human capital. Moreover, they noted, everyone knew the rules when they signed on, and no one had ever sued the company over this practice.

It is no surprise, then, that a few other companies have tried to follow in GE's footsteps. Goodyear was one of the first. Its first efforts identified 2,800 employees making up the worst performers in the company. These workers were then given their walking papers. Not too long afterward, though, Goodyear said it was abandoning the ABC method. Why? The tire maker became the target of an age-discrimination lawsuit that claimed that it singled out too many older employees as bad workers.

Another big company that experimented with—but quickly dropped—the ABC method was Ford Motor Company. The firm paid handsomely for its brief experiment when it agreed to pay $10.6 million to settle an age-discrimination suit filed by a group of fired employees. Since then, most other recent adopters of the ABC system have also dropped it.

One catalyst for the quick demise of the ABC system was when AARP, an advocacy group for

Americans 50 years of age and older committed itself to providing legal resources to those suing Goodyear. The lawsuit named eight plaintiffs aged 55–59, whose annual salaries ranged from $48,700 to 71,700. The lawsuit claimed that hundreds of workers in more than 10 states could join if the case was granted class-action status.

Jim Skykora, 55, the youngest and best-paid plaintiff, said in an interview that he had been designing tires for various Goodyear customers and had had all 11 of his projects approved in the 4 years leading up to his termination. He was graded a B– the first year the system was in place and downgraded to a C the next year. Although, the first lawsuit ended with the court agreeing with Goodyear that the company's practice was not discriminatory, the tire maker still decided to retreat from the ABC system and revert to its old methods.[26]

THINK IT OVER

1. Would you like to work under an ABC system?
2. How would you feel about using the ABC for a group of your own subordinates?

The **forced-distribution method** involves grouping employees into predefined frequencies of performance ratings.

for the employee who might be told that she or he is the "second best" but is not given any information about how to become the best.

A related technique for performance appraisal is forced distribution, a method that has been in practice for many years.[27] The **forced-distribution method** involves grouping employees into predefined frequencies of performance ratings. Those frequencies are determined by the organization in advance and are imposed

254   PART THREE: Managing the Existing Workforce

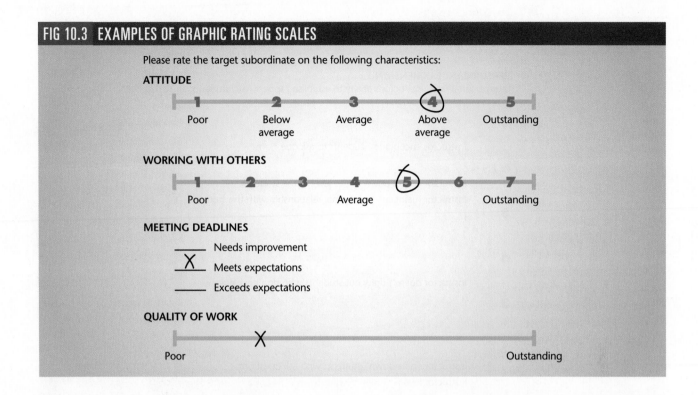

FIG 10.3 EXAMPLES OF GRAPHIC RATING SCALES

Please rate the target subordinate on the following characteristics:

ATTITUDE

1	2	3	4	5
Poor	Below average	Average	Above average	Outstanding

WORKING WITH OTHERS

1	2	3	4	5	6	7
Poor			Average			Outstanding

MEETING DEADLINES

_____ Needs improvement

__X__ Meets expectations

_____ Exceeds expectations

QUALITY OF WORK

Poor — X ———————————————— Outstanding

---

on the rater. For example, an organization could decide, similar to the traditional approach at GE, that approximately 20 percent of the employees are not performing to standard, while 60 percent are meeting expectations and standards, and only 20 percent are truly outstanding. The manager can classify his or her employees into any one of these three groups, but the percentages assigned to each group must be as specified.

An advantage of this system is that it results in a normal distribution of performance ratings, which many people see as inherently fair. In addition, from the organization's perspective, if employees are to receive merit pay increases, a forced distribution ensures control over how much money is spent on merit pay. On the other hand, the distribution that is being imposed may have no relationship to the true distribution of performance in the work group. It is possible, for example, that *all* the employees are performing at acceptable levels, but the forced-distribution methods, as well as the other ranking methods, force the rater to make distinctions that might not really be meaningful. As a result, most organizations rely instead on some type of absolute judgments and employ a system of performance ratings rather than rankings.

10-3b Specific Rating Methods

One of the most popular and widely used performance-appraisal methods is the graphic rating scale. A **graphic rating scale** simply consists of a statement or question about some aspect of an individual's job performance. Following that statement or question is a series of answers; the rater must select the one that fits best. For example, one common set of responses to a graphic rating scale is *strongly agree, agree, neither agree nor disagree, disagree,* and *strongly disagree.* These descriptors or possible responses are usually arrayed along a bar, line, or similar visual representation, and this representation is marked with numbers or letters that correspond to each of the descriptors.

Figure 10.3 illustrates a graphic rating scale. A wide array of performance dimensions can be efficiently tapped with various rating scales on the same form. Each of the descriptors on the rating form is accompanied by a number or a letter for responses. Most graphic rating scales have ranges of one to five or one to seven, although occasionally a scale may use only one to three or perhaps even one to nine. The rater assigns a score for each dimension rated and then can sum these to form a measure of overall performance, or the form might simply add an overall performance scale. The specific dimensions measured by graphic rating scales should be based on job analysis, but this approach is not typically taken. Instead, to have a single instrument that can be used with all or most employees

> A **graphic rating scale** consists of a statement or question about some aspect of an individual's job performance.

FIG 10.4   BEHAVIORALLY ANCHORED RATING SCALES

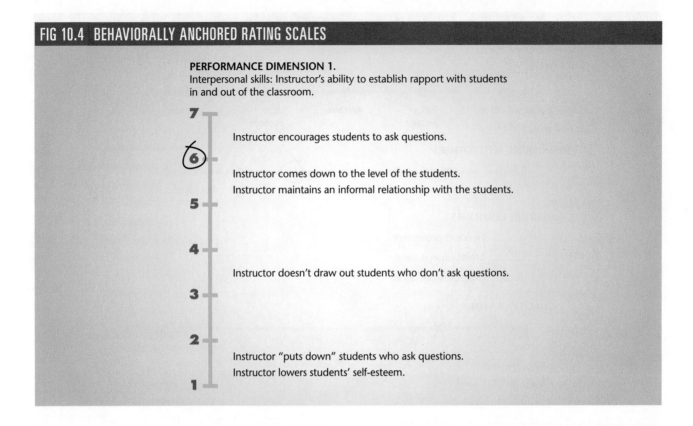

PERFORMANCE DIMENSION 1.
Interpersonal skills: Instructor's ability to establish rapport with students in and out of the classroom.

7

Instructor encourages students to ask questions.

⑥

Instructor comes down to the level of the students.
Instructor maintains an informal relationship with the students.

5

4

Instructor doesn't draw out students who don't ask questions.

3

2

Instructor "puts down" students who ask questions.
Instructor lowers students' self-esteem.

1

in an organization, graphic rating scales typically measure performance relative to traits or behaviors such as initiative or problem-solving capabilities or even attitudes. In addition, a number of problems have been associated with the use of graphic rating scales, but these will be discussed later when we consider various types of rating errors.

A somewhat different type of rating instrument involves the use of the **critical incident method**. (Recall from Chapter 5 that this method can also be used as a job analysis technique.) A critical incident is simply an example or instance of especially good or poor performance on the part of the employee.[28] Organizations that rely on this method often require raters to recall such instances on the job and then describe what the employee did (or did not do) that led to success or failure. Thus, this technique provides rich information for feedback to the employee and defines performance in fairly clear behavioral terms. In other cases, managers are asked to keep a log or diary in which they record examples or critical incidents that they believe reflect good and bad performance on the part of individual employees.[29]

The **critical incident method** relies on instances of especially good or poor performance on the part of the employee.

A **behaviorally anchored rating scale (BARS)** is an appraisal system that represents a combination of the graphic rating scale and the critical incident method.

For example, a critical incident illustrating good performance by a bank teller might read as follows: "On Tuesday, March 5, you were observed helping another teller deal with a difficult transaction. You were also observed going out of your way to help an elderly customer who couldn't understand how to complete a deposit slip." An advantage of the critical incident method is that it allows managers to provide individual employees with precise examples of behaviors that are believed to be both effective and less effective performance. On the other hand, the critical incident method requires considerable time and effort on the part of managers because they must maintain a log or diary of these incidents. In addition, the method may make it difficult to compare one person with another. The sample of behaviors developed from one employee may not be comparable to the sample of behaviors acquired for another.

Another method for appraising performance involves the use of a **behaviorally anchored rating scale (BARS)**.[30] BARS appraisal systems (also known sometimes as *behavioral expectation scales*) represent a combination of the graphic rating scale and the critical incident method. They specify performance dimensions based on behavioral anchors associated with different levels of performance. Figure 10.4 presents an example of a BARS developed by one of the authors to measure one dimension of teacher performance:

iStockphoto.com/DoxaDigital

interpersonal skills. As shown in the figure, the performance dimension has different behavioral examples that specify different levels of performance along the scale.

Developing a BARS is a complicated and often expensive process. Generally, these scales are developed by the same managers who eventually use them to evaluate employees. First, the managers must develop a pool of critical incidents that represent various effective and ineffective behaviors on the job. These incidents are then classified into performance dimensions, and the dimensions that the managers believe represent a particular level of performance are used as behavioral examples, or anchors, to guide the raters when the scales are used. At each step, an incident is discarded unless the majority of managers can agree on where it belongs or what level of performance the incident illustrates.[31] The manager who then uses the scale has to evaluate an employee's performance on each dimension and determine where on the dimension the employee's performance fits best. The behavioral anchors serve as guides and benchmarks in helping to make this determination.

A BARS system has the significant advantage of dramatically increasing reliability by providing specific behavioral examples to reflect effective and less effective behaviors. Because the managers themselves develop the scales, they tend to be more committed to using them effectively, and the process of developing the scales helps raters develop clearer ideas about what constitutes good performance on the job. The process of developing a truly effective BARS is extremely expensive and time-consuming, so these scales are rarely used in their pure form. Instead, some modified BARS procedures are often adopted in an attempt to reap some of the benefits without incurring the costs.

A related measure of performance is the **behavioral observation scale (BOS)**.[32] Like a BARS, a BOS is developed from critical incidents. Rather than using only a sample of behaviors that reflect effective or ineffective behavior, a BOS uses substantially more of the behaviors to define specifically all the measures necessary for effective performance. A second difference between a BOS and a BARS is that a BOS allows managers to rate the frequency with which the individual employee has exhibited each behavior during the rating period. The manager then averages these ratings to calculate an overall performance rating for the individual. Although the BOS approach is an improvement over the limitations of the BARS approach, it takes even more time and can be even more expensive to develop.

Earlier in the chapter, we noted that it might be reasonable to evaluate an employee based on outcomes. In fact, another popular method of appraising performance that does focus on outcomes is a **goal-based** or **management-by-objectives (MBO)** system.[33] Management by objectives is the most

A **behavioral observation scale (BOS)** is developed from critical incidents like a BARS but uses substantially more critical incidents to define specifically all the measures necessary for effective performance.

A **goal-based** or **management-by-objectives (MBO)** system is based largely on the extent to which individuals meet their personal performance objectives.

popular term used for this approach, although many companies develop their own label to describe the system used in their organization. In an MBO system, a subordinate meets with his or her manager, and together they set goals for the subordinate for a coming period of time, often 1 year. These goals are usually quantifiable, objective, and almost always written down. During the year, the manager and the subordinate meet periodically to review the subordinate's performance relative to attaining the goals. At the end of the year, a more formal meeting is scheduled. During that meeting, the actual degree of goal attainment is assessed. The degree of goal attainment then becomes the individual's performance appraisal. If an individual has attained all the goals that she or he set for herself or himself, then employee performance is deemed to be very good. On the other hand, if not all goals were accomplished, and the individual is directly responsible for that performance deficiency, then that employee's performance is judged to be less than adequate or acceptable.

Goal-based systems are often seen as the best alternative available for rating performance, but care must be taken when these systems are used. Specifically, the kinds of behaviors specified in the goal-setting process are exactly what the employee will tend to focus on, so it is critical that the organization really wants to encourage these particular behaviors. For example, a customer service representative may have goals stated in terms of how many customers are served in a day. However, in order to maximize the number of customers served, the representative may need to be curt or even rude to some customers who are taking "too much" time. This may result in lower levels of customer satisfaction, which, in the long run, could be devastating. The only real solution to this type of dilemma is to emphasize the need to be careful in setting goals to make sure that such a situation never arises.

One relatively new innovation in performance-appraisal methods is the use of computer monitoring. Employees can now be monitored electronically to see how they spend their time and how productive they are. These systems are now used widely with customer service representatives and reservations clerks. In fact, you may have heard a telephone recording (after you pressed the right numbers to get the service you wanted) stating, "This call may be monitored for quality purposes." This recording is an indication that electronic monitoring is taking place. For example, it is possible to track how many calls an employee receives, how long each call takes, and (with minimal

Contrast error occurs when we compare people against one another instead of against an objective standard.

input) the outcome of those calls. It is also possible to track when an employee is not at his or her phone station, which has caused some people to raise serious questions about invasions of privacy.[34] Although only a limited number of studies have investigated the effectiveness of this method, it seems as though the approach can be effective without triggering negative reactions on the part of employees—at least under certain circumstances.[35] While we need to know a great deal more about the effects of computer monitoring on individuals, the fact remains that this approach is being used with growing frequency in the workplace, and it is likely to become even more popular in the future.[36]

10-3c Which System Is Best?

Despite the time and effort that have gone into developing and improving performance-appraisal systems, it is difficult to find much advantage for any one system over the others.[37] We will discuss issues of rating errors later in the chapter, and much research has focused on the susceptibility of different types of rating instruments to different types of errors. But this research has been inconclusive, and it is somewhat misguided. As noted at the beginning of this chapter, the ultimate reason for conducting performance appraisal is to improve performance. Therefore, it is difficult to suggest which system is best because it is difficult to predict how a set of employees will react to a given system. The HR manager must take what is known about each type of system and decide how well the system fits into the culture and operations of the organization.

10-4 OTHER ISSUES IN PERFORMANCE APPRAISAL

We noted earlier that all the participants in the appraisal process tend to be dissatisfied with the process. Several issues that arise when we try to appraise performance contribute to this dissatisfaction, and we will discuss some of these problems below, as well as one additional issue that deals more with exactly what should be appraised.

10-4a Rating Errors

Several rating errors have been identified that can affect performance appraisals. Although it is not always clear that these are really "errors," they are nonetheless important to consider as part of our discussion of performance appraisal. One such error is known as **contrast error;**

it occurs when we compare people against one another instead of against an objective standard. For example, suppose a particular employee is a good performer but not an outstanding one. If that individual happens to work in a group of people in which everyone else is a relatively weak performer, then the "average" individual may appear to be a better performer than he or she really is. Likewise, if the same person works in a group of exceptionally strong performers, the person may be seen as a poorer performer than might otherwise be the case.

One of the major criticisms that had been leveled against graphic rating scales is that they were especially prone to a series of **distributional errors**. A distributional error occurs when the rater tends to use only one part of the rating scale.

1. Sometimes the distributional error may be *severity*, which occurs when the manager gives low ratings to all employees by holding them to an unreasonably high standard.

2. The opposite error is *leniency*, which occurs when a manager assigns relatively high or lenient ratings to all employees.[38]

3. A *central tendency* distributional error occurs when the manager tends to rate all employees as average, using only the middle part of a rating scale.

A different type of error that may occur is what is known as either halos or horns. A **halo error** occurs when one positive performance characteristic causes the manager to rate all other aspects of performance positively. For example, suppose a given employee always comes to work early and is always full of energy and enthusiasm at the beginning of the work day. The manager may so appreciate this behavior that he or she gives the employee a high performance rating on all other aspects of performance, even when those other aspects may be only average or merely adequate.[39] The opposite of a halo error is a **horns error**. In this instance, the manager tends to downgrade other aspects of an employee's performance because of a single performance dimension. For example, the manager may feel that a given employee does not dress appropriately and views that characteristic negatively. As a result, the manager may also give the individual low performance ratings on other performance dimensions when higher ratings are justified.

Except for contrast errors, however, it is not always clear that these other "errors" are really errors. Using the term *error* implies that there is a correct rating and that the observed rating in some cases is incorrect. But when we discuss leniency error as indicating that ratings are "too high," we imply that we know how high the ratings really should be—but we don't. Therefore, what we observe might be leniency, or it might simply mean that the employee is really good. Whether or not these are really errors, the presence of these response tendencies can make it difficult to differentiate between different employees or to accurately identify the strengths and weaknesses of a given employee. Furthermore, employees (ratees) might be less likely to perceive a set of lenient ratings as accurately reflecting their performance and so may not be willing to work to improve their performance.

As a result, organizations often do work to reduce rating error. One method for error reduction is to train managers to overcome these weaknesses, even when that means nothing more than pointing out to managers their tendency to commit distributional errors or contrast errors. Rater accuracy training is usually more involved than that, however. Specifically, an approach known as "frame of reference training" attempts to emphasize for managers the fact that performance is multidimensional in nature and to train those managers with the actual content of various performance dimensions.[40] As noted earlier, however, regardless of training or ability, there are cases where a rater simply chooses to be inaccurate. It is critical, therefore, that organizations do whatever they can to reward raters for doing a good job in performance appraisal by reinforcing the fact that these appraisals are important. Perhaps the most important and useful thing an organization can do to improve the quality of performance appraisals is simply to demonstrate to raters how and why it in their own best interests to do the best job they can in appraising employee performance.[41]

10-4b Contextual Performance

Formal performance-appraisal systems assess performance on aspects of one's job. Recently, however, interest has focused on what has been termed *contextual performance*, which brings a different dimension to the question of what should be appraised.[42]

A **distributional error** occurs when the rater tends to use only one part of the rating scale.

A **halo error** occurs when one positive performance characteristic causes the manager to rate all other aspects of performance positively.

A **horns error** occurs when the manager downgrades other aspects of an employee's performance because of a single performance dimension.

Contextual performance refers to tasks an employee does on the job that are not required as part of the job but that nevertheless benefit the organization in some way. These behaviors might include willingly staying late at work to meet deadlines, helping coworkers get their work done, and performing any other task that benefits the general good of the organization. These behaviors are also often referred to as *organizational citizenship behaviors*.[43] Because these behaviors are never stated as formal requirements of the job, the employee is never formally told that he or she is expected to do these tasks. They might be told informally, however, that such behaviors are valued by the organization in general or the manager in particular. In any event, they do benefit the organization, and raters do consider them when conducting employee evaluations.[44]

How important are contextual performance behaviors in determining the overall ratings an employee receives? A recent study indicates that, although they are important, they are not as important as task behaviors (or even as important as counterproductive behaviors), but they do matter.[45] The next question is, how important are these behaviors for organizational effectiveness? Clearly, the organization benefits if someone engages in these behaviors, so they represent part of an employee's overall contribution to the organization. On the other hand, they are not required of anyone. As a result, some, especially union members, argue that it is inherently unfair to evaluate someone on something that is not part of his or her job. Perhaps that assertion is true, but it seems that, consciously or not, raters do take these behaviors into account in making appraisal decisions.

There has also been some recent controversy over the role that contextual performance should play. On one hand, some scholars have argued that organizations should attempt to predict contextual performance among applicants for jobs and make selection decisions on the basis of those predictions.[46] Thus, contextual performance would play a more formal and more critical role in HR than had previously been suggested.

However, on the other hand, there is some evidence that some levels of contextual performance are actually required in many settings; that work-family conflicts may make it more difficult for some employees (especially women with child-care responsibilities) to exhibit these discretionary behaviors; and that women who do exhibit these behaviors may be judged differently from men.[47]

Andresr/Shutterstock.com

10-4c Evaluating the Performance-Appraisal Process

At the beginning of this chapter, we noted the strategic importance of performance appraisal but also noted that several firms had recently been separating performance appraisal from performance management. More specifically, several firms have claimed to have dropped performance appraisals completely and focused entirely on performance management.

Much of the reaction stems from the use of what many companies call "stack ratings," but which is really just the forced distribution method discussed earlier. These systems, say expert consultants, lead to backstabbing, low levels of teamwork, and feelings of frustration as someone must always be rated as a poor performer. The same experts also argue that performance appraisals are too infrequent to really address performance problems.[48]

Companies such as Accenture, Adobe, Netflix, and even GE are dropping their annual appraisals—all based on forced distributions—in favor of systems where managers meet regularly with employees (as often as weekly) to provide personalized feedback and help develop their performance.[49] Thus, the new systems are targeted at collecting more information about employees' performance—not less. New performance management technology makes it possible to collect real-time performance data that is presumably less prone to the biases and errors that plague traditional appraisals as discussed earlier in the chapter. Thus, this is also another area where data analytics is playing a role.

But these trends don't mean that everyone is convinced that eliminating performance appraisals is the answer. These experts note that effective rating systems allow companies to differentiate among employees performing at different levels, although they also acknowledge how biases can cause problems. Interestingly, GE, while dropping their traditional rating system, is retaining some ratings for all but about 8,000 employees who will serve as a pilot group for a "no ratings" system. Others have warned that this new trend is very similar to an earlier trend where everyone began adopting GE's forced distribution system because, if GE did it, it must be good.[50]

How will all this turn out? It seems clear that formal appraisals can be burdensome and problematic, and stack rating may be especially problematic. In addition, it seems clear, as we will discuss in more detail in Chapter 14, that how we work to manage performance is probably more important than actual ratings. Finally, studies indicating that employees react poorly to negative feedback are instructive,[51] but they cannot be interpreted to mean that no one should receive negative feedback—after all, that is the key to improvement—we simply need to find ways to provide feedback more effectively. And, as we will also discuss further in Chapter 14, it is not clear that feedback is the performance management panacea that some managers believe it to be.[52] However, in any case, as we noted at the beginning of this chapter, performance appraisals are used for a number of decisions in organizations. If companies don't rely on some type of ratings to decide who should receive raises or get promoted, how will they decide? Not having some type of documentation could mean serious legal problems for firms that are sued for discrimination. That doesn't mean frequent feedback meetings couldn't be used to generate the data needed to make those decisions, it is just important to recognize that evaluations, under any name, are still evaluations, and they may be important. In the final analysis, however, it is probably not the system or lack thereof that is critical. If managers truly want to develop their employees, they will do so, regardless of the system in place. If they do not want to do so, there is no system that can be devised to force them to do the right thing.

10-4d Legal Issues in Performance Appraisal

When performance appraisals are used as the basis for HR decisions (as in the case of merit pay or promotion decisions), they are considered the same as any other test under the law. This designation includes decisions about layoffs based on performance. Therefore, appraisals that show evidence of disparate impact must be validated the same as any selection technique. This principle was first established in *Brito* v. *Zia Company*[53] and reinforced as part of the decision in the *Albemarle Paper Company* case discussed in Chapter 5.

As noted previously, performance-appraisal decisions are known to suffer from various types of biases and problems. Also noted earlier in the chapter was the fact that ratings based on traits tend to have ambiguous standards, so they are probably more prone to these biases. It is difficult to validate appraisal decisions using the methods described in Chapter 7 (i.e., content validity, construct validity, and criterion-related validity). Therefore, it is critical that the organization can demonstrate that the ratings provided are in areas that are "job related," that raters can observe the behaviors they are rating, and that raters received some training to help them do a better job with rating performance. If an appraisal system is used for providing feedback only, however, it is not subject to these same legal requirements.

We also noted in Chapter 2 that Yahoo was recently sued for layoffs connected with their appraisal program (a "stack rating" program). This case simply emphasizes the variety of decisions that organizations make on the basis of performance appraisals and why they are important. This leads us to believe that although there may be changes in appraisal practices—especially those aimed at streamlining the process—performance appraisals are not dead, and they are not likely to die anytime soon.

As also noted earlier in this chapter, those individuals advocating some alternative performance-management systems argue that most systems ignore the goal of employee development. That is, one of the most important reasons for conducting appraisals is to help employees perform their jobs at the highest level they can and to help them develop themselves and advance their careers. We therefore turn to a more formal discussion of the topic of career management.

10-5 THE NATURE OF CAREERS

Most people have a general idea of the meaning of *career*. For instance, they generally agree that careers have something to do with the work a person does in an organization, but they also recognize that a career is a broader and more general concept than a single job or task in an organization.

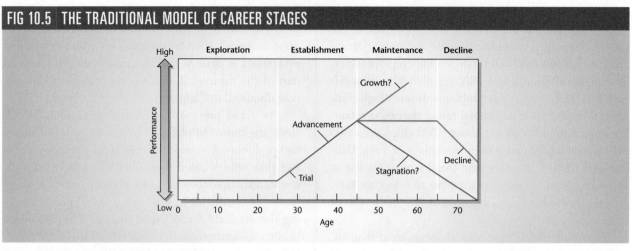

FIG 10.5 | THE TRADITIONAL MODEL OF CAREER STAGES

Source: Adapted from *Careers in Organizations*, by Douglas T. Hall. Copyright © 1976 by Scott, Foresman, and Co. Reprinted by permission of Douglas T. Hall and Lyman Porter.

10-5a The Meaning of Career

We define a **career** as the set of experiences and activities in which a person engages related to his or her job and livelihood over the course of a working life. This definition, then, suggests that a career includes the various specific jobs that a person performs, the kinds of responsibilities and activities that make up those jobs, movements and transitions between jobs, and an individual's overall assessment of and feelings of satisfaction with these various components of her or his career.

Most people have historically thought of the various components making up a person's career as having some degree of interrelation. This perspective stems from the fact that, in the past at least, people generally wanted to work for a single organization and spent most of their work life within that single organization. Presumably, if they performed effectively and were successful at their work, they advanced up the organizational hierarchy. Even when people changed jobs, they tended to work for other organizations in the same industry. For example, Steve Jobs founded Apple in 1976. He left the company in 1985 and started another computer business, NeXT. He also bought a computer-animation business from George Lucas and turned it into Pixar. Jobs eventually rejoined Apple in 1997 and led the company until his death in 2011.

In recent times, however, conceptualizations of careers have become considerably more general. Because of organizational downsizing efforts and innovations in strategies such as outsourcing and shared services, considerably more change has occurred in the work patterns of individuals than in the past.[54] For instance, people are likely to leave an organization in one industry and go to work for an organization in a totally different industry, and they may also spend time between jobs and organizations consulting or working in otherwise independent contractor-type positions.

More and more frequently, people are taking breaks from their work. These breaks include sabbaticals, discretionary periods of unemployment, and similar activities that may make a positive contribution to a person's overall work life but do not involve formal employment by an organization. People who return to school to enhance their education now more than ever before are likely to consider that period of their lives as part of their career.

10-5b Traditional Career Stages

One traditional view, shown in Figure 10.5, suggests that a typical individual progresses through four career stages:

1. The first stage is called **exploration**. During this period in people's lives, they try to identify the kind of work they are interested in doing. This period of a typical person's career starts in the mid- to late teens and lasts through the mid- to late twenties. It generally encompasses the time when he tries to assess his own interests, values, preferences, and career opportunities and to relate them to what he thinks represents a feasible career option. His coursework in school and his first jobs play an important role in the exploration stage of career development. For example, it is not uncommon for someone who anticipates majoring in a certain field of study to change his major after he begins taking

A **career** is the set of experiences and activities that people engage in related to their job and livelihood over the course of their working life.

Exploration is the first traditional career stage and involves identifying interests and opportunities.

courses in that area. Sometimes people take their first jobs in particular fields only to discover they are not what they expected and so begin to look for alternative options. Of course, sometimes people are perfectly happy with the outcome of the exploration stage. They find that the coursework of their field is indeed of interest to them, and their first job assignments are exciting, challenging, and just what they expected them to be.

2. The second stage of a typical career is called the establishment stage. During this period, an individual begins to create a meaningful and relevant role for herself and the organization. She may, for example, become a valuable member of a work team, achieve success and recognition by her superior, and be acknowledged by the organization as someone the company values and wants to retain. There is considerable range in terms of age and time in this stage, but it generally encompasses an individual's late twenties through mid- to late thirties.

3. The maintenance stage is the next stage in a typical career. During this period, the individual begins to reach a level in the organization that optimizes his talents or capabilities. Not everyone can become a chief executive officer, however, and only a small percentage of the total workforce in any organization attains the rank of top executive. For many employees, then, this stage marks a midcareer plateau. Many successful managers, especially in larger companies, may never progress beyond the rank of middle manager and end their careers on this plateau, but they nevertheless enjoy careers considered to be highly productive and worthwhile. Individuals in the maintenance stage of their career must often devote extra effort to learning new job skills and remaining current in their professional skills and abilities. They are also frequently called on to fill mentoring roles in which they help newcomers to the organization get their feet on the ground and launch their own careers.[55]

4. Finally, the fourth stage of a typical career is the disengagement stage. During this period, the individual gradually begins to pull away from her work in the organization, her priorities change, and work may become less important to her. Consequently, she begins thinking more and more about leaving the organization and finding other sources for fulfilling her personal needs and goals. Some employees may evolve toward part-time work status, some

retire from the organization, and some simply cut back on their activities and responsibilities.

10-5c New Views of Career Stages

Of course, in the contemporary era of downsizing and layoffs, sometimes people go through these four stages of career development in a relatively short period of time. People may find themselves disengaging from the organization at a relatively young age, and they may also anticipate beginning the entire process again by seeking new opportunities, new challenges, and new interests.[56] Many experts agree that even though the traditional model of careers summarized above still has conceptual value, new perspectives on careers are better reflections of today's realities. Some experts, for instance, argue that we should think about career ages (how long someone has been on a job) rather than career stages or even chronological age.[57] Furthermore, they suggest that we must directly incorporate the premise of multiple careers into any modern view of careers. At the beginning of each new career, though, the employee begins a process of exploration, trial, and establishment, followed by another period of exploration. This second level of exploration in turn is likely to take the person away from the current career and into a new one where the process begins again.

This perspective also suggests that employees face different types of challenges at each step.[58] At the beginning of one's career, there are issues about making the transition from a student to an employee. This involves questions about one's self-identity, and these questions also influence decisions about exactly what career someone plans to enter. Individuals may choose to enter certain careers because they are considered "hot" or because of general economic trends. They also choose careers because they are more consistent with their own interests, education, and values.

After a career has been chosen and the person begins to build on that career, the issues that emerge often deal with trying to establish the proper balance between work and family life. At this point in one's career, these issues become more salient, and the individual must deal with the potential trade-off between working hard to

The establishment stage of the traditional career model involves creating a meaningful and relevant role in the organization.

The maintenance stage involves optimizing talents or capabilities.

The fourth traditional career stage, disengagement, involves the individual gradually beginning to pull away from work in the organization. Priorities change, and work may become less important.

racorn/Shutterstock.com

is rather mixed and generally weak. For example, although there is evidence of declines in abilities such as motor coordination and dexterity, these effects can be explained by differences in education and job type, and there is no evidence of age-related declines in intelligence, verbal ability, or numerical ability.[60] Perhaps more critically, there is almost no relationship between age and job performance—in fact, some studies have found a curvilinear relationship between age and performance with performance highest when workers are youngest *and* older.[61]

In any event, eventually older workers must confront the decision to retire. In truth, however, the decision to retire is not as simple as it once was. Today, there is really a whole continuum of choices available to a person contemplating retirement. The person can actually retire, take a pension, and begin some other nonwork activities (the traditional view of retirement), but this is becoming less common. More commonly, individuals retire and then take on full-time work at other organizations, or they retire and take on part-time work or work as consultants either at their former employers or elsewhere. Over time, they may reduce the amount of time they spend at work until they gradually move into full retirement, but retirement has become much more of a process than an event.[62]

Nonetheless, many factors are related to the decision to retire (or begin the retirement process). For example, individuals are more likely to retire when they have the financial resources needed to maintain their preretirement lifestyles, and they are more likely to retire when their health makes continuing to work excessively burdensome. Individuals are also more likely to retire when their spouses have retired. In addition, several factors are related to adjustment after retirement. Of course, as noted earlier, many people tend to continue with some type of "bridge work," and these people generally adjust well to retirement. Individuals who have structured leisure activities and those who do volunteer work also tend to adjust better to retirement. But one of the most important factors related to adjustment is one's health. Individuals who avoid serious health problems

build and advance a career and establishing lasting relationships with others, including building a strong family life. In addition, at this stage, decisions are more frequent regarding whether or not the person should remain with a given firm or move to a different organization. The decision as to how best to advance one's career in terms of moving is, of course, also tied to the growing importance of balancing work and family. By the time a person reaches some sort of midcareer point, there are often questions about the worth of continuing to work on one's career, and new questions about self-identity emerge (sometimes leading to a so-called midlife crisis).[59]

10-5d Issues Facing Older Workers and the Decision to Retire

As workers continue to age, they have new career issues to deal with, and some of them relate to potential age discrimination. As noted in Chapter 2, persons age 40 and older are protected by the Age Discrimination in Employment Act, but the fact remains that many people assume that abilities and job performance decline with age. In fact, the evidence regarding such declines

> The Age Discrimination in Employment Act (or ADEA) prohibits discrimination against employees age 40 and older.

adjust better, partly because they can engage in the kinds of activities just outlined. It is important to realize that these and any other issues relating to the decision to retire are likely to become much more important for HR managers as the workforce ages and as lives and productive work careers expand.

10-6 HUMAN RESOURCE MANAGEMENT AND CAREER MANAGEMENT

Most successful organizations and managers today recognize that careers do not simply happen; they must be planned and managed. Most companies with a reputation to be great places to work—such as GE, Disney, and Southwest Airlines—have formal career-planning systems for their managers.[63] Part of the responsibility for this career planning resides with the organization, and the feedback from the appraisal process is a critical factor in this process. But the individual must also play a role in this process.[64] This section examines the organizational and individual perspectives on careers shown in Figure 10.6.

10-6a Organizational and Individual Perspectives on Careers

Organizations are generally responsible for determining the jobs that people will perform for the organization, the pattern of interrelationships between jobs in an organization, the kinds of people who will be hired for those jobs, the development of those individuals to prepare them for more meaningful jobs, and the decisions regarding the movement of people from one job to another. Clearly, it is in the organization's best interest to take an active role in career management for people in the firm, and, for this reason, career management is often part of the larger performance-management process.[65]

The organization can take steps from the outset to facilitate career management. For example, in Chapter 7, we discussed the idea of selecting individuals not because of their match with the requirements of a specific job but because of their fit with the organization. Despite any other problems associated with this selection strategy, it seems helpful for career management because the organization presumably hires individuals who fit different jobs. In fact, even when organizations select individuals for a specific job, it is still possible to do so with subsequent career moves in mind. In other words, if an entry-level position is not particularly demanding, then it is possible for an organization to hire people whose skills and abilities match a higher-level job that they might be expected to move into later. This practice can be defended as long as the employee will likely move up to the higher-level job eventually.

If an organization does indeed help its employees plan and manage their careers more effectively, it can expect to find itself with a larger pool of talented individuals who are generally more satisfied and motivated. On the other hand, if the organization does a poor job with managing the careers of people in the organization, then it will find that the quality of its talent pool might vary in inefficient ways; that is, it might have an abundance or surplus of highly talented and qualified employees in some areas and at some levels of the firm but have a shortage of talented and capable people at other levels or areas of the organization. In addition, the workforce of such an organization might be more dissatisfied and unmotivated because people are not given appropriate promotion opportunities or are not placed in appropriate positions. When the organization needs to transfer

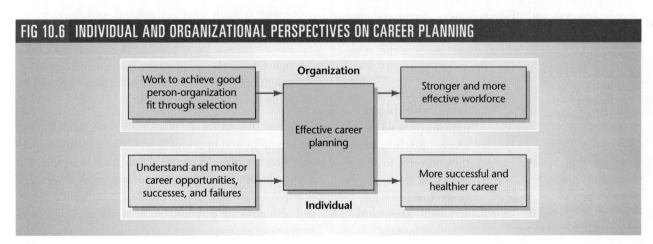

FIG 10.6 INDIVIDUAL AND ORGANIZATIONAL PERSPECTIVES ON CAREER PLANNING

FIG 10.7 STEPS IN CAREER PLANNING

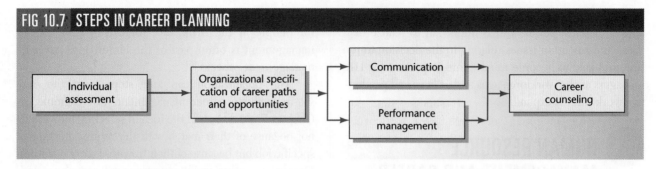

people or lay people off, it may be unsure about who can handle the new assignments.

Individuals obviously have an important stake in their own careers. They experience most directly the benefits and rewards of successful careers and incur the costs and frustrations of unsuccessful careers. A person's perceived and experienced career success or failure is also likely to have a major effect on his or her self-esteem and similar indications of self-worth.

People who understand and carefully monitor their careers are likely to understand the reasons behind their successes and failures. These individuals will know why they have or have not been promoted and will have accurate assessments of future promotion prospects and possibilities. In addition, people who accept responsibility for managing their careers will also be better prepared to deal with unanticipated career setbacks such as job losses and demotions. Unfortunately, many people are surprisingly uninformed and uninvolved in their own careers.

10-6b The Importance of Career Planning

Career planning is clearly important to both organizations and employees. Furthermore, effective career planning requires careful coordination between individual employees and the organization itself. Usually, HR managers represent the organization in the career-planning process. GE and Shell Oil are known to be especially effective with their managers' career planning and development. In general, most career-planning systems involve the steps shown in Figure 10.7.

1. In the **individual assessment phase**, individuals need to analyze carefully what they perceive to be their own abilities, competencies, skills, and goals. Many organizations provide

> The **individual assessment phase** of career planning requires that individuals analyze carefully what they perceive to be their own abilities, competencies, skills, and goals.
>
> **Career counseling** involves interaction between an individual employee or manager in the organization and either a line manager or an HR manager.

employees with forms or questionnaires to help them develop this information.

2. At the same time, the HR manager should be developing a potential career path an employee may take up the corporate ladder.[66] Shell's career-path model, for example, is available to managers on the firm's corporate intranet.

3. Communication is also an important part of this process. For example, the organization may know the paths that are most likely to be followed from one position to another and be able to gauge the probability or likelihood that a specific individual will follow this path or a prescribed path for a promotion to another position. But if this information is not communicated to the individual employee, then it is of little or no value to anyone. At the same time, the organization must also integrate its performance-management system with its career-management system. A person should not expect to progress automatically from one job to another along a certain path but instead recognize that this movement will be determined in part by his or her performance effectiveness.

4. The final step in effective career planning is **career counseling**. As the term suggests, career counseling involves interaction between an individual employee or manager in the organization and either a line manager or an HR manager. This counseling session typically involves frank and open dialogue with the goal of making sure that the individual's assessment and the organization's assessment of the individual's role and prospects in the organization are congruent. We discuss career-counseling programs in more detail in the next section.

Even though career planning is important to both organizations and individuals, and effective career planning benefits both, everyone should also recognize that career planning has limitations and potential pitfalls. For example, no amount of sophisticated forecasting can predict with absolute certainty the level of talent, expertise, motivation, or interest a given individual will have in the future. People experience changes in interests, for example, and they may redefine their priorities. Even though the organization and the individual may expect that the individual will be capable of performing a certain job in the future, it may turn out that both parties are wrong.

The organization's future human resource needs can also change. For example, it may become more or less successful than originally envisioned, or it may decide on new strategies to pursue. New managers may come in and want work done differently than in the past. And new opportunities may present themselves to both the individual and the organization. For instance, an organization may have a certain current member of its workforce who has been tapped to assume an important position in a couple of years. But a substantially stronger individual for that same position may unexpectedly emerge. In this case, the organization may have to alter its original strategy, even at the risk of alienating the individual originally tapped for the job.

Similarly, individuals sometimes find new opportunities at unexpected times. Both an individual and the organization, for instance, may expect that individual to take a certain job in the future. But another organization may appear on the scene to lure the individual away, perhaps at a substantially higher salary. In this instance, the individual is likely to be happy with this turn of events because he or she will have a position and a higher salary. The organization, on the other hand, may face disruption and may have to alter its existing plans.

Unanticipated mergers and acquisitions can also result in changes in career opportunities. For example, when Amoco was acquired by British Petroleum a few years ago, the new organization found itself with a surplus of qualified managers and had to offer early retirement incentives to some of them. Others were presented with unanticipated opportunities for new assignments that were substantially different from what they expected. For example, a senior Amoco manager based in Houston, Texas, had been on a career path that did not include the possibility of an international assignment. Shortly after the integration of the firms, however, this manager was offered a promotion to a new job in London.

10-7 CAREER-DEVELOPMENT ISSUES AND CHALLENGES

Regardless of the career stages for individual employees, many organizations that are sincerely interested in more effective career management for their employees deal with and address various issues and challenges. In this

> "We're living in a different world now in terms of employee needs, and companies have to offer alternative methods for getting the work done. Even under the most difficult circumstances you can have creative flexibility."
>
> —ANNE M. MULCAHY, FORMER CHAIRPERSON AND CEO OF XEROX CORPORATION

section, we introduce and describe some of these issues and challenges in more detail.

10-7a Career-Counseling Programs

As already noted, career-counseling programs are important to an organization interested in career development for its employees. Such programs usually address a wide variety of career-related issues and are readily accessible to people in the organization. Some programs are formal; others are considerably informal.

Formal career-counseling programs usually take the form of workshops, conferences, and career-development centers. In some cases, the organization establishes general-purpose career-counseling programs that are available to all employees. They may also create special programs targeted for certain categories of employees. Among the more popular special programs are counseling programs for fast-track managers, women managers, and minority managers. These special programs serve various purposes in addition to addressing the specific needs of certain categories of employees. They also help to integrate those employees into the mainstream of the overall organization, and they create important networking opportunities for these individuals.

Organizations also have informal counseling programs. Much of this counseling takes the form of one-on-one interactions between an employee and his or her supervisor and typically occurs during the performance-appraisal period. For example, when supervisors appraise and evaluate the performance of a subordinate and then provide performance feedback to that individual, part of the conversation also deals with issues such as promotion prospects, skill development, and so forth. Sometimes employees may simply drop by the HR department for advice on career-related questions and issues. When dropins are common, it is important that the HR department fulfill its center of expertise role and provide useful and accurate information.

10-7b Dual-Career and Work–Family Issues

work

Back in the 1950s and into the 1960s, most married couples in the United States were characterized by roles that gave the male partner career precedence over the female partner; that is, the family tended to live where the husband needed to live. When the husband was given a job transfer, his decision to take it was not usually questioned. And if the wife happened to be employed outside the home, it was assumed that she would resign from her job and that the family would move.

But as increasing numbers of women entered the workforce, primarily beginning in the mid- to late 1960s, this pattern changed substantially. For many married couples now, the wife's career is on an equal footing with the husband's or perhaps may be given precedence over it. Thus, when organizations offer a transfer to an employee, they must be prepared to deal with the complexities associated with another career. The entire process of career planning must take into consideration the fact that another career must often be managed simultaneously.

Perhaps related to this trend is the growing concern over balancing family needs with the demands of work. As noted previously, as dual-career and single-parent employment increases, these concerns pose yet another challenge to career management, especially in the midcareer stages.[67] First, concerns over family-friendly work practices (e.g., child care, elder care, and flexible work schedules) have an influence over the choices that employees make concerning where to work. In fact, many organizations are now advertising their family-friendly practices as a means of competing for employees.[68] It is also increasingly clear that concerns at home and with the family affect an employee's behavior at work. Stress over how to arrange for child care or who will care for an ailing parent can cause the employee problems at work. Relieving these pressures allows the employee to concentrate

more on the job and thus better realize his or her career potential.[69]

Finally, evidence shows that work stressors influence family stress, which in turn is related to long-term health.[70] As the workforce becomes more diverse, organizations thus will have to recognize that both dual-career issues and concerns over work–family balance will become increasingly important factors for determining career success and must be considered as part of career management.

life

patpitchaya/Shutterstock.com

10-7c Evaluating Career-Management Activities

The ultimate goals of career management are to have employees reach their full potential at work, enjoy productive and satisfying work careers, and then make a successful transition to retirement. Full appreciation of career-management activities on the part of the employee may not come until after retirement. But as employees are increasingly unlikely to spend their entire careers in a single organization, success in retirement is much more likely to be a function of the individual's own career-management efforts (as well as the good fortune of remaining healthy through the retirement years). For a large number of employees, especially those in higher-status jobs or those for whom work is an important part of self-image, leaving one's career does not mean the end of work. For these employees, managing the transition to what have been called "bridge" jobs (and eventually to full retirement) is most important for their continued satisfaction.[71]

Therefore, career-management activities can be judged only by their success at any one point in time. If an employee is satisfied with his or her career at this point, then career management must be judged successful up to that point. We have focused primarily on actions the organization can take to manage this process, but clearly a great deal also depends on the employee's efforts at managing his or her career. Employees who go into careers for which they are not well suited (either in terms of abilities or temperament) will obviously be more likely to suffer dissatisfaction with their careers. Although organizational career-management efforts are important, the successful management of one's career depends heavily on the employee's efforts to assess his or her own abilities and interests accurately and to formulate a plan for what a successful career should look like.

CLOSING CASE
Investing In Talent

Some businesses see employee costs such as wages and salaries as an expense. But others see employees as vital resources that can give them a real competitive advantage. Darden Restaurants falls clearly in the second set. Darden operates such popular eateries as Olive Garden, LongHorn Steakhouse, Capital Grill, and others. All told, the firm has about 150,000 employees and 1,500 restaurants (all company owned, not franchised).

Juanmonino/E+/Getty Images

Darden has been named one of the best companies to work for in America by *Fortune* magazine, the only restaurant business that's ever made this list. The firm's annual employee turnover is about 20 percent lower than its industry average, and many Darden top managers started at the bottom and worked themselves up the corporate ladder. In fact, that is one major reason that Darden's employees enjoy working there so much.

Take Mike Stroud, for example. Stroud started as a busboy at a Red Lobster in Georgia in 1973 (at the time Red Lobster was owned by Darden but was recently sold to a private investment group). Today, he is a senior vice president overseeing 215 locations. Likewise, Lisa Hoggs joined the company waiting tables at a LongHorn Steakhouse. Now she is a managing partner, running a $3 million location in Atlanta. About 42 percent of its employees are minorities,

and 39 percent of its managers are women.

What's Darden's secret? For one thing, the company tries to impress upon its employees that working for Darden can be a career and not just a job. The firm invests heavily in talent development and offers extensive career planning to all employees. The company also offers its employees an array of other meaningful benefits as well. For example, it supports a credit union that provides low-interest loans to employees, strong health-care packages, and substantial training and development opportunities.

Darden recently announced plans to open 500 new restaurants in the next 5 years and hire almost 50,000 new employees. Given its track record in hiring, nurturing, and promoting employees, there seems to be little question that it will succeed. And who knows—Olive Garden and Capital Grill may one day soon be as common as McDonald's and Starbucks.[72]

Case Questions

1. What factors have led Darden to take its current approach to employee development and advancement?

2. Darden owns both family-oriented casual restaurants such as Olive Garden and more sophisticated upscale places such as Capital Grill. What effects might this structure have for employee development?

STUDY TOOLS 10

READY TO STUDY?
In the book, you can:

☐ Rip out the chapter review card at the back of the book for a handy summary of the chapter and key terms.

ONLINE AT CENGAGEBRAIN.COM, YOU CAN:

☐ Collect StudyBits while you read and study the chapter.

☐ Quiz yourself on key concepts.

☐ Find videos for further exploration.

☐ Prepare for tests with HR4 Flash Cards as well as those you create.

11 | Managing Labor Relations

After finishing this chapter go to **PAGE 295** for **STUDY TOOLS**

LEARNING OBJECTIVES

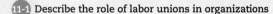

11-1 Describe the role of labor unions in organizations

11-2 Identify and summarize trends in unionization

11-3 Discuss the unionization process

11-4 Describe the collective-bargaining process

11-5 Discuss how labor agreements are negotiated

11-6 Describe how impasses get resolved and agreements are administered

11-7 Discuss emerging labor union issues in the twenty-first century

OPENING CASE
Unionizing in the New Age

Modern labor unions in the United States can trace their origins to the 19th century and started gaining footholds in many major corporations almost a century ago. For example, Boeing signed its first contract with a labor union in 1936, and Ford signed its first labor contract in 1941. Today, unions at those and many other "old-line" businesses still weld significant power and represent thousands of workers.

On the other hand, many newer businesses have successfully avoided unionization among their employees. Their arguments against unions include the following:

- Unions constantly push for higher wages and expensive benefits to the point of reducing business competitiveness.
- Unions usually want businesses to retain and reward workers based on seniority rather than performance.
- Unions aggressively fight job cuts and employee layoffs.
- Unions have the ability to strike, potentially crippling a business for an extended period of time.
- Unions push for highly restrictive work rules, limiting a firm's flexibility to reassign workers to other jobs or change the scope of a worker's job.

Firms such as Walmart, Starbucks, Google, and Amazon are at the forefront of large younger businesses who work consistently to thwart efforts to unionize their employees. Walmart, in particular, has had several major skirmishes. Some Walmart workers complain about low wages, poor benefits, a lack of full-time jobs, and erratic and unpredictable work schedules. For its part, Walmart warns that unionization could mean the end of employee perks such as paid vacation and quarterly bonuses. The United Food and Commercial Workers Union has made Walmart its major battleground and has won several small battles. The union has also had success fighting Walmart in the courts based on various situations in which the retailer has crossed legal lines in trying to avoid unionization. But still, most of Walmart's

> "With the vote against third-party representation, our employees have made it clear that they prefer a direct connection with Amazon."
>
> —MARY OSAKO, AMAZON SPOKESPERSON[1]

employees remain nonunionized, and the UFCW still faces an uphill fight.

Starbucks has also faced union challenges. For its part, the coffee giant has helped minimize unionization interest among its employees by treating them very well. Even part-time workers at Starbucks get benefits, for example, and the firm offers many opportunities for advancement. Still, the Industrial Workers of the World union continues to explore unionization interest among Starbucks employees. The firm recently created a policy that its workers could actually wear a button supporting the union but a limit of a single badge less than one inch in diameter was imposed. The union filed a legal claim against Starbucks, but the company policy was upheld in court.

Various unions, including the International Association of Machinists and Aerospace, a trade union of the AFL-CIO, have also tried to unionize workers at Amazon. Recently, for example, this union managed to gain government approval for a union vote at an Amazon facility. While the majority of workers ended up voting against unionization, the mere fact that they managed to secure the election was seen by the union's leaders as at least a minor victory.[2]

THINK IT OVER

1. Under what employment circumstances might you be interested in joining a union?
2. If you were a manager trying to convince your employees not to form a union what might you say to them?

Walmart, Starbucks, and Amazon are contending with a significant issue that has confronted business leaders for decades: dealing with organized labor in ways that optimize the needs and priorities of both the organization and its employees. When this challenge is handled effectively and constructively, both sides benefit. But when relationships between an organization and its unions turn sour, both sides can suffer great costs. Walmart, for example, has incurred significant costs dealing with its antiunion efforts and the legal battles that have resulted. The firm has also had its image tarnished.

FIG 11.1 A HISTORICAL TIME LINE OF UNIONIZATION IN THE UNITED STATES

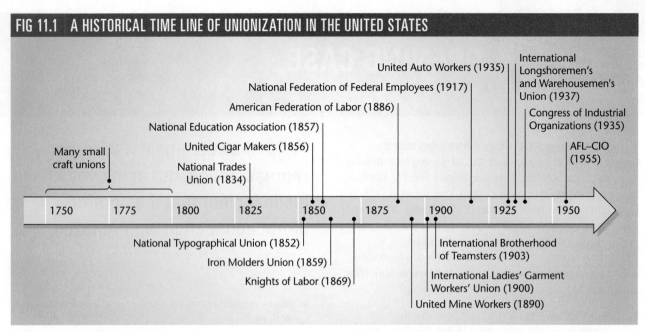

Source: Ricky Griffin and Ronald Ebert, *Business*, 3rd ed., © 1993, p. 264. Reprinted by permission of Pearson Education, Inc., Upper Saddle River, NJ.

In this chapter, we focus on the management of labor relations. We start by assessing the role of labor unions in organizations. We examine trends in unionization and describe the unionization process itself. Collective bargaining is discussed, followed by a description of the issues involved in negotiating labor agreements. The chapter closes with a discussion of the administration of labor agreements.

11-1 THE ROLE OF LABOR UNIONS IN ORGANIZATIONS

Labor relations can be defined as the process of dealing with employees who are represented by a union. A **labor union**, in turn, is a legally constituted group of individuals working together to achieve shared job-related goals. As we will see later, these goals often include issues such as higher wages, enhanced benefits, and/or better working conditions.

Collective bargaining, a specific aspect of labor relations discussed more fully later in this chapter, is the process

by which managers and union leaders negotiate acceptable terms and conditions of employment for those workers represented by the unions.[3] Although *collective bargaining* is a term that technically and properly is applied only in settings where employees are unionized, similar processes often exist in nonunionized settings as well. In these cases, however, they are likely to be labeled *employee relations* rather than labor relations.

11-1a Historical Development of Unions

Figure 11.1 shows the major historical events in the emergence and growth of labor unions in the United States. The historical formation of labor unions actually closely parallels the history of the country itself. For example, the earliest unions in the United States emerged during the Revolutionary War. These associations were called *craft unions*, meaning that each such union limited itself to representing groups of workers who performed common and specific skilled jobs. For example, one of the first unions—the Journeymen Cordwainers Society of Philadelphia—was formed by shoemakers in Philadelphia in 1794. The union's goal was to enhance the pay and working conditions of all shoemakers.

Many of the earliest unions were only local and active in a single place. But in 1834, the first national unions in the United States began to emerge. Throughout the remainder of the 19th century, one major union after another appeared. Among the most significant

Labor relations is the process of dealing with employees who are represented by a union.

A **labor union** is a legally constituted group of individuals working together to achieve shared, job-related goals, including higher pay and shorter working hours.

Collective bargaining is the process by which managers and union leaders negotiate acceptable terms and conditions of employment for those workers represented by the unions.

were the National Typographical Union in 1852, the United Cigar Makers in 1856, and the National Union of Iron Molders in 1859. The 19th century ended with 30 national unions and a combined membership of around 300,000 individuals.

The first major union to have a significant effect in the United States, however, was the Noble and Holy Order of the Knights of Labor, or more commonly, the **Knights of Labor**, which was founded in 1869. Like most other unions, the Knights originally represented crafts and sought to improve the lot of its members. Unlike most other national unions that restricted their organizing activities to a single craft or job, the Knights of Labor expanded its goals and its membership to include workers in many different fields. Their objective was quite simple: leaders of the Knights of Labor believed that if they could control (or represent) the entire supply of skilled labor in the United States, their ability to negotiate favorable wages would be significantly enhanced. Members joined the Knights directly, as opposed to a later model where members joined a separate union that was affiliated with other more specific unions loosely coordinated under an umbrella organization.

The Knights admitted anyone to membership, regardless of race or creed (which typically were important considerations for membership in unions at the time), except for those they considered to be "social parasites" (e.g., bankers). In addition to improving wages, the Knights of Labor sought to replace capitalism with worker cooperatives. The union enjoyed incredible growth for several years, growing from 52,000 members in 1883 to 700,000 members in 1886. But internal strife about goals and disagreement over what should replace the capitalist model all led to the eventual demise of the Knights. The single event that contributed most to its demise, however, was a mass meeting in Chicago's Haymarket Square on May 4, 1886. The meeting was held to protest some earlier violence stemming from an attempt to establish an 8-hour workday. When the May 4 meeting was over, further violence left 200 wounded and resulted in the hanging of several leaders of the Knights. By the end of the century, the Knights of Labor had all but disappeared from the labor scene.

Even as the Knights of Labor union was dying, however, its replacement was already getting stronger. Founded in 1886 by Samuel Gompers, the **American Federation of Labor (AF of L)** was also composed of various craft unions, but unlike the Knights of Labor, the AF of L avoided legislative and political activities and focused instead on improved working conditions and better employment contracts. Also unlike the Knights of Labor, the AF of L served as an umbrella organization, with members joining individual unions affiliated with the AF of L, as opposed to joining the AF of L itself.

While the AF of L focused exclusively on the "business" of unions, several more radical and violent union movements developed after the demise of the Knights of Labor. Under the leadership of Eugene V. Debs, for example, the American Railway Union battled the railroads (especially the Pullman Palace Car Company, which made railroad passenger cars), mostly over wages, and many people were killed during strike violence. Debs also became a leader of the Socialist Party and actually ran for president of the United States on the Socialist ticket in 1920. The Industrial Workers of the World (IWW) consisted mostly of unskilled workers and advocated extreme violence as a means of settling labor disputes. The mining companies and textile mill owners with which they battled also believed in violence as a means of settling labor disputes, and many people were killed during strikes organized by the "Wobblies," as the IWW members were called. The union's opposition to U.S. involvement in World War I led to its prosecution for treason and the jailing of most of its leaders.

For the mainstream organized labor movement, many of these fringe groups were too radical, and workers preferred the businesslike approach of the AF of L. As a result, the federation grew rapidly throughout the early decades of the 20th century, reaching a peak membership of 5 million by the end of World War I. Its membership declined over the next several years, and by the mid-1930s, membership stood at approximately 2.9 million.

One of the AF of L's weaknesses was its continued focus on crafts, accepting only skilled craftspersons for specifically defined jobs. During the 1930s, however, a new kind of unionization began to emerge that focused on industrial unionization. Rather than organizing workers across companies or across industries based on their craft, this new type of union activity focused on organizing employees by industry, regardless of their craft, skills, or occupation.

The **Knights of Labor** was an important early union that expanded its goals and its membership to include workers in numerous fields rather than a single industry.

The **American Federation of Labor (AF of L)** was another early union; it focused its efforts on improved working conditions and better employment contracts rather than getting involved in legislative and political activities.

> The National Labor Relations Act (or Wagner Act) was passed in an effort to control and legislate collective bargaining between organizations and labor unions, to grant power to labor unions, and to put unions on a more equal footing with managers in terms of the rights of employees.

In the late 1930s, John L. Lewis of the United Mine Workers led a dissenting faction of the AF of L to form a new labor organization called the **Congress of Industrial Organizations (CIO)**. The CIO was the first major representative of the new approach to unionization noted earlier. The CIO quickly began to organize the automobile, steel, mining, meatpacking, paper, textile, and electrical industries. By the early 1940s, CIO unions had almost 5 million members.

In the years following World War II, union memberships in the AF of L and the CIO, as well as other unions, gradually increased. However, a series of bitter strikes during that same era led to public resentment and calls for union reform. Congress intervened to curtail the power of unions, and the AF of L and the CIO began to contemplate a merger to consolidate their strength. Eventually, in 1955, the AFL-CIO was formed with a total membership of around 15 million employees. In 2005, however, citing unhappiness with the strategic direction of the AFL-CIO, two of its largest member unions, the Service Employees International Union and the International Brotherhood of Teamsters, withdrew from the parent organization and set out on their own.[4]

11-1b Legal Context of Unions

Partly because of the tumultuous history of labor unions in the United States, a great many laws and regulations have been enacted to deal with unions, and this legislative history is critical to understanding the development of the U.S. labor movement. The earliest legislation simply dealt with the question of whether unions were legal. As early as 1806, the local courts in Philadelphia declared the Cordwainers to be, by its very existence, in restraint of trade and thus illegal. This Cordwainer doctrine, as it became known, dominated the law's view of unions until 1843, when the Massachusetts Supreme Court, in *Commonwealth v. Hunt*, ruled that unions were not by their very nature in restraint of trade but that this issue had to be proven in each individual case. This court decision led to increased union activity, but organizations responded by simply firing union organizers. After the Sherman Antitrust Act was passed in 1890, businesses once again (successfully) sought court injunctions against unions for restraint of trade. By the 1920s, organizations also sought to identify union leaders as communists to reduce public sympathy toward them and to give the government an excuse to control the unions.

By the end of the 1920s, the country was in the grip of the Great Depression, and federal intervention was required to end work stoppages and start the economy on the road to recovery. The first significant piece of legislation was the **National Labor Relations Act**, which was passed in 1935. This act is more commonly referred to as the **Wagner Act** and still forms the cornerstone of contemporary labor relations law (it was discussed earlier in Chapter 2). The basic purpose of the Wagner Act was to grant power to labor unions and put them on a more equal footing with managers in terms of the rights of employees. It gives workers the legal right to form unions, to bargain collectively with management, and to engage in group activities such as strikes to accomplish their goals. This act also forces employers to bargain with properly elected union leaders and prohibits employers from engaging in certain unfair labor practices, including discriminating against union members in hiring, firing, and promotion.

The Wagner Act also established the **National Labor Relations Board (NLRB)** to administer its provisions. The NLRB still administers most labor law in the United States. For example, it defines the units with which managers must collectively bargain and oversees most elections held by employees that will determine whether they will be represented by a union.

In the previous section, we noted congressional activity in the years after World War II that curtailed the power of the unions. The most important piece of

Another important early union was the **Congress of Industrial Organizations (CIO)**, which focused on organizing employees by industry, regardless of their craft, skills, or occupation.

The **National Labor Relations Act** (or **Wagner Act**) administers most labor law in the United States.

The **National Labor Relations Board (NLRB)** administers most labor law in the United States.

> The Labor Management Relations Act (or Taft-Hartley Act) curtails and limits union powers and regulates union actions and their internal affairs in a way that puts them on equal footing with management and organizations.

legislation in this era was the **Labor Management Relations Act**, also known as the **Taft-Hartley Act**, which was passed in 1947. This act was a response to public outcries against a wide variety of strikes in the years following World War II. The basic purpose of the Taft-Hartley Act was to curtail and limit union practices. For example, the act specifically prohibits practices such as requiring extra workers solely as a means to provide more jobs and refusing to bargain with management in good faith. It also outlawed an arrangement called the **closed shop**, which refers to a workplace in which only workers who are already union members may be hired by the employer.

Section 7 of the Taft-Hartley Act also allowed states, if they wished, to restrict union security clauses such as closed-shop agreements. Roughly 20 states took advantage of this opportunity and passed laws that also outlawed **union shop agreements** (where a nonunion member can be hired but must join the union within a specified time to keep his or her job) and various other types of union security agreements. These laws are known as *right-to-work laws*, and the states that have adopted them (predominantly in the Southeast) are known as *right-to-work states*.[5]

States that are not right-to-work states can have an **agency shop agreement**. In such cases, employees can decide whether or not to join the union certified as the bargaining agent: however, if they decide not to join, they must still pay an agency fee, sometimes referred to as a "shared services fee" that is roughly equal to the amount of union dues charged to members. The logic behind such arrangements is that nonunion members benefit from the union's collective bargaining activities and so they should have to help support them. In some states, nonmembers can get a refund for any political activity on the part of the union that is not related to contract negotiations. These arrangements have been firmly in place ever since the Supreme Court's *Abood* decision in 1977.[6]

But, in 2015, a teacher working for the State of California brought suit arguing that such an agency fee violated her free speech rights.[7] The Court of Appeals found for the Teachers, but the case later went to the Supreme Court. This is an important case because if the Supreme Court found for the plaintiff, this would seriously hurt union organizing ability. The opening arguments and questions from the justices led most to believe that the Court was about to decide against the union,[8] but then Justice Scalia died, and a new justice has not been appointed (or even nominated). As a result, in March of 2016, the Supreme Court handed down a 4-4 decision,[9] thus upholding the lower court decision. This was the first real effect of the Supreme Court having to work with eight justices, and the decision (or lack thereof) has upheld a 40-year-old precedent allowing unions to impose dues requirements on nonmembers.

The Taft-Hartley Act also established procedures for resolving strikes deemed threatening to the national interest. For example, the president of the United States has the authority under the Taft-Hartley Act to request an injunction to prohibit workers from striking for 60 days, a so-called cooling-off period in which labor and management have a greater chance of resolving their differences. In February 1997, the union representing the pilots at American Airlines announced that its members had voted to strike. Within minutes of this announcement, President Clinton invoked the Taft-Hartley Act and ordered the union to cancel its strike. His argument was that American Airlines is the nation's largest air carrier and a shutdown would be extremely detrimental to national interests. In addition, the Taft-Hartley Act extended the powers of the NLRB. For example, following passage of the act, the NLRB was also given the power to regulate unfair union practices.

The **Labor Management Relations Act** (or **Taft-Hartley Act**) (1947) was a response to public outcries against a wide variety of strikes in the years after World War II; its basic purpose was to curtail and limit union practices.

A **closed shop** refers to a workplace in which only workers who are already union members may be hired by the employer.

A **union shop agreement** includes various types of union security agreements in addition to a requirement that a nonunion member can be hired, although he or she must join the union within a specified time to keep his or her job.

An **agency shop agreement** is one where employees can decide whether or not to join the union certified as the bargaining agent, but if the employee decides not to join, he or she must still pay a fee roughly equal to the amount of union dues.

FIG 11.2 THE BASIC STRUCTURE OF A UNION

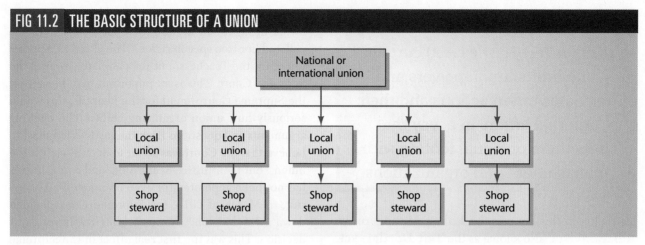

Source: Ricky Griffin and Ronald Ebert, *Business*, 6th ed. © 2002, p. 278. Reprinted by permission of Pearson Education, Inc., Upper Saddle River, NJ.

In Chapter 2, we mentioned the legislation, still floundering in Congress, called the Employee Free Choice Act, or the Union Relief Act. It was first proposed in 2009 as the position of unions in the United States was clearly growing weaker. There are two major provisions of this proposed act worth discussing. First, it would allow a union to be certified if union officials collected the signatures of a majority of workers—eliminating the secret ballot election that is now in place. Second, the bill would require employers and unions to enter binding arbitration if they fail to produce a collective bargaining agreement within 120 days of when the union is certified. The bill also includes increased penalties on employers who discriminate against workers for union involvement. It is unlikely that this bill will pass during President Obama's term as president, and the Democrats would have to win the presidency and control of at least one house of Congress in 2016 for there to be any chance for this law in the near future. Nonetheless, it stands as one of the few developments that seem to favor the union movement in the United States.

A final significant piece of legislation affecting labor relations is the **Landrum-Griffin Act**, which was passed in 1959. Officially called the **Labor Management Reporting and Disclosure Act**, this law focused on eliminating various unethical,

illegal, and undemocratic union practices. For instance, the Landrum-Griffin Act requires that (1) national labor unions elect new leaders at least once every 5 years, and (2) convicted felons cannot hold national union office (which is why Jimmy Hoffa was removed as president of the Teamsters union). It also requires unions to file annual financial statements with the Department of Labor. Finally, the Landrum-Griffin Act stipulates that unions provide certain information regarding their internal management and finances to all members.

11-1c Union Structures

All organizations have their own unique structure, and so do large labor unions. But most unions have some basic structural characteristics in common. Figure 11.2 shows the most common basic structure. The cornerstone of most labor unions, regardless of their size, is the local union, more frequently referred to as a *local*. **Locals** are unions organized at the level of a single company, plant, or small geographic region. Each local has an important elected position called the **shop steward**, who is a regular employee functioning as a liaison between union members and supervisors.

The **Landrum-Griffin Act** (officially called the **Labor Management Reporting and Disclosure Act**) focused on eliminating various unethical, illegal, and undemocratic union practices.

Locals are unions organized at the level of a single company, plant, or small geographic region.

The **shop steward**, an elected position in a local union, is a regular employee who functions as a liaison between union members and supervisors.

> Each local union has an important elected position, the shop steward, who is a regular employee functioning as a liaison between union members and supervisors.

Local unions are usually clustered by geographic region and coordinated by a regional officer. These regional officers in turn report to and are part of a national governing board of the labor union, which then may be involved with some umbrella group such as the AFL-CIO. The national affairs of a large union are generally governed by an executive board and a president. These individuals are usually elected by members of the union themselves. This election takes place at an annual national convention that all union members are invited to and encouraged to attend.

The president is almost always a full-time union employee and may earn as much money as the senior manager of a business. The executive board functions much more like a board of directors and is generally composed of individuals who serve on the board in addition to their normal duties as employees of an organization. Just as large businesses have various auxiliary departments (e.g., a public relations and a legal department), so do large national unions. These auxiliary departments may handle issues such as the legal affairs of the union. They may oversee collective-bargaining issues and may provide assistance and services to the local unions as requested and needed.

 ## 11-2 TRENDS IN UNIONIZATION

While understanding the historical, legal, and structural context of labor unions is important, so too is an appreciation of other trends regarding union membership, union-management relations, and bargaining perspectives. These topics are each discussed in the sections that follow.

11-2a Trends in Union Membership

Union membership in the United States peaked in 1954 with almost 39 percent of all employees belonging to unions or related organizations. Since then, unions have had difficulty in attracting new members, and, in 2015, just over 11 percent of all employees were members. In addition, most of the union members are in the public sector, with only 6.7 percent of employees in the private sector being union members in 2015. The percentage of employees actually represented by unions is slightly higher at 12.3 percent of the total workforce. The overall trends since 1990 are shown in Figure 11.3.

It is also worth noting that men are slightly more likely to be union members than are women (11.5 percent vs. 10.6 percent). Furthermore, black employees are the most likely to be union members with 14.5 percent of black men belonging to unions as opposed to 11.5 percent of white men, 9.2 percent Asian men , and 9.4 percent Hispanic or Latino men. In addition, by age, union membership rates are highest among workers ages 45–64. In 2015, 13.6 percent of workers ages 45–54 and 14.3 percent of those ages 55–64 were union members. In addition, employees in protective service organizations (e.g., police) and education had the highest unionization rates (36.3 percent and 35.5 percent, respectively). New York State has the highest percentage of unionized employees (24.7 percent) and South Carolina has the lowest (2.1 percent). Finally, although the gap has been shrinking, in 2015, the median earnings of nonunion workers ($776) was 79 percent that of union workers ($980), although other factors, such as the cost of living in different states, help explain this gap.

There are other threats to the labor union movement, besides declining numbers. Scott Walker, the governor of Wisconsin, gained national attention when, in 2011, he proposed ending collective bargaining for public employees in his state. He was able to get through massive restrictions in the rights of public sector employees there, and transformed Wisconsin into a right-to-work state (which is even more striking given the progressive history of that state relative to labor issues). He then defeated a recall attempt and, in 2015, announced that he was a candidate for the Republican nomination. Although his candidacy did not generate a great deal of interest, resulting in his dropping his bid by the end of 2015, his speeches as a candidate included his proposals for eliminating unions for employees of the federal government, making all workplaces right-to-work unless individual states vote otherwise, scrapping the NLRB, and generally making it more difficult for unions to organize.[10]

But, despite these trends, it is unlikely that unions will disappear from the U.S. economy. It is likely, however, that the nature of labor unions and the relationship between unions and management will change over the years. In fact, some experts argue that this transformation is already taking place, and the U.S. automobile industry is a good example of those new relationships.

One major reason often cited for the lack of global competitiveness by U.S. automakers is high labor costs. Over a period of decades, companies such as Ford and General Motors (GM) routinely agreed to higher wages and more lucrative benefits to avoid costly strikes. But because foreign competitors—especially those in Asia—have maintained lower labor costs, they can make automobiles for $2,000–4,000 cheaper than their

FIG 11.3 TRENDS IN UNION MEMBERSHIP

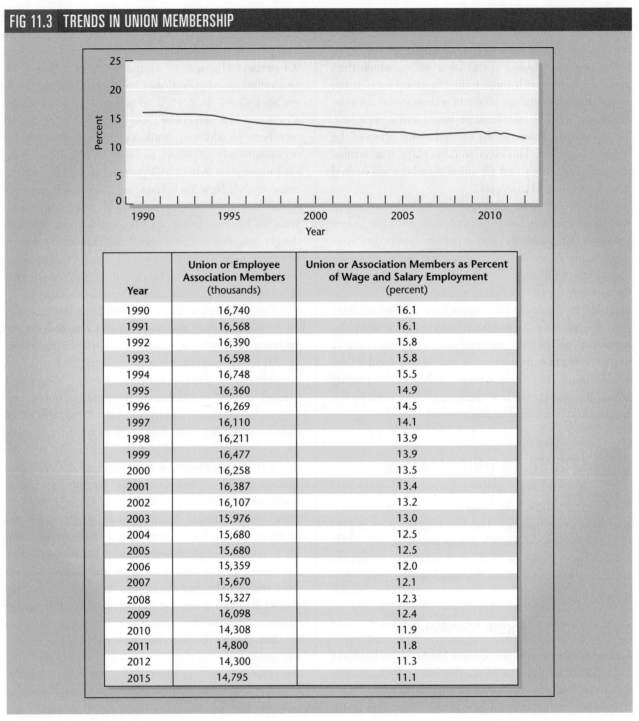

Year	Union or Employee Association Members (thousands)	Union or Association Members as Percent of Wage and Salary Employment (percent)
1990	16,740	16.1
1991	16,568	16.1
1992	16,390	15.8
1993	16,598	15.8
1994	16,748	15.5
1995	16,360	14.9
1996	16,269	14.5
1997	16,110	14.1
1998	16,211	13.9
1999	16,477	13.9
2000	16,258	13.5
2001	16,387	13.4
2002	16,107	13.2
2003	15,976	13.0
2004	15,680	12.5
2005	15,680	12.5
2006	15,359	12.0
2007	15,670	12.1
2008	15,327	12.3
2009	16,098	12.4
2010	14,308	11.9
2011	14,800	11.8
2012	14,300	11.3
2015	14,795	11.1

Sources: U.S. Department of Labor, Bureau of Labor Statistics, 2013.

American competitors. This certainly was a major determinant in GM's decision to declare bankruptcy in 2009, and the general decline of the U.S. automobile industry in 2009–10. But, concessions by unions, cutting costs, and restructuring salaries and pensions have resulted in GM declaring a profit in 2011.

Ford has not been as affected by these issues because earlier in the decade, the company had entered into a creative agreement with its unions.[11] Like its competitors, Ford desperately needed to lower its labor costs, but its powerful unions had negotiated such high levels of job security that Ford found it difficult to either lower wage and benefits costs or reduce the size of its workforce. In response, Ford, working in concert with the United Auto Workers (UAW) and its other unions, devised eight different plans under which it could basically "buy out" workers and end their employment with the company. One option was for workers to accept a one-time cash payment ranging from $35,000 to 140,000 (depending on years of service, age, and how close the employee was to retirement). Another option offered as much as $15,000 per year for 4 years to be applied to college tuition and expenses,

John F. Martin/UPI/Newscomcom

plus half of the employee's salary and benefits for that same 4-year period. Yet another included tuition and 70 percent of salary for 2 years.

During the enrollment period that lasted throughout 2006, 38,000 employees accepted one of the packages—about 46 percent of Ford's unionized workforce. This reduction in force, in turn, had several consequences. Ford incurred short-term costs of several billion dollars but gained flexibility in being able to adjust the size of its workforce that its competitors did not have. Again, this surely contributed to the fact that Ford was in much better shape in 2010 than its U.S. competitors.

The story at GM is also worth considering. After receiving more than $19 billion in federal help, the iconic U.S. automaker realized that it would need to declare bankruptcy.[12] The announcement in June 2009 stunned many Americans who believed that GM was simply too large to fail. But only a few weeks later, in July 2009, GM announced that it was about to emerge from bankruptcy and would repay $50 billion in federal loans faster than required. How did this happen? First of all, GM shed several brands, including Saab, Hummer, Saturn, and Pontiac. The company closed 6,000 dealerships (costing approximately 100,000 additional job losses) and announced the closure of a dozen production facilities around the country. But all of this required the cooperation (or at least nonresistance) of the UAW. In part, the union had no choice but to go along with these changes or else everyone employed at GM could be unemployed, and many of the old master contracts that drove up production costs were abrogated. But the last wrinkle in this reorganization relates to the ownership structure of the new company. Initially, the U.S. government owned a controlling 61 percent interest,[13] but after a historic initial public offering in late 2011, the U.S. government's share is down to 26 percent. Former bondholders and the UAW still retains some ownership as well.

Although the UAW held a seat on Chrysler's board of directors for many years, and although there have been a number of joint ventures between automakers and the union, these recent developments open a new chapter in union involvement in the management of a company. Until the United States gets through the after effects of the financial crisis of 2009–10, similar types of deals may take place. It will be interesting to see how unions react to these new challenges and if relationships such as the one at GM reduces tensions between labor and management—as labor actually becomes a part of management.

Just as union membership has been generally declining, so also has the percentage of successful union-organizing campaigns. In the years immediately after World War II and continuing through the mid-1960s, for instance, most unions routinely won certification elections. In recent years, however, unions are winning certification less than 50 percent of the times when workers are called on to vote. From most indications then, the power and significance of labor unions in the United States, while still quite formidable, is significantly lower than it was just a few decades ago. Several factors explain declining membership.

One common reason is the changing composition of the workforce itself. Traditionally, union members have been predominantly white males in blue-collar jobs, but today's workforce is increasingly composed of women and ethnic minorities. These groups have a much weaker tradition of union affiliation, so their members are less likely to join unions when they enter the workforce. A corollary to these trends has to do with the fact that much of the workforce has shifted toward geographic areas in the South and toward occupations in the service sector that have also been less heavily unionized.

A second reason for the decline in union membership in the United States is more aggressive antiunionization strategies undertaken by businesses.[14] The National Labor Relations Act and other forms of legislation specify strict management practices vis-à-vis labor unions; nevertheless, companies are still free to pursue certain strategies intended to eliminate or minimize unionization. For example, both Motorola and Procter & Gamble now offer no-layoff guarantees for their employees and have created formal grievance systems for all workers. These arrangements were once available only through unions, but because these firms offer them without any union contract, employees are likely to see less benefit from joining a union.

Pacific Press/Getty Images

Some companies have also tried to create a much more employee-friendly work environment and are striving to treat all employees with respect and dignity. One goal of this approach has been to minimize the attractiveness of labor unions for employees. Many Japanese manufacturers that have set up shop in the United States have successfully avoided unionization efforts by the UAW by providing job security, better wages, and a work environment in which employees are allowed to participate in the management of the facilities.

11-2b Trends in Union–Management Relations

The gradual decline in unionization in the United States has been accompanied by significant trends in union–management relations. In some sectors of the U.S. economy, perhaps most notably the automobile and steel industries, labor unions still remain strong. In these areas, unions have a large membership and considerable power vis-à-vis the organizations in which their members work. The UAW, for example, is still one of the strongest unions in the United States today.

In most sectors of the economy, however, labor unions are clearly in a weakened position. As a result, many have had to take more conciliatory stances in their relations with managers and organizations.[15] This contrasts sharply with the more adversarial relationship

that once dominated labor relations in this country. For instance, unions recognize that they do not have as much power as they once held and that it is in their best interests, as well as the best interests of the workers they represent, to work with rather than against management. Hence, union–management relations are in many ways better today than they have been in years. Although this improvement is attributable in large part to the weakened power of unions, most experts would agree that union–management relations have still improved.[16]

None of this means that unions are dead or that unions and management do not still struggle with more basic issues as well as newer issues. A few years ago, for example, Verizon Communications faced a strike by the Communication Workers of America (CWA) and several other unions representing 85,000 employees. The issues were an interesting mix of traditional union concerns and some of the more recent concerns discussed earlier. For example, telephone operators and customer service representatives complained that they were forced to work overtime and that the lack of sufficient break time had led to undue stress on the job. This "stress in the workplace" issue is surely typical of the more recent union issues. There were also problems with pay raises and the fact that the company was shifting jobs to lower-paying regions of the country.

One additional issue at stake never made it to the bargaining table. The CWA, which represents about 75,000 Verizon employees, has been trying to unionize Verizon Wireless as well. The wireless communications sector has thus far resisted unionization, and because that sector is extremely competitive, Verizon has been fighting hard to keep it that way.

The strike lasted for 15 days. Verizon found it difficult to replace the striking high-tech employees and needed to get workers back on the job. As a result, the union won on most issues, including a 14-percent pension increase over 3 years and the right of service reps to "close time," when they could shut down their station to relieve stress. The company also granted stock options to every union employee for the first time in history, although the company did win the right to move around employees as needed in return for certain job-security promises. The issue of unionizing the wireless workers was never addressed. The strike and subsequent settlement illustrate that, while the world of union–management relations is certainly changing, basic issues can still lead to labor problems. The case also suggests that unions may not be quite as powerless as some have suggested.

In fact, there is one sector of the economy where unions have had a much different history and have made important gains. But, here too, recent events suggest that the power has shifted away from the unions.

In 1953, the Major League Baseball Players Association was organized to protect the "nonstars" in baseball by fighting for higher wages, a pension plan, and compensation when a player was unable to play because of an injury. In 1966, the group hired Marvin Miller as their executive director, moving him from his former position as chief negotiator for the United Steel Workers. By 1968, Miller had negotiated the players' first collective-bargaining agreement, doubling the minimum salary for players and introducing arbitration as a means of dispute settlement (this evolved into the system of final-offer arbitration discussed later in this chapter). A short strike by players in 1972 led to the first significant pension benefits for players, with a more significant strike in midseason 1981, but the 1994 players' strike resulted in almost one-third of the baseball season being canceled, including the entire postseason.

Since then, successful contracts have been negotiated, and there have been no other strikes in professional baseball, but these events led players in other professional sports to become more aggressive about pay and benefits and, at least as significantly, convinced owners that they must take the initiative to avoid similar stoppages. In professional football, the NFL Players Association, founded in 1956, was not very active until a threatened strike in 1968. There were brief, not very successful strikes in 1982 and 1987, but things became more serious in Spring 2011 when the collective-bargaining agreement expired. The owners had wanted to make changes such as an extended season, and, when the players threatened action, the owners locked them out (see more about this technique later in this chapter). A judge later invalidated the lockout, and a new agreement was eventually reached, guaranteeing a decade of labor peace for the NFL. But the notion of a lockout by the owners—essentially preventing the players from playing, and thus earning their salaries, and thus being paid—would become an important part of the story of unions in professional sports.

"It was the labor movement that helped secure so much of what we take for granted today. The 40-hour workweek, the minimum wage, family leave, health insurance, Social Security, Medicare, retirement plans. The cornerstones of the middle class security all bear the union label."

—BARACK OBAMA, 44TH PRESIDENT OF THE UNITED STATES

In professional basketball, the first union, the NBA Players Association, was formed in 1954. It didn't get much attention from the owners until a threatened boycott of the NBA All-Star game in 1964. By 1976, players and owners signed the first agreement that eliminated the clauses binding players to their teams (eliminating restrictions to free agency). But, in 1998, issues associated with salary caps and player compensation resulted in a lockout of players, which ended a few months later with a shortened season. Issues around the division of league revenues led to another labor disturbance in 2011 and another lockout by team owners. That lockout ended with a negotiated settlement, leading to another shortened season.

The National Hockey League Players' Associaton was formed in 1967, and the first collective bargaining agreement wasn't signed until 1975. Although the National Hockey League has technically never suffered from a strike, there have been several work stoppages. In 1994, a 103-day lockout by owners resulted in a shortened season. The agreement that was subsequently negotiated was in effect until 2004, when renewed disputes led to a 310-day lockout, the cancellation of the entire 2004–2005 season, and a situation where both sides were worse off than they had been before the lockout.

Thus, although professional sports has been one area where the strength of unions has endured, owners' use of lockouts has been quite effective in keeping that strength in check. Basic issues still are the basis of most labor disputes in this arena, but the use of repeated lockouts—used successfully for the most part—have become an important part of labor–management relations in professional sports. Most recently, the NFL agreed to a $765-million settlement over concussion-related brain injuries among its 18,000 retired players. The settlement came after prolonged mediation and will allow players who have suffered these injuries to be compensated. But the league has only agreed to pay out half over the next 3 years, and the remainder across the next 17 years. Furthermore, the league was not required to acknowledge any causal relationship between playing football and the problems former athletes now face. Finally, the payment will not seriously reduce the $10 billion the league earns every year.[17] Thus, even in the case of this apparent victory for the players' union, a closer analysis would suggest that the NFL has won another victory.

11-2c Trends in Bargaining Perspectives

Building on the trends in membership and union–management relationships, bargaining perspectives have also altered in recent years. For example, previous union–management bargaining situations were usually characterized by union demands for dramatic increases in wages and salaries. A secondary issue was usually increased benefits for union members. But now, unions often bargain for different goals such as job security. Of special interest in this area is the trend toward moving jobs to other countries to take advantage of lower labor costs. Thus, unions might want to restrict job movement, and companies might want to maximize their flexibility by moving jobs to other countries.[18]

As a result of organization downsizing and several years of relatively low inflation in this country, many unions today opt to fight against wage cuts rather than strive for wage increases. Similarly, organizations might be prone to argue for less health care and other benefits for workers, and a common union strategy today is simply preserving what workers currently have. Unions also place greater emphasis on improved job security for their members. This has become an even more serious issue since the financial crisis of 2009. In fact, as discussed earlier, both Ford and GM have been working to reduce their workforces, a real challenge in a heavily unionized environment. An issue that has become especially important in recent years that needed improving was pension programs for employees. The restructuring of GM, however, required retirees to take cuts in pension and health-care benefits, and it will be interesting to see if this becomes a trend in the next few years.

11-3 THE UNIONIZATION PROCESS

The laws discussed earlier, as well as various associated regulations, prescribe a specific set of steps that employees must follow if they want to establish a union. These laws and regulations also dictate what management can and cannot do during an effort by employees to form a union.

11-3a Why Employees Unionize

Why do employees choose to join labor unions? In the simplest of terms, they believe they will somehow be better off as a result of joining a union.[19] More precisely, employees are more likely to unionize when they are dissatisfied with some aspect of their job, they believe that a union can help make this aspect of the job better, and they are not philosophically opposed to unions or collective action.[20]

The real answer is more complex. In the early days of labor unions, people joined them because their working conditions were unpleasant in many cases. In the 18th and 19th centuries, in their quest to earn ever-greater profits, some business owners treated their workers with no respect. They often forced their employees to work long hours, and minimum-wage laws and safety standards did not exist. As a result, many employees worked 12-, 15-, or 18-hour days and sometimes were forced to work 7 days a week. The pay was sometimes just pennies a day, and employees received no vacation time or other benefits. They worked entirely at the whim of their employers; if they complained about working conditions, they were dismissed. So people initially chose to join labor unions because of the strength that lay in the numbers associated with the large-scale labor unions.

In many parts of the United States and in many industries, these early pressures for unionization became an ingrained part of life. Union values and union membership expectations were passed down from generation to generation. This trend typified many industrialized northern cities such as Pittsburgh, Cleveland, and Detroit. In general, parents' attitudes toward unions are still an important determinant for whether or not an employee elects to join a union.[21] As noted earlier, strong unionization pressures still exist in some industries today such as the automobile industry, the steel industry, and other economic sectors relying on heavy manufacturing.

11-3b Steps in Unionization

Several prescribed steps must be followed if employees are to form and join a labor union. These general steps

FIG 11.4 STEPS EMPLOYEES USE TO FORM A UNION

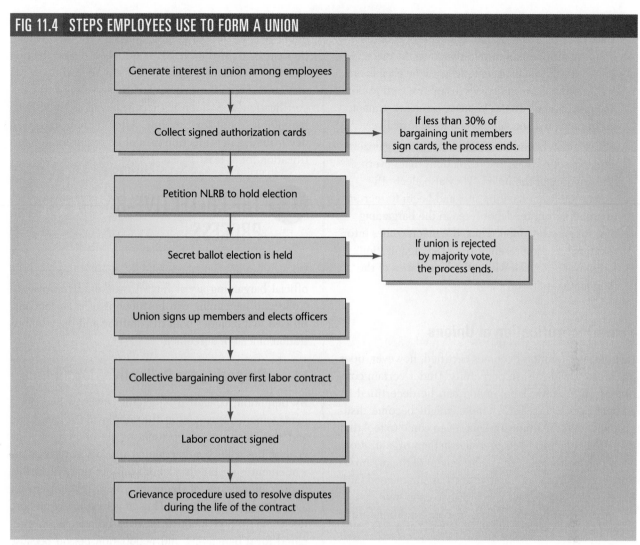

Generate interest in union among employees

Collect signed authorization cards → If less than 30% of bargaining unit members sign cards, the process ends.

Petition NLRB to hold election

Secret ballot election is held → If union is rejected by majority vote, the process ends.

Union signs up members and elects officers

Collective bargaining over first labor contract

Labor contract signed

Grievance procedure used to resolve disputes during the life of the contract

From GRIFFIN, *Management*, 10th ed.

are shown in Figure 11.4 and are described in more detail below.

1. First, employees must have some interest in joining a union. In some cases, this interest may arise from current employees who are dissatisfied with some aspects of the employment relationship. In other instances, existing labor unions may send professional union organizers to nonunionized plants or facilities to generate interest in unionization.[22]

2. If interest in forming a union exists, the NLRB is asked to define the **bargaining unit**, or the specifically defined group of employees who will be eligible for representation by the union. For example, a bargaining unit might be all nonmanagement employees in an organization or perhaps all clerical workers at a specific site within the organization.

3. After the bargaining unit has been defined, organizers must then strive to get 30 percent of the eligible workers within the bargaining unit to sign authorization cards requesting a certification election. Signing an authorization card does not necessarily imply that the individual signing the card wants to join a union; it simply indicates the individual's belief that a union election should be held. If organizers cannot get 30 percent of the workers to sign authorization cards, then the process ends.

4. If the required number of signatures is obtained, the organizers petition the NLRB to conduct an election. The NLRB sends one or more representatives, depending on the size of the bargaining unit, to the facility and

> The **bargaining unit** refers to the specifically defined group of employees who are eligible for representation by the union.

conducts an election. The election is always conducted via secret ballot. If a simple majority of those voting approve union certification, then the union becomes the official bargaining agent of the eligible employees. But if a majority fails to approve certification, the process ends. In this instance, organizers cannot attempt to hold another election for at least 1 year.[23]

5. If the union becomes certified, then its organizers create a set of rules and regulations that govern the conduct of the union. They also elect officers, establish a meeting site, and begin to recruit members from the labor force in the bargaining unit to join the union. Thus, the union comes into existence as a representative of the organization's employees who fall within the boundaries of the bargaining unit.

11-3c Decertification of Unions

Just because a union becomes certified, however, does not mean it will exist in perpetuity. Under certain conditions, an existing labor union can be decertified. A company's workers, for example, might become disillusioned with the union and may even come to feel that they are being hurt by its presence in their organization. They may believe that the management of the organization is trying to be cooperative and bargain in good faith but that the union itself is refusing to cooperate.

For decertification to occur, two conditions must be met.

1. First, no labor contract can currently be in force (i.e., the previous agreement must have expired, and a new one is awaiting approval).

2. Second, the union must have served as the official bargaining agent for the employees for at least 1 year.

If both these conditions are met, then employees or their representatives can again solicit signatures on decertification cards. As with

the certification process, if 30 percent of the eligible employees in the bargaining unit sign the decertification cards, then the NLRB conducts a decertification election. Again, a majority decision determines the outcome. Thus, if a majority of those voting favor decertification, the union is then removed as the official bargaining agent for the unit. After a union has been decertified, a new election cannot be requested for certification for at least 1 year.

11-4 THE COLLECTIVE-BARGAINING PROCESS

When a union has been legally certified, it becomes the official bargaining agent for the workers it represents. Collective bargaining can be thought of as an ongoing process that includes both the drafting and the administration of a labor agreement.

11-4a Preparing for Collective Bargaining

By definition, collective bargaining involves two sides: management representing the employing organization and the labor union representing its employees. The goal of the collective-bargaining process is to produce agreement on a binding labor contract that will define various dimensions of the employment relationship for a specified period of time. Thus, it is incumbent on both management and union leaders to be adequately prepared for a bargaining and negotiation period because the outcome of a labor negotiation will have long-term effects on both parties.

Management can take several actions to prepare for collective bargaining. For example, the firm can look closely at its own financial health to work out a realistic picture of what it can and cannot offer in terms of wages and salaries for its employees. Management can also conduct a comparative analysis to see what kinds of labor contracts and agreements exist in similar companies and what this

Konstantin Chagin/Shutterstock.com

particular labor union has been requesting—and settling for—in the past.

The union can and should undertake several actions to be effectively prepared for collective bargaining. It too should examine the financial health of the company through sources such as public financial records. Like management, the union can also determine what kinds of labor agreements have been reached in other parts of the country and can determine what kinds of contracts other divisions of the company or other businesses owned by the same corporation have negotiated recently.

11-4b Setting Parameters for Collective Bargaining

Another part of preparing for collective bargaining is prior agreement about the parameters of the bargaining session. In general, two categories of items may be dealt with during labor contract negotiations.

1. One set of items, as defined by law, consists of **mandatory items**. Mandatory items include wages, working hours, and benefits. If either party expresses a desire to negotiate one or more of these items, then the other party must agree.

2. Almost any other aspect of the employment relationship is also subject to negotiation, provided both sides agree. These items are called **permissive items**. For example, if the union expresses an interest in having veto power over the promotion of certain managers to higher-level positions and if, for some reason, the company were willing to agree to this demand as a point of negotiation, it would be permissible to enter this point into the negotiations. Many years ago, when one of the authors was a graduate student, a supermarket in Chicago signed a contract with the butchers' union stating that after the butchers went home (around 6 p.m.), the store could not sell any more meat. The store remained open until midnight but covered all its meat cases after 6 p.m. When the company complained to the NLRB that this was unfair and unfavorably affected its business, the NLRB essentially responded that it understood the concern but that because the supermarket had been foolish enough to agree to those terms, it had to live with them. The first issue on the table when the contract was to be renewed was a removal of that provision, and the company managed to get the rule changed 2 years

later. The point is that almost anything is negotiable if the parties agree to discuss it.

Some items are not permissible for negotiation under any circumstances. For example, in a perfect world, management might want to include a clause in the labor contract specifying that the union promises not to strike. However, legal barriers prohibit such clauses from being written into labor contracts, and therefore this item would not be permissible.

11-5 NEGOTIATING LABOR AGREEMENTS

After appropriate preparation by both parties, the negotiation process itself begins. Of course, barriers may also arise during this phase, and bargaining impasses may result in strikes or other actions.

11-5a The Negotiation Process

Generally speaking, the negotiation process involves representatives from management and the labor union meeting at agreed-on times and at agreed-on locations and working together to attempt to reach a mutually acceptable labor agreement. In some instances, the negotiation process itself might be relatively brief and cordial. In other instances, it might be lengthy, spanning weeks or perhaps even months, and it might also be quite acrimonious. For example, the labor agreement reached between the team owners and the union representing baseball players that was settled in late 1996 took several years to negotiate and was interrupted by a strike by the baseball players.

A useful framework for understanding the negotiation process refers to the bargaining zone, which is illustrated in Figure 11.5.[24] During preparations for negotiation, both sides are likely to attempt to define three critical points. For the organization, the bargaining zone and its three intermediate points include the employer's (1) maximum limit, (2) expectation, and (3) desired result on items being negotiated. For example, the organization might have a zero increase in wages and benefits as a desired result (also known as management's *target point*). But it also recognizes that this desired result is unlikely and that it expects to have

> **Mandatory items,** including wages, working hours, and benefits, must be included as part of collective bargaining if either party expresses a desire to negotiate one or more of them.
>
> **Permissive items** may be included in collective bargaining if both parties agree.

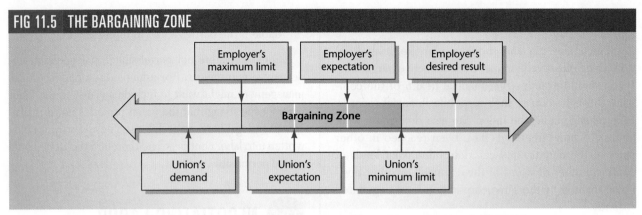

FIG 11.5 THE BARGAINING ZONE

Employer's maximum limit

Employer's expectation

Employer's desired result

Bargaining Zone

Union's demand

Union's expectation

Union's minimum limit

Source: Ricky Griffin and Ronald Ebert, *Business*, 8th ed. © 2006, p. 229. Reprinted by permission of Pearson Education, Inc., Upper Saddle River, NJ.

to provide a modest increase in wages and benefits totaling perhaps 4–5 percent. If preparations are done thoroughly, however, managers also know the maximum amount they are willing to pay, which might be as high as 7 or 8 percent (management's *resistance point*). Note that management in this example would rather suffer through a strike than pay more than an 8-percent pay increase.

On the other side of the table, the labor union also defines a bargaining zone for itself that includes three points: (1) the union's minimum acceptable limit on what it will take from management (the union resistance point may be the settlement level below which the union will strike), (2) its own expectations about what management is likely to agree to, and (3) the most it can reasonably expect to get from management (the union target point). For instance, the labor union might feel that it has to provide a minimum increase of 2–3 percent in wages and benefits to its members. It expects a settlement of around 5 percent but would like to get 9 or 10 percent. In the spirit of bargaining, it may make an opening demand to management of as high as 12 percent.

Hence, during the opening negotiation session, labor might inform management that it demands a 12-percent wage and benefit increase. And the employer might begin by stating emphatically that no increases should be expected. Assuming, however, that some overlap exists between the organization's and the union's demands and expectations in the bargaining zone (a positive settlement zone), and also assuming that both sides are willing to compromise and work hard at reaching an agreement, then an agreement probably will be attained. Where exactly within that range the final agreement falls depends on the relative bargaining power of the two parties. This power is a function of many factors such as negotiating

skills, data on other settlements, and the financial resources needed by the union to call for a strike or by management to survive one.

Much of the actual negotiating revolves around each party trying to discover the other's resistance point without revealing its own. Because this point represents the least favorable settlement the party is willing to accept, the opponent who discovers that point then makes a "final" offer exactly at the resistance point. For example, if the union discovers that management is willing to go as high as 8 percent before breaking off negotiations and facing a strike, the union would then make an offer at 8 percent and indicate that this was its final offer. Management would rather pay 8 percent than have a strike, so it should settle at 8 percent, which is actually the most favorable contract the union could have possibly won. Incidentally, after a party makes a true final offer, it cannot back away from that position without losing face in the negotiations. Parties usually leave themselves some room for further negotiations and use statements such as the following: "I cannot imagine our members accepting anything less than an 8-percent raise, and I'm sure they would walk out on strike if we came back with less."

The resulting agreement is not necessarily the end of the bargaining process. First, the new contract agreement must be ratified by the union membership. If the union membership votes to reject the contract (which typically reflects internal union politics more than anything else), the parties must return to the bargaining table. But even before the union membership votes, a final step in the bargaining process must be followed. As soon as an agreement is reached, both parties begin to make public statements about how tough a negotiator the other party was. Both acknowledge that they really wanted a lot more and that they hope they can live with this agreement, but that the other party was such a good negotiator that this agreement was the best they could come up with. This posturing helps both parties "sell" the agreement to their constituencies and also allows both parties to maintain their image as strong negotiators no matter how one-sided the final agreement might be. Once ratified, this agreement then forms the basis for a new labor contract.

11-5b Barriers to Effective Negotiation

The foremost barrier to effective negotiation between management and labor is the lack of an overlap for the bargaining zones of the respective sides (i.e., there is a negative settlement zone). In other words, if management's upper limit for a wage increase is 3.5 percent, and the union's minimum limit for what it is willing to accept is 5 percent, then no overlap exists in the bargaining zones and the two sides will almost certainly be unable to reach an agreement. Beyond such differences in bargaining zones, however, other barriers to effective negotiation can also come into play.

For example, sometimes a long history of acrimonious relationships between management and labor makes it difficult for the two sides to negotiate in good faith. If, for example, the labor union believes that the management of the firm has a history of withholding or distorting information and that management approaches negotiations from the standpoint of distrust and manipulation, then the union will be suspicious of any proposal made by management and may, in fact, be unwilling to accept almost any suggestion made by management. Of course, the same pattern can occur for the other side, with management exhibiting extreme distrust of the labor union.

Negotiations can also be complicated by inept negotiators and poor communication between negotiators. Effective negotiation is a critical skill that not everyone possesses. Thus, if managers select as a representative someone who does not understand the negotiation process, then difficulties are likely to arise.

As a result of diligent negotiation, however, management and labor should be able to agree on a mutually acceptable labor contract. If, however, management and labor cannot agree on a new contract or one to replace an existing contract after a series of bargaining sessions, then either side or both sides might declare that they have reached an impasse. An **impasse** is simply a situation in which at least one party believes that reaching an agreement is not imminent.

11-6 RESOLVING IMPASSES

If labor and management have reached an impasse, several actions can be taken by either side or both sides in an attempt to break the impasse. The basic objective of most of these tactics is to force the other side to alter or redefine its bargaining zone so that an accord can be reached.

The most potent weapon that the union holds is the potential for a strike. A **strike** occurs when employees walk off their jobs and refuse to work. In the United States, most strikes are called *economic strikes* because they are triggered by impasses over mandatory bargaining items such as salaries and wages. During a strike, workers represented by the union frequently march at the entrance to the employer's facility with signs explaining their reasons for striking. This action is called **picketing** and is intended to elicit sympathy for the union and intimidate management.

Strikes are costly to both parties. Although the company can try to hire strikebreakers, they are likely to lose some if not all their business during a strike—especially when picketers are present at their place of business. Clients and customers then have to look elsewhere for goods and services, and there is no guarantee that they will return after the strike is settled. The union must deal with the fact that members, while out on strike, receive no pay. Unions often pay picketers for their time, and there are often other payments that the union makes to workers while they are out on strike. But these represent true financial costs to the union. In addition, members may become dissatisfied with the union if they believe that the strike could have been averted except for union decisions. Unless the union is clearly triumphant, it usually loses members after a strike.

Strike costs are so important for the process that one of the tactics involved in labor negotiations is directly tied to strike costs. Both parties recognize that each side will suffer costs if there is a strike, so the union, for example, will try to convince management that the union's strike costs are relatively low (because they have built a cash reserve to pay striking workers or because they have a unanimous vote in favor of a strike) and that management's strike costs are higher than they realize

> An **impasse** is a situation in which one or both parties believe that reaching an agreement is not imminent.
>
> A **strike** occurs when employees walk off their jobs and refuse to work.
>
> **Picketing** occurs when workers representing the union march at the entrance to the employer's facility with signs explaining their reasons for striking.

Contemporary Challenges in HR

All Shapes and Sizes

Many people associate unions, union members, collective bargaining, and strikes with blue-collar manufacturing jobs in factories and on assembly lines. But in reality, of course, unions and their members come in all shapes and sizes. For instance, many airline pilots, teachers, firefighters, hotel employees, police officers, and writers belong to unions. So, too, do some people who work in the broadcasting, music, and federal government sectors. And just like factory workers, union members have gone on strike against television networks, airlines, and public school districts.

One of the more interesting—and public—venues for nontraditional labor relations is the world of professional sports. Labor unions represent players and officials in virtually all sports. And within the past 25 years, professional baseball, basketball, and football have all had significant labor crises, ranging from strikes to lockouts and led by players, officials, or team owners.

For example, when the NFL's collective bargaining agreement with its players expired in March 2011, negotiations between the league and its player's union quickly fell apart. The owners, not surprisingly, argued that they were spending too much and wanted to reduce their commitment to the players. But the players scoffed at the notion of accepting salary reductions and a lower share of revenues. They pointed to average profits of more than $30 million per team and to the facts that the league was generating more than $8 billion annually in revenue and that "American-style" football has never been more popular.

AP Images/Bebeto Matthews

As the date for training camps approached, the owners implemented a "lockout." This allowed team owners to shut down their team operations and not allow the players to report for "work." They were also not obligated to pay them until a new labor agreement was reached. The logic was that the owners would lower their costs and exert pressure on players who depended on salary income to cover their living expenses. At the same time, though, the owners also stood to lose revenue if games were not broadcast. An agreement was reached in late July 2011, training camps opened (albeit later than normal), and the league was able to play a full schedule. And as is typical, both sides won some things they wanted but also lost some things. The players, for instance, won greater benefits for retired players, increased minimum salaries, and better medical benefits. The owners got a new salary structure and revised revenue sharing.

But things played out a little differently that same year in the NBA. The situation started out similarly: The existing labor contract expired, a new agreement could not be reached, and the owners locked the players out. But in this case, both sides dug in their heels and refused to compromise. All told, the NBA lockout lasted 161 days and did not end until December 8, 2011. Eventually, though, the two sides did reach an agreement with both sides giving up a few things they wanted. The league also shortened its schedule from the normal 82 games to only 66 games per team.

Interestingly, during this same period another professional sports league averted a similar problem. Team owners and players in the Major League Soccer (MLS) association have managed to play on through a substantive labor disagreement. Fact, when the union contract expired in early 2010, both team owners and players agreed it was in everyone's best interests to keep the games going while negotiators continued to try to reach a new agreement. While the issues are similar—players want more money, team owners want to pay less money—both sides agreed that a work stoppage would be disastrous for everyone. A new agreement was signed in early 2012, but the league nevertheless managed to play over 2 years without a contract.[25]

THINK IT OVER

1. What might most reasonably account for the differences in labor relations at the NFL and the NBA versus the MLS?

2. Some people feel little sympathy for NFL and NBA players, given the large salaries most make. Others defend those salaries in part based on the likelihood of serious injury. What is your opinion?

(because of the misunderstood effect of the picket line or because of information about low inventories of goods). Management, on the other hand, will try to convince the union that management's strike costs are low (because of stockpiled inventory, for example) and that the union's strike costs are high (because replacement workers are readily available). In the vast majority of cases, however, neither party wants a strike.

Two less extreme tactics that unions sometimes use are boycotts and slowdowns.

1. A **boycott** occurs when union members agree not to buy the products of a targeted employer.

2. A **slowdown** occurs when workers perform their jobs but at a much slower pace than normal. A variation on the slowdown occurs when union members agree, sometimes informally, to call in sick in large numbers on certain days, an action called a *sickout*. Pilots at American Airlines once engaged in a massive sickout causing the airline to cancel thousands of flights before a judge ordered the pilots back to work.

Some kinds of strikes and labor actions are illegal. Foremost among these illegal actions is the **wildcat strike**, which occurs when workers suddenly go on strike, without the authorization (presumably) of the striker's union and while a binding labor agreement is still in effect (which is what makes it illegal).

Management also has certain tactics that it may employ in its efforts to break an impasse. One possibility is called a **lockout**, and it occurs when the employer denies employees access to the workplace. The Contemporary Challenges in HR box provides some recent—and interesting—examples of lockouts in the sports world. Managers must be careful when they use lockouts, however, because the practice is closely regulated by the government. A firm cannot lock out its employees simply to deprive them of wages or to gain power during the

labor negotiations. Suppose, however, that the employer can meet a legitimate business need by locking out its employees. If this business need can be carefully documented, then a lockout might be legal. As we noted earlier, the dispute over contracts and terms in the NBA resulted in the owners locking out the players for 161 days in 2011. Earlier there were lockouts at ABC television in 1998,[26] and the NBA had locked out players for several weeks in 1998 as well.[27]

Jaroslav Machacek/Shutterstock.com

In some cases, such as the Verizon case discussed earlier, but NOT the NBA cases, management can try to bring in temporary workers as replacements for striking employees. These individuals are called *strikebreakers* (and sometimes scabs by striking workers), and it is not uncommon for real conflict to break out between strikebreakers and picketing union members. Various tactics described previously are successful in resolving the impasse. For instance, after workers have gone out on strike, the organization may change its position and indeed modify its bargaining zone to accommodate potentially larger increases in pay. After management experiences a strike, it sometimes realizes that the costs of failing to settle are greater than previously believed, so managers are willing to give more to avoid a longer strike (i.e., their resistance

> A **boycott** occurs when union members agree not to buy the products of a targeted employer.
>
> A **slowdown** occurs when workers perform their jobs at a much slower pace than normal.
>
> A **wildcat strike** occurs when workers suddenly go on strike, without the authorization (presumably) of the striker's union and while a binding labor agreement is still in effect.
>
> A **lockout** occurs when an employer denies employees access to the workplace.

point has shifted). In many situations, other alternatives for resolving an impasse are also available. Common alternatives include the use of mediation and arbitration.

In **mediation**, a neutral third party called the *mediator* listens to and reviews the information presented by both sides. The mediator then makes an informed recommendation and provides advice to both parties about what she or he believes should be done. For example, a group of miners might be demanding that the mine owners pay the entire cost of their medical insurance, while the owners have indicated they are only willing to pay half. A mediator would listen to both sides as they defended their positions, and would then review evidence about other settlements in the industry and the financial health of the mine. Based on an analysis of this information, the mediator might then recommend that the mine owners pay two-thirds of the cost of the medical insurance. This recommendation would be provided to both parties, but it is only a recommendation. That is, the miners would be free to reject the recommendation and continue to try to get the owners to pay the full cost of insurance. In many cases, dispute mediation is done through the offices of the Federal Mediation and Conciliation Service. In fact, it is not uncommon for contracts to require mandatory mediation when there is an impasse.

Another alternative to resolving impasses is **arbitration**, or the process in which both sides agree in advance that they will accept the recommendations made by an independent third-party arbitrator. Like a mediator, the arbitrator listens to both sides of the dispute and presents and reviews all the evidence. In arbitration, however, the information that results is placed in the form of a proposed settlement agreement that the parties have agreed in advance to accept. Thus, a settlement is imposed on the parties, and the impasse is ended. But some critics believe that arbitrators tend to impose settlements that "split the difference." If both parties believe that the arbitrator has proposed such a settlement, then they have an incentive to stick to their original positions and not move toward a settlement because such a move shifts the middle further away from their target points.[28] As such, the threat of arbitration may "chill"

the negotiation process and actually make a negotiated settlement less likely. It is becoming more common for contracts to include some form of required arbitration when there is an impasse because both sides in negotiations are beginning to recognize just how costly a strike really is.

An alternative form of arbitration has therefore been proposed that should induce the parties, it is argued, to negotiate a settlement by potentially imposing strike-like costs on both parties.[29] Under **final-offer arbitration**, the parties bargain until impasse. At that point, the two parties' final offers are submitted to the arbitrator. Under traditional arbitration, the arbitrator is then free to impose a settlement at any point he or she wishes. But under final-offer arbitration, the arbitrator has only two choices for the imposed settlement—the two parties' final offers—and the arbitrator must select either one *as the imposed settlement*. Thus, the party that does not bargain in good faith may get everything it wants in the arbitrator's decision but may just as easily lose everything. Under such a system, the parties are more willing to try to reach a settlement on their own rather than go to the arbitrator. Professional baseball uses final-offer arbitration to resolve contract disputes between individual players and owners.

11-6a Administering Labor Agreements

Another key clause in the labor contracts negotiated between management and labor defines how the labor agreement will be enforced. In some cases, enforcement is clear. If the two sides agree that the company will increase the wages it pays to its employees by 3 percent a year over the next 2 years according to a prescribed increase schedule, then there is little opportunity for disagreement. Wage increases can be calculated mathematically, and union members will see the effects in their paychecks. Other provisions of many labor contracts, however, are more subjective in nature and thus more prone to misinterpretation and different perceptions.

For example, suppose a labor contract specifies how overtime assignments are to be allocated in the organization. Such allocation strategies are often relatively complex and suggest that the company may have to take into account various factors such as seniority, previous overtime allocations, and the hours or days in which the overtime work is needed. Now suppose that a supervisor in the factory is attempting to follow the labor contract and offers overtime to a certain employee. This employee, however, indicates that before accepting, he or she must

In **mediation**, a neutral third party called the mediator listens to and reviews the information presented by both sides and then makes an informed recommendation and provides advice to both parties about what she or he believes should be done.

In **arbitration**, both sides agree in advance that they will accept the recommendations made by an independent third-party arbitrator.

Under **final-offer arbitration**, the parties bargain until impasse, and then the two parties' final offers are submitted to the arbitrator.

check with a spouse or partner to learn more about previous obligations and commitments. The supervisor may feel a time crunch and be unable to wait as long as the employee would like. As a result, the supervisor gives the overtime opportunity to a second employee. The first employee may feel aggrieved by this course of action and elect to protest.

When such differences of opinion occur, the individual labor union member takes the complaint to the shop steward, the union officer described earlier in this chapter, who listens to the complaint and forms an initial impression. The shop steward has the option of advising the employee that the supervisor handled the matter appropriately. But other appeal mechanisms are also available so that the employee, even if denied by the shop steward, still has channels for appeal.

Of course, if the shop steward agrees with the employee, she or he may also follow prescribed methods for dealing with the situation. The prescribed methods might include starting with the supervisor to listen to his or her side of the story and then continuing along the lines of appeal up the hierarchy of both the labor union and the company. In some cases, mediation and arbitration may be started to resolve the disagreement. For example, some of the potential resolutions to the grievance described earlier would be to reassign the overtime opportunity to the employee who was asked first. Or the overtime opportunity may stay with the second employee, but the first employee would also receive overtime pay.

 LABOR UNIONS IN THE 21ST CENTURY

Earlier in this chapter, we discussed the historical roots of the U.S. labor movement. We noted that the labor movement in this country focused on bread-and-butter issues such as wages and hours of work, unlike the labor movements in many European countries. Early American unionists were less concerned with social issues, and, partly as a result, a labor party in the United States never drew much interest. Unions and union members supported political candidates who favored their goals, and unions have spoken out on any number of political issues. But for the most part, the issues in which U.S. labor unions became involved were pretty close to the basic issues facing U.S. labor. This situation is clearly changing, however.

One interesting development has involved drivers for "Uber" the fast-growing ride service organization.

Companies such as Uber (and Lyft) have argued that they simply function as an app that allows customers to link with cars. As such, drivers are merely contractors and not employees, and so the company has no obligation to provide benefits, stable pay, or job security. In June of 2015, the California Labor Commissioner ruled that Uber drivers were in fact employees, and, although the case dealt with one specific employee, there is clearly the potential for more litigation.[30] Such cases not only affect companies such as Uber, but also impact many Silicon Valley firms that have focused on hiring contract employees to build flexibility, but this arrangement also serves to eliminate the need to provide basic benefits.

U.S. labor unions have become quite vocal in several areas where they have traditionally been silent, speaking out against child labor in Third World countries and the general exportation of jobs to lower-paying countries. Union positions on these issues reflect their self-interests to some extent; moving manufacturing jobs to Mexico, for example, means that U.S. unions will lose members. But there is more to this issue than obvious self-interest. These public positions have changed the way many people think about unions. Although union membership has declined over the past several decades, these changes can enhance the power of labor unions and thus affect the relationship between unions and management. A wide array of issues has attracted the involvement of the U.S. labor movement, but we will focus on only a few. Note, however, that these issues are simply meant to illustrate the new scope of union interests in this country.

11-7a "Replacement" Sources of Labor

We discussed the trends to export jobs overseas in Chapter 3. The U.S. labor movement has become quite interested in these trends and has generally argued that these trends lead to job losses in the United States. But overseas labor markets are only one source of "replacement" laborers. Labor unions in the United States have also voiced concern over the use of other such sources.

For example, in 2010, there were roughly 1.6 million people serving time in federal or state correctional institutions[31] (we discussed concerns associated with this in Chapter 8). Although many of these inmates work in paid jobs, they are paid much less than the minimum wage, meaning the goods they produce can be sold for less, causing serious problems for unskilled workers in the general population. Furthermore, many critics of the U.S. prison system argue that these prison jobs do not prepare prison inmates for outside jobs after they are released and thus do not lessen the rate of subsequent arrest and incarceration. The U.S. labor movement and its advocates argue that this system needs reform to provide more rights to prison laborers and to ensure that prison labor does not take away civilian population jobs, which in the long run can lead to increased crime.

Unions have become more involved in social issues such as the use of prison labor. Traditionally, prison inmates literally worked on chain gangs or worked sewing clothes or doing laundry. But the range of jobs being done by inmates has expanded considerably. Today, inmates perform a range of jobs in the community, including working to save endangered sea turtles in Florida, and working as firefighters in Oregon and California. Some states do not actually pay inmates, while Oregon's fire crews actually make more than $4.00 an hour. Of course, firefighters on the outside make considerably more than $4.00 an hour, so relying on convict labor saves states a great deal of money, but it also means there are fewer jobs for noninmates (who might be union members), which can also cause problems for a community.[32]

11-7b Contingent Workers

Another source of replacement labor is the pool of contingent workers, which was discussed in Chapter 6. Perhaps it is no surprise that U.S. unions have taken a stand on the topic of contingent workers. Under U.S. labor laws, contingent workers are considered independent contractors or self-employed laborers, and, in 2005, the number of contingent workers who were employed was estimated to be about 5.7 million—or approximately 4 percent of the workforce.[33] As independent contractors, these workers are not covered by most employment and labor laws. In fact, to be covered by almost any legislation related to employment, a person must have some type of employment relationship with an entity, which is not the case for most contingent workers. This problem will become more serious as more organizations turn to contingent workers as a way to manage their demand for labor.

Clearly, organized labor has a vested interest in opposing the reliance on these groups of potential replacement laborers. Although the representatives of the unions focus on the social implications of these practices, and probably are concerned about these social costs, clearly labor unions have more to lose in these cases than do others. Nonetheless, U.S. labor unions have been able to form coalitions with other community groups who oppose the use of prison labor or are concerned about exporting jobs overseas, and they have become very vocal in this movement. As a result, labor unions have gained a great deal of credibility as guardians of middle-class jobs.

11-7c Unions and the Electronic Age

The Internet also presents many interesting challenges for U.S. labor unions. The most obvious one stems from the fact that computers and new technology often mean that work can be done by fewer employees. As noted earlier, companies have been trying to move more production sites to foreign countries where labor costs are lower, and U.S. unions have no input. Thus, unions would lose members. At the same time, the introduction of technology is also reducing the number of workers and the number of union members. Although unions must oppose some of these technological advances for the sake of their members' jobs if nothing else, they cannot simply reject these advances wholesale. Clearly, in many cases, the firms involved will lose business and perhaps even be forced out of business if they cannot keep pace with the technology (and cost controls) of their competitors. Such outcomes are not desirable from the unions' perspective either, and so the U.S. labor movement is in a difficult position.

Changes in technology have also posed a much different set of challenges for unions and for the management of firms with unionized employees. For example, many firms who fear unionization efforts have no-solicitation rules at work. These rules simply mean that no employee can solicit other employees on company time for any cause except United Way campaigns; that is, under such rules, employees cannot sell candy for a high school band, raffle tickets for a new car, or even tickets for a church dinner. An important aspect of these rules is that they also outlaw any attempts by union organizers to solicit employees to sign cards appointing the union as sole bargaining agent. Organizations are usually vigilant about no-solicitation rules because they stop union-organizing efforts at work.

The Internet presents a challenge to these no-solicitation rules. Monitoring solicitation on the Internet is much more difficult, and some of this solicitation may even come from outside the firm. If the company fails to stop these forms of solicitation, then can it still legally stop union solicitation at work? Can unions use the Internet to solicit union membership if they do so from outside the company? Recent NLRB rulings and opinions have not clarified the answers to these questions. For example, if the organization allows employees to use the Internet (even if the computers are company owned) to post thank-you notes, it may be forced to allow union solicitation as well. The NLRB will have to deal with these issues in the coming years, but the key seems to be nondiscrimination. In other words, companies cannot (apparently) forbid employees from using the Internet for union solicitation if companies allow employees to use the Internet for other nonbusiness-related purposes.[34] In any case, the Internet has complicated the problem of solicitation—by any party—on the job.

It seems, however, that unions have generally seen Internet solicitation as a useful tool in a different setting. In many high-tech firms, it is common to outsource work and for people to work at home. In these situations, employees rarely meet face to face. How can a union hope to organize these workers? An article a few years ago pointed out that unions in the Silicon Valley area have been successful in using the Internet for union-organizing campaigns.[35] They have been active in trying to organize a wide variety of contingent workers in the area, and they successfully organized janitorial workers across firms in the Silicon Valley through Internet solicitation. This approach has enabled union organizers to reach workers they could not meet personally, and it plays on the fact that many workers at all levels in this area have easy access to computers. Unions in the Silicon Valley area have also used Internet-based campaigns to mount successful boycotts against some firms.

Finally, unions have found that the Internet has significant effects on the way they conduct their own internal business. Unions in this country can now communicate immediately with union leaders and members from around the world, making unions more democratic in their internal policies. It has also enabled unions to mobilize international resources to deal with issues that all union members face wherever they work such as the lower wages and looser labor regulations associated with agreements under the World Trade Organization.

It remains to be seen how unions will be able to use and be challenged by computers and the electronic age in the coming years. It is already clear, however, that new electronic technology has been a mixed blessing for the U.S. labor movement. Although technology continues to threaten jobs, it also allows unions to reach workers in ways that were never possible before. It is not yet clear that computers will be able to revitalize the union movement in the United States, but they certainly seem capable of breathing new life into that movement.

Very recently, there has been an important development in the area of union-related activity, but that development has taken place somewhere other than in the United States. As noted in Chapter 3, the Chinese economy has seen several sharp downturns after two decades of rapid expansion. As a result of these slowdowns, the Chinese government has instituted widespread wage reductions and labor force reductions. For example, the government recently announced plans to lay off 1.8 million steel and coal workers, and some experts estimate that 3 million Chinese workers in state-owned enterprises may lose their jobs over the next few years. But, today, Chinese workers are better informed than they used to be and are well-aware of developments around the world. These new Chinese workers, facing new insecurities, have taken to the streets to mount protests and actual strikes for back wages, unpaid benefits, and safer working conditions.

Franck Boston/shutterstock.com

In fact, there were 2,700 strikes and protests recorded in 2015, and there had been 500 protests January of 2015 alone.[36]

Is this beginning of an organized labor movement in China? Probably not—at least not in the short term. Although some of the protests have become more pointed, they have not yet turned political or violent. Furthermore, the Chinese government has often responded with crackdowns and imprisonment, and Chinese workers are not allowed to form independent labor unions; they can join only the government controlled All-China Federation of Trade Unions. Finally, the entire situation is embarrassing for Beijing's communist government, which still portrays itself as the socialist guardian of worker rights. Nonetheless, these developments in China prove that the spirit of organized labor continues to exist—even in the most unlikely places.

CLOSING CASE
"Give and Take"

The general view of management and labor unions is that they are antagonists: When one wins, the other loses—and vice versa. In reality, of course, there are many situations where businesses and unions coexist quite peacefully. And there are other situations where businesses and unions find they have little choice but to work together in order for both to survive. During the economic recession of 2009, for example, unions agreed to help out the businesses that employed their members in several cases.

Adriano Castelli/Shutterstock.com

One notable example came from Harley-Davidson, the big motorcycle manufacturer. One of Harley's biggest factories is in York, Pennsylvania. The York plant, one of Harley's oldest, employed about 2,000 nonmanagerial workers. The recession caused a dramatic drop in revenue for Harley, and the firm desperately needed to cut costs. Company officials determined that Harley needed to reduce its overall costs by $120 million to $150 million to remain competitive.

The York factory was a key site for cost reduction. For one thing, the factory was in dire need of modernization. For another, the labor contract governing York workers called for wages well above the industry average; moreover, the factory had more than 60 different job classifications, and the union contract made it nearly impossible to move workers across classifications.

One of the first options Harley considered was simply closing the York plant and moving its jobs to the firm's newest factory in Kentucky. That plant had a more flexible union contract and the newest technology. The International Association of Machinists and Aerospace Workers, however, persuaded the company to negotiate a new arrangement that would allow some of the union's workers to retain their jobs.

Under terms of the new agreement, which took effect in February 2010, about half of the plant's 2,000 jobs would be eliminated. The number of job classifications would also

> "These were changes that had to be made to keep [Harley-Davidson] viable."
>
> —SHARON ZACKFIA, INVESTMENT BANKER

(Continued)

(Closing Case – continued)

be cut from 60 to 5, and Harley would have considerable flexibility to move workers from one classification to another. Moreover, any new employees hired after February 2010 would start at an hourly rate of $19.28, about 20 percent less than the previous starting rate of $24.10. Finally, the 1,000 or so workers who retained their jobs would be divided into two groups. About 750 "first-tier" production workers would retain their full-time jobs with current wages and benefits. The other 250 or so would be classified as "casual" workers; these workers would take a wage cut of about 30 percent and would only work on an as-needed basis.

For its part, Harley agreed to invest $90 million to modernize the plant with the goal of allowing the York factory to be the first one to create new jobs when demand for motorcycles begins to increase. The state of Pennsylvania also agreed to chip in $15 million to support both plant upgrades and new training programs for workers. Finally, Harley also agreed that the 750 first-tier production workers would have their jobs guaranteed for the duration of the 7-year deal.

Many observers saw this new contract as one-sided in favor of Harley-Davidson. One expert, Professor Gary Chaison at Clark University, commented, "This is tying the hands of the union for a long time." In contrast to similar renegotiations, the union does appear to have given up a lot. For instance, the UAW renegotiated its labor contract with GM during the automaker's recent financial problems. Under terms of the new agreement, GM would be allowed to eliminate one-third of its jobs and reduce its retiree health-care obligations by funding a portion of its obligations with stock rather than cash. In exchange, the UAW received job guarantees for two-thirds of the GM workforce, a large equity stake in GM, and a seat on GM's board of directors.[37]

Case Questions

1. Do you think the Harley deal was too one-sided? Why or why not?

2. If you were a Harley or GM employee and union member, would you have voted for the new deal? Why or why not?

3. Do you think it is appropriate for a government entity (e.g., the state of Pennsylvania) to take an active role in union–management negotiations? Why or why not?

STUDY TOOLS 11

READY TO STUDY?

In the book, you can:

☐ Rip out the chapter review card at the back of the book for a handy summary of the chapter and key terms.

ONLINE AT CENGAGEBRAIN.COM YOU CAN:

☐ Collect StudyBits while you read and study the chapter.

☐ Quiz yourself on key concepts.

☐ Find videos for further exploration.

☐ Prepare for tests with HR4 Flash Cards as well as those you create.

AP Images/Greg Wahl-Stephen

12 | Safety, Health, Well-Being, and Security

After finishing this chapter go to **PAGE 314** for **STUDY TOOLS**

LEARNING OBJECTIVES

12-1 Identify and discuss the central elements associated with employee safety and health

12-2 Describe the basic issues involved in the physical work environment

12-3 Discuss stress and stress-management programs in organizations

12-4 Identify and describe the most important HR-related security issues in organizations

AP Images/Greg Wahl-Stephen

OPENING CASE
A Disturbance in the Workforce

In November 2009, Jason Rodriguez, a former employee of an engineering firm in Orlando, Florida, entered the company's offices and opened fire with a handgun, killing one person and wounding five others. Rodriguez had been fired from Reynolds, Smith and Hills less than 2 years earlier and told police that he thought the firm was hindering his efforts to collect unemployment benefits. "They left me to rot," he told a reporter who asked him about his motive.

According to the U.S. Department of Labor, the incidence of workplace violence has actually been trending down over the past few years, in part because employers have paid more attention to the problem and taken successful preventive measures. More and more companies, for example, have set up employee assistance programs (EAPs) to help workers deal with various sources of stress. However, EAP providers report that, in the current climate of economic uncertainty, they're being asked to deal with a different set of problems than those they've typically handled in the past.

In particular, financial problems have replaced emotional problems as employees' primary area of concern, and with unemployment totals remaining high in some industries and in some parts of the country, American workers appear to be more worried about the future than about such conventional stressors as pressing deadlines and demanding bosses. Today, says Sandra Naiman, a Denver-based career coach, "off- and on-the-job stresses feed into one another" to elevate stress levels all around, and workplace stress during the recent recession may reflect this unfamiliar convergence of stressors.

There are as yet no hard data to connect workplace violence with economic downturns, but many professionals and other experts in the field are convinced that the connection is real. ComPsych Corp., an EAP provider in Chicago, reports that calls are running 30 percent above normal. According to Rick Kronberg of Perspectives Ltd., another Chicago-based EAP

"Tough times," he says, "will cause people to do crazy things."

provider, "with the layoffs and the general financial picture, we're getting a lot of reaction . . . [from] people with a high degree of stress." Adds Tim Horner, a managing director at Kroll Inc., a security consulting firm, "There are signs out there that something's going on. It's not unusual that somebody snaps." Kenneth Springer, another security specialist whose job now includes keeping an eye on potentially dangerous ex-employees for their former employers, agrees: "Tough times," he says, "will cause people to do crazy things."

By the same token, says Laurence Miller, a forensic psychologist and author of *From Difficult to Disturbed: Understanding and Managing Dysfunctional Employees*, economic stress alone won't turn someone into a killer, nor is the average coworker likely to turn violent without warning. "People shouldn't be sitting around wondering if someone they've been working with for years who's been a regular guy [with] no real problems is going to suddenly snap and go ballistic on them," says Miller. "It's usually somebody," he warns, "that's had a long streak of problems." Unfortunately, that profile fits Jason Rodriguez, who'd been struggling for years with marital and mental-health problems, unemployment, debt, and smoldering anger. "He was a very, very angry man," reports his former mother-in-law.[1]

THINK IT OVER

1. Have you ever experienced a case of workplace violence?
2. What role, if any, might the organization itself play in instigating workplace violence?
3. Can the threat of workplace violence ever be completely eliminated? Why or why not?

Most people do not think a great deal about their safety or health when they go to work. They assume that their employer has done whatever is possible to make the workplace as safe and as healthy as it can be. Although many people routinely experience stress, many workers do not see it as something they can really control. Unfortunately, while many workplace elements may be beyond their control, a myriad of things—ranging from work hours to pressure to meet high-performance targets—can lead to stress.

The truth is that many accidents do occur in the workplace and that many workplaces are actually not healthy. This chapter is about ways in which organizations and human resource (HR) managers can make the workplace environment safe and healthy. As we will see, some legal pressures (recall the Occupational Safety and Health Act of 1970 we described in Chapter 2) operate to make workplaces safe, and there are also some practical issues that lead HR managers to keep workplaces healthy and secure.

EMPLOYEE SAFETY AND HEALTH

An organization tries to create and maintain a safe and healthy workplace for many reasons. For one thing, it is simply an ethical and socially responsible position; no responsible employer would argue that it is acceptable for employees to get hurt or become ill because of their working conditions. But there are also many other very specific reasons. First, recall from our discussion in Chapter 9 that mandated workers' compensation provides insurance coverage for employees who are hurt or who become ill on the job. The insurance premium an organization pays for this coverage is determined by several factors, including the value of the claims paid out to employees of the firm. Firms that have fewer accidents and workers' compensation claims actually pay lower premiums. In addition, the Occupational Safety and Health Administration (OSHA) can impose fines against organizations that have unsafe workplaces. Finally, lost time from accidents and illness can cost an organization a great deal of money, so it is simply good business to maintain a safe and healthy workplace. An important step in this process is to identify and eliminate safety and health hazards on the job.

Safety hazards are those conditions in the work environment that have the potential to cause harm to an employee. **Health hazards**, on the other hand, are elements of the work environment that more slowly and systematically, and perhaps cumulatively, result in damage to an employee's health. A safety hazard might be a set of metal steps that often get wet and might result in an employee falling down them; an example of a health hazard is toxic fumes, which, when an employee is exposed to them on an ongoing basis, cause various respiratory problems.

These risks are not likely to occur in all types of businesses or occupations. In fact, some types of workers are much more likely to experience injuries than are others. Table 12.1 lists some of the most dangerous occupations in the United States in terms of fatal accidents at work, as well as a few of the less dangerous ones. In 2012, there were 11,562 fatal accidents in trade, transportation, and utilities, with the most frequent cause being transportation related (i.e., accidents going to or from the job or from one place to another on the job). Transportation incidents also accounted for the majority of fatalities in several industries, but workplace violence played a major role in retail, finance, insurance, and auto repair. The total number of fatalities in 2014 (4,679) is down dramatically from the 1995 level of 6,632.

12-1a Common Workplace Hazards and Threats

In this section, we address some of the more frequent causes of accidents and then describe some of the more pervasive health hazards. One major category of factors that can cause accidents in the workplace is the characteristics of the physical environment. At a general level, of course, accidents can happen anywhere. People can slip on wet flooring or a loose piece of carpeting, or they can drop something heavy on a foot in almost any setting. But in manufacturing settings, several specific conditions of the work environment might prove to be potentially dangerous. Among the more common are unguarded or improperly guarded machines. In this instance, "guarding" refers to a shield or other piece of equipment that keeps body parts from contacting moving machine parts such as gears and conveyor belts.

Defective equipment and tools can cause accidents. Poor lighting and poor or improper ventilation can also be dangerous. Improper dress poses a hazard; loose clothing presents the risk of getting caught in the moving parts of a machine. Sharp edges around machinery can be a hazard as well. Finally, poor housekeeping that results in dirty or wet floors, improperly stacked materials, and congested storage areas can result in accidents. Of course, hazards are not restricted to manufacturing settings. They can occur in almost any work setting; home-office safety, for example, must be a concern for businesses that allow telecommuting.[2]

Some personal actions of individual employees also present common workplace hazards. Among the more

Safety hazards are conditions in the work environment that have the potential to cause harm to an employee.

Health hazards are characteristics of the work environment that more slowly and systematically, and perhaps cumulatively, result in damage to an employee's health.

The Occupational Safety and Health Act of 1970 (or OSHA) grants the federal government the power to establish and enforce occupational safety and health standards for all places of employment that directly affect interstate commerce.

TABLE 12.1 MOST DANGEROUS OCCUPATIONS IN THE UNITED STATES, 2014

Industry	No. of Fatalities	Percentage of Total	Most Frequent Cause
Trade, transportation, and utilities	1198	26	Transportation incidents
Construction	874	19	Falls and slips
Transportation and warehousing	749	16	Transportation incidents
Natural resources and mining	749	16	Transportation incidents/contacts with objects
Agriculture, forestry, fishing, and hunting	568	12	Transportation incidents
Professional and business services	418	9	Transportation incidents
Manufacturing	341	7	Contact with objects
Retail trade	267	6	Violence
Leisure and hospitality	207	4	Violence

Source: U.S. Bureau of Labor Statistics, Fatal Occupational Injuries by Industry and Selected Event Exposure, 2015.

frequently described and identified personal actions that lead to accidents are taking unnecessary risks, failing to wear protective equipment such as goggles or gloves, using improper tools and equipment for specific jobs, taking unsafe shortcuts, and simply engaging in foolish horseplay. Any of these actions has the potential to harm or injure people in the workplace quickly and without warning. These kinds of actions caused an excessive number of injuries for years at Georgia-Pacific, until new managers implemented new safety rules and policies. Fatigue can also be a major contributor to workplace hazards. Even without hazardous conditions, a tired employee can still fall or become overly careless.

A separate set of workplace factors may produce negative health effects that appear more gradually. Chemicals, toxic fumes, and similar workplace elements may fall into this category. Secondary smoke may also be a factor. Some buildings themselves have relatively unsafe characteristics, including asbestos insulation and carpeting that has been treated with improper combinations of chemicals and dyes. In many cases, health hazards are occupational. For example, people who work in coal mines and pesticide plants may be especially prone to exposure to potential health hazards. The U.S. Department of Labor has identified seven major categories of occupational illnesses:

1. occupational skin diseases or disorders,
2. dust diseases of the lungs,
3. respiratory conditions due to toxic agents,
4. poisoning,
5. disorders resulting from physical agents,
6. disorders associated with repeated trauma, and
7. other categories of occupational illness.

As discussed later in this chapter, stress is another type of long-term health and safety hazard.

12-1b Organizations and OSHA

Widespread concern about employee safety and health led to the passage in 1970 of the most comprehensive law regarding worker safety. This act is technically known as the Occupational Safety and Health Act of 1970 but is most frequently referred to simply by its initials: OSHA. At the time OSHA was passed, approximately 15,000 work-related deaths occurred in the United States every year.

TABLE 12.2 SAMPLE GENERAL INDUSTRY SAFETY AND HEALTH REGULATIONS FROM OSHA

For drinking water . . .

- Potable water shall be provided in all places of employment.

- The nozzle of a drinking fountain shall be set at such an angle that the jet of water will not splash back down the nozzle; and the end of the nozzle shall be protected by a guard to prevent a person's mouth or nose from coming in contact with the nozzle.

- Portable drinking water dispensers shall be designed and serviced to ensure sanitary conditions, shall be capable of being closed, and shall have a tap. Unused disposable cups shall be kept in a sanitary container, and a receptacle shall be provided for used cups. The "common drinking cup" is prohibited.

For fire protection . . .

- Portable fire extinguishers, suitable to the conditions and hazards involved, shall be provided and maintained in effective operating condition.

- Portable fire extinguishers shall be given maintenance service at least once a year. A durable tag must be securely attached to show the maintenance or recharge date.

- In storage areas, clearance between sprinkler systems deflectors and the top of storage varies with the type of storage. For combustible material, stored over 15 feet, but not more than 21 feet high, in solid piles, or over 12 feet, but not more than 21 feet, in piles that contain horizontal channels, the minimum clearance shall be 36 inches. The minimum clearance for smaller piles, or for noncombustible materials, shall be 18 inches.

For portable ladders . . .

- The maximum length for portable wooden ladders shall be as follows: step, 20 feet; single straight ladders, 30 feet; sectional ladders, 60 feet; trestle ladders, 20 feet; platform stepladders, 20 feet; painter's stepladders, 12 feet; mason's ladders, 40 feet.

- Non-self-supporting ladders shall be erected on a sound base at a 4 to 1 pitch, and placed to prevent slippage.

- The top of a ladder used to gain access to a roof should extend at least 3 feet above the point of contact.

Source: *General Industry Standards and Interpretations*, U.S. Department of Labor, OSHA (Vol. 1, Revised 2008, Part 1914).

OSHA authorized the U.S. government to create and enforce various standards regarding occupational safety and health. The responsibility for enforcing the provisions of OSHA was assigned to the Department of Labor. This enforcement group today is called the Occupational Safety and Health Administration but still operates within the Department of Labor. Somewhat confusingly, then, the acronym "OSHA" can refer to either the original act passed in 1970 or the enforcement group itself.

In concert with the Department of Labor, the Department of Health was also given the task of sponsoring research to establish the criteria for various tasks and occupations and for training employees to comply with the act. Most of this work is conducted by an agency within the Department of Health called the National Institute for Occupational Safety and Health (NIOSH); that is, NIOSH conducts research to help establish appropriate safety and health criteria. These criteria are then communicated to OSHA in the Department of Labor for administration and enforcement. A sample of the guidelines developed from this work is shown in Table 12.2.

Through research and analysis of workplace statistics, OSHA has created various safety standards. These standards are defined as "practices, means, operations, or processes, reasonably necessary to provide safe . . . employment." The various standards that OSHA creates are regularly published and disseminated to employers across the country. Organizations are responsible for keeping current on OSHA standards, which can be difficult because of the length and volume of the various sets of regulations and standards. Each year, new standards, revisions of old standards, or extensions or reinterpretations of various existing standards are published by OSHA in volumes that total hundreds of pages in length. Thus, managers frequently feel that OSHA represents unnecessary regulation of their activities.

To ensure compliance with OSHA, inspectors from the U.S. Department of Labor visit places of employment either randomly or by invitation from an employer, an employee, or a union. If an employee requests an OSHA inspection, then her or his identity is kept confidential. If the OSHA inspector determines that the employer is guilty of major violations, significant penalties can result.

OSHA is both the act that authorized the U.S. government to create various standards regarding occupational safety and health and the administrative agency that enforces those standards.

An employer can be fined $10,000 per violation for willful or repeated major violations. In addition, company officials may be personally fined for failure to comply with OSHA regulations and can conceivably be sentenced to jail time.

OSHA also requires that employers keep highly specific and standardized records of illnesses and injuries that occur in the workplace. These records must be produced and shown to any OSHA compliance officer who requests them. In addition to routine record keeping, employers must also report immediately and directly to OSHA all accidents and illnesses that result in deaths in the workplace or that pose serious health hazards to all employees in the organization. Employers have avenues for appeal; if they disagree with the recommendations of an OSHA compliance officer, they can turn to the Occupational Safety and Health Review Commission. They can also pursue their claims through the federal courts.

Many experts believe that OSHA has not been terribly effective. They argue, for example, that its standards are too comprehensive, too technical, and often too arbitrary. Critics also point out that enforcement of OSHA standards is still relatively uneven. Even in terms of actual measurable effects, OSHA has been less than successful. Although awareness of safety issues has undoubtedly increased, the number of occupational accidents and occupational illnesses has not been significantly diminished.[3]

12-1c Controlling Accidents at Work

Regardless of whether OSHA is involved or not, an organization can take several precautions in its effort to create a safer work environment, especially regarding accidents at work. One important approach is to design more safety into the workplace through a process called *safety engineering*. **Safety engineers** are experts who carefully study the workplace, try to identify and isolate particularly dangerous situations, and recommend solutions for dealing with those situations.

In addition, organizations can sometimes help control workplace accidents by providing protective clothing and safety devices to employees. Among the more common kinds are various types of head protection, eye goggles and face shields, hearing protection for excessively noisy environments, gloves for hand protection, safety shoes for foot protection, waist support belts for people lifting heavy objects, and belts and lifelines for employees who work in high places. In today's technology-driven workplaces, safety equipment also includes wrist and elbow supports and screen filters for people who keyboard several hours a day, as well as properly designed chairs and desk surfaces for people who sit for most of their workday.

In addition, employee training is an important ingredient in controlling accidents at work. Employees should be taught the safest work procedures that the organization can identify, and they should be taught to follow safe work procedures and report unsafe conditions to managers. Finally, providing safety incentives and behavior modification training to employees has also been found effective in reducing the number of accidents on the job.[4]

An organization can try to make the workplace safer in one of two ways. First, it can emphasize a reduction in the number of accidents or in the number of workdays lost to accidents. You may have seen a construction site or facility that has a sign indicating the number of days, weeks, or months since someone missed work because of an accident. Accidents and lost workdays can be counted and so can easily be used to justify whatever measures the organization takes. Second, the organization also can focus on safe behaviors—that is, making the workplace safer—rather than on accidents themselves. An example of an emphasis on safe behavior is providing training and rewards for people who engage in safe behaviors (e.g., wearing their hard hats), with the assumption that this behavior will lead to a decrease in the number of accidents. Although safe behavior is a step removed from reduced numbers of accidents, increasing safe behaviors is clearly a necessary step in reducing accidents. Both approaches can work, but they operate in much different ways.

The kinds of interventions described previously can also be part of a larger safety culture. One of the authors recently observed a group of managers from several companies going down a flight of stairs for lunch during an executive development training session. In one group, all managers held the railing as they went down the stairs, whereas most people just walked down without holding anything. The mangers holding the railing were all employees at various DuPont plants, an organization that has a strong norm for safe behavior.

This idea has been formalized as a construct called *safety climate*. The safety climate of an organization is usually considered to be the perception of the importance and priority an

Kounadeas Ioannhs/Shutterstock.com

> **Safety engineers** are experts who carefully study the workplace, try to identify and isolate particularly dangerous situations, and recommend solutions for dealing with those situations.

organization gives to safety.[5] Basically, the safety climate should influence employees' behavior because they perceive a relationship between their safety behavior and the rewards and punishments meted out by the company. A company with a positive safety climate is one in which employees recognize that they will be rewarded for their safe behaviors and punished for their unsafe behaviors. There is, however, only mixed research support for a relationship between safety climate and accidents at work.[6]

12-1d Controlling Occupational Diseases

Controlling occupational diseases is a bit more complex. The effects of occupational diseases are often observable only after extended periods of time, so it may be difficult for the organization to know if its disease-prevention efforts are effective. For example, following the disaster at the Fukushima Daiichi Nuclear Power Station in Japan, 50 volunteers remained to clean up the plant. These volunteers were exposed to dangerous levels of radiation, as Japan's Health Minister raised the legal limit on how much radiation workers can be exposed to, to a level five times higher than that allowed in the United States. But, although five workers died during the cleanup, experts say that the final impact will be nowhere near that associated with the Chernobyl disaster in 1986. At Chernobyl, more than 6,000 people have been diagnosed with thyroid cancer, associated with drinking contaminated milk. Japanese officials are confident that nothing of this magnitude will occur at Fukushima.[7]

This optimism is due to numerous precautions that the Japanese are taking. These range from daily use of protective gloves and airtight suits, to the daily testing of cleanup workers using both radiation detectors and chemicals, to preventing anyone from drinking either water or milk that may be contaminated. Any organization should take such steps when employees work in an environment that may cause occupational disease. If the hazardous conditions can be reduced or eliminated, the organization should do so, but it must still take precautions even if the hazards cannot be eliminated. These include informing all employees of the exact nature of the various risks and hazards associated with their jobs. This information should enable them to take a larger role in maintaining their own health. Again, in many cases, proper equipment might be helpful. Respiratory shields for breathing, pressurized or rubberized bodysuits, and appropriate safety materials and equipment such as gloves and masks might be helpful.

Circadian rhythms are natural cycles that indicate when a body needs to eat or sleep.

12-2 THE PHYSICAL ENVIRONMENT

The actual physical environment in which an employee works is also extremely important and obviously can affect safety, health, and well-being. In addition, the physical environment can affect how pleasant or unpleasant a work setting is. Although many aspects of the physical environment may affect an employee's attitudes and behavior on the job, we will focus on just a few.

12-2a Hours of Work

In Chapter 14, we will discuss some trends toward nontraditional workweeks as techniques to enhance performance; we note here, however, that the hours worked and how they are distributed can also affect employee safety and well-being. For example, 4 days on, 3 days off a week may be attractive to some people, but not to others. This work schedule can create problems, too. For example, one study found that young males were much more receptive to compressed workweeks than were any other group.[8] Preferences aside, studies of compressed work schedules have also found that construction accidents are more likely to occur later in the day (which would be 10 hours long) because of fatigue on construction jobs, and generally mixed results were found for productivity in jobs with compressed work schedules.[9]

In many industries, the problems of shift work present another challenge to managing the work environment effectively. All human beings are subject to **circadian rhythms**, which tell our bodies when to eat and sleep. When employees work a night shift, their bodies must adapt to sleeping during the day and staying awake at night. Although this change is disruptive, the body adapts and learns to switch day and night. But employees who must work on rotating shifts are never able to establish a new rhythm. As a result, they are more likely to have ulcers than other employees because their bodies struggle to find equilibrium.[10] Nonetheless, other research has indicated that some workers, especially older, more experienced employees, may actually like the variety and can cope with the changes in biological rhythms.[11]

12-2b Illumination, Temperature, and Office and Work Space Design

One phase of the Hawthorne studies conducted in 1924 in a Western Electric plant outside Chicago was concerned with the effects of illumination on productivity.

The results indicated that changes in the level of illumination were not responsible for the changes in productivity observed. This failure discouraged scholars from examining the effects of lighting on workplace behavior for quite some time. Considerable evidence, however, shows that extremes of temperature (in either direction) can affect both attitudes and decision-making on the job.[12] It has even been suggested that ambient temperature helps explain national differences in stress on the job.[13] Research has also shown that different tasks require different levels of optimal lighting and that employees who perceive their work environments as dark are generally less satisfied with their jobs.[14]

Other aspects of the physical work environment that have received attention over the years include the use of music in the workplace. These studies, many of them going back more than 50 years, have indicated that almost any type of background music can improve employee attitudes and performance on the job.[15] A recent study found that the use of personal stereos on the job improved both attitudes and performance, especially on relatively simple jobs.[16] The physical layout of office space and the use of dividers and cubicles also have been found to influence attitudes and behavior at work.[17]

Although many of these studies found that changes in the physical environment affect performance, the physical environment seems to have the strongest effect on attitudes. Even when light, temperature, or office layout did not influence performance, these factors were associated with differences in how employees felt about their jobs and where they worked. Clearly, however, some aspects of the environment can influence employee safety and health, a topic we turn to next.

12-3 STRESS AND STRESS MANAGEMENT AT WORK

Organizations today are also increasingly becoming involved in stress-management and wellness programs for their employees.[18] To see how such programs can be effective, we must first understand the causes and consequences of stress at work. Figure 12.1 notes the major causes and consequences.

FIG 12.1 THE CAUSES AND CONSEQUENCES OF STRESS IN ORGANIZATIONS

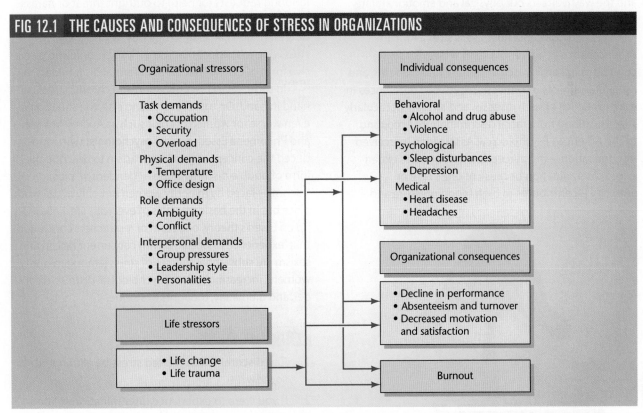

Source: Reprinted from James C. Quick and Jonathan D. Quick, *Organizational Stress and Preventive Management*, McGraw-Hill, 1984, pp. 19, 44, and 76. Copyright © 1984 by The McGraw-Hill Companies. Reprinted with the permission of James C. Quick.

Contemporary Challenges in HR

Diversity Breeds Stress

Audrey Murrell, an African American woman, remembers subtle forms of discrimination when she was in school. White classmates, for example, excluded her from study groups and asserted an implicit privilege in using classroom materials before she was allowed a turn. "You're left with this feeling of 'Is it me or is it them?'" says Murrell. "You know it's them, but it's hard to prove because it's not obvious discrimination." As Murrell learned, however, it takes a toll nevertheless, particularly on the emotional, mental, and even physical health of the young people who suffer from it.

Now a faculty member at the University of Pittsburgh, Murrell is also well aware that the same patterns of discrimination often follow African Americans from the classroom to the workplace. "It can lead to a lot of self-doubt and lack of confidence," she says. "Then you're likely to see withdrawal and detaching oneself from the job, which leads to internal bitterness and anger. . . . Bias and the way it affects our physical and emotional state has very real consequences."

One of those consequences is stress. African Americans are at higher risk than whites for such conditions as cardiovascular disease and diabetes, and research suggests a connection between differences in the prevalence of such diseases and stress—particularly stress resulting from racial discrimination. According to the American Psychological Association, perceived discrimination—the perception that one has experienced discrimination because of one's race or ethnicity—contributes to high blood pressure and diabetes, such unhealthy behaviors as smoking and alcohol/substance abuse, and mental health disorders among African Americans and other minorities.

Specifically, perceived discrimination is a key factor in what's known as chronic stress—that is, long-term stress that results from lingering feelings of despair or hopelessness. When it comes to the workplace, some researchers also distinguish between formal and interpersonal discrimination. According to Sabat, Lindsey, and King (2014), formal discrimination usually occurs as "formal job discrimination" against individuals in such HR processes as "selection, retention, promotion or termination."

On the other hand, interpersonal discrimination occurs in situations that aren't directly related to such "employment outcomes" as being hired or fired. Rather, it occurs in various interpersonal interactions that may be brief or infrequent. It runs the gamut from social distancing (e.g., declining to engage in conversation, ignoring requests for help) to outright threat or harassment. Sabat, Lindsey, and King found that "interpersonal discrimination can lead to high levels of workplace stress due to the fact that it is a more chronic and pervasive form of discrimination than formal discrimination."

In short, racial discrimination and chronic stress go hand in hand. On top of everything else, the situation is even worse for women of color such as Audrey Murrell and Philomena Essed, a social psychologist who introduced the concept of gendered racism to describe the form of double discrimination—"genderism" plus "racism"—faced by minority women not only in the workplace but in the basic activities of everyday life. Following up on Essed's theory, one team of researchers concluded that "experiences associated with concurrent racism and sexism are substantial sources of stress [among minority women], increasing risk for psychological distress, disorder, and ultimately, thoughts of suicide."[19]

Vadymvdrobot/Fotolia

THINK IT OVER

1. Can discrimination-related stress be eliminated? If so, how?

2. If you were to experience discrimination-related stress, how would you respond?

12-3a Causes of Stress at Work

Stress is a person's adaptive response to a stimulus that places excessive psychological or physical demands on him or her. The stimuli that cause stress are called *stressors*. Organizational stressors are various factors in the workplace that can cause stress. We mentioned this topic briefly in Chapter 6 when we discussed the importance of job satisfaction at work. Four general sets of organizational stressors are task demands, physical demands, role demands, and interpersonal demands.

Task demands are stressors associated with the specific job a person performs. By nature, some occupations are more stressful than others. The jobs of surgeon, air traffic controller, and professional football coach obviously are more stressful than those of a general practitioner, an airlines baggage loader, and a football team equipment manager, respectively. Beyond specific task-related pressures, other task demands may pose physical threats to a person's health. Such conditions exist in occupations such as coal mining, toxic-waste handling, and so forth. Security is another task demand that can cause stress. Someone in a relatively secure job is not likely to worry too much about losing that position. On the other hand, if job security is threatened, stress can increase dramatically. For example, stress generally increases throughout an organization during a period of layoffs or immediately following a merger with another firm. Such a phenomenon has been observed at several organizations including Anheuser-Busch, JPMorgan Chase, and AT&T.

Overload is another task demand stressor. It occurs when a person simply has more work to do than he or she can handle. The overload can be either quantitative (the individual has too many tasks to perform or too little time in which to perform them) or qualitative (the person may believe she or he lacks the ability to do the job). More managers report going to their office on weekends to get their jobs done, a direct result of overload.[20]

Advances in information technology may make this problem even worse for some managers. Certainly, new information technology has enabled many HR managers to make decisions better and faster than ever before. And, it also promotes more frequent communication among people, resulting in improved coordination and enhanced organizational flexibility and response times. Managers can keep in constant touch with others, and a manager's boss, colleagues, and subordinates can get in touch anytime. But some trouble also crops up. For example, information technology makes it easier than ever before for HR managers to suffer information overload. Some estimates suggest that managers send or receive more than 400 messages each day. The forms of these messages run the gamut from e-mail to text messages to Post-it Notes. And many HR managers fall into the trap of thinking that because they can always be in touch, they must always be in touch, so they check their e-mail constantly, carry their cell phones on vacation or to the golf course, and keep a BlackBerry or iPhone handy at all times.

We should also note that the opposite of overload may also be undesirable—low task demands can result in boredom and apathy just as overload can cause tension and anxiety. Thus, a moderate degree of workload-related stress is optimal because it leads to high levels of energy and motivation.

Physical demands relate to the job setting. Many of the physical aspects of the work environment that we discussed earlier, such as working in extreme temperatures, have been associated with stress on the job. In addition, office design can be related to stress if its end result is isolation, boredom, or too much interaction with coworkers. Strenuous labor such as loading heavy cargo or lifting packages can also lead to stress, as can poor lighting and inadequate work surfaces.

Role demands can cause stress, too. A role is a set of expected behaviors associated with a position in a group or organization. Stress can result from either role ambiguity or role conflict that people experience in groups. For example, an employee who is feeling pressure from her boss to work longer hours and from her family for more time at home will almost certainly experience stress. A new employee experiencing role ambiguity because of poor orientation and training practices by the organization will also suffer from stress.

Another set of organizational stressors consists of three *interpersonal demands*.

1. Group pressures include pressure to restrict output, pressure to conform to the group's norms, and so forth. For instance, it is quite common for a work group to arrive at an informal agreement about how much each member will produce. Individuals who produce much more or much less than this level may be pressured by the group to get back in line. An individual who feels a strong need to vary from the group's expectations (perhaps to get a pay raise or promotion) will experience a great deal of stress, especially if acceptance by the group is also important to him or her.

2. Leadership style can cause stress. Suppose an employee needs a great deal of social

> **Stress** is a person's adaptive response to a stimulus that places excessive psychological or physical demands on him or her.

support from his leader. The leader, however, is quite brusque and shows no concern or compassion for the employee. This employee will likely feel stressed. Similarly, assume that an employee feels a strong need to participate in decision-making and to be active in all aspects of management. Her boss is autocratic and refuses to consult subordinates about anything. Once again, stress is likely to result.

3. Conflicting personalities and behaviors may cause stress. Conflict can occur when two or more people must work together even though their personalities, attitudes, and behaviors differ. For example, a person with an internal locus of control—that is, who always wants to control events—might get frustrated working with an external person who likes to wait and see what happens.

Table 12.3 provides a subjective list of the most and least stressful jobs. Other relatively high-stress jobs include photojournalist and taxi driver. Other relatively low-stress jobs include furniture upholsterer and electrical technician. In all cases, it is important to realize that the stressors just noted exist against a background of general life stress.

12-3b Differences in How One Experiences Stress

Regardless of the stressors present on any job, different individuals will experience that stress differently. Some individuals respond positively to many types of stress, while others react negatively to any type of stress, so it is important to note some of the factors that influence how one experiences stress.

One factor that is important is personality. Some years ago, a group of medical researchers noticed that patients with certain personality characteristics were more likely to suffer early heart attacks.[21]

1. They identified these patients as having a Type A personality. They are highly competitive, highly focused on their work, and have few interests outside of work.

The **Type A personality** is characterized by being highly competitive and highly focused on work with few interests outside of work.

The **Type B personality** is characterized as being less aggressive, more patient, and more easygoing. In general, individuals with Type B personalities experience less stress and are less likely to suffer some type of illness because of stress than Type A personalities.

Hardiness is an individual difference that allows some individuals to experience less stress when dealing with stressful events and that makes them more effective in dealing with the stress they do experience.

TABLE 12.3 MOST AND LEAST STRESSFUL JOBS

Most Stressful Jobs	Least Stressful Jobs
1. Enlisted military personnel	1. University professor
2. Military general	2. Seamstress/tailor
3. Firefighter	3. Medical records technician
4. Commercial airline pilot	4. Jeweler
5. Public relations executive	5. Medical lab technician
6. Senior corporation executive	6. Audiologist
7. Photojournalist	7. Dietician
8. Newspaper reporter	8. Hair stylist
9. Taxi driver	9. Librarian
10. Police officer	10. Drill press operator

Source: Victoria Brienza, "The Ten Most Stressful Jobs of 2012"; Victoria Brienza, "The Ten Least Stressful Jobs of 2012," on February 2012, www.CareerCast.com.

2. These individuals are often contrasted with the **Type B personality**. They tend to be less aggressive, more patient, and more easygoing. In general, Type A personalities experience more stress and are more likely to suffer some type of illness due to stress than are Type B personalities.[22]

3. Another personality variable that appears to be related to how people experience stress is called **hardiness**. A high degree of hardiness actually reduces the experienced stress associated with stressful events, and so hardy personalities experience less stress overall and are more effective in dealing with the stress they do experience.[23]

4. Individuals high in self-esteem are also less susceptible to the problems associated with stress. They tend to have a more positive outlook on life and are better able to cope with any stress they encounter.[24]

5. Finally, gender appears to be an important factor in determining how one experiences stress. Specifically, women are more likely to experience stress at work, and they are more likely to be absent because of stress-related problems, although these differences may reflect true differences in the stressors that men and women are exposed to at work.[25]

12-3c Consequences of Stress at Work

Stress can lead to several positive and negative consequences. If the stress is positive, then the result may be more energy, enthusiasm, and motivation. Of more concern, of course, are the negative consequences of stress. Three sets of consequences that can result from stress are individual consequences, organizational consequences, and burnout.[26] Individual consequences are as follow:

1. Behavioral consequences of stress are responses that may harm the person under stress or others. One such behavior is smoking. Research has clearly documented that people who smoke tend to smoke more when they experience stress. Other possible behavioral consequences are accident tendencies, violence, and appetite disorders.

2. Psychological consequences of stress relate to an individual's mental health and well-being. When people experience too much stress at work, they may become depressed or find themselves sleeping too much or not enough. Stress may also lead to family problems and sexual difficulties.

3. The medical consequences of stress affect a person's physical well-being. Heart disease and stroke, among other illnesses, have been linked to stress. Other common medical problems resulting from too much stress include headaches, backaches, ulcers and related stomach and intestinal disorders, and skin conditions such as acne and hives.

Clearly, any of the individual consequences just discussed can also affect the organization, but other consequences of stress have even more direct consequences for organizations.

1. One clear organizational consequence of too much stress is a decline in performance. For operating workers, such a decline can translate into poor-quality work or a drop in productivity. For managers, it can mean faulty decision-making or disruptions in working relationships as people become irritable and hard to get along with. As discussed in Chapter 6,

auremar/Shutterstock.com

withdrawal behaviors such as absenteeism and turnover can result from stress on the job.

2. Another direct organizational consequence of employee stress relates to attitudes. As noted, job satisfaction, morale, and organizational commitment can all suffer, along with motivation to perform at high levels. As a result, people may be more prone to complain about trivialities, do only enough work to get by, and so forth. There has been a trend in the United States over the past 30 years that suggests a gradual decline in job satisfaction. Moreover, a major source of the problem seems to be stress-related aspects of the job. Specifically, respondents in a poll conducted by the Conference Board indicated that less than 36 percent of employees expressed contentment with their workload, work–life balance, or communication channels.[27]

Finally, **burnout**, another consequence of stress, has clear implications for both employees and organizations. It is a general feeling of exhaustion that develops when an individual simultaneously experiences too much pressure and too few sources of satisfaction.

Other consequences of stress include various dysfunctional behaviors that detract from, rather than contribute to, organizational performance. Two of the more common are absenteeism and turnover. Some incidents of absenteeism, of course, have legitimate causes, including illness, jury duty, and death and illness in the family. At other times, the employee may feign a legitimate cause as an excuse to stay home. When an employee is absent, legitimately or not, the employee's work does not get done at all or a substitute must be hired to do it. In either case, the quantity or quality of actual output is likely to suffer. Obviously, some absenteeism is expected, but organizations strive to eliminate feigned absenteeism and reduce legitimate absences as much as possible.

Turnover occurs when people leave their jobs. An organization usually incurs costs when replacing workers who have quit; if turnover involves especially productive people, it is even more costly. It seems to result from several factors, including aspects of the job, the organization, the individual, the labor market, and family influences. In general, a poor person–job fit is also a likely cause of turnover. People may also be prone to leave an organization

> **Burnout** is a general feeling of exhaustion that develops when an individual simultaneously experiences too much pressure and too few sources of satisfaction.
>
> **Turnover** refers to people leaving their jobs, whether voluntarily or involuntarily (i.e., through firings).

if its inflexibility makes it difficult to manage family and other personal matters; they may be more likely to stay if an organization provides sufficient flexibility to make it easier to balance work and nonwork considerations.

Other forms of **dysfunctional behavior** may be even more costly for an organization. Theft and sabotage, for example, result in direct financial costs for an organization. Sexual and racial harassment are also costly to an organization, both indirectly (by lowering morale, producing fear, and driving off valuable employees) and directly (through financial liability if the organization responds inappropriately).

Workplace violence and aggression are also growing concerns in many organizations. People who are having problems coping with stress may vent their difficulties by yelling at or harassing their colleagues. They may also engage in other destructive behaviors such as damaging company property or physically assaulting bosses or co-workers. Violence by disgruntled workers or former workers results in dozens of deaths and injuries each year.[28]

It is also possible that stress has some positive effects on behavior at work. Several studies[29] have suggested that not all stress is the same and that some sources of stress can actually lead to positive outcomes at work.[30] In addition, it has been argued that without some stress, employees can become bored.

12-3d Wellness Programs in Organizations

Two basic organizational strategies for helping employees manage stress are institutional programs and collateral stress programs. **Institutional programs** for managing stress are undertaken through established organizational mechanisms. For example, properly designed jobs and work schedules, as discussed earlier, can help ease stress. Shift work, in particular, can cause major problems for employees because they have to adjust their sleep and relaxation patterns constantly. Thus, the design of work and work schedules should be a focus of organizational efforts to reduce stress.

The organization's culture can also be used to help manage stress. Some organizational cultures, for example, have a strong norm against taking time off or going on vacation. In the long run, such norms can cause major stress. To avoid this, the organization should strive to foster a culture that reinforces a healthy mix of work and nonwork activities. Supervision can play an important institutional role in managing stress. A supervisor is a potential major source of overload. Those who are made aware of their potential for assigning stressful amounts of work can do a better job by keeping workloads reasonable.

In addition to their institutional efforts aimed at reducing stress, many organizations are turning to **collateral stress programs**, or programs created specifically to help employees deal with stress. Organizations have adopted stress-management programs, health-promotion programs, and other kinds of programs for this purpose. More and more companies are developing their own programs or adopting existing programs of this type. For example, Lockheed Martin offers screening programs for its employees to detect signs of hypertension, and Hospital Corporation of America offers its employees 4 cents a mile for cycling, 16 cents a mile for walking or jogging, and 64 cents a mile for swimming.

Many firms today also have employee-fitness programs. These kinds of programs attack stress indirectly by encouraging employees to exercise, which in turn is presumed to reduce stress. On the negative side, this kind of effort costs considerably more than stress-management programs because the firm must invest in exercise facilities. Still, more and more companies are exploring this option. Both Raytheon and L. L. Bean, for example, have state-of-the-art fitness centers available for their employees' use.

Organizations try to help employees cope with stress through other kinds of programs. For example, existing career-development programs like that at General Electric are used for this purpose. Other companies use programs promoting everything from humor to massage as antidotes for stress. Of course, little or no research supports some of the claims made by advocates of these programs, so managers must take steps to ensure that any organizational effort to help employees cope with stress is at least reasonably effective.

Given the widespread adoption of wellness and stress-reduction programs, it is important to understand how effective these programs are. Much of the "evidence" supporting their effectiveness is anecdotal, with employees reporting how much better they feel when they are allowed to participate in wellness programs. Such data, although encouraging, cannot substitute for more rigorous evaluations of these programs.

Dysfunctional behavior refers to any behavior at work that is counterproductive. These behaviors may include theft and sabotage, as well as sexual and racial harassment.

Institutional programs for managing stress are undertaken through established organizational mechanisms.

Collateral stress programs are organizational programs created specifically to help employees deal with stress.

Unfortunately, a recent report from the Society for Human Resource Management (SHRM) suggests that many of the programs being established may not be as effective as they could be.[31]

The problem appears to be that many companies, especially smaller firms with more limited resources, do not have comprehensive wellness programs. Instead, they focus on one or two health risks (e.g., high blood pressure), do not continue the programs over the long run, and tend to focus on salaried employees who are already generally healthier than other employees. The report also suggests that top leadership in the organization must support these programs and develop a culture in which employees feel valued if these programs are to be effective. Finally, the report cites several examples of successful programs (e.g., at 3M and at General Mills) where the corporation has partnered with a health-care organization such as the Mayo Clinic to ensure that employees have access to good assessment tools, have programs that can help them deal with specific health problems, and have adequate follow-up. Although it may not be easy for every organization to implement all of these features, it would seem that these are the keys to more effective wellness programs.

12-3e Other Interventions

In 2009, while unemployment inched closer to 10 percent, and major banks disappeared from existence (both causing significant stress), Americans began concerning themselves with a new threat to their well-being. A new and virulent strain of influenza was spreading across the country. Originally and unfortunately called *swine flu,* the H1N1 influenza reached pandemic proportions in 2009, indicating that it had spread across significant areas of the country (technically, a pandemic indicates a disease prevalent throughout an entire country, continent, or the whole world). In fact, by January 2010, the World Health Organization reported confirmed cases of the H1N1 virus in more than 209 countries, including at least 14,142 deaths.[32]

OSHA began issuing statements and testifying before Congress on the ways to deal with the H1N1 virus at work.[33] Here the interventions went far beyond making

medical facilities available. OSHA guidelines called for ordering respirators, fitting employees for these respirators, and training employees in the use of respirators and gloves, as well as programs urging employees to regularly wash their hands and providing sufficient stores of the vaccine. Although this set of events is not typical, it does help illustrate that concerns over safety and health extend beyond the normal threats that occur in work settings.

One last type of threat to safety and health at work also warrants discussion. For the past 25 years or so, acquired immune deficiency syndrome (AIDS) has become a major problem in the world in general—and at work. AIDS is relevant to employers for several reasons. An employee with AIDS must cope with a life-threatening medical issue, but it is also important to that individual's coworkers. Unfortunately, there is no clear-cut solution for dealing with this issue. Individuals who publicly disclose their condition increase the potential for retaliation from coworkers because many people fear the disease and may shun those who have it. And, the organization faces various privacy-related issues.

An organization that wants to deal with this issue must start by developing and implementing a comprehensive AIDS policy. As a premise for developing a policy, however, all employers must keep in mind certain points. First, it is illegal to ask an applicant if she or he has AIDS. Some but not all states allow organizations to require applicants to take an AIDS test. Regardless of the test outcome, an employee can be denied employment only if it is determined that the applicant cannot perform the job. As long as the individual who is already hired is capable of performing the job, then he or she

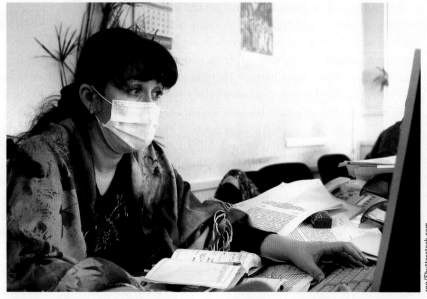

rng/Shutterstock.com

cannot be terminated or placed on leave. All medical information regarding the individual and her or his condition must be kept absolutely confidential.

In general, organizations can adopt three strategies in trying to deal with AIDS from a management perspective. One strategy is to categorize AIDS under a comprehensive life-threatening illness policy. In this instance, AIDS is treated like terminal cancer or any other life-threatening illness. The organization can then apply the same sorts of insurance coverage provisions, early-retirement and leave provisions, and so forth.

Another strategy is to form an AIDS-specific policy. This action is completely legal for an organization to contemplate as long as neither the intent nor the implementation of the policy results in discrimination against people on the basis of an AIDS condition. In general, most companies that form an AIDS-specific policy do so in an affirmative way. The essence of such a policy is to affirm the organization's stance that employees with AIDS are still entitled to work, receive benefits, and be treated comparably to all other employees.

The third approach that some companies take is to have no policy at all, an approach taken by far too many companies. The organization either does not want to confront the necessity for having an AIDS policy, is afraid to confront the need for such a policy, or does not know how to approach such a policy. In any of these events, managerial ignorance can potentially result in serious problems for both the employer and the employees.

12-3f Bullying at Work

In recent years, there has been a lot more attention paid to the problem of bullying. Much of this has focused on bullying in schools, but bullying is an issue in the workplace as well. In general, workplace bullying refers to a persistent pattern of mistreatment from people at work that causes a person some harm.[34] This can include verbal abuse, psychical abuse, psychological abuse, and humiliation, and although most bullying appears to involve someone in authority, it could involve peers or even subordinates. There is no well-accepted definition of bullying beyond this general one, so it is often difficult to determine exactly how widespread a problem bullying really is. It has also meant that bullying at work has been viewed as a social problem rather than one that should be legislated. Nonetheless, workplace bullying is seen as a major source of job stress. In fact, a survey from 2007 indicated that 13 percent of U.S. employees said they were currently being bullied, and 24 percent indicated that had been bullied at work. These statistics also suggest that women are more likely to be bullied at work, as are nonwhite employees.[35]

A recent review[36] of the work in this area has been more specific about the typical bullying behaviors such as taking responsibility away from someone and replacing it with more unpleasant tasks, ignoring someone's opinion, persistently criticizing someone's work, spreading gossip or rumors about a person, excluding someone at work, and hinting that someone should quit their job. This research goes on to suggest that bullying at work is a function of characteristics of the perpetrator (some people are simply bullies), the target (being different), and the situation (stress at work and a culture that allows or encourages bullying). The authors also point out that the costs associated with bullying are both personal (stress and lack of sleep) as well as organizational (lower performance), and they discuss spillover effects on other employees (health problems and aggression toward family members). The paper concludes with recommendations for interventions at the individual and organizational levels but noted that strong organization rules against bullying, which are publicized and fairly enforced, may be the best response.

Incidents reported in the media seem to suggest that this is a growing problem in the workplace although it is not clear if the incidence of bullying is increasing or the likelihood that people report these incidents is increasing. In either case, bullying is an important cause of stress on the job that is different from many of the others discussed, and it is one that needs to be addressed.

12-4 WORKPLACE SECURITY

The need to live in a safe and secure environment is a basic driver of human behavior (as will be discussed in Chapter 13). But security can be threatened (or guaranteed) in many different ways at work. For example, individuals working in organizations with low accident rates are more likely to feel secure about their safety on the job. Even individuals working on relatively dangerous jobs, however, can feel more secure if the organization (or someone else) is concerned about their safety. Thus, employees working at nuclear power facilities may feel quite secure because the organization, as well as the federal government, constantly monitors their environment for any threats.

On the other hand, announcements about impending or actual layoffs are likely to increase feelings of insecurity concerning employment.[37] After layoffs have been announced, many employees will remain feeling insecure for some time as they wonder when the next series of cutbacks will be announced. Potential cuts can lead to increased stress, with all the outcomes that are associated with stress. During times of high unemployment (e.g., 2010), very few employees for any employer feel truly secure about their jobs.

In addition, some organizations are active in allaying employees' fears about an uncertain future in other ways. The whole idea behind private pension plans is to provide employees with some assurance that they will have enough money to live on when they retire. Recall from Chapter 9 that, in the United States, just about every employee is covered by Social Security, but the retirement benefits from this program are not enough for many people to survive on, so they serve more as a safety net to make sure they have *some* pension. Instead, employers set up and contribute to private pension plans to make sure that retired employers can live productive lives after they stop working.

Finally, insurance programs are also designed to provide security in various forms. Health insurance (discussed in Chapter 9) is designed to make sure that an employee can afford the medical services he or she may require. Disability insurance is designed to provide some income for employees who are temporarily unable to work. In fact, there are many programs within the human resource management (HRM) function that are designed to provide some type of security for employees at work.

A different type of security issue has become much more salient to employees in the United States since September 11, 2001. The threat of bombings or kidnappings is not new to the world, but Americans have traditionally felt these concerns only when they were traveling abroad, not when they were at their jobs. During the 1970s, there were many kidnappings of executives visiting Latin America and even in some European countries. Organizations began training drivers in evasion tactics, and firms such as

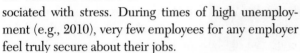

disfera/Shutterstock.com

GTE bought executives inexpensive plastic briefcases to take when they traveled outside the United States, based on the belief that terrorists would target individuals wearing expensive clothes or carrying expensive briefcases. In countries such as Israel, an everyday commute on the bus is far from relaxing because terrorists have repeatedly bombed these buses. In London, for many years, riders on the underground (subway) were often searched in an attempt to stop IRA bombings. Such threats, however, were foreign to U.S. workers.

Of course, there had been an earlier terrorist attack in the United States. On the morning of April 19, 1995, a bomb in a van parked outside the facility exploded at the Alfred P. Murrah Federal Building in downtown Oklahoma City. The explosion killed 168 people in what was then termed the worst terrorist attack on U.S. soil. But that incident did not threaten the basic security of the U.S. population. The bombing could be blamed on one or two irrational men who were certainly not declaring war on the United States. Even the first attack on the World Trade Center in 1993, which killed six people, was not really taken seriously.

The 2001 attack on the World Trade Center, however, changed everything. In the years immediately following this attack, the United States passed various laws and acts dealing with homeland security, as concerns about safety from terrorist actions seemed to overwhelm all other considerations. During the administration of President George W. Bush, the government argued that these security measures prevented other attacks on U.S. citizens, but it is extremely difficult to determine how many attacks would have occurred without these measures in place. The implementation of these measures also triggered intense debates about the trade-offs between privacy and security, and during his presidential campaign, Barack Obama seemed to argue that we had tipped the balance too far in favor of security over privacy.

By the summer of 2013, it had become clear that President Obama had continued and even expanded some of the security measures that had been implemented by President Bush. In August 2013, Edward Snowden, a former contract employee of the National Security Agency

those from the Middle East. In fact, many American universities have also become less willing to recruit students from certain parts of the world, and the U.S. government has made it more difficult for any potential students and employees to obtain visas. The issue with foreign students has become especially serious because several of the attackers at the World Trade Center were in this country on student visas. To the extent that these concerns and practices eliminate potentially qualified employees and students from consideration, they hurt the ability of businesses to recruit the best-qualified people available.

(NSA), revealed that the NSA repeatedly violated the privacy rights of American citizens through its program of widespread wiretapping. That is, it was revealed that the NSA routinely tapped the phone conversations of persons who were "suspected of terrorist activities." The U.S. government argued that, although phone data were being collected, they were not kept or used in any way that would violate anyone's rights to privacy. Instead, these data were simply kept as "metadata" showing trends, as well as the number of calls made and their duration. But throughout the summer and into the fall, more and more reports came out indicating exactly the levels of domestic surveillance that were being conducted by the United States,[38] and, even though the Justice Department upheld the practices that had been revealed so far, it was clear that American citizens were beginning to seriously question how many of their rights they were willing to sacrifice for a greater sense of security.

But, despite these concerns over the loss of privacy, many Americans still feel insecure about their safety relative to potential terrorist acts. It is not surprising, then, that these continuing concerns over security from terrorism have also affected the HRM functions in many organizations. One simple way in which this has occurred is in restricting the labor pool available to U.S. employers. Traditionally, most U.S. firms have been willing to hire non–U.S. citizens for certain types of jobs and to help those new employees attain the proper status with immigration officials. In fact, non-U.S. residents have been an important source for skilled labor especially in some technical fields. That has now changed. Many U.S. companies are now less willing to hire foreigners, especially

Concerns over security have also made many Americans less willing to travel abroad—especially to areas that are potentially dangerous. Although these concerns have been present for quite some time, the new feelings of vulnerability have resulted in U.S. business leaders being even less willing to travel to certain parts of the world on business. This, in turn, has necessitated an increased reliance on teleconferencing and other substitutes for face-to-face meetings. But the reluctance to travel abroad also makes it more difficult to manage overseas operations and more difficult to give managers expatriate assignments.

In addition, most U.S. firms are now engaging in high-level emergency preparedness planning. The World Trade Center attacks wiped out the entire financial records of some firms. In addition, although not a human-made disaster, Hurricane Katrina also destroyed the employee records for many firms in the Gulf Coast area. Many companies have often followed the practice of backing up important records, but those backup files were not always put in safe locations, which made them vulnerable as well. Today, heightened security concerns have led organizations to develop multiple backup systems as well as information technology systems that are not tied to a single location.

Perhaps the greatest impact of September 11 has been on the general sense of well-being. Although the color-coded threat level system was replaced in 2011, we still have the National Terror Advisory System that will focus on specific threats in geographical areas. Because these new warnings inform the public of the exact nature of any threat, the hope is that they will reduce the general stress level caused by the old system, which tended to make people afraid without helping them to prepare. It is interesting to note that concerns over security from terrorist attacks are relevant for people all over the world. What makes the situation in the United States so interesting is that Americans traditionally felt themselves isolated and insulated from such attacks. The United States has now really joined the global community in the sense that Americans realize they are vulnerable and share the same security concerns as most of the rest of the world's population.

In August 2005, Hurricane Katrina struck the Gulf Coast of the United States, breached the levees in New Orleans, and resulted in a large portion of New Orleans being underwater for weeks. In the immediate months following Katrina, surveys of stress in the city of New Orleans indicated that self-reported stress, as well as the incidence of psychosomatic symptoms, had increased dramatically, and security had become a major concern for many New Orleanians. In late 2009, however, the Centers for Disease Control and Prevention published the results of a study conducted on "happiness." Basically, the study involved asking people questions about how satisfied they were with their lives. The results showed that residents of Louisiana were the happiest in the United States.[39] Whatever the explanation, these results seem to suggest that although there is a great deal of stress in the lives of people today, it is possible to be resilient and happy, even in the face of adversity. As more Americans lose their jobs and their homes, perhaps there is something that can be learned from the people of Louisiana that will help us through the recent hard times.

Despite the increased sources of stress in the world, there are always people who can handle stress better than others. For these people, stress is a problem but not a debilitating one. It is not clear why some people are more resilient than others when they deal with stress and physical threats. In January 2010, a major earthquake struck Haiti. Perhaps a quarter of a million people died, but as soon as they could, survivors began rebuilding and getting back to their "normal" lives. The story was the same after the tsunami in Japan, flooding in China and Pakistan, earthquakes in South America in 2011 and 2012, and the terrorist attacks in France in 2015 and 2016. Perhaps there is something about the psychological makeup of all human beings that allows us to handle stress and security threats more easily.

CLOSING CASE
Bullying in the Workplace

While we often associate the term *bullying* with childhood behaviors, considerable research suggests that these behaviors can extend into the workplace. In fact, 28 percent of workers surveyed by CareerBuilder said that they had been bullied at work. The impact of bullying is real—19 percent of these workers left their jobs as a result of the bullying. In addition, workplace bullying has been associated with a number of counterproductive attitudes and behaviors such as disengagement, job dissatisfaction, and symptoms of anxiety, depression, burnout, and psychological distress. Rosemary Haefner, Vice President of Human

Photographee.eu/Shutterstock.com

Resources at CareerBuilder, goes on to explain, "One of the most surprising takeaways from the study was that bullying impacts workers of all backgrounds, regardless of race, education, income, and levels of authority within the organization. Many of the workers who have experienced this don't confront the bully or elect not to report the incidents, which can prolong a negative work experience that leads some to leave their jobs."

You might wonder exactly what bullying looks like in the workplace. It can take many forms, but the most common include being falsely accused of mistakes, constant criticism, gossip, belittling comments, purposeful exclusion from

(Continued)

(Closing Case – continued)

projects or meetings, and even physical intimidation. Bullying is generally a long-term, persistent pattern of behavior intended to cause humiliation, offense, or distress. Bullies tended to be older than the worker and were most commonly their boss or someone else above them in the organization. Interestingly, workers in governmental organizations reported being bullied nearly twice as often as those in corporate settings. Bullying appears to disproportionately affect racial and ethnic minorities, as well as the disabled. It appears that bullying is slightly less common when a worker has a higher level of education or higher pay, although workers at all levels were generally equally likely to have been bullied at some point in their careers.

In light of these statistics, there's a very real chance that you may be the victim of a bully in the future. Of those surveyed, nearly half confronted their bully, but this was successful in remedying the situation only about half the time. Unfortunately, contacting the HR department appears to be even less effective, with no action taken 58 percent of the time. Should you find yourself in this situation, it is important to document incidents of bullying and keep track of what happened and who was present. It may be a good idea to start by speaking directly with the bully—many times a bully may not understand the effects of their actions. Finally, it's important to focus on the resolution, rather than dwelling on what has already happened.[40]

Case Questions

1. What do you think causes bullying in the workplace?

2. As an HR manager, what policies might you implement to reduce or eliminate bullying?

3. Are there ever any circumstances where bullying is appropriate?

STUDY TOOLS 12

READY TO STUDY?

In the book, you can:

☐ Rip out the chapter review card at the back of the book for a handy summary of the chapter and key terms.

ONLINE AT CENGAGEBRAIN.COM YOU CAN:

☐ Collect StudyBits while you read and study the chapter.

☐ Quiz yourself on key concepts.

☐ Find videos for further exploration.

☐ Prepare for tests with HR4 Flash Cards as well as those you create.

13 | Motivation at Work

Francis Vachon/Alamy Stock Photo

After finishing this chapter go to **PAGE 334** for **STUDY TOOLS**

LEARNING OBJECTIVES

13-1 Describe the basic model of performance

13-2 Discuss motivation and human needs

13-3 Identify the basic process models of motivation, and describe an integrative model of motivation

13-4 Describe other related theories and perspectives on motivation

Francis Vachon/Alamy Stock Photo

OPENING CASE
Raising the Bar

Aetna recently made a startling announcement: the insurance giant increased the base wage of its lowest-paid employees to at least $16 per hour, more than double the federal minimum wage. This increase in pay affects 12 percent of Aetna's 48,000 employees and has a significant impact on both the employees and the company. The lowest paid employees, who had a base rate of $12 per hour, received a 33 percent increase in pay, with the average increase of those affected being 11 percent. In addition, the company is extending health insurance benefits to nearly 7,000 employees, lowering their out-of-pocket costs by up to $4,000.

While the employees are no doubt delighted, this increase in compensation and benefits comes with a very high price tag. The total cost of the wage and benefit enhancements was more than $25 million in 2016. What motivated Aetna to make this move? Well, for starters, the company has estimated that turnover costs them about $120 million a year. Research has shown that low-wage workers are more likely to quit than their higher-paid counterparts. The costs associated with recruiting, hiring, and training new employees can be very high, so a high turnover rate comes with significant hidden costs.

In addition, CEO Mark Bertolini thinks that the pay raise will make workers more productive. Many of the lowest-paid workers are employed in the company's call centers. This can be an extremely stressful job, with callers often upset over what is not covered by their insurance or even the events that led up to their claim, whether it's damage to their home or car or an illness or injury. According to Kally Dunn, a call center supervisor from Fresno, "When they call, . . . they're angry. And so it's just a lot of de-escalating, calming them down, . . . reassuring them." On top of the stress of their job, these low-wage workers face the challenges of paying their day-to-day expenses with such low pay. One of the affected employees from the Fresno call center is Fabian Arredondo. He says, "Finance can be one of the main stresses in people's lives. And when you can pull some relief away from that stress, I definitely think it makes for—you know, a happy employee is a productive employee."

This is exactly the logic that led Aetna to take this bold move. Bertolini was surprised to find that many of his employees were on public assistance, such as food stamps and Medicare. He was shocked "that we as a thriving organization, as a successful company, a *Fortune 100* company, should have people that were living like that among the ranks of our employees." Aetna was careful to ensure that the raises that they awarded employees were substantial enough to offset any loss of public assistance benefits, so that they truly ended up in a better financial position after the change.

> "Finance can be one of the main stresses in people's lives. And when you can pull some relief away from that stress, I definitely think it makes for—you know, a happy employee is a productive employee."
>
> —FABIAN ARREDONDO. AETNA EMPLOYEE

Bertolini also believes that Aetna's shareholders, the owners of the company, are supportive of the change. "We positioned it with them on the economics first, but went to this very notion of 'this isn't fair.' We need to invest in our employees. We need to help restore the middle class, and that should be good for the economy as a whole. And so for us it is as much—probably, for me personally, more—a moral argument than it is a financial one."

Economists Justin Wolfers and Jan Zilinsky recently released a study of the impact of this type of pay increase in private-sector businesses in the United States. Wolfers and Zilinsky found research to support the conclusion that higher wages can improve worker productivity and performance. They cited one study which showed that more than half of the cost of a pay increase can be offset by increases in productivity and decreases in turnover-related costs. In addition, by offering higher wages, companies are able to recruit and hire better employees and decrease disciplinary issues. The benefits of higher wages also extend to quality and customer service. A number of recent studies found that employers reported improvements in both customer service and the quality of production.

Aetna is not alone in this strategy. Gap announced that it would raise its lowest hourly wage to $10. The company saw an immediate 10 percent increase in the number of applicants for jobs. And IKEA, the Scandinavian retail giant, recently announced that it was increasing its workers' base pay to $10.76 per hour. Is this a trend that will continue? Will companies increase worker pay to improve performance and cut costs? Only time will tell.[1]

THINK IT OVER

1. Do you agree or disagree with the notion that increasing pay will directly motivate employees to be more productive?

2. Do you think improving employee benefits would have the same effect as raising pay? Why or why not?

Why would one person like a job and another person dislike that same job? Even more germane, if two people are equally capable of performing the same task, why might one consistently outperform the other? We might say that one tries harder or exerts more effort, but what we really mean is that one person is more motivated than the other to perform well. **Motivation** determines how a person will exert his or her effort. More specifically, it represents the forces operating on the person to exert effort, as well as the direction in which that effort will be exerted. One person might work hard at academics while another person might work hard at sports. Both are motivated, but the direction of their motivations are quite different and will produce much different outcomes.

Motivation at work is a critical determinant of what will occur on the job. An effective manager not only must motivate employees to exert *some* effort but also must make sure the effort is exerted in a way that produces organizationally valued outcomes. The human resource (HR) manager must design systems that make it more likely that employees will exert effort in these desirable ways. The key is to understand how we can motivate people to engage in behaviors we desire. As we will discuss, several models or theories of motivation have been proposed as a way to accomplish this. We will review some of these theories and discuss some of their strengths and weaknesses. No one model of motivation, however, is guaranteed to work in all situations for all people. Instead, several models of motivation provide us with insights into how to motivate people; by taking them together, we can formulate a set of clear suggestions about how HR managers could develop systems that improve work motivation, lead to improved performance, and help develop competitive advantage for a firm.

13-1 A BASIC MODEL OF PERFORMANCE

For most of us, the possibility of playing basketball like LeBron James, hitting a tennis ball like Venus Williams, or singing like the most recent winner on *American Idol* has little to do with motivation. We simply lack the necessary talent to perform at those levels (and few people do). Hence, it should be clear that any level of performance on any task is not solely a function of motivation—it is a joint function of ability, motivation, and context. The HR manager must play a critical role in determining two of these critical elements: the ability and the motivation sides of performance. (The third element, context, refers to such things as equipment and materials. Although Venus Williams can certainly hit a tennis ball and might be motivated to do so at any given time, if her racket is improperly strung or there is a defect in her shoes that causes pain when she runs, then she will still not be able to play well. Context, however, is usually not the purview of HR.)

Specifically, the human resource management (HRM) decisions we discussed in Part Two of this book dealt with the determinants of ability on the job. If the HR manager collected the right information about the job requirements, recruited qualified people, selected the best among these recruits, and then trained them on exactly what they were required to do, it is quite likely that all the employees in the firm would be capable of performing their jobs at a reasonably high level of proficiency. The difference between employees who performed at a mediocre level and those who performed at a higher level, would then be a function of motivation alone.

Of course, no HR manager does a perfect job of recruiting, selecting, or training, and so not everyone may be capable of performing at the level the organization desires. For some of these employees, though, they may still be able to reach desired performance levels by exerting an extraordinary level of effort. In other words, high levels of motivation can compensate for lower levels of ability—up to a point. Similarly, if an employee was extremely talented (or able), then she or he might be able to perform at a desired level while exerting little effort. So either ability or motivation can compensate for the other up to a point. But to maximize performance, we need a workforce that is fully capable of doing its various jobs and a system that motivates its workers to exert their highest levels of effort. For the remainder of this chapter, we will assume that the HR manager has staffed the organization with capable people and that the only issue is how to motivate them to do their best work.

Motivation determines how a person will exert his or her effort. It represents the forces operating on the person to exert effort, as well as the direction in which that effort will be exerted.

—THEODORE ROOSEVELT, 26TH PRESIDENT OF THE UNITED STATES

13-2 MOTIVATION AND NEEDS

Everyone has needs they attempt to satisfy. For most of us on a day-to-day basis, these needs are pretty simple and relatively easy to satisfy. We can usually find food and drink when we are hungry or thirsty, and we can usually find shelter when it is raining. Therefore, these types of needs are not really capable of determining long-term behavior. But what would you do if you were shipwrecked on a desert island? Probably the first thing you would do, after you figured out that you could not get off the island, would be to search for food and water. Hunger and thirst, at this level, are critical and basic needs that must be satisfied in order to survive. After you located food and water, you would probably begin working on finding or making a shelter and only then might you begin searching to see if there was anyone else on the island. Through all of this, you would probably not worry much about how you looked or how others might view your behavior if they could see you. All your behavior would be aimed at satisfying basic needs in life, and only after these were satisfied would you begin thinking about other, less critical needs. This view includes several **need-based theories** of motivation.

Some readers will recognize that the preceding discussion is similar to Abraham Maslow's **hierarchy of needs**. Maslow proposed this well-known theory of motivation almost 80 years ago,[2] and it has been quite popular ever since. The basic hierarchy model is presented in Figure 13.1 and illustrates the five categories of needs arranged from the most basic needs at the bottom to the more complex needs at the top. The lowest level of needs, labeled *physiological needs*, includes such things as the need for food or water. The next level of needs, *security needs*, includes anything involving a safe and secure environment. This is followed by *social needs*, which include the need to have meaningful interactions and relationships with others. Next come *esteem needs*, which include the need to have a positive view of oneself, and finally *self-actualization needs*, or the need to reach one's personal potential.

According to the model, only one level of need is capable of motivating behavior at any given time. This level of need is said to be **prepotent**. Thus, if we are truly starving (rather than just in need of a snack), we will not worry about shelter or other people until we get

Gelpi JM/Shutterstock.com

something to eat. Only after we find food and satisfy our physiological needs will we worry about security. Therefore, the other important aspect of the theory is that humans are said to move neatly up the hierarchy, one need at a time. There is some disagreement as to whether the theory suggests that anyone can be completely self-actualized, although at one point in time, Maslow did propose a list of people he suggested were self-actualized, including the pope and Eleanor Roosevelt.

Maslow's theory is useful because it focuses on needs and suggests that not everyone would be motivated by the same set of needs at any one time. Thus, from an organizational point of view, if we tried to motivate employees by meeting their esteem needs (perhaps by assigning grand titles or giving people more prestigious office locations such as the corner office), this would only be effective for employees for whom these needs were important. This plan would not work for employees who were focused on more basic needs that might be satisfied by a pay increase (rather than a larger office).

Considerable research has been done on Maslow's theory,[3] and the results of that research suggest that people are motivated by more than one level of need at any point in time and do not always march neatly up the hierarchy— sometimes they move down the hierarchy as well. In fact, some years later, Clayton Alderfer proposed a variation on Maslow's theory that he called **ERG theory**. Alderfer's theory substituted three levels of needs for Maslow's five (and he labeled them *existence needs*, *relatedness needs*, and *growth needs*). These three levels simply collapse Maslow's five categories into three, but the more important aspect of Alderfer's theory is that he

Need-based theories are theories of motivation that focus on what motivates a person, rather than on how that motivation occurs.

Probably the best known of the need-based theories, the **hierarchy of needs** model proposed by Abraham Maslow, specifies five levels of needs that are capable of motivating behavior: physiological, security, social, esteem, and self-actualization.

According to Maslow's theory, **prepotent** needs are those specific needs (of the five levels in the model) that are capable of motivating behavior at any given point in time.

A need-based theory of motivation proposed by Clayton Alderfer, **ERG theory** involves three rather than five levels of needs, and also allows for someone to regress from a higher-level need to a lower-level need.

FIG 13.1 MASLOW'S HIERARCHY OF NEEDS

Source: Adapted from Abraham H. Maslow, "A Theory of Human Motivation," *Psychological Review*, 1943, vol. 50, pp. 374–396.

suggested people might move either up or down the hierarchy, and he allowed for multiple levels of needs being prepotent. So, after we satisfy our existence needs and move up to relatedness needs, if those relatedness needs are not being satisfied (i.e., they are being frustrated), then we will regress, and existence needs will again be prepotent. Thus, this theory suggests that individuals who cannot find meaningful relationships might spend their time accumulating money instead.

Whichever model we accept, the important thing to remember is that not everyone will be motivated by the same things at any one time and that satisfying needs is an important source of motivation. As discussed in Contemporary Challenges in HR, both work and nonwork forces can be important motivating factors. Managers, therefore, need to help employees balance their work and nonwork activities. Before leaving these models, though, it is worth commenting on the role of money in need-based models of motivation. Money has the potential for satisfying all of the needs proposed by Maslow (and Alderfer). Unless we are on a desert island, we probably satisfy hunger and thirst by buying food and water at the supermarket, which requires money.

Security needs are satisfied by a home (which we must pay for) and by things such as insurance and a pension (which also require money).

Social needs are satisfied by having friends. But money also plays a role. Having money, for instance, allows us to have the leisure time to meet friends as well as to spend time in settings where we might interact with other people. Money also brings us status, which helps to satisfy esteem needs. Furthermore, even if most people are not self-actualized by simply earning more, they may be self-actualized by being able to contribute a new wing to a museum or by paying for an artist to appear at the local opera—activities that require money.

We should also note that there are other need-based theories of motivation as well. The best known is probably Frederick Herzberg's **dual factor theory**,[4] which identifies motivators and hygiene factors as two sets of conditions at work that can satisfy needs. The research on this theory provides little empirical support for the model, however,[5] and so we will not discuss it in any detail. We note, however, that the "motivator" side of this theory provides the basis for much of the work that has been done in the area of job enrichment, which we discuss in some detail in Chapter 14.

Need-based theories only explain part of the story of motivation, however. Needs can help us understand what will motivate someone, but they do not tell us much about how the person becomes motivated or how the person decides where to exert his or her effort. To understand more about that, we need to turn to the various process-based models of motivation.

A need-based theory proposed by Frederick Herzberg, **dual factor theory** identifies motivators and hygiene factors as two sets of conditions at work that can satisfy needs. Research into this theory, however, has provided little empirical support for its model.

Contemporary Challenges in HR

Striving for Balance

The good news is that 60 percent of HR executives are satisfied with the work–life services that their companies offer employees. The bad news is that only 16 percent of their employees agree with them.

According to a study conducted by the Corporate Executive Board (CEB), a global network of business professionals, the disconnect results from the fact that HR managers tend to value different services than employees do. They tend to assume, for example, that such expensive, high-profile services as onsite gyms and health-care options are what employees want in a workplace that claims to promote good work–life balance. In reality, only about 20 percent of employees place any value on such services.

So, what do employees—managers and subordinates alike—really want? The answer seems to be more control over their time. More than 60 percent of the 50,000 workers polled in the CEB study specified flextime schedules as the single most important work–life benefit that an employer can offer. Flexible scheduling, or "flextime," allows employees to adjust the time and/or place for completing their work.

One company that's happy with its experiments in flexible-work programs is KPMG, an Atlanta-based tax and audit consultancy. KPMG is in an industry in which turnover is traditionally higher for women than for men, but the numbers in the financial industry also reflect broader trends in the U.S. workforce. According to a survey reported by the *Harvard Business Review*, for instance, 24 percent of male executives take a career "off-ramp" at

Creatista/Shutterstock.com

some point; that is, they voluntarily leave their careers for a period of time. When it comes to women, the figure is 37 percent; for women with children, it's 43 percent. Among men, 12 percent have interrupted their careers to take care of children or elders; among women, it's the reason cited by 44 percent.

Because of data like these, KPMG launched a campaign a few years ago to transform itself into an "employer of choice" by offering employees a range of options for balancing work and home life. Family-friendly policies fall into such categories as flexibility (flextime/telecommuting, job sharing) and family resources (backup child-care and elder-care, discounts at child-care centers). According to Barbara Wankoff, director of Workplace Solutions, 70 percent of company employees now work flexible hours. "Our employees," she says, "tend to be ambitious and career oriented. They want to develop professionally and build a career, but they also have lives as parents, sons or daughters, and spouses. So, at KPMG, we're promoting a culture of flexibility to help them manage the complexities of work and life."

In one recent year, KPMG managed to improve retention of female employees by 10 percent and to increase the total number of women in its workforce by 15 percent. KPMG also says that if it hadn't offered flexible scheduling to female employees with young children, it would have lost about two-thirds of them. "In order to retain the best and the brightest," says Kristen Piersol-Stockton, one of Barbara Wankoff's regional directors, "we have to be flexible in how, when, and where the work gets done."[6]

"KPMG launched a campaign a few years ago to transform itself into an 'employer of choice' by offering employees a range of options for balancing work and home life."

THINK IT OVER

1. How much value do you put on work–life balance? Does this vary for different people? Why?

2. What do you do (or what will you do if you haven't yet started your career) to achieve a balance between work and life?

13-3 PROCESS THEORIES OF MOTIVATION

Process theories of motivation are concerned with *how* a person becomes motivated to perform in a certain way. These theories also tell only part of the story, so we need to integrate some aspects of need-based theories with some aspects of process theories to understand human motivation better. We attempt such an integration at the end of this chapter.

13-3a Reinforcement Theory

Reinforcement theory is probably the most basic process theory, but its simplicity, as well as its effectiveness and applicability to work settings, make this an important theory to discuss. Stated quite simply, **reinforcement theory**, usually associated with B. F. Skinner,[7] proposes that all behavior is a function of its consequences. Figure 13.2 presents the model of behavior that underlies reinforcement theory. The model has three components only: stimulus, response, and outcomes.

1. The *stimulus* is something in the environment that cues us about a behavior. A bulletin board might advertise a soft drink brand, and this stimulus might remind us we are thirsty and want to buy the beverage.

2. The *response* is the behavior that we exhibit in reaction to the stimulus. In this case, it might involve going into a store and buying the soft drink.

3. The *outcomes* refer to the consequences that follow the response. So after we put a dollar in the machine, several things might happen: The machine might reject the dollar and send it back out; the machine might take the dollar and deposit a soft drink; or the machine might take the dollar and keep it without depositing the beverage.

Reinforcement theory suggests that the response a person makes to the stimulus is a function of what he or she expects will happen. This means that reinforcement theory is really about learning behaviors through some type of experience. So if the last time you deposited a dollar in a soft drink machine you received the beverage you wanted (a positive outcome), the next time you encounter a soft drink machine and feel thirsty, you are likely to deposit a dollar again (i.e., repeat the behavior). If your dollar was rejected the last time you tried (really, no outcome), you might try again, although if your money is rejected over and over, eventually you might stop even trying to buy a soft drink from a machine. If the machine "ate" your dollar last time (a negative outcome), then you will be less likely to repeat the behavior this time and probably will not deposit another dollar.

Note that the key here is that we learn what consequences to expect over time, and these expectations guide our behavior. If we apply this to a work context, we can think about a supervisor asking an employee to stay late to work on a special project. Assuming the employee agrees, it is possible that the supervisor will be grateful, praise the employee, and perhaps even give the employee some time off. This would be a positive outcome for the employee, and this employee would be very likely to volunteer the next time the supervisor asked for someone to stay late.

On the other hand, the supervisor might say and do nothing after the employee's late-night assignment. If this were the case, the employee might or might not be willing to stay late again, but, eventually, if the supervisor continued to ignore the employee's staying late, he or she would no longer be willing to remain and work. Finally, the supervisor could respond by suggesting that because the employee obviously has nothing else to do, she or he should stay late tomorrow night as well. This would represent a negative outcome for the employee, and he or she would not be likely to stay late ever again. Now let us assume that the organization would like all of its employees to be willing to stay late, so that agreeing to work late is a desirable behavior. These scenarios can then be reduced to a simple set of rules as illustrated in Figure 13.3.

1. The first scenario in Figure 13.3 is known as **positive reinforcement** and represents a

---

Process theories are motivation theories that focus on how people become motivated and what they are motivated to do rather than on what motivates them.

Reinforcement theory is a process theory, usually associated with B. F. Skinner, which proposes that all behavior is a function of its consequences.

A term from reinforcement theory, **positive reinforcement** refers to the situation in which a behavior is followed by positive consequences and thus is likely to be repeated.

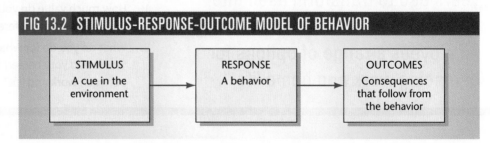

FIG 13.2 STIMULUS-RESPONSE-OUTCOME MODEL OF BEHAVIOR

STIMULUS	RESPONSE	OUTCOMES
A cue in the environment	A behavior	Consequences that follow from the behavior

FIG 13.3 REINFORCEMENT AND BEHAVIOR

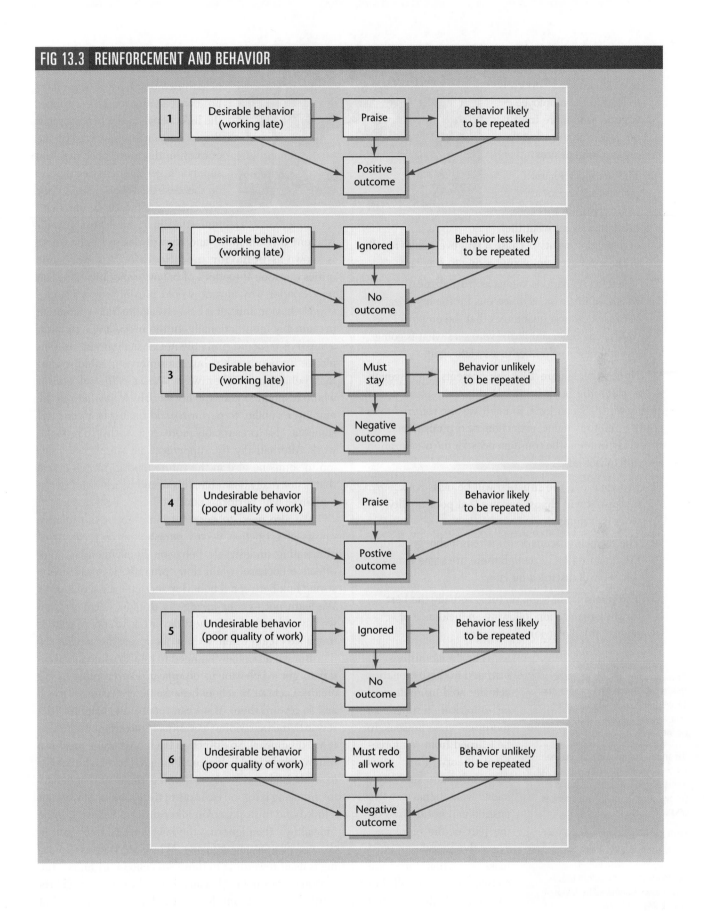

very positive situation from the organization's perspective. The rewards are likely to lead to the employee volunteering more frequently, which is what the organization desires.

iStockphoto.com/Alvarez

2. The second scenario pictured is known as **extinction**; in this case, extinction is not what the organization wants because it will eventually result in the employee not volunteering to stay late.

3. The third scenario is known as **punishment**, which, in this case, is disastrous for the organization because it almost guarantees that the employee (as well as any other employee who sees what is going on) will never volunteer to stay late again.

Notice that Figure 13.3 also presents three scenarios in which the behavior involved is undesirable (poor quality work). Scenarios 4, 5, and 6 are also referred to as positive reinforcement, extinction, and punishment, respectively, but now the consequences for the organization are quite different.

1. In scenario 4, the situation will be disastrous because it will almost en-sure that poor quality work continues.

2. The extinction scenario (5) is reasonably good for the organization (although there are some issues that we will discuss a bit later).

3. The punishment scenario (6) is actually the best for the organization following an incidence of undesirable behavior.

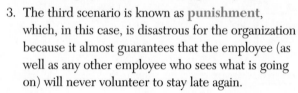

Also a term from reinforcement theory, **extinction** refers to the situation in which a behavior is followed by no consequences and eventually disappears.

Yet another term from reinforcement theory, **punishment** refers to a situation in which a behavior is followed by negative consequences and so is not repeated.

Behavior modification is the combination of positive reinforcement with either punishment or extinction that replaces an undesired behavior with a desired behavior.

The relationships illustrated in these scenarios actually hold up quite well in empirical testing,[8] so there are clear lessons to be learned from reinforcement theory. First, it is critical that the supervisor know what behaviors are desired and not desired on the part of the employee. Then the supervisor must make sure that there are consequences for all behaviors and that desired behaviors are followed by positive consequences and undesired behaviors are followed by negative consequences (or perhaps no consequences). The stronger the links between the behavior and the consequences perceived by the employee, the more likely will the supervisor get the behavior that he or she desires. When a supervisor works to simultaneously eliminate undesired behavior (through punishment or extinction) and reward desired behavior, it is known as **behavior modification**. However, some critics question the ethics of behavior modification. You may wonder why anyone would possibly reward undesired behavior, and yet it happens all the time—although presumably unintentionally. In the preceding examples, a supervisor would probably not actually praise an employee for poor quality, but the supervisor could reward that behavior in other ways. Perhaps the supervisor would respond to poor-quality work by losing faith in the employee's ability to perform good-quality work and ask someone else (presumably more trustworthy) to redo the work. Alternatively, the supervisor may simply assign his job to someone else in the future, and if the job is one that is not really desirable, this would be a reward to the employee who performs poorly.

We also need to say a bit more about the relative merits of extinction versus punishment as a means of eliminating undesirable behavior. Punishment is quite effective because, when done properly, it establishes a strong link between a behavior and a negative outcome. We learn not to over indulge in drinking alcohol when we have a headache the next day; we learn not to eat too much ice cream when we have an upset stomach later.

But we do not always need to punish someone in order to get a behavior to disappear. For example, some children act out in school because their classmates laugh and so reward them. If we can remove the laughter (the reward), the behavior will eventually be extinguished (i.e., it will disappear). So extinction is a more benign means to remove undesired behavior, although it takes a bit longer to work. It also will not work with certain types of behavior. Smoking is a good example of the problem. If we want a loved one to stop smoking (because we believe it to be unhealthy), then ignoring the behavior will not result in the person quitting smoking. Why not? Because smoking is itself rewarding to those who choose to smoke; the person is not smoking because she or he expects to get rewarded by others (surely not in today's environment) but because nicotine is addictive, and smoking satisfies the craving for nicotine. If we ignore the smoking, the person is actually being rewarded because he or she is getting the craved drug. We can only stop someone from smoking by punishing them for it or by finding a substitute source of nicotine that is less harmful (e.g., a nicotine patch).

Note also that punishment (and positive reinforcement) works best when there is a strong link between behavior and consequences. *Every* time the undesired behavior is exhibited, it is punished. But that is quite difficult to manage and requires a great deal of monitoring. Furthermore, if someone realizes that undesired behavior is only punished when it is "caught," then the person is motivated to not get caught rather than to cease the behavior. This is how we explain the fact that motorists often speed until they see a police officer. As a result, it is easier, and more pleasant, if we can change behavior by focusing on positive reinforcement rather than on punishment. Employees are drawn to supervisors who reward them but hide from supervisors who punish them—and it is difficult to supervise employees who are hiding!

Finally, although rewards and punishment are most effective when they are administered following every behavior (also referred to as *continuous reinforcement*), they can still work if they are administered at some times but not others—that is, by **partial reinforcement** (it can be applied to punishment as well, but the reward case is simpler). Specifically, the rewards are administered on some schedule that dictates when the reward is and is not administered. These schedules can vary on two dimensions, so that there are four different schedules of reinforcement that can be used as illustrated in Table 13.1.

First, there are interval schedules versus ratio schedules. **Interval schedules** reinforce behavior as a function of the passage of time. A schedule in which someone is rewarded every 10 minutes as long as they exhibit a desired behavior would be an interval schedule. A **ratio schedule** reinforces behavior as a function of how many times it occurs. For example, rewarding someone every fifth time a desired behavior occurs is an example of a ratio schedule. But in addition, the ratio or the interval can either be fixed or variable; the number of times the behavior must be displayed or the amount of time that must pass before a reward is given can be constant over time or can change. Examples include the following.

1. With a **fixed interval schedule**, employees are paid once every 2 weeks as long as they continue to do their jobs.

2. With a **variable interval schedule**, employees are promoted as a function of time with the firm, but the amount of time between promotions can vary substantially.

3. With a **fixed ratio schedule**, an employee is paid

Audrey Voskressensky/Shutterstock.com

Partial reinforcement means rewarding a behavior only part of the time rather than all the time (it can be applied to punishment as well, but the reward case is simpler).

Interval schedules are partial reinforcement schedules in which behavior is reinforced as a function of the passage of time—for example, rewarding someone every 10 minutes as long as they were exhibiting desired behavior.

Ratio schedules are partial reinforcement schedules in which behavior is reinforced as a function of how many times the behavior occurs—for example, rewarding someone every fifth time a desired behavior occurs.

Fixed interval schedules are interval schedules in which the amount of time that must pass before a reward is given is constant over time.

Variable interval schedules are interval schedules in which the amount of time that must pass before a reward is given can change from one reward period to another.

Fixed ratio schedules are ratio schedules in which the number of times a behavior must occur before it is rewarded remains constant over time.

TABLE 13.1 EFFECTS OF DIFFERENT PARTIAL REINFORCEMENT SCHEDULES

Schedule	Time to Learn	Resistance to Extinction	Productivity[a]
Continuous	Shortest	Least resistant	Average
Fixed interval	Longer	Resistant	Lowest
Variable interval	Longest	Most resistant	Next lowest
Fixed ratio	Longer	Resistant	Next highest
Variable ratio	Longest	Most resistant	Highest

[a]Productivity refers to the number of desired responses or behavior exhibited.

on a piece rate such as $1 for every 10 units produced.

4. With a **variable ratio schedule**, a bonus system is based on performance, with the number of units that must be produced to obtain a bonus varying over time.

From the perspective of the HR manager, or even the general manager, a few things about these partial reinforcement schedules are worth noting. First, if we are trying to shape an employee's behavior through reinforcement, it will take longer for the employee to "learn" the correct behavior under any partial reinforcement schedule as compared to a continuous reinforcement schedule, and it will take even longer for the employee to learn a behavior under any variable schedule. On the other hand, we might also be concerned about a learned behavior disappearing because we fail to reinforce it for a while. Here we are interested in how resistant any learned behavior might be to extinction. Any partial reinforcement schedule is more resistant to extinction than a continuous reinforcement schedule, and furthermore, any variable schedule (i.e., variable ratio or variable interval) is more resistant to extinction than any fixed schedule. Finally, ratio schedules, because they reward individual responses, result in higher levels of behavior (e.g., higher productivity) than do interval schedules, and variable ratio schedules produce more consistent levels of behavior (e.g., output) than do fixed ratio schedules because employees will slow down right after receiving a reinforcement and speed up again as they anticipate the next reinforcement.[9] All of this is summarized in Table 13.1.

13-3b Expectancy Theory

Expectancy theory, sometimes referred to as **VIE theory**,[10] is a fairly complex theory from a cognitive perspective because it casts the employee in the role of decision maker. It developed from early work in psychology,[11] as well as basic economic theory, which assumes that people work to maximize their personal (positive) outcomes. Expectancy theory is concerned with three components and the links among them. The components are termed *effort*, *performance*, and *outcomes* and are used in the usual ways. The links among these three, however, are more central to the theory.

The first link is between effort and performance, and it is sometimes referred to as the *expectancy* term. Specifically, the **effort-to-performance expectancy** is a person's perception of the probability that an increase in effort will result in an increase in performance. This can range from 0 to 1.0. Expectancy is 0 when the employee believes that increasing effort will definitely not increase performance, and this could be the result of a task that is too easy ("I can perform at the highest level with no effort") or a task that is too difficult ("No matter how hard I try, I cannot do any better"). Clearly, ability plays a role in determining this expectancy term because a lack of ability (from poor selection or poor training) will always result in a low level of expectancy.

The second link is between performance and outcomes and is sometimes referred to as the *instrumentality* term. Specifically, the **performance-to-outcomes expectancy (instrumentality)** is the person's perception of the probability that improved performance will lead to certain outcomes. Operationally, this is viewed as a correlation coefficient, indicating that as performance improves, the chances of gaining outcomes can either go up (a positive correlation), remain unchanged (a zero correlation), or go down (a negative correlation). As such, the values can range from +1.0, through 0, to −1.0. We will explain how this works as soon as we discuss the final link in the model.

The final piece of the model is not really a link between two other components but an extra component. **Valence** refers to how attractive or unattractive an outcome looks to a person. Thus, as noted previously, many outcomes might be associated with work, and some of these might be quite attractive, whereas others may be rather unattractive. For example, good performance might be associated with receiving a raise, which would

---

Variable ratio schedules are ratio schedules in which the number of times a behavior must occur before it is rewarded changes over time.

Expectancy theory (or **VIE theory**) is a fairly complex process theory of motivation that casts the employee in the role of decision maker. Basically, an employee decides whether or not to exert effort, depending on the outcomes he or she anticipates receiving for those efforts as based on calculations concerning expectancies, instrumentalities, valences, and the links among these three components.

Effort-to-performance expectancy (or **expectancy**) is a person's perception of the probability that an increase in effort will result in an increase in performance. This can range from 0 to 1.0.

Performance-to-outcomes expectancy (or **instrumentality**) is a person's perception of the probability that improved performance will lead to certain outcomes. Operationally seen as a correlation coefficient indicating that as performance improves, the chances of gaining outcomes can either go up (a positive correlation), remain unchanged (a zero correlation), or go down (a negative correlation).

Valence refers to how attractive or unattractive an outcome is for a person.

be attractive to most people. But poor performance might be associated with being fired, which would presumably be unattractive. Another way of stating this is to suggest that improving performance *increases* the chances of receiving a raise (thus a positive correlation or instrumentality) but *decreases* the chances of being fired (thus a negative correlation or instrumentality), and it has no effect on the chances of winning the lottery (thus, a zero correlation or instrumentality). Valences can thus be positive, negative, or neutral, and it is possible to specify that some outcomes are more positive (or negative) than others.

Note that all the terms in expectancy theory are based on a person's perceptions. In other words, we are less interested in whether, in fact, a person's efforts will result in increased performance and more interested in whether the person believes that to be the case. Of course, if individuals' perceptions are incorrect, then they will learn this over time and adjust their perceptions, but it is essential to remember that we are dealing with perceived links here, not the actual relationships between the components in the model.

Figure 13.4 illustrates the way the model works and indicates that the model is used to estimate the "force" operating on the employee to increase her or his effort. Note that in the example, the expectancy is set at 1.0, suggesting that there is a certainty that increased effort will lead to improved performance. There are also three outcomes in the example: two positive (pay raise and winning the lottery) and one negative (getting fired). Winning the lottery is more attractive than getting a pay raise. The key here, though, is the instrumentality term. Although winning the lottery is attractive, improved performance is not associated with increased chances of winning the lottery, and so this drops from consideration (0 times 3 is 0), suggesting that winning the lottery does not play a role in an employee's decision to increase

effort at work. Notice, too, that getting fired is a negative outcome, but that increased performance decreases the chances of getting fired, producing a negative instrumentality. When we multiply two negatives, we get a positive, suggesting here that increasing performance makes it less likely that an employee will be fired, which is really a benefit of improved performance.

In the example, the force is calculated to be positive, which suggests that the employee should increase effort on the job. We could imagine a situation in which the force would be negative (suggesting there would be no chance of improving effort because it would result in bad things only) or a situation in which the force would be less positive, and so it would be less likely, but still somewhat likely, that the employee would increase effort. If any term in this model goes to 0, the resulting force goes to 0. This also makes sense because there would be no reason for an employee to increase effort if (1) performance was unlikely to improve as a result of that effort, (2) there were no outcomes associated with any improved performance, or (3) increased performance would result in some good outcomes but be canceled out by negative outcomes.

Research on expectancy theory supports the general logic of the theory, but not many of the specific mechanisms, and it suggests that the theory is much more rational and calculating than are most employees.[12] Several variations on expectancy theory also have been proposed,[13] the most comprehensive of which was put forth by Naylor, Pritchard, and Ilgen,[14] and which we discuss later in the context of performance-enhancement interventions. In any case, expectancy theory has important lessons for the HR manager. First, this theory underscores the importance of selecting the right employees for the job and then training them so that they can perform their jobs effectively. The theory also suggests that it is important for the organization to have as

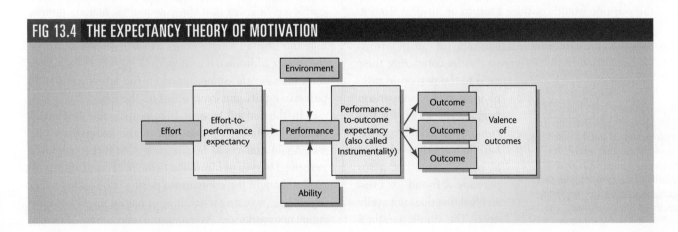

FIG 13.4 THE EXPECTANCY THEORY OF MOTIVATION

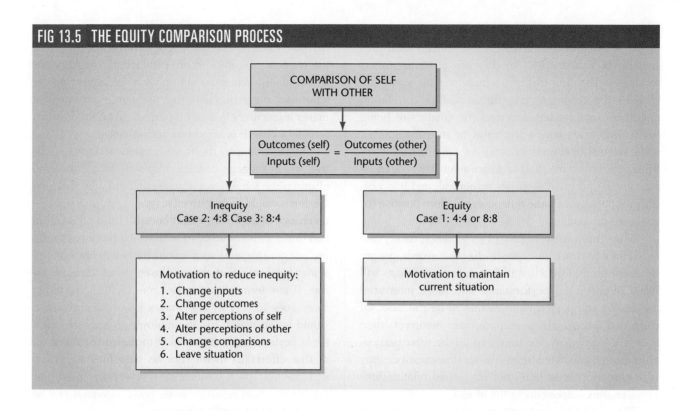

FIG 13.5 THE EQUITY COMPARISON PROCESS

COMPARISON OF SELF
WITH OTHER

$$\frac{\text{Outcomes (self)}}{\text{Inputs (self)}} = \frac{\text{Outcomes (other)}}{\text{Inputs (other)}}$$

Inequity
Case 2: 4:8 Case 3: 8:4

Equity
Case 1: 4:4 or 8:8

Motivation to reduce inequity:
1. Change inputs
2. Change outcomes
3. Alter perceptions of self
4. Alter perceptions of other
5. Change comparisons
6. Leave situation

Motivation to maintain
current situation

many desirable outcomes associated with improved performance as possible. Finally, the theory suggests that organizations can best influence performance by establishing clear links between increased performance and rewards. This will be the basis for our discussion of incentive pay plans in Chapter 14.

13-3c Equity Theory

J. Stacey Adams developed another somewhat narrow but useful process theory called **equity theory**.[15] This theory is most concerned with a person's perceived inputs to a (work) setting and the outcomes he or she receives from that setting. The theory suggests that everyone calculates the ratio of inputs to outcomes, almost the way one would consider a return on any investment. But after individuals calculate this ratio for themselves, they then must determine if their ratio (or rate of return) is "fair." They try to determine this by comparing their ratio to the perceived ratio of some other comparison person. The target for this comparison could be anyone an employee chooses to use—a coworker, a supervisor, a friend, or even an ideal that does not really exist. The employee then

> **Equity theory** is concerned with a person's perceived inputs to a (work) setting and the outcomes received from that setting. The theory suggests that everyone calculates the ratio of inputs to outcomes, similar to considering a return on any investment.

compares his or her input–outcome ratio to the ratio of this other person to determine whether the employee's ratio is fair. Employees are most likely to be motivated when they believe they are being treated fairly, which, in the case of this theory, is defined as *equitably*.

Figure 13.5 illustrates the comparison process and also shows the three potential results of the comparison process. Numbers are provided simply as a matter of clarification because there are really no "scores" for inputs and outcomes. In the first case, the two ratios are the same. Neither the actual inputs nor the actual outcomes need to be the same for the person to perceive equity; instead, it is simply the ratio or rate of return on investment. So an employee may perceive that a coworker is earning more money but still perceive equity if the employee believes that the coworker is making greater inputs to the work setting. These additional inputs could take the form of longer hours worked, greater effort on the job, or additional education or experience. As long as the ratios are the same, however, the employee should perceive equity and exert effort on the job.

In the second case in Figure 13.5, the employee's ratio is less favorable than that of the comparison person. Again, this could be the case even if the employee perceived herself or himself as being paid more, if the employee thought the comparison person was making fewer inputs (e.g., working much less, or having much less education or experience). As long as the ratio, or rate of return,

Marynchenko Oleksandr/Shutterstock.com

was less for the employee, then he or she would be said to perceive underpayment inequity. Not only is an employee not likely to exert effort at work when underpayment inequity is perceived (because the employee feels that any effort will not be "fairly" rewarded) but also the employee will work to restore equity. The employee will try to either reduce his or her inputs (e.g., exert *less* effort), increase his or her outcomes (e.g., ask for a raise), or try to influence the comparison person to either reduce outcomes or increase inputs (unlikely to be successful). Thus, perceived underpayment inequity can present a real problem for a manager trying to enhance performance. In addition, we must note again that this is all based on perceived inequity; in reality, the employee in question might be treated quite fairly, but the fact that the employee does not perceive that to be the case will present problems.

The final example illustrated in Figure 13.5 is a case in which the employee's input–outcome ratio is more favorable than that of the comparison person. The situation is known as *overpayment inequity*. There is some debate about whether anyone really perceives overpayment inequity because it would be easy to justify the overpayment as actually being deserved ("I guess I do work a lot harder"), and research support for overpayment inequity is mixed at best.[16] According to the theory, however, an employee facing overpayment inequity should also seek to restore equity, which would be easiest to do by increasing her or his inputs in the situation.

Equity theory can be quite useful to the HR manager because it makes it clear that any rewards associated with effort or performance will be evaluated, in part, for their fairness as well as their innate attractiveness. In other words, giving someone a raise for a job well done may not be particularly motivating if another employee received a larger raise for a similar job. Whether or not overpayment inequity really exists, the HR manager needs to be aware of this potential problem with underpayment inequity. In addition, if the employee perceiving underpayment inequity were a woman (or a member of any protected class), and the comparison person were a white male, then she would also be likely to sue under the Equal Pay Act (see Chapter 2)—even though she is being paid fairly relative to the male employee. You may recall that equity theory is also the basis for much of the discussion of justice and fairness in Chapter 2, suggesting that this is indeed a useful theory to keep in mind.

Before leaving our discussion of equity theory, however, consider one important point. Our discussion here, as in Chapter 2, revolved around the definition of "fair." In both cases, we are assuming that most people consider equity a good rule for determining fairness; that is, most people assume that the person who contributes more should receive more. But this is really an assumption based on our Western cultural values. There is evidence to suggest that other cultures are more likely to judge fairness using a rule of equality,[17] which would suggest that everyone shares equally in any outcomes regardless of their contributions. Still others have suggested that, in some settings, individuals prefer a rule of need; that is, individuals should share in outcomes according to what they need.[18] We are not suggesting that any one rule is better than the others, but it is important for the HR manager to realize that not everyone judges what is fair in the same way.

13-3d An Integrative Model of Motivation

Although we will discuss a few more models of motivation, need-based models, reinforcement theory, expectancy theory, and equity theory collectively deal with most of the issues facing an HR manager. In each case, we have presented the major aspects of the theory and have commented on the empirical support each has received, but we have said nothing about which theory is better. That is because each has something to offer, and each has weaknesses as well. But we can integrate the useful information provided by each theory to develop a single, integrative model that will make it easier to discuss what the HR manager should understand about motivation.

First, few of these theories actually conflict with each other. They tend to deal with different aspects of the motivational process, and it is rare that two theories would make different predictions about a situation that could not be easily resolved.[19]

Next we note that the five categories of needs from Maslow can be easily mapped onto the three categories used in ERG theory, so the only issue is how many categories of needs we want to consider. Finally, although expectancy theory is much more complex than reinforcement theory, both theories lead us to make the same basic recommendations: that we strengthen the links between performance and gaining valued outcomes.

FIG 13.6   AN INTEGRATIVE MODEL OF MOTIVATION

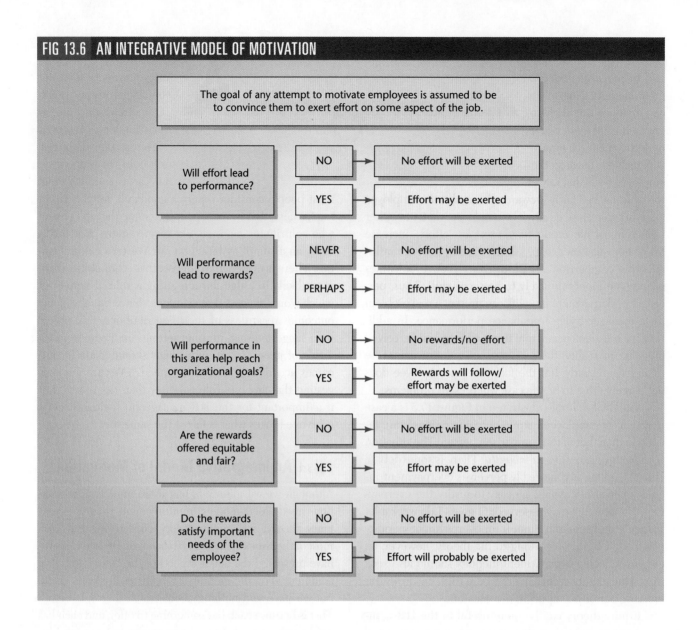

The goal of any attempt to motivate employees is assumed to be to convince them to exert effort on some aspect of the job.

| Will effort lead to performance? | NO → No effort will be exerted |
| | YES → Effort may be exerted |

| Will performance lead to rewards? | NEVER → No effort will be exerted |
| | PERHAPS → Effort may be exerted |

| Will performance in this area help reach organizational goals? | NO → No rewards/no effort |
| | YES → Rewards will follow/ effort may be exerted |

| Are the rewards offered equitable and fair? | NO → No effort will be exerted |
| | YES → Effort may be exerted |

| Do the rewards satisfy important needs of the employee? | NO → No effort will be exerted |
| | YES → Effort will probably be exerted |

With these comments in mind, Figure 13.6 presents a possible integration of the various motivational theories we have discussed thus far.

The basic notion here is that an employee will exert effort on the job *only if* that effort will lead to improved performance, that performance will lead to rewards (which depends on whether or not the improved performance will help the organization meet its goals), and those rewards are considered to be fair *and* satisfy important needs of the employee.

From the perspective of the HR manager, this model suggests that there is a lot to be done to enhance employee motivation. The process really begins with recruitment and selection activities. Organizations must attract and keep the "best" employees. The *best* in this context means employees who desire to work at the organization *and* who can perform the job effectively. If the selection process yields employees who cannot perform effectively, then they will not be able to enjoy the rewards associated with high performance and will actually lose motivation or leave the organization, or both.

Once a person is working at the firm, it is critical that the HR manager apply a compensation system that can recognize good performers. This means creating and using a system that is perceived as fair so that everyone will feel they are being rewarded for their efforts. In addition, this requires a formal appraisal system that fits the culture of the organization and is also perceived as being fair. These two pieces are also combined in setting the tone for incentive pay plans. We will discuss these further in the next chapter, but for now, we can simply state that incentive plans must be designed to reward the "right" behaviors—that is, those that can lead to organizational effectiveness and firm profitability. Finally, that incentive system must include rewards that are truly valued by the employee. If a person is capable of doing a job, believes that she or he is fairly compensated for doing that job, feels that he or she is being evaluated fairly, *and* if those evaluations are closely tied to valued outcomes (e.g., money, recognition, or promotion), then there is every reason to believe that the employee will exert effort on behalf of the organization.

13-4 RELATED THEORIES AND PERSPECTIVES ON MOTIVATION

In addition to the various theories described in the previous section, four other important theories and related perspectives warrant discussion.

13-4a Goal Theory

One of these is **goal theory**, first proposed by Ed Locke.[20] Goal theory is fairly simple because it is based on the premise that people with goals work harder than people without goals. Beyond that, the theory suggests that not all goals are created equal and that goals that are difficult and yet specific and concrete will motivate employees the best. So, for example, a goal to "work harder" is not specific or concrete and is not likely to motivate effort. Goals such as "reducing waste by 10 percent" or "increasing sales by 15 percent," on the other hand, are quite specific and should lead to increased effort because employees will know exactly how to exert effort and exactly what direction that effort should take, and they will also be able to monitor their own progress toward meeting those goals. Difficult goals are also preferable to easy goals because an employee does not need to exert much effort to meet an easy goal. Impossible goals, on the other hand, are not good because eventually the employee will realize that he or she cannot ever attain the goal and will stop trying.

The empirical evidence is rather supportive of goal theory across a wide variety of settings.[21] Goal theory has been used as the basis for some performance-appraisal systems (see Chapter 10) and is very useful as part of a performance management system (which we will discuss in Chapter 14). For

goals to be effective, though, the employee must accept the goal as his or her own. This has led some theorists to suggest that goal setting should be done jointly by managers and their subordinates,[22] although others have argued that joint goal setting is helpful but not essential as long as the employee can be convinced to accept the goal and internalize it.[23] We will discuss other issues associated with the type of goals set in Chapter 14 when we discuss the use of theory in performance-management systems.

13-4b Agency Theory

Another interesting model of motivation is based almost entirely in economics and is known as **agency theory**.[24] This theory is also important for the incentive pay plans we will discuss in Chapter 14, but it is especially useful in the design of incentive plans for executives. Agency theory addresses potential conflicts of interests among different groups of stakeholders in an organization. The name of the theory and some of its basic principles are derived from the fact that the individuals who own most modern organizations do not actually run them on a day-to-day basis. Thus, we can think about the owners (including the stockholders) as being the principals for a firm and the management as being their agents. The theory is concerned with the conflicts that arise from this division, and the fact that what is in the best interests of the principals is not always in the best interests of the managers. Yet when an owner hires a manager, the owner really does assume that the manager will act as his or her agent and work for the best interest of the owner.

In fact, principals and agents differ on several

Yulia Glam/Shutterstock.com

First proposed by Ed Locke, **goal theory** is a fairly simple model of motivation based on the premise that people with goals work harder than people without goals. Beyond that, the theory suggests that not all goals are created equal, and that goals that are difficult and yet specific and concrete will motivate employees best.

Agency theory addresses potential conflicts of interests among different groups of stakeholders in an organization. The name of the theory and some of its basic principles are derived from the fact that, in most modern organizations, the individuals who own a firm do not actually run it on a daily basis. Problems arise when the interests of the owners (the principals) are in conflict with the interests of the managers (agents).

important issues. Agents are less likely than principals to take risks when they make decisions because their livelihood tends to depend on the business being successful; agents are also more likely than principals to focus on a short time horizon because it is usually easier to affect firm performance in the short run, and the agents may not be working for the firm in the long run. Yet it is not easy for the principals to monitor all the decisions made by the agents, and the agents often have more information about the day-to-day business than do the principals.

Empirical research on agency theory is less concerned with supporting the theory, but research has demonstrated that agents do often behave in ways that are inconsistent with the goals of the owners, which is consistent with the theory.[25] As noted, executive compensation and executive incentive plans are the areas in which agency theory is most often applied, but the HR manager can learn more from agency theory than just how to structure executive compensation plans. The basic logic underlying agency theory can be applied to a wide variety of settings where different groups of individuals may have conflicting interests. Managers versus union representatives, supervisors versus hourly employees, and research and development scientists versus accountants are all instances in which we might find groups within an organization that have conflicting goals. Agency theory can provide guidance on how to change some parameters of any such situation so that we can align the interest of the groups involved. This is often done with incentives or even with appraisal systems. However the problem is approached, agency theory provides HR managers with a useful framework for trying to deal with conflicts of interest so that everyone works toward the common organizational goals.

13-4c Intrinsic Motivation

Intrinsic motivation is the motivation to do work because it is interesting, engaging, or possibly challenging rather than because someone is rewarding us to do the work.

Most models and theories of motivation are concerned primarily with extrinsic motivation, which requires an external agent to administer a reward that is separate from the actual task or job being performed. This is in contrast to **intrinsic motivation**. As others have stated it, "Intrinsic motivation is the motivation to do work because it is interesting, engaging, or possibly challenging."[26] The factors usually associated with high levels of intrinsic motivation at work include a sense of self-determination at work (i.e., "I am doing the work because I want to rather than because someone else is rewarding me"), feelings that one's skills are being utilized, and generally positive feelings about the work.[27]

Thus, performing work that is interesting and challenging can be its own reward, and this is the basis for much of the work on job enrichment that is discussed in the next chapter. We can easily think of examples of individuals expending a great deal of time and effort at tasks for which they receive no reward other than the satisfaction of doing something interesting. Typically, we think of these as hobbies or leisure activities, but there are also jobs that people would probably be willing to perform for free if they simply had the opportunity to perform the job.

But what if we added extrinsic rewards, such as contingent pay, to jobs that were already challenging and interesting? At first glance, this seems to represent a great opportunity to improve productivity. It seems reasonable that, if the extrinsic rewards are administered properly (consistent with the theories discussed earlier), this would improve extrinsic motivation, which would then work with the intrinsic motivation that came from the challenging job, and the organization would have a highly motivated employee. Evidence suggests this is not the case, however. In fact, the results from a series of studies[28] suggest that the introduction of extrinsic rewards actually destroys intrinsic motivation. Although there is still room to question this outcome,[29] it is quite clear that intrinsic and extrinsic motivation do not simply interact or add together to form a higher level of motivation.

It is also clear that some types of motivation do not require any intervention on the part of a manager. There are certain types of tasks and jobs for which performing the job is its own reward. This type of motivation does not fit neatly into any of the theories we have discussed, but it will play an important part in the next chapter as we discuss other ways to enhance performance.

13-4d Creativity

At first glance, it might seem that the topic of creativity is misplaced here. After all, only a few highly gifted people are truly creative, and there are very few jobs where one can really be creative on the job. Yet creativity has been suggested as one of the outcomes of intrinsic motivation. Furthermore, and more critically, scholars have begun using a broader definition of creativity at work that encompasses many more employees than we would initially expect.

The most commonly used definition of **creative behavior** at work involves doing things that are innovative and that provide some value for the organization.[30] In general, experts characterize creativity as the process of generating new and useful ideas concerning new products, services, manufacturing methods, and administrative processes.[31] Given this broad definition, almost any employee at almost any job could be creative at work.

In line with this broader view, a great deal of attention has been focused on how to motivate employees to be more creative at work. As noted previously, one factor that has been linked to creativity at work is intrinsic motivation; that is, if we can design jobs to be more challenging and interesting, it is more likely that employees will engage in creative behaviors at work. Interestingly, Amabile has argued that extrinsic motivating factors that serve primarily as information for the employee can also lead to creative behavior at work, as long as they do not threaten the employee's feelings of competency.[32]

Thus, the HR manager can do things to enhance the creativity of any employee. As noted earlier, we will discuss the topic of job enrichment in some detail in the next chapter, but some other factors have been found to be related to creativity at work that can also be affected by HRM policies. For example, informative and constructive feedback has been found to be related to high levels of creativity at work,[33] while another study found that structuring jobs in ways that are consistent with the creativity requirements of those jobs (e.g., allowing more autonomy for jobs requiring more creativity) led to increased satisfaction on the job.[34] In addition, in an interesting development, Zhou and George reported that job dissatisfaction was related to creativity at work under the right circumstances.[35] Specifically, they found that dissatisfied employees, who were also committed to remain with the organization, were more likely to engage in creative behavior at work when they received useful feedback from coworkers and when perceived organizational support for creativity was high.

Clearly, an HR manager can do things to encourage creative behavior from all employees. But before leaving the topic, we need to make one additional point. The definition of creative behavior introduced earlier suggests that ideas or behaviors should be both innovative and useful to the organization. It would seem reasonable, however, that employees might generate a number of ideas that are innovative but not really useful to the organization. It is critical that the organization react to such ideas in a positive way. An employee puts himself or herself at a certain amount of risk when he or she proposes an innovative approach to a problem. If management reacts badly and belittles the employee for an idea that is not very useful, the employee is not likely to come forward with new ideas in the future, and overall creativity is likely to be suppressed. Therefore, it is critical that the organization maintain a climate of openness and make an employee feel comfortable to suggest even a "useless" idea. Only when employees feel safe in this way will they be willing to propose the kinds of creative solutions that the organization needs.[36]

> **Creative behavior** involves doing things at work that are innovative and that provide some value for the organization.

CLOSING CASE
Driving Employee Motivation

Drivers for private truck fleets log about 20,000 miles a year. They drive 82 percent of all medium-duty and heavy-duty vehicles in the United States and account for 52 percent of the total miles traveled by commercial motor vehicles (CMVs).

"The way these employees drive," says veteran industry journalist Mike Antich, "can either increase or decrease fuel economy and greenhouse gas emissions. If you change driving behavior, you have a direct impact on the amount of fuel consumed and

(Continued)

(Closing Case – continued)

the amount of emissions produced. Even small increases in mpg can make a big difference." And, Antich points out that fuel-conscious fleet managers have reported up to 30 percent reductions in fuel consumption by changing driver behavior.

How? By motivating drivers to comply with company sustainability policies. Unfortunately, of course, it's not that simple. Most drivers, according to Antich, "want to do the right thing but don't see sustainability as part of their job responsibilities. In fact, the No. 1 reason corporate sustainability programs are not 'sustainable' is driver noncompliance." According to Antich, a successful sustainability initiative, "requires developing programs that motivate employees to comply." He goes on to argue that effective motivational programs often involve gainsharing—programs designed to share company cost savings with employees.

Again, however, implementing the solution isn't quite as easy as identifying it. Traditionally, observes Antich, gainsharing involves financial incentives, but he admits that "in today's cost-constrained business environment, offering financial incentives [may not be] a realistic option." Consequently, many firms have found that individual recognition can be an effective alternative to financial incentives: "Repeatedly," says Antich, "respondents to employee surveys rate 'individual recognition' as a key factor that motivates them to want to excel or achieve corporate objectives."

Both scientific studies and the experiences of various companies show that the importance of employee recognition—including financial rewards—should not be underestimated in sustainability efforts, primarily because the importance of individual behavior should not be underestimated. According to a report by Jones Lang LaSalle (JLL), a professional-services and investment-management company,

Robert Carner/iStockphoto.com

many companies with active efficiency programs are finding that further improvements in sustainability can be achieved only by turning to the people who are responsible for implementing those programs. "The low-hanging fruit has been plucked," JLL's Michael Jordan advises clients. "You now need the participation of humans."

Nussbaum Transportation, for example, has developed a software program called Driver Excelerator, which collects and analyzes fuel-related data from various sources, including electronic control devices for capturing mpg numbers. Using the resulting data, managers award points to drivers of the 230-truck fleet for beating the company's mpg goal. If, for instance, a driver achieves an average quarterly mpg of 8.5 against a goal of 6.5, he or she receives 200 points, which are allotted according to a three-tier system: Bronze pays $0.50 per point, Silver $5.00 per point, and Gold $8.00 per point. Some drivers in the Gold tier earn an extra $1,600 every three months.

Illinois-based Nussbaum was careful to reject an "all-or-nothing" system in which drivers received a bonus for meeting a target and nothing for falling short. "Our experience," says HR director Jeremy Stickling, "shows that that's a big demotivator" because drivers who miss out tend to blame external circumstances such as weather or load weights. In fact, Nussbaum plans to make mileage-based performance rewards a bigger portion of drivers' base-pay rate. The idea is for drivers to get higher monthly checks instead of big quarterly bonus checks. "Guys want their money now," notes Stickling.[37]

Case Questions

1. How would you assess Nussbaum's incentive program?
2. Which basic motivation concepts and theories are illustrated in this case?
3. If the motivation approach outlined in this case is indeed valid, how might it be used in other settings?

STUDY TOOLS 13

READY TO STUDY?

In the book, you can:

☐ Rip out the chapter review card at the back of the book for a handy summary of the chapter and key terms.

ONLINE AT CENGAGEBRAIN.COM YOU CAN:

☐ Collect StudyBits while you read and study the chapter.

☐ Quiz yourself on key concepts.

☐ Find videos for further exploration.

☐ Prepare for tests with HR4 Flash Cards as well as those you create.

14 | Managing and Enhancing Performance: The Big Picture

John Lund/Sam Diephuis/Blend Images/Jupiter Images

After finishing this chapter go to **PAGE 360** for **STUDY TOOLS**

LEARNING OBJECTIVES

14-1 Describe the relationships among performance measured at different levels within an organization, and discuss how training, development, and job redesign can help improve performance

14-2 Discuss the role of alternative work arrangements in motivating and enhancing performance

14-3 Describe the role of incentive pay, and identify different programs for individual-based and team-based incentive plans

14-4 Discuss the best ways to deliver performance feedback and the issues involved with feedback, and describe the basic operation of the ProMES system

14-5 Discuss how organizations evaluate performance-enhancement programs

14-6 Discuss how recent world events have affected the role of HR

John Lund/Sam Diephuis/
Blend Images/Jupiter Images

OPENING CASE
LEADING IN A VIRTUAL WORLD

One of the most important challenges facing managers today is their ability to lead in a virtual world. Toward this end, the Association for Talent Development (ASTD) explored the challenges facing leaders in a workshop for members in India. Virtual work environments can take many forms—from employees telecommuting on a part-time or full-time basis to a geographically dispersed workforce that crosses cultures and time zones.

For the purposes of this workshop, ASTD conducted a survey to determine the most important leadership skills for a "co-located environment." The top responses included the ability to do the following:

- Set clear goals and measurements for projects.
- Provide a consistent focus on the big picture.
- Operate in a highly complex environment.
- Stimulate organizational commitment.

Some of the challenges facing virtual leaders include the potential feelings of isolation for remote workers. Lack of face-to-face contact can limit the clarity of communication and also can act as a barrier to organizational commitment. Isolation becomes even more of an issue when employees are spread across multiple time zones, challenging the ability of a work team to collaborate effectively.

In spite of the special challenges associated with virtual leadership, some things remain the same. One interviewee for the ASTD study made this clear, stating, "Leadership is leadership. Being authentic, connecting with others, promoting inclusiveness, networking, and all of the interpersonal skills that build relationships and trust are always important." Leaders cannot rely upon frequent, casual contact to build a shared vision in a virtual environment. Instead, leaders must be planned, disciplined, deliberate, and intentional about reaching out to employees on a regular basis.

The ASTD concluded that several best practices are associated with virtual leadership. First, and most important, effective communication is essential. Virtual leaders must learn to use multiple channels to communicate, including phone, e-mail, instant messaging, and video conferencing, and they must appropriately match the media channel to the message.

> "While at first glance it may seem that all the same leadership skills are needed, it may be that leaders in a virtual environment need just a little more of everything: more knowledge of technology, more knowledge of how to work with team dynamics, stronger communication skills, and, of course, a little more patience."
>
> —ASTD REPORT

In addition, communication must be part of a two-way process that includes active listening. The second best practice identified by ASTD was team building. When your team is geographically dispersed, it's essential that leaders plan intentional team-building activities, including structured work-related events as well as more casual social events, if possible.

Finally, leaders must establish the ground rules for their organizations. The unwritten rules of corporate culture are harder to communicate in the virtual world, so it's important to be clear about work-hour expectations as well as risk tolerance. The authors of the ASTD report arrive at a very important conclusion: "While at first glance it may seem that all the same leadership skills are needed, it may be that leaders in a virtual environment need just a little more of everything: more knowledge of technology, more knowledge of how to work with team dynamics, stronger communication skills, and, of course, a little more patience."[1]

THINK IT OVER

1. Do you think virtual leadership requires a different skill set than traditional leadership? Why or why not?
2. How would you feel about working for a boss who lives half way around the world? How might this affect you as an employee?

The previous chapter discussed theories of motivation and, in general terms, things human resource (HR) managers could do to enhance motivation in organizations. Chapter 12 discussed safety and health, noting how stress could interfere with performance on the job. In Chapter 11, we pointed out how some organizations resisted unionization because they believed that it hurt productivity. Chapter 10 outlined procedures for evaluating performance but stated that the ultimate purpose of any performance-appraisal system was to improve performance. In Chapter 9, we discussed how effective compensation systems could attract good employees and how competitive benefit programs could help organizations attract and retain the best employees. Much of our discussion of diversity in Chapter 8 focused on why effectively managing diverse employees could enhance productivity and firm performance, and the major focus of recruitment and selection, as discussed in Chapter 7, was the attraction and retention of employees who could perform well. In fact, an important legal issue in the selection process was to be able to demonstrate how scores on selection techniques were associated with performance on the job.

By now, it should be clear that every decision and activity engaged in by the HR manager is supposed to help improve performance in some way. Of course, employee satisfaction is also important—but important partly because it is related to attrition, and organizations need to retain valued employees. The responsible and professional HR manager does all of this in an ethical way and does not violate the law or anyone's rights; however, the ultimate goal of the HR function is to enhance performance. More specifically, we can assert that the ultimate goal of the HR activities and programs we have described is to enhance *organizational* performance.

This last distinction is important because we are suggesting an ultimate goal of organizational performance rather than simply individual or even group performance. Yet many of the techniques available for performance enhancement that we discuss in this chapter focus on improving the performance of the individual or group; the assumption here is that if the performance of all the individuals working in a firm improves, then so will firm performance Unfortunately, this is not always the case. Therefore, we will begin by discussing some issues associated with the relationship between individual-level and firm-level performance, which will serve as a background for our discussion of specific performance-enhancement techniques, including different kinds of work arrangements, incentive- and performance-based pay, and performance management and rewards. We conclude with a discussion of how managers can best evaluate their performance-enhancement programs.

 14-1 ENHANCING PERFORMANCE AT DIFFERENT LEVELS

Performance in any organization exists at multiple levels. The most basic level of performance is that of the individual employee, and this is the level that most people find easiest to conceptualize. In fact, in Chapter 10, we discussed primarily measures and models of individual-level performance; that is, most appraisal techniques are concerned with determining how many products a person assembles or how many units *individual contributors* sell. We can usually aggregate this up to the group or department level by simply combining sales or productivity data for individuals, but when we move up to the organizational level, things become more complicated. Of course, we can still talk about how many products are produced by the firm, or what a company's total sales are for a quarter, but this is often not very meaningful data.

For example, a server in a restaurant may serve many tables, generate great business for the restaurant, and be very pleasant and earn a lot of tips, but the average bill at the tables she or he serves may not be very high. As a result, that server is doing well but not generating much profit for the restaurant. In fact, it makes little sense to talk about profitability at the level of the individual because profits depend largely on costs, which can only be computed at the firm level. As a result, a performance management or enhancement intervention designed to make the server more efficient or more pleasant might have no effect on firm performance. In fact, there is actually very little evidence to support the idea that improving individual-level performance will lead directly to firm-level performance. The assumption that such a link exists has always been either explicitly or implicitly the basis for working to improve performance appraisals systems so that individual-level performance could be improved. However, although there is ample evidence that performance appraisal and performance management interventions can improve individual-level performance, there is essentially no evidence that this translates into improved firm-level performance.[2] There have surely been suggestions about how this could be accomplished, but no real support to say that any of them work.

Let's begin by stating clearly that it is critical that any performance-enhancement intervention must ultimately improve **firm-level performance**. This is the level that determines the long-term survival of the firm, generates profits for potential profit sharing, and determines the company's stock price. As you read through the rest of this chapter, keep this in mind: Regardless of the level of performance targeted by a specific intervention, these interventions are effective only as long as they also improve organizational performance.

Several recent models[3] suggest that to improve firm-level performance, it is necessary for an organization to create a strong HR system that ensures employees can see how their behavior affects firm performance. A "culture for performance" is then created by coordinating various HR activities (e.g., performance appraisal, selection, and training) in such a way that they have the skills needed to affect firm-level performance, have the opportunity to affect that performance, and are also motivated to do so. Some of these issues are discussed in the remainder of this chapter, but, for now, it is important to stress the idea that all of these activities must be coordinated. The key, then, is finding ways to influence firm-level performance through the use of HR practices. In Chapter 4, we talked about the idea of "strategic human resource management," which advocates that all the HR activities in a firm should be coordinated and should align with corporate strategy. We also noted that research on this approach has shown that firms utilizing bundles of HR practices, know as high-performance work systems, were more successful than their competitors using various measures of firm-level performance. There was also some disagreement about exactly which practices constituted high-performance work systems and some disagreement over exactly how these practices resulted in improved firm-level performance. Nonetheless, this line of research seems to suggest that we can influence firm-level performance but only by implementing a number of coordinated HR practices.

Furthermore, there have been some developments in the area of explaining how high-performance work systems work to influence firm-level performance. Several scholars[4] have suggested a rather straightforward model where HR practices should be focused on ability-enhancing practices (e.g., training and development), motivation-enhancing practices (e.g., incentive compensation), and opportunity-enhancing practices (e.g., job rotation and programs designed to improve voice). Others[5] have emphasized HR practices aimed at converting general knowledge, skills, and abilities (KSAs) into more specific and relevant KSAs that can impact firm-level performance. These transformed KSAs then form the basis of what has been called "human capital resources." Still others[6] have argued for the importance of having a strong culture for performance that is driven by a strong HR system. A strong system is one where employees can see how their behavior affects firm-level performance, and this is what leads to the development of a culture for performance where employees have the ability, motivation, and opportunity to affect firm-level performance.

Thus, it may be less important to worry about the exact nature of the HR practices employed, as long as they are mutually reinforcing so everyone understands what is needed to be successful as both individuals and as a firm. The specifics of the practices involved (e.g., what is evaluated in the appraisals, and what types of employees are selected) probably depend on the strategy the firm uses to compete. Thus, as we discuss various notions of enhancing performance, it is important to remember that we are ultimately interested in enhancing firm-level performance, which can best be accomplished by coordinating the various individual HR practices and making sure they all serve to further the strategic goals of the organization.

Before leaving our discussion of strategic HRM, it is useful to return to a discussion from Chapter 1 concerning "star employees." The issue here is that all employees may not be equally important for achieving a strategic goal, and all employees may not be equally valuable. Thus, it is important to identify those critical or star employees, and make sure that they are well-rewarded and taken care of, in any way possible. In addition, if one of these stars is lost, it is especially critical that the organization replace this person with someone of equal "star power."[7]

14-1a Training and Development

Training and development activities within an organization are a very basic form of performance-enhancement intervention. These topics were discussed in their own right in Chapter 7, and the relevant terms were defined there, but it is worth briefly revisiting the topic in the context of performance enhancement. As we noted in that earlier chapter, the training process begins with some type of needs assessment. The outcome of this assessment provides information about gaps between present and desired levels of performance and therefore provides a road map of what needs to change in order to improve performance.

Firm-level performance is an indication of a firm's chances of long-term survival. Performance at this level generates profits for potential profit sharing and determines the company's stock price.

For example, suppose an online retailer has a group of shipping clerks who are currently taking an average of 2 days to ship a new order. To remain competitive, though, the company has decided it must reduce its shipping time to an average of 1 day. A needs assessment would be conducted to determine what is needed in the way of additional training (and perhaps other things as well) in order to get the clerks to meet this new goal. Perhaps a subsequent training program might deal with efficiency, or it could involve training shipping clerks to use new technology. Assuming that the shipping clerks are capable of working more efficiently and using new technology, this should improve shipping times, move the company toward its new goal, and improve its competitive position.

It is possible to adapt training models to individuals or to groups and teams. It is even possible to adapt training methods to ensure that all team members share mental models of how the team should perform, which is essential for effective teamwork. Training and development activities are a very flexible and, often easy, way to begin the performance improvement process.

14-1b Job Redesign

A much different approach to enhancing organizational performance is through the redesign of jobs. Specifically, this technique involves changing—redesigning— jobs so that the work itself will motivate employees to exert greater effort. This motivation is stimulated by making the job more interesting or more challenging. We will discuss five motivational approaches to the redesign of work: job rotation, job enlargement, job enrichment, job characteristics approach, and work teams. As we will see, the use of work teams is a bit different in its intent. Although a driving consideration is still to motivate employees to work harder, this approach is also concerned with designing more effective ways of doing a job, and it has a great deal of applicability in today's organizations.

> **Job rotation** involves systematically moving employees from one job to another.

> **Job enlargement** was developed to increase the total number of tasks workers perform based on the assumption that doing the same basic task over and over is the primary cause of worker dissatisfaction.

> **Job enrichment** attempts to increase both the number of tasks a worker does and the control the worker has over the job.

Job rotation involves systematically moving employees from one job to another. An employee for a taxi service might work as a driver on Monday, work as a dispatcher on Tuesday, and work on repairs on Wednesday. The jobs do not change, but instead, the employee moves from job to job. For this very reason, however, job rotation has not been very successful in enhancing employee motivation or satisfaction. Jobs that are amenable to rotation tend to be relatively standard and routine. Workers who are rotated to a "new" job may be more satisfied at first, but the novelty soon wanes. Although many companies (among them DuPont, Nucor Steel, Ford, Texas Instruments, Maytag, and Western Electric) have tried job rotation, it is most often used today as a training device to improve worker skills and flexibility.

Based on the assumption that doing the same basic task over and over is the primary cause of worker dissatisfaction, **job enlargement** was developed to increase the total number of tasks that workers perform. As a result, all workers perform a wide variety of tasks, presumably reducing the level of job dissatisfaction. Many organizations have used job enlargement, including IBM, Detroit Edison, AT&T, the U.S. Civil Service, and Maytag. At Maytag, for example, the assembly line for producing washing-machine water pumps was systematically changed so that work originally performed by six workers who passed the work sequentially from one person to another was now performed by four workers, each of whom assembled a complete pump. Although job enlargement does have some positive consequences, they are often offset by several disadvantages: (1) training costs usually rise, (2) unions argue that pay should increase because the worker is doing more tasks, and (3) the work often remains boring and routine even after job enlargement.

A more comprehensive approach, **job enrichment**, assumes that increasing the range and variety of tasks alone is not sufficient to improve employee motivation.[8] Thus, job enrichment attempts to increase both the number of tasks a worker does and the control the worker has over the job. To accomplish this objective, managers remove some controls from the job, delegate more authority to employees, and structure the work in complete, natural units. These changes increase the subordinates' sense of responsibility. Another part of job

"Individual commitment to a group effort— that is what makes a team work, a company work, a society work, a civilization work."

—VINCE LOMBARDI

FIG 14.1 THE JOB CHARACTERISTICS MODEL OF JOB DESIGN

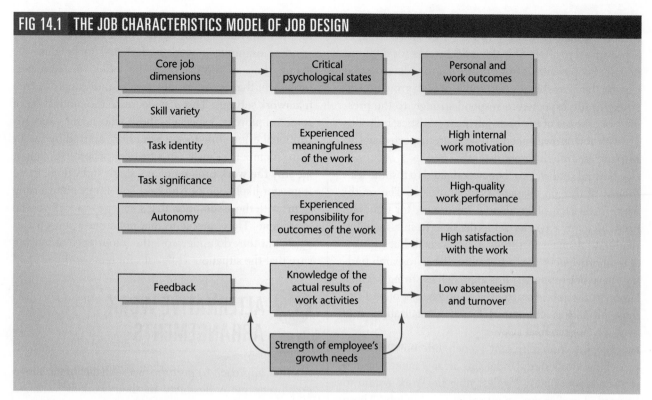

Source: Reprinted from *Organizational Behavior and Human Performance*, Vol. 16, J. R. Hackman and G. R. Oldham, "Motivation Through the Design of Work: Test of a Theory," pp. 250–279, 1976, with permission from Elsevier.

enrichment is to assign new and challenging tasks continually, thereby increasing the employees' opportunity for growth and advancement.

AT&T was one of the first companies to try job enrichment. In one experiment, eight typists in a service unit prepared customer-service orders. Faced with low output and high turnover, management determined that the typists felt little responsibility to clients and received little feedback. The unit was changed to create a typing team. Typists were matched with designated service representatives, the task was changed from 10 specific steps to 3 more general steps, and job titles were upgraded. As a result, the number of orders delivered on time increased from 27 percent to 90 percent, the need for a messenger service was eliminated, accuracy improved, and turnover became practically nil.[9] Other organizations that have tried job enrichment include Lockheed Martin, IBM, and General Foods. Problems have been found with this approach, however. For example, analysis of work systems before enrichment is needed but seldom performed, and managers rarely deal with employee preferences when enriching jobs.

The **job characteristics approach** is an alternative to job specialization in that it does take into account the work system and employee preferences.[10] It is also one of the most widely used and widely studied approaches to job design. As illustrated in Figure 14.1, the job characteristics approach suggests that jobs should be examined and improved along the following five core dimensions.

1. *Skill variety* is the number of tasks a person does in a job.

2. *Task identity* is the extent to which the worker does a complete or identifiable portion of the total job.

3. *Task significance* is the perceived importance of the task.

4. *Autonomy* is the degree of control the worker has over how the work is performed.

5. *Feedback* is the extent to which the worker knows how well the job is being performed.

The higher a job rates on these five dimensions, the more employees will experience various psychological states. Experiencing these states, in turn, presumably leads to high motivation, high-quality

> The **job characteristics approach** is an alternative to job specialization that takes into account the work system and employee preferences; it suggests that jobs should be diagnosed and improved along five core dimensions.

performance, high satisfaction, and low absenteeism and turnover. Finally, a variable called *growth-need strength* is presumed to affect how the model works for different people. People with a strong desire to grow, develop, and expand their capabilities (indicative of high growth-need strength) are expected to respond strongly to the presence or absence of the basic job characteristics; individuals with low growth-need strength are expected not to respond as strongly or consistently.

Several studies have been conducted to test the usefulness of the job characteristics approach. The southwestern division of Prudential Insurance, for example, used this approach in its claims division. Results included moderate declines in turnover and a small but measurable improvement in work quality. Other research findings have not supported this approach as strongly. Thus, although the job characteristics approach is one of the most promising alternatives to job specialization, it is probably not the final answer.

Work teams represent a much different way of approaching job design. Under this arrangement, a group is given responsibility for designing the work system to be used in performing an interrelated set of jobs. These groups are sometimes referred to as *self-directed work teams* or *autonomous work teams*, and they are permanent parts of the organizational architecture. In these teams, the group itself decides how jobs will be allocated. For example, the work team assigns specific tasks to members, monitors and controls its own performance, and exercises autonomy over work scheduling.

The original impetus for the reliance on work teams comes from a famous series of studies conducted in England by the Tavistock Institute and dealing with the coal-mining industry.[11] The researchers determined that it was important for miners to have social interaction, so they suggested that the miners work in teams. The researchers also identified and suggested several changes in the actual coal-mining jobs themselves. As it turned out, the job changes were also conducive to team settings in that they increased the need for coordination. After the jobs were changed and the workers formed into teams, performance in the mines improved considerably, and the miners reported more satisfaction and increased motivation. Hence, in some settings, teams make a great deal of

sense. But work teams are not without problems, and they certainly are not the answer in all cases.

For example, if work is designed to be done by teams, then all rewards must be based on team performance; that is, we cannot reward individuals in true teamwork settings. This may decrease the motivation of some employees, especially those who might exert exceptional effort only to see less effort exerted by fellow team members. Finally, in situations where we cannot identify the work product of any single individual, there is greater likelihood of "shirking," or simply not exerting effort with the assumption that someone else will get the work done. These problems may not argue against teamwork, but they do underscore the importance of making sure that the situation really calls for teamwork.

 14-2 ALTERNATIVE WORK ARRANGEMENTS

Another approach to performance enhancement allows employees more flexibility in their working arrangements. The assumption is that if employees can work in ways that better suit their lifestyles, then they will be less distracted and more likely to be productive. But these interventions are also designed to affect organizational-level performance by simply reducing costs and increasing efficiency. Traditionally, employees came to a specific workplace and were expected to be physically present at work 5 days a week, 8 hours a day, unless the employee was required to spend time on the road. In modern organizations, however, it is becoming increasingly common for people to work on a schedule other than 5 days 40 hours per week or to work at a place other than the office or place of business.

14-2a Alternative Work Schedules

The two most common alternatives to the traditional workweek are programs known as *flexible work hours* and *compressed workweeks*. Employees working under **flexible work hour plans** usually must still work a full 40 hours per week and, typically, 5 days a week. The employees have control, however, over the starting and ending times for work on each day. In almost every case, there is a core time each day when every employee must be at work. During these hours, the organization can schedule meetings or other activities that require coordination among employees. The remaining hours (flextime) can be made up in any way that the employee prefers. For example, if a company's core time is 10 A.M.

A **work team** is an arrangement in which a group is given responsibility for designing the work system to be used in performing an interrelated set of jobs.

Flexible work hour plans are plans in which employees usually must still work 40 hours per week and typically 5 days a week but in which they have control over the starting and ending times for work on each day.

FIG 14.2 FLEXIBLE WORK SCHEDULES

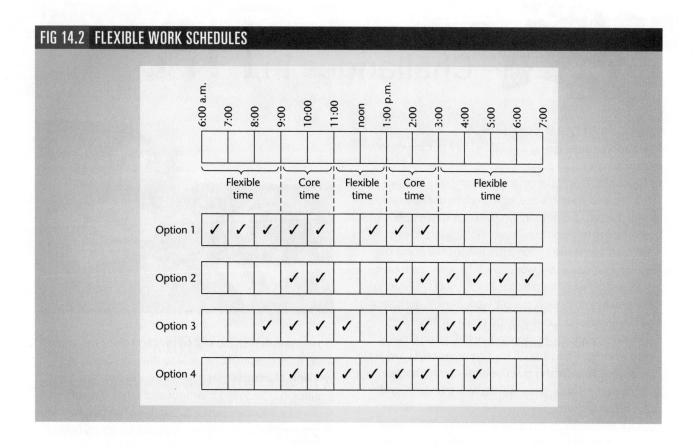

to 2 P.M., then everyone is expected to be at work during those hours. But starting times might be anywhere between 7 A.M. and 10 A.M., and quitting times might be anywhere between 2 P.M. and 7 P.M. Under such a plan, the core time represents 20 hours a week, and the employee is free to work the remaining 20 hours in any fashion within the stated constraints.

Figure 14.2 illustrates how an organization might function with one type of flexible work schedule. This organization has defined 6 A.M.–9 A.M., 11 A.M.–1 P.M., and 3 P.M.–7 P.M. as flexible time, and 9 A.M.–11 A.M. and 1 P.M.–3 P.M. as core time. A worker choosing option 1 (i.e., the early riser) comes to work at 6 A.M., takes an hour for lunch, and is finished for the day at 3 P.M. Option 2, perhaps more attractive for those not considered to be morning people, involves starting work at 9 A.M., taking 2 hours for lunch, and working until 7 P.M. Option 3 is closest to a standard workday, starting at 8 A.M., taking an hour at lunch, and leaving at 5 P.M. Finally, option 4 involves starting at 9 A.M., taking no lunch, and finishing at 5 P.M. In every case, however, each employee works during the core time periods.

These plans are believed to reduce stress because the employee does not have to travel during peak commuting times and can have more control over the commute.[12] They are also believed to increase job satisfaction because the employee is given more control over the work environment and a stronger feeling that he or she is trusted by the organization.[13] They are not as feasible in organizations that place a strong emphasis on teams; otherwise, no serious problems associated with their use are reported. The Contemporary Challenges in HR box provides additional perspectives on flexible work schedules.

Compressed workweeks are arrangements in which the employee works the required number of hours (typically 40) but does so in fewer than 5 days. For example, a 4-day, 10-hour-a-day work schedule is fairly common, and schedules that involve 4 days with 12 hours a day, followed by 4 days off, are also fairly common. The employee gains the flexibility of 3 days off a week, presumably making it less likely that he or she will lose work time to deal with personal business. These schedules are also well suited for employees who work at sites that are difficult to get to such as offshore drilling rigs. These schedules are not for everyone, however, and longer workdays are related to increased accidents in some settings.[14] Nonetheless, compressed workweeks are extremely popular with some employees.

Compressed workweeks are arrangements in which the employee works the required number of hours (typically 40) but does so in fewer than 5 days. For example, a 4-day, 10-hour-a-day work schedule is fairly common.

Contemporary Challenges in HR

Work Is Where You Do It

Once upon a time, "going to work" meant getting dressed in appropriate attire at a predetermined time, driving or using public transportation to get to an office or other work site, and staying there for a predetermined period of time before returning home. But for some people today, "going to work" may mean slipping into shorts and t-shirt and walking down the hall to their home office. Sometimes remote workers live far away from their employer and work from home almost all of the time. In other situations, though, people work from home one or two days a week but come to the office on other days.

More and more organizations are allowing employees to work from home on at least an occasional basis. The general term for this practice is telecommuting. By using e-mail, smartphones, tablets, Web interfaces, and other technology, many employees can maintain close contact with their organization and do as much work at home as they could in their offices. On the plus side, many employees like telecommuting because it gives them added flexibility. By spending one or two days a week at home, for instance, they have the same kind of flexibility to manage personal activities as is afforded by flexible or compressed schedules. Some employees also feel that they get more work done by staying at home because they are less likely to be interrupted. Organizations may benefit for several reasons as well: (1) they can reduce absenteeism and turnover because employees will need to take less "formal" time off, and (2) they can save on facilities such as parking spaces because fewer people will be at work on any given day. There are also environmental benefits, given that fewer cars are on the highways.

On the other hand, although many employees thrive under this arrangement, others do not. Some feel isolated and miss the social interaction of the workplace.

> "…remote workers will tend to work a few more hours…but it's hard to replace face-to-face [interaction]."
>
> —JIM HARTER, CHIEF SCIENTIST, WORKPLACE MANAGEMENT AND WELL-BEING, GALLUP

iStockphoto.com/halbergman

Others simply lack the self-control and discipline to walk away from the breakfast table to their desk and start working. Managers may also encounter coordination difficulties in scheduling meetings and other activities that require face-to-face contact. And there is now a new area of growing concern—cybercrime. Is a company liable if a client's confidential information is stolen because an employee's home computer didn't have hacker protection? What if the employee uses a home computer for business and also peddles online pornography?

Regardless of the downside, the costs seem to be outweighed by the benefits, and the percentage of the workforce that telecommutes is on the upswing. One recent study suggests that almost 10 percent of the U.S. workforce works from home at least one day a week. In some cities, such as Boulder, Santé Fe, and Austin, the percentage is well above the national average. Some companies are also using work at home time as a reward for top performers. And government organizations— federal, state, and local—have also embraced the concept of telecommuting and are increasingly encouraging their employees to work from home on a regular basis.[15]

THINK IT OVER

1. Which do you think you would personally prefer, working in an office all the time, working from home all the time, or a mix of working at an office and home? Why?

2. What complications might exist for managers whose employees work from home all or part of the time?

Both of these alternative schedule plans are growing in popularity, and few problems seem to be associated with them (except as noted). These alternative schedules present some unique challenges to the HR manager, however. As noted previously, flexible schedules are often not feasible in organizations that rely heavily on teams. In fact, whenever one employee's work depends on input from another employee, these schedules may be a problem. Even when they are not a problem, flexible schedules reduce the amount of time that employees interact with their coworkers, which makes it more difficult to develop a strong culture or even a strong esprit de corps.

Although employees are at work the same number of hours as before and have the opportunity to interact with coworkers, compressed workweeks present similar challenges because the stress of longer hours may make social interaction less likely, and the greater number of days off may also affect some social aspects of the job. The HR manager must try to find ways to replace socializing activities with other experiences so that employees, especially new employees, can learn more about their coworkers and become more fully socialized into the organization.

14-2b Alternative Work Sites

In addition to employees working on alternative schedules, employees performing their work at a location other than the place of business, most likely at home, is a growing trend. Home work and telecommuting are two popular variations on this theme. Table 14.1 shows the number and distribution of people currently working under an alternative work arrangement. *Home work programs* include arrangements that are often referred to as *cottage industries*. In the earliest days of the Industrial Revolution, before many factories were built, employees would take parts back home to their cottages, manufacture them, and then return them to a central point where they could be assembled. Similar types of cottage industries still exist for the manufacturing of small and not very complex items.

It is more common, however, to operate in what can be called an *electronic cottage*. Employees take office work home with them and complete it on home computers. They can then return to the office to collect more work. They are connected to that office via servers, VPN, and e-mail. These arrangements can even result in a virtual office and are becoming especially popular with people who want (or need) to work but do not wish to work full-time or who have other responsibilities such as child care or elder care.[16]

Telecommuting is simply the logical extension of the electronic cottage. Under this arrangement, employees may do almost all of their work at home and may receive assignments electronically. This arrangement provides employees with the ultimate in flexibility because they can choose the hours they work and even the location. A growing body of evidence suggests that this arrangement increases job satisfaction and even productivity, and it also allows organizations to use the services of individuals who may not be able to work at a given site.[17] For example, an employee can live many hours from the office if he or she performs most of the work via telecommuting. Finally, larger organizations can save considerable amounts of money if they do not need large (or any) real office space. Cisco Systems, a pioneer in telecommuting, estimates that by allowing employees to work at home, it has boosted productivity by 25 percent, lowered its own overhead by $1 million, and retained key knowledge workers who might have left for other jobs without the flexibility provided by the firm's telecommuting options.[18]

Alternative work sites present a more serious challenge to the HR manager. In the past, the AFL-CIO has complained that work-at-home arrangements allow management to impose unfair working conditions on employees, and it also makes it more difficult for unions to organize workers. So unions continue to oppose these arrangements. As with alternative work schedules, communication among employees is difficult under these arrangements, and it is extremely difficult for a new employee to become socialized. In fact, little socialization may be possible if many of the employees are working under nontraditional work arrangements and many are working at home.

In addition, some individuals may simply lack the self-discipline to get the work done in a completely unconstrained environment, although the available evidence suggests that this outcome is not much of a problem. What does seem to be a problem is that these alternative work sites are likely to increase employees' sense of alienation at work.[19] They have no social connections and no support from coworkers, so loyalty or commitment to the organization is unlikely to develop. Companies are trying, however, to overcome these problems. For example, Merrill Lynch allows potential telecommuters a 2-week dry run to see how they like the arrangement. Aetna assigns each of its telecommuters an office buddy to help those working at home stay in touch with the office. Google and Apple routinely schedule social events to bring together employees who work primarily from home.

TABLE 14.1

EMPLOYED WORKERS WITH ALTERNATIVE WORK ARRANGEMENTS BY OCCUPATION AND INDUSTRY (PERCENTAGE DISTRIBUTION)

Characteristic	Workers with Alternative Arrangements (%)			
	Independent Contractors	On-Call Workers	Temporary Agency Workers	Workers Provided by Contract Firms
Total, 16+ years of age (1,000s)	10,342	2,454	1,217	813
Management, professional, and related occupations	39.9	35.6	20.3	39.6
Service occupations	13.7	22.1	15.6	26.2
Sales and office occupations	20.5	12.6	26.9	7.2
Natural resources, construction, and maintenance occupations	19.7	16.9	7.1	21.8
Production, transportation, and material-moving occupations	6.1	12.7	30.1	5.2
Agriculture and related industries	2.6	0.6	–	0.2
Mining	0.1	1.0	0.5	0.2
Construction	22.0	12.2	3.4	16.5
Manufacturing	3.2	4.8	28.4	14.1
Transportation and utilities	3.9	8.4	3.1	4.0
Wholesale trade	2.1	2.1	5.4	3.4
Retail trade	8.9	5.6	2.1	3.1
Information	2.0	1.8	1.8	4.0
Financial activities	10.4	3.4	4.1	6.8
Professional and business services	2.0	1.8	1.8	4.0
Education and health services	8.7	33.8	11.1	15.7
Leisure and hospitality	4.5	10.4	1.8	4.5
Other services	9.9	3.8	2.9	0.3
Public administrationx	0.3	4.4	2.8	16.6

Source: U.S. Department of Labor, Bureau of Labor Statistics, 2015.

14-3 INCENTIVES AND PERFORMANCE-BASED REWARDS

Yet another approach to enhancing performance is by explicitly tying rewards, especially pay, to performance—that is,

organizations try to reinforce certain types of behaviors and outcomes (recall our discussion in Chapter 13) by tying compensation directly to measures of performance or productivity. Many plans allow this to be done.

The most basic form of incentive compensation is **merit pay**, which generally refers to pay awarded to employees on the basis of the relative value of their contributions to the organization. Employees who make greater contributions are given higher pay than those who make

Merit pay is pay awarded to employees on the basis of the relative value of their contributions to the organization.

lesser contributions. **Merit-pay plans**, then, are formal compensation plans that base at least some meaningful portion of compensation on merit.

The most general form of the merit-pay plan is to provide annual salary increases to individuals in the organization based on their relative merit. Merit, in turn, is usually determined or defined based on the individual's performance and overall contributions to the organization. Recall that in Chapter 10 we discussed various methods for evaluating employee performance. We noted, as well, that performance appraisal had the most meaning to employees if it was subsequently connected with a reward such as a salary increase. However, it is important for the organization to have valid and reliable measures for merit. Merit generally refers to performance, but for the plan to have motivation and performance effects, people throughout the organization must clearly understand what the firm means by the term *merit*. Otherwise, the plan not only will not be effective in improving performance but also may cause problems with employees' perceptions of justice.

Another basic approach is based on systems of *skill-* and *knowledge-based pay.* Recall from Chapter 9 that, under these systems, instead of rewarding employees for increased performance, they are rewarded for acquiring more skills or knowledge. But these skills or this knowledge is related to what the organization believes it will need in the future. Thus, in effect, the organization is rewarding the employee for increasing his or her capacity to perform well in the future, while more traditional merit-pay systems reward employees for achieving some level of performance defined by what the organization needs (or wants) right now. Although problems are associated with these systems and their administration, they offer an alternative to more traditional merit-pay systems and provide a more strategic long-term focus for the organization.[20] In addition, they allow the organization to move employees toward focusing on more than just basic productivity.[21]

Incentive compensation systems are among the oldest forms of performance-based rewards. For example, as noted earlier, some companies used individual piece-rate incentive plans more than 100 years ago.[22] Under a piece-rate incentive plan, the organization pays an employee a certain amount of money for every unit she or he produces. For example, an employee might be paid $1 for every dozen units of product that are completed successfully. But such simplistic systems fail to account for factors such as minimum-wage levels, and they rely heavily on the assumptions that performance is under an individual's complete control and that the individual employee does a single task continuously throughout his or her work time. Thus, most organizations that try to use incentive compensation systems today use more sophisticated methods, which are discussed next.

14-3a Individual Incentive Pay Plans

Generally speaking, **individual incentive plans** reward individual performance on a real-time basis. Rather than increasing a person's **base salary** at the end of the year, an individual instead receives some level of salary increase or financial reward in conjunction with demonstrated outstanding performance in close proximity to when that performance occurred. Individual incentive systems are most likely to be used in cases where performance can be objectively assessed in terms of number of units

Merit-pay plans are compensation plans that formally base at least some meaningful portion of compensation on merit.

Individual incentive plans reward individual performance on a real-time basis.

The **base salary** of an employee is a guaranteed amount of money that the individual will be paid.

of output or similar measures rather than on a subjective assessment of performance by a superior.

Some variations on a piece-rate system are still fairly popular. Although many of these systems still resemble the early plans in most ways, a well-known piece-rate system at Lincoln Electric illustrates how an organization can adapt the traditional model to achieve better results. For years, Lincoln's employees were paid individual incentive payments based on their performance. However, the amount of money shared (or the incentive pool) was based on the company's profitability. A well-organized system allowed employees to make suggestions for increasing productivity. Motivation was provided in the form of a reward equaling one-third of the profits (another third went to the stockholders, and the last third was retained for improvements and seed money). Thus, the pool for incentive payments was determined by profitability, and an employee's share of this pool was a function of his or her base pay and rated performance based on the piece-rate system.

Lincoln Electric was most famous, however, because of the stories (which were apparently typical) of production workers receiving a year-end bonus payment that equaled their yearly base pay.[23] In recent years, Lincoln has partially abandoned its famous system for business reasons, but it still serves as a benchmark for other companies seeking innovative piece-rate pay systems.

Perhaps the most common form of individual incentive is the **sales commission** that is paid to salespeople. For example, sales representatives for consumer products firms and retail sales agents may be compensated under this type of commission system. In general, the person might receive a percentage of the total volume of attained sales as his or her commission for a period of time. Some sales jobs are based entirely on commission, while others use a combination of base minimum salary with additional commission as an incentive. Notice that these plans put a considerable amount

A **sales commission** is an incentive paid to salespeople.

of the salesperson's earnings at risk. Although organizations often have drawing accounts to allow the salesperson to live during lean periods (the person then "owes" this money to the organization), if the employee does not perform well, then he or she will not be paid much. The portion of salary based on commission is simply not guaranteed and is paid only if the employee's sales reach some target level.

Finally, organizations occasionally may use other forms of incentives to motivate employees. For example, a nonmonetary incentive such as additional time off or a special perk might be a useful incentive. A company might establish a sales contest in which the sales group that attains the highest level of sales increase over a specified period of time receives an extra week of paid vacation, perhaps even at an arranged place such as a tropical resort or a ski lodge.[24] At Chipotle restaurants, store managers who groom an employee who eventually also becomes a store manager receive a $10,000 payment. This encourages store managers to recruit talented and motivated employees, and then work to develop them into potential managers.[25]

As with merit systems, incentive compensation systems have some shortcomings and weaknesses. One major shortcoming is that they are practical only when performance can be measured easily and objectively. Most managerial work does not fit this pattern and, in fact, is often characterized by ambiguous performance indicators that are difficult to assess. Thus, it may be much more difficult to provide valid and appropriate incentives for these individuals. Individual incentives are also likely to focus attention on only a narrow range of behaviors, perhaps at the expense of other behaviors. Take, for example, a bank teller who may be able to earn some type of incentive bonus if he or she can sell existing customers additional bank services, such as a safety deposit box. The teller may spend time explaining to the customer why a safety deposit box is so valuable rather than just helping the customer transact business efficiently. The teller may be successful at selling safety deposit boxes, but some customers will

Monkey Business Images/Shutterstock.com

become annoyed because they just want to conduct their business and be on their way. As a result, these customers may move their accounts to another bank. Thus, the teller may maximize his or her earnings but at the cost of increased customer dissatisfaction and loss.

14-3b Team and Group Incentive Plans

In addition to incentive plans designed to improve individual performance, there are plans that focus on group or team performance. These programs are particularly important for managers to understand today because they focus attention on higher levels of performance and because of the widespread trends toward team- and group-based methods of work and organization.[26]

A fairly common type of group incentive system is an approach called **gainsharing**. Gainsharing programs are designed to share the cost savings from productivity improvements with employees. The underlying assumption of gainsharing is that employees and the employer have the same goals and thus should share in incremental economic gains,[27] consistent with our discussion of agency theory in Chapter 13.

In general, organizations that use gainsharing start by measuring team- or group-level productivity. It is important that this measure is valid and reliable and that it truly reflects current levels of performance by the team or group. The team or work group itself is charged with attempting to lower costs and otherwise improve productivity through any measures that its members develop and that its manager approves. Resulting cost savings or productivity gains that the team or group is able to achieve are then quantified and translated into dollar values. A predetermined formula is used to allocate these dollar savings between the employer and the employees themselves. A typical formula for distributing gainsharing savings is to provide 25 percent of the dollar savings to the employees and 75 percent to the company.

One specific type of gainsharing plan is an approach called the **Scanlon plan**. This approach was developed by Joseph Scanlon in 1927. The Scanlon plan has the same basic strategy as gainsharing plans because teams or groups of employees are encouraged to suggest strategies for reducing cost. However, the distribution of these gains is usually tilted much more heavily toward employees, with employees usually receiving between two-thirds and three-fourths of the total cost savings that the plan achieves. The cost savings resulting from the plan are not given just to the team or group that suggested and developed the ideas but are instead distributed to the entire organization.

In addition to gainsharing and Scanlon plans, other systems are also used by some organizations. Some companies, for example, have begun to use true incentives at the team or group level. As with individual incentives, team or group incentives tie rewards directly to performance. And like individual incentives, team or group incentives are paid as they are earned rather than being added to employees' base salaries. The incentives are distributed at the team or group level, however, rather than at the individual level. In some cases, the distribution may be based on the existing salary of each employee, with incentive bonuses being given on a proportionate basis. In other settings, each team or group member receives the same incentive pay.

Some companies also use nonmonetary rewards at the team or group level. These rewards come most commonly in the form of prizes and awards. For example, a company might designate the particular team in a plant or subunit of the company that achieves the highest level of productivity increase, the highest level of reported customer satisfaction, or a similar index of performance. The reward itself might take the form of additional time off (as described earlier in this chapter) or a tangible award such as a trophy or a plaque. In any event, however, the reward is given to the entire team and serves as recognition of exemplary performance by the entire team.

Other kinds of team- or group-level incentives go beyond the contributions of a specific work group. These incentives are generally organization wide. One long-standing method for this approach is **profit sharing**, in which some portion of the company's profits is paid at the end of the year into a shared pool that is distributed to all employees. This amount is either distributed at the end of the year or put into an escrow account, and payment is deferred until the employee retires.

The basic rationale behind profit-sharing systems is that everyone in the organization can expect to benefit when the company does well. During bad economic times, however, when the company is perhaps achieving low or no profits, no profit sharing is paid out. This situation sometimes results in negative reactions from

Gainsharing is a team- and group-based incentive system designed to share the cost savings from productivity improvements with employees.

Scanlon plans are gainsharing plans in which teams or groups of employees are encouraged to suggest strategies for reducing costs; gains are distributed not just to the team that suggested and developed the ideas but to the entire organization.

Profit sharing is an incentive system in which, at the end of the year, some portion of the company's profits is paid into a profit-sharing pool, which is then distributed to all employees.

employees who come to feel that the profit sharing is really part of their annual compensation.

Various types of *stock-based incentives* are also ways to tie incentives to the performance of the firm, although these are more typically used with executive employees rather than hourly employees, as discussed in Chapter 9. For example, in many companies, executives may be given a certain number of *stock options,* which enable them to purchase shares of the company's stock at a fixed price. Thus, under a **stock-option plan,** an executive may be given 1,000 options to purchase the firm's stock at $5 per share (the current trading price) for as long as 1 year. If the stock price rises to $6 a share (presumably because of something the executive did), the employee can exercise his or her option: buy the shares at $5, sell them at $6, and make a $1,000 profit.

Alternatively, some firms offer **stock-purchase plans,** which are typically offered to all the employees of a firm rather than just the executives. Many start-up firms, especially in high-tech sectors, also offer restricted stock plans, which are really used as a retention tool rather than as a performance incentive. Under these plans, employees are entitled to the stock only if they remain with the company for a specified period of time. If they leave before that time, they have no rights to the shares of stock.

Employee stock ownership plans (ESOPs) represent another group-level reward system that some companies use. Under the ESOP, employees are gradually given a major stake in the ownership of a corporation. The typical form of this plan involves the company taking out a loan, which is then used to buy a portion of the company's own stock in the open market. Over time, company profits are then used to pay off this loan. Employees, in turn, receive a claim on ownership of some portion of the stock held by the company based on their seniority and perhaps their performance. Eventually, each individual becomes an owner of the company.

Although group reward systems can be effective in some situations, they are also subject to difficulties. For example, not every member of a group may contribute equally to the group's performance. But if the group-incentive system distributes rewards equally to group members, then people may feel that some factors beyond individual performance dictate the distribution of rewards. In addition, for incentive plans based on firm profitability, employees may not see how their efforts lead to increased profits (often referred to as a *line-of-sight problem*). In fact, many factors that are beyond the employees' control can affect profitability. Thus, the links among effort, performance, and outcomes, as specified by expectancy theory, are often quite weak, resulting in little motivation. In addition, a limitation noted earlier in our discussion on profit sharing is that employees may come to view the group-level incentive as a normal part of their compensation and consequently be unhappy or dissatisfied if that reward is withheld in any given year.

Stock-based programs have special problems because the employees' incentives are tied to the price of the stock. An employee, especially an executive, may therefore make decisions or take actions that might result in a short-term increase in the stock price, while causing long-term problems for firm performance. In addition, stock programs are effective only so long as the price of the stock is rising—or at least not falling. In the example given earlier, if the employee has the option to buy the stock at $5.00 per share, and the price of the stock goes down to $4.00 a share, there is no incentive value and no reason for the employee to exercise the option. In such cases, the stock options are said to be "below water."

A **stock-option plan** is an incentive plan established to give senior managers the option to buy company stock in the future at a predetermined fixed price.

A **stock-purchase plan** is typically offered to all the employees of a firm rather than just the executives to serve more as a retention tool. Under these plans, employees are entitled to the stock only if they remain with the company for a specified period of time. If they leave before that time, they have no rights to the shares of stock.

Employee stock ownership plans (ESOPs) are group-level reward systems in which employees are gradually given a major stake in the ownership of a corporation.

Raywoo/Shutterstock.com

Finally, a few years ago, there was a major scandal about the ways in which organizations can manipulate stock options.[28] A high-tech company, Brocade Systems, Inc., granted employees stock options when they joined the company in 1999. This was a start-up company, and the initial offering price was $2.37, which was also the option price for employees at that time. The stock quickly rose (to more than $133 a share), making those options quite valuable. But then the high-tech bubble burst in 2002, and the share price plummeted. Employees who joined the firm later were also offered options, but at the selling price in effect when they were hired. As the stock price continued to drop, these later options became eventually worthless (i.e., underwater). The management at Brocade then asked employees to change their employment date to make it later than it actually was—at a time when the stock's price was low—so that the employees would qualify for option prices that were low enough for the options to still have some value. The article reporting the scandal noted that similar (but less egregious) practices were carried out by many high-tech firms, but a follow-up piece indicated that the former CEO and several others who were involved were being charged with both civil and criminal securities fraud.[29]

14-4 PERFORMANCE MANAGEMENT AND FEEDBACK

A series of programs and interventions referred to as *performance-management techniques* are somewhat more specific than the programs we have discussed thus far. We discuss two of these that were introduced in Chapter 13—behavior modification and goal setting—and we will also discuss some issues associated with feedback, which is a key component of many of these performance-management interventions.

14-4a Performance-Management Techniques

Recall our discussion of reinforcement theory in Chapter 13. The basic notion underlying this theory is that all behavior is a function of its

consequences—whether actual or anticipated—and so we can shape behavior by arranging for the "right" set of consequences. We also noted that positive reinforcement was designed to reward desirable behaviors that we wanted to see repeated, whereas punishment and extinction were techniques to discourage behaviors that were less desirable. *Behavior modification,* as discussed in the preceding chapter, is the systematic and simultaneous application of positive reinforcement and either punishment or extinction (or both). The basic notion is that it is not enough to eliminate undesirable behaviors unless we can also provide the person with a new set of desirable behaviors.

For example, perhaps an organization is concerned that employees are spending too much time browsing the Internet or checking out friends' Facebook pages. Productivity is suffering because employees are talking and socializing rather than working. The company could begin by taking out the coffee machine (removing an incentive for congregating) and perhaps even install a loud piece of equipment in the space to make it uncomfortable for employees to remain there for long. At the same time, the firm could provide free coffee, delivered to workstations on a cart, but only to people actually working. The idea here would be to discourage congregating and socializing *and* to encourage people to remain at their workstations.

One key to any successful behavior-modification plan is to make sure that the employee can see strong links between his or her behavior and the consequences that can follow. The other, more critical component, however, is to make absolutely sure that desirable behaviors are never punished and that undesirable behaviors are never rewarded. Too often, supervisors reward the wrong behaviors and punish the behaviors they should be rewarding. One of the authors of this text recently had to put together a faculty committee for a task that no one really wanted carried out. When he suggested a certain faculty member, he was told that it was unwise to assign that faculty member to any committees because the person did not usually show up for meetings. Instead, it was

Africa Studio/Shutterstock.com

suggested, he should assign a different faculty member who always showed up for meetings. This apparently had been a long-standing practice and yet no one could understand why it was so difficult to get the first faculty member to perform any service activities. The author, of course, assigned the first faculty member to the committee and actually released the second faculty member from one or two committee assignments.

iStockphoto.com/Kali Nine LLC

We also discussed *goal theory* in the previous chapter and indicated that this theory was very useful for managing performance as well as simply motivating it. Recall that goal theory suggests that employees will exert the greatest effort when they have specific, difficult goals to work toward. Thus, from a performance-management perspective, managers should provide employees with difficult, specific goals, and then reward them when those goals are achieved. The earlier discussion also included consideration of some issues in choosing the "right" goal, but, for the current discussion, it is extremely important that all parties can agree on what is the "right" goal.

Quite often, when employees (and managers) are asked to think about goals, they tend to focus on things that can be readily counted. That is not necessarily bad because such goals are often concrete and specific, but they can simply be wrong. For example, a customer service representative for an airline might be told by his supervisor that he should set a goal of helping 50 customers a day, which is concrete, specific, and presumably difficult. But, if in order to help so many customers, the service rep cuts off customers in the midst of their complaints or simply sends them to someone else who really cannot solve the customers' problems, this will have long-term implications. Customers will be dissatisfied—rude or abrupt customer service reps are not what anyone thinks of when they think of "excellent" customer service. Thus, in the long run, perceptions of customer service would likely decline even though the individual representative is meeting his goals on a daily basis.

Many other examples of goal setting reflect this same type of problem. Think about the telephone repair person whose goal is to fix 50 phones a day (think about what happens if there are only 45 broken phones), or the teacher whose goal is to have the highest percentage of students passing an exam (and therefore has no incentive to fail even the weakest student).

The key here is that any goal chosen as part of a performance-management system must be aligned with the higher-level, strategic goals of the organization. Ideally, one can think about these goals as "cascading down" so that at each level in the organization, the performance goals that are set will influence the goals at the next lower level. In terms of goal accomplishment, we can think about the goals rolling upward so that goals met at one level help the next level to meet its goals and so on up to the strategic level.

Performance feedback plays an important role in both behavior modification and goal setting, and it is also seen as a useful tool in its own right for performance management. But many managers do a poor job in this area, in part because they do not understand how to provide feedback properly and in part because they do not enjoy it. Almost by definition, performance appraisal in many organizations tends to focus on negatives; as a result, managers may have a tendency to avoid giving feedback because they know an employee who hears negative feedback may be angry, hurt, discouraged, or argumentative. But clearly, if employees are not told about their shortcomings, they have no reason to try to improve and have no guidance concerning how to improve. Therefore, it is critical that a rater provide feedback, so he or she must understand how it might be done better.

One method of improving performance feedback is to provide feedback on a regular basis via feedback interviews. Instead of providing feedback annually, in tandem with the annual performance-appraisal interview, it might be more appropriate for managers to provide feedback on an ongoing basis. Feedback might be provided on a daily or weekly basis, depending on the nature of the job, and it should focus on various characteristics of performance, including both effective and ineffective performance.[30] In fact, if managers remember that the goal of performance management is changing employee behavior, then they should also recognize that they clearly are more likely to effect change with more frequent feedback, and this approach is consistent with both behavior modification and goal setting.

Another useful method for improving performance feedback is to have the individual appraise his or her own performance in advance of an appraisal interview. This method involves having employees think about their own performance over the rating period, which helps sensitize them to areas where they have done good and ineffective jobs. This method also lends efficiency to the process because the manager and the subordinate may be able to focus most of their time and effort in a performance-appraisal interview on those areas of performance assessment where they disagree. That is, if the manager and the subordinate both agree that certain elements of the subordinate's performance are very good and that certain other elements need improvement, it may be possible to spend little time discussing those elements and to focus more energy on the performance areas that are in disagreement.

It is also important during a performance feedback interview to encourage participation and two-way communication. Some managers are prone to lecture a subordinate on the outcome of the performance-appraisal interview. The basic nature of the meeting, then, involves the manager telling the subordinate how he or she has been evaluated and then concluding the interview. As a result, the subordinate may feel threatened and that she or he had no voice in the process. Participation and two-way dialogue, however, allow the individual to express her or his own feelings and opinions about job performance and to provide other kinds of feedback as appropriate.[31]

It is also important for the manager to try to balance positive and negative feedback. As already noted, many managers tend to focus on the negative. In reality, however, employees are likely to have many positive characteristics related to performance as well. Thus, even though the manager must clearly address the negative performance characteristics noted in the appraisal, these negative attributes should be balanced against praise and recognition of the positive aspects of the employee's performance.

In addition, throughout the interview and the performance-management process, it is essential that the manager take a developmental and problem-solving orientation to the process. In other words, it is important not to focus on the individual as a person by saying things such as "You are a bad employee." Instead, the focus should be on providing developmental feedback targeted at behavior, not on the individual. A simple distinction between saying things like "You are a poor performer" versus "Your performance is not acceptable" can help keep the focus on behavior and not on the individual.

The performance-appraisal interview should conclude with a future-oriented discussion of what will happen next. This discussion often includes topics such as setting goals for correcting performance deficiencies and discussing the possibility of pay raises, promotion prospects, and similar kinds of awards. Of course, if performance is judged to be deficient, the feedback interview may focus on topics such as the establishment of a probationary period (after which employment may be terminated), the development of a training strategy for improving performance, and so forth. Regardless of the level of current performance, this interview setting should provide a time when the rater and the employee discuss future performance goals for the employee. If the organization uses a goal-based appraisal system, this discussion may be automatic. Even if a different type of appraisal model is used, it is helpful for the employee to have clear and specific goals for improving future performance. These goals, along with continued and regular feedback, should constitute the critical part of any performance-management program.

Even with these recommendations, however, feedback is not always as effective as we would like to believe. Many of today's recommendations and practices are based on the assumption that, if done properly, they will provide employees with feedback about their job performance. Several years ago, however, a study reviewed the research on the effectiveness of feedback interventions, beginning with early studies from the 19th century.[32] This study found that, although feedback was effective in almost two-thirds of the cases, it was not effective in the

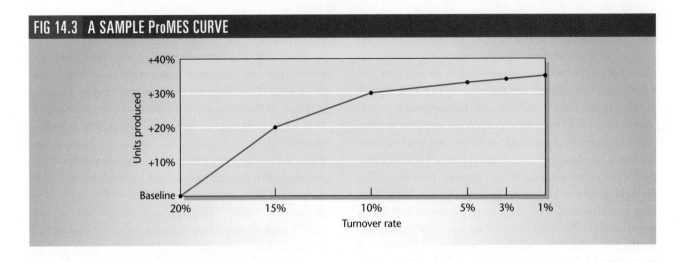

FIG 14.3   A SAMPLE ProMES CURVE

Units produced (y-axis): +40%, +30%, +20%, +10%, Baseline

Turnover rate (x-axis): 20%, 15%, 10%, 5%, 3%, 1%

rest. In fact, in a large number of cases, providing feedback to employees actually lowered subsequent performance. This result was independent of the nature of the feedback (i.e., whether it was positive or negative), which suggests that any feedback can, under certain conditions, have a negative effect on subsequent performance.

The study found that feedback was more likely to have a negative effect when the employee was new to a job, the job was extremely complex, ways to improve performance were not discussed, or goals for the future were not considered. The study also reported that feedback must focus the employee's attention on the task at hand. When feedback is provided so that the employee can take it personally, the feedback is much more likely to interfere with rather than enhance subsequent performance. Thus, the preceding recommendations will help ensure that feedback has the desired effect.

14-4b ProMES

Some of the techniques and interventions we have described are best suited for enhancing individual performance (which hopefully will result in ultimate improvements in firm performance), and others could be used with groups as well. Furthermore, we have been discussing these techniques relative to how they can improve some type of performance, but it is also possible to establish systems that can reduce turnover or absenteeism. These outcomes might also well be related to firm performance, but it is critical that such a link be established. In fact, if any

The **productivity measurement and evaluation system (ProMES)** is a program developed to improve group- or firm-level productivity. This approach incorporates ideas from goal setting with incentives for improvement, and it is based on a model of motivation similar to expectancy theory.

performance-enhancement technique is doing what it was designed to do, the organization as a whole should perform better. One such technique allows for the consideration of a wide range of outcomes and is concerned directly with team or organizational performance.

The **productivity measurement and evaluation system (ProMES)** incorporates ideas from goal setting to feedback, and it includes incentives for improvement.[33] More important, it includes a method for tying performance at the individual and group levels to organizational productivity. Specifically, team members work with outside experts to literally map the relationship between a given outcome and productivity. For example, assume that a group is focusing on reducing turnover. In most cases, reducing turnover will lower costs and boost productivity (as discussed in Chapter 6). In most cases, too, the incremental value of reducing turnover will be greatest when turnover is high; similarly, when turnover is low, further reductions will likely have a smaller impact. This pattern of diminishing returns is shown in the sample ProMES curve in Figure 14.3.

In this hypothetical example, the curve shows that the group has a current annual turnover rate of 20 percent and that there is a known baseline level of units currently being produced (it does not matter what this baseline is, only that it is known). The team has also calculated that if turnover can be reduced from 20 percent to 15 percent, then the number of units produced will increase by 20 percent. An additional reduction in turnover from 15 percent to 10 percent will achieve another 10-percent increase in units produced (a 30-percent increase in total). However, another 5-percent turnover reduction from 10 percent to 5 percent increases the number of units produced by only an additional 3 percent (33 percent total). Further reductions in turnover from 5 percent to 3 percent and 1 percent yields a unit increase of only 1 percent each.

Now, understand that reducing turnover is likely to have costs associated with it such as paying higher wages, paying bonuses for longevity, and so forth. The initial costs of reducing turnover from 20 percent to 15 percent will almost certainly be outweighed by the increased unit production of 20 percent. The additional costs for reducing turnover from 15 percent to 10 percent for an additional 10-percent increase in production may or may not be a cost-effective decision. But almost certainly the cost for reducing turnover from, say, 5 percent to 1 percent for only a 2-percent increase in unit production will end up costing more money than is gained. Of course, the point along the diminishing returns curve where costs begin to outweigh benefits must be calculated for each individual work setting.

The other important part of the ProMES process involves the various "connections" among the components. The procedure is based on a model of motivation[34] that is similar to the expectancy model discussed in the previous chapter. Thus, these connections are concerned with the relationship between effort and performance and between performance and attaining outcomes, as well as the link between obtaining outcomes and satisfying needs. The model and the technique are also based on the assumption that individuals and groups have a pool of resources (and effort) that they can assign to different activities, and the technique is designed to help them understand which activities they should focus on to increase firm productivity. The system has been widely adopted (especially in Europe)[35] and has been quite successful, and it is one of the few performance-enhancement techniques that focuses on performance above the level of the individual.

 14-5 EVALUATING PERFORMANCE-ENHANCEMENT PROGRAMS

When we consider all the ways in which firm performance can be assessed, and all the ways we can evaluate the effectiveness of any performance enhancement technique, it becomes clear that this is another area where data analytics can play a role. It is relatively easy to think about measures of individual performance (units produced or sales dollars), but assessing firm-level performance is much more complex. First, any measure should tie back to the firm's strategic goals, so the most direct way to assess firm performance is to determine whether those goals have been met. However, because there are likely to be many goals present in any organization, it takes large data analytics to even contemplate determining which goals have been met and which have not. There are also a number of general indexes of firm-level performance that could be useful in determining firm performance. These could be used independently or in conjunction with information about goal attainment.

The first set of indexes can be considered HR indicators. These include measures such as turnover rates, absenteeism, accident rates, and even general labor costs. Each of these indicators speaks to how well the organization is managing its human resources, and, given a steady rate of production or sales, changes in these indicators in the desired direction (i.e., lowering them) also translates into higher profitability. In addition, there are measures of profitability, productivity, and controllable costs. These measures actually are related, with specific measures making more sense in some businesses than in others. For example, restaurants often focus on controllable costs, waste, and how frequently they can turn over tables as the major indicators of success, while airlines usually focus on load factors and on-time performance as indicating success.

Finally, organizations also use a set of financial and accounting indicators. One of these is the stock price, which presumably reflects the market's view of a firm's success, although there are surely other factors that could affect stock price as well. Market share is another similar indicator of success, with the assumption that market share translates into market power some ability to influence prices or costs. Indexes such as "return on investment" or "return on assets" are more explicit financial indicators that speak to the rate of return on either corporate investment.

There is no clear rationale for why one of these indexes should be favored over the others, and each provides useful information for a firm trying to measure its success. Therefore, when an organization is interested in gauging the effectiveness of a performance-enhancement technique, it makes sense to examine multiple indicators. One could even think of these as forming a type of hierarchy: If the intervention is working, then individual performance should increase, one or more corporate HR measures should improve, and these should translate into higher rates of return and higher stock prices. An important caveat, however, is to note that many of these indicators can be affected by a wide variety of factors so that changes in any one index may not be a good measure of how effective the intervention has really been.

14-6 HR IN THE HEADLINES

14-6a HR and the Arab Spring

During 2011–2012, an amazing chain of events took place in the Arab world. Tunisia, Egypt, and Libya all saw an overthrow of deeply entrenched governments, dominated (in the last two cases) by strong leaders. These governments were replaced through democratic elections. In the case of Tunisia and Egypt, the parties that appeared to emerge from the turmoil were closely tied to Muslim groups such as the Muslim Brotherhood. Not many models of democratically elected Muslim-oriented governments exist, so there has been a great deal of concern over what is to come. Although most discussions center on world politics, there is also concern over implications for the management of multinationals that operate in these countries, and with the ways in which these developments might influence the HRM process.

Today, there are more than 1.6 billion Muslims in the world, living in more than 200 countries. Most Muslims live in the Middle East and North Africa, but substantial numbers live in India, Pakistan, Afghanistan, and surrounding areas, as well as in Malaysia and Indonesia. In fact, the country with the largest Muslim population is Indonesia.[36]

The first problem we encounter when we discuss HRM in Muslim areas is that cultural differences in various parts of the world affect HRM practices. For example, HRM practices in Turkey are seen as being very similar to those in the West, while practices in Malaysia and Indonesia reflect the multicultural nature of the workforces in both countries.[37] In general, though, HR systems in Muslim countries tend to be value-based and draw heavily

upon The Holy Qur'an (or Koran).[38] In addition, HR systems in Muslim countries rely (to a greater or lesser extent) upon sharia, which is the entire body of Muslim law. Sharia draws upon the Qur'an, and other sources as well. Sharia is not a codified set of laws but, instead, depends upon the opinions of qualified Islamic legal scholars (these opinions are known as *fatwas*). Although we cannot do justice to the entire scope of Sharia law in this text, it is worth noting that these laws forbid the charging of interest; specify the punishment for a number of crimes specifically mentioned in the Qur'an or in the writings of Mohammed; allow men to become divorced at will by just saying it aloud; and specify the dietary restrictions known as halal (very similar to the Jewish laws of kosher).

But values based on the Qur'an itself are the most important part of Muslim (HRM) systems. In fact, Ali et al. identified several implications of the Ten Islamic Commandments for HRM.[39] Most of these were related to issues of fairness and justice because the Qur'an calls for honesty and justice in trade, as well as the equitable distribution of wealth in society. Ahmad goes further, suggesting that HR systems could be based on core Muslim values of piety, morality, and quality (defined as performance excellence). These values, then, result in an HR system where, in hiring, priority should be given to qualified individuals: One can disagree with a supervisor, but it must be done politely; employee layoffs and downsizing should be considered only as the last resort to maintain business survival; it is important to maintain due process when dealing with employee grievances; performance should be the main criteria for evaluation and the basis for compensation; and management should avoid favoritism and nepotism in all aspects of decision-making.

It would seem difficult to argue with these particular HR practices. Concerns for both distributive and procedural justice are clearly important in Muslim societies, but these concerns and the practices would also be quite welcome in most U.S. and Western-based companies. It is true that sharia also specifies the manner of dress for women (actually, for men as well), and that stoning to death is an extreme (but allowable) punishment for fornication and adultery, and these are the examples we usually hear about. But it would seem that an HR system based on the

Mohammed Abed/afp/Getty Images

Qur'an and sharia would not look that different from what we would expect in a (progressive) Western company.

The extent to which the new governments will adopt these practices and values remains to be seen. But it does appear that Western ideas about effective HR practices are quite consistent with Muslim values and law. It will be interesting to see how all this plays out over the next few years.

14-6b Privacy and Cybersecurity in the 21st Century

In Chapter 2, we discussed some of the privacy issues facing organizations today, especially in light of recent revelations about data collection by the National Security Agency (NSA). As you might imagine, privacy and cybersecurity have become much more complex and critical in today's workplace. As a result, HR managers must be more conscientious about protecting the privacy of both business and employee information.

But protection from whom? In today's workplace, every desktop computer, laptop, or handheld device is vulnerable to attack. Intruders hacking into a computer system, malware, lost laptops, and insider threats all combine to present serious challenges to companies. For example, developments in malware have been targeting handheld mobile devices with software that appears to be legitimate but contains code that enables hackers to access secret or sensitive information.[40] Furthermore, data breaches at Target stores and Neiman-Marcus have made it clear that hackers can gain access to huge amounts of sensitive data from presumably sophisticated companies.

These concerns have led to the development of the National Cybersecurity and Critical Infrastructure Protection Act (H.R. 3696), first proposed in 2013 but not yet passed. This Act would provide for the Secretary of Homeland Security to coordinate with government and business leaders to facilitate national efforts to protect sensitive information from cyberthreats. The congressional leaders behind this legislation have also called for all businesses to be aware of the security threats posed by cybercriminals, who are growing more sophisticated every day in their methods to hack into and extract personal records and financial data from companies. They have also urged businesses to practice good cyberhygiene in terms of computer-usage policies, the installation of security software, and assuring that employees do not respond to suspicious e-mails.[41]

In addition, apps for cell phones may also open the door to new types of threats to security and privacy. For example, location-based smartphone games such as Pokemon Go have been used to lure innocent participants to unsafe areas where they have been robbed or assaulted. Further, as myriad social and technological platforms become increasingly blended and blurred, more and more avenues for both mild and vicious acts seem to arise.[42] In fact, developments such as these have led some to suggest that HR screen individuals on the basis of how much of a threat they may pose to the company and to the company's data, based on analyzing a potential employee's workplace traffic on various social media sites. While this idea may seem far-fetched right now, it is clear that new technologies at work will present new challenges for HR.[42]

Legal ambiguity over the ownership of Twitter accounts represents such a new challenge. Specifically, if an employee sets up a Twitter account on the basis of his or her job and attracts many followers, who owns the account if the employee leaves the firm? Based on several recent court decisions, it seems that the answer is not clear, unless the company has a formal policy and written agreements regarding ownership. It is also important to have the company's IT operation control passwords and the administrative rights to them. Otherwise, a departing employee may be able to carry off valuable information.[43]

In addition to these internal and external threats to security and privacy, it is also increasingly clear that the government itself poses a threat, especially in view of its relationship with many top social media companies. In 2013, we learned about PRISM (Planning Tool for Resource Integration, Synchronization and Management), a program used by the NSA. PRISM has been described as a data tool designed to collect and process foreign intelligence that passes through American servers. The program cannot intentionally access information about American citizens, but it *can* access information about them when information is collected "incidentally" as part of a sweep of information about a foreign operative.[44]

Perhaps the most frightening aspect of the PRISM program is that it has been carried out with the apparent cooperation of Microsoft, Yahoo!, Google, Facebook, Paltalk, AOL, Skype, YouTube, and Apple (but not Twitter), and it allows the NSA to collect information from e-mails, video chats, photographs, documents, and connection logs that helps the agency track foreign agents.[45] These companies have denied giving the NSA direct access to their servers, and this appears to be the case. It does also seem, however, that these companies collaborated with the government in developing more efficient methods to share personal data of foreign users in direct response to lawful government requests. Furthermore, requested information was sent to a special, secure server to which the NSA has access and so can obtain that information.[46]

Thus, it seems clear that organizations must be concerned about every aspect of their cybercommunications. Otherwise, sensitive, private information about employees or customers might be at risk, as well as information concerning plans, policies, and technologies that might be of use to competitors. What specific roles should HR play in this process? A big step in protecting information involves training employees about these threats. Training should emphasize vigilance for Internet scams, as well as simple security measures such as locking all devices and keeping passwords secret. Employees should also be trained to understand that business should not be conducted in Internet cafes, hotels, or other public places where security cannot be guaranteed. Policies should also be established prohibiting employees from posting confidential or sensitive business information on social media sites. In addition, there is a need for clear policies and procedures concerning terminated or separated employees to ensure that their accounts are closed and their access to information is immediately terminated as well.[47]

These issues are extremely important for modern organizations, and they will grow in importance in coming years. Cyberthreats are becoming more sophisticated, and HR departments must keep up with them in order to limit a firm's vulnerability. Furthermore, as social media sites become even more important, HR managers must recognize that employees often voluntarily give out information that is either private or sensitive, and they therefore must develop policies to deal with employee usage on these sites without restricting free speech. Finally, given the information-gathering capacity of organizations such as the NSA, we must all realize that assumptions we have made in the past about what is private and what is public are no longer valid. It seems safe to assume that any communications we engage in, using any type of media, are potentially accessible to someone in some form. How companies guard their private and sensitive information in such an environment will present HR managers with a major challenge in the coming years.[48]

14-6c Toward a Two-Class Benefits System?

For decades sociologists have often characterized U.S. society as having three "classes" based on income: upper-, middle-, and lower-class. More sophisticated models also include gradations of each (upper-middle, lower-middle, and so forth). In recent years, though, concerns have been raised about the fact that the middle class (however defined) has been shrinking, leading America toward a two-class system. In blunt terms, some people talk about us becoming a society of "haves" and "have-nots."

In some ways, this same trend may be emerging in the workplace in terms of employee benefits. For example, many firms—especially larger, older businesses—have in recent years systematically reduced many of the benefits they provide to their employees. Among the most common changes are reduced health-care coverage and/or higher health-care premiums and reductions in employer contributions to employee retirement programs. Similarly, businesses that employ fewer full-time employees and use more part-time and/or temporary workers often do so because these employees are paid fewer—or no—benefits. One recent survey found that between 2008 and 2012, approximately 40 percent of all working adults in the United States faced reductions in their employer-sponsored benefits.

At the same time, though, businesses in Silicon Valley are offering increasingly lavish, unusual, and expensive benefits in their efforts to attract and retain talented and mobile employees. Indeed, so scarce is talent that some of these companies are paying a $20,000 "finder's fee" to anyone who refers an employee who subsequently joins the company and stays at least 6 months. But benefits are the real battleground.

Take Google, for example. In addition to "standard" benefits such as insurance and retirement, the company also provides free massages, haircuts, laundry services, shuttles, gourmet meals, and snacks. Not to be outdone, Facebook recently moved into a new office building. The firm ripped out the old cubicles that the previous tenant had used and replaced them with couches and shared work tables. They also installed cafes, eateries, and a pub. Facebook contracted with

Sergio Martinez/Shutterstock.com

a popular local coffee vendor to open kiosks in the building and brew made-to-order coffee drinks. And the firm provides free wash-and-fold laundry services, haircuts, dry cleaning, and concierge services (some of these options, such as dry cleaning, are not free but are very convenient).

Zynga is also in the game. Employees can bring their dogs to work and take advantage of free grooming services. Employees also get access to a free health spa, a full-service gym, and free arcade games scattered throughout the building. Zynga too offers an upscale coffee shop, gourmet food, and an ever-changing menu. Indeed, among the high-tech giants Zynga leads the way in gourmet food options. Its kitchen is run by the former director of the California Culinary Institute. In fact, high-quality food seems to be the current competition among these firms. For instance, when Google's Marissa Mayer was lured to take over Yahoo!, one of her first moves was to hire a new company chef and announce plans to start offering free gourmet meals.

Obviously, such lavish perks are not free. Silicon Valley companies spend far more on employee benefits than do average U.S. employers. As long as these companies are growing rapidly and raking in big profits, they can afford to keep investing in their employees. But there will almost certainly come a time when earnings start to slide; when they do, these perks may well be among the first costs to get trimmed.[49]

14-6d HR in Faith-Based Businesses

Managing so-called faith-based businesses provides some interesting perspectives on how to run a business. A faith-based business is one that is founded and managed in ways that explicitly acknowledge religious beliefs. In the United States, most faith-based businesses incorporate Christian beliefs into their day-to-day management practices. One common practice among faith-based businesses is that they tend to be closed on Sunday. They also tend to be privately owned and to donate a meaningful portion of their profits to churches and/or church-operated charities.

One major faith-based business is Hobby Lobby, a fast-growing retailer that offers an array of products related to various hobbies, crafts, art, and decorating. Hobby Lobby was started in Oklahoma City in 1972 by David Green. Today, the company is run by one of Green's sons, Steven. Another son, Mart, runs an affiliated business called Mardel, a maker of Christian products. Hobby Lobby has about 32,000 employees, annual revenues of about $4 billion, and operates more than 700 stores in 47 states.

Hobby Lobby's website (http://www.hobbylobby.com) actively promotes the religious beliefs of the firm's leadership.

Chick-fil-A, another successful faith-based company, was started in 1967 by Truett Cathy, who still serves as chairman and CEO. His son, Dan, is the current president and heir apparent to the chicken sandwich empire. The company employs about 50,000 people in 2,000 locations in 43 states and has an annual income of about $4.6 billion. Unlike Hobby Lobby, Chick-fil-A (see http://www.chick-fil-a.com) tends to be less aggressive in promoting its religious underpinnings (but more about that later).

Faith-based businesses enjoy certain advantages in terms of recruiting and retaining employees. For instance, regardless of their personal beliefs, some people may be attracted to a retail employer that does not require them to work on Sunday. These firms also tend to provide reasonable compensation and benefits packages for their employees. And some people who themselves have strong religious beliefs may be attracted to an employer who shares those beliefs. But they may also experience some disadvantages as well. Closing on Sunday, for example, may limit sales and provide fewer work hours for employees. In addition, contributions to church also cut into profits, thereby potentially restricting business growth and subsequent career opportunities. Finally, just as some potential employees may be attracted to an organization that espouses their own beliefs, other potential employees with different beliefs may have no interest in working for that same organization.

Sometimes faith-based businesses may also encounter issues they may not have foreseen. For instance, a t-shirt printer in Kentucky is being boycotted because he refused to print shirts promoting an upcoming gay rights parade. And Chick-fil-A recently focused some unwanted attention on its faith-based business practices. In 2012, Dan Cathy was quoted in the media as denouncing same-sex marriage. It was also discovered that the company had made substantial donations to several groups working to limit gay rights. Not surprisingly, critics also pointed out that the firm's benefit packages do not extend coverage to same-sex partners of their employees. In response, politicians such as the mayors of Boston and Chicago indicated that they would try to block Chick-fil-A from expanding into their markets. For its part, Chick-fil-A stresses the fact that while its owner has expressed certain personal views, the firm itself does not discriminate against employees or customers on the basis of their beliefs, gender, creed, race, or sexual orientation. Moreover, the firm's position is that the debate over same-sex marriage belongs in the government and political arenas, not in the business arena.

CLOSING CASE
Creating Humane Work Schedules

Sixty-hour workweeks used to be the norm in the United States; now 80 hours is not uncommon. But working longer hours does not always increase productivity. One recent study showed that U.S. workers were less productive per hour worked than those from countries with shorter workweeks, including France and Germany. Experts hypothesize that overworked employees become tired, stressed, and less motivated. Lowell Bryan, a McKinsey & Company partner, claims, "We've created jobs that are literally impossible. The human cost is profound, and the opportunity cost is also great in terms of organizational effectiveness." Problems made worse by overwork are costly and can include injuries, mistakes, rework, workplace violence, stress-related diseases, absenteeism, and high turnover. The 2009 recession only made things worse as businesses cut jobs but then expected those who were still employed to pick up the slack.

Some companies are now actively seeking ways to offer a more reasonable work–life balance. Fox News, for example, split the job of one senior executive between two individuals who both work full-time and share responsibilities equally. The editorship of the *Los Angeles Times* was once held by one person, but now three workers do the job. Part-time work is another increasingly popular option. JetBlue allows key managers to work part-time schedules in exchange for reduced compensation. In many cases, it is not hard to implement these new working arrangements. Law associates can handle fewer cases, and auditors can work with fewer clients by putting in less time and receiving lower compensation.

It is accepted wisdom that willing workers are plentiful, no matter how demanding the schedule, but most companies note that there is often a shortage of qualified managers. Increasingly, people want time off and are willing to give up money and career advancement to get it. Both men and women now talk freely in many companies about wanting to "have it all," referring to a career and a rewarding life outside of work. As these conversations become more widespread and more intense, perhaps U.S. companies will respond. Alternative, flexible work arrangements are more acceptable to workers, and they can also create a more motivated, productive, and loyal workforce.[51]

Case Questions

1. Do you think working hours will get longer or shorter in the future? Why?
2. Would you be willing to trade off scheduling flexibility and balance for slightly reduced compensation? What factors would be important to you in such an arrangement?

> "We've created jobs that are literally impossible. The human cost is profound, and the opportunity cost is also great in terms of organizational effectiveness."
>
> —LOWELL BRYAN, MCKINSEY & COMPANY PARTNER[50]

NotarYES/Shutterstock.com

STUDY TOOLS 14

READY TO STUDY?
In the book, you can:

☐ Rip out the chapter review card at the back of the book for a handy summary of the chapter and key terms.

ONLINE AT CENGAGEBRAIN.COM YOU CAN:

☐ Collect StudyBits while you read and study the chapter.

☐ Quiz yourself on key concepts.

☐ Find videos for further exploration.

☐ Prepare for tests with HR4 Flash Cards as well as those you create.

ENDNOTES

1

1. Greg Lalicker, President, Hilcorp, *Fortune* (Mar. 16, 2016): 144.

2. "The 100 Best Companies to Work For," *Fortune* (Mar. 15, 2016): 144–165; "The World's Most Admired Companies," *Fortune* (Mar. 1, 2016): 109–116; *Hoover's Handbook of American Business 2016* (Austin: Mergent, Inc., 2016): 45, 337–338, 765–766.

3. Robert M. Grant, "Toward a Knowledge-Based View of the Firm," *Strategic Management Journal* (1996), 17: 109–122.

4. Jeffrey Pfeffer, "Producing Sustainable Competitive Advantage Through the Effective Management of People," *Academy of Management Executive* (Feb. 1995): 55–69; Peter Cappelli and Anne Crocker-Hefter, "Distinctive Human Resources Are Firms' Core Competencies," *Organizational Dynamics* (Winter 1996): 7–22.

5. Jeffrey Pfeffer, *The Human Equation: Building Profits by Putting People First* (Boston: Harvard Business School Press, 1998).

6. Robert E. Lewis and Robert J. Heckman, "Talent Management: A Critical Review," *Human Resource Management Review* (2006), 16: 139–154.

7. Brian E. Becker, Mark A. Huselid, and Richard W. Beatty, *The Differentiated Workforce: Transforming Talent into Strategic Impact* (Boston: Harvard Business School Press, 2009).

8. "Beyond Jobs Numbers, Labor Shortage Looms," *USA Today* (May 7, 2015): B1.

9. "Beyond Jobs Numbers, Labor Shortage Looms," *USA Today* (May 7, 2015): B1; "Pilot Shortage Looms for Airlines," *USA Today* (Jan. 7, 2013): 3B; "Wanted, Desperately: Skills Workers," *USA Today* (Apr. 18, 2012): 2B; "Lack of Workers Plagues Construction Industry," *USA Today* (Nov. 29, 2012): 1B; Heather Long, "Job Cuts Soar 218% in January," *cnn.money.com*, accessed on February 4, 2016.

10. Randall S. Schuler, "Repositioning the Human Resource Function: Transformation or Demise?" *Academy of Management Executive* (Aug. 1990): 49–60.

11. Pamela Babcock, "America's Newest Export: White-Collar Jobs," *HR Magazine* (Apr. 2005): 50–57.

12. For a good discussion of the issues involved with "star" employees, see, Herman Aguinis and Ernest O'Boyle, "Star Performers in Twenty-First Century Organizations," *Personnel Psychology* (2014), 67(2): 313–350.

13. Many of these complexities are discussed in Wayne F. Cascio and Herman Aguinis, "Staffing Twenty-First-Century Organizations," *The Academy of Management Annals* (2008), 2: 133–165.

14. For an excellent review of some of the problems involved in selecting employees in the context of high-security settings, see Paul R. Sackett, Neal Schmitt, Jill E. Ellingson, and Melissa Kabin, "High-Stakes Testing in Employment, Credentialing, and Higher Education," *American Psychologist* (Apr. 2001): 302–418.

15. Daniel Wren, *The Evolution of Management Thought*, 5th ed. (New York: Wiley, 2005).

16. Thomas A. Mahoney, "Evolution of Concept and Practice in Personnel Administration Human Resource Management (PAHRM)," *Journal of Management* (1986), 12 (2): 223–241.

17. Frederick W. Taylor, *Principles of Scientific Management* (New York: Harper, 1911).

18. Oliver E. Allen, "This Great Mental Revolution," *Audacity* (Summer 1996): 52–61.

19. Wren, *The Evolution of Management Thought*.

20. Ibid.

21. Elton Mayo, *The Human Problems of an Industrial Civilization* (New York: Macmillan, 1933).

22. Abraham Maslow, "A Theory of Human Motivation," *Psychological Review* (Jul. 1943): 370–396.

23. Douglas McGregor, *The Human Side of Enterprise* (New York: McGraw-Hill, 1960).

24. James H. Dulebohn, Gerald R. Ferris, and James T. Stodd, "The History and Evolution of Human Resource Management," in Gerald R. Ferris, Sherman D. Rosen, and Harold T. Barnum (Eds.), *Handbook of Human Resource Management* (Cambridge, MA: Blackwell, 1995): 18–41.

25. Katie Hunt and Andrew Stevens, "Key Things to Know about China's Market Meltdown," *CNN Online*, www.cnn.com, accessed on August 24, 2015.

26. Tim Bowler, "Falling Oil Prices: Who Are the Winners and Losers?" *BBC News Online*, www.bbc.com, accessed on January 19, 2016.

27. Larry McShane, "Walmart Closing 269 Store Worldwide, Impacting 10,000 American Employees," *New York Daily News*, (Jan. 15, 2016).

28. This term is most associated with John Mackey, the co-founder of Whole Foods. See John Mackey and Rajendra Sisodia, *Conscious Capitalism: Liberating the Heroic Spirit of Business* (Boston: Harvard Business School Press, 2013).

29. See, for example, John Elkington, *Cannibals with Forks: The Triple Bottom Line of 21st Century Business* (London: Capstone, 1997); and Andrew Savitz and Karl Weber, *The Triple Bottom Line: How Today's Best-Run Companies Are Achieving Economic, Social and Environmental Success—and How You Can Too* (Hoboken, NJ: Jossey-Bass, 2006).

30. Dave Ulrich, "A New Mandate for Human Resources," *Harvard Business Review* (Jan.–Feb. 1998): 124–133.

31. For a fuller discussion of the topic, see Gary S. Becker, "The Age of Human Capital," in Edward P. Lazear (Ed.), *Education in the 21st Century* (Palo Alto, CA: Hoover Institution Press): 3–8.

32. See, for example, Robert Ployhart, Anthony J. Nyberg, Greg Reilly, and Mark Maltarich, "Human Capital Is dead: Long Live Human Capital Resources!" *Journal of Management* (2014), 40: 371–398; and Patrick M. Wright, Russell Coff, and Thomas P. Moliterno, "Strategic Human Capital: Crossing the Great Divide," *Journal of Management* (2014), 40: 353–370.

33. John W. Kendrick, *Understanding Productivity: An Introduction to the Dynamics of Productivity Change* (Baltimore: Johns Hopkins University Press, 1977).

34. Ross Johnson and William O. Winchell, *Management and Quality* (Milwaukee, WI: American Society for Quality Control, 1989).

35. Rudy M. Yandrick, "Help Employees Reach for the Stars," *HR Magazine* (Jan. 1997): 96–100.

36. Michelle Martinez, "Prepared for the Future," *HR Magazine* (Apr. 1997): 80–87.

37. For an interesting contrast between large and small firms and HRM activities, see Allison E. Barber, Michael J. Wesson, Quinetta M. Roberson, and M. Susan Taylor, "A Tale of Two Job Markets: Comparing the Hiring Practices of Large and Small Organizations," *Personnel Psychology* (1999), 52: 841–861.

38. For an excellent review, see John W. Boudreau, "Utility Analysis for Decisions in Human Resource Management," in Marvin D. Dunnette and Leatta M. Hough (Eds.), *Handbook of Industrial and Organizational Psychology*, vol. 2, 2nd ed. (Palo Alto, CA: Consulting Psychologists Press, 1991): 621–745.

39. See, for example, Mark A. Huselid, "The Impact of Human Resource Management Practices on Turnover, Productivity, and Corporate Financial Reporting," *Academy of Management Journal* (1996), 39: 779–801.

40. Lotte Bailyn, "Patterned Chaos in Human Resource Management," *Sloan Management Review* (Winter 1993): 77–89.

41. Martha Finney, "Degrees That Make a Difference," *HR Magazine* (Nov. 1996): 74–82; Bruce Kaufman, "What Companies Want from HR Graduates," *HR Magazine* (Sept. 1994): 84–90.

42. Steve Bates, "Facing the Future," *HR Magazine* (Jul. 2002): 26–32.

43. Brian D. Steffy and Steven D. Maurer, "Conceptualizing and Measuring the Economic Effectiveness of Human Resource Activities," *Academy of Management Review* (1988), 13(2): 271–286.

44. "Walmart vs. Costco," www.bloomberg.com, accessed on October 1, 2013.

2

1. *The Seattle Times* (February 15, 2016) B1.

2. Charlotte Alter, "Millennial Women Are Still Getting Paid Less Than Men," *Time* (Jun. 13, 2015): 56; "Sheryl Sandberg on Ellen Pao: Many Women See Themselves," *The Seattle Times* (Feb. 15, 2016): B1; Kristen Bellstrom, "Female MBAs Face a $400,000 Gender Pay Gap," *Fortune* (Apr. 1, 2016): 46–48.

3. David Israel, "Learn to Manage the Legal Process," *HR Magazine* (July 1993): 83–87.

4. "HR and the Government," *HR Magazine* (May 1994): 43–48. See also J. Ledvinka, *Federal Regulation of Personnel and Human Resource Management* (Boston: Kent, 1982).

5. Jon M. Werner and Mark C. Bolino, "Explaining U.S. Court of Appeals Decisions Involving Performance Appraisal: Accuracy, Fairness, and Validation," *Personnel Psychology* (Spring 1997): 1–24.

6. See Philip E. Varca and Patricia Pattison, "Evidentiary Standards in Employment Discrimination: A View Toward the Future," *Personnel Psychology* (Summer 1993): 239–250.

7. *Diaz v. Pan American World Airways, Inc.*, 442 F. 2d 385 (5th Cir. 1971).

8. James E. Jones, William P. Murphy, and Robert Belton, *Discrimination in Employment*, 5th ed. (American Casebook Series) (St. Paul, MN: West, 1987): 381.

9. *Griggs v. Duke Power Company*, 401 U.S. 424 (1971).

10. Technically, neither guilt nor innocence is determined in civil cases. Instead, the defendant is judged to be either liable or not liable for discrimination. We will use the terms *guilty* and *innocent* occasionally, however, because readers are more comfortable with these terms.

11. *Wards Cove Packing Co., Inc.* v. *Antonio*, U.S. Sup. Ct. 1387 (Jun. 5, 1989).

12. *McDonnell-Douglas Corporation v. Green*, 411 U.S. 792 (1973).

13. "Culture of Racial Bias at Shoney's Underlines Chairman's Departure," *Wall Street Journal* (Dec. 21, 1992): A1.

14. *EEOC v. Abercrombie & Fitch Stores, Inc.*, 135 Sup. Ct. 2028 (2015): 14–86.

15. "When Quotas Replace Merit, Everybody Suffers," *Forbes* (Feb. 15, 1993): 80–102.

16. *Bakke v. The Regents of the University of California at Davis*, 438 U.S. 265 (1978).

17. *United Steelworkers of America, AFL-CIO* v. *Weber*, Sup. Ct. (1979); 443 U.S. 193; 99 S. Ct. 2721; 61 L. Ed. 2d 480.

18. *Wygant v. Jackson Board of Education*, Sup. Ct. (1986); 106 S. Ct. 1842; 90 L. Ed. 2d 260.

19. *Local 93 of the International Association of Firefighters, AFL-CIO, C.L.C.* v. *City of Cleveland*, Sup. Ct. (1986); 106 S. Ct. 3063, 92 L. Ed. 2d 405.

20. *U.S.* v. *Paradise*, Sup. Ct.; 478 US 1019; 106 S. Ct. 3331, 92 L. Ed. 2d737 (1986).

21. *Einsley Branch, NAACP v. Seibels*, 60 F. 3d 717 (11th Cir. 1994).

22. *Hopwood* v. *State of Texas*, 78 F. 3d 932 (5th Cir. 1996).

23. http://scholar.google.com/scholar_case?case=5183084208914209139&q=fisher+v.+university+of+texas&hl=en&as_sdt=8000006&as_vis=1, *Grutter v. Bollinger*, 539 U.S. 306 (2003); http://scholar.google.com/scholar_case?case=6805287674686880550&q=fisher+v.+university+of+texas&hl=en&as_sdt=8000006&as_vis=1, *Gratz v. Bollinger*, 539 U.S. 244, 123 S. Ct. 2411, 156 L.Ed. 2d 257 (2003).

24. *Fisher v. University of Texas*, 133 S. Ct. 2411, U.S. Supreme Court (2013), no. 11–345.

25. Ariane de Vogue, "Supreme Court Divided in University of Texas Affirmative Action Case," *CNN Online* (Dec. 9, 2015).

26. Jonathan A. Segal, "Sexual Harassment: Where Are We Now?" *HR Magazine* (Oct. 1996): 68–73; Gerald D. Block, "Avoiding Liability for Sexual Harassment," *HR Magazine* (Apr. 1995): 91–94.

27. *Meritor Savings Bank, FSB v. Vinson et al.*, Sup. Ct.; 477 U.S. 57 (1986).

28. *Harris v. Forklift Systems* 510 U.S. 17 (1993).

29. Jonathan A. Segal, "Proceed Carefully, Objectively to Investigate Sexual Harassment Claims," *HR Magazine* (Oct. 1993): 91–95.

30. *Scott v. Sears Roebuck*, 798 F. 2d 210 (7th cir. 1986).

31. *Oncale v. Sundowner Offshore Servs.*, 96 Sup. Ct. 568, 523 U.S. 75; S. Ct. 998; 140 L. Ed. 2d 201 (1998).

32. "Justices' Ruling Further Defines Sexual Harassment," *Wall Street Journal* (Mar. 5, 1998): B1.

33. Terry Kingkade, "Notre Dame Stung by 'The Hunting Ground' Is under U.S. Investigation for Sexual Harassment Cases," *The Huffington Post*, www.huffingtonpost.com, accessed on April 17, 2015.

34. Lily Ledbetter Fair Pay Act of 2009, Public Law No. 111-2 (2009).

35. "How to Shrink the Pay Gap," *Business Week* (Jun. 24, 2002): 151.

36. *Johnson v. Mayor and City Council of Baltimore*, Sup. Ct. 105; S. Ct. 2727; 86 l. Ed. 2d 286 (1985).

37. Allen Smith, *EEOC Stats Show Spike in Age Discrimination Charges*. SHRM Report (Nov. 2009).

38. abcnews.com, February 16, 2012, accessed on April 26, 2012.

39. The most noteworthy of these are the *Wards Cove* (1989) case discussed earlier, *Patterson v. McLean Credit Union* [109 S. Ct. 2363 (1989)], and *Pricewaterhouse v. Hopkins* [109 S. Ct. 1775 (1989)].

40. Most of these issues were decided in *EEOC* v. *Arabian American Oil Co.*, 89 Sup. Ct. 1838, 1845; 498 U.S. 808; 111 S. Ct. 40; 112 L. Ed. 2d 17 (1990).

41. Francine S. Hall and Elizabeth L. Hall, "The ADA: Going Beyond the Law," *Academy of Management Executive* (Feb. 1994): 17–26.

42. Albert S. King, "Doing the Right Thing for Employees with Disabilities," *Training & Development* (Sept. 1993): 44–46.

43. "Disabilities Act Abused?" *USA Today* (Sept. 25, 1998): 1B, 2B.

44. Michael Barrier, "A Line in the Sand," *HR Magazine* (Jul. 2002): 35–43.

45. For a review and a discussion of the determinants of this problem, see Adrienne Colella, "Coworker Distributive Fairness Judgments of the Workplace Accommodation of Employees with Disabilities," *Academy of Management Review* (2001), 26(1): 100–116.

46. David Stamps, "Just How Scary Is the ADA?" *Training* (1995), 32: 93–101.

47. "Court Narrows Disability Act," *USA Today* (Jun. 23, 1999): 1A.

48. Michelle Neely Martinez, "FMLA—Headache or Opportunity?" *HR Magazine* (Feb. 1994): 42–45.

49. Jonathan A. Segal, "Traps to Avoid in FMLA Compliance," *HR Magazine* (Feb. 1994): 97–100. See also Timothy Bland, "The Supreme Court Reins in the FMLA (Slightly)," *HR Magazine* (Jul. 2002): 44–48.

50. Randy Albelda and Betty Reid Mandell, "Paid Family and Medical Leave," *New Politics* (Winter 2010), 12(4): Whole No. 48.

51. Jennifer Glass, "Work-Life Policies," in Ann C. Crouter and Alan Booth, *Work-Life Policies*. (Washington, DC: The Urban institute Press, 2009): 232.

52. *Obergefell et al. v. Hodges, Director, Ohio Department of Health, et al.*, No. 14–556, Jun. 26, 2015.

53. John Montoya, "New Priorities for the '90s," *HR Magazine* (Apr. 1997): 118–122.

54. David Israel, "Check EEOC Position Statements for Accuracy," *HR Magazine* (Sept. 1993): 106–109.

55. Allen Smith, *EEOC's Proposed ADA Rule Would List Presumptive Disabilities*. SHRM Report (Sept. 2009).

56. David C. Ankeny and David Israel, "Completing an On-Site OFCCP Audit," *HR Magazine* (Mar. 1993): 89–94.

57. *Hoover's Handbook of American Business 2016* (Austin: Mergent, 2016): 642–642; "Overworked and Underpaid?" *USA Today* (Apr. 16, 2015): 1A, 2A, www.usatoday.com, accessed on April 20, 2016;

"10 Tricks Employers Use to Cheat Workers Out of Overtime," www.jobs.aol.com, accessed on April 20, 2016; "Walmart Fined by Labor Department for Denying Workers Overtime," *Huffington Post* (Mar. 2, 2015): www.huffingtonpost.com, accessed on April 20, 2016.

58. Alejandro Lazo, "Oregon Governor Signs Landmark Minimum Wage Law," *The Wall Street Journal* (Mar. 2, 2016).

59. "Maryland First to OK 'Wal-Mart Bill,'" *USA Today* (Jan. 13, 2006): 1B; "SEC to Propose Overhaul of Rules On Executive Pay," *Wall Street Journal* (Jan. 10, 2006): A1.

60. "Health Care Reform," SHRM Government Affairs News Update (Nov. 2009).

61. Adam Liptak, "Supreme Court Upholds Health Care Law, 5-4, in Victory for Obama, *The New York Times* (Jun. 29, 2012): A1.

62. *Electromation v. NLRB*, US Court of Appeals for the 35 F. 3d 1148 (7th Cir. 1994).

63. *E.I. Du Pont de Nemours and Company* v. *NLRB*, 12 F. 3d 209 (5th Cir. 1993).

64. "Fewer Employers Are Currently Conducting Psych and Drug Tests," *HR Focus* (Oct. 2000): 78.

65. Stephanie Overman, "Splitting Hairs," *HR Magazine* (Aug. 1999): 42–48.

66. "Laws, Juries Shift Protection to Terminated Employees," *USA Today* (Apr. 2, 1998): 1B, 2B.

67. Vindu Goel, "A Yahoo Employee-Ranking System Favored by Marissa Mayer Is Challenged in Court," *The New York Times – Technology* (Feb. 1, 2016).

68. "Sexual Harassment Statistics in the Workplace," www.briancoutour.com, accessed on April 20, 2016; Pamela Mahabeer, "Sexual Harassment Still Pervasive in the Workplace," *AOL Jobs* (Jan. 28, 2011); "Power and Sexual Harassment – Men and Women See Things Differently," *Science Daily* (Apr. 6, 2007): www.sciencedaily.com, accessed on April 20, 2016; "Female Supervisors More Susceptible to Workplace Sexual Harassment," *EurekAlert* (Aug. 8, 2009): www.eurekalert.com, accessed on April 20, 2016.

3

1. "Some Manufacturers Say 'Adios' to China," *USA Today* (Mar. 19, 2013): 7B; "Mexican Manufacturing Rises Again," reuters.com, accessed on April 21, 2016; "Mexico's Manufacturing Base Rebounds," areadevelopment.com, accessed on April 21, 2016; "Mexico's Welcome Mat Attracts Aerospace Manufacturers," aviationweek.com, accessed on April 21, 2016; "Mexico: The New China," *New York Times* (Jan. 26, 2013): B1.

2. "Multinational Corporations in China: Finding and Keeping Talent," report issued by SHRM, www.shrm.org, accessed April 21, 2016.

3. Martha I. Finney, "Global Success Rides on Keeping Top Talent," *HR Magazine* (Apr. 1996): 68–74.

4. Gregory D. Chowanec and Charles N. Newstrom, "The Strategic Management of International Human Resources," *Business Quarterly* (Autumn 1991): 65–70.

5. Ricky W. Griffin and Michael W. Pustay, *International Business*, 8th ed. (Upper Saddle River, NJ: Pearson, 2015).

6. Richard M. Steers, "The Cultural Imperative in HRM Research," in Albert Nedd, Gerald R. Ferris, and Kendrith M. Rowland (Eds.), *Research in Personnel and Human Resources Management* (Supplement 1: International Human Resources Management) (Greenwich, CT: JAI Press, 1989): 23–32.

7. Ibraiz Tarique and Randall S. Schuler, "Global Talent Management: Literature Review, Integrative Framework, and Suggestions for Further Research," *Journal of World Business* (2010), 45(2): 122–133.

8. Geert Hofstede, *Culture's Consequences: Individual Differences in Work-Related Values* (Beverly Hills, CA: Sage Publishers, 1980).

9. Robert J. House, Paul J. Hanges, Mansour Javidan, Peter W. Dorfman, and Vipin Gupta (Eds.), *Culture, Leadership, and Organizations: The GLOBE Study of 62 Societies* (Thousand Oaks, CA: Sage Publications, Inc., 2004).

10. Nakiye Boyacigiller, "The Role of Expatriates in the Management of Interdependence, Complexity, and Risk in Multinational Corporations," *Journal of International Business Studies* (1990), 21(3): 357–382.

11. See Richard Posthuma, Mark Roehling, and Michael Campion, "Applying U.S. Employment Discrimination Law to International Employers: Advice for Scientists and Practitioners," *Personnel Psychology* (Fall 2006): 705–739.

12. "Firms in China Think Globally, Hire Locally," *Wall Street Journal* (Feb. 27, 2013): B1, B3; *Hoover's Handbook of World Business 2016* (Austin, TX: Hoover's Business Press, 2016): 140–141; 322–323.

13. Sakhawat Hossain and Herbert J. Davis, "Some Thoughts on International Personnel Management as an Emerging Field," in Nedd, Ferris, and Rowland (Eds.), *Research in Personnel and Human Resources Management*, 121–136.

14. Griffin and Pustay, *International Business*.

15. Ibid.

16. "The High Cost of Expatriation," *Management Review* (Jul. 1990): 40–41.

17. Cynthia Fetterolf, "Hiring Local Managers and Employees Overseas," *The International Executive* (May–Jun. 1990): 22–26.

18. www.oecd.org/dataoecd/32/50/43948033.pdf; Rebecca Ray and John Schmitt, "No Vacation Nation USA – A Comparison of Leave and Holiday in OECD Countries." European Economic and Employment Policy Brief, No. 3, 2007.

19. Carla Johnson, "Save Thousands per Expatriate," *HR Magazine* (Jul. 2002): 73–77.

20. Winfred Arthur, Jr., and Winston Bennett, Jr., "The International Assignee: The Relative Importance of Factors Perceived to Contribute to Success," *Personnel Psychology* (Fall 1995): 99–113.

21. Anil Gupta and Venkat Govindarajan, "Knowledge Flows within Multinational Organizations," *Strategic Management Journal* (2000), 21: 473–496.

22. Michael Jensen and William Meckling, "Theory of the Firm: Managerial Behavior, Agency Costs and Ownership Structure," *Journal of Financial Economics* (1976), 3: 305–360.

23. C. A. Bartlett and Sumatra Ghosal, *Managing Across Borders: The Trasnational Solution*, 2nd ed. (Boston: Harvard Business School Press, 1998).

24. For more on the role of knowledge contracts and expatriate managers, see Brian Connelly, Micahel Hitt, Angelo DeNisi, and R. Duane Ireland, "Expatriates and Corporate-Level International Strategy: Governing with the Knowledge Contract," *Management Decision* (2007), 45: 564–581.

25. J. Stewart Black, Hal B. Gregersen, and Mark E. Mendenhall, *Global Assignments* (San Francisco: Jossey-Bass, 1992).

26. See, for example, Ian Torbion, "Operative and Strategic Use of Expatriates in New Organizations and Market Structures," *International Studies of Management and Organization* (1994), 24: 5–17.

27. "Global Managers Need Boundless Sensitivity, Rugged Constitutions," *Wall Street Journal* (Oct. 13, 1998): B1.

28. "Firms in Europe Try to Find Executives Who Can Cross Borders in a Single Bound," *Wall Street Journal* (Jan. 25, 1991): B1.

29. "Younger Managers Learn Global Skills," *Wall Street Journal* (Mar. 31, 1992): B1.

30. "As Costs of Overseas Assignments Climb, Firms Select Expatriates More Carefully," *Wall Street Journal* (Jan. 9, 1992): B1, B6.

31. J. Stewart Black and Hal B. Gregersen, "The Right Way to Manage Expats," *Harvard Business Review* (Mar.–Apr. 1999): 52–62; see also Johnson, "Save Thousands per Expatriate."

32. Gary R. Oddou and Mark E. Mendenhall. "Expatriate Performance Appraisal: Problems and Solutions," in Gunter Stahl, Mark Mendenhall, and Gary Oddoun (Eds.), *Readings and Cases in International Human Resource Management and Organizational Behavior*, 5th ed. (New York: Routledge, 2012): 236–245.

33. For examples of proposed assessments based on knowledge transfer, see Dana Minbaeva, "Knowledge Transfer in Multinational Corporations," *Management International Review* (2007), 47: 567–593; or J. Barry Hocking, Michelle Brown, and Anne-Wil Harzing, "A Knowledge Transfer Perspective of Strategic Assignment Purposes and Their Path-Dependent Outcomes," *International Journal of Human Resource Management* (2004), 15(3): 565–586.

34. For example, see Paula Caligiuiri, MaryAnne Hyland, Aparna Joshi, and Allon Bross, "Testing a Theoretical Model for Examining the Relationship Between Family Adjustment and Expatriate Work Adjustment," *Journal of Applied Psychology* (1998), 83: 598–614.

35. Margaret Shaffer and David Harrison, "Expatriates' Psychological Withdrawal from International Assignments: Work, Nonwork, and Family Influences," *Personnel Psychology* (1998), 51: 87–96.

36. See review by Denis Ones and Chockalingam Viswesvaran, "Personality Determinants in the Prediction of Expatriate Job Success," in D. Saunders and Z. Aycan (Eds.), *New Approaches to Employee Management* (1994), 4: 63–92; and the study by Paula Caligiuri, "The Big Five Personality Characteristics as Predictors of Expatriate's Desire to Terminate the Assignment and Supervisor-Rated Performance," *Personnel Psychology* (2000), 53: 67–88.

37. See G. W. Florkowski and D. S. Fogel, "Expatriate Adjustment and Commitment: The Role of Host-Unit Treatment," *International Journal of Human Resource Management* (1999), 10: 783–807.

38. For a more complete discussion of this potential problem, see Soo Min Toh and Angelo DeNisi, "Host Country National Reactions to Expatriate Pay Policies: A Proposed Model and Some Implications," *Academy of Management Review* (2003), 28: 606–621.

39. See, for example, Shaun Pichler, Arup Varma, and Pawan Budhwar, "Antecedents and Consequences of the Social Categorization of Expatriates in India," *International Journal of Human Resource Management* (2012), 23(5): 915–927.

40. Shirley S. Sonesh and Angelo S. DeNisi, "The Categorization of Expatriates and the Support Offered by Host Country Nationals (In Press, 2016)," *Journal of Global Mobility*, 2015; Vol. 4, No. 1, pp. 18–43.

41. "Companies Use Cross-Cultural Training to Help Their Employees Adjust Abroad," *Wall Street Journal* (Aug. 9, 1992): B1, B6.

42. Paul Vanderbroeck, "Long-Term Human Resource Development in Multinational Organizations," *Sloan Management Review* (Fall 1992): 95–99;

see also Carl Fey, Antonina Pavlovskaya, and Ningyu Tang, "A Comparison of Human Resource Management in Russia, China, and Finland," *Organizational Dynamics* (2004), 33(1): 79–97.

43. Kathryn Tyler, "Targeted Language Training Is Best Bargain," *HR Magazine* (Jan. 1998): 61–68.

44. Frank Jossi, "Successful Handoff," *HR Magazine* (Oct. 2002): 48–52.

45. K. Cushner and Richard Brislin, *International Interactions: A Practical Guide* (Thousand Oaks, CA: Sage, 2000).

46. Simca Ronen, "Training the International Assignee," in I. L. Goldstein and Associates, *Training and Development in Organizations* (New York: Jossey-Bass, 1989): 418.

47. Richard M. Hodgetts and Fred Luthans, "U.S. Multinationals' Compensation Strategies," *Compensation & Benefits Review* (Jan.–Feb. 1993): 57–62.

48. Michael J. Bishko, "Compensating Your Overseas Executives, Part 1: Strategies for the 1990s," *Compensation & Benefits Review* (May–Jun. 1990): 33–43.

49. "For Executives Around the Globe, Pay Packages Aren't Worlds Apart," *Wall Street Journal* (Oct. 12, 1992): B1, B5.

50. Stephanie Overman, "In Sync," *HR Magazine* (Mar. 2000): 86–92.

51. See Johnson, "Save Thousands per Expatriate."

52. Robert O'Connor, "Plug the Expat Knowledge Drain," *HR Magazine* (Oct. 2002): 101–107.

53. Andrea Poe, "Welcome Back," *HR Magazine* (Mar. 2000): 94–105.

54. Maria L. Kraimer, Margaret A. Shaffer, and Mark C. Bolino, "The Influence of Expatriate and Repatriate Experiences on Career Advancement and Repatriate Retention," *Human Resource Management* (2009), 48(1): 27–47.

55. See Mila Lazarova and Ibrahim Tarique, "Knowledge Transfer upon Repatriation," *Journal of World Business* (2005), 40(1): 61–73; and Sebastien Reiche, "Knowledge Benefits of Social Capital upon Repatriation: A Longitudinal Study of International Assignees," *Journal of Management Studies* (2012), 49(6): 1052–1077.

56. "In France, Boss Can Become Hostage," *Wall Street Journal* (Apr. 3, 2009): B1, B5.

57. Chevron, "Chevron Angola Employees Train for Future at Southern Alberta Institute of Technology," press release, August 29, 2014, www.chevron.ca, accessed on April 24, 2016; *Hoover's Handbook of World Business 2016* (Austin, TX: Hoover's Business Press, 2016): 467–468; 519–520; Debra Bruno, "Repatriation Blues – Expats Struggle with the Dark Side of Coming Home," *Wall Street Journal* (Apr. 15, 2015): www.wsj.com, accessed on April 24, 2016.

4

1. Kelly Clay, "What Social Media Managers Need to Know about Facebook in 2014," *Forbes.com*, December 29, 2015, accessed on April 24, 2016; Jennifer Beese, "The Top 7 Social Media Stories of 2015," *SproutSocial*, December 27, 2015, accessed on April 24, 2016; The CMO Survey, "Social Media Spend Continues to Soar," March 6, 2015, accessed on April 24, 2016; "Confessions of Big Brand Social Media Managers," *Digiday*, February 11, 2015, accessed on April 24, 2015.

2. Charles R. Greer, *Strategy and Human Resources* (Englewood Cliffs, NJ: Prentice-Hall, 1995).

3. The points in the debate are best explained in Brian Becker and Barry Gerhart, "The Impact of Human Resource Management on Organizational Performance: Progress and Prospects," *Academy*

of Management Journal (Aug. 1996): 779–801. The different sides are represented in Mark A. Huselid, "The Impact of Human Resource Management Practices on Turnover, Productivity, and Corporate Financial Reporting," *Academy of Management Journal* (1995), 38: 635–672; John Delery and D. Harold Doty, "Modes of Theorizing in Strategic Human Resource Management: Tests of Universalistic, Contingency, and Configurational Performance Predictions," *Academy of Management Journal* (1995), 38: 802–835; and Patrick Wright, Dennis Smart, and Gary McMahan, "Matches Between Human Resources and Strategy Among NCAA Basketball Teams," *Academy of Management Journal* (1995), 38(5): 1052–1074.

4. Kaifeng Jiang, David Lepak, Jia Hu, and Judith Baer, "How Does Human Resource Management Influence Organizational Outcomes? A Meta-Analytic Investigation of Mediating Mechanisms," *Academy of Management Journal* (2012), 55(6): 1264–1294.

5. David Bowen and Cheri Ostroff, "Understanding HRM-Firm Performance Linkages: The Role of the 'Strength' of the HRM System," *Academy of Management Review* (2004), 29(2): 203–221.

6. Robert Ployhart and Thomas Moliterno, "Emergence of the Human Capital Resource: A Multilevel Model," *Academy of Management Review* (2011), 36(1): 127–150.

7. For example, see Angelo DeNisi and Caitlin Smith, "Performance Appraisal, Performance Management, and Firm-Level Performance: A Review, a Proposed Model, and New Directions for Future Research," *Academy of Management Annals* (2014), 8: 127–179; as well as Susan Jackson, Randall Schuler, and Kaifeng Jiang, "An Aspirational Framework for Strategic Human Resource Management," *Academy of Management Annals* (2014), 8: 1–56.

8. To read more about this model, see Jay Barney, "Firm Resources and Sustained Competitive Advantage," *Journal of Management* (1991), 17: 99–120; and Jay Barney, "Is the Resource-based 'View' a Useful Perspective for Strategic Management Research? Yes," *Academy of Management Review* (2001), 26: 41–56.

9. See Charles W. L. Hill and Gareth R. Jones, *Strategic Management: An Integrated Approach*, 9th ed. (Stamford, CT: Cengage Learning, 2010).

10. Janine Nahapiet and Sumantra Ghoshal, "Social Capital, Intellectual Capital, and the Organizational Advantage," *Academy of Management Review* (1998), 23: 242–266.

11. Catherine M. Daily and Charles Schwenk, "Chief Operating Officers, Top Management Teams, and Boards of Directors: Congruent or Countervailing Forces?" *Journal of Management* (1996), 22(2): 185–208.

12. S. A. Kirkpatrick and Edwin A. Locke, "Direct and Indirect Effects of Three Core Charismatic Leadership Components on Performance and Attitudes," *Journal of Applied Psychology* (1996), 81: 36–51; see also Harry G. Barkema and Luis R. Gomez-Mejia, "Managerial Compensation and Firm Performance: A General Research Framework," *Academy of Management Journal* (1998), 41: 135–145.

13. See, for example, Donald C. Hambrick and Sidney Finkelstein, "Managerial Discretion: A Bridge Between Polar Views on Organizations," in L. L. Cummings and B. Staw (Eds.), *Research in Organizational Behavior*, Vol. 9 (Greenwich, CT: JAI Press, 1987): 369–406; or Sidney Finkelstein and Donald Hambrick, "Top Management Team Tenure and Organizational Outcomes: The Moderating Role of Managerial Discretion," *Administration Science Quarterly* (1990), 35: 484–503.

14. Eugene F. Fama and Michael C. Jensen, "Separation of Ownership and Control," *Journal of Law and Economics* (1983), 2: 301–325.

15. See, for example, Idalene Kessner and Richard Johnson, "An Investigation of the Relationship Between Board Composition and Stockholder Suits," *Strategic Management Journal* (1990), 15: 327–336; see also Jay Barney, *Gaining and Sustaining Competitive Advantage*, 2nd ed. (Upper Saddle River, NJ: Prentice Hall, 2002): 452–456, for an overview of the role of boards of directors.

16. Lynn Sweet, "Obama Will Move to Block AIG Bonus Payments. Said It Is 'Hard to Understand' Why AIG Traders Deserve Money," *Chicago Sun Times Media* (Mar. 16, 2009).

17. Hill and Jones, *Strategic Management: An Analytical Approach*.

18. Brian Becker and Barry Gerhart, "The Impact of Human Resource Management on Organizational Performance: Progress and Prospects," *Academy of Management Journal* (Aug. 1996), 39(4): 779–801.

19. Donald Laurie, Yves Doz, and Claude Sheer, "Creating New Growth Platforms," *Harvard Business Review* (May 2006): 80–92.

20. Steven Greenhouse, "At Caterpillar, Pressing Labor while Business Booms," *New York Times* (Jul. 22, 2012): www.nytimes.com, accessed April 25, 2016; Drew DeSilver, "For Most Workers, Real Wages Have Barely Budged for Decades," *Pew Research Center*, October 9, 2014, accessed April 25, 2016; Bureau of Labor Statistics, "The Employment Situation – December 2015," press release, www.bls.gov, accessed April 25, 2016; Greenhouse, "Our Economic Pickle," *New York Times* (January 12, 2015): www.nytimes.com, accessed April 25, 2016; Heidi Shierholz and Lawrence Mishel, "A Decade of Flat Wages: The Key Barrier to Shared Prosperity and a Rising Middle Class," Economic Policy Institute (Aug. 21, 2015): www.epi.org, accessed April 25, 2016; Greenhouse, "Caterpillar Workers Ratify Deal They Dislike," *New York Times* (August 17, 2012): www.nytimes.com, accessed April 25, 2016.

21. David M. Schweiger and James P. Walsh, "Mergers and Acquisitions: An Interdisciplinary View," in Kenneth Rowland and Gerald Ferris (Eds.), *Research in Personnel and Human Resource Management*, Vol. 8 (Greenwich, CT: JAI Press, 1990): 41–107.

22. David M. Schweiger and Angelo DeNisi, "Communications with Employees Following a Merger: A Longitudinal Field Study," *Academy of Management Journal* (1991), 34: 110–135.

23. Hill and Jones, *Strategic Management: An Analytical Approach*.

24. Jay Barney and Ricky W. Griffin, *The Management of Organizations* (Boston: Houghton Mifflin, 1992).

25. Russell A. Eisenstat, "What Corporate Human Resources Brings to the Picnic: Four Models for Functional Management," *Organizational Dynamics* (Autumn 1996): 7–21.

26. John O. Whitney, "Strategic Renewal for Business Units," *Harvard Business Review* (Jul.–Aug. 1996): 84–98.

27. Raymond E. Miles and Charles C. Snow, *Organizational Strategy, Structure, and Process* (New York: McGraw-Hill, 1978).

28. Michael Porter, *Competitive Strategy* (New York: Free Press, 1980).

29. Robert L. Cardy and Gregory H. Dobbins, "Human Resource Management in a Total Quality Organizational Environment: Shifting from a Traditional to a TQHRM Approach," *Journal of Quality Management* (1996), 1(1): 5–20.

30. Henry Mintzberg, "Patterns in Strategy Formulation," *Management Science* (Oct. 1978): 934–948.

31. David Fiedler, "Know When to Hold 'Em," *HR Magazine* (Aug. 2002): 89–94.

32. Edilberto F. Montemayor, "Congruence Between Pay Policy and Competitive Strategy in High-Performing Firms," *Journal of Management* (1996), 22(6): 889–912.

33. David Lepak and Scott Snell, "The Human Resource Architecture: Toward a Theory of Human Capital Allocation and Development," *Academy of Management Journal*, 24(1): 31–48; David Lepak and Scott Snell, "Examining the Human Resource Architecture: The Relationships Among Human Capital, Employment, and Human Resource Configuration," *Journal of Management* (2002), 28(4): 517–544; David Lepak and Scott Snell, "Managing the Human Resource Architecture for Knowledge-Based Competition," in Susan Jackson, Michael Hitt, and Angelo DeNisi (Eds.), *Managing Knowledge for Sustained Competitive Advantage: Designing Strategies for Effective Human Resource Management* (San Francisco: Jossey-Bass, 2003).

34. Peter Bamberger and Avi Fiegenbaum, "The Role of Strategic Reference Points in Explaining the Nature and Consequences of Human Resource Strategy," *Academy of Management Review* (Oct. 1996): 926–958.

35. Richard L. Daft, *Organization Theory and Design*, 10th ed. (Stamford, CT: Cengage Learning, 2010).

36. John Purcell and Bruce Ahlstrand, *Human Resource Management in the Multi-Divisional Company* (Oxford, UK: Oxford University Press, 1994).

37. Terrence E. Deal and Allan A. Kennedy, *Corporate Cultures: The Rights and Rituals of Corporate Life* (Reading, MA: Addison-Wesley, 1982).

38. Jay Barney, "Organizational Culture: Can It Be a Source of Sustained Competitive Advantage?" *Academy of Management Review* (Jul. 1986): 656–665.

39. See, for example, David Jemison and Sim Sitkin, "Corporate Acquisitions: A Process Perspective," *Academy of Management Review* (1986), 11(1): 145–163; or Nancy Napier, "Mergers and Acquisitions, Human Resource Issues and Outcomes: A Review and Suggested Typology," *Journal of Management Studies* (1989), 26(3): 271–289.

40. See discussion of this strategy in Bruce Nissen, "The 'Social Movement' Dynamics of Living Wage Campaigns," in Paula Voos (Ed.), *Proceedings of the 53rd Annual Meeting of the Industrial Relations Research Association* (Washington, DC: Industrial Relations Research Association, Jan. 2001): 232–240.

41. Lawrence Hrebiniak, "Obstacles to Effective Strategy Implementation," *Organizational Dynamics* (Fall 2006): 12–31.

42. Gary Johns, "The Essential Impact of Context on Organizational Behavior," *Academy of Management Review* (2006), 31(2): 386–408.

43. Denise Rousseau, "Changing the Deal While Keeping the People," *Academy of Management Executive* (Feb. 1996): 50–61.

44. Elizabeth Wolfe Morrison and Sandra L. Robinson, "When Employees Feel Betrayed: A Model of How Psychological Contract Violation Develops," *Academy of Management Review* (Jan. 1997): 226–256; Sandra Robinson, Matthew Kraatz, and Denise Rousseau, "Changing Obligations and the Psychological Contract," *Academy of Management Journal* (1994): 37(1): 137–152.

45. Murray Barrick and Michael Mount, "The Big Five Personality Dimensions and Job Performance: A Meta-Analysis," *Personnel Psychology* (1991), 44(1): 1–26.

46. Leslie DeChurch and Michelle Marks, "Leadership In Multiteam Systems," *Journal of Applied Psychology* (2006), 91(2): 311–329; Brian Grow, "Renovating Home Depot," *BusinessWeek* (Mar. 6, 2006): 50–58; Jennifer Reingold, "Bob Nardelli Is Watching," *Fast Company* (Dec. 2005): 58–60; George Stalk, Rob Lachenauer, and John Butman, *Hardball: Are You Playing to Play or Playing to Win?* (Cambridge, MA: Harvard Business School Press, 2004).

47. Several critical measurement issues are raised in Barry Gerhart, Patrick Wright, Gary McMahan, and Scott Snell, "Measurement Error in Research on Human Resources and Firm Performance: How Much Error Is There and How Does It Influence Size Estimates?" *Personnel Psychology* (2000), 53(4): 803–834.

48. See, for example, Mark A. Huselid, "The Impact of Human Resource Management Practices on Turnover, Productivity, and Corporate Financial Reporting," *Academy of Management Journal* (1995), 38: 635–672; or Rajiv Banker, Joy Field, Roger Schroeder, and Kingshuk Sinha, "Impact of Work Teams on Manufacturing Performance: A Longitudinal Study," *Academy of Management Journal* (1996), 39(4): 867–890.

49. Sodexo, "Sodexo's Strategic Use of Diversity Metrics to Quantify, Calibrate, and Impact Business Goals Recognized with a Top-Two Spot on DiversityInc's List for Unprecedented 5th Consecutive Year," *Providence (RI) Journal* (Apr. 23, 2014); Annys Shin, "$80 Million Settles Race-Bias Case," *Washington Post* (Apr. 28, 2005); Tanya Aquino, "Even after Lawsuit, Report Reveals Food Service Co. Still Struggles with Diversity," Black Radio Network (Apr. 27, 2010): www.blackradionetwork.com, accessed on April 25, 2016; William Reed, "Diversity Turnaround at Sodexo," *Louisiana Weekly* (Mar. 4, 2013); "Diversity Management: The Chief Diversity Officer's No. 1 Advantage," DiversityInc (n.d.), www.diversityinc.com, accessed on April 25, 2016.

5

1. "Planned Layoffs Jumped in October on Drug, Financial Firm Cutbacks," *Los Angeles Times* (Nov. 6, 2013): 2B. Accessed April 26, 2016.

2. "Planned Layoffs Jumped in October on Drug, Financial Firm Cutbacks," *Los Angeles Times* (Nov. 6, 2013): 2B. Accessed April 26, 2016 "U.S. Retailers Ramp Up Hiring for the Holidays," *USA Today* (Oct. 3, 2015): 1B. Accessed April 26, 2016 "Starbucks Aims to Hire 10,000 Vets, Active-Duty Spouses Over 5 Years," *The Seattle Times* (Nov. 6, 2013): 5C. Accessed April 26, 2016.

3. Lee Dyer, "Human Resource Planning," in K. Rowland and G. Ferris (Eds.), *Personnel Management* (Boston: Allyn & Bacon, 1982): 52–77.

4. R. G. Murdick and F. Schuster, "Computerized Information Support for the Human Resource Function," *Human Resource Planning* (1983), 6(1): 25–35.

5. Taylor H. Cox and Stacy Blake, "Managing Cultural Diversity: Implications for Organizational Competitiveness," *Academy of Management Executive* (Aug. 1991): 45–56.

6. "The Geography of Work," *Time* (Jun. 22, 1998): 98–102.

7. Carla Johnson, "Developing a Strong Bench," *HR Magazine* (Jan. 1998): 92–97.

8. "Firms Plan to Keep Hiring, Spending," *USA Today* (Jan. 26, 1995): B1.

9. "Firms Find Ways to Grow Without Expanding Staffs," *Wall Street Journal* (Mar. 18, 1993): B1, B2.

10. Donald Laurie, Yves Doz, and Claude Sheer, "Creating New Growth Platforms," *Harvard Business Review* (May 2006): 80–92.

11. www.bls.gov/news.release/pdf/ocwage.pdf, accessed on February 2016; "Top 30 Jobs" *Forbes*, May 6, 1996, p. 17. Accessed April 26, 2016.

12. "When UPS Demanded Workers, Louisville Did the Delivering," *Wall Street Journal* (Apr. 24, 1998): A1, A10; *Hoover's Handbook of American Business 2006* (Austin: Hoover's Business Press, 2006): 873–874

13. "Layoffs on Wall Street Will Bruise Big Apple," *USA Today* (Oct. 15, 1998): 1B; "Its Share Shrinking, Levi Strauss Lays Off 6,395," *Wall Street Journal* (Nov. 4, 1997): B1, B8.

14. See especially Roger Griffeth, Peter Hom, and Stefan Gaertner, "A Meta-Analysis of Antecedents and Correlates of Employee Turnover: Update, Moderator Tests, and Research Implications for the Next Millennium," *Journal of Management* (2000), 26: 463–488; and Charlie Trevor, "Interactions Among Actual Ease of Movement Determinants and Job Satisfaction in the Prediction of Voluntary Turnover," *Academy of Management Journal* (2001), 44: 621–638.

15. U.S. Department of Labor, Bureau of Labor Statistics, Local Area Unemployment Statistics, July 2013.

16. Joseph Coombs, "Has Full Employment" become obsolete," *SHRM Reports* (March 7, 2016).

17. For a more detailed discussion of this phenomenon applied to human resource management, see Edward Lazear, *Personnel Economics for Managers* (New York: Wiley, 1998).

18. E. J. McCormick, *Job Analysis: Methods and Applications* (New York: American Management Association, 1979).

19. Charles R. Greer, *Strategy and Human Resources* (Englewood Cliffs, NJ: Prentice Hall, 1995).

20. A. S. DeNisi, "The Implications of Job Clustering for Training Programmes," *Journal of Occupational Psychology* (1976), 49: 105–113.

21. K. Pearlman, "Job Families: A Review and Discussion of Their Implications for Personnel Selection," *Psychological Bulletin* (1980), 87: 1–27.

22. McCormick, *Job Analysis: Methods and Applications.*

23. U.S. Department of Labor, Employment, and Training Administration, *The Revised Handbook for Analyzing Jobs* (Washington, DC: U.S. Government Printing Office, 1991).

24. Frank Landy and Joseph Vasey, "Job Analysis: The Composition of SME Samples," *Personnel Psychology* (1991), 44(1): 27–50.

25. Ibid.

26. Norman Peterson, Michael Mumford, Walter Borman, P. Richard Jeanneret, Edwin Fleishman, Kerry Levin, Michael Campion, Melinda Mayfield, Frederick Morgeson, Kenneth Pearlman, Marilyn Gowing, Anita Lancaster, Marilyn Silver, and Donna Dye, "Understanding Work Using the Occupational Information Network (O°NET): Implications for Practice and Research," *Personnel Psychology* (2001), 54: 451–492.

27. U.S. Department of Labor, Employment, and Training Administration, *The Revised Handbook for Analyzing Jobs.*

28. E. A. Fleishman, *Manual for the Ability Requirements Scale* (MARS, revised) (Palo Alto, CA: Consulting Psychologists Press, 1991).

29. For example, see J. E. Morsh, *Job Types Identified with an Inventory Constructed by Electronics Engineers* (Lackland Air Force Base, San Antonio, TX: U.S. Air Force Personnel Research Laboratory, 1966).

30. S. A. Fine and W. W. Wiley, *An Introduction to Functional Job Analysis* (Kalamazoo, MI: W. E. Upjohn Institute for Employment Research, 1971).

31. E. J. McCormick, P. R. Jeanneret, and R. C. Mecham, "A Study of Job Characteristics and Job Dimensions as Based on the Position Analysis Questionnaire (PAQ)," *Journal of Applied Psychology* (1972), 56: 347–368.

32. McCormick, *Job Analysis: Methods and Applications.*

33. See, for example, McCormick, Jeanneret, and Mecham, " A Study of Job Characteristics and Job Dimensions," or E. J. McCormick, A. S. DeNisi, and J. B. Shaw, "The Use of the Position Analysis Questionnaire (PAQ) for Establishing the Job Component Validity of Tests," *Journal of Applied Psychology* (1978), 64: 51–56.

34. A. S. DeNisi, E. T. Cornelius, and A. G. Blencoe, "A Further Investigation of Common Knowledge Effects on Job Analysis Ratings: On the Applicability of the PAQ for All Jobs," *Journal of Applied Psychology* (1987), 72: 262–268.

35. Walter Tornow and Patrick Pinto, "The Development of a Managerial Job Taxonomy: A System for Describing, Classifying, and Evaluating Executive Positions," *Journal of Applied Psychology* (1976), 61: 410–418.

36. J. C. Flanagan, "The Critical Incident Technique," *Psychological Bulletin*, 51: 327–358.

37. Milan Moravec and Robert Tucker, "Job Descriptions for the 21st Century," *Personnel Journal* (June 1992): 37–40.

38. Karen Cook and Patricia Bernthal, *Job/Role Competency Practices Survey Report* (Bridgeville, PA: Development Dimensions Inc., 1998).

39. For an excellent review of the various issues associated with competency modeling, the reader is referred to Jeffrey Shippman, Ronald Ash, Mariangela Battista, Linda Carr, Lorraine Eyde, Beryl Hesketh, Jerry Kehoe, Kenneth Pearlman, Erich Prien, and Juan Sanchez, "The Practice of Competency Modeling," *Personnel Psychology* (2000), 53: 703–740.

40. See also Adrienne Fox, "At Work in 2020," *HR Magazine* (Jan. 2010): 18–23.

41. Reported in Matt Straz, "Why You Need to Embrace the Big Data Trend in HR," *Entrepreneur* (Apr. 6, 2015): www.entrepreneur.com/article/244326.

42. *Albemarle Paper Co.* v. *Moody*, Sup. Ct. of the U.S., 1975, 422 U.S. 405, 95 S. Ct. 2362, L. Ed. 2d. 280.

43. For a complete discussion of these sources of inaccuracy, see Frederick Morgeson and Michael Campion, "Social and Cognitive Sources of Potential Inaccuracy in Job Analysis," *Journal of Applied Psychology* (1998), 82: 627–655.

44. Richard Arvey, "Sex Bias in Job Evaluation Procedures," *Personnel Psychology* (1986), 39: 315–335.

45. *Electromation Inc.* v. *National Labor Relations Board*, 1992.

46. "Building with Big Data: The Data Revolution Is Changing the Landscape of Business," *The Economist* (May 26, 2011): www.economist.com/blogs/Schumpeter.

47. Read more: www.businessdictionary.com/definition/analytics.html.

48. HADOOP is a free, Java-based programming framework that supports the processing of large data sets in a distributed computing environment. It was developed by the Apache Software Foundation, and is used by such firms as Google, Yahoo, and IBM.

49. "These Six Growth Jobs Are Dull, Dead-End, Sometimes Dangerous," *Wall Street Journal*, (Dec. 1, 1994): A1, A8; *Hoover's Handbook of American Business 2012* (Austin, TX: Hoover's Business Press, 2012). See also the continuing television series *Dirty Jobs*.

6

1. Susan Sorenson, "How Employee Engagement Drives Growth," *Gallup Business Journal* (Jun. 20, 2015): www.gallup.com, accessed on May 29, 2016; Diane Berry, Lily Mok, and Thomas Otter, "CFO Advisory: Employee Engagement Impacts Financial Outcomes and Business Risk@ (Mar. 13, 2013): www.financialexecutives.org, accessed on May 29, 2016; *The Impact of Employee Engagement on Performance*, Harvard Business School Publishing Analytic Services Report (2013): https://hbr.org, accessed on May 29, 2016; Paul Keegan, "The Five New Rules of Employee Engagement," *Inc.* (Dec. 2014/Jan. 2015): www.inc.com, accessed on May 29, 2016.

2. "What to Do with Bad News," *HR Magazine* (Jul. 2002): 58–63.

3. Snapshots, *USA Today* (Dec. 3, 2001): B1.

4. "Cuomo Demands Bonus Data from Eight Big Banks," *New York Times* (Jan. 11, 2010): B1.

5. Araiana Cha and Ellen Nakashima, "Google China Cyberattack Part of Vast Espionage Campaign, Experts Say," *Washington Post* online (Jan. 14, 2010).

6. Anne T. Lawrence, "Google, Inc.: Figuring out How to Deal with China," in Emmanuel Raufflet and Albert Mills, *The Dark Side: Critical Cases on the Downside of Business* (London: Greenleaf, 2009): 257–278.

7. Los Angeles Times Staff, "Story So Far Apple-FBI Battle over San Bernardino Terror Attack Investigation: All the Details," *The Los Angeles Times* online, (Feb. 22, 2016).

8. Katie Reilly, "Bill Gates Seeks Balanced Solution in FBI-Apple iPhone Feud," *Time* online (Feb. 23, 2016).

9. Transparency International: The Global Coalition Against Corruption, Global Report (2012): www.transparency.org.

10. Gilbert Nicholson, "Get Your Benefit Ducks in a Row," *Workforce* (Sept. 2000): 78–84.

11. Lee Phillion and John Brugger, "Encore! Retirees Give Top Performance as Temporaries," *HR Magazine* (Oct. 1994): 74–78.

12. See, especially, David Lepak and Scott Snell, "The Human Resource Architecture: Toward a Theory of Human Capital Allocation and Development," *Academy of Management Review* (1999), 24: 31–48.

13. See Sylvia Roch and Linda Shanock, "Organizational Justice in an Exchange Framework: Clarifying Organizational Justice Distinctions," *Journal of Management* (Apr. 2006): 299–322.

14. J. Stacy Adams, "Inequity in Social Exchange," in L. Berkowitz (Ed.), *Advances in Experimental Social Psychology*, Vol. 2 (New York: Academic Press, 1965): 267–299.

15. Gerald Leventhal, "The Distribution of Rewards and Resources in Groups and Organizations," in L. Berkowitz and W. Walster (Eds.), *Advances in Experimental Social Psychology*, Vol. 9 (New York: Academic Press, 1976): 91–131.

16. Joel Brockner and Batia Wiesenfeld, "An Integrative Framework for Explaining Reactions to Decisions: Integrative Effects of Outcomes and Procedures," *Psychological Bulletin* (1996), 120: 189–298.

17. Robert Bies and Joseph Moag, "Interactional Justice: Communication Criteria of Fairness," in R. Lewicki, B. Sheppard, and M. Bazerman (Eds.), *Research on Negotiations in Organizations*, Vol. 1 (Greenwich, CT: JAI Press, 1986): 43–55.

18. Jerald Greenberg, "The Social Side of Fairness: Interpersonal and Informational Classes of Organizational Justice," in R. Cropanzano (Ed.), *Justice in the Workplace: Approaching Fairness in Human Resource Management* (Hillsdale, NJ: Erlbaum, 1993): 79–103.

19. Bill Roberts, "The Benefits of Big Data," *HR Magazine* (Oct. 2013): 22.

20. "Home is Where the Jobs Are," *Bloomberg Businessweek* (Jan. 6–13, 2014): 15–15; Joshua Brustein, "Fix This Workplace," *Bloomberg Businessweek* (Dec. 23, 2013–Jan. 5, 2014): 82–88.; Bill Roberts, "The Benefits of Big Data," *HR Magazine* (October 2013): 20–30.

21. Wayne Cascio, Clifford Young, and James Morris, "Financial Consequences of Employment Change Decisions in Major U.S. Corporations," *Academy of Management Journal* (1997), 40: 1175–1189.

22. For example, see Dan Worrell, Wallace Davidson, and Varinder Sharma, "Layoff Announcements and Stockholder Wealth," *Academy of Management Journal* (1991), 34: 662–678.

23. Joel Brockner, "The Effects of Work Layoffs on Survivors: Research, Theory and Practice," in B. Staw and L. Cummings (Eds.), *Research in Organizational Behavior*, Vol. 10 (Greenwich, CT: JAI Press, 1988): 213–215.

24. American Management Association, *Corporate Job Creation, Job Elimination, and Downsizing: Summary of Key Findings* (New York: American Management Association, 1997).

25. Towers Watson Consultants, *Looking Forward to Recovery: Focusing on Talent and Rewards* (New York: New York Strategic Rewards Report, Dec. 2009).

26. Fay Hansen, "Employee Assistance Programs (EAPs) Grow and Expand their Reach," *Compensation and Benefits Review* (Mar.–Apr. 2000): 13.

27. See, for example, Meg Bryant, "Testing EAPs for Coordination," *Business and Health* (Aug. 1991): 20–24; or Barbara Pflaum, "Seeking Sane Solutions: Managing Mental Health and Chemical Dependency Costs," *Employee Benefits Journal* (1992), 16: 31–35.

28. James Smith, "EAPs Evolve to Health Plan Gatekeepers," *Employee Benefit Plan Review* (1992), 46: 18–19.

29. M. R. Buckley and W. Weitzel, "Employment at Will," *Personnel Administrator* (1988), 33: 78–80.

30. This approach was pioneered by Union Carbide. See A. B. Chimezie, Osigweh Yg, and William Hutchinson, "To Punish or Not to Punish: Managing Human Resources Through Positive Discipline," *Employee Relations* (Mar. 1990): 27–32. For a more complete picture, see Dick Grove, *Discipline Without Punishment* (New York: American Management Association, 1996).

31. Matt Straz, "Why You Need to Embrace the Big Data Trend in HR," *Entrepreneur* (Apr. 6, 2015): www.entrepreneur.com/article/244326.

32. See, for example, Michael Abelson and Barry Baysinger, "Optimal and Dysfunctional Turnover: Toward an Organizational Level Model," *Academy of Management Review* (1984), 9: 331–341.

33. On the positive side, job satisfaction has been defined as the positive feeling that "results from the perception that one's job fulfills . . . one's important job values." See Edwin Locke, "The Nature and Causes of Job Dissatisfaction," in M. Dunnette (Ed.), *Handbook of Industrial and Organizational Psychology* (Chicago: Rand McNally, 1976): 901–969.

34. For an excellent review of this literature, see Charles Hulin, Mary Roznowski, and Dan Hachiya, "Alternative Opportunities and Withdrawal Decisions," *Psychological Bulletin* (1985), 97: 233–250.

35. The original model was presented in William Mobley, "Intermediate Linkages in the Relationship between Job Satisfaction and Employee Turnover," *Journal of Applied Psychology* (1977), 62: 237–240. A refined model was later presented in Peter Hom and Roger Griffeth, "A Structural Equations Modeling Test of a Turnover Theory: Cross Sectional and Longitudinal Analysis," *Journal of Applied Psychology* (1991), 76: 350–366.

36. John Sheridan and Michael Abelson, "Cusp-Catastrophe Model of Employee Turnover," *Academy of Management Journal* (1983), 26: 418–436.

37. Thomas Lee and Terrence Mitchell, "An Alternative Approach: The Unfolding Model of Voluntary Employee Turnover," *Academy of Management Review* (1994), 19: 51–89.

38. Terrence Mitchell, Brooks Holtom, Thomas Lee, Christopher Sablynski, and Miriam Erez, "Why People Stay: Using Job Embeddedness to Predict Voluntary Turnover," *Academy of Management Journal* (2001), 44: 1102–1121.

39. Richard Arvey, Thomas Bouchard, Neal Segal, and Len Abraham, "Job Satisfaction: Genetic and Environmental Components," *Journal of Applied Psychology* (1989), 74: 187–193.

40. See, for example, Barry Staw, Nancy Bell, and J. Clausen, "The Dispositional Approach to Job Attitudes: A Lifetime Attitudinal Test," *Administrative Science Quarterly* (1986), 31: 56–78; and Timothy Judge, "Does Affective Disposition Moderate the Relationship Between Job Satisfaction and Affective Turnover?" *Journal of Applied Psychology* (1993), 78: 395–401.

41. Barry Gerhart, "How Important Are Dispositional Factors as Determinants of Job Satisfaction? Implications for Job Design and Other Personnel Programs," *Journal of Applied Psychology* (1987), 72: 493–502.

42. See Locke, "The Nature and Causes of Job Dissatisfaction," for a review of the literature on these determinants of job satisfaction.

43. Bruce Meglino, Elizabeth Ravlin, and Cheryl Adkins, "A Work Values Approach to Corporate Culture: A Field Test of the Value Congruence Process and Its Relationship to Individual Outcomes," *Journal of Applied Psychology* (1989), 74: 424–433.

44. For an excellent review of the relationship between leader behavior and employees' reactions, such as satisfaction, see Victor Vroom, "Leadership," in M. Dunnette (Ed.), *Handbook of Industrial and Organizational Psychology* (Chicago: Rand McNally, 1986): 560–663.

45. Rick Hackett and Robert Guion, "A Reevaluation of the Job Satisfaction-Absenteeism Relation," *Organizational Behavior and Human Decision Processes* (1985), 35: 340–381.

46. Richard Mowday, Richard Steers, and Lyman Porter, "The Measurement of Organizational Commitment," *Journal of Vocational Behavior* (1979), 14: 224–247.

47. See, for example, Chester Schriesheim, "Job Satisfaction, Attitudes Towards Unions, and Voting in a Union Representation Election," *Journal of Applied Psychology* (1978), 63: 548–553. For a somewhat more complex model that still focuses on job dissatisfaction, see Stuart Youngblood, Angelo DeNisi, Julie Molleston, and William Mobley,

"The Impact of Worker Attachment, Instrumentality Beliefs, Perceived Labor Union Image, and Subjective Norms on Voting Intentions and Union Membership," *Academy of Management Journal* (1994), 15: 576–590.

48. The original research is summarized in Dennis Organ, *Organizational Citizenship Behavior: The Good Soldier Syndrome* (Lexington, MA: Heath, 1988).

49. See Walter Borman, "Job Behavior, Performance and Effectiveness," in M. Dunnette and L. Hough (Eds.), *Handbook of Industrial and Organizational Psychology*, Vol. 1, 2nd ed. (Palo Alto, CA: Consulting Psychologists Press, 1991): 271–326.

50. See the discussion in Susan Jackson, Donald Schwab, and Randall Schuler, "Toward an Understanding of the Burnout Phenomenon," *Journal of Applied Psychology* (1986), 71: 630–640. For an update and a more complex model, see Evangelia Demerouti, Arnold Bakker, Friedhelm Nachreiner, and Wilmar Schaufei, "The Job Demands-Resources Model of Burnout," *Journal of Applied Psychology* (2001), 86: 499–512.

51. See Locke, "The Nature and Causes of Job Dissatisfaction," for a review.

52. Patricia Smith, Lorne Kendall, and Charles Hulin, *The Measurement of Satisfaction in Work and Retirement* (Chicago: Rand McNally, 1969).

53. Theodore Kunin, "The Construction of a New Type of Attitude Measure," *Personnel Psychology* (1955), 8: 65–78.

54. Spencer Woodman, "Amazon Makes Even Temporary Warehouse Workers Sign 18-Month Non-Competes," *The Verge* (March 26, 2015): www.theverge.com.

55. See review by Gunter Stahl, Mark Mendenhall, Amy Pablo, and Mansour Javidan, "Sociocultural Integration in Mergers and Acquisitions," in Gunter Stahl and Mark Mendenhall (Eds.), *Mergers and Acquisitions: Managing the Culture and Human Resources* (Palo Alto, CA: Stanford University Press, 2005): 3–16.

56. See discussion of various reasons for success and failure of mergers and acquisitions in A. T. Kearney, *White Paper on Post Merger Integration*, KPMG Report, 1998.

57. Tim Arango, "In Retrospect: How the AOL-Time Warner Merger Went So Wrong," *New York Times* (Jan. 11, 2010): B-1.

58. For further discussion of these processes, see H. Tajfel and J. C. Turner, "An Integrative Theory of Intergroup Conflict," in W. Austin and S. Worchel (Eds.), *The Social Psychology of Intergroup Psychology* (Monterey, CA: Brooks-Cole, 1979): 33–47.

59. David Schweiger and Angelo DeNisi, "The Effects of Communication with Employees Following a Merger: A Longitudinal Field Experiment," *Academy of Management Journal* (1991), 34: 110–135.

60. For more details and further discussion of these processes in the context of a merger or acquisition, see Angelo DeNisi and Shung Jae Shin, "Psychological Communication Interventions in Mergers and Acquisitions," in Gunter Stahl and Mark Mendenhall (Eds.), *Mergers and Acquisitions: Managing the Culture and Human Resources* (Stanford, CA: Stanford University Press, 2005): 228–249.

61. Jeffrey Pfeffer and Robert I. Sutton, *Hard Facts, Dangerous Half-Truths, and Total Nonsense: Profiting from Evidence-Based Management* (Cambridge, MA: Harvard Business School Press, 2006); Pfeffer and Sutton, "Evidence-Based Management" (2010): www.evidence-basedmanagement.com, accessed

on March 4, 2011; Donald W. McCormick, "Ethics and the 15-Minute Evidence-Based Manager," *Organization Management Journal*, 7 (2010): www.palgrave-journals.com, accessed on March 4, 2011; J. Pfeffer and R. I. Sutton, "Evidence-Based Management," *Harvard Business Review* (2006) 84(1): 62–74.

7

1. Don Banks, "Black Monday Primer: A Definitive Guide to 2014 Coaching Carousel," http://sportsillustrated.cnn.com/, accessed on January 18, 2014.

2. "NFL Coaching Changes Tracker: Latest Hirings, Firings, Candidates," www.cbssports.com, accessed on January 19, 2016; "College Football Coaching Changes, College Football New Coaches," http://collegefootball.com, accessed on January 18, 2016; "2013-14 FBS Head-Coaching Changes," www.espn.com, accessed on January 18, 2014; Don Banks, "Black Monday Primer: A Definitive Guide to 2016 Coaching Carousel," *Sports Illustrated*, www.si.com, accessed on January 19, 2016.

3. James A. Breaugh, *Recruitment: Science and Practice* (Boston: PWS-Kent, 1992).

4. Robert Bretz, Jr. and Timothy Judge, "The Role of Human Resource Systems in Job Applicant Decision Processes," *Journal of Management* (1994), 20(3): 531–551.

5. Allison Barber, Christina Daly, Cristina Giannatonio, and Jean Phillips, "Job Search Activities: An Examination of Changes over Time," *Personnel Psychology* (1994), 47: 739–750.

6. Timothy Judge and Robert Bretz, "Effects of Work Values on Job Choice Decisions," *Journal of Applied Psychology*, 77(3): 261–271.

7. "Right Here in Dubuque," *Forbes* (Mar. 29, 1993): 86–88.

8. Andy Bargerstock and Hank Engel, "Six Ways to Boost Employee Referral Programs," *HR Magazine* (Dec. 1994): 72–16.

9. Beth McConnell, "Companies Lure Job Seekers in New Ways," *HR News* (Apr. 2002): 1–5.

10. Peter Cappelli, "Making the Most of Online Recruiting," *Harvard Business Review* (Mar. 2001): 139–146.

11. Bill Leonard, "Online and Overwhelmed," *HR Magazine* (Aug. 2000): 37–42.

12. Candee Wilde, "Recruiters Discover Diverse Value in Websites," *Informationweek* (Feb. 7, 2000): 144.

13. Peter Kuhn and Mikal Skuiterud, "Job Search Methods: Internet *versus* Traditional," *Monthly Labor Review* (Oct. 2000): 3–11.

14. Cappelli, "Making the Most of Online Recruiting."

15. J. P. Wanous and A. Colella, "Organizational Entry Research: Current Status and Future Directions," in K. Rowland and G. Ferris (Eds.), *Research in Personnel and Human Resource Management* (Greenwich, CT: JAI Press, 1989).

16. "It's Not Easy Making Pixie Dust," *Business Week* (Sept. 18, 1995): 134.

17. B. M. Meglino and A. S. DeNisi, "Realistic Job Previews: Some Thoughts on Their More Effective Use in Managing the Flow of Human Resources," *Human Resource Planning* (1987), 10: 157–167.

18. Jean Phillips, "Effects of Realistic Job Previews on Multiple Organizational Outcomes: A Meta-Analysis," *Academy of Management Journal* (1998), 41: 673–690.

19. R. A. Dean and J. P. Wanous, "Effects of Realistic Job Previews on Hiring Bank Tellers," *Journal of Applied Psychology* (1984), 69: 61–68.

20. B. M. Meglino, A. S. DeNisi, S. A. Youngblood, and K. J. Williams, "Effects of Realistic Job Previews: A Comparison Using Enhancement and Reduction Previews," *Journal of Applied Psychology* (1988), 73: 259–266.

21. B. M. Meglino, A. S. DeNisi, and E. C. Ravlin, "The Effects of Previous Job Exposure and Subsequent Job Status on the Functioning of Realistic Job Previews," *Personnel Psychology* (1993), 46: 803–822.

22. Paul Crosteau, "Evaluating Your Recruitment Efforts: Some Helpful Metrics," *Legacy Bowes Group* (Jul. 26, 2012): www.legacybowes.com.

23. See Neal Schmitt and Ivan Robertson, "Personnel Selection," *Annual Review of Psychology* (1990), 41: 289–319.

24. Michael Stevens and Michael Campion, "The Knowledge, Skill, and Ability Requirements for Teamwork: Implications for Human Resource Management," *Journal of Management*, (1994), 20(2): 503–530.

25. M. R. Barrick and M. K. Mount, "The Big Five Personality Dimensions and Job Performance: A Meta-Analysis," *Personnel Psychology* (1991), 44: 1–26.

26. It is not always clear that recruiters and interviewers can effectively distinguish between the two types of fit. See, for example, Amy Kristof-Brown, "Perceived Applicant Fit: Distinguishing Between Recruiters' Perceptions of Person-Job and Person-Organization Fit," *Personnel Psychology*, (2000), 53: 643–672.

27. Orlando Behling, "Employee Selection: Will Intelligence and Conscientiousness Do the Job?" *Academy of Management Executive* (Feb. 1998): 77–86.

28. J. E. Hunter and R. F. Hunter, "Validity and Utility of Alternative Predictors of Job Performance," *Psychological Bulletin* (Spring 1984): 72–98.

29. C. J. Russell, J. Mattdson, S. E. Devlin, and D. Atwater, "Predictive Validity of Biodata Items Generated from Retrospective Life Experience Essays," *Journal of Applied Psychology* (1990), 75: 569–580.

30. See "Can You Tell Applesauce from Pickles?" *Forbes* (Oct. 9, 1995): 106–108 for several examples.

31. J. E. Hunter, "Cognitive Ability, Cognitive Aptitudes, Job Knowledge, and Job Performance," *Journal of Vocational Behavior* (1986), 29: 340–362.

32. A. R. Jensen, *Bias in Mental Testing* (New York: Free Press, 1980).

33. M. K. Mount and M. R. Barrick, *Manual for the Personal Characteristics Inventory* (Iowa City, IA University of Iowa Press: 1995).

34. Daniel P. O'Meara, "Personality Tests Raise Questions of Legality and Effectiveness," *HR Magazine* (Jan. 1994): 97–104.

35. See L. M. Hough, "The Big Five Personality Variables–Construct Confusion: Description Versus Prediction," *Human Performance* (1992), 5: 139–155. For an opposing view, see J. E. Hunter and R. F. Hunter, "Validity and Utility of Alternative Predictors of Job Performance," *Psychological Bulletin* (1984), 96: 72–98.

36. "Employers Score New Hires," *USA Today* (Jul. 9, 1997): 1B, 2B.

37. P. R. Sackett, "Integrity Testing for Personnel Selection," *Current Directions in Psychological Science* (1994), 3: 73–76.

38. R. C. Hollinger and J. P. Clark, *Theft by Employees* (Lexington, MA: Lexington Books, 1983).

39. U.S. Congress, Office of Technology Assessment, *The Use of Integrity Tests for Pre-Employment Screening* (Washington, DC: U.S. Government Printing Office, 1990); S. W. Gilliland, "Fairness from the Applicant's Perspective: Reactions to Employee Selection Procedures," *International Journal of Selection and Assessment* (1995), 3: 11–19.

40. Jean Phillips and Stan Gully, *Strategic Staffing*, 2nd ed. (Upper Saddle Rivier, NJ: Pearson Publishing, 2012).

41. "Think Fast!," *Forbes* (Mar. 24, 1997): 146–151.

42. Elaine Pulakos and Neal Schmitt, "Experience-Based and Situational Interview Questions: Studies of Validity," *Personnel Psychology* (1995), 48: 289–308.

43. M. A. McDaniel, D. L. Whetzel, F. L. Schmidt, and S. D. Maurer, "The Validity of Employment Interviews: A Comprehensive Review and Meta-Analysis," *Journal of Applied Psychology* (1994), 79: 599–616.

44. *Watson v. Fort Worth Bank & Trust*, 108 Sup. Ct. 2791 (1988).

45. See Thomas Dougherty, Daniel Turban, and John Callender, "Confirming First Impressions in the Employment Interview: A Field Study of Interviewer Behavior," *Journal of Applied Psychology* (1994), 79(5): 659–665.

46. Paul Falcone, "Getting Employers to Open Up on a Reference Check," *HR Magazine* (Jul. 1995): 58–63.

47. "Think Fast!," *Forbes* (Mar. 24, 1997): 146–151.

48. Annette C. Spychalski, Miguel A. Quinones, Barbara B. Gaugler, and Katja Pohley, "A Survey of Assessment Center Practices in Organizations in the United States," *Personnel Psychology* (Spring 1997): 71–82.

49. Justin Martin, "So, You Want to Work for the Best . . . ," *Fortune* (Jan. 12, 1998): 77–85.

50. Michael Lewis, *Moneyball: The Art of Winning an Unfair Game* (New York: W.W. Norton, 2003); Chris Anderson and David Sally, *The Numbers Game: Why Everything You Know About Soccer Is Wrong* (New York: Penguin Books, 2013).

51. Matt Aberham, "JobsBlog Rewind: Five Ways to Fail My Phone Interview," *The JobsBlog* (April 14, 2010): http://microsoftjobsblog.com, accessed on June 1, 2016.

52. Hugh Anderson, "Phone Interview Tips for Savvy Candidates," *BNet*, 2010, https://www.monster.com/career-advice/article/mastering-the-phone-interview, accessed on June 1, 2016; Anne Fisher, "Fear of Phoning," *Fortune* (September 6, 2005): http://money.cnn.com, accessed on June 1, 2016; Anne Fisher, "How Can I Survive a Phone Interview?" *Fortune* (April 19, 2004): http://money.cnn.com, accessed on June 1, 2016; "Phone Interview Success," *CollegeGrad.com*, www.collegegrad.com, accessed on June 1, 2016; "Need Some Phone Interview Help? Score Big with Our 11 Top Tips," *BNet*, https://www.monster.com/career-advice/article/mastering-the-phone-interview, accessed on June 1, 2016; Aberham, "JobsBlog Rewind: Five Ways to Fail My Phone Interview," *The JobsBlog* (April 14, 2010): http://microsoftjobsblog.com, accessed on June 1, 2016.

53. See especially *Washington v. Davis*, Sup. Ct.; 426 U.S. 229; S. Ct. 2040, L. Ed. 2d 597 (1976).

54. See, for example, *Albermarle Paper Company v. Moody*, Sup. Ct.; 422 U.S. 405; 95 S. Ct. 2362, 45 L. Ed. 2d 280 (1975); *Connecticut v. Teal*, Sup. Ct.; 457 U.S. 440; 102 S. Ct. 2525; L. Ed. 2d 190 (1982); and *Watson v. Fort Worth Bank & Trust*, Sup. Ct.; 487 U.S. 977; 108 S. Ct. 2777; L. Ed. 2d 827 (1988).

55. "Job-Test Ruling Cheers Employers," *Wall Street Journal* (July 1, 2009): B1, B2.

56. C. R. Williams, C. E. Labig, and T. Stone, "Recruitment Sources and Posthire Outcomes for Job Applications and New Hires," *Journal of Applied Psychology* (1993), 78: 163–172.

57. See Chapter 1 in Charles R. Greer, *Strategy and Human Resources* (Englewood Cliffs, NJ: Prentice-Hall, 1995), for an overview of the importance of training and development.

58. Jane Webster and Joseph J. Martocchio, "The Differential Effects of Software Training Previews on Training Outcomes," *Journal of Management* (1995), 21(4): 757–787.

59. Jack Stack, "The Training Myth," *Inc.*, (Aug. 1998): 41–42.

60. "For Some, a Patchwork of Jobs Pays the Bills," www.boston.com, accessed on June 1, 2016; Kristin Kridel, "Overqualified Applying for Temporary Work," Spokesman.com (Mar. 4, 2009): www.spokesman.com, accessed on June 1, 2016; Anne Fisher, "Be a Manager and a Temp?" *CNNMoney.com*: www.cmfassociates.com, accessed on June 1, 2016; U.S. Bureau of Labor Statistics (BLS), "Employer Costs for Employee Compensation," news release, December 2015: www.bls.gov, accessed on June 1, 2016; BLS, "Table 12. Private Industry, by Industry Group and Full-Time and Part-Time Status," News Release (Dec. 2015): www.bls.gov, accessed on June 1, 2016.

8

1. "What Is Assistive Technology?," *AccessIT* (2013): www.washington.edu, accessed on June 7, 2016.

2. "Assistive Technology Reconnects Employees to the Workplace While Recovering from Temporary Disabilities," *Accessibility in Action Case Studies*, www.microsoft.com, accessed on June 7, 2016; National Council on Disability, Empowerment for Americans with Disabilities: Breaking Barriers to Careers and Full Employment (Oct. 2013): www.ncd.gov, accessed on June 7, 2016; "What Is Assistive Technology?," *AccessIT* (2013): www.washington.edu, accessed on June 7, 2016; American Federation for the Blind, "Types of Accommodations," "Cost of Accommodations," *AFB CareerConnect*, (2015): www.afb.org, accessed on June 7, 2016.

3. David A. Thomas and Robin J. Ely, "Making Differences Matter: A New Paradigm for Managing Diversity," *Harvard Business Review* (Sept.–Oct. 1996): 79–90.

4. Dora C. Lau and J. Keith Murnighan, "Demographic Diversity and Faultlines: The Compositional Dynamics of Organizational Groups," *Academy of Management Review* (1998), 23(2): 325–340.

5. The Federation for American Immigration Reform, Immigration Issues (Dec. 2011): www.fairus.org.

6. Frances J. Milliken and Luis L. Martins, "Searching for Common Threads: Understanding the Multiple Effects of Diversity in Organizational Groups," *Academy of Management Review* (1996), 21(2): 402–433.

7. "In a Factory Schedule, Where Does Religion Fit In?" *Wall Street Journal* (Mar. 18, 2013): A1; A14.

8. Adrienne Colella, "The Work Group Perspective: Co-Worker Responses to Group Member Accommodations," in D. Harrison (Chair), "Implementing What Matters Most: Multiple Stakeholders in Accommodating People with Disabilities at Work. All-Academy Symposium," Presented at the Annual Meeting of Academy of Management, San Diego, CA, Aug. 1998.

9. Barbara L. Hassell and Pamela L. Perrewe, "An Examination of Beliefs about Older Workers: Do Stereotypes Still Exist?" *Journal of Organizational Behavior* (1995), 16: 457–468.

10. For a more complete discussion of these dimensions, see Diane L. Stone and Adrienne Colella, "A Model of Factors Affecting the Treatment of Disabled Individuals in Organizations," *Academy of Management Review* (1996), 21: 352–401.

11. *David Baldwin v. Dep't of Transportation*, EEOC Appeal No. 120133080 (Jul. 15, 2015): www.eeoc.gov/decisions/0120133080.pdf.

12. Allen Smith, "EEOC Sexual Orientation Lawsuits Suggest Need for Training," *SHRM Legal Issues* (Mar. 7, 2016).

13. Allen Smith, "Anxiety over Transgender Women in Restrooms Persists," *SHRM Legal Issues* (Mar. 28, 2016).

14. Allen Smith, "EEOC, DOJ Take Aim at North Carolina's 'Bathroom bill'," *SHRM Legal Issues* (May 5, 2016).

15. *Faith Communities Today: Mosque in America: A National Portrait* (Apr. 2001). James R. Lewis and Inga B. Tollefsen (Eds.), *The Oxford Handbook of New Religious Movements*, Vol. 2. (Oxford, UK: Oxford University Press, 2016).

16. U.S. Department of Commerce, United States Census Bureau, "The 2012 Statistical Abstract: Population by Religion," http://www.census.gov/library/publications/2011/compendia/statab/131ed.html.

17. Based on Taylor H. Cox and Stacy Blake, "Managing Cultural Diversity: Implications for Organizational Competitiveness," *Academy of Management Executive* (Aug. 1991): 45–56; see also Gail Robinson and Kathleen Dechant, "Building a Business Case for Diversity," *Academy of Management Executive* (Aug. 1997): 21–30.

18. C. Marlene Fiol, "Consensus, Diversity, and Learning in Organizations," *Organization Science* (Aug. 1994): 403–415.

19. Douglas Hall and Victoria Parker, "The Role of Workplace Flexibility in Managing Diversity," *Organizational Dynamics* (Summer 1993): 5–14.

20. Janice R. W. Joplin and Catherine S. Daus, "Challenges of Leading a Diverse Workforce," *Academy of Management Executive* (Aug. 1997): 32–44.

21. "As Population Ages, Older Workers Clash with Younger Bosses," *Wall Street Journal* (June 13, 1994): A1; A8.

22. "Pursuit of Diversity Stirs Racial Tension at an FAA Center," *Wall Street Journal* (Dec. 3, 1998): A1; A8.

23. "Generational Warfare," *Forbes* (Mar. 22, 1999): 62–66.

24. For a review of these results, see Milliken and Martins, "Searching for Common Threads: Understanding the Multiple Effects of Diversity in Organizational Groups," *Academy of Management Review* (1996), 21: 402–433; or Belle Rose Ragins and Jorge Gonzalez, "Understanding Diversity in Organizations: Getting a Grip on a Slippery Construct," in J. Greenberg (Ed.), *Organizational Behavior: The State of the Science* (Mahwah, NJ: Erlbaum, 2003).

25. See for example, Christopher Earley and Elaine Mosakowski, "Creating Hybrid Team Cultures: An Empirical Test of Transnational Team Functioning," *Academy of Management Journal* (2000), 43: 26–49.

26. Ibid.; Orlando Richard, Tim Barnett, Sean Dwyer, and Ken Chadwick, "Cultural Diversity

in Management, Firm Performance, and the Moderating Role of Entrepreneurial Orientation Dimensions," *Academy of Management Journal* (2004), 47: 255–266.

27. Karen Hildebrand, "Use Leadership Training to Increase Diversity," *HR Magazine* (Aug. 1996): 53–57.

28. Patricia L. Nemetz and Sandra L. Christensen, "The Challenge of Cultural Diversity: Harnessing a Diversity of Views to Understand Multiculturalism," *Academy of Management Review* (1996), 21(2): 434–462.

29. This discussion derives heavily from Taylor H. Cox, "The Multicultural Organization," *Academy of Management Executive* (May 1991): 34–47.

30. The relationship between individual and organizational learning is discussed in much more detail in Lois Tetrick and Nancy Da Silva, "Assessing the Culture and Climate for Organizational Learning," in Susan Jackson, Michael Hitt, and Angelo DeNisi (Eds.), *Managing Knowledge for Sustained Competitive Advantage* (San Francisco: Jossey-Bass, 2003): 333–360.

31. See, for example, Michael Hitt, Barbara Keats, and Sam DeMarie, "Navigating in the New Competitive Landscape: Building Strategic Flexibility and Competitive Advantage in the 21st Century," *Academy of Management Executive* (1998), 12: 22–42; and Angelo DeNisi, Michael Hitt, and Susan Jackson, "The Knowledge-Based Approach to Sustainable Competitive Advantage," in Jackson, Hitt, and DeNisi (Eds.), *Managing Knowledge for Sustained Competitive Advantage*: 3–36.

32. For more on the pressures and challenges facing these firms, see Matthew Jaffe and Scott Mayerowitz, "Unapologetic CEOs: What Did the Bank Do with Your Case?" *ABC News Online* (Feb. 11, 2009).

33. Max Boisot, *Knowledge Assets* (Oxford, UK: Oxford University Press, 1998).

34. M. L. Tushman and C. A. O'Reilly, *Winning Through Innovation* (Cambridge, MA: Harvard Business School Press, 1996).

35. M. A. Von Glinow, *The New Professionals* (Cambridge, MA: Ballinger, 1988).

36. T. W. Lee and S. D. Maurer, "The Retention of Knowledge Workers with the Unfolding Model of Voluntary Turnover," *Human Resource Management Review* (1997), 7: 247–276.

37. J. C. Kail, "Compensating Scientists and Engineers," in D. B. Balkin and L. R. Gomez-Mejia (Eds.), *New Perspectives on Compensation* (Englewood Cliffs, NJ: Prentice-Hall, 1987): 278–281.

38. G. T. Milkovich, "Compensation Systems in High-Technology Companies," in A. Klingartner and C. Anderson (Eds.), *High Technology Management* (Lexington, MA: Lexington Books, 1987).

39. Thomas Stewart, "In Search of Elusive Tech Workers," *Fortune* (Feb. 16, 1998): 171–172.

40. See, for example, the various discussions in the edited volume by Jackson, Hitt, and DeNisi, *Managing Knowledge for Sustained Competitive Advantage*.

41. Beth McConnell, "HR Implements Corporate Social Responsibility Globally," *HR News* (Nov. 28, 2006): 1-2.

42. Angelo DeNisi and Carrie Belsito, "Strategic Aesthetics: Wisdom and HRM" in Eric H. Kessler and James R. Bailey (Eds.), *Handbook of Organizational and Managerial Wisdom* (Thousand Oaks, CA: Sage Publications, 2007).

43. Lynn Gibson, "Implications of the FLSA for Inmates, Correctional Institutions, Private Industry and Labor." Statement before the U.S. Senate Hearings of the Committee on Labor and Human Resources, Oct. 18, 1993.

44. For a more in-depth discussion of these issues, see Ray Marshall, "Industrial Relations and Inmate Labor," *Proceedings of the 53rd Annual Meeting of the Industrial Relations Research Association*, New Orleans (2001): 339–348.

45. Jeffrey Kling and Alan Krueger, "Costs, Benefits, and Distributional Consequences of Inmate Labor," *Proceedings of the 53rd Annual Meeting of the Industrial Relations Research Association*, New Orleans (2001): 349–358.

46. Aimee Pichee. "Why Wal-Mart's Pay Raise Is Backfiring," *CBS Money Watch* (Aug. 7, 2015).

47. Paul LaMonica, "Walmart: Wage Hikes Are Killing Our Profits," *CNN Money* (Oct. 15, 2015).

48. Michael Pearson, Holly Yan, and Arwa Damon, "Migrant Crisis: More Troubles in Hungary as Austria, Germany Near Tipping Point," *CNN On Line* (Sep. 7, 2015): www.cnn.com.

49. See for example, Sandra Waddock, "Building a New Institutional Infrastructure for Corporate Responsibility," *Academy of Management Perspectives* (2008), 22: 87–108.

50. For a more detailed history, see Sandra Waddock, "Parallel Universes: Companies, Academics, and the Progress of Corporate Citizenship," *Business and Society Review* (Mar. 2004), 109: 5–42.

51. Stefan Ambec and Paul Lanoie, "Does It Pay to Be Green? A Systematic Overview," *Academy of Management Perspectives* (2008), 22: 45–62.

52. John Mackey, "The CEO's Blog," *Whole Foods Online* (Dec. 24, 2009).

53. U.S. Department of Commerce, United States Census Bureau, American Community Survey, and the 2010 Census, Washington, DC, (Nov. 2011): http://en.wikibooks.org/w/index.php?title=American_Indians_Today/Current_problems&oldid=2611302 (last revised 2014), accessed on April 1, 2014; "Native American Religious and Cultural Freedom: An Introductory Essay," The Pluralism Project at Harvard University (2015); Keith James, Willie Wolf, Chris Lovato, and Steve Byers, *Barriers to Workplace Advancement Experienced by Native Americans.* Electronic Archive (Ithaca, NY: Catherwood Library, Cornell University); Almanac of Policy Issues, *Civil Rights and the Native Americans* (Washington, DC: U.S. Department of Justice, undated).

9

1. Matthew Boyle, "The Wegmans Way," *Fortune* (Jan. 24, 2015): http://archive.fortune.com, accessed June 10, 2016; Michael Prospero, "Employee Innovator: Wegmans," *Fast Company* (2015): www.fastcompany.com, accessed June 10, 2016; "100 Best Companies to Work For," *Fortune* (2016): www.fortune.com, accessed June 10, 2016.

2. Kathryn Tyler, "Compensation Strategies Can Foster Lateral Moves and Growing in Place," *HR Magazine* (Apr. 1998): 64–69.

3. Emily Pavlovic, "Choosing the Best Salary Surveys," *HR Magazine* (Apr. 1994): 44–48.

4. "How the Internet Is Changing the World of HR," *HR Magazine* (Jan. 19, 2015); "Using the Web to Get Ahead," *USA Today*, January 19, 2016; "Web Transforms Art of Negotiating Raises," *Wall Street Journal* (Jan. 19, 2015).

5. J. Stacey Adams "Inequity in Social Exchange," in L. Berkowitz (Ed.), *Advances in Experimental Social Psychology* (New York: Academic Press, 1965): 267–299.

6. Jeffrey Pfeiffer, "Six Dangerous Myths about Pay," *Harvard Business Review* (May–Jun. 1998): 109–119.

7. See "Is Minimum Wage Minimum Life?" *Associated Press News Story* (Jan. 23 1995), as published in the *Bryan-College Station Eagle* [TX], p. B1.

8. Brian S. Klaas and John A. McClendon, "To Lead, Lag, or March: Estimating the Financial Impact of Pay Level Policies," *Personnel Psychology* (1996), 49(1): 88–98.

9. Edward E. Lawler III, "The New Pay: A Strategic Approach," *Compensation & Benefits Review* (Jul.–Aug. 1995): 145–154.

10. Sandra O'Neal, "Aligning Pay with Business Strategy," *HR Magazine* (Aug. 1993): 76–80.

11. Charles Greer, *Strategy and Human Resources* (Englewood Cliffs, NJ: Prentice-Hall, 1995).

12. "Many Companies Lower Pay Raises," *USA Today* (Apr. 4, 2002): 1B.

13. Judith Collins and Paul Muchinsky, "An Assessment of the Construct Validity of Three Job Evaluation Methods: A Field Experiment," *Academy of Management Journal* (1993), 36(4): 895–904.

14. Ibid.

15. G. D. Jenkins and N. Gupta, "The Payoffs of Paying for Knowledge," *National Productivity Review* (1985), 4: 121–130.

16. Adrienne Colella, Ramona Paetzold, Asghar Zardkoohi, and Michael Wesson, "Exposing Pay Secrecy," *Academy of Management Review* (2007), 32: 35–56.

17. Bureau of National Affairs, *Report on Salary Surveys: 2011 Yearbook* (Arlington VA: Bureau of national Affairs, 2012).

18. "Detroit Meets a 'Worker Paradise,'" *Wall Street Journal* (Mar. 3, 1999): B1; B4.

19. Tamara Lytle, "Six Critical Health Care Reform Issues" *AARP Bulletin Today* (May 13, 2009).

20. Avik Roy, "Delta Air Lines: Next Year, Our Health Care Costs Will Increase by 'Nearly $100 Million," Forbes (Aug. 22, 2013): www.forbes.com.

21. "Health Care Reform," *HR Issues Update* (SHRM) (Jan. 12, 2010).

22. For a recent discussion of these issues, see Maureen Minehan, "Islam's Growth Affects Workplace Policies," *HR Magazine* (Nov. 1998): 216.

23. Mina Westman and Dov Eden, "Effects of Respite from Work on Burnout: Vacation Relief and Fade-Out," *Journal of Applied Psychology* (Aug. 1997): 516–527.

24. Robert Van Glazen, "Paid Leave in Private Industry over the Past 20 Years," *Beyond the Numbers, U.S. Bureau of Labor Statistics, Dept. of Labor* (Aug. 2013).

25. "Employer Benefit Surveys Target Unhealthy Habits," *USA Today* (May 28, 1998): 1B.

26. S. Caudron, "The Wellness Pay Off," *Personnel Journal* (Jul. 1990): 55–60.

27. Shirley Hand and Robert Zawacki, "Family-Friendly Benefits: More Than a Frill," *HR Magazine* (Oct. 1994): 74–79.

28. E. E. Kossek and V. Nichol, "The Effects of On-Site Child Care on Employee Attitudes and Performance," *Personnel Psychology* (1992), 45: 485–509.

29. Rudy Yandrick, "The EAP Struggle: Counselors or Referrers?" *HR Magazine* (Aug. 1998): 90–91.

30. W. J. Sonnenstuhl and H. M. Trice, *Strategies for Employee Assistance Programs: The Crucial Balance* (Ithaca, NY: Cornell University ILR Press, 1990).

31. Melissa Barringer and George Milkovich, "A Theoretical Exploration of the Adoption and Design of Flexible Benefit Plans: A Case of Human Resource Innovation," *Academy of Management Review* (Apr. 1998): 305–324.

32. A. E. Barber, R. B. Dunham, and R. A. Formisano, "The Impact of Flexible Benefits on Employee Satisfaction: A Field Study," *Personnel Psychology* (1992), 45: 55–57.

33. Louise Story, "Goldman Sachs Considers Charity Requirement," *New York Times* (Jul. 11, 2009), business section: 1.

34. Ibid.

35. DealBook, *New York Times* (Jul. 30, 2009).

36. T. A. Steward, "The Trouble with Stock Options," *Fortune* (Jan. 1, 1990): 93–95.

37. Anders Mellin and Brandon Kochkodin, "The Best-Paid U.S. Executives Don't Work on Wall Street," *Bloomberg Business* (Jan. 4, 2016): www.bloomberg.com.

38. "How Perks Stack Up Worldwide" *Forbes*, May 19, 1997, p. 162. Reprinted by permission of *Forbes* Magazine © Forbes, Inc., 1997.; Daniel Fisher, "The Most Outrageous Executive Perks," *Forbes*, July 5, 2012, on Yahoo Finance.

39. Harry Barkema and Luis Gomez-Mejia, "Managerial Compensation and Firm Performance: A General Research Framework," *Academy of Management Journal* (1998), 41(2): 135–145.

40. Rajiv D. Banker, Seok-Young Lee, Gordon Potter, and Dhinu Srinivasan, "Contextual Analysis of Performance Impacts of Outcome-Based Incentive Compensation," *Academy of Management Journal* (1996), 39(4): 920–948.

41. J. Pfeffer and N. Langton, "The Effects of Wage Dispersion on Satisfaction, Productivity and Working Collaboratively: Evidence from College and University Faculty," *Administrative Science Quarterly* (1993), 38: 382–407.

42. R. G. Ehrenberg and M. L. Bognanno, "The Incentive Effects of Tournaments Revisited: Evidence from the European PGA Tour," *Industrial and Labor Relations Review* (1990), 43: 74–88.

43. Allen Smith, "Overtime Overhaul: Review Proposed Changes Now before Final Rule Announced," *SHRM Legal Issues* (May 10, 2016): www.shrm.org.

44. For a more in-depth discussion of the requirements and advantages of qualification, see Michael Sarli, "Nondiscrimination Rules for Qualified Plans: The General Test," *Compensation and Benefits Review* (Sept. 1991): 56–67.

45. H. W. Hennessey, P. L. Perrewe, and W. A. Hochwarter, "Impact of Benefit Awareness on Employee and Organizational Outcomes: A Longitudinal Field Experiment," *Benefits Quarterly* (1992), 8(2): 90–96.

46. M. Wilson, G. B. Northcraft, and M. A. Neale, "The Perceived Value of Fringe Benefits," *Personnel Psychology* (1985), 38: 309–320.

47. "About Us," Nucor Web site (Feb. 22, 2010): www.nucor.com; "The Art of Motivation"; Gretchen Morgenson, "Companies Not Behaving Badly," *New York Times* (Oct. 9, 2005): B3; "Reinventing the Mill," *New York Times* (Oct. 22, 2005): B5.

10

1. "Stores Count Seconds to Cut Labor Costs," *Wall Street Journal* (Nov. 28, 2009): A1, A15.

2. *Hoover's Handbook of Private Companies 2012* (Austin: Hoover's Business Press, 2012) 397–398.

3. A. S. DeNisi and K. R. Murphy, "Performance Management and Appraisal," *Journal of Applied Psychology - Special Centennial Issue* (forthcoming).

4. See Chapter 8 in Charles R. Greer, *Strategy and Human Resources* (Englewood Cliffs, NJ: Prentice-Hall, 1995), for a review of the strategic importance of performance management in organizations.

5. W. Timothy Weaver, "Linking Performance Reviews to Productivity and Quality," *HR Magazine* (Nov. 1996): 93–98.

6. A. S. DeNisi, *Cognitive Approach to Performance Appraisal: A Program of Research* (London: Routledge, 1996).

7. For several excellent reviews of these "cognitive" decision-making processes on the part of the rater, see A. S. DeNisi, T. P. Cafferty, and B. Meglino, "A Cognitive Model of the Performance Appraisal Process," *Organizational Behavior and Human Decision Processes* (1984), 33: 360–396; and D. R. Ilgen and J. M. Feldman, "Performance Appraisal: A Process Focus," in B. Staw and L. Cummings (Eds.), *Research in Organizational Behavior*, Vol. 5 (Greenwich, CT: JAI Press, 1983).

8. Arup Varma, Angelo S. DeNisi, and Lawrence H. Peters, "Interpersonal Affect and Performance Appraisal: A Field Study," *Personnel Psychology* (Summer 1996): 341–360.

9. K. Kraiger and K. Ford, "A Meta-Analysis of Ratee Race Effects in Performance Rating," *Journal of Applied Psychology* (1985), 70: 56–65.

10. See, for example, J. N. Cleveland, R. M. Festa, and L. Montgomery, "Applicant Pool Composition and Job Perceptions: Impact on Decisions Regarding an Older Applicant," *Journal of Vocational Behavior* (1988), 32: 112–125.

11. For example, see the review by V. F. Nieva and B. Gutek, "Sex Effects in Evaluations," *Academy of Management Review* (1980), 5: 267–276.

12. A. Colella, A. S. DeNisi, and A. Varma, "A Model of the Impact of Disability on Performance Evaluations," *Human Resource Management Review* (1997), 7: 27–53.

13. For example, see Kevin R. Murphy and Jeanette N. Cleveland, *Understanding Performance Appraisal: Social, Organizational, and Goal-Based Perspectives* (Thousand Oaks, CA: Sage Publications, 1995).

14. Forest J. Jourden and Chip Heath, "The Evaluation Gap in Performance Perceptions: Illusory Perceptions of Groups and Individuals," *Journal of Applied Psychology* (1996), 81(4): 369–379.

15. Angelo S. DeNisi, W. Alan Randolph, and Allyn G. Blencoe, "Potential Problems with Peer Ratings," *Academy of Management Journal* (1983), 26: 457–467.

16. Leanne Atwater, Paul Roush, and Allison Fischtal, "The Influence of Upward Feedback on Self- and Follower Ratings of Leadership," *Personnel Psychology* (Spring 1995): 35–59.

17. See, for example, Alan Walker and James Smither, "A Five-Year Study of Upward Feedback: What Managers Do with Their Results Matters," *Personnel Psychology* (1999), 52: 393–423.

18. For a good review of the work in this area, see David Waldman and Leanne Atwater, *The Power of 360-Degree Feedback: How to Leverage Performance Evaluations for Top Productivity* (Houston: Gulf Publishing, 2000).

19. James M. Conway, "Analysis and Design of Multitrait-Multirater Performance Appraisal Studies," *Journal of Management*, 22(1): 139–162.

20. For an in-depth discussion of these problems, see Susan Haworth, "The Dark Side of Multi-Rater Assessments," *HR Magazine* (May 1998): 106–112;

or Angelo DeNisi and Avraham Kluger, "Feedback Effectiveness: Can 360-Degree Appraisals Be Improved?" *Academy of Management Executive*, (2000), 14: 129–139.

21. See discussions of these processes in Walter Borman, "Exploring the Upper Limits of Reliability and Validity in Job Performance Ratings," *Journal of Applied Psychology* (1978), 63: 135–144; and DeNisi, Cafferty, and Meglino, "A Cognitive Model of the Performance Appraisal Process."

22. See, for example, H. John Bernardin and C. S. Walter, "Effects of Rater and Training and Diary Keeping on Psychometric Errors in Ratings," *Journal of Applied Psychology* (1977), 62: 64–69; or Angelo DeNisi, Tina Robbins, and Thomas Cafferty, "The Organization of Information Used for Performance Appraisals: The Role of Diary Keeping," *Journal of Applied Psychology* (1989), 74: 124–129.

23. For an excellent review of some relevant court cases, see Jon Werner and Mark Bolino, "Explaining U.S. Courts of Appeals Decisions Involving Performance Appraisal: Accuracy, Fairness, and Validation," *Personnel Psychology* (1997), 50: 1–24.

24. Andrew Likierman, "The Five Traps of Performance Measurement," *Harvard Business Review* (Oct. 2009): 96–105.

25. For a more complete discussion of the proper focus for appraisals in different settings, see Angelo DeNisi, "Performance Appraisal and Control Systems: A Multilevel Approach," in K. Klein and S. Kozlowski (Eds.), *Multilevel Theory, Research, and Methods in Organizations*, SIOP Frontiers Series (San Francisco: Jossey-Bass, 2000): 121–156.

26. "Goodyear to Stop Labeling 10% of Its Workers as Worst," *USA Today* (Sept. 11, 2002): B1; B2; "Goodyear Backs Down," *Beacon Journal* (Sept. 12, 2002): A15; Cathleen Flahardy, "Companies Should Get Their Policies in Order to Avoid Potential Age Discrimination Lawsuits," InsideCounsel.com (Nov. 18, 2006); "Using the ABC Method to Boost Performance," *HR Magazine* (Nov. 2008): 36.

27. E. D. Sisson, "Forced Choice: The New Army Rating," *Personnel Psychology* (1948), 1: 365–381.

28. J. C. Flanagan, "The Critical Incident Technique," *Psychological Bulletin* (1954), 51: 327–358.

29. J. C. Flanagan and R. K. Burns, "The Employee Performance Record: A New Appraisal and Development Tool," *Harvard Business Review* (Sept.–Oct. 1955): 95–102.

30. P. C. Smith and L. M. Kendall, "Retranslation of Expectations: An Approach to the Construction of Unambiguous Anchors for Rating Scales," *Journal of Applied Psychology* (1963), 47: 149–155.

31. H. J. Barnardin, M. B. LaShells, P. C. Smith, and K. M. Alvares, "Behavioral Expectation Scales: Effects of Development Procedures and Formats," *Journal of Applied Psychology* (1976), 61: 75–79.

32. G. P. Latham, C. H. Fay, and L. M. Saari, "The Development of Behavioral Observation Scales for Appraising the Performance of Foremen," *Personnel Psychology* (1979), 33: 815–821.

33. For an excellent review of the variations on these methods, see Chapter 4 in H. J. Bernardin and R. W. Beatty, *Performance Appraisal: Assessing Human Behavior at Work* (Boston: PWS-Kent, 1984).

34. See, for example, Joseph Mishra and Susan Crampton, "Employee Monitoring: Privacy in the Workplace?" *SAM Advanced Management Journal* (1998), 53: 4.

35. See Elizabeth Douthitt and John R. Aiello, "The Role of Participation and Control in the Effects of Computer Monitoring on Fairness Perceptions, Task Satisfaction, and Performance," *Journal of Applied Psychology* (2001), 86: 867–874.

36. American Management Association, *Workplace Monitoring and Surveillance: A 1999 AMA Survey* (New York: American Management Association, 2000).

37. See, for example, reviews by Frank Landy and James Farr, "Performance Rating," *Psychological Bulletin* (1980), 87: 72–102; or Angelo DeNisi, *A Cognitive Approach to Performance Appraisal* (London: Routledge, 1996): 1–20.

38. Jeffrey S. Kane, H. John Bernardin, Peter Villanova, and Joseph Peyrefitte, "Stability of Rater Leniency: Three Studies," *Academy of Management Journal* (1995), 38(4): 1036–1051.

39. Walter C. Borman, Leonard A. White, and David W. Dorsey, "Effects of Ratee Task Performance and Interpersonal Factors on Supervisor and Peer Performance Ratings," *Journal of Applied Psychology* (1995), 80(1): 168–177.

40. Juan I. Sanchez and Phillip De La Torre, "A Second Look at the Relationship Between Rating and Behavioral Accuracy in Performance Appraisal," *Journal of Applied Psychology* (1996), 81(1): 3–10.

41. See also Michael Hammer, "The 7 Deadly Sins of Performance Measurement (And How to Avoid Them)," *MIT Sloan Management Review* (Spring 2009): 36–45.

42. W. C. Borman, "Job Behavior, Performance, and Effectiveness," in M. D. Dunnette and L. Hough (Eds.), *Handbook of Industrial and Organizational Psychology*, Vol. 2, 2nd ed. (Palo Alto, CA: Consulting Psychologists Press, 1991); W. C. Borman and S. J. Motowidlo, "Expanding the Criterion Domain to Include Elements of Contextual Performance," in N. Schmitt and W. Borman (Eds.), *Personnel Selection in Organizations* (San Francisco: Jossey-Bass, 1993).

43. D. W. Organ and K. Ryan, "A Meta-Analytic Review of Attitudinal and Dispositional Predictors of Organizational Citizenship Behavior," *Personnel Psychology* (1995), 48: 775–802.

44. J. M. Werner, "Dimensions That Make a Difference: Examining the Impact of In-Role and Extrarole Behaviors on Supervisory Ratings," *Journal of Applied Psychology* (1994), 79: 98–107.

45. Maria Rotundo and Paul Sackett, "The Relative Importance of Task, Citizenship, and Counterproductive Performance to Global Ratings of Job Performance: A Policy-Capturing Study," *Journal of Applied Psychology* (2002), 87: 66–80.

46. N. P. Podsakoff, S. W. Whiting, P. M. Podsakoff, and P. Mishra, "Effects of Organizational Citizenship Behaviors on Selection Decisions in Employment Interviews," *Journal of Applied Psychology* (2011), 96(2): 310–326.

47. See, for example, E. Vigoda-Gadot, "Compulsory Citizenship Behavior: Theorizing Some Dark Sides of the Good Soldier Syndrome in Organizations," *Journal for the Theory of Social Behavior* (2006), 36: 77–93; M. C. Bolino and W. H. Turnley, "The Personal Costs of Citizenship Behavior: The Relationship Between Individual Initiative and Work Overload, Job Stress, and Work-Family Conflict," *Journal of Applied Psychology* (2005), 90: 740–748; and C. Smith, A. Hall, A. S. DeNisi, "Organizational Citizenship and Selection: Does Candidate Gender Matter?" (paper presented at the Academy of Management Meetings, Philadelphia, PA, Aug. 2014).

48. Claire Suddath, "Performance Reviews: Why Bother?," *Bloomberg Business On Line* (Nov. 7, 2013).

49. Kris Duggan, "Why the Annual Performance Review Is Going Extinct," *Fast Company* (Oct. 20, 2015).

50. Lilian Cunningham and Jena McGregor, "Why Big Business Is Falling Out of Love with the Annual Performance Review," *The Washington Post* (Aug. 17, 2015).

51. Satoris S. Culberston, Jaime B. Henning, and Stephanie C. Payne, "Performance Appraisal |Satisfaction: The Role of Feedback and Goal Orientation," *Personnel Psychology* (2013), 12(4): 189–195.

52. A. N. Kluger and A. S. DeNisi, "The Effects of Feedback Interventions on Performance: Historical Review, Meta-Analysis, a Preliminary Feedback Intervention Theory," *Psychological Bulletin* (1996), 119: 254–284.

53. *Brito v. Zia Company*, 478 F. 2d 1200 (10th Cir. 1973).

54. Manuel London, "Redeployment and Continuous Learning in the 21st Century: Hard Lessons and Positive Examples from the Downsizing Era," *Academy of Management Executive* (Nov. 1996): 67–79.

55. Adrianne H. Geiger-DuMond and Susan K. Boyle, "Mentoring: A Practitioner's Guide," *Training & Development* (Mar. 1995): 51–55.

56. Douglas T. Hall, "Protean Careers of the 21st Century," *Academy of Management Executive* (Nov. 1996): 8–16.

57. Ibid.

58. For a discussion of a wide variety of issues at every stage in one's career, see Daniel Feldman (Ed.), *Work Careers: A Developmental Perspective* (San Francisco: Jossey-Bass, 2002).

59. See Boris Groysberg and Robin Abrahams, "Five Ways to Bungle a Job Change," *Harvard Business Review* (Jan.–Feb. 2010): 137–140.

60. Bruce Avolio and David Waldman, "Variations in Cognitive, Perceptual, and Psychomotor Abilities Across the Working Life Span: Examining the Effects of Race, Sex, Experience, Education, and Occupational Type," *Psychology and Aging* (1994), 9: 430–442.

61. See for example, reviews by Glen McEvoy and Wayne Cascio, "Cumulative Evidence of the Relationship Between Employee Age and Job Performance," *Journal of Applied Psychology* (1989), 74(1): 11–17; and Susan Rhoades, "Age-Related Differences in Work Attitudes and Behavior: A Review and Conceptual Analysis," *Psychological Bulletin* (1970), 93: 328–367.

62. Terry Beehr, "The Process of Retirement: A Review and Recommendations," *Personnel Psychology* (1986), 39(1): 31–55.

63. "The 100 Best Companies to Work For," *Fortune* (Feb. 8, 2010): 75–88.

64. Gregory K. Stephens, "Crossing Internal Career Boundaries: The State of Research on Subjective Career Transitions," *Journal of Management* (1994), 20(2): 479–501.

65. Suzyn Ornstein and Lynn A. Isabella, "Making Sense of Careers: A Review 1989–1992," *Journal of Management* (1993), 19(2): 243–267.

66. Kenneth R. Brousseau, Michael J. Driver, Kristina Eneroth, and Rikard Larsson, "Career Pandemonium: Realigning Organizations and Individuals," *Academy of Management Executive* (Nov. 1996): 52–66.

67. M. Ferber, B. O'Farrell, and L. Allen, *Work and Family: Policies for a Changing Workforce* (Washington, DC: National Academy Press, 1994).

68. H. Morgan and K. Tucker, *Companies That Care: The Most Family-Friendly Companies in America, What They Offer, and How They Got That Way* (New York: Simon & Schuster, 1991).

69. S. Zedeck and K. L. Mosier, "Work in Family and Employing Organizations," *American Psychologist* (1990), 45: 240–251.

70. V. J. Doby and R. D. Caplan, "Organizational Stress as Threat to Reputation: Effects on Anxiety at Work and at Home," *Academy of Management Journal* (1995), 38: 1105–1123.

71. P. B. Doeringer, "Economic Security, Labor Market Flexibility, and Bridges to Retirement," in P. B. Doeringer (Ed.), *Bridges to Retirement* (Ithaca, NY: Cornell University ILR Press, 1990): 3–22.

72. Erika Fry, "Serving Up the American Dream," *Fortune* (May 20, 2013): 34; *Hoover's Handbook of American Business 2016* (Austin, TX: Mergent, Inc., 2016): 247–248.

11

1. "How Amazon Crushed the Union Movement," *Time*, www.business.time.com, accessed on June 11, 2016.

2. "How Amazon Crushed the Union Movement," *Time*: www.business.time.com, accessed on June 11, 2016; "Labor Gets a Foot in the Door at Amazon," *Bloomberg Businessweek* (Dec. 23, 2013– Jan. 5, 2014): 34; "Court Sides with Starbucks in Dispute over Labor Union Pins," *The Consumerist*, www.consumerist.com, accessed on June 11, 2016; "Walmart vs. Union-Backed OUR Walmart," *Bloomberg Businessweek*, www.businessweek.com, accessed on June 11, 2016.

3. David Lipsky and Clifford Donn, *Collective Bargaining in American Industry* (Lexington, MA: Lexington Books, 1981).

4. "Two Rebel Unions Split From AFL-CIO," *USA Today* (Jul. 26, 2005): 1B; 2B.

5. Alabama, Arizona, Arkansas, Florida, Georgia, Idaho, Indiana, Iowa, Kansas, Louisiana, Michigan, Mississippi, Nebraska, Nevada, North Carolina, North Dakota, Oklahoma, South Carolina, South Dakota, Tennessee, Texas, Utah, Virginia, West Virginia, Wisconsin, and Wyoming are right-to-work states, although a state can change its status on this issue at any time.

6. Abood v. Detroit Board of Education, 431 U.S. 209 (1977).

7. Rebecca Friedrichs et al., v. California Teachers Association, et al., No. 14-915.

8. Adam Liptak, "Supreme Court Seems Poised to Deal Unions a Major Setback," *The New York Times* (Jan. 11, 2016): www.nytimes.com, accessed on June 11, 2016.

9. Richard Wolf, "Public Employee Unions Dodge a High Court Bullet," *USA Today* (Mar. 29, 2016): www.usatoday.com, accessed on June 11, 2016.

10. Scott Bauer, "GOP Presidential Candidate Scott Walker to Propose Vast Union Restrictions," *The Huffington Post* (Sep. 14, 2015): www.huffingtonpost.com, accessed on June 11, 2016.

11. "Ford Says 38,000 Have Taken Buyouts," *Wall Street Journal* (Nov. 29, 2006): B1, B14; "38,000 Ford Workers Take Buyout Offers," *USA Today* (Nov. 29, 2006): 1B, 2B.

12. Chris Isidore, "GM Bankruptcy: End of an Ara," *CNN Money.com* (Jun. 2, 2009).

13. "GM Emerges from Bankruptcy," *Associated Press* (reported in *New York Post*) (Jul. 10, 2009).

14. "Companies Counter Unions," *USA Today* (Sept. 1997): 1B, 2B.

15. Edward E. Lawler III and Susan A. Mohrman, "Unions and the New Management," *Academy of Management Executive* (1987), 1(3): 65–75.

16. "Reinventing the Union," *Wall Street Journal* (Jul. 27, 2006): B1; B2.

17. Fujita, Scott, "Mixed feelings over N.F.L. concussion settlement," *New York Times* Online (Sept. 2, 2012).

18. "Why Mexico Scares the UAW," *Business Week* (Aug. 3, 1998): 37–38.

19. Clive Fullagar, Paul Clark, Daniel Gallagher, and Michael E. Gordon, "A Model of the Antecedents of the Early Union Commitment: The Role of Socialization Experiences and Steward Characteristics," *Journal of Organizational Behavior* (1994), 15: 517–533.

20. Stuart Youngblood, Angelo DeNisi, Julie Molleston, and William Mobley, "The Impact of Worker Attachment, Instrumentality Beliefs, Perceived Labor Union Image, and Subjective Norms on Voting Intentions and Union Membership," *Academy of Management Journal* (1984), 27: 576–590.

21. J. Barling, E. K. Kelloway, and E. H. Bremermann, "Pre-Employment Predictors of Union Attitudes: The Role of Family Socialization and Work Beliefs," *Journal of Applied Psychology* (1991), 75: 725–731.

22. "Some Unions Step Up Organizing Campaigns and Get New Members," *Wall Street Journal* (Sept. 1, 1995): A1, A2.

23. See Jeanette A. Davy and Frank Shipper, "Voter Behavior in Union Certification Elections: A Longitudinal Study," *Academy of Management Journal* (1993), 36(1): 187–199, for a discussion of some of the determinants of individual voting behavior in union elections.

24. Adapted from R. E. Walton and R. B. McKersie, *A Behavioral Theory of Labor Negotiations* (New York: McGraw-Hill, 1965). Note that we have used the terminology used by those authors, which is adapted from game theory. The reader might encounter different terms in other treatments of bargaining, but the concepts are the same as those described here.

25. "Dividing Line Is Drawn," *USA Today*, (Mar. 3, 2010): 1C, 2C; "MLS: No Talks, No Posturing," *USA Today*, (Mar. 5, 2010): 2C; *Hoover's Handbook of Private Companies 2129* (Austin, TX: Hoover's Business Press, 2012): 35; "NBA and Players Reach Deal to End Lockout," *New York Times*, (Nov. 26, 2011), accessed on July 4, 2012.

26. "ABC Locks Out Striking Employees," *USA Today* (Nov. 3, 1998): B1.

27. Phil Taylor, "To the Victor Belong the Spoils," *Sports Illustrated* (Jan. 18, 1999): 48–52.

28. H. S. Farber and H. C. Katz, "Interest Arbitration, Outcomes, and the Incentive to Bargain," *Industrial and Labor Relations Review* (1979), 33: 55–63.

29. P. Feuille, "Final Offer Arbitration and the Chilling Effect," *Industrial Relations* (1975), 14: 302–310.

30. Mike Isaac and Natasha Singer, "California Says Uber Driver Is Employee, Not a Contractor," *New York Times: Technology* (Jun. 17, 2015): www .nytimes.com.

31. Bureau of Justice Statistics, "Prisoners in 2010," December 2011.

32. Pauline Vu, "Inmates Gladly Take on Jobs for Low or No Pay," *Stateline.Org*(Feb. 9, 2009).

33. Bureau of Labor Statistics, "Employed Contingent and Non-Contingent Workers," Feb. 2005.

34. For a complete discussion of the issues and the rulings in this area, see Camille Olson and Michael Rybick, "Spotlight on Union Organizing: 'No Solicitation No Distribution' and Related Rules in the Age of E-mail and the Internet," *Legal Report* (published by Society of Human Resource Managers) (May–Jun. 2002): 5–7.

35. Nathan Newman, "Union and Community Mobilization in the Information Age," *Perspectives on Work* (2002), 6(2): 9–11.

36. Javier Hernandez, "Labor Protests Multiply in China as Economy Slows Down, Worrying Leaders," *The New York Times* (Mar. 14, 2016): www .nytimes.com, accessed on June 11, 2016.

37. "Harley Union Makes Concessions," *Wall Street Journal* (Dec. 3, 2009): B3; "GM, UAW Reach Crucial Cost-Cutting Pact," *Wall Street Journal* (May 22, 2009): B1.

12

1. Mark Trumbull, "Orlando Shooting Comes as Trend in Workplace Violence Drops," *Christian Science Monitor* (Nov. 7, 2009): www.csmonitor .com, accessed on July 6, 2012; Ellen Wulhorst, "Recession Fuels Worries of Workplace Violence," *Reuters*, (Apr. 22, 2009): www.reuters.com, accessed on July 6, 2012; Scott Powers and Fernando Quintero, "Jason Rodriguez Profile: 'He Was a Very, Very Angry Man,'" *OrlandoSentinel.com*, (Nov. 6, 2009): www.orlandosentinel.com, accessed on July 6, 2012; Laurence Miller, *From Difficult to Disturbed: Understanding and Managing Dysfunctional Employees* (New York: AMACOM, 2008), http://books. google.com, accessed on July 6, 2012.

2. "Working at Home Raises Job Site Safety Issues," *USA Today* (Jan. 29, 1998): 1A.

3. "Labor Secretary's Bid to Push Plant Safety Runs into Skepticism," *Wall Street Journal* (Aug. 19, 1994): A1, A5.

4. R. S. Haynes, R. C. Pine, and H. G. Fitch, "Reducing Accident Rates with Organizational Behavior Modification," *Academy of Management Journal* (1988), 25: 407–416.

5. Dov Zohar, "Safety Climate in Industrial Organizations: Theoretical and Applied Implications," *Journal of Applied Psychology* (1980), 65: 96–102.

6. See, for example, Andrew Wills, Barry Watson, and Herbert Biggs, "An Exploratory Investigation into Safety Climate and Work-Related Driving," *Work: A Journal of Prevention, Assessment, and Rehabilitation* (1993), 32: 81–94.

7. Keith Bradsher and Hiroko Tabuchi, "Last Defense at Troubled Reactors: 50 Japanese Workers," *New York Times*, (Mar. 15, 2011).

8. Myron D. Fottler, "Employee Acceptance of a Four Day Work Week," *Academy of Management Journal* (1977), 20: 656–668.

9. S. Ronen and S. B. Primps, "The Compressed Work Week as Organizational Change: Behavioral and Attitudinal Outcomes," *Academy of Management Review* (1981), 6: 61–74.

10. A. Purach, "Biological Rhythm Effects of Night Work and Shift Changes on the Health of Workers," *Acta Medica Scandinavia* (1973), 152: 302–307.

11. S. Zedeck, S. E. Jackson, and E. S. Marca, "Shift Work Schedules and Their Relationship to Health, Adaptation, Satisfaction, and Turnover Intentions," *Academy of Management Journal* (1983), 26: 297–310.

12. G. B. Meese, M. I. Lewis, D. P. Wyon, and R. Kok, "A Laboratory Study of the Effects of Thermal Stress on the Performance of Factory Workers," *Ergonomics* (1982), 27: 19–43.

13. E. Van de Vliert and N. W. Van Yperen, "Why Cross National Differences in Role Overload? Don't Overlook Ambient Temperature," *Academy of Management Journal* (1996), 39: 986–1004.

14. D. G. Hayward, "Psychological Factors in the Use of Light and Lighting in Buildings," in J. Lang, C. Burnette, W. Moleski, and D. Vachon (Eds.), *Designing for Human Behavior: Architecture and the Behavioral Sciences* (Stroudsburg, PA: Dowden, Hutchinson, & Ross, 1974): 120–129.

15. R. I. Newman, D. L. Hunt, and F. Rhodes, "Effects of Music on Employee Attitude and Productivity in a Skateboard Factory," *Journal of Applied Psychology* (1956), 50: 493–496.

16. G. R. Oldham, A. Cummings, L. J. Mischel, J. M. Scmidtke, and J. Zhou, "Listen While You Work? Quasi-Experimental Relations Between Personal Stereo Headset Use and Employee Work Responses," *Journal of Applied Psychology* (1995), 80: 547–564.

17. G. R. Oldham, "Effects of Changes in Workspace Partitions and Spatial Density on Employee Reactions: A Quasi-Experiment," *Journal of Applied Psychology* (1988), 73: 253–258.

18. Karen Danna and Ricky W. Griffin, "Health and Well-Being in the Workplace," *Journal of Management* (1999), 19: 125–146.

19. Michelle K. Massie, "The Stress of Workplace Discrimination," *Monster* (2016): www.monster. com/career-advice, accessed on June 12, 2016; American Psychological Association, "Fact Sheet: Disparities and Health" (2015): www.apa.org, accessed on June 12, 2016; Isaac Sabat, Alex Lindsey, and Eden King, "Antecedents, Outcomes, Prevention and Coping Strategies for Lesbian, Gay, and Bisexual Stress," in Pamela L. Perrewé, Christopher C. Rosen, and Jonathon R. B. Halbesleben (Eds.), *The Role of Demographics in Occupational Stress and Well-Being* (Bingley, UK: Emerald Group, 2014): 173–198; American Psychological Association, "Interpersonal Racism: Conceptualization," *Health Psychology* (2015): www.societyforhealth-psychology.org, on June 12, 2016; Brea L. Perry, Erin L. Pullen, and Carrie B. Oser, "Too Much of a Good Thing? Psychosocial Resources, Gendered Racism, and Suicidal Ideation among Low Socio-economic Status African American Women," *Social Psychology Quarterly*, 2012, 75(4): 334–359.

20. "Workplace Demands Taking up More Weekends," *USA Today* (Apr. 24, 1998): 1B.

21. Myron Friedman and Robert Rosenman, *Type A Personality and Your Heart* (New York: Knopf, 1974).

22. James C. Quick and Jonathan D. Quick, *Organizational Stress and Preventive Management* (New York: McGraw-Hill, 1984).

23. David Turnipseed, "An Exploratory Study of the Hardy Personality at Work in the Health Care Industry," *Psychological Reports* (1999), 85: 1199–1218.

24. Daniel Ganster and John Schaubroeck, "Work Stress and Employee Health," *Journal of Management* (1991), 17: 235–271.

25. Debra Nelson and James Quick, "Professional Women: Are Distress and Disease Inevitable?" *Academy of Management Review* (1985), 10: 206–213.

26. Richard S. DeFrank and John M. Ivancevich, "Stress on the Job: An Executive Update," *Academy of Management Executive* (1998), 12(3): 55–67.

27. "U.S Job Satisfaction Declines," *The Conference Board Reports* (Feb. 23, 2007).

28. See Anne O'Leary-Kelly, Ricky W. Griffin, and David J. Glew, "Organization-Motivated Aggression: A Research Framework," *Academy of Management Review* (Jan. 1996): 225–253.

29. See, for example, Wendy Boswell, Julie Olson-Buchanan, and Marcie Cavanaugh, "Investigation of the Relationship between Work-Related Stress and Work Outcomes: The Role of Felt Challenge, Psychological Strain, and Job Control," paper presented at the Academy of Management meetings, Toronto, ON, 2000; and Marcie Cavanaugh, Wendy Boswell, Mark Roehling, and John Boudreau, "An Empirical Examination of Self-Reported Work Stress Among U.S. Managers," *Journal of Applied Psychology* (2000), 85: 65–74.

30. See, for example, Cynthia McCauley, Marian Ruderman, Patricia Ohlott, and Jane Morrow, "Assessing the Developmental Components of Managerial Jobs," *Journal of Applied Psychology* (1994), 79: 544–560.

31. Kathy Gerchiek, "Report Cites Barriers to Wellness Programs' Effectiveness," *HR News* (Jun. 27, 2006).

32. World Health Organization, Global Alert and Response, H1N1 Alert 84 (Jan. 22, 2010).

33. For example, see "Ensuring Preparedness against the H1N1 Flu Virus at School and Work," U.S. Department of Labor, Occupational Safety and health Administration Bulletin (May 7, 2009).

34. See, for example, Charles Rayner and Cary L. Cooper, "Workplace Bullying," in E. Kelloway, J. Barling, and J. Hurrell Jr. (Eds.), *Handbook of Workplace Violence* (Thousand Oaks, CA: Sage, 2006): 47–90.

35. "2007 WBI-Zogby Survey," Workplacebullying .org (Apr. 29, 2011): www.workplacebullying.org /wbiresearch/wbi-2007/, accessed on May 10, 2016.

36. M. Sandy Hershcovis, Tara Reich, and Karen Niven, "Workplace Bullying: Causes, Consequences, and Intervention Strategies," SIOP White Paper Series (Bowling Green, OH: Society for Industrial and Organizational Psychology, 2015).

37. Joel Brockner, Stephen Grover, Thomas Reed, and Rocki DeWitt, "Layoffs, Job Insecurity and Survivors' Work Effort: Evidence of an Inverted-U Relationship," *Academy of Management Journal* (1996), 35: 413–435.

38. "Surveillance of Citizens by Government," *New York Times Online* (Tuesday, Sept. 10, 2013).

39. Randolph Schmid, "Study Ranks States with the Happiest People: Louisiana Ranks First and New York Ranks Last," *Chicago Times Archive* (Dec. 18, 2009).

40. "Dealing with Workplace Bullying," Teller Vision no. 1453: 4–5. Business Source Premier, EBSCOhost, June 12, 2016; Sarah-Geneviève Trépanier, Claude Fernet, and Stéphanie Austin, "A Longitudinal Investigation of Workplace Bullying, Basic Need Satisfaction, and Employee Functioning," *Journal of Occupational Health Psychology* (1996), 20(1): 105–116.

13

1. "Raising the Floor," *Economist*, http://www .economist.com, accessed on May 6, 2016; Justin Wolfers, and Jan Zilinsky, "Economists: Pay Workers a Living Wage to Increase Productivity," *Sott. net*, http://www.sott.net/article/291554-Economists -Pay-workers-a-living-wage-to-increase-productivity, accessed on May 6, 2016; John Ydstie, "Health Insurer Aetna Raises Wages for Lowest-Paid Workers to $16 an Hour," *Nor.org*, http://www.npr .org/2015/04/30/403257223/health-insurer-aetna -raises-wages-for-lowest-paid-workers-to-16-an -hour, accessed on May 6, 2016; Bryce Covert, "Major Insurance Company Announces Large Raises for Lowest-Paid Employees," *Thinkprogress.org*, http://thinkprogress.org/economy/2015/01/14/ 3611357/aetna-raise-wages/, accessed on May 6, 2016.

2. Abraham H. Maslow, "A Theory of Human Motivation," *Psychological Review* (1943), 50: 370–396; Abraham H. Maslow, *Motivation and Personality* (New York: Harper & Row, 1954).

3. Mahmond A. Wahba and Lawrence G. Bridwell, "Maslow Reconsidered: A Review of Research on the Need Hierarchy Theory," *Organizational Behavior and Human Performance* (Apr. 1976): 212–240.

4. Corporate Executive Board, "The Increasing Call for Work Life Balance," *BusinessWeek*, (Mar. 27, 2009): www.businessweek.com, accessed on July 11, 2012; Georgetown University Law Center, "Flexible Work Arrangements: Selected Case Studies," *Workplace Flexibility 2010*, www.law.georgetown. edu on July 11, 2012; Network of Executive Women, "Balancing Acts: People Friendly Policies That Build Productivity," 2007, www.newnewsletter.org on July 11, 2012; Emily Schmitt, "How a Flexible Work Schedule Can Help You Strike the Balance," *Forbes*, (Mar. 16, 2009): www.forbes.com, accessed on July 11, 2012.

5. Frederick Herzberg, Bernard Mausner, and Barbara Synderman, *The Motivation to Work* (New York: John Wiley & Sons, 1959); Frederick Herzberg, "One More Time: How Do You Motivate Employees?" *Harvard Business Review* (Jan.–Feb. 1968): 53–62.

6. Marvin Dunnette, John Campbell, and Milton Hakel, "Factors Contributing to Job Satisfaction and Job Dissatisfaction in Six Occupational Groups," *Organizational Behavior and Human Performance* (May 1967): 143–174; Charles L. Hulin and Patricia Smith, "An Empirical Investigation of Two Implications of the Two-Factor Theory of Job Satisfaction," *Journal of Applied Psychology* (Oct. 1967): 396–402.

7. B. F. Skinner, *Science and Human Behavior* (New York: Macmillian, 1953) and *Beyond Freedom and Dignity* (New York: Knopf, 1972).

8. Alexander D. Stajkovic, "A Meta-Analysis of the Effects of Organizational Behavior Modification on Task Performance, 1975–95," *Academy of Management Journal* (1997): 40(5): 1122–1149.

9. Fred Luthans and Robert Kreitner, *Organizational Behavior Modification and Beyond* (Glenview, IL: Scott, Foresman, 1985).

10. Victor Vroom, *Work and Motivation* (New York: John Wiley & Sons, 1964).

11. Craig Pinder, *Work Motivation in Organizational Behavior* (Upper Saddle River, NJ: Prentice Hall, 1998).

12. See Terence R. Mitchell, "Expectancy Models of Job Satisfaction, Occupational Preference, and Effort: A Theoretical, Methodological, and Empirical Appraisal," *Psychological Bulletin* (1974), 81: 1096–1112; and John P. Campbell and Robert D. Pritchard, "Motivation Theory in Industrial and Organizational Psychology," in Marvin D. Dunnette (Ed.), *Handbook of Industrial and Organizational Psychology* (Chicago: Rand McNally, 1976): 63–130 for reviews.

13. Lyman W. Porter and Edward E. Lawler, *Managerial Attitudes and Performance* (Homewood, IL: Dorsey Press, 1968).

14. James C. Naylor, Robert D. Pritchard, and Daniel R. Ilgen, *A Theory of Behavior in Organizations* (New York: Academic Press, 1980).

15. J. Stacy Adams, "Inequity in Social Exchange," in L. Berkowitz (Ed.), *Advances in Experimental Social Psychology*, Vol. 2 (New York: Academic Press, 1965): 267–299.

16. Craig Pinder, *Work Motivation in Organizational Behavior* (Upper Saddle River, NJ: Prentice Hall, 1998).

17. See Nancy Adler, *International Dimensions of Organizational Behavior*, 3rd ed. (Boston: PWS-Kent, 1997).

18. Priti Pradham Shah, "Who Are Employees' Social Referents? Using a Network Perspective to Determine Referent Others," *Academy of Management Journal* (1998), 41(3): 249–268.

19. Reinforcement theory and expectancy theory seem to be in conflict in some instances, mostly in cases of partial reinforcement schedules. A discussion or attempted resolution of these differences is far beyond the scope of the current discussion.

20. See Edwin A. Locke, "Toward a Theory of Task Performance and Incentives," *Organizational Behavior and Human Performance* (1968), 3: 157–189.

21. Gary P. Latham and Gary Yukl, "A Review of Research on the Application of Goal Setting in Organizations," *Academy of Management Journal* (1975), 18: 824–845.

22. Gary P. Latham and J. J. Baldes, "The Practical Significance of Locke's Theory of Goal Setting," *Journal of Applied Psychology* (1975), 60: 187–191.

23. Gary P. Latham, "The Importance of Understanding and Changing Employee Outcome Expectancies for Gaining Commitment to an Organizational Goal," *Personnel Psychology* (2001), 54: 707–720.

24. See Michael Jensen and William Meckling, "Theory of the Firm: Managerial Behavior, Agency Costs, and Ownership Structure," *Journal of Financial Economics* (1976), 11: 305–360; Eugene Fama, "Agency Problems and the Theory of the Firm," *Journal of Political Economy* (1980), 88: 288–307; and Eugene Fama and Michael Jensen, "Separation of Ownership and Control," *Journal of Law and Economics* (1983), 26: 301–325.

25. See, for example, Richard Johnson, Robert Hoskisson, and Michael Hitt, "Board of Director Involvement in Restructuring: The Effects of Board Versus Managerial Controls and Characteristics," *Strategic Management Journal* (1993), 14: 33–50; Rita Kosnik, "Effects of Board Demography and Directors' Incentives on Corporate Greenmail Decisions," *Academy of Management Journal* (1990), 33: 129–150; or Edward Zajac and James Westphal, "The Costs and Benefits of Managerial Incentives and Monitoring in Large U.S. Corporations: When Is More Not Better?" *Strategic Management Journal* (1994), 15: 121–142.

26. Teresa Amabile, "Stimulate Creativity by Fueling Passion," in E. A. Locke (Ed.), *Handbook of Principles of Organizational Behavior* (Oxford, UK: Blackwell Publishing, 2000): 331.

27. For more information, see Edward Deci and Robert Ryan, *Intrinsic Motivation and Self-Determination in Human Behavior* (New York: Plenum, 1985).

28. For a review of this work, see Teresa Amabile, "Stimulate Creativity by Fueling Passion," in E. A. Locke (Ed.), *Handbook of Principles of Organizational Behavior*, pp. 331–341.

29. For example, see the review by James Cameron and William Pierce, "Reinforcement, Reward, and Intrinsic Motivation: A Meta-Analysis," *Review of Educational Research* (1994), 64: 363–423.

30. Greg Oldham and Anne Cummings, "Employee Creativity: Personal and Contextual Factors at Work," *Academy of Management Journal* (1996), 39: 607–634.

31. Jing Zhou and Jennifer George, "When Job Dissatisfaction Leads to Creativity: Encouraging the Expression of Voice," *Academy of Management Journal* (2001), 44: 682–696.

32. Teresa Amabile, "Motivational Synergy: Toward New Conceptualizations of Intrinsic and Extrinsic Motivation in the Workplace," *Human Resource Management Review* (1993), 3: 185–201.

33. Teresa Amabile and S. Gryskiewicz, "Creativity in the R&D Laboratory," *Technical Report No. 30*

(Greensboro, NC: Center for Creative Leadership, 1987).

34. Christina Shalley, Lucy Gilson, and Terry Blum, "Matching Creativity Requirements and the Work Environment: Effects on Satisfaction and the Intent to Leave," *Academy of Management Journal* (2000), 43: 215–233.

35. Zhou and George, "When Job Dissatisfaction Leads to Creativity: Encouraging the Expression of Voice."

36. For more information, see Todd Dewett, *Differentiating Outcomes in Employee Creativity: Understanding the Role of Risk in Creative Performance* (2002). PhD dissertation submitted to the faculty of the Department of Management, Texas A&M University, College Station, TX.

37. Mike Antich, "Using 'Gainsharing' to Achieve Sustainability Goals," Automotive Fleet, www.automotive-fleet.com, accessed on June 18, 2016; Jones Lang LaSalle, "Employee Sustainability Engagement," www.joneslanglasalle.com, accessed on June 16, 2016; American Transportation Research Institute, "The Role of Truck Drivers in Sustainability," (2015): http://atri-online.org, accessed on June 16, 2016; Aaron Huff, "Performance-Based Pay, Part 1: The Science of Scoring Drivers," *Commercial Carrier Journal*, www.ccjdigital.com, accessed on June 18, 2016.

14

1. "Association for Talent Development (ATD), "Effective Leadership in a Virtual Workforce," *TD Magazine* (Feb. 8, 2013): www.td.org, accessed on October 12, 2016.

2. See conclusions in Angelo DeNisi and Caitlin Smith, "Performance Appraisal, Performance Management, and Firm-Level Performance: A Review, a Proposed Model, and New Directions for Future Research," *Academy of Management Annals* (2014), 8: 127–179; as well as conclusions in Angelo DeNisi and Kevin Murphy, "Performance Management and Appraisal," *Journal of Applied Psychology-Special Centennial Issue*, forthcoming.

3. See the discussion about these practices and systems in David Bowen and Cheri Ostroff, "Understanding HRM-Firm Performance Linkages: The Role of the 'Strength' of the HRM System," *Academy of Management Review*, 29 (2004): 203–221; and Robert Ployhart and Thomas Moliterno, "Emergence of the Human Capital Resource: A Multilevel Model," *Academy of Management Review*, 36 (2011): 127–150.

4. For example, Kaifeng Jiang, David Lepak, Jia Hu, and Judith Baer, "How Does Human Resource Management Influence Organizational Outcomes? A Meta-Analytic Investigation of Mediating Mechanisms," *Academy of Management Journal* (2012), 55(6): 1264–1294.

5. Robert Ployhart and Thomas Moliterno, "Emergence of the Human Capital Resource: A Multilevel Model," *Academy of Management Review* (2011), 36: 127–150.

6. David Bowen and Cheri Ostroff, "Understanding HRM-Firm Performance Linkages: The Role of the 'Strength' of the HRM System," *Academy of Management Review* (2004), 29: 203–221.

7. Brian E. Becker, Mark A. Huselid, and Richard W. Beatty, *The Differentiated Workforce: Transforming Talent Into Strategic Impact.* (Cambridge, MA: Harvard Business Press, 2009); also see Herman Aguinis and Ernest O'Boyle, "Star Performers in Twenty-First Century Organizations," *Personnel Psychology* (2014), 67(2): 313–350.

8. Frederick Herzberg, *Work and the Nature of Man* (Cleveland, OH: World Press, 1966).

9. Robert Ford, "Job Enrichment Lessons from AT&T," *Harvard Business Review* (Jan.–Feb. 1973): 96–106.

10. J. Richard Hackman and Greg R. Oldham, *Work Re-design* (Reading, MA: Addison-Wesley, 1980).

11. Eric Trist and Kenneth Bamforth, "Some Social and Psychological Consequences of the Longwall Method of Coal-Getting," *Human Relations* (1965), 4: 3–38.

12. Joshua Brustein, "Fix This Workplace," *Bloomberg Businessweek*, December 23, 2013-January 5, 2014; "Do Happy Workers Mean Higher Profits?" *USA Today* (Feb. 20, 2013): 1B; "Home Is Where the Job Is," *USA Today* (Oct. 5, 2013): 1B.

13. A. N. Kluger, "Commute Variability and Strain," *Journal of Organizational Behavior* (1998), 19: 147–166.

14. D. Denton, "Using Flextime to Create a Competitive Workforce," *Industrial Management* (Jan.–Feb. 1993): 29–31.

15. J. Pearce and R. Dunham, "The 12-Hour Work Day: A Forty-Eight-Hour,Eight-Day Week," *Academy of Management Journal* (1992), 35: 1086–1098.

16. S. Greengard, "Making the Virtual Office a Reality," *Personnel Journal* (Sept. 1994): 66–79.

17. S. Cauderon, "Working at Home Pays Off," *Personnel Journal* (Nov. 1992): 40–49.

18. "Making Stay-at-Homes Feel Welcome," *Business Week* (Oct. 12, 1998): 155–156.

19. S. D. Atchison, "The Care and Feeding of 'Lone Eagles'," *Business Week* (Nov. 15, 1993): 58.

20. G. D. Jenkins, G. E. Ledford, N. Gupta, and D. H. Doty, *Skill-Based Pay* (Scottsdale, AZ: American Compensation Association, 1992).

21. John L. Morris, "Lessons Learned in Skill-Based Pay," *HR Magazine* (Jun. 1996): 136–142.

22. Daniel Wren, *The Evolution of Management Theory*, 4th ed. (New York: Wiley, 1994).

23. C. Wiley, "Incentive Plan Pushes Production," *Personnel Journal* (Aug. 1993): 91.

24. "When Money Isn't Enough," *Forbes* (Nov. 18, 1996): 164–169.

25. "The Fast-Food Ethicist," *Time* (Jul. 23, 2012): 38–44.

26. Jacquelyn DeMatteo, Lillian Eby, and Eric Sundstrom, "Team-Based Rewards: Current Empirical Evidence and Directions for Future Research," in L. L. Cummings and Barry Staw (Eds.), *Research in Organizational Behavior*, Vol. 20 (Greenwich, CT: JAI Press, 1998): 141–183.

27. Theresa M. Welbourne and Luis R. Gomez-Mejia, "Gain-Sharing: A Critical Review and a Future Research Agenda," *Journal of Management* (1995), 21(3): 559–609.

28. Steve Secklow, "How One Tech Company Played with Timing of Stock Options," *Wall Street Journal* (July 20, 2006): A1, A10.

29. Charles Forelle, James Bandler, and Steve Stecklow, "Brocade Ex-CEO, Two Others Charged in Options Probe," *Wall Street Journal* (July 21, 2006): A1, A8.

30. Kate Ludeman, "To Fill the Feedback Void," *Training & Development* (Aug. 1995): 38–43.

31. Allan H. Church, "First-Rate Multirater Feedback," *Training & Development* (Aug. 1995): 42+.

32. Avraham Kluger and Angelo DeNisi, "Feedback Interventions: An Historical Review, and Meta-Analysis and a Proposed New Model," *Psychological Bulletin* (1996), 119: 254–284.

33. For a full description of the model and its effectiveness, see Robert Pritchard, Steven Jones, Phillip Roth, Karla Stuebing, and Steven Ekeberg, "Effects of Group Feedback, Goal-Setting, and Incentives on Organizational Productivity," *Journal of Applied Psychology* (Monograph) (1988), 73: 337–358; and Robert Pritchard, Steven Jones, Phillip Roth, Karla Steubing, and Steven Ekeberg, "The Evaluation of an Integrated Approach to Measuring Organizational Productivity," *Personnel Psychology* (1989), 42: 69–115.

34. James C. Naylor, Robert D. Pritchard, and Daniel R. Ilgen, *A Theory of Behavior in Organizations* (New York: Academic Press, 1980).

35. For a description of various ProMES projects, see Robert D. Pritchard, H. Holling, F. Lemming, and Barbara Clark (Eds.), *Improving Organizational Performance with the Productivity Measurement and Enhancement System: An International Collaboration* (Huntington, NY: Nova Science, 2002).

36. Hamed Safei-Eldin, "Seeing the Environment Through Islamic Eyes," *Technical Report* (2008), Lubbock, TX, Texas Tech University.

37. J. Hashim, "The Quaran-Based Human Resource Management and Its Effects on Organisational Justice, Job Satisfaction and Turnover Intentions," *Journal of International Management Studies* (2008), 3: 148–159.

38. K. Ahmad, "Challenges and Practices in Human Resource Management of the Muslim World," *The Journal of Human Resources and Adult Education* (2008), 4: 34–42.

39. A. Ali, M. Gibbs, & R. Camp, "Human Resource Strategy: The Ten Commandments Perspective," *Journal of Sociology and Social Policy* (2000), 20: 114–132.

40. Dinah Brin, "Employer Beware: Spyware Comes to Mobile," *SHRM Technology* (Dec. 13, 2012).

41. Bill Leonard, "Cybersecurity a Hot Issue on Capitol Hill," *SHRM Technology* (Feb. 25, 2014).

42. Roy Maurer, "Measuring Social Media Risk," *SHRM Safety and Security* (Nov. 15, 2013).

43. Allen Smith, "Social Media Ownership Relies Partly on Contract Law," *SHRM Legal Issues* (Feb. 26, 2014).

44. Ben Dreyfus and Emily Dreyfus, "What Is the NSA's PRISM Program?" *C/Net News* (Jun. 7, 2013).

45. Barton Gellman, Barton and Laura Poitras, "U.S., British Intelligence Mining Data from Nine U.S Internet Companies in Broad Secret Program," *The Washington Post* (Digital Edition) (Jun. 6, 2013).

46. Connor Simpson, "How Google and Facebook Cooperated with the NSA and PRISM," *The Wire* (Yahoo News) (Jun. 8, 2013).

47. Roy Maurer, "Protect Your Business from Cyberthreats," *SHRM HR Topics and Strategy* (Dec. 31, 2012).

48. Roy Maurer, "Cybersecurity Predictions for 2014," *SHRM Safety and Security* (Jan. 3, 2014).

49. "Welcome to Silicon Valley: Perksville, USA," *USA Today*, July 5, 2012, p 1A; "Employee Benefits Keep Getting Cut," *CNNMoney* (May 31, 2012): cnnmoney.com, accessed on August 17, 2012; "Financially Pinched Companies Snip Employee Benefits," *USA Today*, (Apr. 7, 2010): usatoday.com, accessed on August 17, 2012.

50. "Doing More With Less," *Business Week* (Dec. 17, 2009): 35–38; "Nice Work If You Can Get It," *Business Week* (Jan. 9, 2006): 56–57; Jody Miller and Matt Miller, "Get a Life!" *Fortune* (Nov. 28, 2005): 109–124; Danielle Sacks, "Scenes from the Culture Clash," *Fast Company* (Jan. 2009): 28–31.

Page numbers followed by *f* indicate figure
Page numbers followed by *t* indicate table

PHR/SPHR BODY OF KNOWLEDGE®

Content correlation for DeNisi/Griffin, HR4

The responsibilities and knowledge required for an effective HR professional are listed below. They are also called the "PHR/SPHR Body of Knowledge®." HR subject matter experts create the PHR/SPHR Body of Knowledge®. Their work is guided by research and validated by other HR professionals. The PHR/SPHR Body of Knowledge® is updated regularly to make sure that it represents current practices in the HR profession. The percentages that follow each functional area heading are the PHR® and SPHR® percentages, respectively. The sections in HR4 where specific knowledge areas are covered appear in parentheses following the description of the knowledge.

FUNCTIONAL AREA 01
BUSINESS MANAGEMENT & STRATEGY (11 / 30%)

Developing, contributing to, and supporting the organization's mission, vision, values, strategic goals and objectives; formulating policies; guiding and leading the change process; and evaluating organizational effectiveness as an organizational leader.

Responsibilities:

01 Interpret and apply information related to the organization's operations from internal sources, including finance, accounting, business development, marketing, sales, operations, and information technology, in order to contribute to the development of the organization's strategic plan.

02 Interpret information from external sources related to the general business environment, industry practices and developments, technological advances, economic environment, labor force, and the legal and regulatory environment, in order to contribute to the development of the organization's strategic plan.

03 Participate as a contributing partner in the organization's strategic planning process (e.g., provide and lead workforce planning discussion with management, develop and present long-term forecast of human capital needs at the organizational level). **SPHR ONLY.**

04 Establish strategic relationships with key individuals in the organization to influence organizational decision-making.

05 Establish relationships/alliances with key individuals and outside organizations to assist in achieving the organization's strategic goals and objectives (e.g., corporate social responsibility and community partnership).

06 Develop and utilize business metrics to measure achievement of the organization's strategic goals and objectives (e.g., key performance indicators, balanced scorecard). **SPHR ONLY.**

07 Develop, influence, and execute strategies for managing organizational change that balance the expectations and needs of the organization, its employees, and other stakeholders.

08 Develop and align the human resource strategic plan with the organization's strategic plan. **SPHR ONLY.**

09 Facilitate the development and communication of the organization's core values, vision, mission, and ethical behaviors.

10 Reinforce the organization's core values and behavioral expectations through modeling, communication, and coaching.

11 Provide data such as human capital projections and costs that support the organization's overall budget.

12 Develop and execute business plans (i.e., annual goals and objectives) that correlate with the organization's strategic plan's performance expectations to include growth targets, new programs/services, and net income expectations. **SPHR ONLY.**

13 Perform cost/benefit analyses on proposed projects. **SPHR ONLY.**

14 Develop and manage an HR budget that supports the organization's strategic goals, objectives, and values. **SPHR ONLY.**

15 Monitor the legislative and regulatory environment for proposed changes and their potential impact to the organization, taking appropriate proactive steps to support, modify, or oppose the proposed changes.

16 Develop policies and procedures to support corporate governance initiatives (e.g., whistle-blower protection, code of ethics). **SPHR ONLY.**

17 Participate in enterprise risk management by ensuring that policies contribute to protecting the organization from potential risks.

18 Identify and evaluate alternatives and recommend strategies for vendor selection and/or outsourcing. **SPHR ONLY.**

19 Oversee or lead the transition and/or implementation of new systems, service centers, and outsourcing. **SPHR ONLY.**

20 Participate in strategic decision-making and due diligence activities related to organizational structure and design (e.g., corporate restructuring, mergers and acquisitions [M & A], divestitures). **SPHR ONLY.**

21 Determine the strategic application of integrated technical tools and systems (e.g., new enterprise software, performance management tools, self-service technologies). **SPHR ONLY.**

Knowledge of:

01 The organization's mission, vision, values, business goals, objectives, plans, and processes. (4-1b)

02 Legislative and regulatory processes (2-1, 2-1a)

03 Strategic planning process, design, implementation, and evaluation (4-2b)

04 Management functions, including planning, organizing, directing, and controlling (1-2b)

05 Corporate governance procedures and compliance (for example: Sarbanes-Oxley Act) (4-1d)

06 Due diligence processes (e.g., M & A, divestitures) **SPHR ONLY.**

07 Transition techniques for corporate restructuring, M & A, off-shoring, and divestitures. **SPHR ONLY.**

08 Elements of a cost-benefit analysis during the life-cycle of the business (such as scenarios for growth, including expected, economic stressed, and worst case conditions) and the impact to net-worth/earnings for short-, mid-, and long-term horizons (5-2a)

09 Business concepts (e.g., competitive advantage, organizational branding, business case development, corporate responsibility) (4-1)

10 Business processes (e.g., operations, sales and marketing, data management)

FUNCTIONAL AREA 02
WORKFORCE PLANNING AND EMPLOYMENT (24 / 17%)

Developing, implementing, and evaluating sourcing, recruitment, hiring, orientation, succession planning, retention, and organizational exit programs necessary to ensure the workforce's ability to achieve the organization's goals and objectives.

Responsibilities:

01 Ensure that workforce planning and employment activities are compliant with applicable federal laws and regulations.

02 Identify workforce requirements to achieve the organization's short- and long-term goals and objectives (e.g., corporate restructuring, workforce expansion or reduction).

03 Conduct job analyses to create and/or update job descriptions and identify job competencies.

04 Identify, review, document, and update essential job functions for positions.

05 Influence and establish criteria for hiring, retaining, and promoting based on job descriptions and required competencies.

06 Analyze labor market for trends that impact the ability to meet workforce requirements (e.g., federal/state data reports).

07 Assess skill sets of internal workforce and external labor market to determine the availability of qualified candidates, utilizing third party vendors or agencies as appropriate.

08 Identify internal and external recruitment sources (e.g., employee referrals, diversity groups, social media) and implement selected recruitment methods.

09 Establish metrics for workforce planning (e.g., recruitment and turnover statistics, costs).

10 Brand and market the organization to potential qualified applicants.

11 Develop and implement selection procedures (e.g., applicant tracking, interviewing, reference and background checking).

12 Develop and extend employment offers and conduct negotiations as necessary.

13 Administer post-offer employment activities (e.g., execute employment agreements, complete I-9/e-Verify process, coordinate relocations, and immigration).

14 Develop, implement and evaluate orientation and on-boarding processes for new hires, rehires and transfers.

15 Develop, implement and evaluate employee retention strategies and practices.

16 Develop, implement and evaluate the succession planning process. **SPHR ONLY.**

17 Develop and implement the organization exit/off-boarding process for both voluntary and involuntary terminations, including planning for reductions in force (RIF).

18 Develop, implement and evaluate an affirmative action plan (AAP) as required.

19 Develop and implement a record retention process for handling documents and employee files (e.g., pre-employment files, medical files and benefits files).

Knowledge of:

11 Applicable federal laws and regulations related to workforce planning and employment activities (e.g., Title VII, ADA, EEOC Uniform Guidelines on Employee Selection Procedures, Immigration Reform and Control Act) (2-2b, 2-2e, 1-1, 2-2a, 2-2f)

12 Methods to assess past and future staffing effectiveness (e.g., costs per hire, selection ratios, adverse impact) (7-4d, 2-2a)

13 Recruitment sources (e.g., employee referral, social networking/social media) for targeting passive, semi-active and active candidates (7-1f, 7-1c)

14 Recruitment strategies (7-1)

15 Staffing alternatives (e.g., outsourcing, job sharing, phased retirement) (6-2d, 1-1)

16 Planning techniques (e.g., succession planning, forecasting) (5-1)

17 Reliability and validity of selection tests/tools/methods (7-4c)

18 Use and interpretation of selection tests (e.g., psychological/personality, cognitive, motor/physical assessments, performance, assessment center) (7-2b, 7-4c)

19 Interviewing techniques (e.g., behavioral, situational, panel) (7-2b)

20 Impact of compensation and benefits on recruitment and retention (6-3d, 9-1, 6-3d)

21 International HR and implications of global workforce for workforce planning and employment. **SPHR ONLY.** (3-2)

22 Voluntary and involuntary terminations, downsizing, restructuring, and outplacement strategies and practices (6-2d, 6-3, 4-2a)

23 Internal workforce assessment techniques (for example: skills testing, skills inventory, workforce demographic analysis) (5-1a)

24 Employment policies, practices, and procedures (e.g., orientation, on-boarding, and retention) (6-1)

25 Employer marketing and branding techniques

26 Negotiation skills and techniques (11-5a)

FUNCTIONAL AREA 03
HUMAN RESOURCE DEVELOPMENT (18 / 19%)

Developing, implementing, and evaluating activities and programs that address employee training and development, performance appraisal, and talent and performance management to ensure that the knowledge, skills, abilities, and performance of the workforce meet current and future organizational and individual needs.

Responsibilities:

01 Ensure that human resources development activities are compliant with all applicable federal laws and regulations.

02 Conduct a needs assessment to identify and establish priorities regarding human resource development activities.

03 Develop/select and implement employee training programs (e.g., leadership skills, harassment prevention, computer skills) to increase individual and organizational effectiveness.

04 Evaluate effectiveness of employee training programs through the use of metrics (e.g., participant surveys, pre- and post-testing). **SPHR ONLY.**

05 Develop, implement, and evaluate talent management programs that include assessing talent, developing career paths, and managing the placement of high-potential employees.

06 Develop, select, and evaluate performance appraisal processes (e.g., instruments, ranking and rating scales) to increase individual and organizational effectiveness.

07 Develop, implement, and evaluate performance management programs and procedures (includes training for evaluators).

08 Develop/select, implement, and evaluate programs (e.g., telecommuting, diversity initiatives, repatriation) to meet the changing needs of employees and the organization. **SPHR ONLY.**

09 Provide coaching to managers and executives regarding effectively managing organizational talent.

Knowledge of:

27 Applicable federal laws and regulations related to human resources development activities (e.g., Title VII, ADA, Title 17 [Copyright law]) (2-2b, 1-3d, 1-1, 2-2e)

28 Career development and leadership development theories and applications (e.g., succession planning, dual career ladders) (10-7b, 10-7)

29 Organizational development (OD) theories and applications (7-5b)

30 Training program development techniques to create general and specialized training programs (7-5)

31 Facilitation techniques, instructional methods, and program delivery mechanisms

32 Task/process analysis (5-5a)

33 Performance appraisal methods (e.g., instruments, ranking and rating scales) (10-3a, 6-2c, 10-2)

34 Performance management methods (e.g., goal setting, relationship to compensation, job placements/promotions) (1-3c, 14-4, 14-4a)

35 Applicable global issues (e.g., international law, culture, local management approaches/practices, societal norms). **SPHR ONLY.** (3-2a, 3-2)

36 Techniques to assess training program effectiveness, including use of applicable metrics (e.g., participant surveys, pre- and post- testing)

37 Mentoring and executive coaching

FUNCTIONAL AREA 04
COMPENSATION AND BENEFITS (19 / 13%)

Developing/selecting, implementing/administering, and evaluating compensation and benefits programs for all employee groups in order to support the organization's goals, objectives, and values.

Responsibilities:

01 Ensure that compensation and benefits programs are compliant with applicable federal laws and regulations.

02 Develop, implement, and evaluate compensation policies/programs (e.g., pay structures, performance-based pay, internal and external equity).

03 Manage payroll-related information (e.g., new hires, adjustments, terminations).

04 Manage outsourced compensation and benefits components (e.g., payroll vendors, COBRA administration, employee recognition vendors). **PHR ONLY.**

05 Conduct compensation and benefits programs needs assessments (e.g., bench- marking, employee surveys, trend analysis).

06 Develop/select, implement/administer, update and evaluate benefit programs (e.g., health and welfare, wellness, retirement, stock purchase).

07 Communicate and train the workforce in the compensation and benefits programs, policies and processes (e.g., self-service technologies).

08 Develop/select, implement/administer, update, and evaluate an ethically sound executive compensation program (e.g., stock options, bonuses, supplemental retirement plans). **SPHR ONLY.**

09 Develop, implement/administer and evaluate expatriate and foreign national compensation and benefits programs. **SPHR ONLY.**

Knowledge of:

38 Applicable federal laws and regulations related to compensation, benefits, and tax (e.g., FLSA, ERISA, FMLA, USERRA) (2-3a, 2-2b, 2-2a, 2-1a, 2-3, 2-2e)

39 Compensation and benefits strategies (9-4, 9-1)

40 Budgeting and accounting practices related to compensation and benefits (9-1a)

41 Job evaluation methods (9-2a)

42 Job pricing and pay structures (9-2a)

43 External labor markets and/or economic factors (9-2a)

44 Pay programs (for example: variable, merit) (14-3, 14-1b)

45 Executive compensation methods. **SPHR ONLY.** (9-7a)

46 Non-cash compensation methods (e.g., equity programs, non-cash rewards)

47 Benefits programs (e.g., health and welfare, retirement, Employee Assistance Programs [EAPs]) (9-5, 9-4)

48 International compensation laws and practices (e.g., expatriate compensation, entitlements, choice of law codes). **SPHR ONLY.**

49 Fiduciary responsibilities related to compensation and benefits

FUNCTIONAL AREA 05
EMPLOYEE AND LABOR RELATIONS (20 / 14%)

Developing, implementing/administering, and evaluating the workplace in order to maintain relationships and working conditions that balance employer/employee needs and rights in support of the organization's goals and objectives.

Responsibilities:

01 Ensure that employee and labor relations activities are compliant with applicable federal laws and regulations.

02 Assess organizational climate by obtaining employee input (e.g., focus groups, employee surveys, staff meetings).

03 Develop and implement employee relations programs (e.g., recognition, special events, diversity programs) that promote a positive organizational culture.

04 Evaluate effectiveness of employee relations programs through the use of metrics (e.g., exit interviews, employee surveys, turnover rates).

05 Establish, update, and communicate work- place policies and procedures (e.g., employee handbook, reference guides, or standard operating procedures) and monitor their application and enforcement to ensure consistency.

06 Develop and implement a discipline policy- based on organizational code of conduct/ ethics, ensuring that no disparate impact or other legal issues arise.

07 Create and administer a termination process (e.g., reductions in force [RIF], policy violations, poor performance) ensuring that no disparate impact or other legal issues arise.

08 Develop, administer, and evaluate grievance/ dispute resolution and performance improvement policies and procedures.

09 Investigate and resolve employee complaints filed with federal agencies involving employment practices or working conditions, utilizing professional resources as necessary (e.g., legal counsel, mediation/ arbitration specialists, investigators)

10 Develop and direct proactive employee relations strategies for remaining union-free in non-organized locations. **SPHR ONLY.**

11 Direct and/or participate in collective bargaining activities, including contract negotiation, costing, and administration.

Knowledge of:

50 Applicable federal laws affecting employment in union and nonunion environments, such as laws regarding antidiscrimination policies, sexual harassment, labor relations, and privacy (e.g., WARN Act, Title VII, NLRA) (2-2a, 2-3b, 2-2b, 11-1b, 2-3b, 2-2d, 2-3e)

51 Techniques and tools for facilitating positive employee relations (e.g., employee surveys, dispute/conflict resolution, labor management cooperative strategies) (2-3, 11-1)

52 Employee involvement strategies (e.g., employee management committees, self-directed work teams, staff meetings) (4-4)

53 Individual employment rights issues and practices (for example: employment at will, negligent hiring, defamation) (6-3c, 2-2d)

54 Workplace behavior issues/practices (e.g., absenteeism and performance improvement) (14-1a, 6-4c, 14-1b)

55 Unfair labor practices (2-3b, 11-4)

56 The collective bargaining process, strategies, and concepts (e.g., contract negotiation, costing, and administration) (11-1, 11-4b)

57 Legal disciplinary procedures

58 Positive employee relations strategies and non-monetary rewards (14-3b)

59 Techniques for conducting unbiased investigations

60 Legal termination procedures

FUNCTIONAL AREA 06
RISK MANAGEMENT (8 / 7%)

Developing, implementing/administering, and evaluating programs, procedures, and policies in order to provide a safe, secure working environment and to protect the organization from potential liability.

Responsibilities:

01 Ensure that workplace health, safety, security, and privacy activities are compliant with applicable federal laws and regulations.

02 Conduct a needs analysis to identify the organization's safety requirements.

03 Develop/select and implement/administer occupational injury and illness prevention programs (i.e., OSHA, workers' compensation). **PHR ONLY.**

04 Establish and administer a return-to-work process after illness or injury to ensure a safe workplace (e.g., modified duty assignment, reasonable accommodations, independent medical exam).

05 Develop/select, implement, and evaluate plans and policies to protect employees and other individuals, and to minimize the organization's loss and liability (e.g., emergency response, workplace violence, substance abuse).

06 Communicate and train the workforce on security plans and policies.

07 Develop, monitor, and test business continuity and disaster recovery plans.

08 Communicate and train the workforce on the business continuity and disaster recovery plans.

09 Develop policies and procedures to direct the appropriate use of electronic media and hardware (e.g., e-mail, social media, and appropriate website access).

10 Develop and administer internal and external privacy policies (e.g., identity theft, data protection, workplace monitoring).

Knowledge of:

61 Applicable federal laws and regulations related to workplace health, safety, security, and privacy (e.g., OSHA, Drug-Free Workplace Act, ADA, HIPAA, Sarbanes-Oxley Act) (2-3d, 2-2b, 2-3f, 2-3c, 2-2e)

62 Occupational injury and illness prevention (safety) and compensation programs (12-1)

63 Investigation procedures of workplace safety, health and security enforcement agencies (12-4)

64 Return to work procedures (e.g., interactive dialog, job modification, accommodations) (2-2e)

65 Workplace safety risks (e.g., trip hazards, blood-borne pathogens) (12-1)

66 Workplace security risks (e.g., theft, corporate espionage, sabotage) (12-3c)

67 Potential violent behavior and workplace violence conditions (12-3c)

68 General health and safety practices (e.g., evacuation, hazard communication, ergonomic evaluations) (12-1)

69 Organizational incident and emergency response plans

70 Internal investigation, monitoring, and surveillance techniques (1-2c)

71 Employer/employee rights related to substance abuse (2-3e)

72 Business continuity and disaster recovery plans (e.g., data storage and backup, alternative work locations, procedures) (14-2)

73 Data integrity techniques and technology (e.g., data sharing, password usage, social engineering)

74 Technology and applications (e.g., social media, monitoring software, biometrics) (14-6b)

75 Financial management practices (e.g., procurement policies, credit card policies and guidelines, expense policies) (1-2)

Core Knowledge:

76 Needs assessment and analysis (14-1a)

77 Third-party or vendor selection, contract negotiation, and management, including development of requests for proposals (RFPs) (11-4b, 11-6)

78 Communication skills and strategies (e.g., presentation, collaboration, sensitivity)

79 Organizational documentation requirements to meet federal and state guidelines

80 Adult learning processes

81 Motivation concepts and applications

82 Training techniques (e.g., virtual, classroom, on-the-job) (7-5)

83 Leadership concepts and applications

84 Project management concepts and applications

85 Diversity concepts and applications (e.g., generational, cultural competency, learning styles)

86 Human relations concepts and applications (e.g., emotional intelligence, organizational behavior) (1-2a)

87 Ethical and professional standards

88 Technology to support HR activities (e.g., HR Information Systems, employee self-service, e-learning, applicant tracking systems) (5-1a)

89 Qualitative and quantitative methods and tools for analysis, interpretation, and decision-making purposes (e.g., metrics and measurements, cost/benefit analysis, financial statement analysis)

90 Change management theory, methods, and application

91 Job analysis and job description methods (5-4, 5-5b)

92 Employee records management (e.g., electronic/paper, retention, disposal)

93 Techniques for forecasting, planning, and predicting the impact of HR activities and programs across functional areas (1-1, 5-1a)

94 Types of organizational structures (e.g., matrix, hierarchy)

95 Environmental scanning concepts and applications (e.g., Strengths, Weaknesses, Opportunities, and Threats [SWOT], and Political, Economic, Social, and Technological [PEST])

96 Methods for assessing employee attitudes, opinions, and satisfaction (e.g., surveys, focus groups/panels) (6-4d)

97 Budgeting, accounting, and financial concepts

98 Risk-management techniques

THE LAW

Private Employers, State and Local Governments, Educational Institutions, Employment Agencies, and Labor Organizations

Applicants to and employees of most private employers, state and local governments, educational institutions, employment agencies, and labor organizations are protected under Federal law from discrimination on the following bases:

RACE, COLOR, RELIGION, SEX, NATIONAL ORIGIN

Title VII of the Civil Rights Act of 1964, as amended, protects applicants and employees from discrimination in hiring, promotion, discharge, pay, fringe benefits, job training, classification, referral, and other aspects of employment, on the basis of race, color, religion, sex (including pregnancy), or national origin. Religious discrimination includes failing to reasonably accommodate an employee's religious practices where the accommodation does not impose undue hardship.

DISABILITY

Title I and Title V of the Americans with Disabilities Act of 1990, as amended, protect qualified individuals from discrimination on the basis of disability in hiring, promotion, discharge, pay, fringe benefits, job training, classification, referral, and other aspects of employment. Disability discrimination includes not making reasonable accommodation to the known physical or mental limitations of an otherwise qualified individual with a disability who is an applicant or employee, barring undue hardship.

AGE

The Age Discrimination in Employment Act of 1967, as amended, protects applicants and employees 40 years of age or older from discrimination based on age in hiring, promotion, discharge, pay, fringe benefits, job training, classification, referral, and other aspects of employment.

SEX (WAGES)

In addition to sex discrimination prohibited by Title VII of the Civil Rights Act, as amended, the Equal Pay Act of 1963, as amended, prohibits sex discrimination in the payment of wages to women and men performing substantially equal work, in jobs that require equal skill, effort, and responsibility, under similar working conditions, in the same establishment.

GENETICS

Title II of the Genetic Information Nondiscrimination Act of 2008 protects applicants and employees from discrimination based on genetic information in hiring, promotion, discharge, pay, fringe benefits, job training, classification, referral, and other aspects of employment. GINA also restricts employers' acquisition of genetic information and strictly limits disclosure of genetic information. Genetic information includes information about genetic tests of applicants, employees, or their family members; the manifestation of diseases or disorders in family members (family medical history); and requests for or receipt of genetic services by applicants, employees, or their family members.

RETALIATION

All of these Federal laws prohibit covered entities from retaliating against a person who files a charge of discrimination, participates in a discrimination proceeding, or otherwise opposes an unlawful employment practice.

WHAT TO DO IF YOU BELIEVE DISCRIMINATION HAS OCCURRED

There are strict time limits for filing charges of employment discrimination. To preserve the ability of EEOC to act on your behalf and to protect your right to file a private lawsuit, should you ultimately need to, you should contact EEOC promptly when discrimination is suspected:

The U.S. Equal Employment Opportunity Commission (EEOC), 1-800-669-4000 (toll-free) or 1-800-669-6820 (toll-free TTY number for individuals with hearing impairments). EEOC field office information is available at www.eeoc.gov or in most telephone directories in the U.S. Government or Federal Government section. Additional information about EEOC, including information about charge filing, is available at www.eeoc.gov.

Employers Holding Federal Contracts or Subcontracts

Applicants to and employees of companies with a Federal government contract or subcontract are protected under Federal law from discrimination on the following bases:

RACE, COLOR, RELIGION, SEX, NATIONAL ORIGIN

Executive Order 11246, as amended, prohibits job discrimination on the basis of race, color, religion, sex or national origin, and requires affirmative action to ensure equality of opportunity in all aspects of employment.

INDIVIDUALS WITH DISABILITIES

Section 503 of the Rehabilitation Act of 1973, as amended, protects qualified individuals from discrimination on the basis of disability in hiring, promotion, discharge, pay, fringe benefits, job training, classification, referral, and other aspects of employment. Disability discrimination includes not making reasonable accommodation to the known physical or mental limitations of an otherwise qualified individual with a disability who is an applicant or employee, barring undue hardship. Section 503 also requires that Federal contractors take affirmative action to employ and advance in employment qualified individuals with disabilities at all levels of employment, including the executive level.

DISABLED, RECENTLY SEPARATED, OTHER PROTECTED, AND ARMED FORCES SERVICE MEDAL VETERANS

The Vietnam Era Veterans' Readjustment Assistance Act of 1974, as amended, 38 U.S.C. 4212, prohibits job discrimination and requires affirmative action to employ and advance in employment disabled veterans, recently separated veterans (within three years of discharge or release from active duty), other protected veterans (veterans who served during a war or in a campaign or expedition for which a campaign badge has been authorized), and Armed Forces service medal veterans (veterans who, while on active duty, participated in a U.S. military operation for which an Armed Forces service medal was awarded).

RETALIATION

Retaliation is prohibited against a person who files a complaint of discrimination, participates in an OFCCP proceeding, or otherwise opposes discrimination under these Federal laws.

Any person who believes a contractor has violated its nondiscrimination or affirmative action obligations under the authorities above should contact immediately:

The Office of Federal Contract Compliance Programs (OFCCP), U.S. Department of Labor, 200 Constitution Avenue, N.W., Washington, D.C. 20210, 1-800-397-6251 (toll-free) or (202) 693-1337 (TTY). OFCCP may also be contacted by e-mail at OFCCP-Public@dol.gov, or by calling an OFCCP regional or district office, listed in most telephone directories under U.S. Government, Department of Labor.

Programs or Activities Receiving Federal Financial Assistance

RACE, COLOR, NATIONAL ORIGIN, SEX

In addition to the protections of Title VII of the Civil Rights Act of 1964, as amended, Title VI of the Civil Rights Act of 1964, as amended, prohibits discrimination on the basis of race, color or national origin in programs or activities receiving Federal financial assistance. Employment discrimination is covered by Title VI if the primary objective of the financial assistance is provision of employment, or where employment discrimination causes or may cause discrimination in providing services under such programs. Title IX of the Education Amendments of 1972 prohibits employment discrimination on the basis of sex in educational programs or activities which receive Federal financial assistance.

INDIVIDUALS WITH DISABILITIES

Section 504 of the Rehabilitation Act of 1973, as amended, prohibits employment discrimination on the basis of disability in any program or activity which receives Federal financial assistance. Discrimination is prohibited in all aspects of employment against persons with disabilities who, with or without reasonable accommodation, can perform the essential functions of the job.

If you believe you have been discriminated against in a program of any institution which receives Federal financial assistance, you should immediately contact the Federal agency providing such assistance.

INTRODUCTION

The most successful recruiting organizations approach the hiring process like executive search firms. Their HR recruiting specialists:

- Engage their "clients" aggressively in the beginning of the process
- Capture information required in a streamlined way (minimizing manager time, while maximizing the value of their input)
- Document their understanding of key requirements
- Set expectations regarding time and resources required
- Look for ways to add value in the process using creative and cost effective tools and techniques
- Keep the clients informed throughout the process
- Measure success in meeting client requirements and expectations
- Refine the processes to reflect client evaluations and feedback

That is what the Extreme Hiring Makeover Teams aspire to: Setting new standings for strategic recruiting. This creates exciting opportunities and challenges for the HR professionals that lead recruiting in their organizations. Perhaps the most exciting element of this effort is the chance to reshape the relationship between HR professionals and their leader and manager "clients."

The redefined hiring efforts for all three of our pilot teams include a new "front-end," process that looks more like an executive search firm. In this model, HR recruiting experts conduct a comprehensive interview with managers about their hiring needs and quickly respond with a comprehensive service package. They lead managers through the right strategic thinking about the positions, targeting, marketing and assessment approaches.

Nothing is left to chance, and opportunities for misunderstandings are minimized. Once this step is concluded, the HR teams can launch a much more timely and successful recruiting process. A summary of the key process steps is on the next page.

TASK	Primary Accountability	✔
Launch the Process • Conduct an interview with the hiring manager, executive or administrative officer, and other team members as appropriate	HR Specialist/Hiring Manager	

Evaluate the Opportunity
• Clean up interview notes and exhibits
• Determine whether additional information or steps are required
  – Additional job analysis effort
  – Classification
  – Internal approvals
  – Targeting/marketing research
  – Other
• Work with Hiring Manager to complete package with due speed
• Involve other experts as required
	HR Specialist leads with assistance from hiring teams and other experts as required	

Prepare a package for the hiring manager that includes: • Summary of manager interview notes • Position description • Proposed vacancy announcement • Sourcing/targeting strategies • Marketing/sales pitches for the position • Assessment approach • Manager team resource commitments • Timeline • Special recruitment cost considerations	HR Specialist	
Review, Approve, or Provide Revisions for the Manager Package	Hiring Manager Team	

Create job posting
• Vacancy announcement
• Automated application and assessment process
  – Screening process and questions
  – SME scorecard and process, as appropriate
  – Use of flexibilities—category ranking
	HR Specialist	

Recruit candidates through targeted approaches	HR Spec/Hiring Team	
Close position and complete screening/selection process • Pre-screen candidates • Perform additional screens or assessments • Engage Subject Matter Experts • Consolidate rating information • Produce Certification	HR Spec/Hiring Team, as appropriate	
Notify candidates about progress	HR Spec/Hiring Team, as appropriate	
Conduct interview process/make selection	Hiring Manager Team	
Prepare hiring package and extend offer	HR Specialist	

Continuous Improvement—Assessment of Success of Hire
• Feedback from Managers, New Hires, HR, and Applicants
  – Immediate
  – 90 days
• Incorporate feedback into process improvement
	HR Spec/Hiring Team	

1-1 **Describe the contemporary human resource perspectives.** Human resource management (HRM) is a relatively new functional area in many organizations.

Human resources (HR) are the people an organization employs to carry out various jobs, tasks, and functions in exchange for wages, salaries, and other rewards. (p. 4)

Human resource management (HRM) is the comprehensive set of managerial activities and tasks concerned with developing and maintaining a qualified workforce—human resources—in ways that contribute to organizational effectiveness. (p. 4)

Outsourcing is the process of hiring outside firms to handle basic HRM functions, presumably more efficiently than the organization could. (p. 6)

1-2 **Trace the evolution of the human resource function in organizations.** As today's large organizations began to emerge a little more than a century ago, they found it necessary to establish specialized units to handle the hiring and administration of current employees. These units were usually called personnel departments and were headed by personnel managers. Contemporary HRM deals with different complex and strategic issues.

Scientific management, one of the earliest approaches to management, was concerned with structuring individual jobs to maximize efficiency and productivity. (p. 8)

The **human relations era** supplanted scientific management as the dominant approach to management during the 1930s. (p. 9)

The human relations era was instigated by the **Hawthorne studies**. (p. 9)

Abraham Maslow's **hierarchy of human needs** was developed during the human relations era. (p. 9)

Douglas McGregor's **Theory X** and **Theory Y** framework grew from the human relations movement. (p. 9)

Personnel departments, specialized organizational units for hiring and administering human resources, became popular during the 1930s and 1940s. (p. 10)

Personnel management, a new type of management function, grew from the recognition that human resources needed to be managed. (p. 10)

The manager who ran the personnel department was called the **personnel manager**. (p. 10)

Knowledge workers are employees whose jobs are primarily concerned with the acquisition and application of knowledge. They contribute to an organization through what they know and how they can apply what they know. (p. 12)

1-3 **Identify and discuss the goals of human resource management.** HRM generally has four basic goals to pursue: facilitating organizational competitiveness, enhancing productivity and quality, complying with legal and social obligations, and promoting individual growth and development. Each goal is an important ingredient in organizational effectiveness.

Productivity is an economic measure of efficiency that summarizes and reflects the value of the outputs created by an individual, organization, industry, or economic system relative to the value of the inputs used to create them. (p. 15)

Quality is the total set of features and characteristics of a product or service that bears on its ability to satisfy stated or implied needs. (p. 15)

A **psychological contract** is the overall set of expectations held by the employee with regard to what he or she will contribute to the organization and that are held by the organization with regard to what it will provide to the individual in return. (p. 16)

1-4 **Discuss the setting for human resource management.** Line (or operating) managers and staff managers (or specialized HR managers) typically share the responsibility for effective HRM. Both sets of managers must work to deal with the conflict that often occurs. The owner or general manager still often handles HRM in smaller firms, but as organizations grow, they usually establish separate HR departments. Managers should also adopt a systems perspective on the HR function.

Line managers are those directly responsible for creating goods and services. (p. 17)

Staff managers are those responsible for an indirect or support function that would have costs but whose bottom-line contributions were less direct. (p. 17)

A **human resource management system** is an integrated and interrelated approach to managing human resources that fully recognizes the interdependence among the various tasks and functions that must be performed. (p. 19)

Utility analysis is the attempt to measure, in more objective terms, the impact and effectiveness of HRM practices in terms of such metrics as a firm's financial performance. (p. 20)

1-5 **Describe the job of human resource managers from the perspectives of professionalism and careers.** Today's HR managers are becoming increasingly professional in both their training and orientation toward their work. A variety of career paths are also available for people who want to work in the HR function.

KEY LEGISLATION

Title VII of the Civil Rights Act of 1964: Prohibits discrimination on the basis of an individual's race, color, religious beliefs, sex, or national origin.

California Proposition 8: California state law that banned same-sex marriage. A lower court overturned this law, and the Supreme Court upheld that decision in 2013, essentially allowing California to recognize same-sex marriages, which it did.

Federal Defense of Marriage Act (DOMA): Federal law restricting spousal rights to persons involved in traditional (male–female) marriages. The Supreme Court overturned this act in 2013, granting federal rights to same-sex spouses who were married in states recognizing such marriages.

Key Points for Future Managers

- The effective management of a firm's human resources is probably the most important source of sustained competitive advantage for a modern organization.

- The changing legal environment has made it critical that an organization be aware of the legal requirements involved in all HRM practices. Failure to do so can be quite costly.

- Effective HRM practices support corporate strategic goals.

- Everyone who deals with people has a need to understand some basic notions of HRM.

CHAPTER 2 LEARNING OBJECTIVES / KEY TERMS / KEY LEGISLATION

2-1 **Describe the legal context of human resource management.** The legal context of human resource management (HRM) is shaped by various forces. The first step in this process is the actual creation of new regulation. The second step is the enforcement of those regulations. The third step is the actual practice and implementation of those regulations in organizations. Regulations exist in almost every aspect of the employment relationship.

2-2 **Identify key laws that prohibit discrimination in the workplace, and discuss equal employment opportunity.** The basic goal of all equal employment opportunity regulation is to protect people from unfair or inappropriate discrimination in the workplace. Illegal discrimination results from behaviors or actions by an organization or managers within an organization that cause members of a protected class to be unfairly differentiated from others. Four basic kinds of discrimination are disparate treatment, disparate impact, pattern or practice discrimination, and retaliation. Depending on the specific law, a protected class consists of all individuals who share one or more common characteristic as indicated by that law.

The major laws and related regulations that affect equal employment opportunity include Title VII of the Civil Rights Act of 1964, Executive Order 11246, Executive Order 11478, the Equal Pay Act of 1963, the Age Discrimination and Employment Act (ADEA), the Vocational Rehabilitation Act of 1973, the Vietnam Era Veterans' Readjustment Act of 1974, the Pregnancy Discrimination Act of 1979, the Civil Rights Act of 1991, the Americans with Disabilities Act of 1990 (ADA), the Americans with Disabilities Amendments Act (2008), and the Family and Medical Leave Act of 1993. The enforcement of equal opportunity legislation generally is handled by the Equal Employment Opportunity Commission (EEOC) and the Office of Federal Contract Compliance Procedures (OFCCP).

Illegal discrimination results from behaviors or actions by an organization or managers within an organization that cause members of a protected class to be unfairly differentiated from others. (p. 28)

Disparate treatment discrimination exists when individuals in similar situations are treated differently based on the individual's race, color, religion, sex, national origin, age, or disability status. (p. 28)

A **bona fide occupational qualification (BFOQ)** states that a condition such as race, sex, or other personal characteristic legitimately affects a person's ability to perform the job and therefore can be used as a legal requirement for selection. (p. 29)

A **business necessity** is a practice that is important for the safe and efficient operation of the business. (p. 29)

Disparate impact discrimination occurs when an apparently neutral employment practice disproportionately excludes a protected group from employment opportunities. (p. 30)

The **four-fifths rule** suggests that disparate impact exists if a selection criterion (e.g., a test score) results in a selection rate for a protected class that is less than four-fifths (80 percent) of that for the majority group. (p. 30)

Geographical comparisons involve comparing the characteristics of the potential pool of qualified applicants for a job (focusing on characteristics such as race, ethnicity, and gender) with those same characteristics of the present employees in the job. (p. 31)

The **McDonnell-Douglas test** is used as the basis for establishing a prima facie case of disparate impact discrimination. (p. 31)

Pattern or practice discrimination is similar to disparate treatment but occurs on a classwide basis. (p. 31)

A **protected class** consists of all individuals who share one or more common characteristics as indicated by that law. (p. 33)

Affirmative action represents a set of steps taken by an organization to actively seek qualified applicants from groups underrepresented in the workforce. (p. 34)

A **utilization analysis** is a comparison of the racial, sex, and ethnic composition of the employer's workforce compared to that of the available labor supply. (p. 34)

Quid pro quo harassment is sexual harassment in which the harasser offers to exchange something of value for sexual favors. (p. 36)

A **hostile work environment** is one that produces sexual harassment because of a climate or culture that is punitive toward people of a different gender. (p. 36)

2-3 **Discuss legal issues in compensation, labor relations, and other areas in human resource management.** The most far-reaching law dealing with total compensation is the Fair Labor Standards Act, which was passed in 1938. This law established a minimum hourly wage for jobs. Another important piece of legislation that affects compensation is the Employee Retirement Income Security Act of 1974 (ERISA). The National Labor Relations Act, or Wagner Act, was passed in 1935 in an effort to control and legislate collective bargaining between organizations and labor unions. Congress subsequently passed the Taft-Hartley Act in 1947 and the Landrum-Griffin Act in 1959 to regulate union actions and their internal affairs.

2-4 **Discuss the importance to an organization of evaluating its legal compliance.** Several related areas of HRM are affected by laws and associated legal issues. These related areas include employee safety and health (especially as related to the Occupational Safety and Health Act, or OSHA), various emerging areas of discrimination law (especially sexual harassment), and ethics. In addition, several recent Supreme Court decisions have addressed some controversial issues as same-sex marriage rights and retaliation, and the Affordable Care Act will have a major impact on how company's administer their health care benefits. Finally, recent debates over rights of privacy versus the government's need to protect the citizens from terrorism will likely become more heated.

CHAPTER 2 LEARNING OBJECTIVES / KEY TERMS / KEY LEGISLATION

KEY LEGISLATION

The ADA Amendments Act (ADAAA) of 2008 broadens the protection offered to persons with disabilities at work by defining certain disabilities as "presumptive," thus negating several court cases that had ruled certain persons having disabilities as not qualifying for coverage under the ADA.

The Age Discrimination and Employment Act (ADEA) prohibits discrimination against employees age 40 and older.

The Americans with Disabilities Act of 1990 (ADA) prohibits discrimination based on disability and all aspects of the employment relationship such as job application procedures, hiring, firing, promotion, compensation, and training, as well as other employment activities such as advertising, recruiting, tenure, layoffs, leave, and fringe benefits.

The Civil Rights Act of 1964 The most significant single piece of legislation specifically affecting the legal context for HRM to date has been Title VII of the Civil Rights Act of 1964.

The Civil Rights Act of 1991 makes it easier for individuals who feel they have been discriminated against to take legal action against organizations and provides for the payment of compensatory and punitive damages in cases of discrimination under Title VII.

The Drug-Free Workplace Act of 1988 was passed to reduce the use of illegal drugs in the workplace.

Executive Order 11478 requires the federal government to base all of its own employment policies on merit and fitness and specifies that race, color, sex, religion, and national origin should not be considered.

Executive Order 11246 prohibits discrimination based on race, color, religion, sex, or national origin for organizations that are federal contractors and subcontractors.

The Employee Free Choice Act (EFCA) would make it easier for unions to be recognized as sole bargaining agents, eliminating the need for secret ballot elections.

The Employee Retirement Income Security Act of 1974 (ERISA) guarantees a basic minimum benefit that employees could expect to be paid at retirement.

The Equal Pay Act of 1963 requires that organizations provide men and women who are doing equal work the same pay.

The Fair Labor Standards Act of 1938 established a minimum hourly wage for jobs.

The Family and Medical Leave Act of 1993 requires employers having more than 50 employees to provide as many as 12 weeks unpaid leave for employees after the birth or adoption of a child; to care for a seriously ill child, spouse, or parent; or if the employee is seriously ill.

The Genetic Information Nondiscrimination Act (GINA) of 2009 prohibits employers from obtaining genetic information about employees.

The Labor Management Relations Act (or Taft-Hartley Act) curtailed and limited union powers when enacted and currently regulates union actions and their internal affairs in a way that puts them on equal footing with management and organizations.

The Landrum-Griffin Act focused on eliminating various unethical, illegal, and undemocratic practices within unions themselves.

The Lilly Ledbetter Fair Pay Act of 2009 clearly outlaws differential pay for male and female employees doing essentially the same job.

The National Labor Relations Act (or Wagner Act) was passed in an effort to control and legislate collective bargaining between organizations and labor unions, to grant power to labor unions, and to put unions on a more equal footing with managers in terms of the rights of employees.

The Occupational Safety and Health Act of 1970 (OSHA) grants the federal government the power to establish and enforce occupational safety and health standards for all places of employment directly affecting interstate commerce.

The Patriot Act expanded the rights of the government or law enforcement agencies to collect information about and pursue potential terrorists.

The Pregnancy Discrimination Act of 1979 protects pregnant women from discrimination in the workplace.

The Privacy Act of 1974 allows federal employees to review their personnel files periodically to ensure that the information contained in them is accurate.

The Reconstruction Civil Rights Acts of 1866 and 1871 further extended protection offered to people under the Thirteenth and Fourteenth Amendments.

The Vocational Rehabilitation Act of 1973 requires that executive agencies and subcontractors and contractors of the federal government receiving more than $2,500 a year from the government engage in affirmative action for disabled individuals.

The Worker Adjustment and Retraining Notification (WARN) Act of 1988 stipulates that an organization employing at least 100 employees must provide notice at least 60 days in advance of plans to close a facility or lay off 50 or more employees.

Key Points for Future Managers

- The law represents a major constraint on corporate HR practices.

- The Civil Rights Act is probably the single most important piece of legislation that addresses which HR practices are allowed under the law.

- Under the Civil Rights Act, policies that are applied equally to all employees but have a different (and adverse) effect on employees based on race, gender, religion, color, or national origin are potentially illegal.

- Sexual harassment is outlawed under the Civil Rights Act, and the scope of activities covered here is quite broad.

- Laws also outlaw discrimination on the basis of disability and age.

- Still other laws regulate how people are paid, how organizations deal with unions (or attempts to unionize), and worker safety and privacy.

- No HR decision should be made without consulting someone knowledgeable about the legal implications of the action. These consultations should include a professional HR manager as well as a lawyer.

CHAPTER 3 LEARNING OBJECTIVES / KEY TERMS / KEY LEGISLATION

3-1 **Describe the growth of international business.**
Organizations can adopt a wide variety of strategies for competing in the international environment. One strategy is exporting, which is the process of making a product in the firm's domestic marketplace and then selling it in another country. In licensing, a company grants its permission to another company in a foreign country to manufacture or market its products in the foreign country's local market. Direct investment occurs when a firm headquartered in one country builds or purchases operating facilities or subsidiaries in a foreign country. In a joint venture or strategic alliance, two or more firms cooperate in the ownership or management of an operation, often on an equity basis.

3-2 **Identify and discuss the global issues in international human resource management.** Various global issues in international human resource management (HRM) must be addressed by any international firm. One issue is the development of an international HRM strategy. Another is developing an understanding of the cultural environment of HRM. A third is developing an understanding of the political and legal environment of international business.

The **ethnocentric staffing model** primarily uses parent-country nationals to staff higher-level foreign positions. (p. 61)

The **polycentric staffing model** calls for the dominant use of host-country nationals throughout the organization. (p. 61)

The **geocentric staffing model** puts parent-country, host-country, and third-country nationals all in the same category, with the firm attempting to always hire the best person available for a position. (p. 61)

Culture refers to the set of values that helps an organization's members understand what it stands for, how it does things, and what it considers important. (p. 62)

3-3 **Discuss the human resource management function in international business.** The international HRM function must deal with several fundamental management challenges in international business. The first major set of challenges relates to differences that may exist in culture, levels of economic development, and legal systems that typify the countries where the firm operates. A second fundamental HRM challenge in international business is the determination of the most appropriate source of employees: the host country, the home country, or a third country. Third, international businesses must also deal with different complex training and development challenges. Yet another important international HRM question relates to working conditions, compensation, and the cost of living.

Exporting is the process of making a product in the firm's domestic marketplace and then selling it in another country. Exporting can involve both goods and services. (p. 70)

Licensing involves one company granting its permission to another company in a foreign country to manufacture or market its products in its local market. (p. 70)

Direct foreign investment occurs when a firm headquartered in one country builds or purchases operating facilities or subsidiaries in a foreign country. (p. 70)

In a **joint venture (strategic alliance)**, two or more firms cooperate in the ownership or management of an operation on an equity basis. (p. 71)

3-4 **Identify and discuss the domestic issues in international human resource management.** All firms dealing in foreign markets must also confront three sets of domestic issues in HRM. These domestic issues are local recruiting and selection, local training, and local compensation.

3-5 **Describe the issues involved in managing international transfers and assignments.** International HRM must also pay close attention to the various issues involved in the effective management of expatriate employees. Key areas of importance include selecting, training, and compensating expatriates.

Expatriates are employees who are sent by a firm to work in another country; they may be either parent-country or third-country nationals. (p. 73)

A **hardship premium** (also called a **foreign service premium**) is an additional financial incentive offered to individuals to entice them to accept a "less than attractive" international assignment. (p. 78)

3-6 **Summarize the issues in international labor relations.** Labor relations are the processes of dealing with employees who are organized into labor unions. In the United States, membership in labor unions has steadily declined in recent years, and labor relations are heavily regulated by laws. Different situations exist, however, in other countries.

KEY LEGISLATION

The **North American Free Trade Agreement (NAFTA)** reduced trade barriers among Canada, the United States, and Mexico. NAFTA also includes separate labor agreements among the three countries.

Key Points for Future Managers

- It is critical that a firm develop an international HRM strategy for dealing with overseas business.

- An important part of this strategy is to determine the appropriate mix of host-country nationals (HCNs), expatriates, and third-country nationals who will staff operations in a given country.

- It is critical for an organization to understand the cultural, political, and legal environments in a country where it is considering doing business.

- It is critical that a firm develop an international business strategy that includes consideration of the relative importance of exporting, licensing, direct investment, and joint ventures for doing business in a given country or region.

- Policies for recruiting, selecting, training, and compensating expatriate managers must consider the impact these practices have on HCNs because they must help the expatriate adjust to his or her new environment, and they may be less likely to do so if they feel resentment toward the expatriate manager.

- A strategic approach to expatriation must include a strategy for repatriation.

4-1 **Describe the competitive environment of human resource management.** All firms operate in a competitive environment and formulate a strategy to determine how they will compete. The strategic context of human resource management (HRM) plays an important role in determining the effectiveness of not only the human resource (HR) function but the entire organization as well. Understanding the organization's purpose and its mission guides HR managers as they formulate their strategy. They must also recognize the role of the top management team.

An organization's **purpose** is its basic reason for existence. (p. 89)

An organization's **mission** is a statement of how it intends to fulfill its purpose. (p. 89)

The **top management team** of an organization refers to the group of senior executives responsible for the overall strategic operation of the firm. (p. 89)

4-2 **Identify three types of strategies, and relate each to human resource management.** Corporate strategy involves decisions about which markets or businesses the firm intends to address, whereas business strategy deals with competitive issues within a particular market or business. The firm's HR strategy is an important functional strategy that must be integrated with marketing, finance, operations, and other relevant functional strategies.

Corporate strategy deals with determining what businesses the corporation will operate. (p. 92)

Business strategy deals with how the firm will compete in each market where it conducts business. (p. 92)

Functional strategy deals with how the firm will manage each of its major functions such as marketing, finance, and human resources. (p. 92)

Growth strategy focuses on growing and expanding the business. It can be pursued internally by opening additional locations or externally through mergers, joint ventures, or the acquisition of other businesses. (p. 92)

A **retrenchment** or **turnaround strategy** occurs when an organization finds that its current operations are not effective, and major changes are usually needed to rectify the problem. In most cases, this strategy involves rightsizing the organization by closing operations, shutting down factories, and terminating employees in order to get back on the right track. (p. 94)

Stability strategy essentially calls for maintaining the status quo. A company that adopts a stability strategy plans to stay in its current businesses and intends to manage them as they are already being managed. The organization's goal is to protect itself from environmental threats. A stability strategy is frequently used after a period of retrenchment or after a period of rapid growth. (p. 95)

A **diversification strategy** is used by companies that are adding new products, product lines, or businesses to their existing core products, product lines, or businesses. (p. 95)

Related diversification is used when a corporation believes it can achieve synergy among the various businesses that it owns. (p. 95)

Unrelated diversification is used when a firm attempts to operate several unique businesses in different, unrelated markets. The basic logic behind unrelated diversification is that a company can shield itself from the adverse effects of business cycles, unexpected competition, and other economic fluctuations. (p. 95)

The **adaptation model** is one popular approach to business strategy where a business seeks ways to adapt to its environment. (p. 96)

A company that uses a **differentiation strategy** attempts to develop an image or reputation for its product or service that sets the company apart from its competitors. (p. 97)

A **cost leadership strategy** is one that focuses on minimizing the costs as much as possible. (p. 97)

The **focus strategy** is undertaken when an organization tries to target a specific segment of the marketplace for its products or services. (p. 98)

4-3 **Discuss human resource strategy formulation and relevant organizational factors.** The actual process of formulating HR strategy results in separate but consistent strategies for staffing, employee development, and compensation. To enact HR strategy effectively, it must be closely coordinated with the particular form of organization design the firm uses, the culture it creates, and the impact of unionization and collective bargaining.

Organization design refers to the framework of jobs, positions, clusters of positions, and reporting relationships among positions that are used to construct an organization. (p. 100)

An organization's **culture** refers to the set of values that helps its members understand what the organization stands for, how it accomplishes what it wants to accomplish, and what it considers important. (p. 101)

4-4 **Discuss the processes through which human resource strategy is implemented.** The implementation of HR strategy requires an understanding of fundamental individual and interpersonal behavioral processes. Individual processes include psychological contracts, individual personality traits, employee attitudes, motivation, and stress. Interpersonal processes include group behavior, leadership, and communication.

A **psychological contract** is the overall set of expectations held by an individual with respect to what he or she will contribute to the organization and what the organization will provide the individual in return. (p. 102)

Personality is the relatively stable set of psychological attributes or traits that distinguish one person from another. Some organizations believe that one or more particular personality traits may relate to how well an employee can perform a certain job or type of job. (p. 103)

Motivation is the set of forces that causes people to behave in certain ways. Individual motivation is also a major determinant of individual performance, but motivation is at the heart of what causes an employee to choose to expend the effort that will support any organizational activity. (p. 103)

Stress is a person's adaptive response to a stimulus that places excessive psychological or physical demands on that person. It is important for HR managers understand the causes of stress, the processes by which stress affects individuals, and how organizations and individuals can cope better with stress in organizational settings. (p. 103)

4-5 **Discuss how the human resource function in organizations can be evaluated.** Managers should attempt to evaluate the effectiveness of the HR function and its role in helping the organization attain its strategic goals. This evaluation usually focuses on specific HR practices. However, recent evidence suggests that bundles of so-called best practices may be a viable alternative approach.

KEY LEGISLATION

Key Points for Future Managers

- Corporate and business strategies define how an organization will operate and compete in the market.

- Common strategies at the corporate level include a growth strategy, a retrenchment (or turnaround) strategy, and a stability strategy.

- A diversification strategy is one in which an organization decides to operate different related or unrelated businesses.

- The adaptation strategy model suggests that organizations should match their strategy to the environment. The model includes defender, prospector, analyzer, and reactor strategies.

- Major competitive strategies include differentiation, cost leadership, and focus strategies (i.e., targeting a specific segment of the market).

- HRM strategy is determined by organizational-level strategy as well as by organizational design, culture, technology, and the workforce.

- Certain specific HR practices may be capable of providing a competitive advantage to organizations.

5-1 Describe human resource planning as a source of information for decision-making. Human resource (HR) executives rely on many sources of information to make decisions and to manage human capital. HR planning, for example, draws from forecasts of the supply of human resources, labor force trends and issues, and forecasts of the demand for human resources.

Human resource planning is the process of forecasting the supply and demand for human resources within an organization and developing action plans for aligning the two. (p. 110)

A **human resource information system** is an integrated and increasingly automated system for maintaining a database regarding the employees in an organization. (p. 111)

Executive succession involves systematically planning for future promotions into top management positions. (p. 113)

5-2 Discuss strategy as a source of information for making human resource decisions. The organization's strategy is also a critical information source. Growth, stability, and reduction strategies, for example, each carry substantially different implications for HR managers.

5-3 Discuss economic conditions as a source of information for making human resource decisions. Another important source of information comes from various economic conditions. Unemployment rates, market wage rates, and human capital investments each provide useful information to HR executives.

The **rate of unemployment** is calculated by the Bureau of Labor Statistics as the percentage of individuals looking for and available for work who are not currently employed. (p. 116)

The **market wage rate** is the prevailing wage rate for a given job in a given labor market. (p. 117)

Human capital investments are investments people make in themselves to increase their value in the workplace. These investments might take the form of additional education or training. (p. 118)

5-4 Describe job analysis as a source of information for making human resource decisions. Job analysis is one of the building blocks of the HR planning process and a fundamental source of information for that same planning process. Job analysis involves the gathering and organizing of detailed information about various jobs within the organization so that managers can better understand the processes through which jobs are most effectively performed. Job analysis provides input to the HR planning process by helping planners better understand exactly what kinds of work must be performed.

Job analysis is the process of gathering and organizing detailed information about various jobs within an organization so that managers can better understand the processes through which they are performed most effectively. (p. 119)

Knowledge, skills, and abilities (KSA) are the fundamental requirements necessary to perform a job. (p. 120)

5-5 Discuss the job-analysis process, and identify and summarize common job-analysis methods. Job analysis itself generally follows a three-step process: determining information needs, determining methods for obtaining information, and determining who will collect information. The responsibility of analysis is jointly shared by line managers, the HR group or department, and job analysts. Commonly used methods of job analysis include the narrative approach, Fleishman job-analysis system, task-analysis inventory, functional job analysis, Position Analysis Questionnaire (PAQ), Management Position Description Questionnaire (MPDQ), and critical incidents approach. The Occupational Information Network (O*NET), while not technically a job-analysis procedure, provides advanced job-analysis information. Job analysis results in a job description and a job specification. The changing nature of work and of jobs must also be understood and appreciated by managers. Finally, there are also important legal implications related to job analysis.

Job analysts are individuals who perform job analysis in an organization. (p. 121)

A **subject matter expert (SME)** is an individual presumed to be highly knowledgeable about a particular job and who provides data for job analysis. An SME may be an existing job incumbent, a supervisor, or another knowledgeable employee. (p. 122)

Occupational Information Network (O*NET) is technically not a job-analysis procedure but a database that provides both basic and advanced job-analysis information; as such, IT can be viewed as an alternative to conducting job analysis. (p. 122)

The **Fleishman job-analysis system** is a job-analysis procedure that defines abilities as the enduring attributes of individuals that account for differences in performance; it relies on the taxonomy of abilities that presumably represents all the dimensions relevant to work. (p. 123)

The **task-analysis inventory** is a family of job-analysis methods, each with unique characteristics; each focuses on analyzing all the tasks performed in the focal job. (p. 123)

The **Position Analysis Questionnaire (PAQ)** is a standardized job-analysis instrument consisting of 194 items that reflect work behavior, working conditions, and job characteristics that are assumed to be generalizable across a wide variety of jobs. (p. 124)

Management Position Description Questionnaire (MPDQ) is a standardized job-analysis instrument, similar in approach to the PAQ, that also contains 197 items. The MPDQ's focus, however, is on managerial jobs, and the analysis is done in terms of 13 essential components of all managerial jobs. (p. 125)

The **critical incidents approach** to job analysis focuses on critical behaviors that distinguish effective from ineffective performers. (p. 125)

A **job description** lists the tasks, duties, and responsibilities for a particular job. It specifies the major job elements, provides examples of job tasks, and provides some indication of their relative importance in the effective conduct of the job. (p. 126)

A **job specification** focuses on the individual who will perform the job and indicates the knowledge, abilities, skills, and other characteristics that an individual must have to be able to perform the job. (p. 126)

KEY LEGISLATION

The Americans with Disabilities Act (ADA) prohibits discrimination based on disability and all aspects of the employment relationship such as job application procedures, hiring, firing, promotion, compensation, and training, as well as other employment activities such as advertising, recruiting, tenure, layoffs, leave, and fringe benefits.

Key Points for Future Managers

- Planning is as important for human resource management (HRM) as for any other function in an organization.

- HRM should be an integral part of the organization's strategy.

- Job analysis is and should be the basic cornerstone for all other HRM functions.

- It is essential to understand the strengths and weaknesses of different job analysis approaches because one is not better than the others.

- Competency modeling is concerned with identifying broader sets of requirements that may cut across individual jobs within an organization.

WWW.CENGAGEBRAIN.COM

6-1 **Discuss the role of ethics in human resource decision-making.** Ethics are formed by the social context in which people and organizations function. Managers from every part of the organization must take steps to ensure that their behavior is both ethical and legal. Some organizations develop codes of conduct or ethical statements in an attempt to communicate publicly their stance on ethics and ethical conduct.

Ethics refers to an individual's beliefs about what is right and wrong and what is good and bad. Ethics are formed by the societal context in which people and organizations function. (p. 134)

6-2 **Describe the concept of rightsizing, and identify organizational strategies for rightsizing.** Organizations strive to maintain the right number of employees. Options for such rightsizing include hiring new employees when there is a long-term need for more employees (discussed in the next chapter), responding to temporary demands for additional employees using various methods, and reducing the size of the organization's workforce. When organizations have temporary or short-term needs for additional employees, managers can generally use overtime, temporary workers, leased employees, or part-time employees instead of hiring permanent workers.

Rightsizing is the process of monitoring and adjusting the composition of the organization's workforce to its optimal size. (p. 136)

Overtime refers to hours worked above the normal 40-hour workweek, for which there is usually a pay premium. (p. 137)

Employee leasing involves an organization paying a fee to a leasing company that provides a pool of employees who are available on a temporary basis.

This pool of employees usually constitutes a group or crew intended to handle all or most of the organization's work needs in a particular area. (p. 137)

Part-time workers refers to individuals who are regularly expected to work less than 40 hours a week. They typically do not receive benefits and afford the organization a great deal of flexibility in staffing. (p. 138)

Distributive justice refers to perceptions that the outcomes a person faces are fair when compared to the outcomes faced by others. (p. 139)

Procedural justice refers to perceptions that the process used to determine the outcomes were fair. (p. 140)

Interactional justice refers to the quality of the interpersonal treatment people receive when a decision is implemented. (p. 140)

6-3 **Describe how to manage termination and retention.** Organizations that need to reduce the number of employees can achieve these reductions through early retirement and plans to encourage early retirement or through layoffs. Layoffs can bring legal problems (especially concerning potential age discrimination), and the survivors of layoffs often experience guilt. Furthermore, evidence suggests that downsizing is not an effective strategy. A final way to reduce the size of the labor force is through termination—that is, some people can be fired. Although employment at will is the law, there are enough exceptions to this doctrine that organizations are often sued for wrongful termination.

Involuntary turnover is terminating employees whose services are no longer desired. (p. 143)

Punishment simply refers to following unacceptable behavior with some type of negative consequences. (p. 144)

Discipline refers to the system of rules and procedures for how and when punishment is administered and how severe the punishment should be. (p. 144)

Progressive disciplinary plans are organizational disciplinary programs where the severity of the punishment increases over time or across the problem. (p. 144)

Verbal warnings —the first step in most progressive disciplinary programs—are cautions conveyed orally to the employee. (p. 145)

Written warnings —the second step in most progressive disciplinary programs—are more formal warnings. They are given to the employee in writing and become part of the employee's permanent record. (p. 145)

As part of a progressive disciplinary program, a **suspension** is a temporary layoff, usually with pay, when there is an ongoing investigation. (p. 145)

As part of a progressive disciplinary program, **termination** is an act by the organization to end the employment relationship. (p. 145)

Employment at will states that an employer can terminate any employee, at any time, for any reason (good or bad), or for no reason at all. (p. 145)

6-4 **Describe the elements of voluntary turnover.** Even as organizations seek to eliminate some employees, they must also strive to retain valued employees. This process involves reducing voluntary turnover and requires an understanding of the causes of voluntary turnover. The major determinant of voluntary turnover is usually job dissatisfaction, or being unhappy in one's job. Several models of the voluntary turnover process exist, but these models usually focus on helping us understand how job dissatisfaction results in turnover. One model, however, focuses on job embeddedness and helps us understand why some dissatisfied employees choose to remain on their jobs. In addition to relating to turnover, job satisfaction can lead to other outcomes, and it is therefore a major concern for organizations that seek to monitor levels of employee satisfaction and dissatisfaction. For example, higher levels of employee satisfaction are related to higher levels of employee commitment and a greater frequency of behaviors known as organizational citizenship behaviors (OCBs).

OCBs are behaviors that are not required of an employee but are important for the functioning of the organization.

Job dissatisfaction is the feeling of being unhappy with one's job. It is a major cause of voluntary turnover. (p. 147)

Job embeddedness refers to the fact that some people stay in their jobs, even when they decide they are unhappy and should leave. Other ties in the community or obligations keep the employee in the job. (p. 148)

Organizational commitment is the degree to which an employee identifies with an organization and is willing to exert effort on behalf of the organization. (p. 150)

Organizational citizenship behaviors (OCBs) include employee behaviors that are beneficial to the organization but are not formally required as part of an employee's job. (p. 150)

Realistic job previews (RJPs) are preemployment previews that provide accurate and realistic information to the job applicant. They can also be used with new employees as a means of socializing them in their new job roles, and they are effective in reducing turnover. (p. 151)

Stock options are rights given to employees to purchase a certain number of shares of stock at a given price. (p. 152)

6-5 **Discuss the key human resource issues during mergers and acquisitions.** Finally, it is important that managers understand the role and importance of human resources (HR) during and after a merger or an acquisition. A failure to do so will greatly increase the chances that the merger or acquisition will fail to meet its intended goals or, worse, result in outright failure.

KEY LEGISLATION

The Fair Labor Standards Act (FLSA) stipulates that hourly workers must be compensated at a rate of 1.5 times their normal hourly rate for work in excess of 40 hours per week.

The Worker Adjustment and Retraining Notification (WARN) Act requires at least 60 days' notice for a facility closure or a mass layoff.

Key Points for Future Managers

- Rightsizing of the workforce may involve hiring new permanent employees, temporarily increasing the size of the workforce, or downsizing (reducing the workforce).

- Temporary needs for additional employees can be achieved through overtime, the use of temporary or leased employees, or the use of part-time workers.

- When possible, reductions should be made by relying on natural attrition and early retirement rather than on layoffs because layoffs can lead to legal problems and have been shown to be relatively ineffective at reducing costs.

- Although employment at will is the common-law rule, it is not acceptable to terminate employees without cause. The various exceptions to employment at will can result in serious legal problems.

- While trying to reduce the workforce, it is also necessary to retain valued employees. The best way to retain valued employees is to monitor and improve job satisfaction.

- Job satisfaction is related to absenteeism and turnover, but it is also related to organizational commitment.

- Job satisfaction is also related to organizational citizenship behaviors. These behaviors are not the responsibility of employees; if someone does not carry them out, however, the organization suffers.

- It is very important that general managers actively involve their HR colleagues during a merger or acquisition.

CHAPTER 7 LEARNING OBJECTIVES / KEY TERMS / KEY LEGISLATION

7-1 **Describe the recruiting process, including internal and external recruiting and the importance of realistic job previews.** Recruiting is the process of developing a pool of qualified applicants who are interested in working for the organization and from which the organization might reasonably select the best individual or individuals to hire for employment. Organizational goals in recruiting are to optimize, in various ways, the size of the pool of qualified applicants and to offer an honest and candid assessment to prospective applicants of what kinds of jobs and what kinds of opportunities the organization can potentially make available to them. Internal recruiting is the process of looking inside the organization for existing qualified employees who might be promoted to higher-level positions. The two most common methods used for internal recruiting are job posting and supervisory recommendations. External recruiting involves looking to sources outside the organization for prospective employees. Different methods are likely to be used by an organization engaged in external recruiting. These include the general labor pool, direct applicants, referrals, advertisements, employment agencies, and colleges and universities. Many organizations today are finding that it is increasingly important to provide prospective employees with what is called a *realistic job preview*. Realistic job previews might involve providing job applicants with an opportunity to actually observe others performing the work.

Recruiting is the process of developing a pool of qualified applicants who are interested in working for the organization and from which the organization might reasonably select the best individual or individuals to hire. (p. 158)

Internal recruiting is the process of looking inside the organization for existing qualified employees who might be promoted to higher-level positions. (p. 159)

Job posting is a mechanism for internal recruiting in which vacancies in the organization are publicized through various media such as company newsletters,

bulletin boards, internal memos, and the firm's intranet. (p. 159)

Using **supervisory recommendations**, a mechanism for internal recruiting, a manager solicits nominations or recommendations for a position that needs to be filled from supervisors in the organization. (p. 160)

External recruiting is the process of looking to sources outside the organization for prospective employees. (p. 160)

In **word-of-mouth recruiting**, the organization simply informs current employees that positions are available and

encourages them to refer friends, family members, or neighbors for those jobs. (p. 161)

A **headhunter** is an individual working for an executive search firm who seeks out qualified individuals for higher-level positions. (p. 162)

A **realistic job preview (RJP)** is an effective technique for ensuring that job seekers understand the actual nature of the jobs available to them. (p. 164)

7-2 **Discuss the steps in the selection process and the basic selection criteria used by most organizations.** The selection process involves three clear, distinct steps: gathering information about the members of the pool of qualified recruits, evaluating the qualifications of each applicant from among the recruiting pool, and making the actual decision about which candidate or candidates will be offered employment with the organization. The basic selection criteria that most organizations use in deciding whom to hire are education and experience, skills and abilities, and personal characteristics. Firms must also decide whether to focus on fit or skills.

Selection is concerned with identifying the best candidate or candidates for a job from among the pool of qualified applicants developed during the recruiting process. (p. 164)

Education refers to the formal classroom training an individual has received in

public or private schools and in a college, university, or technical school. (p. 166)

Experience is the amount of time the individual has spent working in either a general capacity or a particular field of study. (p. 166)

The **big five personality traits**—neuroticism, extraversion, openness to experience, agreeableness, and conscientiousness—tend to be more behavioral than cognitive or emotional and are likely to be more important for job performance than more traditional personality traits. (p. 166)

7-3 **Identify and discuss popular selection techniques that organizations use to hire new employees.** Organizations use various techniques for gathering information about job candidates. The most common are employment applications and background checks, employment tests, work simulations, and employment interviews. Each technique has its unique strengths and weaknesses but also can play an important role in selection.

An **employment application** asks individuals for various bits of information pertaining to their personal background. (p. 168)

A **weighted application blank** relies on numerical indexes to determine the relative importance of various personal factors for predicting a person's ability to perform a job effectively. (p. 168)

Biodata application blanks focus on the same type of information that is found in a regular application but go into more complex and detailed assessments about that background. (p. 168)

An **employment test** is a device for measuring the characteristics of an individual such as personality, intelligence, and aptitude. (p. 168)

Cognitive ability tests measure mental skills. (p. 168)

Psychomotor ability tests measure physical abilities such as strength, eye–hand coordination, and manual dexterity. (p. 172)

Personality tests measure traits, or tendencies to act, that are relatively unchanging in a person. (p. 172)

A **self-report inventory** is a paper-and-pencil measure in which an applicant responds to a series of statements that might or might not apply to him or her. (p. 172)

The **projective technique** involves showing an individual an ambiguous stimulus, such as an inkblot or a fuzzy picture, and then asking what he or she "sees." (p. 172)

Integrity tests attempt to assess an applicant's moral character and honesty. (p. 173)

Work simulations (or **work samples**) involve asking the prospective employee to perform tasks or job-related activities that simulate or represent the actual work for which the person is being considered. (p. 173)

In-basket exercises are special forms of work simulations for prospective managers. They consist of collections of hypothetical memos, letters, and notes that require responses. (p. 173)

In the **structured employment interview** the interviewer either prepares or receives from others a list of standard questions to be asked during the interview. All interviewers ask the same questions of each candidate to achieve consistency across interviews. (p. 173)

A **semistructured employment interview** involves advance preparation of major or key questions that all applicants will be asked. However, the interviewer is also given the prerogative to ask additional follow-up questions to probe the interviewee's specific answers. (p. 173)

An **unstructured employment interview** involves relatively little advance preparation. The interviewer may have a general idea about what she or he wants to learn about the job applicant but has few or no advance questions that are formally constructed. (p. 174)

The **situational interview** is a type of interview, growing in popularity, in which the interviewer asks the applicant questions about a specific situation to see how the applicant reacts. (p. 174)

A **first-impression error** occurs when an interviewer makes a decision too early in the interview process. This error may significantly affect a decision even when subsequent information indicates the first impression may have been wrong. (p. 174)

A **contrast error** occurs when the interviewer is unduly influenced by other people who have been interviewed. For example, suppose an interviewer meets with one candidate who is extremely good or extremely bad. The next person interviewed may suffer or benefit by the contrast with this person. (p. 174)

A **similarity error** occurs when the interviewer is unduly influenced by the fact that the interviewee is similar to the interviewer in one or more important ways. As a result of the perception of similarity, the interviewer may be more favorably disposed toward the candidate than the candidate's credentials warrant. (p. 175)

Nonrelevancy is a type of error that occurs when an interviewer is influenced by information that is not relevant to an individual's ability to perform the job. (p. 175)

7-4 **Describe the selection decision, including potential selection errors and reliability and validity.** After subjecting the pool of qualified applicants to the organization's selection process, it is then necessary to make a final selection decision. Most organizations choose to rely on several selection techniques and, in fact, may use all or most of the selection techniques discussed in this chapter. Managers also strive to avoid various selection errors. The organization needs to understand the legal context in which it can recruit and select new employees and evaluate its selection and placement activities periodically.

False positives are applicants who are predicted to be successful and are hired but who ultimately fail. (p. 177)

False negatives are applicants who are predicted to fail and are not hired, but if they had been hired would have been successful. (p. 177)

Reliability is the consistency of a particular selection device—that is, it measures whatever it is supposed to measure without random error; this is not the same as accuracy. (p. 179)

Test **validity** means that scores on a test are related to performance on a job. This must be determined empirically, and it is critical to defending against charges of discrimination in hiring. (p. 179)

Criterion-related validity is the extent to which a selection technique accurately predicts elements of performance.

It is most typically demonstrated by establishing a correlation between a test or measured performance in a simulated work environment and measures of actual on-the-job performance. (p. 180)

Utility analysis is an attempt to determine the extent to which a selection system provides real benefit to the organization. (p. 181)

7-5 **Discuss how organizations train and develop new employees to better enable them to perform effectively.** After the new employees are hired, it is common for organizations to submit them to training and development activities, deigned to improve their performance on the job. Training is more concerned with short-term and specific job skills, while development activities focus on less specific and long-term managerial skills. Organizational development is aimed at improving the functioning of the entire organization, so we can discuss organizational learning as a process where these developmental activities become part of the entire organization.

Training is a planned attempt by an organization to facilitate employee learning of job-related knowledge, skills, and behaviors. (p. 182)

Development refers to teaching managers and professionals the skills needed for both present and future jobs. (p. 182)

Work-based programs tie training and development activities directly to performance of the tasks. (p. 183)

Apprenticeships involve a combination of on-the-job training and classroom instruction. (p. 183)

On-the-job training involves having employees learn the job while they are actually performing it. (p. 183)

Vestibule training involves a work-simulation situation in which the job is performed under a condition that closely simulates the real work environment. (p. 183)

Organizational development is a system-wide effort, managed from the top of the organization, to increase the organization's overall performance through planned interventions. (p. 184)

Organizational learning refers to the process by which an organization "learns" from past mistakes and adapts to its environment. (p. 185)

KEY LEGISLATION

The Civil Rights Act of 1964, Title VII, is the most significant single piece of legislation specifically affecting the legal context for HRM to date. Court cases based on this law have helped to define how and why organizations should develop and validate their selection systems.

Key Points for Future Managers

- The goal of recruiting is to generate qualified applicants for jobs.

- Recruiting can be either internal or external, and each has advantages and disadvantages.

- Decisions about the best methods for external (or internal) recruiting should be based on the kind of applicants the firm wants to attract.

- Electronic recruiting is revolutionizing the recruiting field. It is cost-effective and allows the firm to reach a broad range of applicants, but it can increase administrative costs.

- Realistic job previews involve telling applicants both the positive and negative aspects of the job. Some applicants may be frightened by this information, but these are people who would not have been successful anyway. The use of realistic job previews has been linked to more positive attitudes about the job, higher performance, and lower turnover rates for a wide variety of jobs.

- Applicants decide which jobs to apply for and to accept based on the extent to which they feel they will fit with the company (in addition to considering basic issues such as compensation, benefits, and terms of employment).

- Selection is one of the most important functions carried out by the HR department.

- No selection system is perfect, and decisions have to be made about which types of errors are the most and the least costly.

- Selection systems should be based on careful job-analysis information.

- Decisions must be made about the basis for selection decisions. It is especially important to decide the extent to which people should be selected on the basis of their fit with the organization.

- Many techniques are available for selecting individuals. Each has advantages and drawbacks. An ideal system combines several of these techniques into a single system, but there is no one best way to select people. When any technique is used for making a selection decision, including interviews, it is treated as a "test" for legal purposes and must be validated.

- Using tests that are not valid (and not reliable) is irrational and can lead to serious legal problems.

- Methods are available, all falling under the general category of utility analysis, that can allow an assessment of whether the costs of a selection system are justified by increased productivity or decreased costs.

- Training activities are aimed at improving specific job skills of employees so they can perform their jobs more effectively.

- Development activities usually involve managers and are focused on more broadly defined managerial skills that will help the manager in the long run.

- Organizational learning refers to the process by which these developmental activities are spread throughout the company and everyone learns new ways of doing their jobs. some basic notions of HRM.

CHAPTER 8 LEARNING OBJECTIVES / KEY TERMS / KEY LEGISLATION

8-1 **Discuss the nature of diversity, and distinguish among diversity management, equal employment opportunity, and affirmative action.** Diversity exists in a group or organization when its members differ from one another along one or more important dimensions. Diversity is increasing in organizations today due to changing demographics, the desire by organizations to improve their workforces, legal pressures, and increased globalization. Diversity management and equal employment opportunity may appear to be the same, but they are actually quite different. Equal employment opportunity is intended to eliminate discrimination in the workplace; management diversity focuses on recognizing and accommodating differences among people. Affirmative action simply refers to positive steps an organization takes to attract qualified applicants from underrepresented groups. Its ultimate goal is to increase the diversity of the workforce.

Diversity exists in a group or organization when its members differ from one another along one or more important dimensions. (p. 190)

Equal employment opportunity means treating people fairly and equitably and taking actions that do not discriminate against people in protected classes on the basis of some illegal criterion. (p. 191)

Diversity management places a much heavier emphasis on recognizing and appreciating differences among people at work and attempting to provide accommodations for those differences to the extent that is feasible and possible. (p. 191)

8-2 **Identify and describe the major dimensions of diversity in organizations.** Diversity involves several key dimensions. Four of the more common are age, gender, ethnicity, and disability. The overall age of the workforce is increasing. More women are also entering the workplace, although a glass ceiling still exists in many settings. In the United States, more Hispanics are entering the workplace as the percentage of whites in the general population gradually declines.

The **glass ceiling** describes a barrier that keeps many females from advancing to top management positions in many organizations. (p. 194)

Ethnicity refers to the ethnic composition of a group or organization. (p. 195)

8-3 **Discuss the primary impact of diversity on organizations.** Diversity affects organizations in many different ways. It also serves as a force for social change. Many organizations are realizing that diversity can be a major force for competitive advantage. Finally, diversity can also be a significant source of conflict. More recent views of this potential trade-off seem to suggest that further increases in diversity might lead to more positive outcomes and fewer problems with conflict.

8-4 **Describe individual and organizational strategies and approaches to coping with diversity, and discuss the multicultural organization.** Managing diversity in organizations can be done by both individuals and the organization itself. Individual approaches to dealing with diversity include understanding, empathy, tolerance, and communication. Major organizational approaches are through policies, practices, diversity training, and culture. Few, if any, organizations have become truly multicultural. The key dimensions that characterize organizations as they eventually achieve this state are pluralism, full structural integration, full integration of the informal network, an absence of prejudice and discrimination, no gap in organizational identification based on a cultural identity group, and low levels of intergroup conflict attributable to diversity. Ultimately, the people of any country with a diverse population such as the United States must decide if a model of pluralism will also work on the national level.

Diversity training is specifically designed to enable members of an organization to function better in a diverse workplace. (p. 205)

The **multicultural organization** is one that has achieved high levels of diversity, can capitalize fully on the advantages of the diversity, and has few diversity-related problems. (p. 206)

8-5 **Discuss the basic issues in managing knowledge workers.** Managers increasingly recognize that they need to address the knowledge function in their organizations in order to be successful. The knowledge function starts with an understanding of both organizational learning and organizational memory. Human resource (HR) managers may play an especially important role in managing knowledge workers.

Organizational learning is the process by which an organization "learns" from past mistakes and adapts to its environment. (p. 208)

Organizational memory is the collective, institutional record of past events. (p. 209)

Knowledge workers are employees who add value simply because of what they know. (p. 209)

8-6 **Relate human resource management to social issues.** Human resource management (HRM) is also becoming increasingly linked to social issues. Key examples include prison labor, a living wage, immigration, and social responsibility and social entrepreneurship.

CHAPTER REVIEW

CHAPTER 8 LEARNING OBJECTIVES / KEY TERMS / KEY LEGISLATION

KEY LEGISLATION

Key Points for Future Managers

- Managing diversity is critical for the company that wants to remain competitive in the new century. Extremely effective diversity management can lead to a strong competitive advantage as a firm becomes more attractive to a broader set of applicants, has easier access to a broader set of markets, and increases creativity within the firm.

- Effective diversity management is a full-time job and requires strong and consistent support from top management.

- Although managing the knowledge function is an organization-wide imperative, HR managers need to be included in specific issues associated with knowledge workers.

9-1

Describe the basic issues involved in developing a compensation strategy. Compensation and benefit programs have several fundamental purposes and objectives. One fundamental purpose is to provide an adequate and appropriate reward system for employees so that they feel valued and worthwhile as organizational members and representatives. Firms, however, can adopt one of three basic strategies when it comes to compensation: pay above-market compensation rates, pay at-market compensation rates, or pay below-market compensation rates. Several different factors contribute to the compensation strategy that a firm develops. The critical source of information that many organizations use in developing compensation strategies is pay surveys.

Compensation is the set of rewards that organizations provide to individuals in return for their willingness to perform various jobs and tasks within the organization. (p. 220)

Benefits generally refer to various rewards, incentives, and other things of value that an organization provides to its employees beyond their wages, salaries, and other forms of direct financial compensation. (p. 220)

Internal equity in compensation refers to comparisons made by employees to other employees within the same organization. (p. 220)

External equity in compensation refers to comparisons made by employees to others employed by different organizations performing similar jobs. (p. 221)

Pay surveys are surveys of compensation paid to employees by other employers in a particular geographic area, industry, or occupational group. (p. 221)

Wages generally refer to hourly compensation paid to operating employees; the basis for wages is time. (p. 223)

Salary is income paid to an individual on the basis of performance, not on the basis of time. (p. 223)

A **maturity curve** is a schedule specifying the amount of annual increase a person will receive. (p. 224)

9-2

Discuss how organizations develop a wage and salary structure. After an overall strategy has been chosen, human resource (HR) managers must determine what any given job should be paid. The starting point in this effort is job evaluation, which is a method for determining the relative value or worth of a job to the organization so that individuals who perform that job can be compensated adequately and appropriately. Several job evaluation techniques and methods have been established, although alternative approaches to compensation such as pay for knowledge and skill-based pay are increasingly popular.

Job evaluation is a method for determining the relative value or worth of a job to the organization so that individuals who perform that job can be compensated adequately and appropriately. (p. 226)

The **classification system** for job evaluation attempts to group sets of jobs together into clusters, which are often called grades. (p. 227)

The **point system** for job evaluation requires managers to quantify, in objective terms, the value of the various elements of specific jobs. (p. 227)

The **point manual**, used to implement the point system of job evaluation, carefully and specifically defines the degrees of points from first to fifth. (p. 228)

The **factor-comparison method** for job evaluation assesses jobs, on a factor-by-factor basis, using a factor-comparison scale as a benchmark. (p. 228)

Pay for knowledge involves compensating employees for learning specific information. (p. 229)

Skill-based pay rewards employees for acquiring new skills. (p. 229)

9-3 **Identify and describe the basic issues involved in wage and salary administration.** Continued administration of the wage and salary structure in an organization requires consideration of how to deal with such things as pay secrecy and general market conditions, including those resulting in pay compression.

Wage and salary administration is the ongoing process of managing a wage and salary structure. (p. 230)

Pay secrecy refers to the extent to which the compensation of any individual in an organization is secret or the extent to which information on compensation is formally made available to other individuals. (p. 230)

Pay compression occurs when individuals with substantially different levels of experience, performance abilities, or both are paid wages or salaries that are relatively equal. (p. 230)

In **pay inversion**, the external market changes so rapidly that new employees are actually paid more than experienced employees. (p. 230)

9-4 **Discuss the basic considerations in understanding benefit programs.** Benefits take up an ever-larger portion of employers' total compensation costs. Organizations sustain these costs because they believe that competitive benefits packages attract better applicants and help the company retain the employees they have already hired. Although benefits costs are high in the United States, levels of mandated benefits are much higher in Europe and elsewhere. The kinds of benefits that are attractive or appropriate to employees around the world differ considerably. Several laws provide guidelines for how benefits plans should be administered.

9-5 **Identify and describe mandated benefits.** Additional laws mandate that all employees must have certain benefits such as Social Security, unemployment insurance, and workers' compensation. In addition, many organizations offer optional protection plans such as health and dental insurance coverage and private pension plans. The recent passage of the Affordable Care Act has, in essence, made health insurance a mandated benefit as well.

Unemployment insurance, a mandated protection plan, is intended to provide a basic subsistence payment to employees who are between jobs. (p. 232)

Social Security (officially the **Old Age Survivors and Disability Insurance Program**), another mandated program, was originally designed to provide limited income to retired individuals to supplement their personal savings, private pensions, part-time work, and so forth. (p. 232)

Workers' compensation, another mandated protection program, is insurance that covers individuals who suffer a job-related illness or accident. (p. 233)

9-6 **Identify and describe nonmandated benefits.** Paid time off is another important benefit. The most common forms of paid time off are vacation time, holidays, religious days, sick leave, and personal time. This benefit, in particular, varies widely from country to country. Organizations are also becoming more likely to offer benefits in areas such as wellness programs, child care, elder care, and employee assistance programs (EAPs). Finally, some benefits provided by organizations are services and perks that the employee would otherwise have to pay for.

Private pension plans are prearranged plans administered by the organization that provides income to employees at their retirement. (p. 235)

Defined benefit plans are private pension plans in which the size of the benefit is precisely known and is usually based on a simple formula using input such as years of service. (p. 235)

Defined contribution plans are private pension plans in which the size of the benefit depends on how much money is contributed to the plan. (p. 235)

Wellness programs are special benefits programs that concentrate on keeping employees from becoming sick rather than simply paying expenses when they do become sick. (p. 237)

Cafeteria-style benefits plans allow employees to choose those benefits they really want. (p. 237)

9-7 **Discuss contemporary issues in compensation and benefits.** Because needs and preferences differ, some organizations offer cafeteria-style benefits plans in which the employee gets to pick and choose the benefits desired. These programs are expensive to run, but they result in employees getting exactly what they want, which makes the benefits program more cost-effective. Executive compensation issues have attracted considerable attention in recent years. This attention was increased when executives in the financial sector received substantial bonuses even after their firms received large infusions of government bail-out funds in 2009. There are also numerous ongoing legal issues that confront managers as they manage their organizations' compensation and benefits programs. Given the enormous cost of compensation and benefits packages to an organization, it is clearly important that managers also carefully assess the advantages of those packages to the organization. In other words, they need to assess the effectiveness of the firm's compensation structure to ensure that organizational and employee interests are optimized.

Vesting rights are guaranteed rights to receive pension benefits. (p. 241)

KEY LEGISLATION

Affordable Care Act of 2010

The Employee Retirement Income Security Act of 1974 (ERISA) guarantees a basic minimum payment that employees could expect to be paid upon retirement.

The Equal Pay Act of 1962 states that men and women who perform essentially the same job must be paid the same.

The Fair Labor Standards Act (FLSA) established a minimum hourly wage for jobs and further stipulated that wages for hourly workers must be paid at a rate of 1.5 times the normal rate for work in excess of 40 hours per week.

The Social Security Act of 1935, among other things, provides social welfare and social insurance coverage for retired workers.

Key Points for Future Managers

- Critical strategic decisions relate to determining what should be paid to employees and what that rate should be relative to market rates.

- The decision concerning what to pay employees for is probably the most critical, and new pay-for-knowledge and skill-based pay systems advocate paying employees for what they know rather than what they do.

- All decisions to pay wages and salaries at rates below, above, or at the going market rate should be made with full knowledge of the implications of each decision.

- Indirect compensation and benefits represent a large portion of total compensation costs. Many of the benefits are required by law; others (e.g., vacations and medical insurance) have become such a strong part of employee expectations that they cannot easily be eliminated.

- Cafeteria-style benefits plans may allow the company to spend its benefits dollars so that the plan has the greatest impact on employee satisfaction, although these plans have some disadvantages.

- Executive compensation and the legal context of compensation and benefits are important issues that affect businesses.

- Communication is a key part of the indirect compensation strategy, but the link between indirect compensation and organizational-level outcomes is unclear.

10-1

Describe the purposes of performance appraisal in organizations. Performance appraisal and career management are two tools used by organizations to begin the process of performance improvement. Performance appraisal is the specific and formal evaluation of an employee conducted to determine the degree to which the employee is performing his or her job effectively. Careers are the set of experiences that one has through his or her work life. The management of that career is critical for employee development.

Performance appraisals are important because they ensure that recruiting and selection processes are adequate, they play an important role in training, they can help link performance with rewards, they demonstrate that important employment-related decisions are based on performance, and they can promote employee motivation and development. They also provide valuable and useful information to the organization's human resources (HR) planning process. The ultimate goal for any organization using performance appraisals is to improve performance on the job.

A **performance appraisal** is the specific and formal evaluation of an employee to determine the degree to which the employee is performing his or her job effectively. (p. 245)

Performance management is the general set of activities carried out by the organization to change (improve) employee performance. (p. 246)

10-2

Summarize the performance-appraisal process in organizations. The organization, primarily through the work of its HR function, develops the general performance-appraisal process, including issues of timing, for its managers and employees to use. The organization is also responsible for ensuring that clear and specific performance standards are available to managers and employees. Both the rater and the ratee have specific responsibilities. Raters can include the supervisor, peers, colleagues, coworkers, subordinates of the individual being appraised, the individual himself or herself, and customers and clients. When all of these raters are used, the appraisal is called 360-degree feedback.

In a **360-degree appraisal**, performance information is gathered from people on all sides of the manager: above, beside, below, and so forth. (p. 251)

10-3

Identify and describe the most common methods that managers use for performance appraisal. Several methods can be used to assess performance, ranging from ranking systems to rating systems employing behaviorally anchored rating scales (BARS), behavioral observation scales (BOS), and goal-based or management-by-objectives systems. All of these methods are subject to one or more weaknesses or deficiencies, and no system is ideal for all settings.

The **simple ranking method** involves having the manager rank-order each member of a particular work group or department from top to bottom or from best to worst. (p. 253)

In the **paired-comparison method** of performance appraisal, each individual employee is compared with every other individual employee, two at a time. (p. 253)

The **forced-distribution method** involves grouping employees into predefined frequencies of performance ratings. (p. 254)

A **graphic rating scale** consists of a statement or question about some aspect of an individual's job performance. (p. 255)

The **critical incident method** relies on instances of especially good or poor performance on the part of the employee. (p. 256)

A **behaviorally anchored rating scale (BARS)** is an appraisal system that represents a combination of the graphic rating scale and the critical incident method. (p. 256)

A **behavioral observation scale (BOS)** is developed from critical incidents like a BARS but uses substantially more critical incidents to define specifically all the measures necessary for effective performance. (p. 257)

A **goal-based** or **management-by-objectives (MBO)** system is based largely on the extent to which individuals meet their personal performance objectives. (p. 257)

10-4 **Discuss other general issues involving performance appraisal in organizations.** Regardless of the approach used, after the appraisal is completed, the next major activity is the provision of feedback to the employee with the goal of improving performance and guiding the employee's self-development. Part of that self-development must be focused on career management.

Contrast error occurs when we compare people against one another instead of against an objective standard. (p. 258)

A **distributional error** occurs when the rater tends to use only one part of the rating scale. (p. 259)

A **halo error** occurs when one positive performance characteristic causes the manager to rate all other aspects of performance positively. (p. 259)

A **horns error** occurs when the manager downgrades other aspects of an employee's performance because of a single performance dimension. (p. 259)

Contextual performance refers to tasks an employee does on the job that are not required as part of the job but that still benefit the organization in some way. (p. 260)

10-5 **Describe the nature of careers in organizations.** A career is the set of experiences and activities that people engage in related to their job and livelihood over the course of their working life. Traditionally, individuals were seen as progressing through a series of career stages that include exploration, establishment, maintenance, and disengagement. A more recent perspective refocuses career stages on career age and acknowledges the likelihood of multiple careers, and this more recent perspective also recognizes that retirement is a part of the career progression.

A **career** is the set of experiences and activities that people engage in related to their job and livelihood over the course of their working life. (p. 262)

Exploration is the first traditional career stage and involves identifying interests and opportunities. (p. 262)

The **establishment** stage of the traditional career model involves creating a meaningful and relevant role in the organization. (p. 263)

The **maintenance** stage involves optimizing talents or capabilities. (p. 263)

The fourth traditional career stage, **disengagement**, involves the individual gradually beginning to pull away from work in the organization. Priorities change, and work may become less important. (p. 263)

10-6 Discuss human resource management and career management. Successful careers don't just happen; they must be planned and managed by both the organization and the individual employee. Career planning requires careful coordination between individual employees and the organization itself. Even though career planning is important and beneficial to both organizations and individuals, everyone should also recognize that career planning has limitations and potential pitfalls.

In many ways, the early career stages are the most tumultuous. Regardless of whether they are taking their first jobs or moving into one job after a long period of employment elsewhere, new entrants into an organization always feel a certain degree of uncertainty and apprehension about their new employer. Thus, an important starting point for HR managers interested in managing the careers of their employees more effectively is understanding some of the early career problems that such employees often encounter.

The **individual assessment phase** of career planning requires that individuals analyze carefully what they perceive to be their own abilities, competencies, skills, and goals. (p. 266)

Career counseling involves interaction between an individual employee or manager in the organization and either a line manager or an HR manager. (p. 266)

10-7 Identify and discuss basic career-development issues and challenges. After an individual completes the first few years of a job successfully, many of the early career problems may have been addressed. However, some problems still loom on the horizon for these individuals after they reach the midcareer stage. The most common midcareer problem faced by most individuals in corporations today is what is generally referred to as the midcareer plateau. In the latter stages of a person's career, it is perhaps even more important for the organization to provide career-management services. Many of these services try to solve the problems people face in the later stages of their careers. Many of these problems revolve around issues associated with retirement.

Regardless of the career stage of each employee, many organizations that are sincerely interested in more effective career management for their employees deal with and address various issues and challenges. Career-counseling programs are important to an organization interested in career development for its employees. Such programs usually address a wide variety of career-related issues and are readily accessible to people in the organization. Dual-career and work–family issues are also an important part of today's career-management activities and concerns. The success of career management activities can only be judged according to their success at any one point in time. If an employee is satisfied with his or her career at one point, then career management must be judged successful up to that point.

KEY LEGISLATION

The Age Discrimination in Employment Act (ADEA) prohibits discrimination against employees over the age of 40.

Key Points for Future Managers

- Appraisal systems should always be designed so that they have the greatest likelihood of improving individual and organizational performance.

- Raters must be convinced that it is in their best interests to be fair and accurate in appraisals. No type of system can replace rater motivation to do a good job.

- Although 360-degree appraisals are popular, evidence does not support their effectiveness relative to other, less-expensive methods, and using 360-degree appraisals is problematic for decision-making.

- In team settings, decisions must be made about whether appraisals and feedback should focus on the whole team or on individual members.

- Contextual performance refers to those behaviors that we do not evaluate formally but that must occur for the organization to function effectively. Decisions have to be made about how to treat contextual performance.

- Clear evidence shows that one appraisal system is not more effective than any other type of appraisal system, although there is some reason to believe that goal-based systems may offer some advantages over the alternatives.

- Feedback does not always have the desired effect on performance. Sometimes providing feedback can hurt subsequent performance.

- Although the traditional career may be dead, it is still critical to think through and plan an employee's entire career and help the employee to manage that career.

CHAPTER 11 LEARNING OBJECTIVES / KEY TERMS / KEY LEGISLATION

11-1 **Describe the role of labor unions in organizations.** Managing labor relations is the process of dealing with employees who are represented by a union. A labor union is a legally constituted group of individuals working together to achieve shared job-related goals. Collective bargaining is the process by which managers and union leaders negotiate acceptable terms and conditions of employment for those workers represented by the unions. Many laws and other regulations have been passed regarding unions; some are intended to promote unionization and union activities, while others are intended to limit or curtail union activities. Like any large organization, labor unions also have structures that facilitate their work.

Labor relations is the process of dealing with employees who are represented by a union. (p. 272)

A **labor union** is a legally constituted group of individuals working together to achieve shared, job-related goals, including higher pay and shorter working hours. (p. 272)

Collective bargaining is the process by which managers and union leaders negotiate acceptable terms and conditions of employment for those workers represented by the unions. (p. 272)

The **Knights of Labor** was an important early union that expanded its goals and its membership to include workers in numerous fields rather than a single industry. (p. 273)

The **American Federation of Labor (AF of L)** was another early union; it focused its efforts on improved working conditions and better employment contracts rather than getting involved in legislative and political activities. (p. 273)

Another important early union was the **Congress of Industrial Organizations (CIO)**, which focused on organizing employees by industry, regardless of their craft, skills, or occupation. (p. 274)

The **National Labor Relations Act** (or **Wagner Act**) administers most labor law in the United States. (p. 274)

The **National Labor Relations Board (NLRB)** administers most labor law in the United States. (p. 274)

The **Labor Management Relations Act** (or **Taft-Hartley Act**) (1947) was a response to public outcries against a wide variety of strikes in the years after World War II; its basic purpose was to curtail and limit union practices. (p. 275)

A **closed shop** refers to a workplace in which only workers who are already union members may be hired by the employer. (p. 275)

A **union shop agreement** includes various types of union security agreements in addition to a requirement that a nonunion member can be hired, although he or she must join the union within a specified time to keep his or her job. (p. 275)

An **agency shop agreement** is one where employees can decide whether or not to join the union certified as the bargaining agent, but if the employee decides not to join, he or she must still pay a fee roughly equal to the amount of union dues. (p. 275)

The **Landrum-Griffin Act** (officially called the **Labor Management Reporting and Disclosure Act**) focused on eliminating various unethical, illegal, and undemocratic union practices. (p. 276)

Locals are unions organized at the level of a single company, plant, or small geographic region. (p. 276)

The **shop steward**, an elected position in a local union, is a regular employee who functions as a liaison between union members and supervisors. (p. 276)

11-2 **Identify and summarize trends in unionization.** Since the mid-1950s, labor unions in the United States have experienced increasing difficulty in attracting new members. Indeed, while millions of U.S. workers still belong to labor unions, union membership as a percentage of the total workforce has continued to decline at a steady rate. Unions recognize that they don't have as much power as they once held and that working *with* instead of *against* management is in the unions' best interests, as well as the best interests of the workers they represent. Bargaining perspectives have also altered in recent years.

11-3 **Discuss the unionization process.** Employees must follow a specific set of steps if they want to establish a union. First, employees must express some interest in joining a union. If interest exists in forming a union, then the National Labor Relations Board (NLRB) is asked to define the bargaining unit. After the bargaining unit has been defined, organizers must then strive to get 30 percent of the eligible workers within the bargaining unit to sign authorization cards requesting a certification election. If organizers cannot get 30 percent of the workers to sign authorization cards, the unionization process ends. However, if the required number of signatures is obtained, then organizers petition the NLRB to conduct an election. If the union becomes certified, its organizers create a set of rules and regulations that will govern the conduct of the union. Under certain conditions, an existing labor union may be decertified.

The **bargaining unit** refers to the specifically defined group of employees who are eligible for representation by the union. (p. 283)

11-4 **Describe the collective-bargaining process.** Collective bargaining involves management representing the employing organization and the labor union representing its employees. The collective bargaining process is aimed at agreement on a binding labor contract that will define various dimensions of the employment relationship for a specified period. One important part of preparing for collective bargaining is prior agreement on the parameters of the bargaining session.

Mandatory items, including wages, working hours, and benefits, must be included as part of collective bargaining if either party expresses a desire to negotiate one or more of them. (p. 285)

Permissive items may be included in collective bargaining if both parties agree. (p. 285)

11-5 **Discuss how labor agreements are negotiated.** The negotiation process involves representatives from management and the labor union meeting at agreed-on times and locations and working together to attempt to reach a mutually acceptable labor agreement. A useful framework for understanding the negotiation process is the bargaining zone. Of course, numerous barriers to effective negotiation exist, and several methods are available for both management and labor to use in their attempts to overcome an impasse.

An **impasse** is a situation in which one or both parties believe that reaching an agreement is not imminent. (p. 287)

11-6 **Describe how impasses get resolved and agreements are administered.** A key clause in the labor contracts negotiated between management and labor defines how the labor agreement will be enforced. Although some enforcement issues are relatively straightforward, others may rely heavily on a formal grievance procedure.

A **strike** occurs when employees walk off their jobs and refuse to work. (p. 287)

Picketing occurs when workers representing the union march at the entrance to the employer's facility with signs explaining their reasons for striking. (p. 287)

A **boycott** occurs when union members agree not to buy the products of a targeted employer. (p. 289)

A **slowdown** occurs when workers perform their jobs at a much slower pace than normal. (p. 289)

A **wildcat strike** occurs when workers suddenly go on strike, without the authorization (presumably) of the striker's union and while a binding labor agreement is still in effect. (p. 289)

A **lockout** occurs when an employer denies employees access to the workplace. (p. 289)

In **mediation**, a neutral third party called the mediator listens to and reviews the information presented by both sides and then makes an informed recommendation and provides advice to both parties about what she or he believes should be done. (p. 290)

In **arbitration**, both sides agree in advance that they will accept the recommendations made by an independent third-party arbitrator. (p. 290)

Under **final-offer arbitration**, the parties bargain until impasse, and then the two parties' final offers are submitted to the arbitrator. (p. 290)

11-7 **Discuss emerging labor union issues in the twenty-first century.** The labor movement in the United States focused on bread-and-butter issues such as wages and hours of work, unlike the labor movements in many European countries. U.S. labor unions have become quite vocal in several areas where they have traditionally been silent, speaking out against child labor in Third World countries and the general exportation of jobs to lower paying countries.

KEY LEGISLATIONS

The Labor Management Relations Act (or Taft-Hartley Act) curtailed and limited union powers when enacted and now regulates union actions and their internal affairs in a way that puts them on equal footing with management and organizations.

The Landrum-Griffin Act (officially called the Labor Management Reporting and Disclosure Act) focused on the elimination of various unethical, illegal, and/or undemocratic practices within unions themselves.

The National Labor Relations Act (or Wagner Act) passed in an effort to control and legislate collective bargaining between organizations and labor unions, to grant power to labor unions, and to put unions on a more equal footing with managers in terms of the rights of employees.

Key Points for Future Managers

- Unions have traditionally played an important role in improving working conditions for U.S. workers, and many workers still view unions in this light. Therefore, if a firm has a union, it may be difficult to vote it out; if a firm does not have a union, it may be more difficult than some managers believe to keep a union out.

- Some firms have found unions to be helpful partners as they explore new ways to organize work, while others have found unions to be tenacious opponents to any change. It is important to think seriously about the kind of relationship management wants to have with unions.

- A well-developed legal framework is in place to guide management in dealing with unions, and enforcement of these laws has been consistent over the years.

- Unions have become effective at calling for social reform, and such actions have increased their popularity in the media.

12-1 **Identify and discuss the central elements associated with employee safety and health.** There are many reasons why modern organizations are more concerned about employee safety and health issues than ever before. Lost work time and increased insurance costs are among the most important of these reasons, but organizations also are very interested in ways of keeping employees safe, healthy, and secure.

Safety hazards are conditions in the work environment that have the potential to cause harm to an employee. (p. 298)

Health hazards are characteristics of the work environment that more slowly and systematically, and perhaps cumulatively, result in damage to an employee's health. (p. 298)

OSHA is both the act that authorized the U.S. government to create various standards regarding occupational safety and health and the administrative agency that enforces those standards. (p. 300)

Safety engineers are experts who carefully study the workplace, try to identify and isolate particularly dangerous situations, and recommend solutions for dealing with those situations. (p. 301)

12-2 **Describe the basic issues involved in the physical work environment.** As such, organizations are interested in managing the work environment to make it safer. Basic issues involve actions that the organization can and should take to control or eliminate safety hazards and health hazards. Safety hazards refer to those conditions in the work environment that have the potential to cause harm to an employee. Health hazards are those characteristics of the work environment that more slowly and systematically—perhaps cumulatively—result in damage to an employee's health. The Occupational Safety and Health Act (OSHA) authorized the U.S. government to create and enforce various standards regarding occupational safety and health.

In addition, the actual physical environment in which an employee works is extremely important. Many aspects of the physical environment may affect an employee's attitudes and behavior on the job and can affect employee health and well-being. Work hours reflect one such aspect. Illumination, temperature, and office and work-space design are also important.

Circadian rhythms are natural cycles that indicate when a body needs to eat or sleep. (p. 302)

12-3 **Discuss stress and stress-management programs in organizations.** Stress is a person's adaptive response to a stimulus that places excessive psychological or physical demands on him or her. The stimuli that cause stress are called *stressors*. Organizational stressors are various factors in the workplace that can cause stress. Four general sets of organizational stressors are task demands, physical demands, role demands, and interpersonal demands. If the stress is positive, the result may be more energy, enthusiasm, and motivation. Three other sets of consequences that can result from stress are individual consequences, organizational consequences, and burnout. However, it is important to note that not everyone experiences stress in the same way, and there are also individual differences in the effects that stress has on employees. Two basic organizational strategies for helping employees manage stress are institutional programs and collateral stress programs. In addition, organizations develop programs to reduce the threat of various diseases at work, including AIDS.

Stress is a person's adaptive response to a stimulus that places excessive psychological or physical demands on him or her. (p. 305)

The **Type A personality** is characterized by being highly competitive and highly focused on work with few interests outside of work. (p. 306)

The **Type B personality** is characterized as being less aggressive, more patient, and more easygoing. In general, individuals with Type B personalities experience less stress and are less likely to suffer some type of illness because of stress than Type A personalities. (p. 306)

Hardiness is an individual difference that allows some individuals to experience less stress when dealing with stressful events and that makes them more effective in dealing with the stress they do experience. (p. 306)

Burnout is a general feeling of exhaustion that develops when an individual simultaneously experiences too much pressure and too few sources of satisfaction. (p. 307)

Turnover refers to people leaving their jobs, whether voluntarily or involuntarily (i.e., through firings). (p. 307)

Dysfunctional behavior refers to any behavior at work that is counterproductive. These behaviors may include theft and sabotage, as well as sexual and racial harassment. (p. 308)

Institutional programs for managing stress are undertaken through established organizational mechanisms. (p. 308)

Collateral stress programs are organizational programs created specifically to help employees deal with stress. (p. 308)

12-4 **Identify and describe the most important HR-related security issues in organizations.** Finally, security concerns have emerged as a real issue for employees. The United States has probably seen the greatest change in stress due to security concerns because such concerns were not salient to Americans in the past. Especially since the September 11 attacks, U.S. firms have become much more security conscious, as have most Americans.

KEY LEGISLATION

The Occupational Safety and Health Act of 1970 (OSHA) grants the federal government the power to establish and enforce occupational safety and health standards for all places of employment directly affecting interstate commerce.

Key Points for Future Managers

- Employee safety is not only a matter of the law but also good business because it reduces costs and increases productivity.

- The physical work environment is critical for productivity, health, safety, and employee attitudes.

- Stress on the job could be the result of job demands, physical demands, role demands, and interpersonal demands.

- Stress can have many negative effects, although there are individual differences in how people experience stress.

- Security concerns at work have become much more important, especially in the United States.

CHAPTER 13 LEARNING OBJECTIVES / KEY TERMS / KEY LEGISLATION

13-1 **Describe the basic model of performance.** *Motivation* refers to the efforts employees exert at work. An individual's performance is a function of both ability to perform a task and motivation to exert effort on that task. Thus, it is critical that human resource (HR) managers understand how they might motivate employees to exert effort toward reaching an organization's strategic goals.

Motivation determines how a person will exert his or her effort. It represents the forces operating on the person to exert effort, as well as the direction in which that effort will be exerted. (p. 318)

13-2 **Discuss motivation and human needs.** A number of models or theories of motivation can provide some help. Need-based theories are more concerned with *what* motivates people, and Maslow's hierarchy of needs is the best known of these theories. The most important lesson an HR manager can learn from these need theories is that, at any one time, different employees may be motivated by different things as they try to satisfy different needs.

Need-based theories are theories of motivation that focus on what motivates a person, rather than on how that motivation occurs. (p. 319)

Probably the best known of the need-based theories, the **hierarchy of needs** model proposed by Abraham Maslow, specifies five levels of needs that are capable of motivating behavior: physiological, security, social, esteem, and self-actualization. (p. 319)

According to Maslow's theory, **prepotent** needs are those specific needs (of the five levels in the model) that are capable of motivating behavior at any given point in time. (p. 319)

A need-based theory of motivation proposed by Clayton Alderfer, **ERG theory** involves three rather than five levels of needs, and also allows for someone to regress from a higher-level need to a lower-level need. (p. 319)

A need-based theory proposed by Frederick Herzberg, **dual factor theory** identifies motivators and hygiene factors as two sets of conditions at work that can satisfy needs. Research into this theory, however, has provided little empirical support for its model. (p. 320)

13-3 **Identify the basic process models of motivation, and describe an integrative model of motivation.** Process theories of motivation are more concerned with how people become motivated. Reinforcement theory, expectancy theory, and equity theory are three process theories that can be useful to HR managers. The insights from these three theories plus the insights from need-based theories can be combined to form a more integrative view of motivation at work. In this view, employees will be motivated to exert effort on their jobs when they believe their effort can lead to improved performance and that improved performance will be rewarded with fair outcomes that can satisfy basic needs.

Process theories are motivation theories that focus on how people become motivated and what they are motivated to do rather than on what motivates them. (p. 322)

Reinforcement theory is a process theory, usually associated with B. F. Skinner, which proposes that all behavior is a function of its consequences. (p. 322)

A term from reinforcement theory, **positive reinforcement** refers to the situation in which a behavior is followed by positive consequences and thus is likely to be repeated. (p. 322)

Also a term from reinforcement theory, **extinction** refers to the situation in which a behavior is followed by no consequences and eventually disappears. (p. 324)

Yet another term from reinforcement theory, **punishment** refers to a situation in which a behavior is followed by negative consequences and so is not repeated. (p. 324)

Behavior modification is the combination of positive reinforcement with either punishment or extinction that replaces an undesired behavior with a desired behavior. (p. 324)

Partial reinforcement means rewarding a behavior only part of the time rather than all the time (it can be applied to punishment as well, but the reward case is simpler). (p. 325)

Interval schedules are partial reinforcement schedules in which behavior is reinforced as a function of the passage of time—for example, rewarding someone every 10 minutes as long as they were exhibiting desired behavior. (p. 325)

Ratio schedules are partial reinforcement schedules in which behavior is reinforced as a function of how many times the behavior occurs—for example, rewarding someone every fifth time a desired behavior occurs. (p. 325)

Fixed interval schedules are interval schedules in which the amount of time that must pass before a reward is given is constant over time. (p. 325)

Variable interval schedules are interval schedules in which the amount of time that must pass before a reward is given can change from one reward period to another. (p. 325)

Fixed ratio schedules are ratio schedules in which the number of times a behavior must occur before it is rewarded remains constant over time. (p. 325)

Variable ratio schedules are ratio schedules in which the number of times a behavior must occur before it is rewarded changes over time. (p. 326)

Expectancy theory (or **VIE theory**) is a fairly complex process theory of motivation that casts the employee in the role of decision maker. Basically, an employee decides whether or not to exert effort, depending on the outcomes he or she anticipates receiving for those efforts as based on calculations concerning expectancies, instrumentalities, valences, and the links among these three components. (p. 326)

Effort-to-performance expectancy (or **expectancy**) is a person's perception of the probability that an increase in effort will result in an increase in performance. This can range from 0 to 1.0. (p. 326)

Performance-to-outcomes expectancy (or **instrumentality**) is a person's perception of the probability that improved performance will lead to certain outcomes. Operationally seen as a correlation coefficient indicating that as performance improves, the chances of gaining outcomes can either go up (a positive correlation), remain unchanged (a zero correlation), or go down (a negative correlation). (p. 326)

Valence refers to how attractive or unattractive an outcome is for a person. (p. 326)

Equity theory is concerned with a person's perceived inputs to a (work) setting and the outcomes received from that setting. The theory suggests that everyone calculates the ratio of inputs to outcomes, similar to considering a return on any investment. (p. 328)

13-4 Describe other related theories and perspectives on motivation. Goal theory and agency theory are two other theories of motivation that can be useful to the HR manager. Finally, it is important to realize that all motivation at work does not follow from the introduction of some type of reward. Intrinsic motivation is an important source of motivation at work, and this motivation is derived from having people work on jobs that are challenging and interesting. Intrinsic motivation is also related to creative behavior at work, which can be exhibited by almost any employee. Creativity also depends on informative feedback and a climate where it is safe for people to make mistakes.

First proposed by Ed Locke, **goal theory** is a fairly simple model of motivation based on the premise that people with goals work harder than people without goals. Beyond that, the theory suggests that not all goals are created equal, and that goals that are difficult and yet specific and concrete will motivate employees best. (p. 331)

Agency theory addresses potential conflicts of interests among different groups of stakeholders in an organization. The name of the theory and some of its basic principles are derived from the fact that, in most modern organizations, the individuals who own a firm do not actually run it on a daily basis. Problems arise when the interests of the owners (the principals) are in conflict with the interests of the managers (agents). (p. 331)

Intrinsic motivation is the motivation to do work because it is interesting, engaging, or possibly challenging rather than because someone is rewarding us to do the work. (p. 332)

Creative behavior involves doing things at work that are innovative and that provide some value for the organization. (p. 333)

KEY LEGISLATION

Key Points for Future Managers

- Employee motivation is essential for organizational success.
- Reward systems must be designed to motivate the behaviors that the organization really desires.
- Managing employee behavior is easiest when there is a strong link between desired behaviors and outcomes that are important to the employee.
- It *is* possible to motivate employees by increasing intrinsic motivation.
- It *is* possible to increase creativity at work.

14-1 **Describe the relationships among performance measured at different levels within an organization, and discuss how training, development, and job redesign can help improve performance.** Performance in any organization exists at multiple levels. The most basic level of performance is at the level of the individual employee, and this is the level that most people find easiest to conceptualize. However, performance-enhancement techniques are ultimately aimed at improving firm-level performance. Moving from performance enhancement at the level of the individual to performance enhancement at the level of the firm requires a systems approach where all human resource (HR) activities are coordinated to create a performance culture that allows employees to work to enhance firm-level performance.

One specific approach to enhancing organizational performance is through the use of the training and development activities described in Chapter 7. A much different approach to enhancing organizational performance is through the redesign of jobs. Specifically, this technique involves changing—redesigning—jobs so that the work itself will motivate employees to exert greater effort. This motivation is stimulated by making the job more interesting or challenging. There are five motivational approaches to the redesign of work: job rotation, job enlargement, job enrichment, job characteristics, and work teams.

Firm-level performance is an indication of a firm's chances of long-term survival. Performance at this level generates profits for potential profit sharing and determines the company's stock price. (p. 339)

Job rotation involves systematically moving employees from one job to another. (p. 340)

Job enlargement was developed to increase the total number of tasks workers perform based on the assumption that doing the same basic task over and over is the primary cause of worker dissatisfaction. (p. 340)

Job enrichment attempts to increase both the number of tasks a worker does and the control the worker has over the job. (p. 340)

The **job characteristics approach** is an alternative to job specialization that takes into account the work system and employee preferences; it suggests that jobs should be diagnosed and improved along five core dimensions. (p. 341)

A **work team** is an arrangement in which a group is given responsibility for designing the work system to be used in performing an interrelated set of jobs. (p. 342)

14-2 **Discuss the role of alternative work arrangements in motivating and enhancing performance.** Another approach to performance enhancement comes with allowing employees more flexibility in their working arrangements. The two most common alternatives to the traditional workweek are programs known as *flexible work hours* and *compressed workweeks*. Employees working under flexible work hour plans usually must still work a full 40 hours per week and typically 5 days a week. Compressed workweeks are arrangements in which the employee works the required number of hours (typically 40) but does so in fewer than 5 days. Allowing employees to perform their work at a location other than the place of business, most likely at home, is a growing trend.

Flexible work hour plans are plans in which employees usually must still work 40 hours per week and typically 5 days a week but in which they have control over the starting and ending times for work on each day. (p. 342)

Compressed workweeks are arrangements in which the employee works the required number of hours (typically 40) but does so in fewer than 5 days. For example, a 4-day, 10-hour-a-day work schedule is fairly common. (p. 343)

14-3 **Describe the role of incentive pay, and identify different programs for individual-based and team-based incentive plans.** Yet another approach to enhancing performance is by explicitly tying rewards, especially pay, to performance. There are many plans to allow this to be done. These include merit pay, skill-based and knowledge-based pay, individual incentive plans, and group or team incentive plans. The latter include gainsharing and the Scanlon plan. Organization-wide methods include profit sharing, stock option plans, stock-purchase plans, and employee stock ownership plans (ESOPs).

Merit pay is pay awarded to employees on the basis of the relative value of their contributions to the organization. (p. 346)

Merit-pay plans are compensation plans that formally base at least some meaningful portion of compensation on merit. (p. 347)

Individual incentive plans reward individual performance on a real-time basis. (p. 347)

The **base salary** of an employee is a guaranteed amount of money that the individual will be paid. (p. 347)

A **sales commission** is an incentive paid to salespeople. (p. 348)

Gainsharing is a team- and group-based incentive system designed to share the cost savings from productivity improvements with employees. (p. 349)

Scanlon plans are gainsharing plans in which teams or groups of employees are encouraged to suggest strategies for reducing costs; gains are distributed not just to the team that suggested and developed the ideas but to the entire organization. (p. 349)

Profit sharing is an incentive system in which, at the end of the year, some portion of the company's profits is paid into a profit-sharing pool, which is then distributed to all employees. (p. 349)

A **stock-option plan** is an incentive plan established to give senior managers the option to buy company stock in the future at a predetermined fixed price. (p. 350)

A **stock-purchase plan** is typically offered to all the employees of a firm rather than just the executives to serve more as a retention tool. Under these plans, employees are entitled to the stock only if they remain with the company for a specified period of time. If they leave before that time, they have no rights to the shares of stock. (p. 350)

Employee stock ownership plans (ESOPs) are group-level reward systems in which employees are gradually given a major stake in the ownership of a corporation. (p. 350)

14-4 Discuss the best ways to deliver performance feedback and the issues involved with feedback, and describe the basic operation of the ProMES system. There are also a series of programs and interventions that are referred to as performance-management techniques. These include behavior modification and goal setting. Performance feedback plays an important role in both behavior modification and goal setting and is also seen as a useful tool in its own right for performance management. The productivity measurement and evaluation system (ProMES) incorporates ideas from goal setting to feedback, and it includes incentives for improvement.

The **productivity measurement and evaluation system (ProMES)** is a program developed to improve group- or firm-level productivity. This approach incorporates ideas from goal setting with incentives for improvement, and it is based on a model of motivation similar to expectancy theory. (p. 354)

14-5 Discuss how organizations evaluate performance-enhancement programs. First, any true measure of organizational success must tie back the organization's strategic goals. In addition, several more general indexes of firm-level performance could be used to help evaluate the effectiveness of these interventions. The first set of indexes can be considered HR indicators. These include measures such as turnover rates, absenteeism, accident rates, and even general labor costs. In addition, there are measures of profitability, productivity, and controllable costs. These measures actually are related, with specific measures making more sense in some businesses than in others.

14-6 Discuss how recent world events have affected the role of HR. Privacy and cybersecurity have become much more complex and critical in today's workplace. As a result, HR managers must be more conscientious about protecting the privacy of both business and employee information. In today's workplace, every desktop computer, laptop, or handheld device is vulnerable to attack. Intruders hacking into a computer system, malware, lost laptops, and insider threats all combine to present serious challenges to companies.

KEY LEGISLATION

Key Points for Future Managers

- Improving individual-level performance does not automatically result in improved corporate-level performance.

- Redesigning jobs along certain lines can improve motivation without increasing pay.

- There are pros and cons associated with both individual- and group-level incentives.

- Feedback is not always effective.

- Some organizational-level interventions have been shown to be effective in improving performance.

- Any performance-enhancement technique must be evaluated as to its effectiveness.

- The world around us is constantly changing, and it is important to think about how these changes affect the ways we manage human resources in organizations.